The Tree of Liberty

The Tree

A Documentary History of Rebellion
and Political Crime in America

REVISED EDITION

A Legal, Historical, Social, and
Psychological Inquiry into
Rebellions and Political Crimes,
Their Causes, Suppression,
and Punishment in the United States

# of Liberty

edited by Nicholas N. Kittrie
and Eldon D. Wedlock, Jr.

Volume 1

Colonial Era to
World War II

The Johns Hopkins University Press
Baltimore and London

© 1986, 1998 The Johns Hopkins University Press
All rights reserved. First edition 1986
Revised edition 1998
Printed in the United States of America on acid-free paper
07 06 05 04 03 02 01 00 99 98   5 4 3 2 1

The Johns Hopkins University Press
2715 North Charles Street, Baltimore, Maryland 21218-4319
The Johns Hopkins Press Ltd., London

Permissions are on pages lxxvi-lxxvii, which are a continuation of the
copyright page.

Library of Congress Cataloging-in-Publication Data will be found
at the end of this book.
A catalog record for this book is available from the British Library.

ISBN 0-8018-5812-7   ISBN 0-8018-5643-4 (pbk.: v. 1)
ISBN 0-8018-5811-9 (pbk.: v. 2)

For
Leon Felhendler
who led the righteous in rebellion (Sobibor, 1943)

and

in memory of
Eldon D. Wedlock
(1908-1983)
who freed minds and liberated hearts

I hold it that a little rebellion now and
then is a good thing, and as necessary in
the political world as storms in the physical. . . . It is a medicine necessary for the
sound health of government.

God forbid we should ever be twenty
years without such a rebellion.

*   *   *

What signify a few lives lost in a century or
two? The tree of liberty must be refreshed
from time to time with the blood of patriots
and tyrants. It is its natural manure.

—Thomas Jefferson

The struggle between Liberty and Authority
is the most conspicuous feature in . . . history.

—John Stuart Mill

Contents

Illustrations follow pages 222, 351, and 569

Detailed Contents

Volume 1

Contents xiii

Preface to the Revised Edition

The past decade has witnessed increased communal discontent and an escalation in the incidence of rebellion and public strife, both in the United States and elsewhere. In the Introduction to this book's first edition, published in 1986, we identified major eruptions of political rebellion and militance as expressions of protest against alleged abuses of power by governmental agencies or by powerful elites. The protests have frequently been fueled by the attempts of those excluded from the prevailing "social contract" to gain political, economic, and social empowerment. We further attributed the escalating political tensions to conflicts of allegiance within marginalized groups or individuals. The traditional loyalty that citizens owe their country or state, nourished by appeals to national pride and honor and enforced by the power of the existing law, often finds itself in conflict with allegiances owed to some other community—be it racial, ethnic, tribal, clannish, religious, ideological, economic, sexual, or linguistic. When such competing allegiances cannot be reconciled through existing political institutions, protest, violence, and domestic warfare may erupt. These internal tensions are even more likely to flare up when the existence of external, or international, threats declines, as seen at the conclusion of the cold war.

The emerging domestic struggles consist not merely of resistance, civil disobedience, and martial contests but also of appeals to the minds and hearts of the people. The mass media, with their influence over modern society, are frequently used as a vehicle, or courted as allies, by the combating camps. Ironically, both those in power and their challengers sometimes base the legitimacy of their causes on identical or related sources. This commonality is frequently manifested in the United States by appeals to the Constitution. Opponents often challenge the government, arguing that it and its agents have betrayed their oaths, have strayed from the path of the Founders, and have exceeded the powers devolved upon them by the Constitution. American political offenders, as a consequence, frequently perceive no "disloyalty," "treason," or "fundamental disso-

nance" in their quest for the "true meaning of the Constitution" and their struggle to dispossess those in power who have allegedly "abused or perverted" the Constitutional scheme. While in other countries the primary contest might be between such extremes as religious fundamentalism and secular democracy, and the antagonists might agree on no common ideological principles or national objectives, in the United States the hallowed image of the Constitution has made both the government and its political opponents point to that document's language and intent for the legitimation of their claims.

The worldwide political strife of the past decade (in such diverse settings as Afghanistan, Cambodia, Canada, East Timor, Mexico, Liberia, Rwanda, Somalia, and the former Yugoslavia and Soviet Union) helps to demonstrate the many close relationships between the international scene and domestic disorder. Domestic rebellion and militancy are evidently dampened when foreign threats are perceived as more dangerous to the common well-being than the injustices practiced by the existing government in power. Grossly disaffected communities or groups may, nevertheless, succumb to dangerous adventuring and variations of the maxim "The enemy of my enemy is my friend," and may seek to advance their group's causes through questionable foreign alliances. But most will eschew such extremes, to submerge for a time the more militant measures for proclaiming or correcting existing grievances. The relative domestic calm that prevailed within the countries of both the Eastern and Western blocs during much of the twentieth century, an era of mortal confrontations between the proponents of democracy and the forces of Nazism, Fascism, and "Godless Communism," well illustrates this inverse relationship between the presence of external enemies and the emergence of domestic militancy.

It was shortsightedness, therefore, that suggested to many pundits of international affairs that the end of the cold war heralded the arrival of a global peace. Similar lack of vision led to claims that the racial and political struggles of the 1960s and 1970s would lead to domestic tranquility, as well. This optimism was clearly ill-placed. In a world community containing few nation-states (a term suggesting sovereign entities consisting of homogeneous nations or peoples) but composed instead of patchwork countries made up of diverse ethnic, religious, racial, or tribal communities, each with distinct objectives and expectations, the removal of external threats has not brought about conciliation and peace at home. Indeed, when the external threats that cement these pluralistic and diverse communities vanish, new as well as old and long-suppressed grievances surface with renewed vigor and cruelty. The removal of the East-West divide did not begin the end of history but rather renewed the traditional rivalries that have occupied peoples over the millennia.

Evidence of similar developments in the United States, a country made up of an ever-changing pluralistic mix, is abundantly supplied in this revised edition. Not only the rekindling of recent grievances but also the emergence of forgotten concerns, as well as totally new ones, is illustrated. These include the surfacing of both individual and collective militance in the country's heartland, among the "dispossessed" people of the nation's farm belt and the "forgotten" former members of the country's armed services. Accusations that uncontrolled immigration has turned America into an "alien nation" and suspicions that the United Nations is seeking to impose a New World Order have done little to quiet the fears and discontents of a country in the midst of a painful search for a just, appropriate, and broadly encompassing consensus for the third century of its evolution.

The new documents added to this revised edition of *The Tree of Liberty* clearly demonstrate that even the United States, this great leader of the democratic camp, is far from reaching its own peaceful utopia. The struggles in the nation's urban ghettoes and in front of its abortion clinics, the fires that gut religious institutions, the deep discontent in mid-America, and the disorder spreading through streets, schools, and families readily testify to the fact that the ongoing war against authority is likely to continue. To paraphrase Thomas Jefferson's memorable words, the roots of the tree of liberty must continue to be "refreshed" until its fruits truly meet the pluralistic tastes and expectations of America—a country made up of a richly diverse people.

Acknowledgments to the Revised Edition

The Johns Hopkins University Press is owed a debt of gratitude for its recognition of *The Tree of Liberty*'s unique character and its classic potential as a record of the role of rebellion and political militance in the creation and democratic development of the United States. Particular thanks are due to the press's director, Willis Regier; former director, Jack Goellner; associate director, Doug Armato; and executive editor, Henry Tom. Our deep appreciation is due also to Miriam Kleiger, senior manuscript editor. To make the volume more readily available to history and politics enthusiasts and to facilitate its use as a sourcebook for classroom instruction, this new, updated, and enlarged edition appears in a two-volume paperback edition as well as in a one-volume hardcover edition.

The editors wish to express their deep appreciation to Dean Claudio Grossman and to former dean Elliott Milstein, of American University's Washington College of Law, for the further nourishing of this project. Asnat Davidi, Sharon Maerten, and Lesley Rein, all students at the law school, earned our thanks for their thorough and dedicated research and editing work. Donna Bradley, Elma Gates, Robert Kelso, Christopher Stearns, and Mark Williams, members of the law school staff, carried out the complex production and copying tasks under great pressure and with great devotion.

Alan Fisher, a recent graduate of the Washington College of Law who is currently an attorney working for the United States government, is gratefully acknowledged both as an active participant in and as the chief coordinator of all the research, writing, and editing connected with the preparation of this revised edition.

Georgette J. Sobel has earned special recognition for her selfless and tireless care and feeding of the participating "troops," as well as her timely and exceptional carrying out of all requisite coordination and managerial duties.

Acknowledgments

This collection was initiated in 1980 during a visiting fellowship extended to Dr. Kittrie by the National Institute of Justice of the United States Department of Justice. A previous grant to him by the National Endowment for the Humanities, in 1973, helped in the initial planting of the seeds for this project. Warm thanks are due to our colleagues at the National Endowment for the Humanities and the National Institute for Justice, particularly Winifred L. Reed and Patrick Langan, for their professional challenges, material support, and personal confidence. Several research assistants worked loyally with Dr. Kittrie in the collection of and commentary on these documents. Patrice Fitzgerald, William Pesch, Eric Pomeranz, Elizabeth Buck, and Daniel B. Seferian are owed a particular debt of gratitude. Beth Levenson, a recent graduate of the American University Law School, carried out the demanding final tasks of review and editing. Several seminar groups at the American University both utilized and analyzed earlier versions of these materials. For their commentary we wish to express our thanks to Mary Schwemle, Jill Rosenfeld, Bob Burkholder, George May, Richard Cohen, Ruth Jamison, May Farber, Tony Bornstein, Ingrid Yellick, Rick Gondelman, Sara Chenetz, Rick Lazio, Tom Kass, Steven Kantor, Keith Costa, Jessica Indig, Karen Shapiro, William Sharp, Bruce Waterhouse, Linda Harrison, Bruce Bender, Joy Schwan, and Sharon Gross. Dean Thomas Buergenthal of the American University has nourished the project, recognizing its contributions to the cause of human rights, and Professor Burton D. Wechsler generously shared with us his sensitive understanding of constitutional law and history. Thanks are also due to Dean Harry M. Lightsey, Jr., and the University of South Carolina for continuing staff and service support to Professor Wedlock during his sabbatical. Finally, we must express our gratitude to Michal R. Belknap of the University of Georgia for a thorough and critical review of the manuscript, to Henry Tom and Carol Ehrlich of the Johns Hopkins University Press for their invaluable editorial contributions, and to Georgette J. Sobel for her untiring effort in supervising the technical production of this volume. Professor Henry Steele Commager supplied enthusiastic encouragement for the comprehensive breadth of this undertaking. Shirley Green was responsible for the creative character of the historical photographs and illustrations; Stina C. Wedlock assisted with the graphic research; and Jonathan Dolger supplied invaluable assistance as the editors' literary agent. Recognition is due also to Norda and Zachary Kittrie for their assistance with the Bibliography and to Elizabeth Kelne and Mary Wason for carrying out the complex typing and photocopying tasks.

Introduction

The terms *political crime* and *political criminals* are rarely found in the American literature of the social and political sciences, history, criminology, or law. In 1979, *Webster's New Collegiate Dictionary* for the first time defined the political criminal as one "involv[ed] or charged . . . with acts against the government or a political system." This obviously impoverished definition provides a point of departure for the subject matter of this book.

Political criminals need not necessarily engage in acts; their crimes might be their failure to perform legally imposed duties. Failure to swear allegiance or to register for the draft is such a crime. Speech or writing concerning a prohibited subject matter can be criminal. The crimes of sedition and treason are examples. To be political a crime need not seek to overthrow the government or to depose its leaders. Proposing change or attempting reform of entrenched political policies, such as the advocacy of liberty for blacks and the exercise of the franchise by women, may be criminal.

To comprehend political criminality, one must view the term *political* quite liberally. Many actions or omissions motivated by religious, economic, social, or racial concerns may be perceived as threatening the political authority of the state. The recent refusal by Christian ministers in Nebraska to submit their schools to certification by the secular government resulted in court injunctions and the arrests of the offending fundamentalists. Moreover, even an offense against nongovernmental institutions, persons, or practices may be deemed political. Violence or even discrimination against an ethnic or racial group, as well as a proscribed labor strike or picketing against a private employer, can be perceived as a political crime when those in power see such conduct as undermining the political stability of the state.

A political offender, finally, need not be charged with a crime or be dealt with through criminal sanctions. Politically suspect individuals may be subjected to other burdens and liabilities. Restrictions on public employment and officeholding have been impcsed not only on Communists but on others whose allegiance to the government was in doubt. Limitations on travel and association, curfew, and exile have been applied not only to the Japanese-Americans during World War II but also to Native Americans throughout our national history.

We have sought in this collection to bring together materials that broadly survey these various aspects of political crime. Our task has been complicated by the fact that the conventional vision of American history and growth strongly rejects the utility of studying the meaning and role of political criminality. Given the paucity of discussion and analysis of the concept of political criminality among American scholars, we have chosen to proceed in a broad exploratory fashion, without a strict definition. We have developed, in the lexicon of the mathematicians, an open rather than a closed set of materials. The boundary of the open set is indefinite, vague, amorphous, and indiscernible, while in the latter it is definitively fixed and firm. It may be possible sometime in the future to elaborate a precise and complete definition of political crime, but to do so at this point in our knowledge would be to truncate prematurely the investigation of this important arena.

Pilgrims in the Promised Land

The story of America's success in molding a pluralistic society has been told and retold in numerous variations. Most accounts have sought out or dwelled on harmonizing elements and influences. Few have viewed the initial hardships or the continuing internal conflicts as more than temporary roadblocks and digressions on the path toward national unity. Yet one may advance the thesis that America's unique success and its peculiar sensitivity to questions of justice and equality stem from the stress of this historical adversity and strife. It is therefore with no apologies that this account of America's internal tensions and upheavals is presented.

Severe challenges confronted the first English settlers on these shores. When in December of 1606 three small ships—the *Susan Constant*, the *Godspeed*, and the *Discovery*—sailed down the Thames River on their way to settle the distant colony of Virginia, storms prevented them from promptly leaving the English Channel. Numbering approximately 105 men, not including the crews of the three ships, the Virginia settlers later made several stops in the Canaries and in the islands of the West Indies, further delaying their arrival in the New World and diminishing their stores of supplies.

From their very first landing on a spring day in 1607, the settlers, in addition to battling the physical and economic hardships of colonizing a wilderness (for which the gentlemen-adventurers were ill prepared), became embroiled in constant political strife. Natives attacked an exploring party of the English empire builders even before they had selected a place for their permanent colony. Within the first year, George Kendall, one of the seven councillors initially put in charge of the colony by King James's authority, was charged, convicted, and shot for conspiring against the colony. In 1622, the struggling colony was almost obliterated during a mass Indian uprising in which more than 350 white settlers of all ages and both sexes perished (blacks were left unharmed). In 1635 long-brewing controversies between the settlers, their council, and their governor, Sir John Harvey, appointed by the Crown, erupted into open revolt. The critics of the governor and leaders of the opposition were arrested on the governor's orders and were held to be tried under martial law. In the ensuing confrontation with the council, the governor charged a councillor with treason against His Majesty the King. The council summoned forty musketeers previously planted around the chamber into action, and the conflict did not subside until Governor Harvey departed in haste for England— this possibly constituting the first coup d'état in the new colonies. Indeed, not until after the bloody suppression of the popular rebellion of 1676, commanded by Nathaniel Bacon, an aristocratic Cambridge-educated member of the council who led opposition to another royal governor, did Virginia achieve a temporary political respite.[1]

The pattern of remonstrance, rebellion, and response was evident elsewhere in the colonies, if not as dramatically so. It culminated in two civil wars and several insurrections. Challenges to constituted authority in America and the government's need to mold timely response continued with every wave of immigration, with every thrust westward, with every stage in economic development, with every new assertion of racial, gender, or class claims, and with every American involvement in conflicts beyond its boundaries. This volume presents the evidentiary record for the thesis that political criminality is an integral part of an ongoing historical process of challenge and response which accounts for many of the liberties and for much of the societal diversity for which America is most admired.

The Denial of Political Crime in America

Dissent, protest, disobedience, violence, and rebellion—in pursuit of political change or in opposition to it—have been major forces in the recent history of the nations of the world. This compilation is the first comprehensive documentation of the historical causes and outcomes—from the colonial period to the present—of the political struggle by individuals and groups in America against governmental authority. Although many excellent documentary histories of particular reformist or activist movements and of the United States generally exist, they are either too narrow in the former case or too broad in the latter. The common trends among all resisters to authority—as well as repeated patterns of governmental response—are not treated; or if they are, tend to be lost.

Problems of definition and historical diffusion greatly complicated the task of researching, documenting, and analyzing, under the rubric of political criminality, the phenomena that constitute the core events in this book. One frequently encounters events of political turmoil, kidnappings, bombings, and terrorism in other countries. One is often exposed to the campaigns of the International Red Cross or Amnesty International on behalf of political prisoners elsewhere. But reference to "political crimes and criminals in America" usually brings a puzzled look to the faces of an American audience. Presenting the notion that the concept of political crime might have a place in American social science or law brings forth either a denial of the validity of the concept or the opposite assertion that all crimes are at root political. Neither of these responses is particularly helpful in assessing or addressing the very real problems associated with the existence of unorthodox political beliefs or with the resort to unlawful methods for attaining political ends.

Despite the inability of the public, the social sciences, or the law to articulate some general, neutral, and acceptable definitions of the phenomenon, the archives of United States history are full of evidence of political violence and struggle from the beginning of this continent's colonization. The public's lingering suspicion that political crime—however inadequate its definition—indeed exists in our midst has been fed further by a series of governmental measures designed to combat "royalists," "traitors," "seditionists," "political prisoners," "anarchists," "syndicalists," "communists," and other breeds of dissidents.

Nevertheless, Americans have long adhered to the contradictory belief that the history of this country has differed radically, and for the better, from the heritage of the less civilized countries and even that of other Western nations. Europe, despite its advanced civilization, was conceded to have had a violent foundation and a convulsive history. In both scholarly and public opinion it is admitted, therefore, that

> [a]s comforting as it is for civilized people to think of barbarians as violent and of violence as barbarian, Western civilization and various forms of collective violence have always been close partners. . . . Historically, collective violence has flowed regularly out of the central political processes of Western countries. . . . The oppressed have struck in the name of justice, the privileged in the name of order, those in between in the name of fear. Great shifts in the arrangements of [European] power have ordinarily produced—and have often depended on—exceptional movements of collective violence.[2]

In contrast, both political leaders and social commentators have painted the United States as being endowed with a manifest destiny and a distinct governmental style. "[A]mericans since the Puritans have historically regarded themselves as a latter-day 'chosen people' sent on a holy errand to the wilderness, there to create a new Jerusalem," wrote historian Hugh Davis Graham and political scientist Ted Robert Gurr.[3] On the new continent settlers were to attain the Peaceable Kingdom, the restored Eden that nineteenth-century American

painter Edward Hicks so frequently portrayed. Within its boundaries the true realization of Isaiah's prophetic promise was to occur. "The wolf and lamb shall feed together, and the lion shall eat straw like the bullock; and dust shall be the serpent's food. They shall not hurt nor destroy in all my holy mountain. . . ."[4]

With characteristic faith and optimism the American nation—said by Benjamin Franklin to be founded by the design of providence to cultivate the new earth[5]—was believed to be the agent of destiny in the realization of humanity's utopian ideals and progress. There developed, concurrently, what historian Richard E. Rubenstein called "The Myth of Peaceful Progress."[6] The myth professed that the United States, alone among nations, was the place in which extremely diverse groups had learned to compromise their differences peaceably. American society, it was held, had been blessed by a blurring of divisions between its multiple economic, social, political, and ethnic groups. This achievement was attributed to a combination of factors, including the fertility of the land and the richness of its resources, the tendency of the people to be hardworking, the fact that neither a true aristocracy nor an impoverished proletariat grew roots on this soil, and finally, the ability of the Constitution and the two-party system to provide an ideal instrument for political compromise. There was a general conviction that "any sizeable domestic group could gain its proper share of power, prosperity and respectability merely by playing the game according to the rules."[7] In an America which had, through the design of destiny, constitutional doctrines, and pragmatic politics, perfected the unique art of peaceful power sharing and transference, so necessary for continuing change and progress, there was no need for violent political, social, or economic conflicts.

But the riots in the urban ghettoes and the student and Vietnam-connected unrest of the 1960s produced an awareness of the uses of political dissent and violence and a revision of the traditional or change-through-consensus view of United States history. When black activist H. Rap Brown asserted that mass political violence was "as American as apple pie," the public was shocked. Serious scholars, however, soon joined in debunking the myth of peaceful progress. The Reverend Theodore Parker's voice was a daring and lonely one when he proclaimed in 1848: "We are a rebellious nation; our whole history is treason; our blood was attainted before we were born." Yet, well over a century later, prominent historians and social scientists have embraced his claim.

"For more than two hundred years . . . the United States has experienced regular episodes of serious mass violence related to the social, political, and economic objectives of insurgent groups," Richard E. Rubenstein asserted.[8] The Staff Report to the National Commission on the Causes and Prevention of Violence reached similar conclusions. There has been a vast amount of violence, pointed out the report, "connected with some of the most constructive, positive, and indeed, among the noblest chapters in our national history."[9] But some of the most ignoble, destructive, and undemocratic chapters of American history have likewise been connected with political violence, disorder, and subversion.

The Founding Fathers were political offenders all. But although traitors in contemporary English judgment, they were patriots in their own eyes and in the subsequent view of history. This resort to illegal or extralegal political means, however, did not come to an end in America with the founding of the new nation or the Republic. Crimes committed for political ends manifested by rebellions, treasons, assassinations, homicides, hostage taking, bomb throwings, seditions, draft evasions, and widespread civil disobedience have influenced and continue to affect dramatically the political life of the nation.

Despite America's virtually unbroken tradition of political dissent, crime, and violence, American criminal law and jurisprudence, following the dictum of English Common Law, refuse to take account of assertions of political motive, ideology, conviction, or demands of conscience as a justification, excuse, or defense. Obscured by the precept of criminal law that only intent to commit the prohibited act is important and that motive—evil or benign—has no bearing on guilt, political criminality has not been recognized by the American police, courts, or corrections system as a unique category of offenses.

This has resulted in a failure formally to accord political offenders a differential standing and treatment by the government and its agencies. Thus, while the laws of most European countries, as well as international law generally, grant political offenders a special and "honorable" status—by virtue of which they are exempted from demeaning penalties and from international extradition—the domestic law of the United States has continued to view political offenders no differently from common criminals. The argument that one was acting for a political motive or in adherence to the demands of a higher law or the values of one's conscience and beliefs has not officially penetrated American jurisprudence.

Author Brendan Behan, in his autobiographical *Borstal Boy*, reflected on this peculiarly Anglo-Saxon anomaly. As an adolescent Behan was active with the Irish Republican Army. After his arrest he was placed in confinement together with common offenders. To this he responded: "I knew . . . it was the usual hypocrisy of the English not giving anyone political treatment, and then being able to say that alone among the empires she had no political prisoners."[10]

American law and the American criminal justice system never have denominated any portion of the country's massive criminal problem as "political crime." Even though the only crime defined in the United States Constitution, treason, is a political offense, neither this nor the other criminal offenses erected and used to preserve political order and governmental authority have ever been so designated. Never have these offenses been grouped together for common consideration, analysis, or criticism. Indeed, for a long time the country's legal and criminal justice experts failed to profess any interest in this compelling subject. So little concern have Anglo-American criminal justice scholars manifested for political criminality that when renowned Italian criminologist Cesare Lombroso published his major study of political and revolutionary offenses in 1890 (*Il Delitto Politico e le Rivoluzioni*), the topic was considered so irrelevant that no English translation was undertaken.

Neither a Nation of Lawlessness nor One of Oppression

American law's resistance to any doctrine of political criminality is not surprising. The colonies were conceived in political exile; the nation was born of treason and midwifed by violent revolution. From the perspectives of stability and political order, the United States has not overcome the fear of the skeletons in its closet. It is no wonder that to counter the lessons of its own origins, responsible leaders and politicians fostered the dogma that all evils of the past were the result of the tyrannical monarch, that in a democratic republic obedience to the law was the unquestionable duty of all citizens, and that existing political mechanisms were ample for peaceful reform. The proposition that ends might sometimes justify extralegal means became an intolerable heresy. Nevertheless, our national original sin was never quite expiated, and as is eminently apparent from the materials in this collection, extralegal, illegal, and violent methods are significant factors in weaving freedom, justice, and equality into the fabric of the American social order.

American law over the years has responded vigorously to real as well as to imagined challenges to authority. The law has prohibited various types of political or politically-motivated conduct—from treason and sedition to the education of blacks, from the advocacy of anarchy to voting by women, from office-holding by Communists to picketing and striking by workers, from interstate and international travel by dissidents and subversives to continued residence by suspect aliens and citizens. Diverse mechanisms and criminal or quasi-criminal sanctions for the control of political offenses and the punishment of political offenders likewise have been established. Federal and state laws have relied not only on penal sanctions but also on loyalty oaths, security investigations, the exclusion and expulsion of politically suspect aliens, the calling up of the military, the imposition of martial law, and the confinement of suspect populations in special camps as tools to maintain political order.

Political offenses in America have not necessarily consisted of overt actions. Failure to act, when required under law, has oftentimes constituted an offense. The law not only has prohibited direct opposition or attacks upon the state (by traitors, secessionists, or anarchists) but also has sanctioned those unwilling to render active service or offer verbal adherence to the state and its endeavors (conscientious objectors, refusers of loyalty oaths, and the like). From time to time the state has sought to protect not only its own agencies but also the interests of its power elites. Criminal penalties as well as court injunctions were utilized to ward off attacks against the Southern institution of human bondage and the Northern menace of labor organization. At times the people's resort to rights now considered guaranteed under the Constitution (freedom of speech, assembly, and association) were punished as sedition and criminal conspiracy. Finally, and frequently, political offenses have consisted of nothing more than the very act of being. Singled out on the basis of gender, color, race, ethnicity, or nationality, some populations were selected for adverse treatment—through criminal or other state sanctions—because of their perceived collective threat. Native Americans, blacks, women, and Japanese-Americans thus became political offenders by virtue of their nature rather than their deeds.

Unlike its doctrine, in actual implementation the American justice system frequently has differentiated between political offenses and offenders and common ones. Offenders motivated by political, ideological, or other convictions sometimes have been granted certain benefits, usually through the executive rather than the judicial agencies of government. Most amnesties and pardons granted by American presidents have been issued for the benefit of former political offenders—especially those who criminally resisted the prosecution of international wars or participated in domestic insurrections or civil wars. But differentiation has not necessarily resulted in more lax or benevolent treatment. From time to time, the political nature of the offense has triggered harsher sanctions and more oppressive policing measures. Through reliance on either explicit or implicit constitutional authority, the executive has employed measures against political offenders which are impermissible in the struggle against common crime, including suspension of the writ of habeas corpus, imposition of martial law, use of the militia for quelling mass disorders, trial by military tribunals without the protection of the Bill of Rights, the exclusion of civilian populations from militarily proclaimed defense zones, and the undertaking of comprehensive surveillance programs against suspect populations, without compliance with the warrant requirement or other constitutional safeguards.

We set out to thoroughly collect documents surrounding the major events and actors of political criminality in the United States, whether manifested in purely political or in social, economic, religious, racial, or gender struggles.

The resulting sourcebook unequivocally demonstrates that the vigorous pursuit of life, liberty, and happiness has been a particular and ongoing undertaking of the American people beginning even before the nation's independence. Given endorsement by the Declaration of Independence, this pursuit has not always been satisfied with the available legally prescribed methods for political action and change. American history reflects frequent and continuing resort to unlawful means for political ends. Yet, despite this constant dissidence and fervor, America has become neither a nation of lawlessness nor one of oppression. Instead, spurred by the people's constant vigilance for liberty and equality and protected from severe oppressions of government, many competing nations, ideologies, races, religions, and economic systems have found here their best haven in the memory of human history.

Approaches to a Definition: Conflicts of Allegiance

The definitional problem of political crime has troubled the editors no less than others, and we do not attempt to present a complete solution to it. Instead, we have sought to provide in one collection basic materials from which further research and reflection may lead to a better understanding, if not a consensus, about political crime in the United States. Of course, the process of selecting documents requires that some parameters be set, and some preliminary analysis is in order.

It may be that an objective and neutral definition of political crime is impossible, because the term seems to involve relativistic relationships between the motives and acts of individuals and the perspectives of government toward their conduct and allegiances. Thus, on the one hand, an individual may claim to be committing acts of violence against the state out of political motivations but be relegated to the status of common criminal by the government. On the other hand, an individual may profess firm allegiance to the state yet be subjected to the pains and penalties of criminality because the government perceives his status or professed ideals to be inimical to its interests. Sometimes the perspectives of the parties coalesce, and a common agreement that particular people are political criminals is reached.

Furthermore, a third party, a neutral country or an eye detached from events by the distance of time, may designate particular activity as a political offense.

Another complication in any attempt to define political criminality revolves around the nature of the act that makes up the crime. Mere membership by birth in a suspect population, or voluntary adherence to a proscribed political party, may suffice as an "act." More frequently, engaging in prohibited speech or, conversely, refusal to swear an oath of allegiance may cause the application of criminal penalties. All these nonviolent activities are usually referred to, in international law, as pure political offenses. In addition, there are common criminal acts, such as murder, assault, and kidnapping, which, when directed against political figures and motivated by political goals, are known as complex political crimes. Finally, there are criminal acts perpetrated against innocent and private parties, allegedly for the purpose of sustaining, financing, or publicizing political opposition, and whose connection with political goals or change is tangential at best.

It should always be remembered that unlike a strict documentary history of a well-defined topic or phenomenon, this collection is charting new territory. Many of the entries relate to incidents that do not result in a direct resort to traditional criminal laws and sanctions; there are documents that relate to activities that many would consider primarily economic, racial, or social rather than political; there are documents regarding unsuccessful attempts by government to regulate conduct and to impose sanctions upon the nonconforming; and there are memoirs, speeches, letters, and other communications intended to give insights into the political offender and his or her pursuits. Not all of these appear immediately and obviously connected with political criminality. However, they all contribute to the understanding of the roles and methods of political criminals and the reciprocal governmental attempts, through resort to penal as well as nonpenal sanctions, to control them.

The power and compulsion of the state have also operated, and do operate, through sanctions other than those contained in penal codes, such as capital or corporal punishment, restraint of liberty, and fines. In many cases exclusion, expulsion, exile, curfews, confiscation, confinement, and diverse licensing burdens become the tools of the coercive power of the state. The withdrawal of passports and licenses and the withholding of eligibility for officeholding, voting, and government employment are resorted to, in addition, to enforce governmentally prescribed norms. The use of restraining orders and civil injunctions further serves to expand the state's coercion into areas of economic and social conflict such as labor and racial disputes. Indeed, in its warfare against political criminality the state possesses the particularly dangerous option of making selective use of these alternative approaches, rather than relying solely on criminal sanctions, for the attainment of its ends.

Economic, social, and racial dissent often is the vanguard of political criminality. Materials relating to the preliminary stages of societal ferment are necessary to establish the matrix from which political criminality arises. After the methods of peaceful change are exhausted (and sometimes before), the proponents of reform often turn to extralegal activity and rebellion. But even before that point is reached, oftentimes the government, in an abundance of caution, takes upon itself the burden of extinguishing even the mildest voices for reform, making otherwise innocuous activities criminal. Prohibiting the education of blacks, making the distribution of abolitionist literature illegal, and proscribing the display of the red flag all fall within this category. Political criminality can thus arise from the most passive manifestations.

The importance of a government's attempt, albeit eventually unsuccessful, to make some political activity illegal must not be overlooked. Many of the selected materials relate to failed efforts to limit political activism and opposition, and we should be alert to the reasons for these failures. In these materials are contained the seeds of a methodology for understanding the processes whereby the state power combating political crime has been constrained in the United States. It is also important to identify these failed state efforts, because in many instances they have continued in effect for long periods of time, exerting a "chilling effect" upon the struggle for political and civil rights in this country.

Ultimately, political crime arises from perceived irreconcilable conflicts of allegiance. Individuals may profess an adherence to different racial, religious, ethnic, familial, or economic

groups. There may be philosophical, ethical, social, or political ideals that claim one's attention and passion as well. The need to balance the claims of the various allegiances and ideals is left mostly to the conscience and conduct of the individual. Inevitably, however, conflicts will arise between the central principles and requirements of the different groups making claims upon the individual. The more pluralistic a society is, the more likely these conflicts are. For the most part, these conflicts are resolved within the privacy of the individual's conscience or through efforts within or between groups to remove incompatibilities. Individuals, alternatively, may be expelled from or choose to abandon one or more of the incompatible groups. While often deeply troubling to the individuals involved, the resolution of these conflicts is, nevertheless, generally an informal and private matter.

The conflict of allegiances cannot be as easily resolved when it involves the state. Having access to the power of the law to compel obedience and adherence to its norms, the state is usually unwilling to tolerate an accommodation with a conflicting allegiance. Thus, when an individual to whose allegiance the state makes a claim is confronted with an uncompromisable conflict between the demands of the state and the principles of another group or belief, an informal compromise is not possible. The state demands total obedience and frequently exacts punishment not only for the betrayal but even for doubting the primacy of the allegiance owed to it.

In nation-states evolving from relatively homogeneous ethnic, linguistic, racial, and cultural societies, conflicts of allegiances may not be too evident. In the more recently created nations, where populations may have little in common other than that they share geographical boundaries designated by colonial powers, conflicts may be all too common. The United States is lodged midway between these categories, and this collection well documents the process whereby conflicts of allegiance were resolved in a New World composed of a variety of peoples with many conflicting affiliations and aspirations.

There are in this collection at least two categories of documents that flow unambiguously from conflicts with the demands of the state. Ironically, they represent the opposite ends of the continuum of criminal conduct: the passive type manifested in refusals to offer service demanded by the state (conscientious objection, draft resistance, failing to swear allegiance) and the aggressive type reflecting direct attack upon the state in the interest of a competing group or allegiance (treason, secession, anarchy).

The conflict of allegiances may manifest itself in yet other ways. This collection offers several instances of special state controls and sanctions against groups identified by some attributes that cast doubts upon the political "maturity," "patriotism," or commitment of their members to the state. Slaves, blacks, Native Americans, Japanese-Americans, Communists, and women have been so singled out and thus qualify for attention and study in a volume on political crime. State sanctions and disabilities have been imposed upon these groups whether or not individual members have committed discrete offenses against the law. For an understanding of the reaches of political crime it is important not to confuse one phenomenon, the punishment of individual violations of laws, with the other, the oppression of peoples whose allegiance to the status quo is suspect. While there is a certain interrelationship in a causal sense between actors against the regime and dissatisfied groups who may precipitate such actions, the two are different phenomena. Important items on the agenda of research and analysis in the new arena of political criminality are the connections and disconnections between these distinct manifestations of political crime.

Finally, some of the materials in this collection document the uses of criminal and other state sanctions in upholding certain widely (but not universally) shared principles, ideals, or even biases that might be challenged in the nation's social and economic evolutionary process. The resort to criminal and noncriminal sanctions for the suppression of labor organizations and strikes, the preservation of abolition of slavery and racial discrimination, the prohibition or permission of abortions, illustrate the practice of recruiting the state as arbiter of intracommunity value conflicts. Unlike the earlier classifications, these materials do not deal directly with the issues of allegiance. Instead, they reflect political and legal structures that permit certain groups or interests to utilize the compulsory and sanctioning power of the state to bear upon groups not sharing their particular interests or practices. The documents reflecting the struggles of labor and the civil rights movement fall within this category.

Rebels, Reformers, Madmen, and Renegades

The study of political criminality in large measure brings together the investigation of two unorthodoxies—unorthodox politics and unorthodox crimes. To students of politics, the political offender is one who deviates from the orthodox or authorized political procedures in order to secure his ends. Since legitimate means of political action have varied throughout the history of the United States, a deviant is a person who resorts to political methods beyond those recognized by the positive law at any given period of time. A political criminal of one period or place therefore may not constitute an offender at another time or location. Yet despite this definitional relativism, the existing authorities continue to prevent and punish criminally any such political unorthodoxy and deviations from the permissible.

Criminologists characterize political offenders as unorthodox criminals, for they often admit to violation of the positive law but deny guilt and culpability—professing adherence to values higher than, or transcending those served by, the law. Political criminals lay claim to the authority of justice and morality, which ordinarily is presumed to lie behind the law. In their unorthodoxy they disown the egotistic mantle of the common criminal and assert the altruistic goal of the social reformer. To counteract this heroic stance, the government often seeks deliberately to trivialize and personalize the goals and deeds of political offenders.

Because of this, we have gone beyond the official portrayal of political offenders and their offenses, as contained in legislation, administrative rulings, and judicial cases, and have sought to elucidate the motivations and present the self-images of those acting in opposition to authority. These considerations dictated the inclusion, among the more traditional historical and legal sources, of materials that reflect sociological, psychological, and philosophical perspectives.

A corollary problem is posed by the instinctive urge for either deification or vilification of political criminality and criminals. The law's failure to recognize the existence of the political offender, or to respond to his or her offer of noble motives, perversely translates into a negative comment upon the system of justice and its punishment of someone who might popularly be accepted as acting for the common good. But it is important to divorce the judgments of morality and history from the day-to-day questions posed by political criminality. Political criminals have been both heroes and villains upon the stage of politics. Thus we have George Washington, traitor to his king, and Benedict Arnold, recanting his treason and adhering once again to his sovereign lord; John Brown, leader of an armed raid upon the armory of the United States at Harpers Ferry, seeking to incite a slave rebellion, and Jefferson Davis, constitutional scholar and leader of the rebellion against the Union. There are other colorful figures in the play as well: Susan B. Anthony, confined to prison for her militant urging of women's suffrage; Eugene V. Debs, labor leader, disobedient to court injunctions and underminer of the World War I effort; Martin Luther King, Jr., leading unlawful demonstrations in Selma, Alabama; Philip Berrigan and Daniel Ellsberg, who broke the law to expose what they saw as the truth about the Vietnam War; Julius and Ethel Rosenberg, convicted of communicating atom bomb secrets to the Soviet Union; and Philip Agee, who sought to divulge the names of America's secret agents abroad. But however these figures ultimately are disposed of by the judgment of the ages, their activities at first glance meet the criteria of political crimes, although it might be said in some cases that such status is tenuous.

Resistance to "oppressive" taxes and to military conscription provided a rich source of political criminality in earlier American history, but can the modern tax protest movement or the opposition to Selective Service registration be so considered? And then there are the psychiatrically borderline assassins—John Wilkes Booth, Sirhan Sirhan, Arthur Bremer, and John Hinckley. Can their crimes be called political?

In eschewing an attempt at definitiveness, we have preferred to err on the side of inclusion rather than exclusion. Since this is not a doctrinaire thesis but an exploratory sourcebook, we urge readers to develop their own views and conclusions as to the meaning of the materials. But we believe that a thorough review will demonstrate that the concept of political crime is not without content, and that we have

cause to regret that the peculiar problems it presents have not, heretofore, been addressed in a dispassionate manner. As the nation moves ahead and encounters new challenges to the existing order, we would do well to have a firmer grasp than we currently do on the role and limits of political crime and the government's response to it.

First, admitting and then understanding our own record of political dissent, disobedience, protest, and violence also may help reshape our perception of political turmoil in other nations. We have frequently been appalled and our foreign policy thrown into imbalance by the sight of internal disruptions in other countries. Our own myth of peaceful change has obscured our vision and made us insensitive and intolerant to the complex moral as well as pragmatic issues raised by the conflict between just ends and unlawful means in a less than perfect world. A more realistic assessment of our past might aid not only in understanding internal conflicts in other places but in the shaping of a more consistent, just, and pragmatic American position in the international arena.

Two characteristics of American political dissent and criminality unambiguously emerge from these materials. First, the resort to unorthodox and extralegal political means in America may be described generally as a manifestation of a reformist rather than an insurrectionary mission. Political disorder in this country has usually been directed to modifying the use of power by government, not overthrowing it.[11] Moreover, much of our political violence, as pointed out by historian Richard Hofstadter, "has taken the form of action by one group of citizens against another group rather than by citizens against the State."[12] When governmental authority is enlisted to defend one group's interests, the strife usually changes from social or economic to political. Undoubtedly the political diffusion and the governmental decentralization of America, coupled with the notion that it is not the government's structure but its abusers that must be guarded against, have caused public dissatisfaction and political crimes to be directed not so much against "government" itself but against its "agents," its subdivisions, or individuals and groups representing some social, political, or economic "establishment" or power base.

Second, this book demonstrates the constant yet dramatic shift from rebellions, violent assemblies, and direct action to militant advocacy in the legislative halls and particularly in the courts. This may be described as a progression from militant deeds to litigiousness. The dominance of judicial cases in the second part of this volume is testimony of this trend.

Finally, the collection readily demonstrates that the ascendancy of nationalism and self-determination cannot be counted on to produce an end to political turmoil and violent fervor, in this country or elsewhere. From the war-like beginnings of Swiss independence and the American revolution to Garibaldi's and the Irish campaigns against foreign rule, and on to the contemporary struggles for national liberation, self-determination rarely has been achieved without illegal and violent means. Yet the hope that once self-determination and self-rule are attained, political continuity and change would be achieved through peaceful means has not been fulfilled in most countries. Discontented political, regional, tribal, ethnic, religious, lingual, economic, and racial factions frequently have set out to accomplish their unsatisfied claims through acts of dissent, subversion, violence, and rebellion, and the record of the present day shows no improvement.

Since they attained independence, during the post-World War II years, some two-thirds of Africa's forty-five nations have seen their regimes toppled by unlawful or extralegal means. In Latin America fourteen out of twenty-eight existing governments have come into power through means other than those constitutionally prescribed. Central America, in particular, has become the virtual powder keg of unor-

thodox political activism. Manifestations of political strife and disorder are evident, not only in Africa, Latin America, and Asia, but also among the European nations claiming long and established traditions of relatively peaceful political life and transition. Basques in Spain, Corsican zealots in France, ethnic dissidents in Yugoslavia, royalist insurgents in Albania, Scottish Nationalists in the United Kingdom, the Red Brigade in Italy, the Bader-Meinhof group in West Germany, and the IRA in Northern Ireland are a mere sampling of the diverse political activists in contemporary Europe.

Although comparisons are inherently suspect, we believe that these materials demonstrate that our experience with manifestations of political crime is not wholly unlike that of other nations. Thus it may be that careful analysis of the treatment of political offenders in foreign countries would be useful in forging a principled American response to domestic political crime. The similarity suggests also that the study of our experience might be fruitful for others, for despite our definitional myopia, our inability to achieve the Peaceable Kingdom, and our failure to solve internal problems without resort to unlawfulness and violence, the stern and severe governmental responses thereto have stayed within civilized boundaries and have never thrown this nation into a reign of terror or long-term irreversible oppression—such as occurred in revolutionary France, in the twentieth-century Soviet Union, Nazi Germany, and Fascist Italy, and in an increasing number of post-World War II regimes worldwide.

---

1. Virginius Dabney, *Virginia: The New Dominion* (Garden City, N.Y.: Doubleday, 1971), 1-68.

2. Charles Tilly, "Collective Violence in European Perspective," in National Commission on the Causes and Prevention of Violence, vol. 1, *Violence in America: Historical and Comparative Perspectives* (Washington, D.C.: U.S. Government Printing Office, 1969), 5.

3. Hugh Davis Graham and Ted Robert Gurr, "Conclusion," in vol. 2, *Violence in America*, 624. *See* n. 2, above.

4. Isaiah 65:25.

5. Rollo May, *Power and Innocence: A Search for the Sources of Violence* (New York: Norton, 1972), 51.

6. Richard E. Rubenstein, *Rebels in Eden: Mass Political Violence in the United States* (Boston: Little, Brown, 1970), 2.

7. Id., 5.

8. Id., 7.

9. Richard Maxwell Brown, "Historical Patterns in Violence in America," in vol. 1, *Violence in America*, 35. *See* n. 2, above.

10. Brendan Behan, *Borstal Boy* (New York: Knopf, 1959), 271.

11. National Advisory Committee on Criminal Justice Standards and Goals, *Disorders and Terrorism* (Washington, D.C.: U.S. Government Printing Office, 1977), 1.

12. Richard Hofstadter and Michael Wallace, eds., *American Violence: A Documentary History* (New York: Vintage Books, 1971), 10.

Note to Readers and Users

This comprehensive collection offers a historical survey of political criminality (including rebellion and terrorism) and of governmental responses to it in America. The comprehensive approach—which brings together instances of political, social, economic, racial, gender, and religious unrest—is designed to permit discussion and analysis of the common issues raised by various types and forms of political crime.

The chapters as well as the documents in this sourcebook have been organized in chronological order. Only the last three chapters (Chap. 11, "Contemporary Political Conflicts and Domestic Security," Chap. 12, "International Terrorism and Human Rights," and Chap. 13, "Towards the Third Millennium") depart from this pattern. To permit special attention to a number of major contemporary issues (such as government secrecy and related questions of domestic security, or topics raised by the growth of international political criminality), these two chapters have been set apart and include documents that otherwise would have been treated in previous chapters.

Although the ordering of the material is chronological, special efforts were made by the editors to permit the volume's ready utilization by those primarily or exclusively interested in specific issues relating to political crime. To simplify the task of the reader and user who seeks information about a particular topic (e.g., the status of Native Americans or the requirement of loyalty oaths), a subject-matter guide (Concordance), is supplied in addition to the more traditional Proper Name Index and the Table of Cases at the back of the volume. The Concordance is a compilation of major concepts and subjects, each followed by a list of documents (designated by number). For example, one interested in civil disobedience could find all the documents treating the subject listed under that heading. In addition, each document is likely to be listed under more than one heading. A document dealing with the status of blacks, for instance, might appear both under "Blacks, Slavery, and Civil Rights" and "Advocacy of Unlawful Acts or Disobedience to Law." The Concordance headings, moreover, seek to bring together many related subjects. For example, executive clemency is treated under the heading "Amnesty, Pardon, and Clemency." Cross-references are provided for the user's convenience.

Abridgment

Most of the documents have been abridged. Asterisks indicate deletions of one or more paragraphs—or, in some instances, several pages. The editors sought in these abridgments to maintain the historical flavor of the original writings. Nevertheless, since the goal of this collection has been to focus the reader's attention on matters relating to political dissent and disorder, material extraneous to these ends was deleted.

Legal Materials—Cases and Statutes

Because the in-text citations typically found in legal documents interfere with the flow of the material and are of limited interest in the context of this collection, we have omitted most of them. We have kept only those that make it easier for the reader to refer to another document in this book and some to relevant materials that we have had to omit. We have similarly deleted most footnotes to the texts. Interested readers may find the fully cited original texts in any law library by utilizing the references or citations given for the document in the Table of Cases.

Most of the cases included are from decisions of the Supreme Court of the United States. These are compiled in the United States Reports and are cited as "U.S." The first number in the citation is the volume, the second number is the page number, and the year of the decision is in parentheses. For example, *Adler v. Board of Education*, 342 U.S. 485 (1952), denotes that the named opinion may be found in the 342d volume of the United States Reports at page 485, and that the case was decided in 1952.

Citations to cases decided by other courts follow the same format of volume, law reporter system, page, and date. In addition to the United States Reporter we have included cases from The Federal Reporter (F.), The Federal Reporter, Second Series (F.2d), The Federal Supplement (F. Supp.), Federal Cases (F. Cas.), and various state reporters, the identity of which is obvious from the abbreviations (Mass., N.H., Va., Ill., Ala., etc.). The second citation for state cases refers to the West regional reporter system—for example, N.E. denotes Northeastern; So., Southern. State cases are from that state's highest court unless otherwise noted.

Citations to the federal reporters include within parentheses the level and territorial jurisdiction of the court rendering the decision. For example, *McSurley v. Ratliff*, 282 F. Supp. 848 (E.D. Ken. 1967) advises, in addition to the location and year of the case, that it was decided by a U.S. district (or trial) court in the Eastern District of Kentucky. *Levy v. Parker*, 478 F.2d 772 (3d Cir. 1973) designates a decision by the United States Court of Appeals for the Third Circuit.

Most of the statutes included are enactments of the United States Congress. We have referenced them to the Statutes at Large (Stat.), the original chronological compilation of all Acts of Congress. Although some of the federal laws in the collection subsequently appeared in the compiled United States Code, we have viewed the original reference as preferable for historical accuracy and research purposes. As with the case citations, the number preceding the "Stat." reference is the volume, and the number following is the page. With the

more modern statutes we have parenthetically indicated the current United States Code Sections. The date appears parenthetically. The treatment of state statutory material follows this system.

Internet Documents

Chapter 13 of this book contains several documents culled from the Internet. Given the ephemeral nature of the medium, the reader is advised that the addresses given for these works may not be valid when this book goes to print. This is regrettable, albeit unavoidable, and it is recommended that the reader use any of the various search engines available to find these documents in their new locations.

Format, Variant Spellings, Errors, Sources

Certain aspects of diverse formats occurring in the collected documents have been harmonized by the editors (e.g., the styling of salutations and closings in letters, internal headings). Variant and archaic spellings in the earlier documents of the colonial and national periods have been retained, with either a [sic] or a bracketed correction if considered necessary. Punctuation was not standardized. Obvious typographical errors in the original documents were corrected without specific notation. The editors have attempted to provide citations to modern sources of material, when available, to assist the interested reader.

The Tree of Liberty

CHAPTER 1

The Colonial Heritage

1352-1750

NO sooner did the colonists set out for the shores of the Promised Land in search of liberty than they found it necessary to delineate the boundaries between freedom and authority.

This first set of materials presents some of the organic documents of the English colonial period in America. These fall into two basic categories. The first traces the bases of the assertion of European authority in North America. The king's colonists were given the legal and moral authority to conquer the land and to subjugate all native inhabitants. The Crown's representatives, whether styled as companies under a royal charter or as lords of a proprietary grant, were accorded full authority in the new lands, to be breached only upon pain of the penalty for treason—death and attainder. Secondly, the colonists themselves, in the exercise of considerable self-government and often under royal urging, formed law-making associations of their own to manage their internal and day-to-day affairs.

Ultimate allegiance was always stoutly sworn to the king, but often the more immediate concerns of the colonists were at odds with those of the overseas sovereign. Several of the documents relate to the clashes between the economic interests of the overlords and the survival problem faced by the colonists. The rash of uprisings in Virginia over the colonial governor's abuse and neglect provided the first example of the harsh methods used by the government in America to deal with popular unrest.

The next focus of this chapter is on the use of the law to define the relations among the different ethnic and religious groups newly constituting the population of the eastern seaboard of North America. The religious minorities that founded some colonies erected barriers of religious intolerance of their own. Additionally, the tensions between the Native Americans and the English erupted into open warfare at various points, prompting John Smith to conclude that there was full justification to pursue a policy of extermination toward the Native Americans. Other materials, nevertheless, demonstrate a more congenial, conciliatory, and respectful political attitude toward the aboriginal populations. William Penn's letter and the laws of certain colonies reflected a respect for their right to maintain their self-governing societies. Virginia, in contrast, presumed a more intrusive authority.

Effort was made everywhere, however, to maintain the segregation of the Native American and white populations by imposing burdens, punishments, and restraints upon Native Americans inhabiting the areas of white settlement. At the same time efforts were made to preserve aboriginal lands from unauthorized encroachment. When it became clear the local Native American societies had been weakened, the colonists enacted other legislation exercising paternalistic and quasi-assimilative authority over the remaining communities and individuals. Nevertheless, the strict line between white and Native American remained. Indeed, the law frequently classified the Native Americans together with that other unfortunate race of American history—African blacks.

Race relations have from our earliest times been the object of extensive legislative attention in America's North as well as South. It was extremely important to white society that the relationship between the "colored peoples" and whites be clearly delineated and subject to strict regulation. Detailed laws were enacted to make sure the social interaction between these peoples was highly structured and formalized. The divisions, while ostensibly based on the need to regulate slaves, swept within this stricture all men and women of color—free as well as enslaved. From these beginnings flowed the race wars and riots of our later history, as well as the oppressive use of the law against emerging social and economic groups considered dangerous by the majority.

We have focused on documents defining the crime of treason and recording its use in these early times. It should be noted that this most heinous of crimes was often invoked to assert the righteousness of an interest the government sought to advance or protect rather than merely to guard the safety of government itself. It also should be noted how quickly the appellations "traitor" and "treason" were abandoned when the government perceived the threat to have subsided. Special attention also should be paid to the procedural requirements accompanying this offense—demonstrating awareness of the potential for abuse contained in the accusation of treason, were it to be used against political opponents. The early use of the military in maintaining political order is documented, as well as the traditional American concern regarding the injection of the military into the country's social and political mainstream.

The materials in this section finally expose the roots of the greatest American rebellion and political criminality. Throughout the earlier period God and the Gospels supplied the main foundations for judging the righteousness and accepting the authority of political governance in the colonies. So, too, did divine authority provide much of the justification for contradicting the commands of law. But new, secular standards for judging political authority were increasingly being advanced before the Revolution. The documents in the chapter reflect the

intensity of the colonial commitment to righteousness: the remonstrance against practices approved by law but condemned by the rules of a higher morality; the assertion of a duty of disobedience to a government that perpetuates injustice; the use of the press to communicate the odiousness of governmental practices; civil disobedience in the name of religious and political liberty; and riot and rebellion to compel a distant and unheeding government to attend to the needs of the people. These are practices and techniques that we will see repeated and refined throughout future chapters—and so shall we see the corresponding efforts of government to curtail them through the use of law.

---

1 King Edward III's Treason Law (1352)

Arriving at the shores of the "New Jerusalem"—an epithet sometimes applied to the English colonies of America—the settlers nevertheless found themselves still bound to the legal commands of the mother country, England. Uppermost among these was the law of treason, which articulated the political loyalty of all the Crown's subjects, whether settled in England or colonizing the new realms, to their sovereign.

King Edward III's statute of 1352—being "A declaration [upon] which offenses shall be adjudged Treason"—was the first codification of the English treason law. The law of treason always stood in the center of the broad legal effort to protect the Crown and the country against external as well as internal enemies. Prior to the statute of 1352, the English courts applied vague and overly broad criteria to this offense, making even mere speech, such as criticism and ridicule of the Crown, tantamount to treason. In the struggle to consolidate royal authority and to wrest political power from the nobility, the Crown frequently resorted to the elastic treason laws as an oppressive weapon against its opponents. Treason was not only a capital offense but also punishable by the forfeiture of the offender's estate to the king.

Intended to reform the abuses of the treason law, the 1352 statute was passed at a time when Edward III was particularly vulnerable. Taking advantage of the king's weakness—the result of financial overextension caused by the support of foreign wars, harlots, and court pageantry—Parliament forced a reform of the treason law. The new statute reflected the close affinity between the state and the sover-

eign—punishing conduct against the realm as well as against the king's kin. But the effort to curtail the overreach of the treason law was short-lived. The king's courts soon resorted to their old practices of unduly broadening the law through judicial interpretation. Yet the restraining principles of the English statute remained as a model for America's own eventual treason law. Phrases from Edward's law (such as levying war or "adhering" to the enemies, giving them "aid and comfort") were incorporated into the United States Constitution (Art. III, Sec. 3) and have continued in American legal and political language for over three hundred years.

☆1 A Declaration Which Offenses Shall Be Adjudged Treason (23 Edward III [1352])

Reprinted in C. Stephenson and F. Marcham, eds., *Sources of English Constitutional History* (New York: Harper & Bros., 1937), 227.

ITEM, Whereas divers Opinions have been before this Time in what Case Treason shall be said, and in what not; (2) the King, at the Request of the Lords and of the Commons, hath made a Declaration in the Manner as hereafter followeth; that is to say, When a Man doth compass or imagine the Death of our Lord the King, or of our Lady his Queen, or of their eldest Son and Heir; (3) or if a Man do violate the King's Companion, or the King's eldest Daughter unmarried, or the Wife of the King's eldest Son and Heir; (4) of if a Man do levy War against our Lord the King in his Realm, or be adherent to the King's Enemies in his Realm, giving to them Aid and Comfort in the Realm, or elsewhere, and thereof be probably attainted of open Deed by the People of their Condition. (5) And if a Man counterfeit the King's Great or

Privy Seal, or his Money; (6) and if a Man bring false Money into this Realm, counterfeit to the Money of *England*, as the Money called *Lushburgh*, or other like to the said Money of England, knowing the Money to be false, to merchandise or make Payment in Deceit of our said Lord the King and of his People; (7) and if a Man flee the Chancellor, Treasurer, or the King's Justices of the one Bench or the other, Justices in Evre, or Justices of Assise, and all other Justices assigned to hear and determine, being in their Places, doing their Offices. (8) And it is to be understood, that in the Cases above rehearsed, that ought to be judged Treason which extends to our Lord the King, and his Royal Majesty: (9) And of such Treason the Forfeiture of the Escheats pertaineth to our Sovereign Lord, as well of the Lands and Tenements holden of other, as of himself. (10) And moreover there is another Manner of Treason, that is to say, when a Servant slayeth his Master, or a Wife her Husband, or when a Man Secular or Religious slayeth his Prelate, to whom he oweth Faith and Obedience; (11) and of such Treason the Escheats ought to pertain to every Lord of his own Fee. (12) And because that many other like Cases of Treason may happen in Time to come, which a Man cannot think nor declare at this present Time; it is accorded, That if any other Case, supposed Treason, which is not above specified, doth happen before any Justices, the Justices shall tarry without any going to Judgment of the Treason, till the Cause be shewed and declared before the King and his Parliament, whether it ought to be judged Treason or other Felony. (13) And if percase any Man of this Realm ride armed covertly or secretly with Men of Arms against any other, to slay him, or rob him, or take him, or retain him till he hath made Fine or Ransom for to have his Deliverance, it is not the Mind of the King nor his Council, that in such Case it shall be judged Treason, but shall be judged Felony or Trespass, according to the Laws of the Land of old Time used, and according as the Case requireth.

*   *   *

2 Authority to Subjugate America's Natives (1496)

On March 5, 1496, Henry VII, King of England, France, and Ireland, granted letters patent to Giovanni Caboto, a native of Genoa, who set sail from Bristol to find lands hitherto unknown to the Christians of Europe. These letters authorized Caboto, better known by his anglicized name, John Cabot, to discover the provinces "of the heathens and infidels," subdue them, and take possession of all towns and lands on behalf of the Crown. Overlooking the wishes as well as the potential opposition of the native inhabitants of the unexplored lands, the charter decreed the extension of English sovereignty in the New World (to be administered by Cabot and his company) to English settlers and Native Americans alike. It is against the background of this assertion of authority that the Native American rebellions and wars of the ensuing years must be viewed.

☆ 2 Letters Patent of Henry VII to John Cabot

Reprinted in F. Thorpe, ed., *Federal and State Constitutions* (Washington, D.C.: U.S. Government Printing Office, 1909), 1:46-47.

The Letters patents of King Henry the seuenth granted vnto Iohn Cabot and his three sonnes, Lewis, Sebastian, and Sancius for the discouerie of new and vnknowen lands.

Henry, by the grace of God, king of England and France, and lord of Ireland, to all to whom these presents shall come, Greeting.

Be it knowen that we haue giuen and granted, and by these presents do giue and grant for vs and our heires, to our welbeloued Iohn Cabot citizen of Venice, to Lewis, Sebastian, and Santius, sonnes of the sayd Iohn, and to the heires of them, and euery of them, and their deputies, full and free authority, leaue, and power to saile to all parts, countreys, and seas of the East, of the West, and of the North, vnder our banners and ensignes, with fiue ships of what burthen or quantity soeuer they be, and as many mariners or men as they will haue with them in the sayd ships, vpon their owne proper costs and charges, to seeke out, discouer, and finde whatsoeuer isles, countreys, regions or prouinces of the heathen and infidels whatsoeuer they be, and in what part of the world soeuer they be, which before this time haue bene vnknowen to all Christians: we haue granted to them, and also to euery of them, the heires of them, and euery of them, and their deputies, and haue giuen them licence to set vp our banners and ensignes in euery village, towne, castle, isle, or maine land of them newly found. And that the aforesayd Iohn and his sonnes, or their heires and assignes may subdue, occupy and possesse all such townes, cities, castles and isles of them found, which they can subdue, occupy and possesse, as our vassals, and lieutenants, getting vnto vs the rule, title, and iurisdiction of the same villages, townes, castles, & firme land so found. Yet so that the aforesayd Iohn, and his sonnes and heires, and their deputies, be holden and bounden of all the fruits, profits, gaines, and commodities growing of such nauigation, for euery their voyage, as often as they shall arriue at our port of Bristoll (at which port they shall be bound and holden onely to arriue) all manner of necessary costs and charges by them made, being deducted, to pay vnto vs in wares or money the fift part of the capitall gaine so gotten. We giuing and granting vnto them and to their heires and deputies, that they shall be free from all paying of customes of all and singular such merchandize as they shall bring with them from those places so newlie found.

And moreouer, we haue given and granted to them, their heires and deputies, that all the firme lands, isles, villages, townes, castles and places whatsoeuer they be that they shall chance to finde, may not of any other of our subjects be frequented or visited without the licence of the foresayd Iohn and his sonnes, and their deputies, vnder payne of forfeiture as well of their ships as of all and singular goods of all them that shall presume to saile to those places so found. Willing, and most straightly commanding all and singular our subjects as well on land as on sea, appointed officers, to giue good assistance to the aforesaid Iohn, and his sonnes and deputies, and that as well in arming and furnishing their ships or vessels, as in prouision of quietnesse, and in buying of victuals for their money, and all other things by them to be prouided necessary for the sayd nauigation, they do giue them all their help and fauour. In Witnesse whereof we have caused to be made these our letters of patents. Witnesse our selfe at Westminster, the fifth day of March, in the eleventh yeere of our reigne.

3 "all Liberties, Franchises, and Immunities" (1606)

The actual English colonization of America did not commence until the end of the sixteenth century. In 1584, Sir Walter Raleigh received a royal charter pursuant to which he organized five expeditions to the New World. His short-lived colony on Roanoke Island, Virginia (now part of North Carolina), was the first to demonstrate the practicability of establishing permanent English settlements in America.

In 1606, King James I granted a charter to the Virginia Company, and 120 settlers planted the first permanent English colony in America—at Jamestown on May 14, 1607. The royal charter inaugurated the first English council in North America, which was nevertheless under the supervision of a similar council resident in England. By extending to all settlers, and their children born in the colony all the rights they would enjoy had they been natives and residents of England, the king firmly asserted for the populations of the New World the primacy of the Crown and the allegiance owed to it. Further authority, in the name of evangelism, was granted to the settlers to bring the Indian populations into "civility and ... settled [English] government."

☆ 3 First Charter of Virginia (April 10, 1606)

Reprinted in B. P. Poore, ed., The Federal and State Constitutions, Colonial Charters, and Other Organic Laws of the United States (Washington, D.C.: U.S. Government Printing Office, 1877), pt. 2:1889 ff.

I, JAMES, by the Grace of God, King of England, Scotland, France, and Ireland, Defender of the Faith, &c. WHEREAS our loving and well-disposed Subjects, Sir Thomas Gates, and Sir George Somers, Knights, Richard Hackluit, Clerk, Prebendary of Westminster, and Edward-Maria Wingfield, Thomas Hanham, and Ralegh Gilbert, Esqrs. William Parker, and George Popham, Gentlemen, and divers others of our loving Subjects, have been humble Suitors unto us, that We would vouchsafe unto them our Licence, to make Habitation, Plantation, and to deduce a Colony of sundry of our People into that Part of America, commonly called VIRGINIA, and other Parts and Territories in America, either appertaining unto us, or which are not now actually possessed by any Christian Prince of People, situate, lying, and being all along the Sea Coasts, between four and thirty Degrees of Northerly Latitude from the Equinoctial Line, and five and forty Degrees of the same Latitude, and in the main Land between the same four and thirty and five and forty Degrees, and the Islands thereunto adjacent, or within one hundred Miles of the Coast thereof;

And to that End, and for the more speedy Accomplishment of their said intended Plantation and Habitation there, are desirous to divide themselves into two several Colonies and Companies; The one consisting of certain Knights, Gentlemen, Merchants, and other Adventurers, of our City of London and elsewhere, which are, and from time to time shall be, joined unto them, which do desire to begin their Plantation and Habitation in some fit and convenient Place, between four and thirty and one and forty Degrees of the said Latitude, alongst the Coasts of Virginia and Coasts of America aforesaid; And the other consisting of sundry Knights, Gentlemen, Merchants, and other Adventurers, of our Cities of Bristol and Exeter, and of our Town of Plimouth, and of other Places, which do join themselves unto that Colony, which do desire to begin their Plantation and Habitation in some fit and convenient Place, between eight and thirty Degrees and five and forty Degrees of the said Latitude, all alongst the said Coast of Virginia and America, as that Coast lyeth:

We, greatly commending, and graciously accepting of, their Desires for the Furtherance of so noble a Work, which may, by the Providence of Almighty God, hereafter tend to the Glory of his Divine Majesty, in propagating of Christian Religion to such People, as yet live in Darkness and miserable Ignorance of the true Knowledge and Worship of God, and may in time bring the Infidels and Savages, living in those Parts, to human Civility, and to a settled and quiet Government; Do, by these our Letters Patents, graciously accept of, and agree to, their humble and well-intended Desires;

AND do therefore, for US, our Heirs, and SUCCESSORS, GRANT and agree, that the said Sir Thomas Gates, Sir George Somers, Richard Hackluit, and Edward-Maria Wingfield, Adventurers of and for our City of London, and all such others, as are, or shall be, joined unto them of that Colony, shall be called the first Colony....

AND we do likewise ... GRANT and agree, that the said Thomas Hanham, and Ralegh Gilbert, William Parker, and George Popham, and all others of the Town of Plimouth in the County of Devon, or elsewhere, which are, or shall be, joined unto them of that Colony, shall be called the second Colony....

*   *   *

AND we do also ordain ... that each of the said Colonies shall have a Council, which shall govern and order all Matters and Causes, which shall arise, grow, or happen, to or within the same several Colonies, according to such Laws, Ordinances, and Instructions, as shall be, in that behalf, given and signed with Our Hand or Sign Manual, and pass under the Privy Seal of our Realm of England; Each of which Councils shall consist of thirteen Persons, to be ordained, made, and removed, from time to time, according as shall be directed and comprised in the same instructions....

AND that also there shall be a Council established here in England, which shall, in like Manner, consist of thirteen Persons, to be, for that Purpose, appointed by Us, ... which shall be called our Council of Virginia; And shall, from time to time, have the superior Managing and Direction, only of and for all Matters, that shall or may concern the Government, as well of the said several Colonies, as of and for any other Part or Place, within the aforesaid Precincts....

AND moreover, we do GRANT that the said several Councils, of and for the said several Colonies, shall and lawfully may, by Virtue hereof, from time to time, without any Interruption of Us ..., give and take Order, to dig, mine, and search for all Manner of Mines of Gold, Silver, and Copper, as well within any part of their said several Colonies, as for the said main Lands on the Backside of the same Colonies ... YIELDING therefore, to Us ... the fifth Part only of all the same Gold and Silver, and the fifteenth Part of all the same Copper, so to be gotten or had....

Giving and granting, by these Presents, unto the said Sir Thomas Gates ... and their Associates of the said first Colony, and unto the said Thomas Hanham ... and their Associates of the said second Colony ... Power and Authority to take and surprise, by all Ways and Means whatsoever, all and every Person and Persons, with their Ships, Vessels, Goods and other Furniture, which shall be found trafficking, into any Harbour or Harbours, Creek or Creeks, or Place, within the Limits or Precincts of the said several Colonies and Plantations, not being of the same Colony, until such time, as they, being of any Realms or Dominions under our Obedience, shall pay, or agree to pay, to the Hands of the Treasurer of that Colony, within whose Limits and Precincts they shall so traffick, two and a half upon every Hundred, of any thing, so by them trafficked, bought, or sold; And being Strangers, and not Subjects under our Obeysance, until they shall pay five upon every Hundred, of such Wares and Merchandises, as they shall traffick, buy, or sell, within the Precincts of the said several Colonies, wherein they shall so traffick, buy, or sell as aforesaid....

Also we do ... DECLARE ... that all and every the Persons, being our Subjects, which shall dwell and inhabit within every or any of the said several Colonies and Plantations, and every of their children, which shall happen to be born within any of the Limits and Precincts of the said several Colonies and Plantations, shall HAVE and enjoy all Liberties, Franchises, and Immunities, within any of our other Dominions, to all Intents and Purposes, as if they had been abiding and born, within this our Realm of England, or any other of our said Dominions....

*   *   *

4 "combine ourselves together into a civil Body Politick" (1620)

A group of London and Yorkshire separatists, religious dissenters who had exiled themselves to Amsterdam and Leyden to escape persecution, applied to the Virginia Company for a patent to immigrate to the New World. To assure the English king of their loyalty and docility, they drafted the Leyden Agreement in 1618:

> The King's Majesty wee acknoledge for Spreame Governer in his Dominion in all causes and over al parsons, and ye none maye decklyne or apeale from his authority or judgement in any cause whatsoever, but y in all thinges obedience is dewe unto him, ether active, if ye thing commanded be not agaynst God's woord, or passive yf itt bee....

Finally securing a patent for a private plantation, the Leyden Pilgrims, reinforced by some seventy persons from London, sailed from Plymouth, England in September 1620. Since some of the London recruits, described as an "undesirable lot," rebelled against the authority of the Virginia Company and threatened to "use their owne libertie," the Pilgrim leaders drew up the Mayflower Compact. Although ultimate allegiance was sworn to the king, the document provided for the formation of a governing unit based on mutual consent of the signatories, to which all would submit. The compact not only advanced for the first time the concept of self-determination in the New World but provided an alternative allegiance to that of the overseas sovereign—one that was more likely to respond to the needs and grievances of the governed.

☆4 The Mayflower Compact (November 11, 1620)

Reprinted in B. P. Poore, ed., *The Federal and State Constitutions, Colonial Charters, and Other Organic Laws of the United States* (Washington, D.C.: U.S. Government Printing Office, 1877), pt. 1:931.

IN The Name of God, Amen. We, whose names are underwritten, the Loyal Subjects of our dread Sovereign Lord King James, by the Grace of God, of Great Britain, France, and Ireland, King, Defender of the Faith, &c. Having undertaken for the Glory of God, and Advancement of the Christian Faith, and the Honour of our King and Country, a Voyage to plant the first colony in the northern Parts of Virginia; Do by these Presents, solemnly and mutually in the Presence of God and one another, covenant and combine ourselves together into a civil Body Politick, for our better Ordering and Preservation, and Furtherance of the Ends aforesaid; And by Virtue hereof do enact, constitute, and frame, such just and equal Laws, Ordinances, Acts, Constitutions, and Offices, from time to time, as shall be thought most meet and convenient for the general Good of the Colony; unto which we promise all due Submission and Obedience. In WITNESS whereof we have hereunto subscribed our names at Cape Cod the eleventh of November, in the Reign of our Sovereign Lord King James of England, France, and Ireland, the eighteenth and of Scotland, the fifty-fourth. Anno Domini, 1620.

MR. JOHN CARVER	JOSES FLETCHER
MR. WILLIAM BRADFORD	JOHN GOODMAN
MR. EDWARD WINSLOW	MR. SAMUEL FULLER
MR. WILLIAM BREWSTER	MR. CHRISTOPHER MARTIN
ISAAC ALLERTON	MR. WILLIAM MULLINS
MILES STANDISH	MR. WILLIAM WHITE
JOHN ALDEN	MR. RICHARD WARREN
JOHN TURNER	JOHN HOWLAND
FRANCIS EATON	MR. STEPHEN HOPKINS
JAMES CHILTON	DIGERY PRIEST
JOHN CRAXTON	THOMAS WILLIAMS
JOHN BILLINGTON	GILBERT WINSLOW

EDMUND MARGESSON	JOHN RIDGATE
PETER BROWN	EDWARD FULLER
RICHARD BITTERIDGE	RICHARD CLARK
GEORGE SOULE	RICHARD GARDINER
EDWARD TILLY	MR. JOHN ALLERTON
JOHN TILLY	THOMAS ENGLISH
FRANCIS COOKE	EDWARD DOTEN
THOMAS ROGERS	EDWARD LIESTER
THOMAS TINKER	

5 We Now Have Just Cause to Destroy Them by All Means (1622)

Seeking in the New World a haven from England's religious, economic, and political oppressions, the settlers did not arrive at a continent barren of populations. A wide range of Native American tribes in various stages of economic, social, and political development inhabited areas throughout most of North America. The Native Americans never were able to articulate effectively or organize their political opposition to the invasion of their lands by alien colonizers, but resistance to assertions of English sovereignty nevertheless was manifested from time to time in acts of violence, which the settlers conceived to be further evidence of the "brutishness" of these "beasts." The apparent cause of the 1622 massacre of 347 settlers in Virginia, recorded by Captain John Smith, describing himself as President of Virginia and Admiral of New England, was the killing of a Native American who resisted arrest and trial for the murder of an Englishman. The uprisings provided the moral justification for the English to oust the Native Americans from their lands.

☆5 The Massacre upon the Two and Twentieth of March

Reprinted in E. Arber, *Travels and Works of Captain John Smith* (New York: Burt Franklin, 1910), pt. 2:572-79.

THE Prologue to this Tragedy, is supposed was occasioned by *Nemattanow*, otherwise called *Iack of the Feather*, because hee commonly was most strangely adorned with them; and for his courage and policy, was accounted amongst the Saluages their chiefe Captaine, and immortall from any hurt could bee done him by the *English*. This Captaine coming to one *Morgans* house [*in March* 1622], knowing he had many commodities that hee desired, perswaded *Morgan* to goe with him to *Pamau[n]ke* to trucke, but the Saluage murdered him by the way; and after two or three daies returned againe to *Morgans* house, where he found two youths his Seruants, who asked for their Master: *Iack* replied directly he was dead; the Boyes suspecting as it was, by seeing him weare his Cap, would haue had him to Master

Thorp: But *Iack* so moued their patience, they shot him; so he fell to the ground, [they] put him in a Boat to haue him before the Gouernor, then seuen or eight miles from them. But by the way *Iack* finding the pangs of death vpon him, desired of the Boyes two things: the one was, that they would not make it knowne hee was slaine with a bullet; the other, to bury him amongst the *English.*

At the losse of this Saluage, *Opechankanough* much grieued and repined, with great threats of reuenge; but the *English* returned him such terrible answers, that he cunningly dissembled his intent, with the greatest signes he could of loue and peace: yet within fourteene daies after he acted what followeth.

Sir *Francis Wyat* at his arriuall [*Oct.* 1621] was aduertised, he found the Countrey setled in such a firme peace, as most men there thought sure and vnuiolable, not onely in regard of their promises, but of a necessitie. The poore weake Saluages being euery way bettered by vs, and safely sheltred and defended, whereby wee might freely follow our businesse: and such was the conceit of this conceited peace, as that there was seldome or neuer a sword, and seldomer a peece [used], except for a Deere or Fowle; by which assurances the most plantations were placed straglingly and scatteringly, as a choice veine of rich ground inuited them, and further from neighbours the better. Their houses [were] generally open to the Saluages, who were alwaies friendly fed at their tables, and lodged in their bed-chambers; which made the way plaine to effect their intents, and the conuersion of the Saluages as they supposed.

Hauing occasion to send to *Opechankanough* about the middle of March, hee vsed the Messenger well, and told him he held the peace so firme, the sky should fall or he dissolued it; yet such was the treachery of those people, when they had contriued our destruction, euen but two daies before the massacre, they guided our men with much kindnesse thorow the woods, and one *Browne* that liued among them to learne the language, they sent home to his Master. Yea, they borrowed our Boats to transport themselues ouer the Riuer, to consult on the deuillish murder that insued, and of our vtter extirpation, which God of his mercy (by the meanes of one of themselues conuerted to Christianitie) preuented; and as well on the Friday morning that fatall day, being the two and twentieth of March [1622], as also in the euening before, as at other times they came vnarmed into our houses, with Deere, Turkies, Fish, Fruits, and other prouisions to sell vs: yea in some places sat downe at breakfast with our people, whom immediatly with their owne tooles they slew most barbarously, not sparing either age or sex, man woman or childe; so sudden in their execution, that few or none discerned the weapon or blow that brought them to destruction. In which manner also

they slew many of our people at seuerall works in the fields, well knowing in what places and quarters each of our men were, in regard of their familiaritie with vs, for the effecting that great master-peece of worke their conuersion: and by this meanes fell that fatall morning vnder the bloudy and barbarous hands of that perfidious and inhumane people, three hundred forty seuen men, women and children; most[l]y by their owne weapons; and not being content with their liues, they fell againe vpon the dead bodies, making as well as they could a fresh murder, defacing, dragging, and mangling their dead carkases into many peeces, and carrying some parts away in derision, with base and brutish triumph.

Neither yet did these beasts spare those amongst the rest well knowne vnto them, from whom they had daily receiued many benefits; but spightfully also massacred them without any remorse or pitie: being in this more fell than Lions and Dragons, as Histories record, which haue preserued their Benefactors; such is the force of good deeds, though done to cruell beasts, to take humanitie vpon them, but these miscreants put on a more vnnaturall brutishnesse then beasts, as by those instances may appeare.

6 "to be drawn and hanged" (1630)

Less than one generation passed between the Jamestown settlement in Virginia and the first reported political trial in the colony.

Patterned after the English treason law, with its feudal origins, the colonial treason statutes and court cases similarly reflected the social stratification of the Middle Ages. Treason in England consisted not only of an act of betrayal against the country's highest sovereign (the king, his family, his seal, and his realm) but also of offenses against others in the social order — i.e., those to whom one owed feudal allegiance. Accordingly, petit treason applied when a servant slew his master; or a wife, her husband. The 1630 Virginia conviction of Matthewes not only established the colonial acceptance of petit treason but also demonstrated its gravity by the barbarity of the punishment inflicted — drawing and hanging. The Cugley conviction further reflected the period's intolerance of dissent from governmental policy or administration. The concept of a "loyal opposition" hardly had been broached in either England or the colonies, and speech critical of government officials was viewed as a grave threat to the social and political order. Repentant prodigals, however, were welcomed back.

☆6 Extract from the Minutes of the Judicial
Proceedings of the Governor and Council of
Virginia

Reprinted in W. Hening, ed., *Virginia Statutes at Large,
1619-1660* (Charlottesville: University Press of Virginia,
1969), 146.

July 13th, 1630. William Matthewes servant to
Henry Booth, indicted and found guilty of petit treason, by fourteen jurors. Judgment to be drawn and
hanged.

For scandalous speeches against Governor and
Councell, Daniel Cugley sentenced to be pilloryd,
but was forgiven.

7 "Subversion of our Fundamental Frame" (1636)

The 1636 laws of New Plymouth reflected the settlers' dual cultural heritage: the biblical Judaeo-
Christian and the English. The crimes of idolatry
and blasphemy were founded on the biblical prohibitions contained in Exodus, Deuteronomy, and Le-
viticus. The crime of treason incorporated the 1352
English protection for the person of the king and his
estates in the New World. But the New Plymouth
statute voiced a new commitment to the preservation of the established government or its "fundamental frame and constitution." Thus the form of
government, in addition to the person of the sovereign and his realm, was recognized as deserving of
protection by the harsh law of treason.

☆7 The Capital Laws of New Plimouth

Reprinted in *The Book of the General Laws of the Inhabitants of the Jurisdiction of New Plymouth* (Boston: Samuel
Green, 1685), chap. 4.

It is Enacted by this Court, and the Authority
thereof, That if any Person having had the knowledge of the true God, openly and manifestly, have or
worship any other God but the Lord God, he shall be
put to Death. Exod. 22.20. Deut. 13.6, 10.

2. If any Person within this Jurisdiction professing the True God, shall wittingly and willingly presume to Blaspheme the Holy Name of God the Father, Son, or Holy Ghost, with direct, express,
presumptious, high-handed Blasphemy, either by
wilful or obstinate denying of the True God, or his
Creation, or Government of the World, or shall
curse God the Father, Son or Holy Ghost, such Persons shall be put to Death. Levit. 24.15, 16.

3. Treason against the Person of our Soveraigne
Lord the King, the Realm and Common-wealth of
England, shall be punisht by Death.

4. That whosoever shall Conspire and Attempt

any invasion, Insurrection, or publick Rebellion
against this Jurisdiction and His Majesties Authority here established, or surprize any Town, Plantation, Fortification or Amunition therein provided for
the safety thereof; or shall treacherously and profi-
deously attempt and endeavor the Alteration and
Subversion of our Fundamental Frame and Constitution of this Government, every such Person shall
be put to Death.

*   *   *

8 "to come adhere or confederate with the Indians" (1638)

The Maryland Act for Treasons reflected special colonial concerns. Unlike earlier colonies, which exper-
imented with new, autonomous forms of government, Maryland, established by the English Crown,
was a proprietorship of Sir George Calvert, Lord
Baltimore. The land was divided into manors, and
their "lords" had nearly feudal control over their
estates.

The Maryland General Assembly passed the
Treasons Act against a background of ever-increasing hostility between its citizens and those of Virginia. The rich fisheries and fertile lands of the Chesapeake region made Virginians covetous of the new
colony. The fact that Maryland had been carved
from land originally under the Virginia Charter did
not diminish the envy, and the "Oyster Wars"
resulted.

Marylanders thus were particularly sensitive to
treasonous activities of the inhabitants which might
adversely affect the feudal inheritance of the "Lord
Proprietary." In addition to securing the feudal hier-
archy in Maryland, the law also brought association
with the Indians within the scope of political betrayal. The act imposed on traitors the most severe
penalties known to the English law — drawing, hanging, burning, and quartering, as well as the forfeiture of lands and the corruption of the offenders'
bloodline.

☆8 An Act for Treasons [Maryland]

Reprinted in W. Brown, ed., *Proceedings and Acts of the
General Assembly of Maryland, January 1637-1638* (Baltimore: Press of Isaac Friedenwald, 1883), 70.

AN ACT FOR TREASONS

Be it Enacted By the Lord proprietarie of this Province of and with the advice and approbation of the
freemen of the same   That these offences following
in this act shall be adjudged offences of Treason
within this Province   To Compasse or conspire the
death of his Majestie the King of England or the

Queen his wife or of his son and heir or to levie warre against his Majestie or to counterfeit the Kings great or privy Seal or his coin or to come or adhere to any forreine prince or State being a professed and declared enemy of his Majesties in any practice or attempt against his said Majestie

Or to Compass conspire and cause the death of the Lord proprietarie within this Province or of his Leiutenant Generall for the time being (in the absence of the Lord Proprietarie) or to levy warre against the Lord Proprietarie or his Leiutent Generall for the time being (in absence of the Lord proprietarie) or to come adhere or confederate with the Indians of these parts or any forreing prince or Governour to the invadeing of this Province or disheriting the Lord Proprietarie of his Seignory and dominion therein And all offences of treason shall be punished by drawing hanging and quartering of a man by drawing and burning of a Woman and the offenders blood shall be corupted and the offender shall forfeit to the Lord Proprietary all his or her Lands tenements goods franchises and all that may be forfeited Provided That punishment of death shall be inflicted on a Lord of a Mannour by beheading This Act to Continue to the end of the next Generall Assembly.

9 The Memory of Charles I in Virginia (1649)

The laws of the remote American colonies frequently reflected the political turmoil and wars of the mother country. At the commencement of the conflict between Charles I and the Parliamentarians under Cromwell, the Virginians asserted their loyalty to the Crown. The Virginia Assembly voiced its concern over the trial, conviction, and execution of Charles I and the resultant disruption to the English Crown. The assembly sought not only to protect the king's memory and honor by prohibiting any "discourse or argument" in defense of the Puritan regime but also to reinforce the royal claim of Charles II (who did not ascend to the throne until 1660) and the authority of Virginia's royalist government by outlawing "false reports and malicious rumors." The arbitrary nature of political offenses is herein demonstrated. While, in England, royalists were traitors to the Cromwell regime, in Virginia, an English colony, it was treasonous to utter any words in favor of the ruling power of England. The problem became even more complex when the Puritan colonies of Connecticut and Massachusetts gave refuge to the regicides who fled England after the Restoration.

☆9 Act I of a Grand Assembly (Held at James City the 10th Day of October 1649)

Reprinted in W. Hening, ed., *Virginia Statutes at Large, 1619-1660* (Charlottesville: University Press of Virginia, 1969), 358-61.

WHEREAS divers out of ignorance, others out of malice, schisme and faction, in pursuance of some designe of innovation, may be presumed to prepare mens' minds and inclinations to entertaine a good liking of their contrivement, by casting blemishes of dishonour upon the late most excellent and now undoubtedly sainted king, and to those close ends vindicating and attesting the late proceedings against the said blessed King (though by so much as they may seeme to have colour of law, and forme of justice, they may be truly and really said to have the more and greater height of impudence.) And upon this foundation of asserting the cleerness and legality of the said unparalel'd treasons, perpetrated on the said King, doe build hopes and inferrences to the high dishonour of the regall estate, and in truth to the utter disinherison of his sacred Majesty that now is, and the devesting him of those rights, which the law of nature and nations and the knowne lawes of the kingdom of England have adjudged inherent to his royall line, and the law of God himself (if sacred writ may be soe stiled which this age doth loudly call in question) hath consecrated unto him. And as arguments easily and naturally deduced from the aforesaid cursed and destructive principles, with much indeavour, they press and perswade the power of the comission to be void and null, and all magistracy and office thereon depending to have lost their vigor and efficacy, but such means assuredly expecting advantages for the accomplishment of their lawless and tyrranous intentions,

Be it therefore declared and enacted and it is hereby enacted by Governour, Council and Burgesses of this Grand Assembly, and the authority of the same, That what person soever, whether stranger or inhabitant of this collony, after the date of this act, by reasoning, discourse or argument shall go about to defend or maintain the late traiterous proceedings against the aforesaid King of most happy memory, under any notion of law and justice, such person using reasoning, discourse or argument, or uttering any words or speeches to such purpose or effect, and being proved by competent witnes, shall be adjudged an accessory post factum, to the death of the aforesaid King, and shall be proceeded against for the same, according to the knowne lawes of England: or whoever shall go about by irreverent or scandalous words or language to blast the memory and honour of that late most pious King, (deserving ever altars and monuments in the hearts of all good men,) shall, upon conviction, suffer such censure and punishment as shall be thought fitt by the Governour and Council. And be it further enacted, That what person soever shall by words or speeches indeavour to insinuate any doubt, scruple or question of or concerning the undoubted and inherent right of his Majesty that now is to the collony of Virginia, and all other his majesties dominions and countryes as King and Supream Governour, such words and speeches shall be adjudged high treason: And it is also enacted, That what person soever, by false reports and malicious rumors shall spread abroad, among the people, any thing tending to change of government, or to the lessening of the power and authority of the Governor or government either in civill or ecclesiasticall causes (which this Assembly hath and doth declare to be full and plenarie to all intents and purposes) such persons not onely the authors of such reports and rumours, but the reporters and divulgers thereof, (unless it be done by way of legall information before a magistrate) shall be adjudged equally guilty, and shall suffer such punishment even to severity as shall be thought fitt, according to the nature and quality of the offence.

*   *   *

10 Popular Agitation in Virginia (1653)

The Virginians' sympathy for King Charles in his war with Parliament was shared by Sir William Berkeley, who had been Virginia's governor since 1641. In 1652, when Parliament sent a fleet to secure the royalist colony, the residents decided the wisest course was to surrender to the mission. Richard Bennett, a Puritan, was appointed governor. He and his Puritan successors continued to govern until Berkeley was restored to office in 1660. Nevertheless, the change of governors did not reduce the growing conflict between the outlying, less privileged populations and the aristocratic plantation families who controlled the House of Burgesses. Popular petitions calling for a freer land-grant system and a more popular governmental assembly chosen by all freeholders were not entertained sympathetically by the oligarchical Burgesses. The tensions that eventually erupted in the rebellion of Nathaniel Bacon were manifested initially in popular agitation followed by repressive legislation. This document prescribed a punishment for "subscription" or signing of a petition critical of the government. Disabling individuals with suspect allegiances from office holding was a common method of preserving political orthodoxy.

☆ 10 Laws of Virginia

Reprinted in W. Hening, ed., *Virginia Statutes at Large, 1619-1660* (Charlottesville: University Press of Virginia, 1969), 380.

WHEREAS the paper subscribed by name of the inhabitants of Northampton countie is scandalous and seditious and hath caused much disturbance in the peace and government of that county, It is therefore ordered by this present Grand Assembly, That all the subscribers of the said paper bee disabled from bearing any office in this countery, and that Leift. Edmund Scarbrough who hath been an assistant and instrument concerneing the subscribeing of the same bee also disabled from bearing any office vntill he hath answered therevnto, and the honourable Governour & Secretarie be intreated to go over to Accomack with such assistants as the house shall think fitt, for the settlement of the peace of that countie, and punishinge delinquents.

11 "subversion of the frame of policy" (1656)

The colonial settlers, many of whom were fugitives from the English law of treason or its ecclesiastical counterpart, heresy, sought to create new societies. Nevertheless, they were intent on protecting the security and fundamental structure of their new governments against subversion. New Haven Colony, an offshoot of the Massachusetts settlement, reflected its foundations by relying upon the Bible as authority for its political structure. But in seeking to make every person a bulwark against rebellion, the law punished not only those actively conspiring or attempting rebellion but also those aware of the political threat who failed to report it to the authorities.

☆ 11 Capital Laws of New Haven

Reprinted in J. D. Cushing, ed., *The Earliest Laws of the New Haven and Connecticut Colonies, 1639-1673* (Wilmington, Del.: Michael Glazier, 1977), 19 20.

If any person shall conspire, and attempt any invasion, insurrection, or publick Rebellion against this Jurisdiction, or shall endeavour to surprize, or seize any Plantation, or Town, any Fortification, Platform, or any great Guns, provided for the defence of the Jurisdiction, or any Plantation therein; or shall treacherously and perfidiously attempt the alteration and subversion of the frame of policy, or fundamentall Government laid, and setled for this Jurisdiction, he or they shall be put to death. Num. 16. 2 Sam. 18. 2 Sam. 20. Or if any person shall consent unto any such mischievous practice, or by the space of foure and twenty houres conceale it, not giving notice thereof to some Magistrate, if there be any Magistrate in the Plantation, or place where he liveth, or if none, to some Deputy for the Jurisdiction, or to the Constable of the place, that the publick safety may be seasonably provided for, he shall be put to death, or severely punished, as the Court of Magistrates weighing all circumstances shall determine.

12 "rebelliously returning" (1660)

The new settlers of Massachusetts Bay and Plymouth colonies were disturbed by the intrusions of members of other dissident sects and the emergence of heresies. Although victims of persecution themselves, their reaction to any threat to their religiously orthodox government was harsh. In 1635 Roger Williams was banished for advocating liberty of conscience, supporting separation of church and state, and denouncing the practice of settling on Native American lands without payment. Ann Hutchinson was banished in 1638 for religious reasons. The settlements they subsequently founded on lands purchased from the Narragansett Indians (Hutchinson's Rhode Island settlement and Williams's Providence Plantations) were chartered specifically as a separate colony by Charles I in 1644. But expulsion and exclusion of those professing unorthodox belief persisted in the older colonies.

With the English Revolution of 1649 and the rise of Puritan power in England, members of the Society of Friends, or Quakers, became the target of persecution. They found little refuge in Puritan New England. In 1656, the first Quakers to arrive in Boston were promptly reembarked to England. That same year the General Court of Massachusetts Bay directed that Quakers be jailed after being "severly whipt." In 1658, government officials banished Quakers from Massachusetts Bay upon pain of death, and in 1660 Mary Dyer, a Quaker, was condemned to death and hanged. Three others suffered her fate. Public reaction to the executions, however, caused the repeal of the law in 1661. While expelling Quakers from their midst the General Court, nevertheless, gave haven in the colony to two of the signers of the death warrant of Charles I; they sought refuge in the colonies after the Restoration in England.

Massachusetts was not the only colony to conduct religious prosecutions. Even Maryland, Catholic and relatively liberal, reserved its religious toleration for Christians professing a belief in the Trinity—excluding Jews, Unitarians, Quakers, and other religious groups from full privileges. Conformity of religious belief was a prime requisite for full enjoyment of political and civil rights.

Only Rhode Island provided refuge for heretics and infidels. In 1659, Dutch Jews who were unwelcome in the colony of New Amsterdam (New York) migrated to Newport, where they established the first synagogue in America in 1763. Even though it had been excluded from the surrounding confederation known as the United Colonies of New England because of its refusal to yield to the hegemony of Massachusetts, Rhode Island prospered, earning its nickname, "Rogue's Island," by welcoming the exiles of the other colonies.

☆ 12 The Second Sentence of Mary Dyer

4 Mass. Ct. Rec., part 1:419 (1660), reprinted in E. Powers, *Crime and Punishment in Early Massachusetts, 1620-1692* (Boston: Beacon Press, 1966), 343.

The whole Court mett together sent for Mary Dyer, who rebelliously, after sentence of death past against hir, returned into this jurisdiction. Being come before the Court, she acknowledged hirself to be Mary Dyer, the person, & was condemned by this Court to death. Being asked what she had to say why the sentence should not be executed, she gave no other answ[r] but that she denied our lawe, came to beare witnes against it, & could not choose but come & doe as formerly. The whole Court mett together voted, that the said Mary Dyer, for hir rebelliously returning into this jurisdiction, (notwithstanding the favor of this Court towards hir,) shall be, by the marshall generall, on the first day of June, about nine of the clocke in the morning, carried to the place of execution, and according to the sentence of the Generall Court in October last, be put to death; that the secretary issue out warrant accordingly; which sentence the Governor declared to hir in open Court; & warrant issued out accordingly to Edward Michelson, marshall generall, & to Captain James Oliver, & his order, as formerly.

13 "illegal and clandestine purchases" (1663)

The Indian tribes were generally viewed as independent, self-governing societies. Relations between settlers and Native Americans were under the political control of the colonial governments. Rhode Island, accordingly, outlawed the purchase of Native American lands by its settlers without authorization by the General Assembly. All cession of lands by Native Americans to whites was subject to political negotiation and supervision.

☆ 13 Rhode Island Indian Land Purchase Law

Reprinted in J. D. Cushing, ed., *Rhode Island Colony Laws, 1647-1719* (Wilmington, Del.: Michael Glazier, 1977), 139.

Made and Past by the General Assembly . . . Begun . . . the first day of March 1662. . . .

*   *   *

AN ACT FOR THE PREVENTING OF ILLEGAL AND
CLANDESTINE PURCHASES OF THE NATIVE
INDIANS IN THIS COLONY

Forasmuch as divers persons have made purchases
of lands in this Colony of the Indians, without the
consent or approbation of the General Assembly,
which manifestly tends to the defrauding and manifest injury of such native Indians, as well as defeating the just rights of this Colony:

*Be it therefore enacted by the General Assem-
bly, and the authority of the same,* That no person or
persons, for the future, shall purchase any lands or
islands within this Colony, of or from the native Indians within the same, but such only as are so allowed
to do by the General Assembly, upon penalty of forfeiting all such lands or islands so purchased, to this
Colony; and to pay for every such purchase by them
so made, the sum of twenty pounds, as a fine to and
for the use of the Colony; and all such purchases
shall be esteemed and adjudged null, void, and of
none effect.

14 Beginnings of Black Bondage (1664)

The colonists brought the first black "servants" to
Jamestown, Virginia, in 1619, the same year in
which they established the House of Burgesses, the
instrument of their own local government and self-
determination. In the early seventeenth century,
American planters and landlords did not seek black
labor. They preferred white settlers and servants
who would continue the patterns of master-servant
relations familiar to feudal Europe. But in the passage of time the black immigrant, not initially differentiated from other servants, became an important
resource in the land-rich, population-poor New
World.

The scarcity of labor in the colonies tempted
landowners into subjugating the native populations
as well as the African immigrant workers. Although
blacks originally shared with other servants the opportunities for emancipation, the last part of the seventeenth century marked the beginning of a particularly racist policy which inaugurated black bondage
durante vita and enforced it through criminal and
civil law.

From this document, it is apparent that some in-
terracial marriages existed. For the betrayal of
their race, free white women who married slaves became slaves themselves, as did their children. They
thus were rendered civilly impotent as well as socially outcast.

☆14 An Act concerning Negroes and Other Slaves [Maryland]

Proceedings and Acts of the General Assembly of Maryland, September 1664, 28-29, reprinted in Albert P. Blaustein & Robert Zangrando, eds., *Civil Rights and the American Negro: A Documentary History* (New York: Trident
Press, 1968), 8-9.

Be it enacted by the Right Honorable the Lord Proprietary by the advise and consent of the upper and
lower house of this present Generall Assembly, that
all Negroes or other slaves already within the province, and all Negroes and other slaves to be hereafter imported into the province, shall serve *durante
vita.* And all children born of any Negro or other
slave shall be slaves as their fathers were, for the
term of their lives. And forasmuch as divers freeborn English women, forgetful of their free condition and to the disgrace of our nation, marry Negro
slaves, by which also divers suits may arise touching
the issue of such women, and a great damage befalls
the masters of such Negroes for prevention whereof, for deterring such freeborn women from such
shameful matches. Be it further enacted by the authority, advise, and consent aforesaid, that whatsoever freeborn woman shall marry any slave from
and after the last day of this present Assembly shall
serve the master of such slave during the life of her
husband. And that all the issue of such freeborn
women so married shall be slaves as their fathers
were. And be it further enacted, that all the issues of
English or other freeborn women that have already
married Negroes shall serve the masters of their
parents till they be thirty years of age and no longer.

15 Native Americans as Rebels (1665)

Despite the general tendency of the Native Americans and the English colonists to live apart, there
were continual interactions between them. While
most colonies had legislation regulating commerce
with Native Americans and punishing them for
crimes against whites within the colony, this Virginia enactment attempted to assert overall political
control over the Native Americans as a people. The
act deprived them of self-government and designated as rebellion any Native American refusal to
obey the commanders appointed by the colonial authorities. It is the first instance of an attempt
through law to break the social and political order of
the Native Americans and supplant it with colonial
control.

☆15 An Act concerning Indians [Virginia]

Reprinted in W. Hening, ed., *Virginia Statutes at Large,
1660-1682* (Charlottesville: University Press of Virginia,
1969), 21.

WHEREAS, at a Grand Assemblie, held at James City, September 10th, 1663, it was provided that where any murther was committed by the Indians upon the English, the nexte turne of the Indians was, to use their utmost endeavours for discovering the actors and doers thereof, and in regard the said act was only lymited upon the northern Indians: *This Grand Assembly have thought fit to enact, and it being enacted,* That the said law be a generall law against all Indians whatsoever, and where any murthers be committed upon the English, the next turne is to use all their care and diligence in finding the doers and actors of the said murthers.

And be it further enacted, That if any Englishmen is murthered, the nexte turne shall be answerable for it with their lives or liberties to the use of the publique.

And be it further enacted by this Grand Assembly, That the said Indians shall not have power within themselves to elect or constitute their owne *werowance* or Chiefe Commander, but the present Honourable Governour, and his successors from time to time shall constitute and authorize such persons in whose fidelity they may finde the greatest cause to repose a confidence, to be the Commander of the respective townes, and in case the Indians shall refuse their obedience to, or murther such persons, then that nation of Indians soe refusing or offending to be accompted enemies and rebels and to be proceeded against accordingly.

And whereas the careless manner of the English, in going unarmed into churches, courts, and other publique meetings, may probably in time invite the Indians to make some desperate attempt upon them,

It is further enacted, That the Honourable the Governour, be requested to issue his commands to the officers of the malitieo to take care to prevent the same.

And it is further enacted, That any person or persons that shall harbour, entertaine, or employ any Indian, shall be fined five thousand pounds of tobacco, or suffer one year's imprisonment without baile or maineprise, unless such as shall give sufficient security to the county courts, and upon such security, obteyne a certificate from the said court, and upon that certificate a lysence from the Governour.

And whereas by the former articles of agreement, it was provided, that no Indians which are seated on the South side of James river, should come over the *Black water* or the Southerne branches thereof,

It is hereby enacted, That the said bounds, from the head of *Black water* to the Apamatack Indian towne, and thence cross to the Monikon towne, be the bounds of the Indians on the South side of James river.

16 Removing "the guilt of blood from the land" (1672)

Although the English Crown claimed dominion over all discovered lands, colonial existence depended on the sufferance and often the assistance of the powerful Native American tribes and nations that inhabited the territory. The colonies traded with and purchased land from the tribes, but as their populations grew, frictions with the Native Americans developed.

The surge of settlers into the Connecticut Valley from both New England and New Amsterdam (and the resulting competition between the English and the Dutch) stirred the Pequot tribe to fight the white migration. After failing to enlist the aid of the powerful Narragansetts or Mohicans, the Pequots undertook the task alone. The Massachusetts colony sent aid to the settlers, and in a surprise raid from the sea upon the Pequot stockade on the Mystic River, the settler forces killed over one thousand men, women, and children of the tribe. Those escaping were hunted down and killed or enslaved. Remnants of the tribe were assimilated into other tribes, and the Pequots' history as a cohesive people came to an end.

The colonists began to regulate more carefully their relations with the Native Americans. It was unusual, nevertheless, for the whites to assert jurisdiction, as here, with respect to affairs that involved Native American aggression upon other Native Americans. More common were the restrictions on trade, particularly of liquor and armaments—and not without cause. In 1675, Metacomet (or King Philip as he was known to the whites), son of Massasoit, who first welcomed the colonists, began a war that was to last three years and to rage through Massachusetts, Rhode Island, and Connecticut. Thirteen towns were destroyed and six hundred whites and three thousand Wampanoags, Narragansetts, and Nipmucks were killed. The war ended when King Philip was assassinated by another Native American. With the defeat, the threat Native Americans posed to the existence of these colonies ended.

☆16 An Act for the Well Ordering of the Indians [Connecticut]

Reprinted in E. M. Coleman, ed., *Laws of the Colonial And State Governments Relating to Indians and Indian Affairs, from 1633-1831 Inclusive* (Washington, D.C.: Thompson and Homans, 1832), 37-40.

That some means may be used to convey the knowledge of God, and of his word, to the Indians and natives among us,

Be it enacted by the Governor, Council, and Representatives, in General Court assembled, and by

the authority of the same, That one or more of the teaching Elders of the churches in this jurisdiction, with the help of an able interpreter, shall be desired, as often as he may, in every year, to go among the neighboring Indians, and endeavor to make known to them the councils of the Lord; thereby to draw and stir them up to direct and order all their ways and conversations according to the rules of his word: and the Governor and Deputy Governor, and other magistrates, are desired to take care and see the thing attended, and, with their own presence, so far as may be convenient, to encourage the same.

And it is further enacted, by the authority aforesaid, That where any company of Indians do sit down near any town or English plantation, they shall declare who is their Sachem, or Chief; and that the said Sachem, or Chief, shall pay to the English such trespasses as shall be committed by any Indian or Indians in the said plantations adjoining, either by spoiling or killing of cattle or swine, either with guns, traps, dogs, or arrows, or by any other means, although they plead it was done by strangers, unless they can produce the party, and deliver him, or his goods, into the custody of the English; and that they shall pay double damage if it were done wittingly and voluntarily; the like engagement this Court also makes to them, in case of wrong or injury done to them by the English, which shall be paid by the party by whom it was done, if it can be made to appear, or else by the town in whose limits such facts are committed.

And to prevent inconveniences and troubles that may arise by the Indians coming into the English towns and plantations in the night season, and supplying themselves with liquors and prohibited goods,

It is further enacted by the authority aforesaid, That all and every Indian and Indians that shall be found passing and repassing in any town in this Colony, after the shutting in of the evening, (except he or they shall give sufficient reason that there was necessity thereof) shall forfeit and pay the sum of *twenty shillings*, whereof *fifteen shillings* shall be to the county treasury, and *five shillings* to the complainer or complainers; or be whipt, not exceeding *six stripes*: any one assistant or justice of the peace, before whom any such complaint shall come, shall be, and is hereby, empowered to secure every such Indian or Indians, by committing them to prison, or setting a watch upon them, till he may hear and issue such complaints.

And be it further enacted, by the authority aforesaid, That no person or persons whomsoever, shall, directly or indirectly, sell, truck, barter, give, or deliver, to any Indian, any strong beer, ale, cyder, perry, wine, rum, brandy, or other strong liquors, by what name or names soever called or known, on pain of forfeiting the sum of *twenty shillings* for every

pint, and proportionable for any greater or lesser quantity so sold, trucked, bartered, given, or delivered, to any Indian, directly or indirectly, as aforesaid, upon conviction thereof before any assistant or justice of the peace, where the penalty doth not exceed *forty shillings*, and if it exceed that sum, at the county court to be holden for the same county where the offence is committed; two-third parts of all such forfeitures to be to the county treasury, the remaining third part to him or them that shall prosecute the same by bill, plaint, or information: *Provided*, This act shall not be intended, or extend to restrain any act of charity for relieving any Indian (*bona fide*) in any sudden exigent of faintness, or sickness, not to exceed one or two drams, or by the allowance of an assistant or justice of the peace.

And it is further enacted, by the authority aforesaid, That every Indian or negro, servant or slave, that shall be convicted of the breach of this law, shall be openly whipt, not exceeding *ten stripes*, unless the master of such servant or slave shall answer the law by paying his or her fine: and every Indian convicted of drunkenness in the Colony, shall forfeit and pay the sum of *ten shillings*, whereof one half shall be to the complainer or complainers, and the other half to the County Treasury, where the offence is committed, or else be openly whipped, not exceeding *ten stripes* for one offence, as the assistant or justice of the peace, before whom such conviction is, shall determine.

And for preventing of the breach of the Sabbath, by the Indians within this Colony:

It is further enacted by the authority aforesaid, That, if any Indian or Indians shall labour or play on the Sabbath day, within the limits of any English town, every such Indian, being thereof duly convicted, shall pay a fine of *five shillings*, whereof the one-half shall be to the complainer, the rest to the county treasury, or else set in the stocks *one hour*; any one assistant or justice of the peace to hear and determine the same.

And be it further enacted by the authority aforesaid, That no Indian or Indians shall, at any time, pawaw, or perform outward worship to false gods, or to the devil, within this Colony, on pain of forfeiting the sum of *five pounds* to the public treasury of this Colony, for every time any Indian or Indians shall be convicted of performing or doing the same.

And if any person or persons, of the age of twenty years or upwards, shall, at any time, be present at any Indian play or pawawing, at any of their general meetings, every such person shall forfeit the sum of *forty shillings*; and if any person shall join in playing with any Indian or Indians, or shall lay any wager with, or for, any Indian, about or concerning any such play or game, he shall forfeit and pay a fine of *ten pounds*; one moiety of these fines and forfeitures to be to the complainer, or complainers, and the other moiety to the treasury of the county in which such offence is committed.

And whereas, it is too manifest, that the Indians, notwithstanding all council and advice to the contrary, have committed, and still do proceed to commit murder, and kill one another, within the English plantations in this Colony, and take no course that such justice be executed on such malefactors as may take off the guilt of blood from the land: Which to prevent—

It is further enacted by the authority aforesaid, That, if any Indian or Indians, within this Colony, shall wilfully and violently fall upon any Indian or Indians, within this Colony, and upon the English land, (except it be such as they are at open war with) and murder him or them, and be thereof legally convicted, every such Indian and Indians shall suffer the pains of death: And if the Indians shall not do just execution upon such murderer, or murderers, speedily, the next assistant or justice of the peace shall, forthwith, cause him or them to be apprehended, and without bail or mainprize, commit him or them to the common gaol, there to be secured for a trial, at the next court of assistants.

*   *   *

17 Nathaniel Bacon's Rebellion (1676-1677)

An aristocratic, English-born Cambridge graduate, Nathaniel Bacon, sailed for Virginia in 1673, where he acquired several estates and received an appointment to the governor's council. Virginia's western settlers were dissatisfied with rule by privileged families and the failure of the government to protect them against Native American raids. (Sir William Berkeley, the royal governor, was alleged to have benefited greatly from the Native American fur trade.) Bacon took up the cause of pacifying the borders. In the Battle of Bloody Run, Bacon's unofficial military expedition defeated and severely punished the Native Americans.

Governor Berkeley quickly outlawed Bacon, who then marched on the colonial capital demanding recognition for his forces as the official colonial army. In the civil war that followed, Berkeley was defeated and Jamestown was burned. But Bacon fell ill in the midst of the campaign, and with his death in October 1676, the rebellion collapsed.

The House of Burgesses declared Bacon and his followers guilty of high treason without trial. The episode concluded with wholesale executions and confiscations of the rebels' estates by the royal governor. To prevent future unrest, the legislature also passed an act prohibiting any spoken or written sentiments supporting Bacon's on any other rebellion or

in any way treating contemptuously the governor, his council, the justices of the peace, or the official militia. The prescribed penalties included fines of one thousand pounds of tobacco, a stint in the pillory, and, for women offenders, whipping on the naked back.

The act of attainder or outlawry was an important tool used to punish individuals for political dissent. An attainder, as here, was usually a legislative adjudgment and punishment for a past treason. Lesser penalties were prescribed prospectively for people engaging in activities not amounting to treason but nevertheless considered inimical to the welfare of the colony.

☆ 17 Acts against Wicked and Desolute Persons [Virginia]

W. Hening, ed., *Virginia Statutes at Large, 1660-1682* (Charlottesville: University Press of Virginia, 1969), 366-87.

☆ 17a Act II. An Act of Attainder, etc.

WHEREAS Nathaniel Bacon the younger, having by many false and wicked pretences drawn to his party many other wicked and desolute persons within this his majesties collony of Virginia, and haveing together with some other his desperate accomplices plotted and contrived the ruine of this his majesties country, and to draw and persuade many of his most sacred majesties subjects from theire due allegiance and obedience to his majestie, and the government under him established, under which this collony hath bin soe long happy and flourished, in order to which plotts and contrivances, the said Nathaniel Bacon junior, and his desperate accomplices in a most traiterous and rebellious manner, haveing putt themselves in armes and under pretence of the said Indian warr by threats and menaces of killing and destroying the whole grand assembly, haveing by force procured a commission to make the said Nathaniel Bacon generall for the said Indian warr, did in prosecution of the said traytorous and rebellious plotts themselves contrive and take most traiterous and rebellious oathes against and contrary to their allegiance to his most sacred majestie and with their armed men, and otherwayes did inforce many of his majesties subjects to take the same traiterous and rebellious oathes, and proceeded with his said armed acomplices to the seizing and imprisoning many of his majesties loyall subjects, and threatening his majesties governour and many of his loyall subjects with death, soe as they were inforced to departe from their habitations, whereupon the said Nathaniell Bacon did with the said wicked ayders and assisters, robb and dispoile many of his majesties subjects of their estates, and murthered and killed many of them; in the height of their monstrious rebellion, it pleased Almighty God of his infinite mercy and goodnes to this poore country, by a just and most exemplary death, to take the said Nathaniell Bacon out of this world, and his said wicked accomplices still continueing their said treasons and rebellions against his sacred majestie, did prosecute the said rebellion, destroying their estates and endeavouring to kill and destroy many his majesties loyall subjects, untill God Almighty, by his infinite mercy and goodnesse was pleased soe to blesse the just endeavours of the right honourable Sir William Berkeley, his majesties governour of this colony, and the loyall party under his command, that the said traitors and rebells were reduced to their allegiance, and enforced to submit to the right and good government established by his most sacred majestie. *And whereas* the said Nathaniell Bacon the younger died in open rebellion against his most sacred majestie, and Edmund Cheesman a principall ayder and abetter with the said Nathaniell Bacon in the said rebellion, being taken in armes and brought prisoner dyed before his tryall, and William Hunt, another principal ayder and abetter of the said Nathaniell Bacon, dyed alsoe before the rebells were reduced to their allegiance to his majestie by which said meanes the said Nathaniell Bacon, junr. Edmund Cheeseman and William Hunt have escaped their due and just demerritts for their wicked and unheard of treasons and rebellions; *Bee it therefore enacted by the governour, councell and burgesses of this grand assembly, and the authoritie thereof*, that the said Nathaniell Bacon, junr. Edmund Cheesman and William Hunt, and every and either of them shall by vertue of this act be adjudged to be convicted and attainted of high treason to all intents and purposes, as if they and every of them had been attainted respectively in their lives. *And whereas* alsoe Thomas Hansford, Thomas Wilsford, William Carver, Wm. Drummond, James Crewes, John Johnson, George ffarloe, Thomas Hall, Thomas Young, Henry Page, James Wilson, John Baptista, William Cockson and John Digby, all notorious actors and confederates with the said Nathaniell Bacon, junr. in the said rebellions and treasons, and endeavoured to continue the same after his death, who were some of them taken in the height of, and all of them taken in open rebellion against the kings majestie, and were all of them tryed found guilty, and deservedly adjudged to death by the right honourable the governour and a councell of warre of the cheife commanders of the country, which sentance for their said treasons and rebellions against his sacred majestie accordingly executed upon them and every of them. *And be it further enacted by the authority aforesaid*, that the said Thomas Hansford, Thomas Wilsford, William Carver, William Drummond, James Crewes, John Johnson, George ffarloe,

Thomas Hall, Thomas Young, Henry Page, James Wilson, John Baptista, William Cockson and John Digby, and every or either of them, shalby vertue of this act be adjudged to be convicted and attainted of high treason to all intents and purposes. And that William West and John Turner, two notorious actors and confederates with the said Nathaniell Bacon, junr. in the said wicked treasons and rebellions, and endeavoured to continue the same after his death, and were taken in open rebellion against his most sacred majestie, and for such their treasons and rebellions, before the right honourable the governour and a councell of warr, were tryed, found guilty and deservedly adjudged to death, but before justice was executed upon them, they made their escapes out of prison and are fled; *Bee it therefore further enacted by the authority aforesaid*, that the said William West and John Turner, and either of them shall by vertue of this act stand, and be adjudged to be convicted and attainted of high treason to all intents and purposes. And whereas William Rookins, a very notorious actor and confederate with the said Nathaniell Bacon in the said rebellions and treasons, and endeavouring to continue the same after his death, was taken in open rebellion against his most sacred majestie, and for such his treasons and rebellions before the right honourable the governour and a councell of warr, was tryed, found guilty and deservedly adjudged to suffer death, but before justice was executed upon him, he the said William Rookins dyed in prison; *Bee it therefore enacted by the authority aforesaid*, that the said William Rookins shall by vertue of this act be adjudged to be convicted and attainted of high treason to all intents and purposes. And whereas Richard Lawrence, Thomas Whaley and John fforth, three of the most notorious ayders and assisters of the said Nathaniell Bacon in the said horrid rebellions and treasons, and three of the principall actors in continueing of the same, are fled from justice, not dareing to abide a legall tryall; *Bee it further enacted by the authority aforesaid*, that the said Richard Lawrence, Thomas Whaley and John fforth, and either of them, shall by vertue of this act be adjudged to be convicted and attainted of high treason to all intents and purposes, and that all and every the messuages, lands, tenements, rents, remainders, interests and all other the hereditaments, chattles, reall goods, debts and other principall estate, and other things of that nature whatsoever that be of them the said Nathaniell Bacon, junr., Edmund Cheesman, William Hunt, Thomas Hansford, Thomas Wilsford, William Carver, William Drummond, James Crewes, John Johnson, George ffarloe, Thomas Hall, Thomas Younge, Henry Page, James Willson, John Baptista, William Cookson, William West, John Turner, John Digby, William Rookins, Richard Lawrence, Thomas Whaley and John fforth, which they or either of them, or any other person or persons to their or any of their uses or interests, for them or either of them were seized or possessed of the ffirst day of October last past, or at any time since, shall stand and be forfeited to the kings most sacred majestie, his heires and successors, and shalbe deemed vested, and adjudged to be in the actuall and reall possession of the kings majestie without any office or inquisition thereof hereafter to be taken or found.

*   *   *

☆ 17b Act V. An Act for the Reliefe of Such Loyall Persons As Have Suffered Losse by the Late Rebells

*   *   *

Bee it enacted by this present grand assembly, and the authority thereof, and it is hereby enacted, that if any person or persons, not being a women covert shall presume to speake, write, disperse or publish by words, writeing or otherwise, any matter or thing tending to rebellion, or in favour of the late rebells or rebellion, and shall thereof be lawfully convict, then such persons for the ffirst such offence shall be fined one thousands pounds of tobacco and caske, and stand upon the pillory two howers with capitall letters of their crimes affixed on their foreheads or brest, and for such second offence pay double the fine and stand in the pillory two howres with capitall letters of their crimes fixed as aforesaid, and for the third such offence be prosecuted as a rebell and a tratour to his most sacred majestie. And if any woman covert that comitt such offence as is before recited, then to be whipped on the bare back with twenty lashes, for the first offence, and for the second offence thirty lashes, except she can redeeme herselfe from the said corporall punishments by payment of the ffine or ffines before mentioned, for such first and second offences. *And be it further enacted,* that if any woman under covert shall a third tyme committ such offence, to be prosecuted against as a rebell and traytor to his most sacred majestie. And whereas it hath beene frequent for rude and ill disposed persons to contemne and revile authority and magistrates, as well in words as in actions; *Bee it therefore enacted by this present grand assembly, and by the authority thereof,* that all and every person and persons that shall from the tyme to come presume to speake and utter mutinous or contemptuous words, or shall by any wayes or meanes abuse the right honourable the governour or any of the councell, justices of the peace or commissionated militia officers, and shall be thereof lawfully convict, shall for his such offence, if against the right honourable the governour, be whipped on the bare back with thirty lashes, or pay eight hundred pounds of

tobacco and caske, if against any of the honourable councell, that then he shalbe whipped on the bare back with twenty fowre lashes, or pay six hundred pounds of tobacco and caske, and if against any justice of the peace or comissionate field officer, then to be whipped on the bare back with twenty lashes, or pay fowre hundred pounds of tobacco and caske, and the like for such second offence, being likewise thereof lawfully convict. And if any person or persons, male or female, shall be convicted a third tyme of such mutany or contemptious or villifying words writeing or otherwise, abuseing or scanduliseing the right honourable the governour or any of the honourable councell or any justice of the peace or commissionated militia ffield officer, then to be whipped on the bare back with thirty nine lashes, and stand in the pillowry two howers, or pay double the before recited ffines, all which said ffines as aforesaid shalbe and belong the one halfe to the informer, if he shall sue for the same, and the other halfe to the county, where the offending party then dwells or resides, which said ffines to be levyed by distresse or otherwise, and collected or destrayned for by the sherriffe or collector for the publique and county levyes. ... *And* whereas by a branch of an act of assembly made in March last, liberty is granted to all persons to carry their armes wheresoever they goe, which liberty hath beene found to be very prejudiciall to the peace and wellfaire of this colony. *Bee it therefore further enacted by this present grand assembly, and the authority thereof, and it is hereby enacted,* that if any person or persons shall, from and after publication of this act, presume to assemble together in armes to the number of five or upwards without being legally called together, that for such convention, or assembling together in armes the number of ffive or upwards, they be held deemed and adjudged as riotous and mutinous, and that they be proceeded against and punished accordingly.

*   *   *

18 "seduced from their allegiance" (1680)

The brutal sanctions Governor Berkeley imposed on Bacon's followers resulted in Berkeley's censure by Charles II. Berkeley sailed to England to set forth his defense, but he died in London in 1677 without having seen the king. Seeking a reconciliation with the rebels, both Charles II and the General Assembly of Virginia in 1680 granted a comprehensive pardon to those who had participated in Bacon's Rebellion—with certain exceptions. This amnesty set the course for similar reconciliations following future rebellions in America. Nevertheless, this "generall pardon" was unwilling to overlook the "lycentiousnesse" of those who in the future might defame the government and its officials. It prescribed less severe penalties for those who would spread false and scandalous reports or otherwise would dishonor or defame the colony's councillors, judges, or officers.

☆ 18 An Act of Free and Generall Pardon, Indennitie and Oblivion [Virginia]

W. Hening, ed., *Virginia Statutes at Large, 1660-1682* (Charlottesville: University Press of Virginia, 1969), 458-64.

THE Kings most excellent majestie haveing taken into his serious and gratious consideration the present state and condition of his colony of Virginia, and reflecting on the late rebellion raised there by Nathaniell Bacon junr. deceased, his complices and abettors, and how many of his good subjects were drawne into the same and seduced from their allegiance by the specious pretences sett forth by the said Nathaniell Bacon, who have since by their dutifull behaviour shewed themselves sencible thereof, and repenting for the same, and to the intent that noe crime whatsoever comitted against his said majestie and government may hereafter rise into judgment or be brought in question against any of them to their least endamagement, either in lives, liberties, estates or to the prejudice of their reputations, by any reproach or terme of distinctions, and to turne all seeds of future discords and the remembrances thereof in utter oblivion, as well in his majesties owne breast as in the breasts of his majesties subjects one towards another, and out of an earnest desire to put an end to all suites, quarrells and controversies whatsoever that by occasion of the said rebellion and late destractions have arisen and may arise betweene any of his majesties subjects and in pursuance of his gratious proclamation of pardon hearing date the seaven and twentyeth day of October 1676, and in the eight and twentyeth yeare of his raigne, is gratiously pleased *that it may be enacted, and be it encted by the kings most excellent majestie by and with the consent of the generall assembly*, that all and all manner of treasons, misprision of treasons, murders, fellonies, crimes and misdeameanors comitted, acted, councelled or done by any person or persons whatsoever upon or at any tyme before the sixteenth day of January, 1676, in the 28th yeare of his majesties raigne, other then the persons hereafter excepted.... *And be it further enacted by the authority aforesaid*, that all and every such person and persons, their and every of their heires, executors and administrators (except as hereafter excepted) that were actually ingaged in ayding, assisting, adviseing, abetting or councelling the said rebellion shall have and enjoy all and every their lands, tenements, hereditaments, goods, and chattells, whatsoever forfeited to his majestie, his heires and successors for any of the crimes aforesaid in the same manner, and as freely to all intents and purposes as if they had not been forfeited, yet soe that they may and every of them and their estates both reall and personall, shalbe subject and lyable to pay all and singuler their just debts in the same manner as if they had comitted noe rebellion, crimes or offences, *except and always foreprized out* of this act, the above named *Nathaniell Bacon, junr.* the principall contriver, beginner and maintainer of the said rebellion who haveing taken up armes under pretence of an Indian warr, assumed unto himselfe the title of generall, and did afterwards chase the then governor, there rob, kill and continue to destroy severall other of his majesties loyall subjects that refused to take the detestible oaths imposed by the said Bacon, untill it pleased the Allmighty to send him the said *Bacon* an infamous and exemplary death, whereby he hath escaped the punishment in this world soe justly due to his person; *Bee it therefore enacted, and it is hereby enacted by the authority aforesaid*, that the said Nathaniell Bacon junior shalbe by virtue of this act, and is hereby adjudged to be convict and attainted of high treason to all intents and purposes as if he had been convict and attainted thereof by due course of law in his life time, and that all the estate reall and personall, whereof he was seized or possessed upon the ffifth day of June 1676, or at any tyme after within the colony of Virginia shalbe forfeited to the kings majestie, his heires and successors, and is hereby declared to be vested in his majesty, his heires and successors without any office or inquisition thereof to be hereafter taken or found; *Provided always, and be it enacted* that this act nor any thing therein contained shall extend to pardon, discharge or give any other benefitt whatsoever unto [certain named individuals] but that the persons last aforesaid and their estates are out of this act wholly excepted and fforeprized.

Provided alsoe, and it is hereby enacted and declared by the authority aforesaid, that if Joseph Ingram, Gregory Walklett, Thomas Whaley, John fforth and John Langston shall at any tyme after the passing of this act accept or exercise any publique office whatsoever within the said colony of Virginia, that then such of them as doe soe, accept or exercise aforesaid, shall to all intents and purposes stand as if he or they had beene totally excepted by name out of this act.... *Provided always* that noe further punishment, satisfaction or damages shalbe recovered or inflicted on any christian servants that have deserted their masters or bin active in the late rebellion, then that the time incurring betweene the said ffirst day of May and the said sixteenth of January shalbe accompted noe part of their tyme of service. *And be it further enacted by the authority aforesaid* that noe verdicts, judgments, indictments, informations, decrees, sentences, probatts of wills, adminis- trations, writts or actings, or returne of writts, or- ders or other proceedings whatsoever in law or equity had, made, given, taken or done or depending in any courts or before any judges whatsoever within the said colony of Virginia. . . . *And whereas* during the lycentiousnesse of the late tymes several ill disposed persons tooke upon them to asperse the government and defame the governor and cheife magistrates of the said colony, raising false and scandalous reports, without which our good subjects there could not have been soe easily led away, which cannot but tend to the future disturbance of the peace and welfare thereof if not tymely prevented, by inflicting punishments proportionate to the greateness of the crime. *Bee it therefore enacted by the authority aforesaid*, that whosoever shall after passing of this act, malitiously and advisedly by writeing, speakeing or otherwise expresse, publish, utter or declare any word, sentence or thing or things to incite or stir up the people to the dislike of any person appointed by his majestie to be governor or comander in cheife of the said colony, or tending to the dishonour or defameing the said governour or comander in cheife for the tyme being, and being thereof legally convicted shalbe imprisoned during one yeare without bayle or mainprize, and incurr such forfeiture as shalbe adjudged, not exceeding the sume of 500*l.* to the kings most excellent majes- tie, his heires and successors, *And it is in like man- ner enacted*, that whosoever shall malitiously and advisedly by writing, speaking or otherwise ex- presse, publish, utter or declare any words, senten- ces or other things to incite or stirr up the people to the dislike of his majesties councellors, judges, or other principall officers within the said colony, or tending to the dishonour or defameing of the said councellors, judges or principall officers, and being thereof legally convicted shalbe imprisoned three months without bayle or mainprise and incurr such forfeiture as shalbe adjudged, not exceeding the sume of one hundred pounds, to the kings most ex- cellent majestie, his heires and successors, any act or acts, order or orders to the contrary in any wise notwithstanding.

19 "not to devour and destroy one another" (1681)

In 1681 Charles II granted a charter to his friend William Penn—in settlement of a debt owed by the king to Penn's father—to permit the founding of a haven for Penn's fellow Quakers in the New World. Originally interested in settling New Jersey, Penn accepted instead the fertile lands along the west bank of the Delaware River. Charles himself be- stowed the name *Pennsylvania* upon this territory. Being a remarkable proprietor, Penn set out not only to permit the people of the colony to formulate their own laws but also to seek an accommodation with the land's native people.

References exist to a Great Treaty entered into by Penn with the Native Americans in 1682 to bring about mutual cooperation between the colonizers and the natives. This treaty was to guarantee the founding in America of the Peaceable Kingdom fore- cast in biblical times by the prophet Isaiah. No copy of the treaty has survived, and its existence is doubted. But Penn's sensitivity toward the native population is reflected in a letter written to the Na- tive Americans of Pennsylvania a year earlier. The communication is in sharp contrast to the attitudes of other colonists (including John Smith, rescued by Pocahontas) and calls for relations based upon mu- tual respect between equals. Tension between these two fundamentally radical attitudes toward the Na- tive Americans has long persisted.

☆ 19 William Penn's Letter to the Native Americans of Pennsylvania (October 18, 1681)

Reprinted in Catherine O. Peare, *William Penn: A Biogra- phy* (Ann Arbor: University of Michigan Press, 1956), 223- 24.

MY FRIENDS:

There is one great God and power that hath made the world and all things therein, to whom you and I and all people owe their being and well-being, and to whom you and I must one day give an account, for all that we do in the world; this great God hath written His law in our hearts, by which we are taught and commanded to love and help, and do good to one an- other, and not to do harm and mischief one unto an- other. Now this great God hath been pleased to make me concerned in your parts of the world, and the King of the country where I live hath given unto me a great province therein; but I desire to enjoy it with your love and consent, that we may always live together as neighbors and friends, else what would the great God say to us, who hath made us not to devour and destroy one another, but live soberly and kindly together in the world? Now I would have you well observe, that I am very sensible of the un- kindness and injustice that hath been too much exer- cised toward you by the people of these parts of the world, who have sought themselves, and to make great advantages by you, rather than be examples of justice and goodness unto you, which I hear, hath been matter of trouble to you, and caused great grudgings and animosities, sometimes to the shed- ding of blood, which hath made the great God angry. But I am not such a man, as is well known in my own country, I have great love and regard towards you, and I desire to win and gain your love and friendship by a kind, just and peaceable life, and the people I send are of the same mind, and shall in all things behave themselves accordingly; and if in any thing any shall offend you or your people, you shall have a full and speedy satisfaction for the same, by an equal number of just men on both sides, that by no means you may have just occasion of being offended against them. I shall shortly come to you myself, at what time we may more largely and freely confer and discourse of these matters; in the meantime, I have sent my commissioners to treat with you about land, and a firm league of peace; let me desire you to be kind to them and the people, and receive these presents and tokens which I have sent to you, as a testimony of my good will to you, and my resolution to live justly, peaceably and friendly with you.

I am your loving friend,

WILLIAM PENN

20 The Tobacco Treason (1684)

Until William and Mary's succession to the British throne in 1688, a bitter struggle continued between the privileged landowners, joined by the English officials, and the poorer population. Popular dissatisfaction frequently was vented by the destruction of the tobacco crop upon which the colonial government relied for revenue. In 1684, the General Assembly of Virginia, during the governorship of Lord Howard, perceived that the cutting up, pulling up, or other destruction of a tobacco plant, primarily an act of protest against private property, was a threat to the political order of the colony. The General Assembly decreed such acts to be treason punishable by death. The economic interests in the state thus were granted special protection from attack by the less fortunate segments of the populace.

☆ 20 An Act for the Better Preservation of the Peace of Virginia, and Preventing Unlawfull and Treasonable Associations

Reprinted in W. Hening, ed., *Virginia Statutes at Large, 1682-1710* (Charlottesville: University Press of Virginia, 1969), 9-12.

*   *   *

WHEREAS, many evill and ill-disposed persons inhabitants of this his majesties collony and dominion of Virginia, contrary to their duty and allegiance, on or about the first of May, in the thirty-fourth yeare of his majesties raigne (1682), and divers other dayes, and times tumultously and mutinously assembled and gathered together to cut up and destroy all tobacco plants, and to perpetrate the same in a trayterous and rebellious manner, with force

and armes entered the plantations of many his majesties good subjects of this his collony, resolving by open force, a generall and totall destruction of all tobacco plants within this his majesties dominion, to the hazarding the subvertion of the whole government, and ruine and destruction of his majesties good subjects. . . . *And bee it enacted by the governour, councill and burgesses of this assembly,* That if any person or persons whatsoever, to the number of eight or above, being assembled together, shall at any time after the first day of June now next ensueing, intend, goe about, practice or put in use with force, unlawfully to cut, pull up or destroy any tobacco plants, either in bedds or hills, growing within the said collony, or to destroy the same, either cureing or cured, either before the same is in hogsheads or afterwards, or to pull downe, burne or destroy the houses or other places where any such tobacco shall be, or to pull downe the fences or enclosures of any tobacco plants, with intent to cut up or destroy the same, (and such person or persons being commanded or required in his majesties name by the governour or other commander in chief, or any one of the councell, or one or more of the justices of the peace of the said collony, commanding and requireing such persons to disperse themselves, and peaceably to depart to their habitations) shall continue together by the space of four houres after such proclamation made, at or nigh the place where such persons shall be soe assembled; that then every such persons soe willingly assembled, in forceable manner, to doe any of the acts before mentioned and soe continuing together as aforesaid, and being thereof lawfully convicted, shall be deemed, declared and adjudged to be traytors, and suffer paines of death, and alsoe and forfeite as in cases of high treason. *Provided always,* that noe person or persons whatsoever shall incurr the pains and penalties hereby inflicted, unlesse he or they be prosecuted and indicted thereupon, within twelve months after the offence committed. Any thing herein contained to the contrary notwithstanding.

*   *   *

21 "against the traffic of men-body" (1688)

In William Penn's colony, founded as a haven for the oppressed Quakers and perceived as tolerant of national, ethnic, and religious diversity, the first protest against black enslavement resounded. The Germantown Mennonites argued that the slave trade was inhuman and contrary to Christian principles and should not be permitted in Pennsylvania. Despite the fact that the existing law required subservient acquiescence by the slave to his condition, the

Mennonites stated the moral case justifying breach of the law in defense of one's freedom.

☆ 21 Resolution of the Germantown, Pennsylvania, Mennonites

Reprinted in P. Mode, ed., *Source Book and Bibliographical Guide for American Church History* (Menasha, Wis.: George Banta, 1921), 552-53.

This is to the monthly meeting held at Richard Worrell's:

These are the reasons why we are against the traffic of men-body, as followeth: Is there any that would be done or handled at this manner? viz., to be sold or made a slave for all the time of his life? How fearful and faint-hearted are many at sea, when they see a strange vessel, being afraid it should be a Turk, and they should be taken, and sold for slaves into Turkey. Now, what is *this* better done, than Turks do? Yea, rather it is worse for them, which say they are Christians; for we hear that the most part of such negers are brought hither against their will and consent, and that many of them are stolen. Now, though they are black, we cannot conceive there is more liberty to have them slaves, as it is to have other white ones. There is a saying, that we should do to all men like as we will be done ourselves; making no difference of what generation, descent, or colour they are. And those who steal or rob men, and those who buy or purchase them, are they not all alike? Here is liberty of conscience, which is right and reasonable; here ought to be likewise liberty of the body, except of evil-doers, which is another case. But to bring men hither, or to rob and sell them against their will, we stand against. In Europe there are many oppressed for conscience-sake; and here there are those oppressed which are of a black colour. And we who know that men must not commit adultery — some do commit adultery *in* others, separating wives from their husbands, and giving them to others: and some sell the children of these poor creatures to other men. Ah! do consider well this thing, you who do it, if you would be done at this manner — and if it is done according to Christianity! You surpass Holland and Germany in this thing. This makes an ill report in all those countries of Europe, where they hear of [it], that the Quakers do here handel men as they handel there the cattle. And for that reason some have no mind or inclination to come hither. And who shall maintain this your cause, or plead for it? Truly, we cannot do so, except you shall inform us better hereof, viz.: that Christians have liberty to practice these things. Pray, what thing in the world can be done worse towards us, than if men should rob or steal us away, and sell us for slaves to strange countries; separating husbands from their wives and children. Being now this is not done in the manner we would be done at; therefore, we contradict, and are against this traffic of men-body. And we who profess that it is not lawful to steal, must, likewise, avoid to purchase such things as are stolen, but rather help to stop this robbing and stealing, if possible. And such men ought to be delivered out of the hands of the robbers, and set free as in Europe. Then is Pennsylvania to have a good report, instead, it hath now a bad one, for this sake, in other countries; Especially whereas the Europeans are desirous to know in what manner *the Quakers* do rule in *their* province; and most of them do look upon us with an envious eye. But if this is done well, what shall we say is done evil?

If once these slaves (which they say are so wicked and stubborn men,) should join themselves — fight for their freedom, and handel their masters and mistresses, as they did handel them before; will these masters and mistresses take the sword at hand and war against these poor slaves, like, as we are able to believe, some will not refuse to do? Or, have these poor negers not as much right to fight for their freedom, as you have to keep them slaves?

Now consider well this thing, if it is good or bad. And in case you find it to be good to handel these blacks in that manner, we desire and require you hereby lovingly, that you may inform us herein, which at this time never was done, viz., that Christians have such a liberty to do so. To the end we shall be satisfied on this point, and satisfy likewise our good friends and acquaintances in our native country, to whom it is a terror, or fearful thing, that men should be handelled so in Pennsylvania.

This is from our meeting at Germantown, held ye 18th of the 2d month, 1688, to be delivered to the monthly meeting at Richard Worrell's.

GARRET HENDERICH
DERICK OP DE GRAEFF
FRANCIS DANIEL PASTORIUS
ABRAM OP DE GRAEFF

22 No Appearance of Any Domestic Rebellion (1691)

Under a charter granted to the Earl of Clarendon and seven other royal favorites in 1663, Charles II established Carolina as a proprietary colony. Its two early settlements were Albemarle (1670) and Charleston (1680). Theoretically North and South Carolina constituted a single colony, but after 1712 each part of the province had its own governor. For this province, the "Lords Proprietors" were to legislate "by and with the advice, assent, and approbation of the freeman."

The Lords Proprietors' rule met with much popular opposition. In their eagerness to combat popular unrest, the governor of the southern province and several leaders of the military declared martial law over that portion of the colony in 1690. As part of English common law and practice, colonial governments had the power to impose martial law to and suspend the traditional liberties and political rights of citizens whenever an emergency necessitated such measures. Martial law, an exception to the rule of law, permitted the military to resort to whatever measures it deemed necessary to meet the emergency.

Although concerned with the colony's protection against treason and rebellion, Carolina's legislature was mindful of the potential abuses of citizen's rights under the guise of an impending emergency. The colonial legislature, therefore, acted promptly to curtail the military's power. Pointing to the absence of a foreign invasion or a domestic rebellion that would have justified the termination of civil government and the imposition of martial law, the legislators set out to bar the offending officers from holding any future public office, "military or civil." This document then reflected on several subjects relating to political criminality: the temptation to resort to military power to suppress political dissention; the duty of responsible government to sanction those who betray and exceed their political authority; and the beginning of an American policy to keep the military out of political strife.

Proprietary rule in the Carolinas weakened, and in 1719 local dissatisfaction finally led to a rebellion against the existing government in Charleston and to the popular election of James Moore as governor. England accepted this outcome, and the colony, denominated South Carolina, came thereafter under royal rule until it achieved independence and statehood in 1776. Albemarle, denominated North Carolina in 1691, became a royal colony in 1729.

☆22 An Act for the Disabling of the Several Persons That Did Sett Up & Advise the Setting Up and Executing Martial Law [South Carolina]

Reprinted in T. Cooper, ed., *Statutes of South Carolina, 1682-1716* (Columbia, S.C.: A. S. Johnston, 1837), 49-50.

WHEREAS, Lieut. Col. Ste. Bull, Major Charles Colleton, Paul Grimball, Esq. together with Landgrave James Colleton, late Governor of this part of the Province, did make articles of warr and erect and establish Martiall Law, and the same cause to be published at the head of every company of the militia of this part of the Province, under the paines of death and other penaltys as in the said articles is sett downe and required, and the same did enforce and put in execution against divers of theire Majesties

peaceable subjects inhabiting in this province, to the apparent breach of libertys, propertys and privileges, and to the dread and terrour of theire Majesty's subjects, notwithstanding at the time there was noe appearance of any forraigne invasion or any domestick rebellion, tumult or sedition, and that at the same tyme all the Courts of Justice were opened and alwayes after continued to be so. And whereas, Thomas Smith, senior, Esq. did by composing, inventing, writing and publishing, as by him confest a certaine Petition, entitled The Petition of divers of theire Majesty's subjects and inhabitants of Charlestowne and parts adjacent, and by other means move, stirr, encourage, advise and persuade the said Stephen Bull, Charles Colleton, Paul Grimball and James Colleton, to exercise and establish law martiall, contrary to law and the priviledges of theire Majesty's subjects as aforesaid.

Be it therefore enacted by the Pallatine and the rest of the Lords and absolute Proprietors of this Province, by and with the advice and consent of the Commons of this present Parliament assembled, and by the authority of the same, that the said Stephen Bull, Charles Colleton, Paul Grimball and Thomas Smith, shall not att any tyme after the ratifycation of this Act, exercise any publick office or charge, either military or civill, either of honour, profit or trust in this Province, but shall be utterly disabled and are hereby rendered and made incapable to exercise the same by him or themselves, theire substitutes or deputys. And if any one of the aforesaid persons in any way offend contrary to this Act or any clause therein contained, he or they shall forfeit the summe of one thousand pounds sterling, one moyety whereof shall be disposed of by the Parliament, and the other moyety to him or them that shall sue for the same by any action of debt, bill, plaint, or information. . . .

23 "burned with a hot iron on the most visible part of the left cheek" (1704)

The colonial legislatures spelled out in great detail the conduct of slaves and the responsibilities of freemen toward them. Slaves departing from permitted conduct suffered harsh physical punishment, and erring freemen incurred severe financial penalties. In addition, laws were enforced in large measure by offering rewards to informants in the populace, a prime technique in combating political crime. The New Jersey enactment of 1704 was typical of colonial practices, but in 1709 the Lord Commissioners for Trade and Plantations recommended the repeal of this law on the grounds that it imposed "inhumane penalties on Negroes."

☆ 23 An Act for Regulating Negro, Indian,
and Mulatto Slaves within the Province of
New Jersey

Laws of New Jersey, chap. IX (1704).

Whereas it is found by daily experience, that Negro, Indian, and mulatto slaves, under pretense of trade, or liberty of traffic, frequently steal from their masters, mistresses, or others what they expose to sale at a difference from their habitations; and it being a known truth, that without a receiver, the thief would soon desert his practice, be it therefore enacted by the Governor, Council, and Assembly now met and assembled, and by the authority of the same, that all and every person or persons inhabiting within this province, who shall at any time after publication hereof buy, sell, barter, trade, or traffic with any Negro, Indian, or mulatto slaves, for any rum, wine, beer, cider, or other strong drink, or any other chattels, goods, wares, or commodities whatsoever within this province of Nova Casaria, or New Jersey, shall pay for the first offense five pounds, and for the second and every other offense, ten pounds current money of this province, one-half to the informer, the other half to the use of the poor of that place where the fact is committed....

*   *   *

And be it further enacted by the authority aforesaid, that if any Negro, Indian, or mulatto slaves of or belonging to any other province, without license under the hand of his or her master or mistress, shall be taken up by any person within this province, he, she, or they so taken up shall be whipped at the public whipping post belonging to the place where the said Negro, Indian, or mulatto slaves shall be taken up, not exceeding twenty lashes on the bare back, and to be committed by a warrant from a justice of the peace where the fact shall arise to the jail of that county; and the person so taking them up and carrying them to be whipped, shall have for his reward the sum of ten shillings for each slave, paid by the master or mistress of the said slaves, and to remain in prison till it be paid, with all other charges that shall accrue thereby.

And be it further enacted by the authority aforesaid, that if any Negro, Indian, or mulatto slave shall steal to the value of sixpence, or above, and under the sum of five shillings, and be thereof convicted before two justices of the peace, one whereof to be of quorum, upon the oath or solemn affirmation of one or more witnesses, such Negro, Indian, or mulatto slave shall be whipped on the bare back, at the public whipping place, with forty lashes by the constable of such township or place where the offense was committed, or by such person as he shall appoint. And, that if any Negro, Indian, or mulatto slave shall steal to the value of five shillings, or above, and under the sum of forty shillings, and be thereof convicted in manner as aforesaid, such Negro, Indian, or mulatto slave shall be whipped on the bare back with forty stripes, as aforesaid, and be likewise burned with a hot iron on the most visible part of the left cheek, near the nose, with the letter T, by the constable, as aforesaid; the said constable shall receive for the whipping of each Negro, Indian, or mulatto slave five shillings, and for burning each Negro, Indian, or mulatto slave ten shillings, to be paid by the master or mistress of the said slave; and in default of payment, to be levied by warrant from any justice of the peace, out of the goods of the said master or mistress; and that every constable who shall neglect or refuse to do his duty herein shall forfeit the sum of forty shillings, to be levied by warrant of any justice of the peace, directed to whom he shall appoint, out of the goods and chattels of the said constable.

And if any Negro, Indian, or mulatto slave shall attempt by force or persuasion to ravish or have carnal knowledge of any white woman, maid or child, and be thereof convicted by the verdict of twelve men of the neighborhood before two justices of the peace, one whereof to be of the quorum, such Indian, Negro, or mulatto shall be castrated at the care and charge of his master or mistress, and the Negro to continue in jail at the charge of his master or mistress till execution be performed.

And whereas the baptizing of slaves is thought by some to be a sufficient reason to set them at liberty, which being a groundless opinion and prejudicial to the inhabitants of this province, be it further enacted by the authority aforesaid, that the baptizing of any Negro, Indian, or mulatto slave shall not be any reason or cause for setting them, or any of them, at liberty; nor shall they nor any of them have or procure their or any of their liberty by virtue thereof.

And be it enacted by the authority aforesaid, that all the children that have been or shall be born in the county of such Negro, Indian, or mulatto slaves as have been formerly or may hereafter be set at liberty, and all their posterity shall be and are hereby forever after rendered incapable of purchasing or inheriting any lands and tenements within this province.

And be it further enacted by the authority aforesaid, that any person or persons within this province, who shall knowingly keep or entertain any Negro, Indian, or mulatto slave in his or their house, or otherwise, for above the space of two hours, without their master's or mistress' leave, or some other reasonable cause or occasion, shall forfeit the sum of one shilling for each hour to the master or mistress of such slave, to be recovered before any one of Her Majesty's justices of the peace, in the manner aforesaid; and if above forty shillings, then before the Court of Common Pleas, as aforesaid.

24 "a convenient dwelling place in this their native country" (1704)

As the population of the colonies grew, the settlers pressed into aboriginal lands with or without the approval of the colonial governments. New legislation was enacted to protect the lands held by Native Americans against incursions by whites. Significantly, while confirming the property rights of the Native Americans, this law also affirmed the higher sovereignty of Maryland's Lord Proprietor, to whom a yearly rent of a beaver skin was to be paid. Under this claim of a dominant sovereignty over the land, Native American self-governance became predicated upon English suffrance.

☆ 24 An Act for Ascertaining the Bounds of a Certain Tract of Land to the Use of the Nanticoke Indians so Long as They Shall Occupy and Live upon the Same [Maryland]

Reprinted in J. D. Cushing, ed., *Laws of the Province of Maryland (1718)* (Wilmington, Del.: Michael Glazier, 1977), 38.

It being most just that the Indians, the ancient inhabitants of this province, should have a convenient dwelling place in this their native country, free from the encroachments and oppressions of the English, more especially the Nanticoke Indians, in Dorchester county, who, for these many years, have lived in peace and concord with the English; and, in all matters, in obedience to the government of this Province; we, the burgesses and delegates of this present General Assembly, therefore, do pray that it may be enacted,

SEC. 2. *And be it enacted by the Queen's most Excellent Majesty, by and with the advice and consent of Her Majesty's Governor, Council, and Assembly, of this Province, and the authority of the same,* That all the land, [herein described] is confirmed and assured unto Panquash and Annotoughquan, and the people under their government or charge, and their heirs and successors forever, any law, usage, custom, or grant, to the contrary, in anywise, notwithstanding, to be held of the lord proprietary, and his heirs, lord proprietary, or lords proprietaries, of this province, under the yearly rent of one beaver skin, to be paid to his said lordship, and his heirs, as other rents in this province by the English used to be paid.

SEC. 3. *Provided always,* That it shall or may be lawful for any person or persons, that hath formerly taken up and obtained any grants from the Lord Baltimore, for any tracts or parcels of land within the aforesaid boundaries, upon the Indians deserting or leaving the said land, to enter, occupy, and enjoy the same; any thing in this law to the contrary notwithstanding.

SEC. 4. *And be it further enacted by the authority aforesaid,* That it may not, nor shall be lawful for the Lord Baltimore to ask, have, or demand, any rent or service for any of the said tracts or dividends as may or have been taken up as aforesaid, within the said Indian boundaries, until such time that the takers up, or owners aforesaid, do enjoy or possess the same, any law, usage, or custom, to the contrary notwithstanding. . . .

25 Sunday Arrests for Treason (1705)

While recognizing the gravity of the offense of treason, the colonists nevertheless insisted upon procedural safeguards for those accused. The 1705 Virginia laws that prohibited any sheriff or other officer from serving a legal writ on the Lord's Day excepted from this limitation the arrest of specified offenders, including those suspected of treason or riot. Extraordinary procedural mechanisms were a hallmark of combating the political offender.

☆ 25 An Act Prescribing the Method of Appointing Sheriffs; and for Limiting the Time of Their Continuance in Office and Directing Their Duty Therein [Virginia]

Reprinted in W. Hening, ed., *Virginia Statutes at Large, 1682-1710* (Charlottesville: University Press of Virginia, 1969), 250.

*   *   *

VI. *Provided always,* That it shall not be lawful for any sheriff, or his officer, or deputy, to execute any writ or precept upon the Lord's Day, commonly called Sunday, nor upon any person attending or doing his duty at any muster of the militia, or at any election of burgesses. And the execution of any writ or precept, contrary to the true meaning hereof, is hereby declared to be null and void; any thing herein contained, or any law, custom, or usage to the contrary, notwithstanding.

VII. *Provided nevertheless,* That it shall and may be lawful for the sheriff, his officer, and deputy, at any time and place whatsoever, to arrest and apprehend any person for treason, or felony, or suspicion of felony, or being accessory thereto; or for any riot, or breach of the peace; or upon any escape out of prison; any thing herein contained to the contrary thereof, notwithstanding.

*   *   *

26 Any Person May Be Outlawed and Thereby Attainted (1712)

To protect their population against unfounded and false charges of treason, England's lawmakers relied not only on the early statute of Edward III (1352) which narrowly defined the offense but also on a 1696 enactment under William and Mary which established procedural requirements for treason trials. Following the 1696 English reform, South Carolina set out, in 1712, to lessen the "terror and dread" of this accusation by requiring that all treason indictments be returned by a grand jury within three years of the commission of the offense, testimony be given by two lawful witnesses in open court, and the accused be accorded the right to two court-appointed lawyers. Those charged with treason thus were accorded the right to counsel over 250 years before the United States Supreme Court extended this safeguard to felons generally (*Gideon v. Wainwright*, 372 U.S. 335 [1963]).

☆26 An Act for Regulating of Trials in Cases of Treason and Misprision of Treason [South Carolina]

Reprinted in T. Cooper, ed., *Statutes of South Carolina, 1682-1716* (Columbia, S.C.: A. S. Johnston, 1837), 539-41.

WHEREAS, nothing is more just and reasonable, than that persons prosecuted for high treason and misprision of treason, whereby the liberties, lives, honour, estates, blood, and posterity of the subjects, may be lost and destroyed, should be justly and equally tried, and that persons accused as offenders therein should not be debarred of all just and equal means for defence of their innocencies in such cases; in order thereunto, and for the better regulation of trials of persons prosecuted for high treason and misprision of such treason, be it enacted by the King's most excellent majesty, by and with the advice and consent of the lord's spiritual and temporal, and the commons, in this present parliament assembled, and by the authority of the same, That from and after the 25th day of March, in the year of our Lord 1696, all and every person and persons whatsoever, that shall be accused and indicted for high treason, whereby any corruption of blood may or shall be made to any such offender or offenders, or to any heir or heirs of any such offender or offenders, or for misprision of such treason, shall have a true copy of the whole indictment, but not the names of the witnesses, delivered unto them, or any of them, five days at the least before he or they shall be tried, for the same, whereby to enable them, and any of them respectively, to advise with counsel thereupon, to plead and make their defence, his or their attorney or attornies, agent or agents, or any of them, requiring the same, and paying the officer his reasonable fees for writing thereof, not exceeding 5s. for the copy of every such indictment; and that every such person so accused and indicted, arraigned or tried for any such treason, as aforesaid, or for misprision of such treason, from and after the said time, shall be received and admitted to make his and their full defence, by counsel learned in the law, and to make any proof that he or they can produce by lawful witness or witnesses, who shall then be upon oath, for his and their just defence in that behalf; and in case any person or persons so accused or indicted shall desire counsel, the court before whom such person or persons shall be tried, or some judge of that court, shall and is hereby authorized and required immediately, upon his or their request, to assign to such person and persons such and so many counsel, not exceeding two, as the person or persons shall desire, to whom such counsel shall have free access at all seasonable hours; any law or usage to the contrary notwithstanding.

II. And be it further enacted, That from and after the said 25th day of March, in the year of our Lord 1696, no person or persons whatsoever shall be indicted, tried, or attainted, of high treason, whereby any corruption of blood may or shall be made to any such offender or offenders, or to any the heir or heirs of any such offender or offenders, or of misprision of such treason, but by and upon the oaths and testimony of two lawful witnesses, either both of them to the same overt act, or one of them to one, and the other of them to another overt act of the same treason; unless the party indicted, and arraigned, or tried, shall willingly, without violence, in open court, confess the same, or shall stand mute, or refuse to plead, or in cases of high treason shall peremptorily challenge above the number of 35 of the jury; any law, statute, or usage, to the contrary notwithstanding.

III. Provided always, That any person or persons, being indicted, as aforesaid, for any of the treasons, or misprisions of the treasons aforesaid, may be outlawed, and thereby attainted of or for any of the said offences of treason, or misprision of treason; and in cases of the high treasons aforesaid, where by the law, after such outlawry the party outlawed may come in, and be tried, he shall, upon such trial, have the benefit of this Act.

IV. And be it further enacted and declared by the authority aforesaid, That if two or more distinct treasons of divers heads or kinds shall be alleged in one bill of indictment, one witness produced to prove one of the said treasons, and another witness produced to prove another of the said treasons, shall not be deemed or taken to be two witnesses to the same treason, within the meaning of this Act.

V. And to the intent that the terror and dread of such criminal accusations may in some reasonable time be removed, be it further enacted by the authority aforesaid, That ... no person or persons whatsoever shall be indicted, tried or prosecuted, for any such treason ... unless the same indictment be found by a grand jury within three years next after the treason or offence done or committed.

VI. And that no person or persons shall be prosecuted for any such treason, . . . always provided and excepted, That if any person or persons whatsoever, shall be guilty of designing, endeavouring or attempting, any assassination on the body of the King, by poison or otherwise, such person or persons may be prosecuted at any time, notwithstanding the aforesaid limitation.

VII. And that all and every person or persons, who shall be accused, indicted, and tried for such treason . . . shall have copies of the panel of the jurors who are to try them, . . . two days at the least before he or they shall be tried for the same; and that all persons so accused and indicted for any such treason . . . shall have the like process of the court where they shall be tried, to compel their witnesses to appear for them at any such trial or trials, as is usually granted to compel witnesses to appear against them.

VIII. And be it further enacted, That no evidence shall be admitted or given of any overt act that is not expressly laid in the indictment, against any person or persons whatsoever.

*   *   *

27 To Acquaint Indians with the Laws of Government (1717)

Native American proximity to the colonies not only caused concern regarding their adherence to the white man's law and order but also resulted in an evangelizing effort. While continuing to recognize the self-governing nature of the Native American tribes, the new laws began a movement to undermine aboriginal social order and tribal authority by replacing dependence upon tribal resources with individual and familial "self-reliance."

☆ 27 An Act for the More Effectual Well Ordering of the Indians and for the Bringing of Them to the Knowledge of the Gospel [Connecticut]

Reprinted in *Laws of the Colonial and State Governments, Relating to Indians and Indian Affairs, 1633-1831 Inclusive* (Standfordville, N.Y.: E. M. Coleman, 1979), 42-43.

Whereas, pursuant to an act of the Assembly, holden in Hartford on the ninth day of May, in the present year one thousand seven hundred and seventeen: The Governor and Council have laid before this Assembly several measures for bringing the Indians in this Colony to the knowledge of the gospel, which was the avowed design of those that obtained the patent for this corporation, to hold the land and government of the Colony:

Upon consideration of which measures, the Gov-

ernor and Company of this, his Majestie's colony, in General Court assembled, desirous of pursuing in the best manner the solemn professions of our predecessors, have enacted,

And it is hereby enacted by the Governor, Council, and Representatives, in General Court assembled, and by the authority of the same, That care be taken annually, by the authority of each town, to convene the Indians inhabiting in each town, and acquaint them with the laws of the Government for punishing such immoralities as they shall be guilty of, and make them sensible that no exemption from the penalties of such laws lies for them, any more than for other his Majesty's subjects.

*   *   *

And forasmuch as idleness appears to be a great obstruction to the Indians receiving the gospel of truth, and it might very much conduce to their reformation, in that particular, if they were, by easy and agreeable methods, brought off from their pagan manner of living, and encouraged to make settlements in convenient places, in villages, after the Eglish manner:

It is hereby resolved, That measures shall be used to form villages of the natives, wherein the several families of them should have suitable portions of land appropriated to them, so that the said portions shall descend from the father to his children, the more to encourage them to apply themselves to husbandry, and good diligence therein, for their support.

*   *   *

28 "publishing a false, scandalous, and seditious libel" (1735)

John Peter Zenger's trial generally is considered the first important test for the political freedom of the press in American colonies. It occurred at a time when the right to political opposition was not widely recognized. In 1733, German-born printer Zenger began publishing the *New York Weekly Journal*. Virtually every issue of the *Journal* contained scathing attacks on the policies of the colonial governor, William Cosby. Zenger had been publishing the *Journal* for two months when Governor Cosby decided to silence him.

Chief Justice James DeLancey unsuccessfully sought indictments for seditious libel from a grand jury. The governor's council then carried out the campaign against Zenger on its own. On November 2, 1734, it decided that four issues of the *Journal* were seditious and should be burned, and that the attorney general would be instructed to prosecute the authors of the controversial articles as well as Zenger, the printer. Zenger was arrested on November 17, and bail was set at £400—an unusually large sum. Unable to raise bail, Zenger remained in the city jail until the conclusion of his trial.

Zenger's trial did not take place until August 4, 1735. Prior to that time, the hostile court had disbarred his counsel. New counsel volunteered to represent the accused—including Andrew Hamilton of Philadelphia, then reputed to be the best lawyer in America.

Hamilton offered to prove the truth of the statements that had appeared in Zenger's paper. But the judge, in accordance with English law, instructed the jury that truth was not a defense to seditious libel, and that the legal decision of whether the statements were libelous could be left for the court rather than the jury to decide. Hamilton, nevertheless, urged the jury to consider itself competent to decide not only whether Zenger, in fact, published the statements but also whether they were legally libelous.

When the arguments were concluded at the end of the day, the jury took only a few minutes before returning a verdict of not guilty. Despite the ultimate vindication, the government was successful in silencing Zenger for the period of his incarceration—and similar treatment could be expected for future dissidents, as the law of sedition remained generally viable. This document is one of the few to highlight the role of the jury in nullifying the reach of the law in political cases.

☆ 28 The Trial of John Peter Zenger [New York]

Reprinted in James Alexander, *A Brief Narrative of the Case and Trial of John Peter Zenger* (Cambridge, Mass.: Harvard University Press, Belknap Press, 1963), 58-79.

MR. ATTORNEY GENERAL opened as follows: ... May it please Your Honors, and you, gentlemen of the jury; the information now before the Court, and to which the Defendant Zenger has pleaded not guilty, is an information for printing and publishing a false, scandalous and seditious libel, in which His Excellency the Governor of this Province, who is the King's immediate representative here, is greatly and unjustly scandalized as a person that has no regard to law nor justice; with much more, as will appear upon reading the information. This of libeling is what has always been discouraged as a thing that tends to create differences among men, ill blood among the people, and oftentimes great bloodshed between the party libeling and the party libeled. There can be no doubt but you gentlemen of the jury will have the same ill opinion of such practices as the judges have always shown upon such occasions: But I shall say no more at this time until you hear the information, which is as follows:

... Be it remembered that Richard Bradley, Esq., Attorney General of our sovereign lord the King, for the Province of New York, who for our said lord the King in this part prosecutes ... gives the Court here to understand and be informed that John Peter Zenger, late of the City of New York, printer (being a seditious person and a frequent printer and publisher of false news and seditious libels, ... [designed] to bring into suspicion and the ill opinion of the subjects of our said lord the King residing within the said Province) the twenty-eighth day of January, ... did falsely, seditiously and scandalously print and publish, and cause to be printed and published, a certain false, malicious, seditious scandalous libel, entitled The New York Weekly Journal, containing the Freshest Advices, Foreign and Domestic; in which libel (of and concerning His Excellency the said Governor, and the ministers and officers of our said lord the King, of and for the said Province) among other things therein contained are these words:

Your appearance in print at last gives a pleasure to many, though most wish you had come fairly into the open field, and not appeared behind *retrenchments* made of the supposed laws against libeling and of what other men have said and done before; these *retrenchments*, gentlemen, may soon be shown to you and all men to be weak, and to have neither law nor reason for their foundation, so cannot long stand you in stead: Therefore, you had much better as yet leave them, and come to what *the people of this City and Province* ... think are the points in question (to wit) *They ... think as matters now stand that their LIBERTIES and PROPERTIES are precarious, and that SLAVERY is like to be entailed on them and their posterity if some past things be not amended, and this they collect from many past proceedings.* (Meaning many of the past proceedings of His Excellency the said Governor, and of the ministers and officers of our said lord the King, of and for the said Province.)

*   *   *

And the said Attorney general ... likewise gives the Court here to understand and be informed that the said John Peter Zenger ... did falsely, seditiously and scandalously print and publish, and cause to be printed and published, another false, malicious seditious and scandalous libel entitled The New York Weekly Journal, containing the Freshest Advices, Foreign and Domestic. In which libel ... among other things therein contained was these words:

One of our neighbors (one of the inhabitants of New Jersey meaning) *being in company, observing the strangers* (some of the inhabitants of New York meaning) *full of complaints, endeavored to persuade them to remove into Jersey; to which it was replied that would be leaping out of the frying pan into the fire, for, says he, we both are under the same Governor* (His Excellency the said

Governor meaning) *and your Assembly have shown with a witness what is to be expected from them; one that was then moving to Pennsylvania,* (meaning one that was then removing from New York with intent to reside at Pennsylvania) *to which place it is reported several considerable men are removing* (from New York meaning) *expressed, in terms very moving, much concern for the circumstances of New York* (the bad circumstances of the Province and people of New York meaning) *seemed to think them very much owing to the influence that some men* (whom he called tools) *had in the administration* (meaning the administration of government of the said Province of New York) *said he was now going from them, and was not to be hurt by any measures they should take, but could not help having some concern for the welfare of his countrymen, and should be glad to hear that the Assembly* (meaning the General Assembly of the Province of New York) *would exert themselves as became them, by showing that they have the interest of their country more at heart than the gratification of any private view of any of their members, or being at all affected by the smiles or frowns of a governor* (His Excellency the said Governor meaning), *both which ought equally to be despised when the interest of their country is at stake. You, says he, complain of the lawyers, but I think the law itself is at an end; WE* (the people of the Province of New York meaning) *SEE MEN'S DEEDS DESTROYED, JUDGES ARBITRARILY DISPLACED, NEW COURTS ERECTED WITHOUT CONSENT OF THE LEGISLATURE* (within the Province of New York meaning) *BY WHICH, IT SEEMS TO ME, TRIALS BY JURIES ARE TAKEN AWAY WHEN A GOVERNOR PLEASES* (His Excellency the said Governor meaning), *MEN OF KNOWN ESTATES DENIED THEIR VOTES CONTRARY TO THE RECEIVED PRACTICE, THE BEST EXPOSITOR OF ANY LAW: Who is then in that Province* (meaning the Province of New York) *that call* (can call meaning) *anything his own, or enjoy any liberty* (liberty meaning) *longer than those in the administration* (meaning the administration of government of the said Province of New York) *will condescend to let them do it, for which reason I have left it* (the Province of New York meaning), *as I believe more will.*

To the great disturbance of the peace of the said Province of New York, to the great scandal of our said lord the King, of His Excellency the said Governor, and of all others concerned in the administration of the government of the said Province, and against the peace of our sovereign lord the King his crown and dignity, etc. Whereupon the said Attorney General of our said lord the King, for our said lord the King, prays the advisement of the Court here, in the premises, and the due process of the law, against him the said John Peter Zenger, in this part

to be done, to answer to our said lord the King of and in the premises, etc.

R. BRADLEY, ATTORNEY GENERAL

To this information the Defendant has pleaded not guilty, and we are ready to prove it. . . .

MR. HAMILTON. May it please Your Honor; I cannot think it proper for me (without doing violence to my own principles) to deny the publication of a complaint which I think is the right of every free-born subject to make when the matters so published can be supported with truth; and therefore . . . I do (for my client) confess that he both printed and published the two newspapers set forth in the information, and I hope in so doing he has committed no crime.

*   *   *

MR. ATTORNEY. [A]s Mr. Hamilton has confessed the printing and publishing these libels, I think the jury must find a verdict for the King; for supposing they were true, the law says that they are not the less libelous for that; nay indeed the law says their being true is an aggravation of the crime.

MR. HAMILTON. Not so neither, Mr. Attorney, there are two words to that bargain. I hope it is not our bare printing and publishing a paper that will make it a libel: You will have something more to do before you make my client a libeler; for the words themselves must be libelous, that is, false, scandalous, and seditious or else we are not guilty.

*   *   *

MR. ATTORNEY. The case before the Court is whether Mr. Zenger is guilty of libeling His Excellency the Governor of New York, and indeed the whole administration of the government? Mr. Hamilton has confessed the printing and publishing, and I think nothing is plainer than that the words in the information are scandalous, and tend to sedition, and to disquiet the minds of the people of this Province. And if such papers are not libels, I think it may be said there can be no such thing as a libel.

*   *   *

MR. CHIEF JUSTICE. Mr. Attorney, you have heard what Mr. Hamilton has said, and the cases he has cited, for having his witnesses examined to prove the truth of the several facts contained in the papers set forth in the information, what do you say to it?

MR. ATTORNEY. The law in my opinion is very clear; they cannot be admitted to justify a libel; for, by the authorities I have already read to the Court, it is not the less a libel because it is true. I think I need not trouble the Court with reading the cases over again; the thing seems to be very plain, and I submit it to the Court.

MR. CHIEF JUSTICE. Mr. Hamilton, the Court is of opinion, you ought not to be permitted to prove the facts in the papers: These are the words of the book, "It is far from being a justification of a libel, that the contents thereof are true, or that the person upon whom it is made had a bad reputation, since the greater appearance there is of truth in any malicious invective, so much the more provoking it is."

MR. HAMILTON. These are Star Chamber cases, and I was in hopes that practice had been dead with the Court.

... MR. HAMILTON. I thank Your Honor. Then, gentlemen of the jury, it is to you we must now appeal for witnesses to the truth of the facts we have offered and are denied the liberty to prove; and let it not seem strange that I apply myself to you in this manner, I am warranted so to do both by law and reason. The law supposes you to be summoned out of the neighborhood where the fact is alleged to be committed; and the reason of your being taken out of the neighborhood is because you are supposed to have the best knowledge of the fact that is to be tried. And were you to find a verdict against my client, you must take upon you to say the papers referred to in the information, and which we acknowledge we printed and published, are false, scandalous and seditious. . . .

*   *   *

MR. CHIEF JUSTICE. No, Mr. Hamilton; the jury may find that Zenger printed and published those papers, and leave it to the Court to judge whether they are libelous; you know this is very common; it is in the nature of a special verdict, where the jury leave the matter of law to the Court.

MR. HAMILTON. I know, may it please Your Honor, the jury may do so; but I do likewise know they may do otherwise. I know they have the right beyond all dispute to determine both the law and the fact, and where they do not doubt of the law, they ought to do so. This of leaving it to the judgment of the Court whether the words are libelous or not in effect renders juries useless (to say no worse) in many cases; . . .

For though I own it to be base and unworthy to scandalize any man, yet I think it is even villainous to scandalize a person of public character, and I will go so far into Mr. Attorney's doctrine as to agree that if the faults, mistakes, nay even the vices of such a person be private and personal, and don't affect the peace of the public, or the liberty or property of our neighbor, it is unmanly and unmannerly to expose them either by word or writing. But when a ruler of a people brings his personal failings, but much more his vices, into his administration, and the people find themselves affected by them, either in their liberties or properties, that will alter the case mightily, and all the high things that are said in favor of rulers, and of dignities, and upon the side of power, will not be able to stop people's mouths when they feel themselves oppressed, I mean in a free

government. It is true in times past it was a crime to speak truth, and in that terrible Court of Star Chamber, many worthy and brave men suffered for so doing; and yet even in that Court and in those bad times, a great and good man durst say, what I hope will not be taken amiss of me to say in this place, to wit, The practice of informations for libels is a sword in the hands of a wicked king and an arrant coward to cut down and destroy the innocent; the one cannot because of his high station, and the other dares not because of his want of courage, revenge himself in another manner.

*   *   *

29 "A riot, and insult upon the King's government" (1747)

Not all disagreements between the colonists and the English authorities were viewed or were articulated as political conflicts. Many of the conflicts were related, however, to a growing difference between the mother country and its colonies regarding the power of government and the rights of the people. "Pressing" unwilling sailors into service in the British navy gave rise to some early conflicts. Press gangs who seized merchant seamen plagued Boston in the 1740s, and sympathetic townspeople often joined in the resistance to the practice. Despite strong protests at the town meeting, impressment, which hurt Boston's trade, continued. On November 16, 1747, several hundred townspeople made up of sailors, laborers, and blacks seized a navy lieutenant under Commodore Charles Knowles, assaulted a sheriff who came to his aid, and stormed the General Court. The local militia failed to respond to Governor William Shirley's order to put down the riot. Impressment in America, despite popular opposition, continued until after the War of 1812.

A report of the riots was contained in Governor Shirley's letter to the Lords of Trade in London.

☆ 29 Letter by Governor William Shirley to the Lords of Trade regarding the Knowles Riot (December 1, 1747)

Reprinted in Richard Hofstadter and Michael Wallace, eds., *American Violence: A Documentary History* (New York: Knopf, 1970), 60-63.

A riot, and insult upon the King's government lately happen'd here of so extraordinary a nature, that I think it my duty to give your Lordships an account of it.

It was occasion'd by an impress made on the sixteenth of November at night out of all the vessels in this harbour, by order of Commodore Knowles, then on board the Canterbury, for manning his Squadron. . . .

The first notice, I had of the mob, was given me between nine and ten o'clock in the forenoon by the Speaker of the House of Representatives, who had pick'd up in the streets Captain Derby of his Majesty's Ship Alborough, and the Purser of the Canterbury, and brought 'em under his Protection to me for shelter in my house acquainting me at the same time, that the mob consisted of about three hundred seamen, all strangers, (the greatest part Scotch) with cutlasses and clubs, and that they had seiz'd and detain'd in their custody a Lieutenant of the Lark, whom they met with at his lodgins on shoar; The next notice I had was about half an hour after by the Sheriff of the County, who with some of his officers had been in pursuit of the mob in order to recover the Man of War's Lieutenant, and to endeavour to disperse 'em; and who coming up with four of 'em separated from the others, had wrested a cutlass from one and seiz'd two of 'em; but being overtaken by the whole mob, (who were appriz'd of this), as he was carrying those two to goal, was assaulted, and grievously wounded by 'em, and forc'd to deliver up his two prisoners, and leave one of his deputies in their hands, for whose life he assur'd me he was in fear.

Thereupon I immediately sent orders to the Colonel of the Regiment to raise the militia of the town and suppress the mob by force, and, if need was, to fire upon 'em with ball; which were scarcely deliver'd to him, when they appear'd before my gates, and part of 'em advanc'd directly through my court yard up to my door with the Lieutenant, two other sea officers, that part of the mob which stay'd at the outward gate crying out to the party at my door not to give up any of their prisoners to me. Upon this I immediately went out to 'em and demanded the cause of the tumult, to which one of 'em arm'd with a cutlass answer'd me in an insolent manner it was caus'd by my unjustifiable impress warrant; whereupon I told 'em that the impress was not made by my warrant, nor with my knowledge; but that he was a very impudent rascal for his behaviour; and upon his still growing more insolent, my son in law who happen'd to follow me out, struck his hat off his head, asking him if he knew, who he was talking to; this immediately silenced their clamour, when I demanded of 'em, where the King's Officers were, that they had seiz'd; and they being shewn to me, I went up to the Lieutenant and bid him go into my house, and upon his telling me the mob would not suffer him, I took him from among 'em, and putting him before me caus'd him to go in, as I did likewise the other three and follow'd 'em without exchanging more words with the mob, that I might avoid making any promises or terms with 'em. . . .

[T]he mob now increas'd and join'd by some inhabitants came to the Town House (just after candle light) arm'd as in the morning, assaulted the Council Chamber (myself and the Council being then sitting there and the House of Representatives a minute or two before by accident adjourn'd) by throwing stones and brickbatts in at the windows, and having broke all the windows of the lower floor, where a few of the Militia Officers were assembled, forcibly enter'd into it, and oblig'd most of the officers to retire up into the Council Chamber; where the mob was expected soon to follow 'em up; but prevented by some few of the officers below, who behav'd better.

*   *   *

. . . The day following Mr. Knowles upon hearing of these outrages wrote me word, that he purpos'd to bring his whole squadron before the town the next morning, but I dissuaded him from it, by an immediate answer to his letter: In the evening the mob forcibly search'd the Navy Hospital upon the Town Common in order to let out what seamen they could find there belonging to the King's ships; and seven or eight private houses for officers, and took four or five petty officers; but soon releas'd 'em without any ill usage, as they did the same day Captain Erskine, whom they had suffer'd to remain in a gentleman's house upon his parole, their chief intent appearing to be, from the beginning, not to use the officers well any otherwise than by detaining 'em, in hopes of obliging Mr. Knowles to give up the impress'd men.

*   *   *

30 "punishing their secret Plots and dangerous Combinations" (1748)

Between 1680 and 1776, the British colonies of America and the West Indies imported more than two million African slaves. The British slave trade reached its peak shortly before the War of American Independence.

During the first half of the eighteenth century, several slave rebellions occurred in South Carolina, Virginia, and New York. Colonial slaveowners attempted to keep news of conspiracies or uprisings from spreading so as not to incite slaves in other places. It is known, however, that thirty-four slave ship revolts took place from 1700 to 1776. Among the colonial rebellions, the Cato uprising of 1739-40 in South Carolina and the New York slave insurrection scare of 1741 are particularly noteworthy. By the mid-eighteenth century, the laws in southern states began to reflect considerable anxiety regarding slave conspiracies and insurrections. In attempting to combat the perceived threat, the law began to sweep within its proscriptions free blacks, who, for reasons of racial affinity, might be in sympathy with the plight of slaves.

☆30 An Act Directing the Trial of Slaves Committing Capital Crimes, and for the More Effectual Punishing Conspiracies and Insurrections of Them, and for the Better Government of Negroes, Mulattoes, and Indians, Bond or Free [Virginia]

Reprinted in *The Acts of Assembly Now in Force in the Colony of Virginia 1661-1769* (Williamsburg: Rind, Purdie, and Dixon, 1769), 258-59.

I. WHEREAS it is absolutely necessary that effectual Provision should be made for the better ordering and governing of Slaves, free Negroes, Mulattoes, and Indians, and detecting and punishing their secret Plots and dangerous Combinations, and for the speedy Trial of such of them as commit capital Crimes:

II. BE it therefore enacted, by the Lieutenant Governour, Council, and Burgesses of this present General Assembly, and it is hereby enacted, by the Authority of the same, that if any Negro, or other Slaves, shall at any Time consult, advise or conspire to rebel or make Insurrection, or shall plot or conspire the Murder of any Person or Persons whatsoever, every such consulting, plotting, or conspiring, shall be adjudged and deemed Felony, and the Slave or Slaves convicted thereof, in Manner herein after directed, shall suffer Death, and be utterly excluded all Benefit of Clergy.

III. AND whereas many Negroes, under Pretence of practicing Physick, have prepared and exhibited poisonous Medicines, by which many Persons have been murdered, and others have languished under long and tedious Indispositions, and it will be difficult to detect such pernicious and dangerous Practices if they should be permitted to exhibit any Sort of Medicine, Be it therefore further enacted, that if any Negro or other Slave, shall prepare, exhibit, or administer, any Medicine whatsoever, he or she so offending shall be judged guilty of Felony, and suffer Death without Benefit of Clergy.

IV. PROVIDED always, that if it shall appear to the Court, before which such Slave shall be tried, that the Medicine was not prepared, exhibited, or administered, with an ill Intent, not attended with any bad Consequences, such Slave shall have the Benefit of Clergy.

V. PROVIDED also, that nothing herein contained shall be construed to extend to any Slave or Slaves administering Medicines by his or her Master's or Mistress's Order, in his or her Family, or the Family of another, with the mutual Consent of the Owner of such Slave, and the Master or Mistress of such Family.

VI. AND be it further enacted, by the Authority aforesaid, that every Slave committing such Offence as by Law is punishable with Death, or Loss of Member, shall be forthwith committed to the common Gaol of the County wherein such Offence shall be done, there to be safely kept, and upon such Commitment the Sheriff of such County shall certify the same, with the Cause thereof, to the Governour or Commander in Chief of this Dominion for the Time being, who is thereupon desired and empowered to issue a Commission of Oyer and Terminer to such Persons as he shall think fit, which Persons, forthwith after Receipt of such Commission, are empowered and required to cause the Offender to be publickly arraigned and tried at the Courthouse of the said County, and to take for Evidence the Confession of the Offender, the Oath of one or more credible Witnesses, or such Testimony of Negroes, Mulattoes, or Indians, bond or free, with pregnant Circumstances, as to them shall seem convincing, without the Solemnity of a Jury; and the Offender being by them found guilty, to pass such Judgment upon such Offender as the Law directs for the like Crimes, and on such Judgment to award Execution.

VII. PROVIDED always, that if at such Trial the Court be divided in Opinion whether the accused be guilty or not guilty, in that Case he, she, or they, shall be acquitted: Provided also, that when Judgment of Death shall be passed upon any such Offender there shall be ten Days at least between the Time of passing Judgment and the Day of Execution, except in Cases of Conspiracy, Insurrection, or Rebellion.

*   *   *

31 "Rulers have no authority from God to do mischief" (1750)

The foundation of the American position on civil disobedience owes much to Jonathan Mayhew, who, from 1747 to 1766, served as minister of Boston's West Church. Mayhew thought of himself as a true and loyal Englishman committed to the beloved, though unwritten, British constitution. Yet he opposed the doctrine of the divine rights of kings. The legitimacy of secular authority, he believed, was contingent on its commitment to advance the happiness and well-being of the people.

Having borrowed his theories from John Locke, Mayhew was not an original thinker but was nevertheless a very prominent and influential speaker in America. Preaching on the anniversary of the death of Charles I, Mayhew spoke in support of the people's right to overthrow a tyrannical government. But his sermon went beyond the question of communal opposition to tyranny and disclosed a sensitivity toward the duties of the individual citizen confronted by unjust rulers. His most succinct support of dissent was contained in an earlier sermon where he stated:

It indeed is often a sin to transgress human laws; but not universally so. It is possible for human legislators who are sometimes wicked, and always fallible, to enact unrighteous laws; to enjoin things that are in their own nature unlawful; and to forbid things that are in their own nature good and commendable. Now when iniquity comes to be thus established by a law, it can not be any iniquity to transgress that law by which it is established. On the contrary, it is a sin not to transgress it. . . . It is universally better to obey God than Man when the laws of God and Man clash and interfere with one another.

These premises, having firm roots in the colonies' reliance upon biblical authority and their experience with consensual government, provided a process by which to test the legitimacy of law and political authority. In the contest between allegiances, Mayhew advocated the supremacy of God's law and righteousness over the iniquities of the state.

☆ 31 Discourse concerning Unlimited Submission and Non-Resistance to the Higher Powers (Jonathan Mayhew)

Reprinted in J. W. Thornton, ed., *The Pulpit of the American Revolution: Or the Political Sermons of the Period of 1776* (Boston: Gould & Lincoln, 1860), 73-86.

Rulers have no authority from God to do mischief. . . . It is blasphemy to call tyrants and oppressors God's ministers. They are more properly "the messengers of Satan to buffet us." No rulers are properly God's ministers but such as are "just, ruling in the fear of God." When once magistrates act contrary to their office, and the end of their institution—when they rob and ruin the public, instead of being guardians of its peace and welfare—, they immediately cease to be the ordinance and ministers of God, and no more deserve that glorious character than common pirates and highwaymen.

If magistrates are unrighteous, . . . the main end of civil government will be frustrated. And what reason is there for submitting to that government which does by no means answer the design of government? "Wherefore ye must needs be subject not only for wrath, but also for conscience' sake." Here the apostle [Paul] argues the duty of a cheerful and conscientious submission to civil government from the nature and end of magistracy, as he had before laid it down; *i.e.*, as the design of it was to punish evil-doers, and to support and encourage such as do well; . . . if the motive and argument for submission to government be taken from the apparent usefulness of civil authority,—it follows, that when no such good end can be answered by submission, there remains no argument or motive to enforce it; . . . And therefore, in such cases, a regard to the public welfare ought to make us withhold from our rulers

that obedience and submission which it would otherwise be our duty to render to them. If it be our duty, for example, to obey our king merely for this reason, that he rules for the public welfare (which is the only argument the apostle makes use of), it follows, by a parity of reason, that when he turns tyrant, and makes his subjects his prey to devour and destroy, instead of his charge to defend and cherish, we are bound to throw off our allegiance to him, and to resist; and that according to the tenor of the apostle's argument in this passage. Not to discontinue our allegiance in this case would be to join with the sovereign in promoting the slavery and misery of that society, the welfare of which we ourselves, as well as our sovereign, are indispensably obliged to secure and promote, as far as in us lies. It is true the apostle puts no case of such a tyrannical prince; but, by his grounding his argument for submission wholly upon the good of civil society, it is plain he implicitly authorizes, and even requires us to make resistance, whenever this shall be necessary to the public safety and happiness. . . .

But, then, if unlimited submission and passive obedience to the higher powers, in all possible cases, be not a duty, it will be asked, "How far are we obliged to submit? If we may innocently disobey and resist in some cases, why not in all? Where shall we stop? What is the measure of our duty? This doctrine tends to the total dissolution of civil government, and to introduce such scenes of wild anarchy and confusion as are more fatal to society than the worst of tyranny."

But . . . similar difficulties may be raised with respect to almost every duty of natural and revealed religion. To instance only in two, both of which are near akin, and indeed exactly parallel to the case before us: It is unquestionably the duty of children to submit to their parents, and of servants to their masters; but no one asserts that it is their duty to obey and submit to them in all supposable cases, or universally a sin to resist them. Now, does this tend to subvert the just authority of parents and masters, or to introduce confusion and anarchy into private families? No. How, then, does the same principle tend to unhinge the government of that larger family the body politic? . . . Now, there is at least as much difficulty in stating the measure of duty in these two cases as in the case of rulers and subjects; so that this is really no objection—at least, no reasonable one—against resistance to the higher powers. Or, if it is one, it will hold equally against resistance in the other cases mentioned.

We may very safely assert these two things in general, without undermining government: One is, that no civil rulers are to be obeyed when they enjoin things that are inconsistent with the commands of God. All such disobedience is lawful and glorious; . . . All commands running counter to the declared will of the Supreme Legislator of heaven and earth are null and void, and therefore disobedience to them is a duty, not a crime. Another thing that may be asserted with equal truth and safety is, that no government is to be submitted to at the expense of that which is the sole end of all government—the common good and safety of society. . . .

Now, as all men are fallible, it cannot be supposed that the public affairs of any state should be always administered in the best manner possible, even by persons of the greatest wisdom and integrity. Nor is it sufficient to legitimate disobedience to the higher powers that they are not so administered, or that they are in some instances very ill-managed; for, upon this principle, it is scarcely supposable that any government at all could be supported, or subsist. Such a principle manifestly tends to the dissolution of government, and to throw all things into confusion and anarchy. But it is equally evident, upon the other hand, that those in authority may abuse their trust and power to such a degree, that neither the law of reason nor of religion requires that any obedience or submission should be paid to them; but, on the contrary, that they should be totally discarded, and the authority which they were before vested with transferred to others, who may exercise it more to those good purposes for which it is given. Nor is this principle, that resistance to the higher

powers is in some extraordinary cases justifiable, so liable to abuse as many persons seem to apprehend it. . . . Mankind in general have a disposition to be as submissive and passive and tame under government as they ought to be. . . . While those who govern do it with any tolerable degree of moderation and justice, and in any good measure act up to their office and character by being public benefactors, the people will generally be easy and peaceable, and be rather inclined to flatter and adore than to insult and resist them. . . . [P]eople know for what end they set up and maintain their governors, and they are the proper judges when they execute their trust as they ought to do it. . . . Till people find themselves greatly abused and oppressed by their governors, they are not apt to complain; and whenever they do, in fact, find themselves thus abused and oppressed, they must be stupid *not* to complain. To say that subjects in general are not proper judges when their governors oppress them and play the tyrant, and when they defend their rights, administer justice impartially, and promote the public welfare, is as great treason as ever man uttered. 'T is treason, not against one *single* man, but the state—against the whole body politic; 't is treason against mankind, 't is treason against common sense, 't is treason against God. . . .

CHAPTER 2

The Revolutionary War

1765-1781

T HE American Revolution has meant various things to different observers and commentators: some have seen it primarily as a political rebellion, others as an economic protest or a social uprising. But in the context of this collection the Revolution represented the first major collaborative—indeed, nation-wide—manifestation of political crime in America. By and large, the modern conception of the Revolutionary War is that of a unified country fighting a relatively brief war of national liberation against an exploitive and foreign power. Similarly, the Declaration of Independence has been perceived, for the most part, as a domestic preamble for the rights and goals of national self-government. However, a closer examination of contemporary documents reveals wavering and conflicting bonds of allegiance, first to the king and later to the local colonial governing bodies that ultimately promulgated the Revolution. Nowhere is the status of the new national American sovereign clearly defined. The Declaration of Independence likewise represents more than a mere domestic document; it is indeed the first national and international statement articulating the right to lawful revolution.

The years spanning this chapter are replete with well-known instances of political dissent and violence, such as the Boston Tea Party in 1773. Their number and our limited space prevents inclusion of them all. This collection focuses instead on the more revealing though less dramatic documents associated with the enunciation of disobedience to the overseas king and the enforcement of allegiance to the embryonic local political sovereignty. This emphasis, not on acts of dissent and violence, but on the theories and machinery utilized both in support of and in opposition to political criminality, should enhance the understanding of the jurisprudence of political crime.

Both sides of the Atlantic were aware of the law of treason and the requirement of oaths (including adherence to the Articles of War) as mechanisms for the assertion of sovereignty and political dominion over people. The pains and penalties for treason were applied and misapplied in like manner, although for opposite reasons, by the contending powers in North America. Once, it was the colonists who remonstrated against the excesses of General Gage, who, acting in response to Bostonian intransigence, expanded the reach of the law of treason beyond that of the English law. Later, the newly independent states enacted laws that abandoned the jealously guarded procedural protections surrounding those accused of treason for continuing to adhere to the English king. Other methods of investigating the loyalties of an ambivalent citizenry and of purging those suspected of royalist sympathies were utilized by the states as well.

Thus, the requirement of oaths of allegiance and the formulation of the law of treason provide the main instruments for examining the process whereby, in the eighteen-year period from the Stamp Act (1765) to the Treaty of Paris (1783), the loyalties of the citizenry officially and gradually were changed from the king to the sovereign United States. The materials, in addition, relate the asserted grievances that provided the incentive for the colonists' abandoning not only the obligation to obey the laws of Parliament but ultimately the allegiance to the king himself. The chapter, finally, supplies some references to demonstrate that while the Revolutionary War was going on, the foundations for new and future dissent, unrest, and political criminality were beginning to evolve.

---

32 "We can no longer forbear" (1765)

In 1760, England's seven-year-long French and Indian War, waged to expand English colonial rule in America, concluded, with France ceding to Britain her territories in Canada in the 1763 Treaty of Paris. Even though the proportion of English to French colonists was approximately fifteen to one, the more numerous but disunited English colonials initially were no match for the Frenchmen and their Native American allies, both superior wilderness fighters. But with his ascension to power in England in 1758, William Pitt made adequate finances and capable commanders available to change the course of events in America. The actual hostilities ceased with the British conquest of Quebec in 1759 under the command of Major General James Wolfe and the surrender of Montreal in 1760 to Colonel Jeffrey Amherst.

The English Parliament's demands for colonial

contributions to the defense costs of the American continent gave rise to a number of conflicts between the colonists and the mother country. Parliament, in March 1765, passed the Stamp Act, imposing a tax on all formal documents such as deeds, diplomas, bills, and newspapers. The artisans and shopkeepers of Boston led the popular resistance to the new tax, and the houses of several government officials were attacked, including that of Andrew Oliver, the Stamp Collector-designate. Although the violence was limited and no one was killed, the tax united the colonies for the first time, in the Stamp Act Congress, in opposition to English law.

The colonial objections to the Stamp Act were summarized in the instructions of the Town of Braintree, Massachusetts, drafted by John Adams.

☆32 Instructions of the Town of Braintree

Reprinted in C. F. Adams, ed., *The Works of John Adams* (New York: AMS Press, 1971), 3:465-67.

To Ebenezer Thayer, Esq.

Sir, — ... We can no longer forbear complaining, that many of the measures of the late ministry, and some of the late acts of Parliament, have a tendency, in our apprehension, to divest us of our most essential rights and liberties. We shall confine ourselves, however, chiefly to the act of Parliament, commonly called the Stamp Act, by which a very burthensome, and, in our opinion, unconstitutional tax, is to be laid upon us all; and we subjected to numerous and enormous penalties, to be prosecuted, sued for, and recovered, at the option of an informer, in a court of admiralty, without a jury.

We have called this a burthensome tax, because the duties are so numerous and so high, and the embarrassments to business in this infant, sparsely-settled country so great, that it would be totally impossible for the people to subsist under it, if we had no controversy at all about the right and authority of imposing it. Considering the present scarcity of money, we have reason to think, the execution of that act for a short space of time would drain the country of its cash, strip multitudes of all their property, and reduce them to absolute beggary. And what the consequence would be to the peace of the province, from so sudden a shock and such a convulsive change in the whole course of our business and subsistence, we tremble to consider. We further apprehend this tax to be unconstitutional. We have always understood it to be a grand and fundamental principle of the constitution, that no freeman should be subject to any tax to which he has not given his own consent, in person or by proxy. And the maxims of the law, as we have constantly received them, are to the same effect, that no freeman can be separated

from his property but by his own act or fault. We take it clearly, therefore, to be inconsistent with the spirit of the common law, and of the essential fundamental principles of the British constitution, that we should be subject to any tax imposed by the British Parliament; because we are not represented in that assembly in any sense, unless it be by a fiction of law, as insensible in theory as it would be injurious in practice, if such a taxation should be grounded on it.

But the most grievous innovation of all, is the alarming extension of the power of courts of admiralty. In these courts, one judge presides alone! No juries have any concern there! The law and the fact are both to be decided by the same single judge, whose commission is only during pleasure, and with whom, as we are told, the most mischievous of all customs has become established, that of taking commissions on all condemnations; so that he is under a pecuniary temptation always against the subject. ... We have all along thought the acts of trade in this respect a grievance; but the Stamp Act has opened a vast number of sources of new crimes, which may be committed by any man, and cannot but be committed by multitudes, and prodigious penalties are annexed, and all these are to be tried by such a judge of such a court! ... We cannot help asserting, therefore, that this part of the act will make an essential change in the constitution of juries, and it is directly repugnant to the Great Charter itself; for, by that charter, "no americament shall be assessed, but by the oath of honest and lawful men of the vicinage;" and, "no freeman shall be taken, or imprisoned, or disseized of his freehold, or liberties of free customs, nor passed upon, nor condemned, but by lawful judgment of his peers, or by the law of the land." So that this act will "make such a distinction, and create such a difference between" the subjects in Great Britain and those in America, as we could not have expected from the guardians of liberty in "both."

As these, sir, are our sentiments of this act, we, the freeholders and other inhabitants, legally assembled for this purpose, must enjoin it upon you, to comply with no measures or proposals for countenancing the same, or assisting in the execution of it, but by all lawful means, consistent with our allegiance to the King, and relation to Great Britain, to oppose the execution of it, till we can hear the success of the cries and petitions of America for relief.

We further recommend the most clear and explicit assertion and vindication of our rights and liberties to be entered on the public records, that the world may know, in the present and all future generations, that we have a clear knowledge and a just sense of them, and, with submission to Divine Providence, that we never can be slaves. ...

33 " 'you shall die then' " (1766)

Colonial America witnessed several instances of domestic economic struggle. The accumulation of large estates in New York created a quasi-feudal class with single-family possessions sometimes exceeding one million acres. The owners of these estates often were granted criminal jurisdiction, the authority to appoint magistrates, and the right to name representatives to the assembly of the colony. Cultivated by tenants who paid rent in kind, the estates flourished while the workers chafed against the system. Tenant complaints at times erupted into violence. The climax came in the Agrarian Rebellion of 1766, when the sheriff of Albany County attempted to dispossess settlers on the John Van Renselear land. Some seventeen hundred armed settlers closed the courts and opened the jails in Poughkeepsie. In response to the landowners' call for help, the government declared the insurrection's leaders guilty of high treason.

An account of the initial June 26, 1766, confrontation between the settlers and the forces of law was printed in the *Boston Gazetteer.*

☆33 New York Agrarian Rebellion (July 14, 1766)

Boston Gazetteer or *Country Journal*, reprinted in Richard Hofstadter and Michael Wallace, eds., *American Violence: A Documentary History* (New York: Knopf, 1970), 116-17.

. . . [T]he inhabitants of a place called Nobletown and a place called Spencer-Town lying west of Sheffield, Great Barrington, and Stockbridge, who has purchased of the Stockbridge Indians the lands they now possess; by virtue of an order of the General Court of this province, and settled about two hundred families; John Van Renselear Esq., pretending a right to said lands, had treated the inhabitants very cruelly, because they would not submit to him as tenants, he claiming a right to said lands by virtue of a patent from the Government of New York; that said Van Renselear some years ago raised a number of men and came upon the poor people, and pulled down some houses killed some people, imprisoned others, and has been constantly vexing and injuring the people. That on the 26th of last month said Renselear came down with between two and three hundred men, all armed with guns, pistols and swords; that upon intelligence that 500 men armed were coming against them, about forty or fifty of the inhabitants went out unarmed, except with sticks, and proceeded to a fence between them and the assailants, in order to compromise the matter between them. That the assailants came up to the fence, and Hermanus Schuyler the Sheriff of the County of Albany, fired his pistol down . . . upon them and three others fired their guns over them. The inhabitants thereupon desired to talk with them, and they would not harken; but the Sheriff, it was said by some who knew him, ordered the men to fire, who thereupon fired, and killed one of their own men, who had got over the fence and one of the inhabitants likewise within the fence. Upon this the chief of the inhabitants, unarmed as aforesaid, retreated most of them into the woods, but twelve betook themselves to the house from whence they set out and there defended themselves with six small arms and some ammunition that were therein. The two parties here fired upon each other. The assailants killed one man in the house, and the inhabitants wounded several of them, whom the rest carried off and retreated, to the number of seven, none of whom at the last accounts were dead. That the Sheriff shewed no paper, nor attempted to execute any warrant, and the inhabitants never offered any provocation at the fence, excepting their continuing there, nor had any one of them a gun, pistol or sword, till they retreated to the house. At the action at the fence one of the inhabitants had a leg broke, whereupon the assailants attempted to seize him and carry him off. He therefore begged they would consider the misery he was in, declaring he had rather die than be carried off, whereupon one of the assailants said "you shall die then" and discharging his pistol upon him as he lay on the ground, shot him to the body, as the wounded man told the informant; that the said wounded man was alive when he left him, but not like to continue long. The affray happened about sixteen miles distant from Hudson's River. It is feared the Dutch will pursue these poor people for thus defending themselves, as murderers; and keep them in great consternation.

34 "The alarming cries of the oppressed" (1769)

Colonial America was not a classless society, and the dissatisfaction of the backcountry and its nonslaveholding small farmers with the aristocratic and privileged landed gentry frequently surfaced. Economically deprived, politically unrepresented, and religiously unorthodox, the dissenting frontiersmen were particularly vocal in North and South Carolina. The political history during the colonial period can be depicted as a constant struggle between representatives of the people and the representatives of the crown. These disputes were over local government corruption, scarcity of money, stiff taxation, restraints on commerce, burdensome land policies, and religious intolerance. Organized into formal associations known as the "Regulators," these country yeomen from the Blue Ridge Mountain settlements petitioned the authorities for reform, but in the eyes of the officials the demands constituted sedition. When the 1769 Regulator petitions (calling for ballot voting, taxation in proportion to wealth, collection of taxes in local commodities, and the regular publishing of laws) were ignored, the exasperated Regulators interfered with the collection of rents and taxes and with the operation of the courts. The assembly responded by imposing the death penalty upon members of any crowd of ten or more who failed to disperse when so ordered.

Even earlier, armed partisans in 1765 and 1766 prevented the enforcement of the Stamp Act in North and South Carolina, whose population numbered less than three hundred thousand. There were several other armed conflicts that culminated in the Battle of Alamance (1771) between the Regulators and the forces of Governor William Tryon, the Crown representative. The Regulators forced the governor to lead two military expeditions against them in 1768 and in 1771. The latter campaign required a government force of approximately one thousand men and officers. The Regulator troops consisted of twice that number, but their lack of arms and discipline resulted in defeat. Seven rebel prisoners were executed for treason. Thousands of frontiersmen were required to take an oath of allegiance to the colonial government, and many moved further west to avoid the requirement. The hostility between the western settlers and the eastern seaboard establishment led many of the backcountry population to support the Loyalists rather than their exploitative local gentry at the time of the revolution.

☆ 34 Petition of the Inhabitants of Anson County, North Carolina (October 9, 1769)

Reprinted in W. Saunders, ed., *The Colonial Records of North Carolina* (Raleigh: Josephus Daniel, 1890), 3:75.

MR. SPEAKER AND GENTLEMEN OF THE ASSEMBLY:

The Petition of the Inhabitants of Anson County, being part of the Remonstrance of the Province of North Carolina, HUMBLY SHEWETH, That the Province in general labour under general grievances, and the Western part thereof under particular ones; which we not only see but very sensibly feel, being crouch'd beneath our sufferings: and, notwithstanding our sacred priviledges, have too long yielded ourselves slaves to remorseless oppression.—Permit us to conceive it to be our inviolable right to make known our grievances, and to petition for redress; as appears in the Bill of Rights pass'd in the reign of King Charles the first, as well as the act of Settlement of the Crown of the Revolution. We therefore beg leave to lay before you a specimen

thereof, that your compassionate endeavours may tend to the relief of your injured Constituents, whose distressed condition calls aloud for aid. The alarming cries of the oppressed possibly may reach your Ears; but without your zeal how shall they ascend the throne. How relentless is the breast without sympathy, the heart that cannot bleed on a View of our calamity; to see tenderness removed, cruelty stepping in; and all our liberties and priviledges invaded and abridg'd by (as it were) domesticks who are conscious of their guilt and void of remorse. O how daring! how relentless! whilst impending Judgments loudly threaten and gaze upon them, with every emblem of merited destruction.

A few of the many grievances are as follows, viz.,

1. That the poor Inhabitants in general are much oppress'd by reason of disproportionate Taxes, and those of the western Counties in particular; as they are generally in mean circumstances.

2. That no method is prescribed by Law for the payment of the Taxes of the Western counties in produce (in lieu of a Currency) as is in other Counties within this Province; to the Peoples great oppression.

3. That Lawyers, Clerks, and other pentioners, in place of being obsequious Servants for the Country's use, are become a nuisance, as the business of the people is often transacted without the least degree of fairness, the intention of the law evaded, exorbitant fees extorted, and the sufferers left to mourn under their oppressions.

4. That an Attorney should have it in his power, either for the sake of ease or interest or to gratify their malevolence and spite, to commence suits to what Courts he pleases, however inconvenient it may be to the Defendant: is a very great oppression.

5. That all unlawful fees taken on Indictment, where the Defendant is acquitted by his Country (however customary it may be) is an oppression.

6. That Lawyers, Clerks, and others extorting more fees than is intended by law; is also an oppression.

7. That the violation of the King's Instructions to his delegates, their artfulness in concealing the same from him; and the great Injury the People thereby sustains: is a manifest oppression.

And for remedy whereof, we take the freedom to recommend the following mode of redress, not doubting audience and acceptance; which will not only tend to our relief, but command prayers as a duty from your humble Petitioners.

1. That at all elections each suffrage be given by Ticket & Ballot.

2. That the mode of Taxation be altered, and each person to pay in proportion to the profits arising from his Estate.

3. That no future tax be laid in Money, untill a currency is made.

4. That there may be established a Western as

well as a Northern and Southern District, and a Treasurer for the same.

5. That when a currency is made it may be let out by a Loan office on Land security, and not to be call'd in by a Tax.

6. That all debts above 40*s*. and under £10 be tried and determined without Lawyers, by a jury of six freeholders impanneled by a Justice, and that their verdict be enter'd by the said Justice, and be a final judgment.

7. That the Chief Justice have no perquisites, but a Sallary only.

8. That Clerks be restricted in respect to fees, costs, and other things within the course of their office.

9. That Lawyers be effectually Barr'd from exacting and extorting fees.

10. That all doubts may be removed in respect to the payment of fees and costs on Indictments where the Defendant is not found guilty by the jury, and therefore acquitted.

11. That the Assembly make known by Remonstrance to the King, the conduct of the cruel and oppressive Receiver of the Quit Rents, for omitting the customary easie and effectual method of collecting by distress, and pursuing the expensive mode of commencing suits in the most distant Courts.

12. That the Assembly in like manner make known that the Governor and Council do frequently grant Lands to as many as they think proper without regard to head rights, notwithstanding the contrariety of His Majesties Instructions; by which means immense sums has been collected and numerous Patents granted, for much of the most fertile lands in this Province, that is yet uninhabited and uncultivated, environed by great numbers of poor people who are necessitated to toil in the cultivation of bad Lands whereon they hardly can subsist, who are thereby deprived of His Majesties liberality and Bounty: nor is there the least regard paid to the cultivation clause in said Patent mentioned, as many of the said Council as well as their friends and favorites enjoy large Quantities of Lands under the above-mentioned circumstances.

* * *

16. That every denomination of People may marry according to their respective Mode, Ceremony, and custom, after due publication or Licence.

17. That Doctr Benjamin Franklin or some other known patriot be appointed Agent, to represent the unhappy state of this Province to His Majesty, and to solicit the several Boards in England. . . .

* * *

35 "I heard the word 'fire' " (1770)

The repeal of the Stamp Act reduced tensions temporarily. But the colonies met the Townshend Acts, which imposed new import duties and created both customs boards and vice-admiralty courts for their collection and enforcement, with new hostility. A boycott against the importation of British goods was instituted, and the Massachusetts House of Representatives called for united colonial resistance. Five British regiments were sent to Boston in response.

On March 5, 1770, a local crowd attacked some British sentries. The evidence of what happened was contradictory; in response to the hurling of snowballs the soldiers shot into the crowd, killing three people instantly, with two others dying shortly thereafter. The leader of the troops, Captain Thomas Preston, and six of his men were arrested and tried for murder. Preston and four soldiers, defended by John Adams and Josiah Quincy, were acquitted, and the remaining two were convicted of manslaughter. To the local patriots the incident supplied a major focus for anti-British propaganda.

☆ 35 The Horrid Massacre in Boston

Richard Palmes, "A Short Narrative of the Horrid Massacre in Boston (1770)," reprinted in Richard Hofstadter and Michael Wallace, eds., *American Violence: A Documentary History* (New York: Knopf, 1970), 116–17.

I, Richard Palmes, of Boston, of lawful age, testify and say, that between the hours of nine and ten o'clock of the fifth instant, I heard one of the bells ring, which I supposed was occasioned by fire, and enquiring where the fire was, was answered that the soldiers were abusing the inhabitants; I asked where, was first answered at Murray's barracks. I went there and spoke to some officers that were standing at the door, I told them I was surprised they suffered the soldiers to go out of the barracks after eight o'clock; I was answered by one of the officers, pray do you mean to teach us our duty; I answered I did not, only to remind them of it. One of them then said, you see that the soldiers are all in their barracks, and why do you not go to your homes. Mr. James Lamb and I said, Gentlemen, let us go home, and were answered by some, home, home. Accordingly I asked Mr. William Hickling if he was going home, he said he was; I walked with him as far as the post-office, upon my stopping to talk with two or three people, Mr. Hickling left me; I then saw Mr. Pool Spear going towards the townhouse, he asked me if I was going home, I told him I was; I asked him where he was going that way, he said he was going to his brother David's. But when I got to the town-pump, we were told there was a rumpus at the Custom-house door; Mr. Spear said to me you had better not go, I told him I would go and try to make peace. I immediately went there and saw Capt. Preston at the head of six or eight soldiers in a circular form, with guns breast high and bayonets fixed; the said Captain stood almost to the end of their guns. I went immediately to Capt. Preston (as soon as Mr. Bliss had left him), and asked him if their guns were loaded, his answer was they are loaded with powder and ball; I then said to him, I hope you do not intend they shall fire upon the inhabitants, his reply was, by no means. When I was asking him these questions, my left hand was on his right shoulder; Mr. John Hickling had that instant taken his hand off my shoulder, and stepped to my left, then instantly I saw a piece of snow or ice fall among the soldiers on which the soldier at the officer's right hand stepped back and discharged his gun at the space of some seconds the soldier at his left fired next, and the others one after the other. After the first gun was fired, I heard the word "fire," but who said it I know not. After the first gun was fired, the said officer had full time to forbid the other soldiers not to fire, but I did not hear him speak to them at all; then turning myself to the left I saw one man dead, distant about six feet; I having a stick in my hand made a stroke at the soldier who fired, and struck the gun out of his hand. I then made a stroke at the officer, my right foot slipped, that brought me on my knee, the blow falling short; he says I hit his arm; when I was recovering myself from the fall, I saw the soldier that fired the first gun endeavoring to push me through with his bayonet, on which I threw my stick at his head, the soldier starting back, gave me an opportunity to jump from him into Exchange lane, or I must been inevitably run through my body. I looked back and saw three persons laying on the ground, and perceiving a soldier stepping round the corner as I thought to shoot me, I ran down Exchange lane, and so up the next into King Street, and followed Mr. Gridley with several other persons with the body of Capt. Morton's apprentice, up to the prison house, and saw he had a ball shot through his breast; at my return I found that the officers and soldiers were gone to the main guard. To my best observation there were not seventy people in King street at the time of their firing, and them very scattering; but in a few minutes after the firing there were upwards of a thousand. . . .

36 "enemy to the liberties of America" (1773-1774)

The East Indian Company's importation and sale of tea in the colonies was greatly assisted by Parliamentary concessions as well as by effective merchandizing practices. An act of May 1773 authorized the East India Company to sell tea directly to the colonies free from other duties except a three-penny tax payable in America. The distribution of the imported tea in the colonies was through the company's exclusive agents. Both the local tax and the monopolistic distribution system aroused suspicion and hostility. The colonists devised opposition tactics, as the accompanying document illustrates. In Philadelphia and New York, ships bearing tea were forced to turn back. In Boston, attempts to land tea resulted in the Boston Tea Party of December 16, 1773. In response to these disturbances the British Parliament passed a number of emergency measures, known collectively in the colonies as the "Intolerable Acts"; one of these, the Administration of Justice Act, permitted the transfer of controversial trials from local courts to England.

☆ 36 The Boston Tea Party and Its Aftermath

☆ 36a Sons of Liberty Resolutions on Tea (December 15, 1773)

Reprinted in Hezekiah Niles, *Chronicles of the American Revolution*, ed. Alden T. Vaughn. (New York: Grosset & Dunlap, 1965), 66-67.

. . . To prevent a calamity which, of all others, is the most to be dreaded—slavery, and its terrible concomitants—we, subscribers being influenced from a regard to liberty, and disposed to use all lawful endeavors in our power, to defeat the pernicious project, and to transmit to our posterity, those blessings of freedom which our ancestors have handed down to us; and to contribute to the support of the common liberties of America, which are in danger to be subverted, *do*, for those important purposes, agree to associate together, under the name and style of the *sons of liberty of New York*, and engage our honor to, and with each other, faithfully to observe and perform the following *resolutions, viz.*

1st. *Resolved*, That whoever shall aid, or abet, or in any manner assist in the introduction of tea, from any place whatsoever, into this colony, while it is subject, by a British act to parliament, to the payment of a duty, for the purpose of raising a revenue in America, he shall be deemed an enemy to the liberties of America.

2d. *Resolved*, That whoever shall be aiding, or assisting, in the landing, or carting, of such tea, from any ship or vessel, or shall hire any house, storehouse, or cellar or any place whatsoever to deposit the tea, subject to a duty as aforesaid, he shall be deemed an enemy to the liberties of America.

3d. *Resolved*, That whoever shall sell, or buy, . . . tea, or shall aid . . . in transporting such tea, . . . from this city, until the . . . revenue act shall be totally and clearly repealed, he shall be deemed an enemy to the liberties of America.

4th. *Resolved*, That whether the duties on tea, imposed by this act, be paid in Great Britain or in America, our liberties are equally affected.

5th. *Resolved*, That whoever shall transgress any of these resolutions, we will not deal with, or employ, or have any connection with him.

☆36b Administration of Justice Act (May 20, 1774)

Reprinted in H. S. Commager, ed., *Documents of American History* (New York: Meredith Corp., 1973), 1:73-74.

An act for the impartial administration of justice in the cases of persons questioned for any acts done by them in the execution of the law, or for the suppression of riots and tumults, in the province of the Massachuset's Bay, *in* New England.

WHEREAS *in his Majesty's province of* Massachuset's Bay, *in* New England, *an attempt hath lately been made to throw off the authority of the parliament of* Great Britain *over the said province, and an actual and avowed resistance, by open force, to the execution of certain acts of parliament, hath been suffered to take place, uncontrouled and unpunished ...: and whereas, in the present disordered state of the said province, it is of the utmost importance ... to the reestablishment of lawful authority throughout the same, that neither the magistrates acting in support of the laws, nor any of his Majesty's subjects aiding and assisting them therein, or in the suppression of riots and tumults, ... should be discouraged from the proper discharge of their duty, by an apprehension, that in case of their being questioned for any acts done therein, they may be liable to be brought to trial for the same before persons who do not acknowledge the validity of the laws, in the execution thereof, or the authority of the magistrate in support of whom, such acts had been done: in order therefore to remove every such discouragement from the minds of his Majesty's subjects, and to induce them, upon all proper occasions, to exert themselves in support of the public peace of the province, and of the authority of the King and Parliament of* Great Britain *over the same;* be it enacted ... , That if any inquisition or indictment shall be found, or if any appeal shall be sued or preferred against any person, for murther, or other capital offence, in the province of the *Massachuset's Bay*, and it shall appear, by information given upon oath to the governor ... of the said province, that the fact was committed by the person against whom such inquisition or indictment shall be found, or against whom such appeal shall be sued or preferred, as aforesaid, either in the execution of his duty as a magistrate, for the suppression of riots, or in the support of the laws of revenue, or in acting in his duty as an officer of revenue, or in acting under the direction and order of any magistrate, for the suppression of riots, or for the carrying into effect the laws of revenue, or in aiding and assisting in any of the cases aforesaid; and if it shall also appear, to the satisfaction of the said governor ... that an indifferent trial cannot be had within the said province, in that case, it shall and may be lawful for the governor ... , to direct, with the advice and consent of the council, that the inquisition, indictment, or appeal, shall be tried in some other of his Majesty's colonies, or in *Great Britain;* and for that purpose, to order the person against whom such inquisition or indictment shall be found, ... to be sent, under sufficient custody, to the place appointed for his trial, or to admit such person to bail, taking a recognizance ... from such person, with sufficient sureties, ... in such sums of money as the said governor ... shall deem reasonable, for the personal appearance of such person, if the trial shall be appointed to be had in any other colony, before the governor, ... of such colony; and if the trial shall be appointed to be had in *Great Britain*, then before his Majesty's court of *King's Bench*, at a time to be mentioned in such recognizances; and the governor, ... or court of *King's Bench*, where the trial is appointed to be had in *Great Britain*, upon the appearance of such person, according to such recognizance, or in custody, shall either commit such person, or admit him to bail, until such trial. ...

37 "our lawful and rightful Sovereign" (1774)

Colonial dissatisfaction with taxes imposed by a Parliament with no colonial representation mounted. In 1772, Boston and other Massachusetts towns, at the proposal of Samuel Adams, organized Committees of Correspondence to formulate American rights and grievances. Other colonies followed suit, and relations with England worsened. By 1774, General Thomas Gage, commander in chief of the English colonial troops, arrived to govern Massachusetts. The Committees of Correspondence called for an intercolonial congress. The First Continental Congress convened in Philadelphia on September 5, 1774.

Although the Instructions by the Virginia Convention to Their Delegates expressed "true Allegiance to his Majesty King George the Third, our lawful and rightful Sovereign," they sounded a new and more independent chord concerning the political relationship between England and her American colonies. The Instructions laid the grievances at the feet of a malevolent Parliament. But while seeking royal relief, the Instructions' endorsement of a total embargo conveyed an assertion of political sovereignty.

Particular note should be taken of the reaction of the English to these threats. Although not a time of generalized civil disorder, the civil authorities had been supplanted by General Gage's military authority. In addition, the crime of treason had, by military edict, been extended beyond the provisions of the existing English statutory authority contained in 25 Edward III. These two responses—imposition of military rule and expansion of the crime of treason (or its surrogate)—have characterized governmental response to political crime ever since.

☆ 37 Instructions by the Virginia Convention to Their Delegates in Congress (August 1-6, 1774)

Reprinted in J. Boyd, ed., *The Papers of Thomas Jefferson* (Princeton: Princeton University Press, 1950) 1:141-43.

THE unhappy Disputes between Great Britain and her American Colonies, which began about the third Year of the Reign of his present Majesty, and since, continually increasing, have proceeded to Lengths so dangerous and alarming as to excite just Apprehensions in the Minds of his Majesty's faithful Subjects of this Colony that they are in Danger of being deprived of their natural, ancient, constitutional, and chartered Rights, have compelled them to take the same into their most serious Consideration; and, being deprived of their usual and accustomed Mode of making known their Grievances, have appointed us their Representatives to consider what is proper to be done in this dangerous Crisis of American Affairs. It being our Opinion that the united Wisdom of North America should be collected in a General Congress of all the Colonies, we have appointed the Honourable PEYTON RANDOLPH, Esquire, RICHARD HENRY LEE, GEORGE WASHINGTON, PATRICK HENRY, RICHARD BLAND, BENJAMIN HARRISON, and EDMUND PENDLETON, Esquires, Deputies to represent this Colony in the said Congress, to be held at Philadelphia on the first Monday in September next.

And that they may be the better informed of our Sentiments touching the Conduct we wish them to observe on this important Occasion, we desire that they will express, in the first Place, our Faith and true Allegiance to his Majesty King George the Third, our lawful and rightful Sovereign; and that we are determined, with our Lives and Fortunes, to support him in the legal Exercise of all his just Rights and Prerogatives. And however misrepresented, we sincerely approve of a constitutional Connexion with Great Britain, and wish most ardently a Return of that Intercourse of Affection and commercial Connexion that formerly united both Countries, which can only be effected by a Removal of those Causes of Discontent which have of late unhappily divided us.

It cannot admit of a Doubt but that British Subjects in America are entitled to the same Rights and Privileges as their Fellow Subjects possess in Britain; and therefore, that the Power assumed by the British Parliament to bind America by their Statutes, in all Cases whatsoever, is unconstitutional, and the Source of these unhappy Differences.

The End of Government would be defeated by the British Parliament exercising a Power over the Lives, the Property, and the Liberty of the American Subject; who are not, and, from their local Circumstances, cannot, be there represented. Of this Nature we consider the several Acts of Parliament for raising a Revenue in America, for extending the Jurisdiction of the Courts of Admiralty, for seizing American Subjects and transporting them to Britain to be tried for Crimes committed in America, and the several late oppressive Acts respecting the Town of Boston and Province of the Massachusetts Bay.

The original Constitution of the American Colonies possessing their Assemblies with the sole Right of directing their internal Polity, it is absolutely destructive of the End of their Institution that their Legislatures should be suspended, or prevented, by hasty Dissolutions, from exercising their legislative Powers.

Wanting the Protection of Britain, we have long acquiesced in their Acts of Navigation restrictive of our Commerce, which we consider as an ample Recompense for such Protection; but as those Acts derive their Efficacy from that Foundation alone, we have Reason to expect they will be restrained so as to produce the reasonable Purposes of Britain, and not injurious to us.

To obtain Redress of these Grievances, without which the People of America can neither be safe, free, nor happy, they are willing to undergo the great Inconvenience that will be derived to them from stopping all Imports whatsoever from Great Britain after the first Day of November next, and also to cease exporting any Commodity whatsoever to the same Place after the tenth Day of August 1775.... [I]t is our Desire that you cordially co-operate with our Sister Colonies in General Congress in such other just and proper Methods as they, or the Majority, shall deem necessary for the Accomplishment of these valuable Ends.

The Proclamation issued by General Gage, in the Government of the Province of the Massachusetts Bay, declaring it Treason for the Inhabitants of that Province to assemble themselves to consider of their Grievances and form Associations for their common Conduct on the Occasion, and requiring the Civil Magistrates and Officers to apprehend all such Persons to be tried for their supposed Offences, is the most alarming Process that ever appeared in a British Government; that the said General Gage hath thereby assumed and taken upon himself Powers denied by the Constitution to our legal Sovereign; that he, not having condescended to disclose by what Authority he exercises such extensive and unheard of Powers, we are at a Loss to determine whether he intends to justify himself as the Representative of the King or as the Commander in Chief of his Majesty's Forces in America. If he considers himself as acting in the Character of his Majesty's Representative, we would remind him that the Statute 25th Edward III has expressed and defined all treasonable Offences, and that the Legislature of

Great Britain hath declared that no Offence shall be construed to be Treason but such as is pointed out by that Statute, and that this was done to take out of the Hands of tyrannical Kings, and of weak and wicked Ministers, that deadly Weapon which constructive Treason had furnished them with, and which had drawn the Blood of the best and honestest Men in the Kingdom; and that the King of Great Britain hath no Right by his Proclamation to subject his People to Imprisonment, Pains, and Penalties.

That if the said General Gage conceives he is empowered to act in this Manner, as the Commander in Chief of his Majesty's Forces in America, this odious and illegal Proclamation must be considered as a plain and full Declaration that this despotick Viceroy will be bound by no Law, nor regard the constitutional Rights of his Majesty's Subjects, whenever they interfere with the Plan he has formed for oppressing the good People of the Massachusetts Bay; and therefore, that the executing, or attempting to execute, such Proclamation, will justify Resistance and Reprisal.

38 "whereas hostilities have actually been commenced" (1775)

The First Continental Congress, convened in Philadelphia on September 5, 1774, approved resistance to the Intolerable Acts of Parliament and expressed the view that all colonies should support Massachusetts if the British sought execution of their laws by force. It also approved the Declaration of Rights and Resolves, which called for rights of assembly and petition, trial by peers, freedom from a standing army, and the right to be consulted on the imposition of taxes. The Congress threatened to reconvene in Philadelphia in May 1775 unless the British redressed colonial grievances. When Parliament met at the close of 1774, the king and his ministers expressed the view that the First Continental Congress constituted illegal assembly and that Massachusetts was, in fact, in a state of rebellion.

As a conciliatory measure, former prime minister William Pitt, now earl of Chatham, proposed that Parliament agree not to levy any tax upon the colonies. Lord North, then prime minister, secured passage of another conciliatory resolution, but these efforts proved futile. The two parties drifted steadily toward war. Suspecting the Massachusetts militia was gathering arms, British General Gage directed 700 troops to Concord on April 18, 1775, to seize military stores. The following day, at Lexington, the Minutemen stood their ground against the approaching force, and the first blood of the American Revolution was shed.

The Second Continental Congress met on May 10, 1775. The previous month the revolution had begun in Lexington and Concord. On June 17, fighting resumed at the Battle of Bunker Hill, and George Washington took command of the Continental Army on June 23, 1775.

The Preamble to the Articles of War, a proclamation of fidelity to the English king, preceded the regulations for the new army that would fight the royal forces. The Articles dramatically illustrated the Revolutionary War's conflict of loyalties—the old loyalty to the Crown versus the new loyalty to the emerging United States.

☆ 38 Articles of War for the Continental Army (June 30, 1775)

Reprinted in W. C. Ford, ed., *Journals of the Continental Congress* (Washington, D.C.: U.S. Government Printing Office, 1906), 2:120.

The Congress met according to adjournment.

The consideration of the articles of war being resumed, Congress agreed to the same:

RULES AND REGULATIONS

Whereas his Majesty's most faithful subjects in these Colonies are reduced to a dangerous and critical situation, by the attempts of the British Ministry, to carry into execution, by force of arms, several unconstitutional and oppressive acts of the British parliament for laying taxes in America, to enforce the collection of these taxes, and for altering and changing the constitution and internal police of some of these Colonies, in violation of the natural and civil rights of the Colonies.

And whereas hostilities have been actually commenced in Massachusetts Bay, by the British troops, under the command of General Gage, and the lives of a number of the inhabitants of that Colony destroyed; the town of Boston not only having been long occupied as a garrisoned town in an enemy's country, but the inhabitants thereof treated with a severity and cruelty not to be justified even towards declared enemies.

And whereas large reinforcements have been ordered, and are soon expected, for the declared purpose of compelling these colonies to submit to the operation of the said acts, which hath rendered it necessary, and an indispensable duty, for the express purpose of securing and defending these Colonies, and preserving them in safety against all attempts to carry the said acts into execution; that an armed force be raised sufficient to defeat such hostile designs, and preserve and defend the lives, liberties and immunities of the Colonists: for the due regulating and well ordering of which;—

Resolved, That the following Rules and Orders be attended to, and observed by such forces as are or may hereafter be raised for the purpose aforesaid.

Article I. That every officer who shall be retained, and every soldier who shall serve in the Continental Army, shall, at the time of his acceptance of his commission or inlistment, subscribe these rules and regulations.

Article II. It is earnestly recommended to all officers and soldiers, diligently to attend Divine Service; and all officers and soldiers who shall behave indecently or irreverently at any place of Divine Worship, shall, if commissioned officers, be brought before a court-martial.

*   *   *

Article IV. Any officer or soldier, who shall behave himself with contempt or disrespect towards the General or Generals, or Commanders in chief of the Continental Forces, or shall speak false words, tending to his or their hurt or dishonour, shall be punished according to the nature of his offence, by the judgment of a general court-martial.

Art. V. Any officer or soldier, who shall begin, excite, cause, or join in any mutiny or sedition, in the regiment, troop or company to which he belongs, or in any other regiment, troop or company of the Continental Forces, either by land or sea, or in any party, post, detachment, or guard, on any pretence whatsoever, shall suffer such punishment, as by a general court-martial shall be ordered.

Art. VI. Any officer, non-commissioned officer, or soldier, who being present at any mutiny or sedition, does not use his utmost endeavours to suppress the same, or coming to the knowledge of any mutiny, or intended mutiny, does not, without delay, give information thereof to the commanding officer, shall be punished by order of a general court-martial, according to the nature of his offence.

Art. VII. Any officer or soldier, who shall strike his superior officer, or draw, or offer to draw, or shall lift up any weapon, or offer any violence against him, being in the execution of his office, on any pretence whatsoever, or shall disobey any lawful commands of his superior officer, shall suffer such punishment as shall, according to the nature of his offence, be ordered by the sentence of a general court-martial.

*   *   *

Art. XII. Every officer, commanding in quarters or on a march, shall keep good order, and, to the utmost of his power, redress all such abuses or disorders which may be committed by any officer or soldier under his command: If upon any complaint [being] made to him, of officers or soldiers beating, or otherwise ill-treating any person, or of committing any kind of riot, to the disquieting of the inhabitants of this Continent: he the said commander, who shall refuse or omit to see justice done on the offender or offenders, and reparation made to the party or parties injured, as far as the offender's

wages shall enable him or them, shall, upon due proof thereof, be punished as ordered by a general court-martial, in such manner as if he himself had committed the crimes or disorders complained of.

Art. XIII. If any officer should think himself to be wronged by his colonel or the commanding officer of the regiment, and shall, upon due application made to him, be refused to be redressed, he may complain to the General or Commander in chief of the Continental Forces, in order to obtain justice, who is hereby required to examine into said complaint, and see that justice be done.

*   *   *

Art. XXV. Whatsoever officer or soldier shall shamefully abandon any post committed to his charge, or shall speak words inducing others to do the like, in time of an engagement, shall suffer death immediately.

Art. XXVI. Any person belonging to the Continental Army, who shall make known the watchword to any person who is not entitled to receive it, according to the rules and discipline of war, or shall presume to give a parole, or watch-word, different from what he received, shall suffer death, or such other punishment as shall be ordered by the sentence of a general court-martial.

Art. XXVII. Whosoever belonging to the Continental Army, shall relieve the enemy with money, victuals, or ammunition, or shall knowingly harbour or protect an enemy, shall suffer such punishment as by a general court-martial shall be ordered.

Art. XXVIII. Whosoever belonging to the Continental Army, shall be convicted of holding correspondence with, or of giving intelligence to, the enemy, either directly or indirectly, shall suffer such punishment as by a general court-martial shall be ordered.

*   *   *

Art. XXXI. If any commander of any post, intrenchment, or fortress, shall be *compelled*, by the officers or soldiers under his command, to give it up to the enemy, or to abandon it, the commissioned officer, non-commissioned officers, or soldiers, who shall be convicted of having so offended, shall suffer death, or such other punishment as may be inflicted upon them by the sentence of a general court-martial.

*   *   *

Art. LI. That no persons shall be sentenced by a court-martial to suffer death, except in the cases expressly mentioned in the foregoing articles; nor shall any punishment be inflicted at the discretion of a court-martial, other than degrading, cashiering, drumming out of the army, whipping not exceeding thirty-nine lashes, fine not exceeding two months pay of the offender, imprisonment not exceeding one month.

*   *   *

39 "We have pursued every temperate, every respectful measure" (1775)

Shortly after granting the command of the Continental Army to George Washington and drafting Articles of War for the army's conduct, the Continental Congress established a committee to draw up a justification for the colonies' resort to arms. Benjamin Franklin of Pennsylvania, John Jay of New York, Edward Rutledge of South Carolina, Robert R. Livingston of New York, William Samuel Johnson of Connecticut, Thomas Jefferson of Virginia, and John Dickinson of Delaware constituted the committee. The final document, addressing the "Necessity of Taking up Arms," was the work of Dickinson and Jefferson.

☆ 39 Declaration of the Causes and Necessity of Taking Up Arms (July 6, 1775)

Reprinted in W. C. Ford, ed., *Journals of the Continental Congress* (Washington, D.C.: U.S. Government Printing Office, 1906), 2:140.

If it was possible for men, who exercise their reason to believe, that the divine Author of our existence intended a part of the human race to hold an absolute property in, and an unbounded power over others, marked out by his infinite goodness and wisdom, as the objects of a legal domination never rightfully resistible, however severe and oppressive, the inhabitants of these colonies might at least require from the parliament of Great Britain some evidence, that this dreadful authority over them, has been granted to that body. But a reverence for our great Creator, principles of humanity, and the dictates of common sense, must convince all those who reflect upon the subject, that government was instituted to promote the welfare of mankind, and ought to be administered for the attainment of that end. The legislature of Great Britain, however, stimulated by an inordinate passion for a power not only unjustifiable, but which they know to be peculiarly reprobated by the very constitution of that kingdom, and desperate of success in any mode of contest, where regard should be had to truth, law, or right, have at length, deserting those, attempted to effect their cruel and impolitic purpose of enslaving these colonies by violence, and have thereby rendered it necessary for us to close with their last appeal from reason to arms. Yet, however blinded that assembly may be, by their intemperate rage for unlimited domination, so to slight justice and the opinion of mankind, we esteem ourselves bound by obligations of respect to the rest of the world, to make known the justice of our cause.

Our forefathers, inhabitants of the island of Great Britain, left their native land, to seek on these shores a residence for civil and religious freedom. At the expense of their blood, at the hazard of their fortunes, without the least charge to the country from which they removed, by unceasing labour, and an unconquerable spirit, they effected settlements in the distant and inhospitable wilds of America, then filled with numerous and warlike nations of barbarians. Societies or governments, vested with perfect legislatures, were formed under charters from the crown, and an harmonious intercourse was established between the colonies and the kingdom from which they derived their origin.

... [But] these devoted colonies were judged to be in such a state, as to present victories without bloodshed, and all the easy emoluments of statuteable plunder. The uninterrupted tenor of their peaceable and respectful behaviour from the beginning of colonization, their dutiful, zealous, and useful services during the [French and Indian] war, though so recently and amply acknowledged in the most honourable manner by his majesty, by the late king, and by parliament, could not save them from the meditated innovations. Parliament [has] undertaken to give and grant our money without our consent, though we have ever exercised an exclusive right to dispose of our own property; statutes have been passed for extending the jurisdiction of courts of admiralty, and vice-admiralty beyond their ancient limits; for depriving us of the accustomed and inestimable privilege of trial by jury, in cases affecting both life and property; for suspending the legislature of one of the colonies; for interdicting all commerce to the capital of another; and for altering fundamentally the form of government established by charter, and secured by acts of its own legislature solemnly confirmed by the crown; for exempting the "murderers" of colonists from legal trial, and in effect, from punishment; for erecting in a neighbouring province, acquired by the joint arms of Great Britain and America, a despotism dangerous to our very existence; and for quartering soldiers upon the colonists in time of profound peace. It has also been resolved in parliament, that colonists charged with committing certain offences, shall be transported to England to be tried.

But why should we enumerate our injuries in detail? By one statute it is declared, that parliament can "of right make laws to bind us in all cases whatsoever." What is to defend us against so enormous, so unlimited a power? Not a single man of those who assume it, is chosen by us; or is subject to our controul or influence; but, on the contrary, they are all of them exempt from the operation of such laws, and an American revenue, if not diverted from the ostensible purposes for which it is raised, would actually lighten their own burdens in proportion, as they increase ours. ...

We have pursued every temperate, every respectful measure: we have even proceeded to break off our commercial intercourse with our fellow subjects, as the last peaceable admonition, that our attachment to no nation upon earth should supplant our attachment to liberty. This, we flattered ourselves, was the ultimate step of the controversy: but subsequent events have shewn, how vain was this hope of finding moderation in our enemies.

*   *   *

Fruitless were all the entreaties, arguments, and eloquence of an illustrious band of the most distinguished peers, and commoners, who nobly and stren[u]ously asserted the justice of our cause, to stay, or even to mitigate the heedless fury with which these accumulated and unexampled outrages were hurried on....

... General Gage, who in the course of the last year had taken possession of the town of Boston, in the province of Massachusetts Bay, ... on the 19th day of April, sent out from that place a large detachment of his army, who made an unprovoked assault on the inhabitants of the said province, at the town of Lexington ... murdered eight of the inhabitants, and wounded many others. From thence the troops proceeded in warlike array to the town of Concord, where they set upon another party of the inhabitants of the same province, killing several and wounding more, until compelled to retreat by the country people suddenly assembled to repel this cruel aggression. Hostilities, thus commenced by the British troops, have been since prosecuted by them without regard to faith or reputation. The inhabitants of Boston being confined within that town by the general their governor, and having, in order to procure their dismission, entered into a treaty with him ... but in open violation of honour, in defiance of the obligation of treaties, which even savage nations esteemed sacred, ... detained the greatest part of the inhabitants in the town, and compelled the few who were permitted to retire, to leave their most valuable effects behind....

The General ... proceeds to "declare them all, either by name or description, to be rebels and traitors, to supersede the course of the common law, and instead thereof to publish and order the use and exercise of the law martial." His troops have butchered our countrymen, have wantonly burnt Charlestown, besides a considerable number of houses in other places; our ships and vessels are seized; the necessary supplies of provisions are intercepted, and he is exerting his utmost power to spread destruction and devastation around him.

We have received certain intelligence, that General Carleton, the Governor of Canada, is instigating the people of that province and the Indians to fall upon us; and we have but too much reason to apprehend, that schemes have been formed to excite domestic enemies against us. In brief, a part of these colonies now feel, and all of them are sure of feeling, as far as the vengeance of administration can inflict them, the complicated calamities of fire, sword, and famine. We are reduced to the alternative of choosing an unconditional submission to the tyranny of irritated ministers, or resistance by force. The latter is our choice. We have counted the cost of this contest, and find nothing so dreadful as voluntary slavery. Honour, justice, and humanity, forbid us tamely to surrender that freedom which we received from our gallant ancestors, and which our innocent posterity have a right to receive from us. We cannot endure the infamy and guilt of resigning succeeding generations to that wretchedness which inevitably awaits them, if we basely entail hereditary bondage upon them.

Our cause is just. Our union is perfect. Our internal resources are great, and, if necessary, foreign assistance is undoubtedly attainable. We gratefully acknowledge, as signal instances of the Divine favour towards us, that his Providence would not permit us to be called into this severe controversy, until we were grown up to our present strength, had been previously exercised in warlike operation, and possessed of the means of defending ourselves.... The arms we have been compelled by our enemies to assume, we will, in defiance of every hazard, with unabating firmness and perseverance, employ for the preservation of our liberties; being with one mind resolved to die freemen rather than to live slaves.

Lest this declaration should disquiet the minds of our friends and fellow subjects in any part of the empire, we assure them that we mean not to dissolve that union which has so long and so happily subsisted between us, and which we sincerely wish to see restored. Necessity has not yet driven us into that desperate measure, or induced us to excite any other nation to war against them. We have not raised armies with ambitious designs of separating from Great Britain, and establishing independent states. We fight not for glory or for conquest. We exhibit to mankind the remarkable spectacle of a people attacked by unprovoked enemies, without any imputation or even suspicion of offence. They boast of their privileges and civilization, and yet proffer no milder conditions than servitude or death.

In our own native land, in defence of the freedom that is our birth-right, and which we ever enjoyed till the late violation of it — for the protection of our property, acquired solely by the honest industry of our fore-fathers and ourselves, against violence actually offered, we have taken up arms. We shall lay them down when hostilities shall cease on the part of the aggressors, and all danger of their being renewed shall be removed, and not before.

40 "misled by dangerous and ill designing men" (1775)

Despite continuing pitched battles, the moderates in the Continental Congress continued to hope for a peaceful solution. On June 18, 1775, two days after Bunker Hill, John Dickinson of Delaware, the leader of the moderates, introduced the draft of a final petition to the king. After approval of the draft on July 8, William Penn was to present it in London. Nevertheless, the conciliatory voices in England were growing weak, and the news of American resistance moved the king on August 23, 1775, to proclaim a state of rebellion, declaring its adherents to be traitors and ordering his loyal subjects to inform upon those who corresponded or expressed sympathy with the rebels.

☆ 40 A Proclamation by the King for Suppressing Rebellion and Sedition (August 23, 1775)

Reprinted in P. Force, ed., *American Archives*, 4th ser. (Washington, D.C.: M. St. Clair Clarke & P. Force, 1837), 3:240.

Whereas many of our subjects in divers parts of our Colonies and Plantations in North America, misled by dangerous and ill designing men, and forgetting the allegiance which they owe to the power that has protected and supported them; after various disorderly acts committed in disturbance of the publick peace, to the obstruction of lawful commerce and to the oppression of our loyal subjects carrying on the same; have at length proceeded to open and avowed rebellion, by arraying themselves in a hostile manner, to withstand the execution of the law, and traitorously preparing, ordering and levying war against us: And whereas, there is reason to apprehend that such rebellion hath been much promoted and encouraged by the traitorous correspondence, counsels and comfort of divers wicked and desperate persons within this realm: To the end therefore, that none of our subjects may neglect or violate their duty through ignorance thereof, or through any doubt of the protection which the law will afford to their loyalty and zeal, we have thought fit, by and with the advice of our Privy Council, to issue our Royal Proclamation, hereby declaring, that not only all our Officers, civil and military, are obliged to exert their utmost endeavours to suppress such rebellion, and to bring the traitors to justice, but that all our subjects of this Realm, and the dominions thereunto belonging, are bound by law to be aiding and assisting in the suppression of such rebellion, and to disclose and make known all traitorous conspiracies and attempts against us, our crown and dignity; and we do accordingly strictly charge and command all our Officers, as well civil as military, and all others

our obedient and loyal subjects, to use their utmost endeavours to withstand and suppress such rebellion, and to disclose and make known all treasons and traitorous conspiracies which they shall know to be against us, our crown and dignity; and for that purpose, that they transmit to one of our principal Secretaries of State, or other proper officer, due and full information of all persons who shall be found carrying on correspondence with, or in any manner or degree aiding or abetting the persons now in open arms and rebellion against our Government, within any of our Colonies and Plantations in North America, in order to bring to condign punishment the authors, perpetrators, and abetters of such traitorous designs.

*   *   *

God save the King.

41 Amendments to the Articles of War (1775)

The American War of Independence began on April 19, 1775, with the skirmishes at Lexington and Concord. In May, Ethan Allen's Green Mountain Boys took Fort Ticonderoga; the conquest became America's first military victory. George Washington was named commander in chief of the Continental Army in June, and the British issued the Royal Proclamation of Rebellion on August 23. The establishment of an American navy followed in October.

The original Articles of War, enacted on June 30, 1775, appeared inadequate for the conduct of an independent and wartime army. The colonies were no longer willing to proclaim their loyalty to the Crown. The Amendments to the Articles of War, dated November 7, 1775, extended the death penalty to offenses not so punished originally, including treacherous correspondence, sedition, desertions, and mutiny.

☆ 41 Additions and Alterations to the Rules of the Continental Army (November 7, 1775)

Papers of the Continental Congress, 1, no. 152:155, reprinted in W. C. Force, ed., *Writings of George Washington* (New York: Putnam 1889), 190.

A letter from General Washington, No. 11, was read.

The secretary having digested in order the resolutions of Congress, as far as they have gone on the report of the Committee of Conference, produced the same, which being read, and agreed to as follows:

Resolved, That the following additions and alterations or amendments, be made in the RULES and REGULATIONS of the continental Army, viz.

1. All persons convicted of holding a treacherous correspondence with, or giving intelligence to the enemy, shall suffer death, or such other punishment as a general court-martial shall think proper.

*   *   *

4. In all cases where a commissioned officer is cashiered for cowardice or fraud, it be added in the punishment, that the crime, name, place of abode, and punishment of the delinquent be published in the news papers, in and about the camp, and of that colony from which the offender came, or usually resides: after which it shall be deemed scandalous in any officer to associate with him.

5. Any officer or soldier, who shall begin, excite, cause, or join in any mutiny or sedition in the regiment, troop, or company to which he belongs, or in any other regiment, troop, or company of the continental forces, either by land or sea, or in any party, post, detachment or guard, on any pretence whatsoever, shall suffer death, or such other punishment, as a general court-martial shall direct.

6. Any officer or soldier, who shall desert to the enemy, and afterwards be taken, shall suffer death, or such other punishment, as a general court-martial shall direct.

7. Whatsoever commissioned officer shall be found drunk on his guard, party, or other duty under arms, shall be cashiered and drummed out of the army with infamy; any non-commissioned officer or soldier, so offending, shall be sentenced to be whipt, not less than twenty, nor more than thirty-nine lashes, according to the nature of the offence.

*   *   *

10. Whatsoever officer or soldier shall misbehave himself before the enemy, or shamefully abandon any post committed to his charge, or shall speak words inducing others to do the like, shall suffer death.

*   *   *

16. All officers and soldiers who shall wilfully, or through negligence, disobey any general or special orders, shall be punished at the discretion of a regimental court-martial, where the offence is against a regimental order, and at the discretion of a general court-martial, where the offence is against an order given from the commander in chief, or the commanding officer of any detachment or post, and such general court-martial can be had.

42 "Ye that dare oppose not only the tyranny but the tyrant" (1776)

When the time arrived, the cause of the American Revolution had many willing and courageous soldiers and an even greater number of supporters. But no one had a larger role in the planting and nour-

ishment of the seeds of independence than Patrick Henry, a native Virginian who came to be called "The Tongue of the Revolution," and Thomas Paine, a transplanted Englishman who best articulated the need for the break from the mother country in *Common Sense*.

Patrick Henry's (1736-99) fame was derived from his initial 1765 oration against the Stamp Act, when shouts of "treason" resounded from his fellow burgesses at Williamsburg. A decade later in Richmond, his cry for "liberty or death" helped galvanize further the emerging nation. After the Revolution Thomas Paine (1737-1809) became a French citizen and a member of the National Convention. But the French revolutionary upheaval resulted in Paine's disaffection; and labeled a reactionary, he was imprisoned and condemned by Robespierre. Upon the fall of Robespierre, Paine was released from jail; and after a six-year stay in France, he returned to America in 1802 at the invitation of President Jefferson. Paine died alone and neglected.

☆ 42 Common Sense

Reprinted in R. Heffner, ed., *A Documentary History of the United States* (New York: Mentor, 1952), 13-15.

Volumes have been written on the subject of the struggle between England and America. Men of all ranks have embarked in the controversy, from different motives, and with various designs; but all have been ineffectual, and the period of debate is closed. Arms as the last resource decide the contest; the appeal was the choice of the King, and the Continent has accepted the challenge. . . .

The Sun never shined on a cause of greater worth. 'Tis not the affair of a City, a County, a Province, or a Kingdom; but of a Continent—of at least one-eighth part of the habitable Globe. 'Tis not the concern of a day, a year, or an age; posterity are virtually involved in the contest, and will be more or less affected even to the end of time, by the proceedings now. Now is the seedtime of Continental union, faith and honour. The least fracture now will be like a name engraved with the point of a pin on the tender rind of a young oak; the wound would enlarge with the tree, and posterity read in it full grown characters. . . .

I have heard it asserted by some, that as America has flourished under her former connection with Great Britain, the same connection is necessary towards her future happiness, and will always have the same effect. Nothing can be more fallacious than this kind of argument. We may as well assert that because a child has thrived upon milk, that it is never to have meat, or that the first twenty years of our lives is to become a precedent for the next twenty. But even this is admitting more than is true; for I answer roundly that America would have flourished as much, and probably much more, had no European power taken any notice of her. The commerce by which she hath enriched herself are the necessaries of life, and will always have a market while eating is the custom of Europe.

But she has protected us, say some. That she hath engrossed us is true, and defended the Continent at our expense as well as her own, is admitted; and she would have defended Turkey from the same motive, *viz.* for the sake of trade and dominion.

Alas! we have been long led away by ancient prejudices and made large sacrifices to superstition. We have boasted the protection of Great Britain, without considering, that her motive was *interest* not *attachment*; and that she did not protect us from *our enemies* on *our account*; but from *her enemies* on *her own account*, from those who had no quarrel with us on any *other account*, and who will always be our enemies on the *same account.* Let Britain waive her pretentions to the Continent, or the Continent throw off the dependence, and we should be at peace with France and Spain, were they at war with Britain....

But Britain is the parent country, say some. Then the more shame upon her conduct. Even brutes do not devour their young, nor savages make war upon their families.... Europe, and not England, is the parent Country of America....

I challenge the warmest advocate for reconciliation to show a single advantage that this Continent can reap by being connected with Great Britain. I repeat the challenge; not a single advantage is derived. Our corn will fetch its price in any market in Europe, and our imported goods must be paid for, buy them where we will.

But the injuries and disadvantages which we sustain by that connection, are without number; and our duty to mankind at large, as well as to ourselves, instructs us to renounce the alliance: because, any submission to, or dependence on, Great Britain, tends directly to involve this Continent in European wars and quarrels, and set us at variance with nations who would otherwise seek our friendship, and against whom we have neither anger nor complaint. As Europe is our market for trade, we ought to form no partial connection with any part of it. It is the true interest of America to steer clear of European contentions, which she never can do, while, by her dependence on Britain, she is made the makeweight in the scale of British politics....

'Tis repugnant to reason, to the universal order of things, to all examples from former ages, to suppose that this Continent can long remain subject to any external power. The most sanguine in Britain doth not think so. The utmost stretch of human wisdom cannot, at this time, compass a plan, short of separation, which can promise the Continent even a year's security. Reconciliation is *now* a fallacious dream. Nature hath deserted the connection, and art cannot supply her place. For, as Milton wisely expresses, "never can true reconcilement grow where wounds of deadly hate have pierced so deep." ...

To talk of friendship with those in whom our reason forbids us to have faith, and our affections wounded thro' a thousand pores instruct us to detest, is madness and folly. Every day wears out the little remains of kindred between us and them; and can there be any reason to hope, that as the relationship expires, the affection will encrease, or that we shall agree better when we have ten times more and greater concerns to quarrel over than ever?

Ye that tell us of harmony and reconciliation, can ye restore to us the time that is past? Can ye give to prostitution its former innocence? neither can ye reconcile Britain and America. The last cord now is broken, the people of England are presenting addresses against us. There are injuries which nature cannot forgive; she would cease to be nature if she did. As well can the lover forgive the ravisher of his mistress, as the Continent forgive the murders of Britain....

O! ye that love mankind! Ye that dare oppose not only the tyranny but the tyrant, stand forth! Every spot of the old world is overrun with oppression. Freedom hath been hunted round the Globe. Asia and Africa have long expelled her. Europe regards her like a stranger, and England hath given her warning to depart. O! receive the fugitive, and prepare in time an asylum for mankind....

43 "required to take the following Oath" (1776)

Not all colonists favored the war against the English sovereign. A significant portion of the colonial population was English-born. Many others belonged to the Tory ranks and continued to profess their allegiance to the king.

Still other Americans, sympathetic to the cause of independence, were reluctant to risk a failed revolution and trial for treason. Until almost its very close, the colonial military campaign of 1776 appeared to be a disheartening failure. By the end of the year, the colonies possessed only five thousand poorly equipped troops.

But others who were more ambivalent in their support apparently desired to modify this zeal in the hopes of not altogether forswearing a reconciliation. This North Carolina oath requirement reflected these competing claims on the allegiance of the civil population. In addition, it recorded the fact that the old backwoods parochial conflicts were not subsumed totally by the greater rebellion.

☆ 43 Resolution of the Provincial Council of
North Carolina, March 5, 1776

Reprinted in W. Saunders, ed., *The Colonial Records of
North Carolina* (Raleigh: Josephus Daniel, 1890), 10:475-76.

The [Provincial Council of North Carolina] met according to Adjournment Tuesday, 5th March 1776.

*　　　*　　　*

Resolved, That all persons who shall be disarmed
by the Town and County Committees and other suspected persons who have not taken up Arms against
this Colony shall be required to take the following
Oath on pain of imprisonment viz:

I do solemnly and sincerely swear on the holy
Evangelists of Almighty God that during the present unhappy contest between Great Britain and
America, I will not under any pretence whatever oppose or take up Arms to oppose the Measures of the
Continental or provincial Congresses or any Troops
raised by or acting under the Authority of either,
nor will I directly or indirectly, either personally or
by letter, Counsel, advise or give Intelligence to any
of his Majesty's Governors, General Officers, Soldiers, or others employed by Land or sea to carry
into execution and enforce Obedience to the several
Acts of British Legislature, deemed oppressive to
these Colonies: I will not by example, opinion, advice
or persuasion, endeavour to prejudice the people or
any of them in favour of Parliamentary Measures or
against those recommended by the General and provincial Congresses until it shall please God to restore peace and good understanding to the contending powers.

*　　　*　　　*

That the thanks of this Council be given to Col.
James Moore and all the Brave Officers and Soldiers
of every denomination for their late very important
services rendered their country in effectually suppressing the late daring and dangerous insurrection
of the Highlanders and Regulators, and that this Resolve be published in the North Carolina gazette.

Resolved, That Col. Robert Howe is justly in-
titled to the most honourable Testimony of the Approbation of this Council for his important services
while in the Colony of Virginia rendered in the common cause of American Liberty, and that the President transmit the warmest thanks of this Board in
the fullest and most honorable terms to Colonel
Howe and all the Brave Officers and Soldiers under
his command for their spirited conduct, having acquitted themselves greatly to their Country.

44 "all persons abiding within any of
the United Colonies" (1776)

Not until the adoption of the United States Constitution in 1787 was there a nationwide law respecting

treason against the newly created American political entity. At the start of the Revolution, the laws of
various colonies defined treason as adherence to the
enemies of the English sovereign. Thus, there was
no law prohibiting treason against the United Colonies or any individual colony by supporters of the
Loyalist cause. The Second Continental Congress
acted to remedy this legal anachronism by setting
forth the foundations of allegiance and treason for
the several colonies.

The Resolution on Spies, passed before the Declaration of Independence, acknowledged the preemi-
nence of the colonial governments over the Crown in
America by referring to those adhering to the king
as "guilty of treason." The document also reflected
the incompetence of the Continental Congress to
pass laws binding within the various colonies.

☆ 44 Resolution on Spies (June 24, 1776)

Reprinted in W. C. Ford, ed., *Journals of the Continental
Congress* (Washington, D.C.: U.S. Government Printing Office, 1906), 5:475.

The Congress took into consideration the report of
the Committee on Spies; Whereupon,

Resolved, That all persons abiding within any of
the United Colonies, and deriving protection from
the laws of the same, owe allegiance to the said laws,
and are members of such colony; and that all persons
passing through, visiting, or make a temporary stay
in any of the said colonies, being entitled to the protection of the laws during the time of such passage,
visitation or temporary stay, owe, during the same
time, allegiance thereto:

That all persons, members of, or owing allegiance
to any of the United Colonies, as before described,
who shall levy war against any of the said colonies
within the same, or be adherent to the king of Great
Britain, or others the enemies of the said colonies, or
any of them, within the same, giving to him or them
aid and comfort, are guilty of treason against such
colony:

That it be recommended to the legislatures of the
several United Colonies, to pass laws for punishing,
in such manner as to them shall seem fit, such persons before described, as shall be proveably attainted of open deed, by people of their condition, of
any of the treasons before described.

*　　　*　　　*

45 "the right of the people to alter or
to abolish" Forms of Government
(1776)

The country had not yet attained an international
standing, and its independence could not be secured

without military victories against the world's great-est naval power, Britain, well-supported by veteran British armies. To some, a claim of independence seemed an act of utmost recklessness. Yet on June 4, Richard Henry Lee of Virginia introduced in the Continental Congress a resolution that "these united Colonies are and of right ought to be free and independent states" and that a plan of confederation should be carried out. A committee to prepare such a declaration formed, consisting of John Adams, Benjamin Franklin, Thomas Jefferson, Robert R. Livingston, and Roger Sherman. On July 4, 1776, the Congress adopted the declaration, substantially as drafted by Thomas Jefferson, and John Hancock as president of the Congress signed it. The New York delegation abstained from the vote, and two dele-gates from Pennsylvania stayed away so as not to have to cast votes.

The abuses heretofore blamed on Parliament and wicked ministers were laid directly to the king. The Declaration gave effect to the twin political themes articulated from earliest colonial times: that govern-ments derive their just powers from the consent of the governed and that the people have a right and a duty to revolt against abusive government.

☆ 45 Declaration of Independence (July 4, 1776)

THE UNANIMOUS DECLARATION OF THE THIRTEEN
UNITED STATES OF AMERICA

WHEN, in the course of human events, it becomes necessary for one people to dissolve the political bands which have connected them with another, and to assume, among the powers of the earth, the sepa-rate and equal station to which the laws of nature and of nature's God entitle them, a decent respect to the opinions of mankind requires that they should declare the causes which impel them to the separation.

We hold these truths to be self-evident: that all men are created equal; that they are endowed, by their Creator, with certain unalienable rights; that among these are life, liberty, and the pursuit of hap-piness. That to secure these rights, governments are instituted among men, deriving their just powers from the consent of the governed; that whenever any form of government becomes de-structive of these ends, it is the right of the people to alter or to abolish it, and to institute a new govern-ment, laying its foundation on such principles, and organizing its powers in such form, as to them shall seem most likely to effect their safety and happi-ness. Prudence, indeed, will dictate, that govern-ments long established, should not be changed for light and transient causes; and accordingly all expe-rience hath shown, that mankind are more disposed to suffer, while evils are sufferable, than to right themselves by abolishing the forms to which they are accustomed. But when a long train of abuses and

usurpations, pursuing invariably the same object, evinces a design to reduce them under absolute des-potism, it is their right, it is their duty, to throw off such government, and to provide new guards for their future security. Such has been the patient suf-ferance of these colonies; and such is now the neces-sity which constrains them to alter their former sys-tems of government. The history of the present King of Great Britain is a history of repeated inju-ries and usurpations, all having in direct object the establishment of an absolute tyranny over these states.

*   *   *

46 The Revolution in Literature (1776-1777)

Described as the First American Civil War, the con-test between the competing American political forces—the Patriots and the Loyalists—took place in the streets, the legislative arenas, and the artistic and religious forums. But even here, the references often were to legal rights and obligations. A Loyalist song of 1776 warned against the sedition of the Con-tinental Congress and foresaw "scenes of blood," while Patriot literature, taking the text of Judges 5:23, drew biblical support for violent opposition to oppression.

☆ 46 Loyalists and Patriots

☆ 46a The Congress

A Song
wrote in the spring of the year 1776
TUNE: "Nancy Dawson"

Reprinted in W. Sargent, *The Loyalist Poetry of the Revo-lution* (Boston: Milford House, 1972), 70-74.

> YE Tories all rejoice and sing
> Success to George our gracious king;
> The faithful subjects tribute bring
>   And execrate the Congress.
>
> These hardy knaves and stupid fools;
> Some apish and pragmatic mules;
> Some servile acquiescing tools;
>   These, these compose the Congress.
>
> *   *   *
>
> Time serving priests to zealots preach,
> Who king and parliament impeach;
> Seditious lessons to us teach
>   At the command of Congress.
>
> Good Lord! disperse this venal tribe;
> Their doctrine let no fools imbibe;
> Let Balaam no more asses ride
>   Nor burdens bear to Congress.
>
> *   *   *

There's Washington and all his men—
Where Howe had one, the goose had ten—
March'd up the hill, and down again;
    And sent returns to Congress.

Prepare, prepare, my friends prepare,
For scenes of blood, the field of war;
To royal standard we'll repair,
    And curse the haughty Congress.

☆ 46b An Antidote against Toryism (Nathaniel Whittaker)

Reprinted in L. F. S. Upton, ed., *Revolutionary versus Loyalist: The First American Civil War, 1774-1784* (Waltham: Blaisdell, 1968), 85.

JUDGES V, 23

Curse ye Meroz, said the Angel of the Lord,
Curse ye bitterly the inhabitants thereof,
    because they came not to the help of the Lord,
    to the help of the Lord, against the mighty. . . .

        *   *   *

From this view of the text and context, we may deduce the following doctrinal observations:

I. That the cause of Liberty is the cause of God and Truth.

II. That to take arms and repel force by force, when our Liberties are invaded, is well pleasing to God.

III. That it is lawful to levy war against those who oppress us, even when they are not in arms against us.

IV. That indolence and backwardness in taking arms, and exerting ourselves in the service of our Country, when called thereto by the public voice in order to recover and secure our freedoms, is a heinous sin in the sight of God.

V. That God requires a people, struggling for their Liberties, to treat such of the community who will not join them, as open enemies, and to reject them as unworthy of the privileges which others enjoy. . . .

        *   *   *

47 "dark and criminal designs of enslaving America" (1777)

The law passed by the Maryland General Assembly in 1777 sought to punish those who were "still pursuing their dark and criminal designs of enslaving America." The act coincided with similar attempts throughout the states to clarify the duties as well as the rights of the citizenry by means of state treason laws, bills of rights, and constitutions.

Pockets of Toryism remained strong, particularly in states like Maryland where pro-British populations and economic interests were pronounced.

The new law prohibited any citizen, under penalty of five years' imprisonment or banishment for life, from maintaining that the king or Parliament had any authority over the United States. Oaths of allegiance were imposed on all voters. Citizens adjudged guilty of treason against the state were to be put to death without benefit of clergy, and their estates were forfeited to the state. The 1777 law was replete with several of the controversial practices which were reenacted in later periods of political stress in America: the requirement of loyalty oaths; the prohibition of seditious speech; the limitation of travel; the detention of suspicious individuals; and the suspension of habeas corpus—the legal writ that serves to protect individuals from unlawful imprisonment.

☆ 47 An Act to Punish Certain Crimes and Misdemeanors, and Prevent the Growth of Toryism [Maryland]

1777-80 Maryland Laws (Annapolis: Frederick Green, 1777), chapter 20.

WHEREAS the clemency of this state towards such of its subjects and inhabitants as are inimical to its freedom and independence, has not had the desired effect of reclaiming them from their evil practices, but still pursuing their dark and criminal designs of enslaving America, they continue to encourage and promote the operations of our enemies: And whereas every hope of uniting to the interest of their country the affections of these its unnatural and implacable enemies is extinguished, and great disadvantages have arisen, and still more dangerous consequences may be apprehended, from a delay of effectual measures to suppress or remove them from the society of a free people, constrained by oppression to declare their independence, and determined at all events to maintain the fame;

II. BE it therefore enacted, by the General Assembly of Maryland, That if any subject or inhabitant of this state shall, within or without the same, and if any person whatever, being an inhabitant of any other of the United States; shall, within this state, levy war against the United States, or any of them, or shall adhere to any person bearing arms, or employed in the service of Great Britain, against the United States, or any of them, or shall afford such persons, or any of them, any aid or comfort, or shall give them, or any of them, or any subject of Great Britain, any intelligence of the warlike preparations or designs of the United States, or any of them, and shall be thereof convicted in the general court of this state, or shall stand mute, or peremptorily challenge above the number of twenty of the pannel [*sic*], shall be adjudged guilty of treason against this state, and shall suffer death without benefit of clergy, and forfeit all the estate which he had at the time of the commission of the crime, to the use of this state; and the several crimes aforesaid shall receive the same constructions that have been given to each of the said crimes as are enumerated in the statute of Edward the third, commonly called the statute of treasons. . . .

III. AND be it enacted, That if any subject or inhabitant of this state has knowledge of the actual commission of any of the crimes aforesaid, about to be treason, shall conceal the same, and shall not, as soon as convenient be, disclose and make the same known to the governor, or some one of the judges or justices of this state for the time being, such person, on conviction thereof in the general court, shall be adjudged guilty of a misprision of treason, and shall forfeit all the estate which he had, at the time of the commission of the crime, to the use of this state.

IV. AND be it enacted, That if any subject or inhabitant of this state shall, by any word, open deed, writing, printing, or other act, advisedly and willingly declare, affirm, maintain or defend, that the king or parliament of Great Britain hath any authority, power or jurisdiction, in or over the United States, or any of them, or that any allegiance is due from any of the subjects or inhabitants of the United States, or any of them, to the king of Great Britain, his heirs or successors, or shall wickedly, corruptly or seditiously, persuade or entice any of the subjects or inhabitants of this state, to return to or acknowledge any dependence on the crown and parliament of Great Britain, or to own any allegiance or obedience to the King of Great Britain, his heirs or successors, and shall be thereof convicted in the general court, such person shall be fined not exceeding ten thousand pounds current money, and be imprisoned not more than five years, in the discretion of the court, or be banished from this state for ever.

V. AND be it enacted, That if any subject or inhabitant of this state shall, by any word, open deed, writing, printing, or other act, persuade or excite any of the inhabitants of this state to resist the present government thereof by force, or to oppose, or in any manner obstruct, with force, the execution of any of the laws of this state, such person being convicted thereof in the general court, shall be fined not exceeding two thousand pounds current money, and be imprisoned not more than two years, in the discretion of the court.

VI. AND be it enacted, That if any subject or inhabitant of this state shall know of any intention, design or attempt, to commit any of the crimes declared by this act to be treason against this state, and shall not reveal the same, as soon as conveniently may be, to the governor, or some one of the judges or justices of this state for the time being, such person, on conviction thereof in the general court, shall be fined not exceeding one thousand pounds current money, and imprisoned not more than one year, in the discretion of the court.

VII. AND be it enacted, That if any subject or inhabitant of this state, shall advisedly and maliciously, with an intention to obstruct the service, dissuade, discourage or obstruct, any person from enlisting or engaging in the army or navy of the United States, or any of them, such person, on conviction thereof in the general court, shall be fined not exceeding one thousand pounds current money, in the discretion of the court.

VIII. AND be it enacted, That if any subject or inhabitant of this state shall, by any word, open deed, writing, printing or other act, wickedly, corruptly or seditiously, dissuade, discourage or terrify, any of the people of this state from supporting the independency of the United States, or any of them, or shall directly or indirectly endeavour to support or justify the measures taken by the king and parliament of Great Britain against the United States, or any of them, and shall be thereof convicted in the general court, such person shall be fined not exceeding one thousand pounds current money, in the discretion of the court.

IX. AND be it enacted, That if any subject or inhabitant of this state, shall write or convey any letter, or send or carry any message, to any person employed in the service of Great Britain against the United States, or any of them, without the leave of the governor of this state, or some one of the general officers of the army of the United States, or shall knowingly receive or bring any letter or message from any such person, and shall not deliver or communicate the same, as soon as conveniently may be, to the governor, or some one of the judges or justices of the peace within this state, and shall be thereof convicted in any county court of this state, such person shall be fined not exceeding one hundred pounds current money, in the discretion of the court.

*   *   *

XII. AND be it enacted, That in case this state shall be invaded by the enemy, the governor for the time being, with the advice of the council, shall have full power and authority to arrest, or order to be arrested, all persons whose going at large the governor and council shall have good grounds to believe may be dangerous to the safety of this state, and the same persons to confine during such invasion, to such places as the governor and the council shall think proper, or to limit such persons to particular districts in this state, or in their discretion to discharge such persons on security; and that during any invasion of this state by the enemy, the habeas corpus act shall be suspended, as to all such persons arrested by the order of the governor and council.

*   *   *

XV. AND be it enacted, That every voter for delegates of sheriffs, or for electors of the senate, if required, and every other person required by law to take the oath of fidelity and support to this state, shall take, repeat and subscribe, the same oath, or if a quaker, menonist or dunker, shall solemnly, sincerely and truly, declare and affirm thereto in the words thereof.

XVI. AND be it enacted, That if any person shall travel into or pass through or from this state to any other, without a pass of safe conduct, signed by some member of congress, or by the governor, or some judge or justice of this state, or of the state of which he is a subject or resident, he shall be liable to be apprehended and carried before some judge or justice for examination, who may commit him to the public gaol, if an offender against the laws, or dangerous person to this state, or to the United States, or any of them, there to remain till discharged by due course of law, and if not an offender or dangerous as aforesaid, the said judge or justice may discharge him and give him a pass.

XVII. WHEREAS several persons, late inhabitants of this state, have, since the fourteenth day of August, seventeen hundred and seventy-five, deserted the defence of this country in the present just and necessary war, BE IT ENACTED, That no person whatsoever, who hath deserted as aforesaid, or any person who since the said time hath left this state without leave, shall at any time hereafter (unless he returns to this state within twelve months, and during the present war, and takes and subscribes the oath of fidelity aforesaid within ten days after his return) be capable of holding any office of trust or profit within this state; nor shall any person, now a resident of this state, who hath refused or neglected to subscribe the association, and shall not take the said oath of fidelity on or before the first day of August next, be capable of holding any office as aforesaid.

XVIII. PROVIDED always, That nothing herein contained shall extend to such persons who from religious principles have not subscribed or shall not subscribe the association.

XIX. AND be it enacted, That this act shall be publicly read by the clerk of the general court, and by the clerk of every county court in this state, at their next court respectively, immediately after empannelling the grand jury, and also by every minister, teacher or preacher of the gospel, immediately after divine service, at every church, chapel or meeting-house, where they officiate, on some Sunday in the month of May next; and every clerk, minister, teacher or preacher, failing so to do, shall forfeit and pay the sum of five pounds, to be recovered with costs by the informer before any justice of the peace of the county where the offence shall be committed.

*   *   *

48 "Dangers Which May Arise from Persons Disaffected to the State" (1777-1780)

In 1777, North Carolina responded to the Continental Congress's Resolution on Spies by stiffening its oath-taking requirement and making continued allegiance to the English sovereign an act of treason. The law prohibited the continuation of the public debate on the issues of war and independence and made treasonous any efforts to persuade people "to return to a dependence on the Crown" or to spread "false and dispiriting news." Although attending to the forms of earlier English treason law, the act broadened the definitions of treason and misprision of treason. The General Assembly also established an elaborate oath-taking procedure for those suspected of Loyalist connections. Individuals who continued to acknowledge allegiance to the king were subject to exile from the state. By 1780, so many were accused of treason that problems arose in the administering of the statute. In response, the legislature simplified the legal process for the trial of alleged traitors by eliminating many procedural protections of the accused.

☆ 48 All Persons Accused of Treason

☆ 48a An Act to Amend an Act for Declaring What Crimes and Practices against the State Shall Be Treason, and What Shall Be Misprision of Treason, and Providing Punishments Adequate to Crimes of Both Classes, and for Preventing the Dangers Which May Arise from Persons Disaffected to the State [North Carolina]

Chap. 3, 1777 N.C. Sess. Laws 11.

I. Be it Enacted by the General Assembly of the State of North Carolina, and it is hereby Enacted by the Authority of the same, That all and every Person or Persons (Prisoners of War excepted) now inhabiting or residing within the Limits of the State of North Carolina, or who shall voluntarily come into the same hereafter to inhabit or reside, do owe and shall pay Allegiance to the State of North Carolina.

II. And be it further Enacted, by the Authority aforesaid, That if any Person or Persons belonging to, or residing within this State, and under the protection of its Laws, shall take a Commission or Commissions from the King of Great Britain, or any under his Authority, or other the Enemies of this State, or the United States of America, or shall levy War against this State, or the Government thereof, or knowingly and wilfully shall aid or assist any Enemies at open War against this State, or the United States of America, by joining their Armies, or by inlisting, or procuring or persuading others to inlist for that Purpose, or by furnishing such Enemies with Arms, Ammunition, Provision, or any other Article for their Aid or Comfort, or shall form, or be in any wise concerned in forming, any Combination, Plot or Conspiracy, for betraying this State, or the United States of America, into the Hands or Power of any Foreign Enemy, or shall give any Intelligence to the Enemies of this State for that Purpose, every Person so offending, and being thereof legally convicted by the Evidence of Two sufficient Witnesses, or standing mute, or peremptorily challenging more than Thirty Five Jurors, in any Court of Oyer and Terminer, or other Court that shall and may be established for the Trial of such Offences, shall be adjudged guilty of High Treason, and shall suffer Death without the Benefit of Clergy, and his or her Estate shall be forfeited to the State. Provided, That the Judge or Judges of the Court wherein such Conviction may be, shall and may order and appropriate so much of the Traitor's Estate as to him or them may appear sufficient for the Support of his or her Family.

III. And be it further Enacted, by the Authority aforesaid, That if any Person or Persons within this State shall attempt to convey intelligence to the Enemies of this State, or of the United States, or shall Publickly and deliberately speak or write against the Public Defence, or shall maliciously and advisedly endeavour to excite the People to resist the Government of this State, or persuade them to return to a Dependence on the Crown of Great Britain, or shall knowingly spread false and dispiriting News, or maliciously and advisedly terrify and discourage the People from inlisting into the Service of this State, or the United States, or shall stir up or excite Tumults, Disorders, or Insurrections in the State, or dispose the People to favour the Enemy, or oppose, or endeavour to prevent the Measures carrying on in Support of the Election of the Freedom and Independence of the said United States, every such Person or Persons, being thereof legally convicted by the Evidence of Two or more creditable Witnesses, or other sufficient Testimony, shall be adjudged guilty of Misprision of Treason, and shall suffer Imprisonment during the War, and forfeit to the State one Half of his, her, or their Lands, Tenements, Goods and Chattels.

*   *   *

V. And whereas the safety of the State, and the present critical Situation of Affairs, make it necessary that all Persons who owe or acknowledge Allegiance or Obedience to the King of Great Britain should be removed out of the State; Be it Enacted, by the Authority aforesaid, That all the late Officers of the King of Great Britain, and all Persons (Quakers excepted) [Quakers to make a similar Affirmation], being Subjects of this State, and now living therein, or who shall hereafter come to live therein, who have traded immediately to Great Britain or

Ireland within Ten Years last Past, in their own Right, or acted as Factors, Storekeepers or Agents, here or in any of the United States of America or Ireland, shall take the following Oath of Abjuration or Allegiance, or depart out of the State, viz.

I will bear faithful and true Allegiance to the State of North Carolina, and will truly endeavour to support, maintain, and defend the independent Government thereof, against George the Third, King of Great Britain, and his Successors, and the Attempts of any other Person, Prince, Power, State or Potentate, who by secret Arts, Treasons, Conspiracies, or by open Force, shall attempt to subvert the same, and will in every Respect conduct myself as a peaceful orderly Subject; and that I will disclose and make known to the Governor, some Member of the Council of State, or some Justice of the Superior Courts or of the Peace, all Treasons, Conspiracies, and Attempts, committed or intended against the State, which shall come to my knowledge.

*   *   *

And the said Oath or Affirmation shall be taken and subscribed in open Court, in the County where the Person or Persons taking the same shall or do usually reside.

VI. And be it further Enacted, by the Authority aforesaid, That the County Courts in each and every County, and every Justice of the Peace in each respective County, shall have full Power to issue Citations against Persons coming within the above Description. . . .

And if any Person so cited (due proof being made thereof), shall fail or neglect to attend, or attending shall refuse to take the said Oath or Affirmation (as the Case may be) then the said Court shall and may have full Power and Authority to order such Person to depart out of this State, to Europe or the West Indies, within Sixty Days. . . .

VII. And be it further Enacted, That if any Person so departing, or sent off from this State, shall return to the same, then such Persons shall be adjudged guilty of Treason against the State, and shall and may be proceeded against in like Manner as is herein directed in Cases of Treason. . . .

VIII. And whereas . . . some Scruples have arisen with Respect to the Manner by Law required for the Service of such Citations [for appearance at the court for the taking of the oath] and as by many it has been held that a Service upon the Person of him intended to be cited was necessary, before his Attendance in Court could be legally compelled, as many suspected Persons, by continual Absence from their Place of Abode, or frequently removing from thence, have rendered the Service of such personal Citations difficult, and in some Cases impracticable, whereby they evade the Intentions of the said Act, and cannot be obliged to take the said Oath prescribed, nor be made subject to the Penalties ordained for neglecting or refusing the same: And whereas there is great Reason to believe that there are divers persons whose intentions are inimical to the State, who would in Case of Invasion by our Enemies, or the Expectation of immediate Support of them, carry such Intentions into Practice, but who artfully in their open Demeanor and Deportment betray no such Design, whereby from not incurring particular Suspicion, they have escaped being cited; ... Be it further Enacted, by the Authority aforesaid, That [there be established districts in each county in] which said Justices within their respective Districts are hereby enjoined and required to administer such Oath of Allegiance or Affirmation, as the Case may be, to all free Male Persons above Sixteen Years of Age (Persons non compos Mentis, Prisoners of War, only excepted) and ... post and publish a Notice in Writing of the Places and Times when and where he or they will attend within their respective Districts to administer such Oath or Affirmation; and all such Persons who are inhabitants of the said Districts respectively (and it is declared that a Residence of one Week shall in this Instance constitute any Person an Inhabitant, seafaring Persons and foreign Traders excepted) being above the Age of Sixteen Years, and of sound Mind, shall at such Time attend upon such Justice of the Peace, and take the Oath or Affirmation required, as the case may be, and subscribe the same in a Book ..., and if any Person (such only as are by this Act excepted) shall fail to attend, or attending at such Time and Place as he shall have been warned by such public Notice, shall refuse to take the Oath, or make such Affirmation, as the case may be, except as excused by Sickness or unavoidable Necessity, or other sufficient Reason ..., [he] shall be ordered by the said County Court next after such Failure or Neglect, to take the said Oath, or quit the State, and depart to the West Indies or Europe in Sixty Days; or permit[ted] to remain within the State.

IX. And be it further Enacted, by the Authority aforesaid, That all Persons failing or refusing to take the Oath of Allegiance, and permitted by the County Courts, as immediately aforesaid, to remain in the State, shall be adjudged incapable and disabled in Law to have, occupy or enjoy, any Office, Appointment, Licence, or Election of Trust or Profit, civil or Military, within this State, and shall not be capable of being elected to, or aiding by their Votes to elect another to be a Member of Assembly, and shall not by themselves, or by Deputy, Attorney or Trustee, execute any such Office, Trust or Appointment, and shall be disabled to prosecute any Suit at Law or Equity, or to be Guardians, Executors or Administrators, or capable of any Legacy, or Deed of Gift of Lands, and shall be disabled from taking any Lands by Descent or Purchase, or conveying Lands to oth-

ers for any Term longer than for one year, and shall not keep Guns or other Arms within his or their house, but the same may be seized by a written Order of a Justice of the County in which he or they reside; and after the Expiration of the said Sixty Days, he or they shall not be permitted to depart this State without Permission first had and obtained from the Governor and Council; and in Case of being suffered to depart, shall give Bond and sufficient Security, if such shall be required, not to be aiding to the Enemies of the State during his or their Absence; and in Case of their Departure without such Permission had, he or they shall forfeit all their Goods and Chattels, Lands and Tenements, to the Use of the State. ...

X. And be it further Enacted, by the Authority aforesaid, That if any Person who has been banished this State for not having taken the Oath of Allegiance, or made the Affirmation agreeable to the aforesaid Act ... shall return hither, or who may be banished in Consequence of this Act, then such Persons shall and may be dealt with in like Manner as is herein directed in Cases of Treason.

*　　　*　　　*

☆ 48b An Act for the Speedy Trial of All Persons Accused of Treason against This and the United States and for Other Purposes [North Carolina]

Chap. 3, 1780 N.C. Sess. Laws 4.

I. Whereas most of the county gaols in this State are insufficient to contain any number of prisoners, as well with respect to their size as their strength, and where there are district gaols, the most of them are already crowded with prisoners of divers kinds, and whereas the armies of the enemy, now in the State of South Carolina, preparing to carry the war into this State, makes it highly necessary that some method for the speedy trial of traitors should be adopted and enforced.

II. Be it therefore enacted by the General Assembly of the State of North Carolina, and it is hereby enacted by the authority of the same, that when any person or persons, shall hereafter be accused of treason ... it shall be lawful for the magistrates of any county in this State, although such county shall be distant from, or in a different district, from that in which such person or persons may be taken, or have committed such treasonable crime, or any three of them ... to hear, try and determine, all treasons against this State, and against the United States, which shall be committed within their jurisdiction, and shall pass sentence on, and order immediate execution, if necessary, of all such offenders who shall be convicted or stand mute.

III. And be it further enacted, by the authority aforesaid, that in case of a default of jurors attending at any of the said courts, it shall be lawful for such courts to direct the sheriff or coroner of the county, as the case may require, to summon of the bystanders other persons, being freeholders, to complete the said juries or any of them; and that on the trial by the petit jury no challenges shall be allowed, unless the causes be shewn, any law or usage to the contrary notwithstanding.

IV. And be it further enacted, by the authority aforesaid, that counsel shall not be allowed on trial in any of the said courts either for or against the prisoner, nor shall any prisoner arrest judgment for any defect or want of form in the bill of indictment, or other proceedings so that there is sufficient substance to convict such prisoner. Provided always, that every prisoner shall be at liberty to make his own defence, and to demand summonses to inforce the attendance of his witnesses, and a reasonable time to prepare for his trial.

*   *   *

49 To Invite Tribes to Form a State (1778)

After the Declaration of Independence, the Continental Congress appointed commissioners to carry out the relations of the new nation with the several Native American tribes. Some tribes, including the powerful Cherokee Nation, fought on the side of the Crown in the Revolutionary War. Other tribes fought with the rebels. Securing Native American sympathy and support was important to both parties in the conflict.

In 1778, the United States ratified its first treaty with a Native American nation, complying with the forms of international law and plainly speaking in the terms of equal sovereignty which had been the basis of William Penn's attitude toward Native American relations. The hint of statehood appeared to offer an additional incentive for Native American collaboration. The premises of this treaty, however, did not provide the foundation for subsequent policy of the United States toward the Native Americans.

☆ 49 United States Treaty with the Delawares, September 17, 1778

7 Stat. 13 (1778).

Articles of agreement and confederation, made and entered into by Andrew and Thomas Lewis, Esquires, Commissioners for, and in Behalf of the United States of North-America of the one Part, and Capt. White Eyes, Capt. John Kill Buck, Junior, and Capt. Pipe, Deputies and Chief Men of the Delaware Nation of the other Part.

Article I. That all offences or acts of hostilities by one, or either of the contracting parties against the other, be mutually forgiven, and buried in the depth of oblivion, never more to be had in remembrance.

Article II. That a perpetual peace and friendship shall from henceforth take place, and subsist between the contracting parties aforesaid, through all succeeding generations: and if either of the parties are engaged in a just and necessary war with any other nation or nations, that then each shall assist the other in due proportion to their abilities, till their enemies are brought to reasonable terms of accommodation: and that if either of them shall discover any hostile designs forming against the other, they shall give the earliest notice thereof, that timeous measures may be taken to prevent their ill effect.

Article III. And whereas the United States are engaged in a just and necessary war, in defence and support of life, liberty and independence, against the King of England and his adherents, and as said King is yet possessed of several posts and forts on the lakes and other places, the reduction of which is of great importance to the peace and security of the contracting parties, and as the most practicable way for the troops of the United States to some of the posts and forts is by passing through the country of the Delaware nation, the aforesaid deputies, on behalf of themselves and their nation, do hereby stipulate and agree to give a free passage through their country to the troops aforesaid, and the same to conduct by the nearest and best ways to the posts, forts or towns of the enemies of the United States, affording to said troops such supplies of corn, meat, horses, or whatever may be in their power for the accommodation of such troops. . . .

*   *   *

Article VI. Whereas the enemies of the United States have endeavored, by every artifice in their power, to possess the Indians in general with an opinion, that it is the design of the States aforesaid, to extirpate the Indians and take possession of their country: to obviate such false suggestion, the United States do engage to guarantee to the aforesaid nation of Delawares, and their heirs, all their territorial rights in the fullest and most ample manner, as it hath been bounded by former treaties, as long as they the said Delaware nation shall abide by, and hold fast the chain of friendship now entered into. And it is further agreed on between the contracting parties should it for the future be found conducive for the mutual interest of both parties to invite any other tribes who have been friends to the interest of the United States, to join the present confederation, and to form a state whereof the Delaware nation shall be the head, and have a representation in Congress: Provided, nothing contained in this article to be considered as conclusive until it meets with the approbation of Congress. And it is also the intent and meaning of this article, that no protection or countenance shall be afforded to any who are at present our enemies, by which they might escape the punishment they deserve.

In witness whereof, the parties have hereunto interchangeably set their hands and seals, at Fort Pitt, September seventeenth, anno Domini one thousand seven hundred and seventy-eight.

ANDREW LEWIS,   [L. S.]
THOMAS LEWIS,   [L. S.]
WHITE EYES, HIS X MARK,   [L. S.]
THE PIPE, HIS X MARK,   [L. S.]
JOHN KILL BUCK, HIS X MARK,   [L. S.]

In presence of—
LACH'N MCINTOSH, brigadier-general, commander the Western Department
DANIEL BRODHEAD, colonel Eighth Pennsylvania Regiment
W. CRAWFORD, colonel
JOHN CAMPBELL
JOHN STEPHENSON
JOHN GIBSON, colonel Thirteenth Virginia Regiment
A. GRAHAM, brigade major
LACH. MCINTOSH, JR., major brigade
BENJAMIN MILLS
JOSEPH L. FINLEY, captain Eighth Pennsylvania Regiment
JOHN FINLEY, captain Eighth Pennsylvania Regiment

50 The Treason of Malin (1778)

Pennsylvania indicted Malin, a British sympathizer, for the crime of treason. Malin's prosecution furnished one of the early American judicial decisions demonstrating the strict evidentiary requirements necessary to prove this offense. The laconic acquittal in the face of the evidence indicates a reluctance on the part of the jury to convict one of treason in these times of ambivalent loyalties.

☆ 50 *Respublica v. Malin*

1 U.S. (1 Dall.) 33 (1778).

INDICTMENT for High Treason. The prisoner, mistaking a corps of American troops for British, went over to them. And now the Attorney-General offered evidence of words spoken by the defendant, to prove this mistake, and his real intention of joining and adhering to the enemy.

This was opposed by the counsel for the defendant, who contended that, as words did not amount to treason, no general evidence could be given of a man's sentiments; but that the intention expressed by any words offered in evidence, must relate immediately to the overt act laid and proved on the indictment; that although an adherence to the British troops was treason, yet, an adherence to American troops, even under a supposition that they were British, did not amount to that crime; and that the opinion, that words joined with actions made treason, however ingeniously supported, failed in point of law.

The Attorney-General, on the other hand, admitted that words alone do not amount to treason; but, he insisted that they were proper evidence to explain the defendant's actions on a trial for that crime. For, though barely being within the enemy's camp might be innocent, yet, if it could be shown that the intention of going thither was to join and adhere to them, the evidence ought to be received.

BY THE COURT. No evidence of words, relative to the mistake of the American troops, can be admitted, for any adherence to them, though contrary to the design of the party, cannot possibly come within the idea of treason. But, as it appears that the prisoner was actually with the enemy, at another time, words indicating his intention to join them are proper testimony, to explain the motives upon which that intention was afterwards carried into effect.

The Attorney-General then called a witness to prove that the defendant was seen parading with the enemy's light horse in the city of Philadelphia. But to this, also, his counsel objected; for, they urged, that every criminal act must be tried in the county in which it is committed. And that the circumstance of merely joining the enemy's army, being neither treason, nor misprision of treason, unless done with a traitorous intention, no overt act had been proved in Chester, which was a pre-requisite to any evidence being heard of an overt act committed in any other county. To evince that this was, likewise, the sense of the legislature, the defendant's counsel read the act of assembly giving the supreme court a special power to try offenders in Lancaster, for crimes committed in the counties of Chester and Philadelphia.

The Attorney-General answered, that when an overt act is proved in the county where the trial is held, corroborative evidence may be given of overt acts committed in any other county. And that having established the prisoner's presence with the British army, nothing, but the proof of actual force, and its continuance, could excuse him from the charge of adhering to the enemies of the commonwealth. [J]oining the army of an enemy, has always been held prima facie evidence of an overt act. And—

BY THE COURT, it was accordingly ruled, that evidence might be given of an overt act, committed in another county, after an overt act was proved to have been committed in the county where the indictment was laid and tried.

The defendant was acquitted.

51 The Execution of Abraham Carlisle (1778)

Abraham Carlisle served as a gatekeeper for the city of Philadelphia while it was under British occupation. The Commonwealth's laws made it an act of treason to take a commission from the king of Great Britain. Carlisle was tried, promptly convicted, and executed. The case demonstrates the perils confronting one's choice of loyalties during the Revolution, even as to discharging a civil office under the wrong authority.

☆ 51 *Respublica v. Carlisle*

1 U.S. (1 Dall.) 35 (1778).

This was an indictment for high treason which was set forth in the following words:

"The jurors for the commonwealth of Pennsylvania, upon their oaths and affirmations do present, That Abraham Carlisle, late of the city of Philadelphia, in the county of Philadelphia, carpenter; being an inhabitant of and belonging to and residing within the state of Pennsylvania, and under the protection of its laws, and owing allegiance to the same state he owed wholly withdrawing, and with all his might intending the peace and tranquility of this commonwealth of Pennsylvania to disturb, and war and rebellion against the same to raise and move, and the government and independency thereof, as by law established, to subvert, and to raise again and restore the government and tyranny of the king of Great Britain within the same commonwealth: On the first day of January, in the year of our Lord one thousand seven hundred and seventy-eight, and at divers days and times, as well before as after, at the city of Philadelphia, in the county aforesaid, with force and arms, did falsely and traitorously take a commission or commissions from the king of Great Britain, and then and there, with force and arms did falsely and treacherously also take a commission or commissions from Gen. Sir William Howe, then and there acting under the said king of Great Britain, and under the authority of the same king, to wit, a commission to watch over and guard the gates of the city of Philadelphia, by the said Sir William Howe, erected and set up for the purpose of keeping and maintaining the possession of the said city, and of shutting and excluding the faithful and liege inhabitants and subjects of this state and of the United States from the said city: And then and there also maliciously and traitorously, with a great multitude of traitors and rebels, against the said commonwealth, (whose names are as yet unknown to the jurors) being armed and arrayed in a hostile manner, with force and arms did falsely and traitorously assemble and join himself against this commonwealth, and then and there, with force and arms, did falsely

and traitorously, and in a warlike and hostile manner, array and dispose himself against this commonwealth; and then and there in pursuance and execution of such his wicked and traitorous intentions and purposes aforesaid, did falsely and traitorously prepare, order, wage and levy a public and cruel war against this commonwealth; then and there committing and perpetrating a miserable and cruel slaughter of and amongst the faithful and liege inhabitants thereof, and then and there did, with force and arms, falsely and traitorously aid and assist the king of Great Britain being an enemy at open war against this state, by joining his armies, to wit, his army under the command of Gen. Sir William Howe, then actually invading this state; and then and there maliciously and traitorously (with divers other traitors to the jurors aforesaid unknown) with force and arms, did combine, plot and conspire to betray this state and the United States of America into the hands and power of the king of Great Britain being a foreign enemy to this state and to the United States of America, at open war against the same; and then and there did with force and arms, maliciously and traitorously give and send intelligence to the same enemies for that purpose, against the duty of his allegiance, against the form of the act of Assembly in such case made and provided and against the peace and dignity of the commonwealth of Pennsylvania."

The Attorney General offering a witness to prove, that the defendant had taken a quantity of salt from persons, whom he termed rebels, as they were passing out of the city of Philadelphia; and that he had a power of granting passes; his Counsel objected, that this was impertinent to the overt act laid in the indictment, and therefore not admissible. It was urged that at common law, no evidence could be given of a fact, which was not stated in the declaration. And that this caution, with respect to the allegata et probata, in a civil cause, ought, a fortiori, to be exercised in a capital prosecution. The overt act must be particularly laid, and strictly proved. For, justice requires that the Defendant should be fully apprized of the charge, so that he may have an opportunity of encountering it with his evidence.

The Attorney General, in reply, observed that by the pleadings in a civil action, the issue must be reduced to a single point, and he admitted that in all indictments for treason, an overt act must be laid and proved. But, he contended, that it was unnecessary to fill the indictment with a detail of the whole evidence in support of the prosecution; for, if the charge is reduced to a reasonable certainty, it is all that justice can require, and it is all that is to be found in any former precedent. Divers overt acts may, also, be laid in the same indictment; and, though, some of them are faulty, if one be well proved, it is sufficient to entitle the commonwealth to a verdict.

THE CHIEF JUSTICE delivered the opinion of the Court to the following effect:

M'KEAN, Chief Justice. There are three species of treason in Pennsylvania; First, To take a commission or commissions from the king of Great Britain or any under his authority; second, To levy war against the state or government thereof; and third, Knowingly and willingly to aid and assist any enemies at open war against this state or the United States of America. With respect to this third species of treason, the legislature has further explained the meaning of the words, aiding and assisting, to be, "by joining the armies of the enemy, or by enlisting, or procuring, or persuading others to enlist for that purpose; or by furnishing such enemies with arms or ammunition, provision, or any other article, or articles, for their aid or comfort, or by carrying on a traitorous correspondence with them." All these several species of treason are laid in this indictment.

It is here particularly stated, that the defendant took a commission, under the king of Great Britain, to watch and guard the gates of the city of Philadelphia; and the offense is certain enough in this description, though, without some overt act, it would not be sufficient for a conviction. In order to prove an overt act however, evidence has been offered to show, that the prisoner had a power of granting passes into, and out of the city, which was at that time in the possession of the enemy.... The court, on the present occasion ... are of opinion, that the evidence which is offered, ought to be received, but not as conclusive proof of the defendant's having taken a commission. Nor will the evidence of seizing the salt, or any act of disarming the inhabitants whom the defendant called rebels, apply to this species of treason; however they may support the allegation, of his having joined the armies of the king of Great Britain.

We think it is sufficient, also, to lay in the indictment, that the defendant sent intelligence to the enemy, without setting forth the particular letter, or its contents: And, though the charge of levying war is not, of itself, sufficient; yet assembling, joining and arraying himself with the forces of the enemy, is a sufficient overt act levying war.

BY THE COURT: Let the witness be sworn.

The Attorney General and Reed for the commonwealth—Ross and Wilson for the defendant.

The defendant being convicted by the verdict of the jury, his counsel filed the following reasons in arrest of judgment:

1st. For that the indictment is vague and uncertain, there being no overt act expressly or particularly ascertained, as the prisoner is advised it ought to be.

2d. For that the formal part of the indictment is not drawn with sufficient precision.

3d. For that the several facts are so uncertainly charged, that the prisoner could not be apprized of the particulars urged against him. And

4th. That the whole wants form and substance.

These reasons were elaborately discussed on the 5th of October, 1778, by the same counsel on both sides: But, upon mature consideration, they were finally overruled by the court, who gave judgment for the commonwealth; and the defendant, a short time afterwards, was accordingly executed.

52 The Treason of Benedict Arnold (1780)

From the first proclamation of the Declaration of Independence in Philadelphia on July 9, 1776, the road to victory over the English army and the Loyalist faction was long and painful. Throughout the war, the allegiances of the people, and even of the leading patriots, were often in doubt.

At the end of 1777, General William Howe captured Philadelphia, driving Congress out of the city. A group of disgruntled army officers and members of Congress plotted to remove Washington from his command, hoping to place General Horatio Gates in charge of the American forces. The plot was exposed, and Washington retired his army into winter quarters at Valley Forge, Pennsylvania.

In 1778 Sir Henry Clinton, the newly appointed British commander, organized a new offensive, abandoning Philadelphia and attempting to reach New York. The American troops dashed out in pursuit, but American general Charles Lee ordered a retreat, thus permitting Clinton to extricate his English troops. Rumors of treason by General Lee circulated. The British once again sought support from Native Americans and Loyalists. In 1779, they moved the major scene of the battle into the southern states, where substantial Loyalist sympathy prevailed. The American troops spent their winter in Morristown in great gloom. The British gained substantial control over Georgia and South Carolina in the beginning of 1780, but the substantial support expected from southern Loyalists failed to materialize. Difficulties within the American ranks greatly troubled General Washington.

On September 21, 1780, with the arrest by New York militiamen of Major John Andre, an adjutant of General Clinton, the plot of Benedict Arnold to deliver his command, West Point, to the British was exposed. Arnold fled to the British ranks. They commissioned him a brigadier general, and he led a British raiding expedition into Virginia. He moved to London at the end of 1781, then immigrated to Canada, and from there returned to England, where he lived on a military pension and the six hundred pounds that he had received for his treason.

☆ 52 Correspondence of Washington

Reprinted in S. Commins, ed., *Basic Writings of George Washington* (New York: Random House, 1948), 406-7.

[To General William Heath, September 26, 1780.]

DR SIR: In the present situation of things I think it necessary that You should join the Army, and request that You will do it. I write to the Count de Rochambeau by this conveyance and I trust that your coming away now will not be attended with any material inconvenience to him.

I cannot conclude without informing You of an event which has happened here which will strike You with astonishment and indignation. Major General Arnold has gone to the Enemy. He had had an interview with Major Andre, Adjutant Genl. of the British Army, and had put into his possession a state of our Army; of the Garrison at this post; of the number of Men considered as necessary for the defence of it; a Return of the Ordnance, and the disposition of the Artillery Corps in case of an Alarm. By a most providential interposition, Major Andre was taken in returning to New York with all these papers in General Arnold's hand writing, who hearing of the matter kept it secret, left his Quarters immediately under pretence of going over to West point on Monday forenoon, about an hour before my arrival, then pushed down the river in the barge, which was not discovered till I had returned from West point in the Afternoon and when I received the first information of Mr. Andre's captivity. Measures were instantly taken to apprehend him, but before the Officers sent for the purpose could reach Verplank's point, he had passed it with a Flag and got on board the Vulture Ship of War, which lay a few miles below. He knew of my approach and that I was visiting with the Marquiss, the North and Middle Redoubts, and from this circumstance was so strained in point of time that I believe, he carried with him but very few if any material papers, tho he has a very precise knowledge of the Affairs of the post.

The Gentlemen of General Arnold's family, I have the greatest reason to believe, were not privy in the least degree to the measures he was carrying on, or to his escape. I am etc.

G? WASHINGTON

[To Count de Rochambeau, September 27, 1780.]

SIR: General Arnold, who has sullied his former glory by the blackest treason, has escaped to the enemy. This is an event that occasions me equal regret and mortification; but traitors are the growth of every country and in a revolution of the present nature, it is more to be wondered at, that the catalogue is so small than that there have been found a few.

The situation of the army at this time will make General Heath's presence with us useful. . . . I hope his removal will be attended with no inconvenience to your Excellency. With the greatest regard etc.

G? WASHINGTON

53 Sentence to Be Served on a Ship of War (1781)

During the early part of 1781, the British controlled the seas and occupied or blockaded most major American ports. But toward August two powerful French fleets appeared, breaking the British siege. By September the forces of Washington and Rochambeau had combined to form a sixteen-thousand-man American-French army, which the British mistakenly believed to be intent on striking New York. The American-French troops instead traveled down the Chesapeake Bay to Yorktown, where they surprised General Cornwallis and his seven thousand British troops. Cornwallis's surrender on October 19 sealed the English hopes of recapturing rebellious America.

Yet, American gloom and destitution had marked much of the earlier part of the year. The English held the city of New York, and the American lack of naval support made recapture impossible. The American army suffered from mutiny and desertion. Although the country's Articles of Confederation and Perpetual Union had been declared in effect after Maryland entered its ratification, the Loyalists continued challenging the revolutionary cause. The New York law of March 30, 1781, supplemented its existing treason law by creating a new felony. At the same time, a special penalty provision was enacted to meet the shortage of seamen in the naval service of the United States as well as to mitigate the sentence of death for the offense. This practice of mitigating the harshness of declared sentences is a recurring theme of political criminality.

Despite the surrender of General Cornwallis, the war continued along the eastern seaboard, in the west, and in the northwest. Indeed, remnants of a stubborn British army lingered, refusing to evacuate New York completely until the end of 1783.

☆ 53 An Act More Effectually to Punish Adherence to the King of Great Britain within This State [New York]

Reprinted in *Laws of the State of New York, 1777-1784* (Albany: Weed, Parsons, 1886), 1:370-71.

WHEREAS, altho' adhering to the enemies of this State is by law high treason against the people of this State: yet in order more effectually to prevent an adherence to the king of Great Britain it is deemed requisite that farther provision should be made by law.

Be it therefore enacted by the People of the State of New York represented in Senate and Assembly and it is hereby enacted by the authority of the same. That if any person, being a citizen or subject of this State or of any of the United States of America and abiding or residing within this State, shall maliciously advisedly and directly be preaching, teaching speaking writing or printing declare or maintain that the king of Great Britain hath or of right ought to have any authority or dominion in or over this State or the inhabitants thereof, or shall maliciously and advisedly seduce or persuade or attempt to seduce or persuade any inhabitant of this State to renounce his or her allegiance to this State or to acknowledge allegiance or subjection to the king or crown of Great Britain, or shall maliciously and advisedly declare or affirm that he or she doth owe allegiance to the king or crown of Great Britain, and be convicted thereof shall he be adjudged guilty of felony and shall suffer the pains and penalties pre-scribed by law in cases of felony without benefit of clergy. . . .

Provided nevertheless that it shall and may be lawful for the court before whom such offender shall be convicted if such court shall deem it proper instead of giving judgment of death to order and direct that such offender shall be sent as soon as conveniently may be to serve for the term of three years on board of any ship of war belonging to this State or to the United States or to an ally of the United States and if any offender so ordered by any such court to be sent to serve on board any such ship of war for the term aforesaid shall desert from such service and be found within this State or any other of the United States the person so deserting shall be liable to be punished as a person attainted of felony without benefit of clergy and execution may and shall be awarded against such offender accordingly any thing in this act to the contrary notwithstanding.

CHAPTER 3

The Dawn of the Republic

———

1785-1815

AS the United States emerged victorious from the Revolution, new and difficult problems faced the loosely allied peoples of the nation. Foremost among these was the structure of the federal government and its relationship to the several states. Fearful that the recently experienced excesses of government under the king of England might be repeated, the new country's political leaders originally opted for a confederation with a virtually powerless central government. When this arrangement proved unsatisfactory, the Constitution of the United States was drafted and adopted. But since the document was one of compromise, many questions were left unanswered concerning the reach of the federal government's power.

Many of the documents in this chapter relate to the disputes concerning the extension of federal authority. To the extent that actions of the federal government were perceived as exceeding its delegated authority and therefore as unconstitutional, they were considered void, and at times were defied openly, a reaction not without some contemporary parallels. As the concept of judicial review for constitutionality was not yet established firmly, the major forums for testing the validity of federal law were the state legislatures, the political arena (including the press), and the battlefield.

The materials in this chapter trace the developments of the central dispute over the primacy of sovereignty (state versus federal) through the remonstrances of the legislatures, state flirtations with secession, fulminations of the press, and open rebellions in defiance of the law. Mostly, these materials reflect on the nature of the governmental response to these perceived threats to national security. The Alien and Sedition Laws, the resort to the military to suppress insurrections, and the trials of rebellion leaders for treason and their eventual pardons by executive authority reflect the many ways in which the government responded to political crime.

In reading these materials, one should be alert to the contrasting attitudes of the executive at the beginning and the end of a particular incident. Also, the judicial and executive responses to the treatment of participants in the various insurrections should be compared. In addition, the reader should note how the early and fearfully expansive interpretations of the law of treason were truncated and constrained in the later *Burr* case when national security seemed less threatened. Overall, it was an uncertain and fractious thirty years; the people and governments of the United States sorted out the balance of power between the federal and state authority, often through breaches of the criminal law and responses thereto. Although the bitterness in the debate drained away as the Jeffersonian ideals of a democratic republic were victorious at the ballot box, the ultimate issues of state and federal power, as well as the question of the individual's and the community's right to resist oppression, were not resolved—only stored away.

---

54 "restore all the prisoners taken" (1785)

Although the 1783 Treaty of Paris had terminated all English claims to the territory of the former colonies, as well as to the territory east of the Mississippi, it did not determine the status of the Native American nations residing therein. The Cherokees, in particular, did not recognize the Treaty of Paris as concluding the war with them, and they continued to maintain their ties with the English Crown. In a 1763 proclamation, George III had previously guaranteed to Native Americans protection of their lands from pressure by western settlers. This guarantee was affirmed by the United States in the Treaty of Hopewell, in return for Native American consent in concluding the war and relinquishing land titles. It was around this treaty and its guarantees that United States policy toward the Native Americans evolved over the next half-century, culminating in the Trail of Tears.

☆ 54 United States Treaty with the Cherokees, November 28, 1785

7 Stat. 18 (1785).

Articles concluded at Hopewell on the Keowee, between Benjamin Hawkins, Andrew Pickens, Joseph Martin and Lachlan M'Intosh, Commissioners Plenipotentiary of the United States of America, of the one part, and the head men and warriors of all the Cherokees of the other.

The Commissioners Plenipotentiary of the United States, in Congress assembled, give peace to all the Cherokees, and receive them into the favour and protection of the United States of America, on the following conditions:

ARTICLE I. The Head-Men and Warriors of all the Cherokees shall restore all the prisoners, citizens of the United States, or subjects of their allies, to their entire liberty: They shall also restore all the Negroes, and all other property taken during the late war from the citizens, to such person, and at such time and place, as the Commissioners shall appoint.

ARTICLE II. The Commissioners of the United States in Congress assembled, shall restore all the prisoners taken from the Indians, during the late war, to the Head-Men and Warriors of the Cherokees, as early as is practicable.

ARTICLE III. The said Indians for themselves and their respective tribes and towns do acknowledge all the Cherokees to be under the protection of the United States of America, and of no other sovereign whosoever.

*   *   *

ARTICLE IX. For the benefit and comfort of the Indians, and for the prevention of injuries or oppressions on the part of the citizens or Indians, the United States in Congress assembled shall have the sole and exclusive right of regulating the trade with the Indians, and managing all their affairs in such manner as they think proper.

ARTICLE X. Until the pleasure of Congress be known, respecting the ninth article, all traders, citizens of the United States, shall have liberty to go to any of the tribes or towns of the Cherokees to trade with them, and they shall be protected in their persons and property, and kindly treated.

*   *   *

ARTICLE XIII. The hatchet shall be forever buried, and the peace given by the United States, and friendship re-established between the said states on the one part, and all the Cherokees on the other, shall be universal; and the contracting parties shall use their utmost endeavours to maintain the peace given as aforesaid, and friendship re-established.

In witness of all and every thing herein determined, between the United States of America, and all the Cherokees, We, their underwritten Commissioners, by virtue of our full powers, have signed this definitive treaty, and have caused our seals to be hereunto affixed.

Done at Hopewell, on the Keowee, this twenty-eighth of November, in the year of our Lord one thousand seven hundred and eighty-five.

BENJAMIN HAWKINS
ANDW. PICKENS

JOS. MARTIN
LACH'N M'INTOSH
KOATOHEE, OR CORN TASSEL OF TOQUE
SCHOLAUETTA, OR HANGING MAN OF CHOTA
OOSK-WHA, OR ABRAHAM OF CHILKOWA
KOLAKUSTA, OR PRINCE OF NOTH
NEWOTA, OR THE GRITZS OF CHICAMAGA
KONATOTA, OR THE RISING FAWN OF HIGHWASSAY
CHOKASATAHE, CHICASAW KILLER TASONTA
ONANOOTA, OF KOOSOATEE
OOKOSETA, OR SOWER MUSH OF KOOLOQUE
UMATOOETHA, THE WATER HUNTER, CHOIKAMAWGA
WYUKA, OF LOOKOUT MOUNTAIN
TULCO, OR TOM OF CHATUGA
WILL, OF AKOHA
NECATEE, OF SAWTA
AMOKONTAKONA, KUTCLOA
TUCKASEE, OR YOUNG TARRAPIN OF ALLAJOY
TOOSTAKA, OR THE WAKER OF OOSTANAWA
UNTOOLA, OR GUN ROD OF SETECO
UNSUOKANAIL, BUFFALO WHITE CALF NEW CUFFEE
KOSTAYEAK, OR SHARP FELLOW WATAGA
CHONOSTA, OF COWE
CHESCOONWHO, BIRD IN CLOSE OF TOMOTLUG
TUCKASEE, OR TARRAPIN OF HIGHTOWA
CHESETOA, OR THE RABBIT OF TLACOA
CHESECOTETONA, OF YELLOW BIRD OF THE PINE LOG
SKETALOSKA, SECOND MAN OF TILLICO
KOWETATAHEE, IN FROG TOWN
KEUKUCH, TALKOA
TULATISKA, OF CHAWAY
WOOALUKA, THE WAY-LAYER, CHOTA
TATLIUSTA, OR PORPUS OF TILASSI
JOHN, OF LITTLE TALLICO
SKELELAK
AKONOLUCHTA, THE CABIN
CHEANODA, OF KAWETAKAC
YELLOW BIRD

IN PRESENCE OF
WM. BLOUNT
SAML. TAYLOR, *Major*
JOHN OWEN
JESS WALTON
JNO. COWAN, *Capt. Commandant*
THOS. GEGG
W. HAZZARD
Sworn Interpreters, JAMES MADISON, ARTHUR COODEY

55 Shays's Rebellion (1786)

In April of 1783, some seven thousand loyalists sailed from the port of New York, heading for Canada. Altogether, over 120,000 loyalists departed from the United States during the War of Independence. On September 3, Great Britain and the United States signed the Treaty of Paris, formally ending the war. Although independent, the United States was united in name only. A loose confederation of thirteen states with competing economic interests, strong tariff barriers, and a deep distaste for centralized power, the country could not meet its growing obligations—domestic and international. When the revolutionary forces disbanded at the end of 1783, the nation remained obligated to them for unpaid wages.

The nation's central government proved ineffectual. Under the Articles of Confederation, Congress had no power to levy or collect taxes. In 1785, inflation reached new heights. By 1786, a major depression severely afflicted the country's business. Currency was considered unstable, prices were falling, and the shipping industry was at a standstill. From the following documents, it is evident that the newly won independence had done little to remedy the grievances of the unprivileged. Note also the disclaimer that the grievances were British-inspired.

In the fall of 1786, against this backdrop of economic near-chaos and governmental indifference, Captain Daniel Shays led a rebellion to stop court foreclosures of the farms of impoverished soldiers and farmers who failed to pay taxes. The rebellion threatened the federal arsenal at Springfield, Massachusetts, and demonstrated further the weakness of the Confederation. The uprising was declared to be treason by Massachusetts, and the state militia crushed it. Nevertheless, all participants were pardoned for their offense by 1788, and many of the reforms here advocated eventually were enacted by the Massachusetts legislature.

☆ 55 Communications regarding the Insurrection

☆ 55a An Address to the People of the Several Towns in the County of Hampshire, Now at Arms [Massachusetts]

Reprinted in G. R. Minot, *History of the Insurrection in Massachusetts* (Boston: James W. Burditt, 1810), 82.

GENTLEMEN,

We have thought proper to inform you of some of the principal causes of the late risings of the people, and also of their present movement, viz.

1st. The present expensive mode of collecting debts, which by reason of the great scarcity of cash, will of necessity fill our gaols with unhappy debtors; and thereby a reputable body of people rendered incapable of being serviceable either to themselves or the community.

2d. The monies raised by impost and excise being appropriated to discharge the interest of governmental securities, and not the foreign debt, when these securities are not subject to taxation.

3d. A suspension of the writ of Habeas Corpus, by which those persons who have stepped forth to assert and maintain the rights of the people, are liable to be taken and conveyed even to the most distant part of the Commonwealth, and thereby subjected to an unjust punishment.

4th. The unlimited power granted to Justices of the Peace and Sheriffs, Deputy Sheriffs, and Constables, by the Riot Act, indemnifying them to the prosecution thereof; when perhaps, wholly actuated from a principle of revenge, hatred, and envy.

Furthermore, Be assured, that this body, now at arms, despise the idea of being instigated by British emissaries, which is so strenuously propagated by the enemies of our liberties: And also wish the most proper and speedy measures may be taken, to discharge both our foreign and domestic debt.

Per Order,

DANIEL GRAY, Chairman of the Committee

☆ 55b To the Printer of the Hampshire Herald

Reprinted in G. R. Minot, *History of the Insurrection in Massachusetts* (Boston: James W. Burditt, 1810), 82.

SIR,

It has some how or other fallen to my lot to be employed in a more conspicuous manner than some others of my fellow citizens, in stepping forth on defense of the rights and privileges of the people, more especially of the county of Hampshire.

Therefore, upon the desire of the people now at arms, I take this method to publish to the world of mankind in general, particularly the people of this Commonwealth, some of the principal grievances we complain of. . . .

In this first place, I must refer you to a draught of grievances drawn up by a committee of the people, now at arms, under the signature of Daniel Gray, chairman, which is heartily approved of; some others also are here added, viz.

1st. The General Court, for certain obvious reasons, must be removed out of the town of Boston.

2d. A revision of the constitution is absolutely necessary.

3d. All kinds of governmental securities, now on interest, that have been bought of the original owners for two shillings, and the highest for six shillings and eight pence on the pound, and have received more interest than the principal cost the speculator who purchased them—that if justice was done, we verily believe, nay positively know, it would save this Commonwealth thousands of pounds.

4th. Let the lands belonging to this Commonwealth, at the eastward, be sold at the best advantage to pay the remainder of our domestick debt.

5th. Let the monies arising from impost and excise be appropriated to discharge the foreign debt.

6th. Let that act, passed by the General Court last June by a small majority of only seven, called the Supplementary Act, for twenty-five years to come, be repealed.

7th. The total abolition of the Inferiour Court of Common Pleas and General Sessions of the Peace.

8th. Deputy Sheriffs totally set aside, as a useless set of officers in the community; and Constables who are really neccessay, be empowered to do the duty, by which means a large swarm of lawyers will be banished from their wonted haunts, who have been more damage to the people at large, especially the common farmers, than the savage beasts of prey.

To this I boldly sign my proper name, as a hearty well-wisher to the real rights of the people.

THOMAS GROVER
Worcester, December 7, 1786

56 The Constitution and Political Crime (1787)

To many, it was intolerable that the Commonwealth of Massachusetts had to relieve the national arsenal at Springfield, Massachusetts, from Shays's forces. The growing recognition of the inadequacy of the Confederation, reinforced by this event, soon produced a movement for the reform of the national government. In 1787, a convention, with George Washington presiding, met in Philadelphia "for the sole and express purpose of revising the Articles of Confederation." The result was a new United States Constitution.

The Constitution, in its various articles, set up the branches of a unified and stronger central government. But safeguards against federal abuse of power abounded throughout the document. Article I limited the arbitrary power of government by guaranteeing to citizens the protection of the writ of habeas corpus. Article III purposefully defined treason against the United States, thus making that offense the only constitutionally defined crime, as a safeguard against the overreach of the federal government. As for the states, each was obliged to aid the others in the apprehension of traitors, criminals, and runaway slaves. The new Constitution ordained the republican form of government as the new political orthodoxy for members of the Union.

☆ 56 United States Constitution

*   *   *

Art. I, Section 9, cl. 2. The Privilege of the Writ of Habeas Corpus shall not be suspended, unless when in Cases of Rebellion or Invasion the public Safety may require it.

*   *   *

Art. III, Section 3. Treason against the United States, shall consist only in levying War against them, or in adhering to their Enemies, giving them Aid and Comfort. No Person shall be convicted of Treason unless on the Testimony of two Witnesses to the same overt Act, or on Confession in open Court.

The Congress shall have Power to declare the Punishment of Treason, but no Attainder of Treason shall work Corruption of Blood, or Forfeiture except during the Life of the Person attained.

*   *   *

Art. IV, Section 2. A Person charged in any State with Treason, Felony, or other Crime, who shall flee from Justice, and be found in another State, shall on Demand of the executive Authority of the State from which he fled, be delivered up, to be removed to the State having Jurisdiction of the Crime.

No Person held to Service or Labour in one State, under the Laws thereof, escaping into another, shall, in Consequence of any Law or Regulation therein, be discharged from such Service or Labour, but shall be delivered up on Claim of the Party to whom such Service or Labour may be due.

*   *   *

Art. VI, Section 4. The United States shall guarantee to every State in this Union a Republican Form of Government, and shall protect each of them against Invasion; and on Application of the Legislature, or of the Executive (when the Legislature cannot be convened) against domestic Violence.

57 "a general constitution, in subversion of that of the state" (1787)

The convention that assembled in Philadelphia on May 25, 1787, to revise the Articles of Confederation had representatives from all the original states except Rhode Island. The fifty-five delegates were described as "clear-headed, moderate men, with positive views of their own and firm purpose but with a willingness to compromise." The document that was produced differed from that of the Confederation in many respects, principally by giving the national government direct power over individual citizens. Some of the delegates, including Edmund Randolph and George Mason of Virginia and Elbridge Gerry of Massachusetts, refused to sign the Constitution. Of New York's three delegates, two walked out prior to the signing of the Constitution, and Alexander Hamilton alone from that state gave his consent. The two New York dissenters, Robert Yates and John Lansing, represented the intense opposition which existed in New York to the proposed Constitution. In the end, New York ratified the document after the requisite nine states already had done so. To these opponents, participating in the presentation of the proposed Constitution would amount to an act of subversion against the state. Allegiance to the primary sovereignty of the several states thus provided the legal justification for refusal to support the new order. Despite its apparent resolution by the ratification of the new Constitution, this is a theme that echoes and reechoes for the next two centuries and provides much authority for resistance to the federal government.

☆ 57 Letter from Robert Yates and John Lansing to the Governor of New York

Reprinted in J. Elliot, ed., *Debates in the Several State Conventions on the Adoption of the Federal Constitution* (Philadelphia: Lippincott, 1907), 1:480-82.

*   *   *

... We beg leave, briefly, to state some cogent reasons, which, among others, influenced us to decide against a consolidation of the states. These are reducible into two heads:—

1st. The limited and well-defined powers under which we acted, and which could not on any possible construction, embrace an idea of such magnitude as to assent to a general constitution, in subversion of that of the state.

2nd. A conviction of the impracticability of establishing a general government, pervading every part of the United States, and extending essential benefits to all.

Our powers were explicit, and confined to the sole and express purpose of revising the Articles of Confederation, and reporting such alterations and provisions therein, as should render the Federal Constitution adequate to the exigencies of government, and the preservation of the Union.

From these expressions, we were led to believe that a system of consolidated government could not, in the remotest degree, have been in contemplation of the legislature of this state; for that so important a trust, as the adopting measures which tended to deprive the state government of its most essential rights of sovereignty, and to place it in a dependent situation, could not have been confided by implication; and the circumstance, that the acts of the Convention were to receive a state approbation in the last resort, forcibly corroborated the opinion that our powers could not involve the subversion of a Constitution which, being immediately derived from the people, could only be abolished by their express consent, and not by a legislature, possessing authority vested in them for its preservation. Nor could we suppose that, if it had been the intention of the legislature to abrogate the existing confederation, they would, in such pointed terms, have directed the attention of their delegates to the revision and amendment of it, in total exclusion of every other idea.

Reasoning in this manner, we were of opinion that the leading feature of every amendment ought to be the preservation of the individual states in their uncontrolled constitutional rights, and that, in reserving these, a mode might have been devised of granting to the Confederacy, the moneys arising from a general system of revenue, the power of regulating commerce and enforcing the observance of foreign treaties, and other necessary matters of less moment.

Exclusive of our objections originating from the want of power, we entertained an opinion that a general government, however guarded by declarations of rights, or cautionary provisions, must unavoidably, in a short time, be productive of the destruction of the civil liberty of such citizens who could be effectually coerced by it, by reason of the extensive territory of the United States, the dispersed situation of its inhabitants, and the insuperable difficulty of controlling or counteracting the views of a set of men (however unconstitutional and oppressive their acts might be) possessed of all the powers of government, and who, from their remoteness from their constituents, and necessary permanency of office, could not be supposed to be uniformly actuated by an attention to their welfare and happiness; that, however wise and energetic the principles of the general government might be, the extremities of the United States could not be kept in due submission and obedience to its laws, at the distance of many hundred miles from the seat of government; that, if the general legislature was composed of so numerous a body of men as to represent the interests of all the inhabitants of the United States, in the usual and true ideas of representation, the expense of supporting it would become intolerably burdensome; and that, if a few only were vested with a power of legislation, the interests of a great majority of the inhabitants of the United States must necessarily be unknown; or, if known, even in the first stages of the operations of the new government, unattended to.

These reasons were, in our opinion, conclusive against any system of consolidated government: to that recommended by the Convention, we suppose most of them very forcibly apply. . . .

*   *   *

58 "to put to death or capture the said Indians" (1787)

Native Americans were subject to the white man's rules when visiting his territory and, according to federal treaty, they were purportedly autonomous in their own territory. But the states sought to exercise jurisdiction over Native Americans within their boundaries as well.

Particularly with regard to the western territory England ceded to the United States in the Treaty of Paris, the controversy between the federal government, the state authorities, and the indigenous populations grew extremely intense. The federal government claimed the territory as the sovereign successor to the king of England. This position was accepted by those states (Rhode Island, New Hampshire, New Jersey, Pennsylvania, Delaware, and Maryland) that, as colonies, had fixed western boundaries. The states without a colonial western border claimed sovereignty over the same territory at least as far as Mississippi. This dispute accounted in part for the delay between the adoption of the Articles of Confederation in 1777 and their ratification in 1781. Most of the states finally ceded their claims to the lands west of the Eastern Continental Divide to the federal government during the 1780s. Georgia, nevertheless, did not relinquish its claim until 1802.

With the jurisdiction over these lands in dispute, western settlers moved into aboriginal territories, an act that produced skirmishes with Native Americans. Despite the protection accorded by treaty to Native American territory by the United States, Georgia, in effect, declared war in 1787 on the Creek Nation that occupied most of what is now Georgia and Alabama.

☆ 58 An Act for Suppressing the Violences of the Indians

Reprinted in E. M. Coleman, ed., *Laws of the Colonial and State Governments Relating to Indians and Indian Affairs, from 1633-1831 Inclusive* (Washington: Thompson and Homans, 1832), 186-87.

Be it enacted by the Representatives of the Freemen of the state of Georgia, in General Assembly met, and by the authority of the same, That from and immediately after the passing of this act, the Creek Indians shall be considered as without the protection of this state; and it shall be lawful for the government and people of the same to put to death or capture the said Indians wheresoever they may be found within the limits of this state, except such tribes of the said Indians which have not, or shall not hereafter, commit hostilities against the people of this state, or which the commanding officer shall judge.

SEC. 2. *And be it further enacted,* That fifteen hundred men be enlisted as soon as may be, to serve until peace is established with the Indians. . . .

*   *   *

SEC. 8. And whereas, it may so happen, that certain persons have run and surveyed lands without the limits of the respective counties of this State, as established by law, and for which grants may have been surreptitiously claimed: *Be it enacted,* That all lands without the limits aforesaid, are hereby declared to be vacant, any warrant, survey, or grant, to the contrary notwithstanding; and that a tract of land herein described shall be reserved, and, at the cessation of the hostilities with the Indians, appropriated to and for the allowances and bounties of and for the said officers and troops; and no warrant, survey, or grant, shall be obtained for any part of the lands within the said reserve, by any person whatever, until such hostilities shall cease; and all such officers or troops shall have a preference in laying their bounties within the said reserve.

SEC. 9. *And be it also enacted,* That the said bounties shall not interfere with a certain quantity of land in the vicinity of those Indian towns which are, and shall continue to be, friendly, which quantity shall be determined by a future legislature. . . .

*   *   *

59 The United States Treason Statute (1790)

In the new American nation, the political leadership consisted of persons formerly condemned as traitors by the British as well as by some of their fellow Americans. Having been so tarred, these political leaders responded to the issue of loyalty with some delicacy. The question of where primary allegiance lay — to the United States or to a particular state — remained unresolved for a long time. The United States Congress enacted the Treason Statute of 1790 in accordance with the power granted to it in the Constitution. The Constitution had defined the crime of treason, but not its punishment. Although the statute retained the death penalty for treason, it ordained hanging as a less barbaric sanction than the English drawing and quartering, and abolished corruption of blood and forfeiture. The enactment implemented the procedural safeguards previously developed under English and colonial law. The statute also created and defined other offenses against the government of the United States, including the lesser crime of misprision of treason and piracy.

☆ 59 An Act for the Punishment of Certain Crimes against the United States

1 Stat. 112 (1790).

SECTION 1. *Be it enacted by the Senate and House of Representatives of the United States of America in Congress assembled,* That if any person or persons, owing allegiance to the United States of America, shall levy war against them, or shall adhere to their enemies, giving them aid and comfort within the United States or elsewhere, and shall be thereof convicted, on confession in open court, or on the testimony of two witnesses to the same overt act of the treason whereof he or they shall stand indicted, such person or persons shall be adjudged guilty of treason against the United States, and shall suffer death.

SEC. 2. *And be it [further] enacted,* That if any person or persons, having knowledge of the commission of any of the treasons aforesaid, shall conceal and not as soon as may be disclose and make known the same to the President of the United States, or some one of the judges thereof, or to the president or governor of a particular state, or some one of the judges or justices thereof, such person or persons on conviction shall be judged guilty of misprision of treason, and shall be imprisoned not exceeding seven years, and fined not exceeding one thousand dollars.

* * *

SEC. 8. *And be it [further] enacted,* That if any person or persons shall commit upon the high seas, or in any river, haven, basin or bay, out of the jurisdiction of any particular state, murder or robbery, or any other offence which if committed within the body of a county, would by the laws of the United States be punishable with death; or if any captain or mariner of any ship or other vessel, shall piratically and feloniously run away with such ship or vessel, or any goods or merchandise to the value of fifty dollars, or yield up such ship or vessel voluntarily to any pirate; or if any seaman shall lay violent hands upon his commander, thereby to hinder and prevent his fighting in defence of his ship or goods committed to his trust, or shall make a revolt in the ship; every such offender shall be deemed, taken and adjudged to be a pirate and felon, and being thereof convicted, shall suffer death; and the trial of crimes committed on the high seas, or in any place out of the jurisdiction of any particular state, shall be in the district where the offender is apprehended, or into which he may first be brought.

SEC. 9. *And be it [further] enacted,* That if any citizen shall commit any piracy or robbery aforesaid, or any act of hostility against the United States, or any citizen thereof, upon the high seas, under colour of any commission from any person, such offender shall, notwithstanding the pretence of any such authority, be deemed, adjudged and taken to be a pirate, felon, and robber, and on being thereof convicted shall suffer death.

* * *

SEC. 24. *Provided always,* and be it enacted, That no conviction or judgment for any of the offences aforesaid, shall work corruption of blood, or any forfeiture of estate.

* * *

SEC. 29. *And be it [further] enacted,* That any person who shall be accused and indicted of treason, shall have a copy of the indictment, and a list of the jury and witnesses, to be produced on the trial for proving the said indictment, mentioning the names and places of abode of such witnesses and jurors, delivered unto him at least three entire days before he shall be tried for the same; and in other capital offences, shall have such copy of the indictment and list of the jury two entire days at least before the trial: And that every person so accused and indicted for any of the crimes aforesaid, shall also be allowed and admitted to make his full defence by counsel learned in the law; and the court before whom such person shall be tried, or some judge thereof, shall, and they are hereby authorized and required immediately upon his request to assign to such person such counsel, not exceeding two, as such person shall desire, to whom such counsel shall have free access at all seasonable hours; and every such person or persons accused or indicted of the crimes aforesaid, shall be allowed and admitted in his said defence to make any proof that he or they can produce, by lawful witness or witnesses, and shall have the like process of the court where he or they shall be tried, to compel his or their witnesses to appear at his or their trial, as is usually granted to compel witnesses to appear on the prosecution against them.

SEC. 30. *And be it further enacted,* That if any person or persons be indicted of treason against the United States, and shall stand mute or refuse to plead, or shall challenge peremptorily above the number of thirty-five of the jury; or if any person or persons be indicted of any other of the offences herein before set forth, for which the punishment is declared to be death, if he or they shall also stand mute or will not answer to the indictment, or challenge peremptorily above the number of twenty persons of the jury; the court, in any of the cases aforesaid, shall notwithstanding proceed to the trial of the person or persons so standing mute or challenging, as if he or they had pleaded not guilty, and render judgment thereon accordingly.

SEC. 31. *And be it further enacted,* That the benefit of clergy shall not be used or allowed, upon conviction of any crime, for which, by any statute of the United States, the punishment is or shall be declared to be death.

SEC. 32. *And be it further enacted,* That no person or persons shall be prosecuted, tried or punished for treason or other capital offence aforesaid, wilful murder or forgery excepted, unless the indictment for the same shall be found by a grand jury within three years next after the treason or capital offence aforesaid shall be done or committed; . . . *Provided,* That nothing herein contained shall extend to any person or persons fleeing from justice.

SEC. 33. *And be it further enacted,* That the

manner of inflicting the punishment of death, shall be by hanging the person convicted by the neck until dead.

Approved, April 30, 1790.

60 The Bill of Rights (1791)

Fears of abuse of power by the stronger central government proposed in the Constitution led many states to ratify the Constitution with requests for the adoption of a declaration of rights (restraints) upon the exercise of federal power. On September 25, 1789, Congress placed twelve proposals before the states as amendments to the Constitution. The first two, dealing respectively with the ratio of representatives to population and the compensation of members of Congress, never received the requisite number of ratifications. Thus, the first amendment to the Constitution was actually the third one that Congress proposed. On December 15, 1791, Virginia became the eleventh of fourteen states to ratify the Bill of Rights, completing the amendment process.

Although ultimately a supporter of the Bill of Rights, James Madison earlier had expressed doubts regarding its wisdom. He was concerned that the specific definitions of rights would lend themselves to narrowing constructions and that, in any event, "experience proves the inefficacy of a bill of rights on those occasions when its control is most needed. Repeated violations of these parchment barriers have been committed by overbearing majorities in every state. . . . Whenever there is an interest and power to do wrong, wrong will generally be done and not less readily by a powerful and interested party than by a powerful and interested prince." Apparently, Jefferson's response to Madison, particularly the argument that a bill of rights would place an instrument in the hands of a hopefully independent, learned, and honest judicial department which would check overreaching legislative and executive authorities, persuaded Madison to change his position. The change was probably due also to political consideration: Madison's desire to weaken the cause of the anti-Federalists, who agitated for the recognition of these rights, and to forestall demands for a second constitutional convention which might weaken the new central government.

In conformity with Jefferson's views, the speech and press clauses of the First Amendment as well as the procedural protections of the Fourth, Fifth, and Sixth Amendments have sometimes played an important role in limiting the government's reaction to political crimes. At other times Madison's more cynical view has prevailed.

☆ 60 United States Constitution, Amendments I-X

AMENDMENT I

Congress shall make no law respecting an establishment of religion, or prohibiting the free exercise thereof; or abridging the freedom of speech, or of the press; or the right of the people peaceably to assemble, and to petition the Government for a redress of grievances.

AMENDMENT II

A well regulated Militia, being necessary to the security of a free State, the right of the people to keep and bear Arms, shall not be infringed.

AMENDMENT III

No Soldier shall, in time of peace be quartered in any house, without the consent of the Owner, nor in time of war, but in a manner to be prescribed by law.

AMENDMENT IV

The right of the people to be secure in their persons, houses, papers, and effects, against unreasonable searches and seizures, shall not be violated, and no Warrants shall issue, but upon probable cause, supported by Oath or affirmation, and particularly describing the place to be searched, and the persons or things to be seized.

AMENDMENT V

No person shall be held to answer for a capital, or otherwise infamous crime, unless on a presentment or indictment of a Grand Jury, except in cases arising in the land or naval forces, or in the Militia, when in actual service in time of War or public danger; nor shall any person be subject for the same offence to be twice put in jeopardy of life or limb; nor shall be compelled in any criminal case to be a witness against himself, nor be deprived of life, liberty, or property, without due process of law; nor shall private property be taken for public use, without just compensation.

AMENDMENT VI

In all criminal prosecutions, the accused shall enjoy the right to a speedy and public trial, by an impartial jury of the State and district wherein the crime shall have been committed, which district shall have been previously ascertained by law, and to be informed of the nature and cause of the accusation; to be confronted with the witness against him; to have compulsory process for obtaining witnesses in his favor, and to have the Assistance of Counsel for his defense.

AMENDMENT VII

In Suits at common law, where the value in controversy shall exceed twenty dollars, the right of trial by jury shall be preserved, and no fact tried by jury, shall be otherwise re-examined in any Court of the United States, than according to the rules of the common law.

AMENDMENT VIII

Excessive bail shall not be required, nor excessive fines imposed, nor cruel and unusual punishments inflicted.

AMENDMENT IX

The enumeration in the Constitution, of certain rights, shall not be construed to deny or disparage others retained by the people.

AMENDMENT X

The powers not delegated to the United States by the Constitution, nor prohibited by it to the States, are reserved to the States respectively, or to the people.

61 Fugitives from Law and from Slavery (1793)

The United States Constitution gave legal validity to slavery, restrained states from emancipating slaves escaped from other states, and articulated the right to repossess fugitive slaves. The detailed machinery for the execution of this right, the Fugitive Slave Act, was created by the Second Congress on February 12, 1793. Upheld by the Supreme Court in *Prigg v. Pennsylvania*, 41 U.S. (16 Pet.) 539 (1842), the 1793 act was later amended by the Fugitive Slave Law of 1850, a more severe measure resulting from a series of compromise resolutions proposed by Senator Henry Clay of Kentucky.

Congress relied on state authorities for rendering fugitives from the law but invoked federal process for the repossession of runaway slaves. Thus, the power of the United States government sustained the institution of slavery outside the boundaries of the slave states. Additionally, those who acted to hinder the recapture of slaves were subject to criminal punishment by the United States. The vigor with which this law was or was not enforced provided one point of friction between the Union and the various states, as well as among states.

☆ 61 An Act respecting Fugitives from Justice, and Persons Escaping from the Service of Their Masters

1 Stat. 302 (1793).

SECTION 1. *Be it enacted by the Senate and House of Representatives of the United States of America in Congress assembled*, That whenever the executive authority of any state in the Union, or of either of the territories northwest or south of the river Ohio, shall demand any person as a fugitive from justice, of the executive authority of any such state or territory to which such person shall have fled, and shall moreover produce the copy of an indictment found, or an affidavit made before a magistrate of any state or territory as aforesaid, charging the person so demanded, with having committed treason, felony, or other crime, certified as authentic by the governor or chief magistrate of the state or territory from whence the person so charged fled, it shall be the duty of the executive authority of the state or territory to which such person shall have fled, to cause him or her to be arrested and secured, and notice of the arrest to be given to the executive authority appointed to receive the fugitive, and to cause the fugitive to be delivered to such agent when he shall appear. . . .

SEC. 2. *And be it further enacted*, That any agent, appointed as aforesaid, who shall receive the fugitive into his custody, shall be empowered to transport him or her to the state or territory from which he or she shall have fled. And if any person or persons shall by force set at liberty, or rescue the fugitive from such agent while transporting, as aforesaid, the person or persons so offending shall, on conviction, be fined not exceeding five hundred dollars, and be imprisoned not exceeding one year.

SEC. 3. *And be it also enacted*, That when a person held to labour in any of the United States, or in either of the territories on the northwest or south of the river Ohio, under the laws thereof, shall escape into any other of the said states or territory, the person to whom such labour or service may be due, his agent or attorney, is hereby empowered to seize or arrest such fugitive from labour, and to take him or her before any judge of the circuit or district courts of the United States, residing or being within the state, or before any magistrate of a county, city or town corporate, wherein such seizure or arrest shall be made, and upon proof to the satisfaction of such judge or magistrate, either by oral testimony or affidavit taken before and certified by a magistrate of any such state or territory, that the person so seized or arrested, doth, under the laws of the state or territory from which he or she fled, owe service or labour to the person claiming him or her, it shall be the duty of such judge or magistrate to give a certificate thereof to such claimant, his agent or attorney, which shall be sufficient warrant for removing the said fugitive from labour, to the state or territory from which he or she fled.

SEC. 4. *And be it further enacted*, That any person who shall knowingly and willingly obstruct or hinder such claimant, his agent or attorney in so seizing or arresting such fugitive from labour, or shall rescue such fugitive from such claimant, his agent or attorney when so arrested pursuant to the authority herein given or declared; or shall harbor or conceal such person after notice that he or she was a fugitive from labour, as aforesaid, shall, for either of the said offences, forfeit and pay the sum of five hundred dollars. Which penalty may be recovered by and for the benefit of such claimant, by action of debt, in any court proper to try the same, saving moreover to the person claiming such labour or service, his right of action for or on account of the said injuries or either of them.

Approved, February 12, 1793.

62 The Whiskey Rebellion (1791-1794)

In 1790, at the suggestion of Secretary of the Treasury Alexander Hamilton, the federal government assumed the entire domestic debt from the Revolutionary War, which the states had not been able to service. The undertaking of this substantial load compelled government to seek new revenues.

The March 3, 1791, excise tax on domestically produced spirits stirred up the western counties of Pennsylvania, which contained a quarter of the nation's stills. The backcountry farmers considered the tax, ranging from nine to twenty-five cents per gallon, particularly unjust, because it affected the sole product that they were able to transport profitably over the rugged Alleghany mountains to the markets of Philadelphia and the East Coast. The tax also reminded the settlers of hated English excises including the odious Stamp Act, opposition to which had fueled the movement toward revolution. The fact that western distillers accused of violating the excise law were to be tried in Philadelphia aggravated the situation. The trip was time consuming and expensive, and the law was reminiscent of the acts of Parliament requiring that certain crimes in the colonies be tried in England. In 1794, Congress provided that these charges could be heard in the local state court, as well as the federal court in Philadelphia, but it was too late. A series of summonses commanding appearance in Philadelphia had already been issued and subsequently served. Angry western settlers directed their wrath at the federal marshals seeking to serve process. Several were tarred and feathered and forced to swear not to serve federal process in the western counties. The following report from a trial arising out of the Whiskey Rebellion sets out subsequent events in graphic detail. Prior to his appointment as a tax inspector, General Neville had been a popular state politician.

In reading this and the documents that follow, it should be kept in mind that these events occurred a scant few years after the ratification of the Constitution, characterized by its opponents as vesting in a central government powers that could as easily be abused as those previously held by the English king and Parliament.

☆ 62 *United States v. Insurgents*

26 F. Cas. 449 (C.C.D. Pa. 1795) (No. 15,443).

The act of congress of the 3rd of March, 1791, which imposed a duty upon spirits distilled within the United States, produced at once great opposition, both in and out of congress. . . . It was branded with the name of excise, a term very hateful to the people, as connected with the former oppressions of the British government. It was declared unnecessary and tyrannical. The legislatures of Maryland, Pennsylvania, Virginia, and North Carolina united in solemn declarations of rooted dislike, and of resistance, in some cases hardly to be reconciled with constitutional opposition; and by the latter state a position was assumed, which in later days would have been called nullification. But it was in the western parts of Pennsylvania and Virginia, and particularly in the counties of Alleghany, Washington, Fayette, and Westmoreland, in the first-mentioned state, that resistance to the bill was most violent, and it was there an agitation was started which, in the course of a few years, ripened into an organized insurgation and involved its leaders in the crime of treason.

*   *   *

The act of 1791 came up for revision before the congress which assembled in October of the same year. By an act passed May 8, 1792, several material alterations were thereto made; the duties were reduced to so moderate a rate as to obviate any complaint on that score. The other changes were also favourable to distillers.

The act of 1792 required that there should be an office for collection in every county. It was therefore supposed, on the part of the discontented, that if the establishment of these offices was prevented, a material point would be gained. A plan of intimidation was accordingly pursued, directed against those who might be disposed to allow their houses to be used for the obnoxious purpose. Threats of personal violence and of destruction of property were made, and in some cases actually executed. It became, therefore, in a short time, almost impossible to obtain suitable places for the revenue offices. After much difficulty, in August, 1792, General Neville obtained the house of one William Faulkner, a captain in the army, for an office of inspection in Washington county. Soon after this, Captain Faulkner was met by a large number of people, in the same neighbourhood where Johnson had been maltreated the preceding year. A knife was put at his throat, and the assailants threatened to scalp, tar and feather him, and to burn his house, unless he would promise to prevent its further use as an office. He was compelled to make the promise; and, in consequence, wrote a letter to the inspector, countermanding the permission to use his house.

General Neville had received warnings for some time previous, that an attack was intended on his house. . . . Acting on these intimations, he had had his house prepared for resistance. The windows were filled up with thick plank, and the negroes abundantly supplied with arms and ammunition. These precautions were not idle. About day-break on the 10th [July, 1794], the party from the meeting [at Couche's Fort] under the command of one John Holcroft, counting about forty guns, appeared at the house of the inspector. On being asked what they wanted, and replying in a suspicious manner, they were fired upon from the house. They returned the fire, but being unexpectedly attacked by the negroes in the out-houses, they precipitately retired, with six of their number wounded and one killed. The inspector's family received no injury. Though thus far entirely successful, General Neville had every reason to suppose that the business would not terminate thus, and to anticipate a renewed and more dangerous attack. He accordingly made application to the judges, generals of militia, and sheriff of the county for protection. A reply to this application, on the part of these officers, informed him that the laws could not be executed, so as to afford him protection, owing to the too general combination of the people in that part of Pennsylvania, to oppose the revenue law; and expressed a fear, that should the posse comitatus be ordered out in support of the civil authority, very few could be found who were not of the party of the rioters. A detachment of eleven men, regulars, was obtained, however, from Fort Pitt, and command was taken by Major Kirkpatrick, a relative of General Neville. On the day following the attack, the rioters assembled again at Couche's Fort, a few miles from the residence of General Neville, to the number of five or six hundred men. [They conceived a plan to march to the General's house, compel his resignation, and seize the tax records. Upon arriving at the house, they sent a messenger with a flag to demand the papers. Informed that the General had left,] the flag was sent a second time, requiring the inspector to resign, and that six good, reputable citizens should be admitted to examine and seize the papers, promising that in that case no further injury should be done. This was refused at once. Notice was given, by a third flag, for the women and children to withdraw. The attack then commenced.

In about a quarter of an hour the defenders of the house was ceased firing, and a call was heard thence, which was mistaken by the assailants for a parley. Their leader, McFarlane, then stepped from behind a tree, where he had for greater safety posted himself, to order the firing to stop, when he was hit in the groin by a musket-ball from the house, and instantly killed. The firing then recommenced, and a message was sent to the committe to know whether the house should not be stormed. In the meantime the out-houses and the adjacent buildings were set fire to. The intensity of the heat, and the danger of an immediate communication of the conflagration to the house, compelled Major Kirkpatrick and his small party to come out and surrender themselves. The attack lasted for about an hour, during which the assailants had two killed and several wounded; and three of the soldiers were wounded. The privates were suffered to depart without injury, but Major Kirkpatrick was arrested, and ordered to give up his musket. He refused to do so, whereupon one presented a gun at his breast, and was about to fire, when he dropped upon his knees and asked quarter. The mansion was then set on fire, and it and the out-buildings were consumed, except a small out-house, which was preserved at the request of the negroes, as containing their bacon. While the house was burning, the rioters broke open the cellar, and drunk up the wine, and many things of value were supposed to be stolen therefrom. The marshal, with Colonel Presley Neville (the son of General Neville) and several others, were taken on their way to the house. They were arrested and put under guard. After a short time, all but the two former were permitted to escape. Colonel Neville begged to be permitted to go on, and engaged that all their demands should be complied with. He was refused, however, and was compelled to remain during the period of the attack in sight of the house; in painful uncertainty as to the fate of his father and family. [The insurgents finally forced General Neville and the Marshall to leave Pittsburgh. The insurgents threatened to attack the town in an attempt to compel Neville's resignation and forced the surrender of the processes held by the Marshall.]

Before separating, after the attack on the inspector's, the insurgents appointed a meeting to be held on the 23rd of July, at Mingo Creek Meeting House, in Washington county. At this meeting, which was composed of those who had been engaged in the attack, and a large number from the neighbouring counties . . . managed to show them that they had committed acts of treason, and to persuade them against any precipitate action, without endangering his safety, and without appearing to be adverse to their cause. It was finally determined to postpone their final determination to a more general assemblage. The following call for another meeting was made, and published in the Pittsburgh Gazette of the 26th July: "By a respectable number of citizens who met on Wednesday, the 23rd instant, it is recommended to the townships of the four Western

Pennsylvania counties, and its neighbouring counties of Virginia to meet and choose representatives, to meet at Parkinson's Ferry, on the Monongahela, on the 11th of August next to take into consideration the situations of the Western country."

*   *   *

63 "combinations to defeat the execution of the laws" (1794)

Under the leadership of David Bradford, a deputy state's attorney, the masses of the Whiskey Army mustered at Braddock's Field and marched into Pittsburgh. Note that while the state officials could not provide protection for the federal officers, the uprising was limited to opposition to the enforcement of a single law. The civil authorities were otherwise in control of matters, and presumably there was no generalized disorder. Nevertheless, President Washington characterized the situation as insurrection and anarchy. Clearly the resistance was a test of the newly created government's ability to enforce federal law. In his first proclamation, Washington exhorted the insurgents to disperse. The ultimate calling of the militia was in acquiescence to Hamilton's recommendation that forceful action was necessary or else the "spirit of disobedience will naturally extend."

☆ 63 Proclamations of President Washington on the Whiskey Rebellion

☆ 63a August 7, 1794

Reprinted in J. Richardson, ed., *A Compilation of the Messages and Papers of the Presidents* (New York: Bureau of National Literature, 1897), 150-52.

Whereas combinations to defeat the execution of the laws laying duties upon spirits distilled within the United States and upon stills have from the time of the commencement of those laws existed in some of the western parts of Pennsylvania; and

Whereas the said combinations, proceeding in a manner subversive equally of the just authority of government and of the rights of individuals, have hitherto effected their dangerous and criminal purpose by the influence of certain irregular meetings whose proceedings have tended to encourage and uphold the spirit of opposition by misrepresentations of the laws calculated to render them odious; by endeavors to deter those who might be so disposed from accepting offices under them through fear of public resentment and of injury to person and property, and to compel those who had accepted such offices by actual violence to surrender or forbear the execution of them; by circulating vindictive menaces against all those who should otherwise, directly or indirectly, aid in the execution of the said laws, or who, yielding to the dictates of conscience and to a sense of obligation, should themselves comply therewith, by actually injuring and destroying the property of persons who were understood to have so complied; by inflicting cruel humiliation punishments upon private citizens for no other cause than that of appearing to be the friends of the laws; by intercepting the public officers on the highways, abusing, assaulting, and otherwise ill treating them; by going to their houses in the night, gaining admittance by force, taking away their papers, and committing other outrages, employing for these unwarrantable purposes the agency of armed banditti disguised in such manner as for the most part to escape discovery; and

Whereas the endeavors of the Legislature to obviate objections to the said laws by lowering the duties and by other alterations conducive to the convenience of those whom they immediately affect . . . and the endeavors of the executive officers to conciliate a compliance with the laws by explanations, by forbearance, and even by particular accommodations founded on the suggestion of local considerations, have been disappointed of their effect by the machinations of persons whose industry to excite resistance has increased with every appearance of a disposition among the people to relax in their opposition and to acquiesce in the laws, insomuch that many persons in the said western parts of Pennsylvania have at length been hardy enough to perpetrate acts which I am advised amount to treason, being overt acts of levying war against the Unites States, . . . avowing as the motives of these outrageous proceedings an intention to prevent by force of arms the execution of the said laws, . . . to withstand by open violence the lawful authority of the Government of the United States, and to compel thereby an alteration in the measures of the Legislature and a repeal of the laws aforesaid; and

Whereas by a law of the United States entitled "An act to provide for calling forth the militia to execute the laws of the Union, suppress insurrections, and repel invasions," it is enacted "that whenever the laws of the United States shall be opposed or the execution thereof obstructed in any State by combinations too powerful to be suppressed by the ordinary course of judicial proceedings . . . it shall be lawful for the President of the United States to call forth the militia of such State to suppress such combinations and to cause the laws to be duly executed. And if the militia of a State where such combinations may happen shall refuse or be insufficient to suppress the same, it shall be lawful for the President, if the Legislature of the United States shall not be in session, to call forth and employ such numbers of the militia of any other State or States most convenient thereto as may be necessary; . . . Provided always, that whenever it may be necessary in the judgment of the President to use the military force hereby directed to be called forth, the President shall forthwith, and previous thereto, by proclamation, command such insurgents to disperse and retire peaceably to their respective abodes within a limited time," ... and

Whereas it is in my judgment necessary under the circumstances of the case to take measures for calling forth the militia in order to suppress the combinations aforesaid, and to cause the laws to be duly executed; and I have accordingly determined so to do, feeling the deepest regret for the occasion, but withal the most solemn conviction that the essential interests of the Union demand it, that the very existence of Government and the fundamental principles of social order are materially involved in the issue, and that the patriotism and firmness of all good citizens are seriously called upon, as occasions may require, to aid in the effectual suppression of so fatal a spirit:

Wherefore, and in pursuance of the proviso above recited, I, George Washington, President of the United States, do hereby command all persons being insurgents as aforesaid, and all others whom it may concern, on or before the 1st day of September next to disperse and retire peaceably to their respective abodes. And I do moreover warn all persons whomsoever against aiding, abetting, or comforting the perpetrators of the aforesaid treasonable acts, and do require all officers and other citizens, according to their respective duties and the laws of the land, to exert their utmost endeavors to prevent and suppress such dangerous proceedings. ...

G.° WASHINGTON

☆ 63b September 25, 1794

Reprinted in J. Richardson, ed., *A Compilation of the Messages and Papers of the Presidents* (New York: Bureau of National Liberature, 1897), 1:153-54.

Whereas from a hope that the combinations against the Constitution and laws of the United States in certain of the western counties of Pennsylvania would yield to time and reflection I thought it sufficient in the first instance rather to take measures for calling forth the militia than immediately to embody them, but the moment is now come when the overtures of forgiveness, with no other condition than a submission to law, have been only partially accepted; when every form of conciliation not inconsistent with the being of Government has been adopted without effect; ... when the opportunity of examining the serious consequences of a treasonable opposition has been employed in propagating principles of anarchy, ... and inviting similar acts of insurrection; when it is manifest that violence would

continue to be exercised upon every attempt to enforce the laws; when, therefore, Government is set at defiance, the contest being whether a small portion of the United States shall dictate to the whole Union, and, at the expense of those who desire peace, indulge a desperate ambition:

Now, therefore, I, George Washington, President of the United States, in obedience to that high and irresistible duty consigned to me by the Constitution "to take care that the laws be faithfully executed," deploring that the American name should be sullied by the outrages of citizens on their own Government, ... resolved to reduce the refractory to a due subordination to the law, do hereby declare and make known that, ... a force which, according to every reasonable expectation, is adequate to the exigency is already in motion to the scene of disaffection; that those who have confided or shall confide in the protection of Government shall meet full succor under the standard and from the arms of the United States; that those who, having offended against the laws, have since entitled themselves to indemnity will be treated with the most liberal good faith if they shall not have forfeited their claim by any subsequent conduct, and that instructions are given accordingly.

And I do moreover exhort all individuals, officers, and bodies of men to contemplate with abhorrence the measures leading directly or indirectly to those crimes which produce this resort to military coercion; to check in their respective spheres the efforts of misguided or designing men to substitute their misrepresentation in the place of truth and their discontents in the place of stable government, and to call to mind that, as the people of the United States have been permitted, under the Divine favor, in perfect freedom, after solemn deliberation, and in an enlightened age, to elect their own government, so will their gratitude for this inestimable blessing be best distinguished by firm exertions to maintain the Constitution and the laws.

And, lastly, I again warn all persons whomsoever and wheresoever not to abet, aid, or comfort the insurgents aforesaid, as they will answer the contrary at their peril, and I do also require all the officers and other citizens, according to their several duties, as far as may be in their power, to bring under the cognizance of the laws all offenders. ...

G.° WASHINGTON

64 The Treasons of Mitchell and Vigol (1795)

Thirteen thousand troops advanced to crush the Whiskey Rebellion. Alexander Hamilton secured George Washington's permission to join the punitive expedition and wrote: "Those ... who preach doctrines or set examples which underwrite or subvert the authority of the law, lead us from freedom to slavery. They incapacitate us from a government of laws and consequently prepare the way for one of force, for mankind must have government of one sort or another."

Prepared for a protracted war, the federal army arrived to find that most of the insurgents had departed. Many former rebels were seeking the benefits of an amnesty offer that required subscription to a loyalty oath. By and large, the more moderate forces had established control. While the use of military force to suppress the resistance was not untoward, the incident exemplified some of the perils of using the military to support domestic authority. (One historical commentator claims that "[t]he conduct of the Army in the disaffected territory is a sorry page in United States military history. Wholesale and indiscriminate arrests, harsh treatment of prisoners, inhumanity as Standard Operating Procedure — best describes it.")

The main leaders of the rebellion had either escaped or received amnesty. (David Bradford sought refuge in the Spanish territory, and although pardoned in 1799, he continued the life of a planter in Natchez.) The federal troops took twenty prisoners to Philadelphia. Only two lowly members of the rebellious forces were convicted of treason: John Mitchell, who came voluntarily before General Daniel Morgan to confess his guilt; and Philip Weigel, appearing in the court records as Vigol, who was reportedly a mad Pennsylvania Dutchman. Although the events of the rebellion were well established, questions remained whether these individuals had participated in the rebellion and whether their conduct was treasonous or merely riotous. Note how the court characterized organized resistance to the operation of a law as constituting treason and the distinction between conspiracy and treason.

Mitchell and Vigol were sentenced to hang. Nevertheless, President Washington pardoned them because of their obvious incapacities.

☆ 64 A Madman and a Moron

☆ 64a *United States v. Mitchell*

26 F. Cas. 1277 (C.C.D. Pa. 1795) (No. 15,788).

Indictment for high treason, by levying war against the United States. It was alleged that the prisoner was one of the party that assembled at Couche's Fort, armed; that he proceeded thence to Gen. Neville's and assisted at the burning of the general's house; that he attended with great zeal at the meeting at Bradock's field; and that on the day prescribed for signing a submission to the government he was intoxicated, refused to sign himself, and was active in dissuading others from signing.

PATERSON, Circuit Justice. . . . Let it be granted that to compel Congress to repeal a law, by . . . violence, or intimidation, is treason . . . it does not follow, that resisting the execution of a law, or attempting to coerce an officer into the resignation of this commission, will amount to the same offence. Let it be granted, also, that an insurrection, for the avowed purpose of suppressing all the excise offices in the United States, may be construed into an act of levying war against the government . . . it does not follow that an attempt to oblige one officer to resign, or to suppress all the offices in one district, will be a crime of the same denomination.

*   *   *

[I]t has been argued, that Congress has provided a specific punishment for the offence of resisting or obstructing the service of process, obviously distinguishing it from treason; and that it is as much treason to resist the execution of one law as another; to resist the marshall of a court, as much as the supervisor of a district. The analogy is, in a great measure, just. In either case, if the resistance is made by a few persons, in a particular instance, and under the impulse of a particular interest, the offence would not amount to high treason; but, if, in either case, there is a general rising of a whole county, to prevent the officer from discharging his duty in relation to the public at large, the offence is, unquestionably, high treason.

Again, it has been urged, that the criminal intention must point to the suppression of all the excise offices in the United States, or it cannot amount to high treason. If it is meant by this argument, that the insurgents of Pennsylvania must have contemplated a march from Georgia to New Hampshire, it is extravagant and absurd: but, in another view, it is perfectly correct; for, if it was intended that, by their lawless career and example, congress should be forced into a repeal of the obnoxious law, it necessarily followed, that, from the same cause, the offices of excise would be suppressed throughout the Union. That universality of object, which the books require, was inseparable from the nature of the opposition; for, it was impossible to contemplate the repeal of the excise law in one survey, or in one state, without effecting it in every survey, and in every state. The truth is, however, that the insurgents did not entertain a personal dislike for Gen. Neville; but in every stage of their proceedings at Couche's Fort, at the general's house, and at Bradock's field, they were actuated by one single, traiterous motive, a determination, if practicable, to frustrate and prevent the execution of the excise law. The whole was one great insurrection; and it is immaterial at what point of time, or place, from its commencement to its termination, any man became an agent in carrying it on. Many persons, indeed, may have attended innocently at Couche's Fort, as was the case with Porter; but those would not remain long, after the purpose of the meeting was developed. To render any man criminal, he must not only have been present, but he must have taken part with the insurgents; yet, whether he was present at Couche's Fort on the march to Gen. Neville's, or at the burning of the general's house, if his intention was traiterous, his offence was treason.... The overt act laid in the indictment ... is levying war; and war may be levied, though not actually made.... It is agreed that this overt act must be proved by two witnesses; but there is a difference as to what constitutes the act itself. Now, it is manifest from every authority, that to assemble in a body, armed and arrayed, for some treasonable purpose, is an act of levying war; this was the case at Couche's Fort; and the prisoner's active attendance there is proved by a number of witnesses. It is not required that every witness should have seen him at the same spot, at the same moment, and in the same act; but if they see him at the place and time of rendezvous, exhibiting the same species of traiterous conduct, the law is satisfied. The conspiracy to levy war being effected, all the conspirators are guilty, though, they did not all attend at Gen. Neville's house.... Besides, the meeting at Bradock's field is a distinct and substantive act of treason: and the prisoner is proved by four witnesses to have been there. The design of the meeting, was, avowedly, to oppose the execution of the excise law, to over-awe the government, to involve others in the guilt of the insurrection, to prevent the punishment of the delinquents, to banish unpopular individuals from the town, and to attack the garrison of Pittsburgh. The hasty declarations of the quo animo, proceeding from the prisoner himself, ought not to have much weight, were they not so strongly corroborated by other testimony.

PATERSON, Circuit Justice (charging jury). The first question to be considered is, what was the general object of the insurrection? If its object was to suppress the excise offices, and to prevent the execution of an act of congress, by force and intimidation, the offence, in legal estimation, is high treason; it is an usurpation of the authority of government; it is high treason by levying of war. Taking the testimony in a rational and connected point of view, this was the object: It was of a general nature, and of national concern.

Let us attend, for a moment, to the evidence. With what view was the attack made on General Neville's house? Was it to gratify a spirit of revenge against him as a private citizen, as an individual? No: as a private citizen he had been highly respected and beloved; it was only by becoming a public officer that he became obnoxious: and it was on account of his holding the excise office alone, that his house had been assailed, and his person endangered. On the

first day of attack, the insurgents were repulsed; but they rallied, returned with greater force, and fatally succeeded in the second attempt. They were arrayed in a military manner; they affected the military forms of negotiation by a flag; they pretended no personal hostility to General Neville; but they insisted on the surrender of his commission. Can there be a doubt, then, that the object of the insurrection was of a general and public nature?

The second question to be considered, is—how far was the prisoner traiterously connected with the insurgents? It is proved by four witnesses, that he was at Couche's Fort, at a great distance from his own home, and that he was armed.... Of the overt act of treason, there must, undoubtedly, be proof by two witnesses: and it is equally clear, that the intention and the act, the will and the deed, must concur; for, a bare conspiracy is not treason.

☆ 64b *United States v. Vigol*

28 F. Cas. 376 (C.C.D. Pa. 1795) (No. 16,621).

Indictment for high treason, in levying war against the United States. The prisoner was one of the most active of the insurgents in the western counties of Pennsylvania, and had accompanied the armed party, who attacked the house of the excise officer (Reigan) in Westmoreland, with guns, drum, &c., insisted upon his surrendering his official papers, and extorted an oath from him, that he would never act again in the execution of the excise law. The same party then proceeded to the house of Wells, the excise officer in Fayette county, swearing that the excise law should never be carried into effect, and that they would destroy Wells and his house. On their arrival, Wells had fled and concealed himself; whereupon they ransacked the house: burned it, with all its contents, including the public books and papers; and afterwards discovering Wells, seized, imprisoned, and compelled him to swear, that he would no longer act as excise officer. Witnesses were, likewise, examined to establish that the general combination and scope of the insurrection, were to prevent the execution of the excise law by force; and in the course of the evidence, the duress of the marshal of the district, the assembling at Couche's, the burning of General Neville's house, &c., were prominent features.

As no question of law arose upon the trial, but the case rested entirely on a proof of the overt acts by two witnesses, M. Levy and Lewis, for the defendant, and the attorney of the district agreed, without argument, to submit to the decision of the jury, under the charge of the court, which was delivered to the following effect:

PATERSON, Circuit Justice. The first point for consideration is the evidence which has been given to establish the case stated in the indictment; the second point turns upon the criminal intention of the party; and from these points, — the evidence and intention — the law arises.

With respect to the evidence, the current runs one way. It harmonizes in all its parts. It proves that the prisoner was a member of the party who went to Reigan's house, and, afterwards, to the house of Wells, in arms, marshalled and arrayed; and who, at each place, committed acts of violence and devastation.

With respect to the intention, likewise, there is not, unhappily, the slightest possibility of doubt. To suppress the office of excise in the Fourth survey of this state, and particularly, in the present instance, to compel the resignation of Wells, the excise officer, so as to render null and void, in effect, an act of congress, constituted the apparent — the avowed — object of the insurrection, and of the outrages which the prisoner assisted to commit. Combining these facts and this design, the crime of high treason is consummate in the contemplation of the constitution and law of the United States.

The counsel for the prisoner have endeavored, in the course of a faithful discharge of their duty, to extract from the witnesses some testimony which might justify a defence upon the ground or duress and terror. But in this they have failed, for the whole scene exhibits a disgraceful unanimity; and, with regard to the prisoner, he can only be distinguished for a guilty pre-eminence in zeal and activity. It may not, however, be useless on this occasion to observe that the fear which the law recognizes as an excuse for the perpetration of an offence must proceed from an immediate and actual danger, threatening the very life of the party. The apprehension of any loss of property, by waste or fire, or even an apprehension of a slight or remote injury to the person, furnish no excuse. If, indeed, such circumstances could avail, it would be in the power of every crafty leader of tumults and rebellion to indemnify his followers by uttering previous menaces; an avenue would be forever open for the escape of unsuccessful guilt, and the whole fabric of society must, inevitably, be laid prostrate.

A technical objection has, also, been suggested in favor of the prisoner. It is said that the offence is not proved to have been committed on the day, nor the number of the insurgent party to be so great, as the indictment states. But both these exceptions, even if well founded in fact, are immaterial in point of law. The crime is proved, and laid to have been committed, before the charge was presented; and whether it was committed by one hundred or five hundred cannot alter the guilt of the defendant. If, however, the jury entertain any doubt upon the matter, they may find it specially.

Verdict, guilty.

65 "a full, free, and entire pardon" (1795)

President Washington had proved the presidential authority granted under the new Constitution in the campaign against the Whiskey rebels. The speedy and successful quashing of the rebellion demonstrated that the new federal government's power extended to all citizens throughout the nation, and that national laws could be enforced. Having survived the test, the new government could afford to be magnanimous. In 1795, the president issued a general amnesty to all those who gave bona fide assurance of allegiance to the United States. He restored tranquility in western Pennsylvania without the shedding of blood or the exacting of vengeance.

☆ 65 Washington's Presidential Proclamation (July 10, 1795)

Reprinted in J. Richardson, ed., *A Compilation of the Messages and Papers of the Presidents* (New York: Bureau of National Literature, 1897), 1:173.

PROCLAMATION

Whereas the commissioners appointed by the President of the United States to confer with the citizens in the western counties of Pennsylvania during the late insurrection which prevailed therein, by their act and agreement bearing date the 2d day of September last, in pusuance of the powers in them vested, did promise and engage that, if assurances of submission to the laws of the United States should be bona fide given by the citizens resident in the fourth survey of Pennsylvania, in the manner and within the time in the said act and agreement specified, a general pardon should be granted on the 10th day of July then next ensuing of all treasons and other indictable offenses against the United States committed within the said survey before the 22d day of August last, excluding therefrom, nevertheless, every person who should refuse or neglect to subscribe such assurance and engagement in manner aforesaid, or who should after such subscription violate the same, or willfully obstruct or attempt to obstruct the execution of the acts for raising a revenue on distilled spirits and stills, or be aiding or abetting therein; and

Whereas I have since thought proper to extend the said pardon to all persons guilty of the said treasons, misprisions of treasons, or otherwise concerned in the late insurrection within the survey aforesaid who have not since been indicted or convicted thereof, or of any other offense against the United States:

Therefore be it known that I, George Washington, President of the said United States, have granted, and by these presents to grant, a full, free, and entire pardon to all persons (excepting as is hereinafter excepted) of all treasons, misprisions of treason, and other indictable offenses against the United States committed within the fourth survey of Pennsylvania before the said 22d day of August last past, excepting and excluding therefrom, nevertheless, every person who refused or neglected to give and subscribe the said assurances in the manner aforesaid (or having subscribed hath violated the same) and now standeth indicted or convicted of any treason, misprision of treason, or other offense against the said United States, hereby remitting and releasing unto all persons, except as before excepted, all penalties incurred, or supposed to be incurred, for or on account of the premises.

66 "the doctrine of nonresistance is . . . slavish" (1797)

Despite the dramatic suppression of the Whiskey Rebellion, the revolutionary tradition of the United States continued, finding authority not only in the Declaration of Independence but also in Article X of the New Hampshire Constitution. This article is a clear reminder that at the conclusion of the first decade of the federal government's existence—a decade of political strife—the American people's commitment to the "Social Contract" continued to be reserved and conditional.

The legal efficacy of New Hampshire's permissiveness must be weighed, however, against the federal Constitution's provision in Article VI, Section 2, that laws made "under the authority of the United States, shall be the supreme law of the land; . . . any thing in the Constitution or laws of any state to the contrary notwithstanding." Nevertheless, New Hampshire's "Right of Revolution" might provide the foundation for a defense to charges of treason against the state for resisting the enforcement of some "odious" law.

☆66 New Hampshire Constitution, Article X

*   *   *

10th [Right of Revolution]. Government being instituted for the common benefit, protection, and security, of the whole community, and not for the private interest or emolument of any one man, family, or class of men; therefore, whenever the ends of government are perverted, and public liberty manifestly endangered, and all other means of redress are ineffectual, the doctrine of nonresistance against arbitrary power, and oppression, is absurd, slavish, and destructive of the good and happiness of mankind.

*   *   *

67 "dangerous to the peace and safety of the United States" (1798)

The French Revolution, a rebellion in Ireland, and political unrest in England caused an influx of large numbers of political activists into the new American nation. The administration of President John Adams was preparing for war with France. In domestic politics, the relations between the Federalist and the Jeffersonian Republicans grew tense. Thus, seven years after the adoption of the First Amendment protection of free speech, press, and assembly, Congress passed a series of laws which seriously punished expression of views critical of the government or its laws. Some argued that the acts were compatible with the First Amendment, since they imposed no prior restraint on what might be expressed.

Collectively known as the Alien and Sedition Acts, these laws "concerning aliens" (June 25), "respecting alien Enemies" (July 6), and "for the punishment of certain crimes against the United States" (July 14) reflected fears of threats to American security. The Alien Acts gave the president unbridled discretion to deport "dangerous" aliens. The Sedition Act prohibited not only the counseling of or the attempt "to procure any insurrection, riot, unlawful assembly" but also the printing and uttering of any "false" and "scandalous" writings with intent to defame the president, congress, or the government.

The sedition law was enforced vigorously and discriminatorily against newspaper editors and officeholders who challenged the policies of Adams's Federalist administration. It expired by its own terms on March 3, 1801.

☆67 Alien and Sedition Laws (June 25-July 14, 1798)

☆67a An Act concerning Aliens

1 Stat. 570 (1798).

SECTION 1. *Be it enacted by the Senate and House of Representatives of the United States of America in Congress assembled,* That it shall be lawful for the President of the United States at any time during the continuance of this act, to *order* all such *aliens* as he shall judge dangerous to the peace and safety of the United States, or shall have reasonable grounds to suspect are concerned in any treasonable or secret machinations against the government thereof, to depart out of the territory of the United States, within such time as shall be expressed in such order, which order shall be served on such alien by delivering him a copy thereof, or leaving the same at his usual abode. . . . *Provided always, and be it further enacted,* that if any alien so ordered to depart shall prove to the satisfaction of the President

... that no injury or danger to the United States will arise from suffering such alien to reside therein, the President may grant a *license* to such alien to remain within the United States for such time as he shall judge proper, and at such place as he may designate. ...

*   *   *

Approved, June 25, 1798.

☆ 67b An Act respecting Alien Enemies

1 Stat. 577 (1798).

SECTION 1. *Be it enacted by the Senate and House of Representatives of the United States of America in Congress assembled*, That whenever there shall be a declared war between the United States and any foreign nation or government, or any invasion or predatory incursion shall be perpetrated, attempted, or threatened against the territory of the United States, by any foreign nation or government, ... all natives, citizens, denizens, or subjects of the hostile nation or government, being males of the age of fourteen years and upwards, who shall be within the United States, and not actually naturalized, shall be liable to be apprehended, restrained, secured and removed, as alien enemies. And the President of the United States shall be, and he is hereby authorized, in any event, as aforesaid, by his proclamation thereof, or other public act, to direct the conduct to be observed, on the part of the United States, towards the aliens who shall become liable, as aforesaid; the manner and degree of the restraint to which they shall be subject, and in what cases, and upon what security their residence shall be permitted, and to provide for the removal of those, who, not being permitted to reside within the United States, shall refuse or neglect to depart therefrom; and to establish any other regulations which shall be found necessary in the premises and for the public safety: Provided, that aliens resident within the United States, who shall become liable as enemies, in the manner aforesaid, and who shall not be chargeable with actual hostility, or other crime against the public safety, shall be allowed, for the recovery, disposal, and removal or their goods and effects, and for their departure, the full time which is, or shall be stipulated by any treaty, ... and where no such treaty shall have existed, the President of the United States may ascertain and declare such reasonable time as may be consistent with the public safety, and according to the dictates of humanity and national hospitality. ... And the President may also require of such alien to enter into a bond to the United States, in such penal sum as he may direct, with one or more sufficient sureties to the satisfaction of the person authorized by the President to take the same, conditioned for the good behavior of such alien during his residence in the United States,

and not violating his license, which license the President may revoke, whenever he shall think proper.

*   *   *

Approved, July 6, 1798.

☆ 67c An Act for the Punishment of Certain Crimes against the United States

1 Stat. 596 (1798).

SECTION 1. *Be it enacted by the Senate and House of Representatives of the United States of America, in Congress assembled*, That if any persons shall unlawfully combine or conspire together, with intent to oppose any measure or measures of the government of the United States, which are or shall be directed by proper authority, or to impede the operation of any law of the United States, or to intimidate or prevent any person holding a place or office in or under the government of the United States, from undertaking, performing or executing his trust or duty; and if any person or persons, with intent as aforesaid, shall counsel, advise or attempt to procure any insurrection, riot, unlawful assembly, or combination, whether such conspiracy, threatening, counsel, advice, or attempt shall have the proposed effect or not, he or they shall be deemed guilty of a high misdemeanor, and on conviction, before any court of the United States having jurisdiction thereof, shall be punished by a fine not exceeding five thousand dollars, and by imprisonment during a term not less than six months nor exceeding five years; and further, at the discretion of the court may be holden to find sureties for his good behaviour in such sum, and for such time, as the said court may direct.

SEC. 2. *And be it further enacted*, That if any person shall write, print, utter or publish, or shall cause or procure to be written, printed, uttered or published, or shall knowingly and willingly assist or aid in writing, printing, uttering or publishing any false, scandalous and malicious writing or writings against the government of the United States, or either house of the Congress of the United States, or the President of the United States, with intent to defame the said government, or either house of the said Congress, or the said President, or to bring them, or either of them, into contempt or disrepute; or to excite against them, or either or any of them, the hatred of the good people of the United States, or to stir up sedition within the United States, or to excite any unlawful combinations therein, for opposing or resisting any law of the United States, or any act of the President of the United States, done in pursuance of any such law, or of the powers in him vested by the constitution of the United States, or to resist, oppose, or defeat any such law or act, or to aid, encourage or abet any hostile designs of any foreign nation against the United States, their people

or government, then such person, being thereof convicted before any court of the United States having
jurisdiction thereof, shall be punished by a fine not
exceeding two thousand dollars, and by imprisonment not exceeding two years.

SEC. 3. *And be it further enacted and declared,*
That if any person shall be prosecuted under this
act, for the writing or publishing any libel aforesaid,
it shall be lawful for the defendant, upon the trial of
the cause, to give in evidence in his defence, the
truth of the matter contained in the publication
charged as a libel. And the jury who shall try the
cause, shall have a right to determine the law and
the fact, under the direction of the court, as in other
cases.

SEC. 4. *And be it further enacted,* That this act
shall continue and be in force until the third day of
March, one thousand eight hundred and one, and no
longer: *Provided,* that the expiration of the act shall
not prevent or defeat a prosecution and punishment
of any offence against the law, during the time it
shall be in force.

Approved, July 14, 1798.

68 "blush and weep over our
sedition law" (1798)

Jefferson's early wariness of federal power was exemplified in his letter to John Taylor, a member of
the Virginia House of Delegates and a leading political philosopher. It was Taylor, the foremost apolo-
gist for Jeffersonian democracy, who introduced the
doctrine of state's rights (manifested in the Kentucky and Virginia Resolutions) into the Virginia legislature. At this point in the history of the new republic, the Constitution seemed ineffective in
constraining its exercise of powers. The worst fears
of the Jeffersonian Republicans were becoming reality.

☆ 68 Letter from Thomas Jefferson
to John Taylor

Reprinted in W. Parker, ed., *Letters and Addresses of
Thomas Jefferson* (New York: United Book Publishing,
1905), 126.

Monticello, November 26, 1798

I wish it were possible to obtain a single amendment
to our Constitution. I would be willing to depend on
that alone for the reduction of the administration of
our government to the genuine principles of its Constitution; I mean an additional article, taking from
the federal government the power of borrowing.

For the present, I should be for resolving the
alien and sedition laws to be against the Constitu-

tion and merely void, and for addressing the other
States to obtain similar declarations. . . .

I inclose you a column, cut out of a London paper,
to show you that the English, though charmed with
our making their enemies our enemies, yet blush
and weep over our sedition law.

*   *   *

69 "ridiculous pomp, foolish adulation,
and selfish avarice" (1798)

The first case brought under the Sedition Act was
against Matthew Lyon, a Republican congressman
from Vermont. He was charged with publishing two
letters critical of the Adams administration's domestic and foreign policies. Lyon's newspaper, *The
Scourge of Aristocracy,* labeled the president a
bully.

At Lyon's trial, the presiding judge's charge to
the jury reflected the fear that the jury, which
lacked sympathy with the law, might acquit the defendant. The judge's sentence plainly favored en-
hancement of the punishment because of the political nature of the controversy and the defendant.
Lyon was fined one thousand dollars and jailed for
four months. The prosecution and the resultant public outcry subsequently helped to reelect Lyon to
Congress by an overwhelming majority. When Jefferson assumed the presidency, he pardoned Lyon
and all others convicted under the act.

☆ 69 *Lyon's Case*

15 F. Cas. 1183 (C.C.D. Vt. 1798) (No. 8,646).

[This was an indictment, under the act of July 14,
1798, against Matthew Lyon, for the publication of a
seditious libel.]

The indictment which was found on October 5,
1798, contained three counts, the first of which, after
averring the intent to be "to stir up sedition, and to
bring the president and government of the United
States into contempt," laid the following libelous
matter:

"As to the executive, when I shall see the efforts
of that power bent on the promotion of the comfort,
the happiness, and accommodation of the people,
that executive shall have my zealous and uniform
support: but whenever I shall, on the part of the executive, see every consideration of the public welfare swallowed up in a continual grasp for power, in
an unbounded thirst for ridiculous pomp, foolish adu-
lation, and selfish avarice; when I shall behold men
of real merit daily turned out of office, for no other
cause but independency of sentiment; when I shall
see men of firmness, merit, years, abilities, and experience, discarded in their applications for office,

for fear they possess that independence, and men of meanness preferred for the ease with which they take up and advocate opinions, the consequence of which they know but little of — when I shall see the sacred name of religion employed as a state engine to make mankind hate and persecute one another, I shall not be their humble advocate."

The second count consisted of having maliciously, &c., and with intent, &c., published a letter, said to be a letter from a diplomatic character in France, containing two paragraphs in the words following:

"The misunderstanding between the two governments (France and the United States), has become extremely alarming; confidence is completely destroyed, mistrusts, jealousy, and a disposition to a wrong attribution of motives, are so apparent, as to require the utmost caution in every word and action that are to come from your executive. I mean, if your object is to avoid hostilities. Had this truth been understood with you before the recall of Monroe, before the coming and second coming of Pinckney; had it guided the pens that wrote the bullying speech of your president, and stupid answer of your senate, at the opening of congress in November last, I should probably had [sic] no occasion to address you this letter. — But when we found him borrowing the language of Edmund Burke, and telling the world that although he should succeed in treating with the French, there was no dependence to be placed on any of their engagements, that their religion and morality were at an end, that they would turn pirates and plunderers, and it would be necessary to be perpetually armed against them, though you were at peace: we wondered that the answer of both houses had not been an order to send him to a mad house. Instead of this the senate have echoed the speech with more servility than ever George III experienced from either house of parliament."

The third count was for assisting, counseling, aiding, and abetting the publication of the same.

*   *   *

PATERSON, Circuit Justice (charging jury). "You have nothing whatever to do with the constitutionality or unconstitutionality of the sedition law. Congress has said that the author and publisher of seditious libels is to be punished; and until this law is declared null and void by a tribunal competent for the purpose, its validity cannot be disputed. Great would be the abuses were the constitutionality of every statute to be submitted to a jury, in each case where the statute is to be applied. The only question you are to determine is, that which the record submits to you. Did Mr. Lyon publish the writing given in the indictment? Did he do so seditiously? On the first point, the evidence is undisputed, and in fact, he himself concedes the fact of publication as to a large portion of libellous matter. As to the second point, you will have to consider whether language such as

that here complained of could have been uttered with any other intent than that of making odious or contemptible the president and government, and bringing them both into disrepute. If you find such is the case, the offence is made out, and you must render a verdict of guilty. Nor should the political rank of the defendant, his past services, or the dependent condition of his family, deter you from this duty. Such considerations are for the court alone in adjusting the penalty they will bestow. The fact of guilt is for you, for the court, the grade of punishment. As to yourselves, one point, in addition, in exercising the functions allotted to you, you must keep in mind; and that is, that in order to render a verdict of guilty, you must be satisfied beyond all reasonable substantial doubt that the hypothesis of innocence is unsustainable. Keeping these instructions in your mind, you will proceed to deliberate on your verdict."

At about eight o'clock in the evening of the same day, after about an hour's absence, the jury returned with a verdict of guilty.

The defendant being called up for sentence, a postponement was obtained till the next morning, when, after upon a representation of his circumstances, it appearing that he was almost insolvent, Judge PATERSON addressed him as follows: "Matthew Lyon, as member of the federal legislature, you must be well acquainted with the mischiefs which flow from an unlicensed abuse of government, and of the motives which led to the passage of the act under which this indictment is framed. No one, also, can be better acquainted than yourself with the existence and nature of the act. Your position, so far from making the case one which might slip with a minimal fine through the hands of the court, would make impunity conspicuous should such a fine alone be imposed. What, however, has tended to mitigate the sentence which would otherwise have been imposed, is, what I am sorry to hear of, the reduced condition of your estate. The judgment of the court is, that you stand imprisoned four months, pay the costs of prosecution, and a fine of one thousand dollars, and stand committed until this sentence be complied with."

*   *   *

70 "no rampart now remains against the passions and the power of a majority of Congress" (1798)

The Alien and Sedition Acts, noted historian Nathaniel Weyl, were weapons of internal political warfare designed to disintegrate the opposition party. Although the Supreme Court never addressed the constitutionality of the Alien and Sedition Acts, three Supreme Court justices sitting on circuit upheld the Sedition Act as merely codifying the existing common law of seditious libel. Supporters also argued that authority to pass the law derived from Article I, Section 8 (18) of the Constitution, the "necessary and proper" clause, and claimed that it did not violate the First Amendment's proscription, since it imposed no prior restraint upon speech.

Twenty years after the Revolution, the problems of sovereignty which caused the near collapse of the government under the Articles of Confederation remained unresolved. The case for states' rights, or, more properly, the primacy of state sovereignty and a limited national government, was strongly stated in the resolution drafted by Jefferson and passed by the Kentucky Legislature. James Madison drafted a similar resolution for the state of Virginia. Primarily, these resolutions declared that federal legislation was void whenever Congress assumed "undelegated powers"; the First Amendment was only secondarily relied upon as a limit on congressional authority to pass the Sedition Act.

The opposition by the states proved unsuccessful. Not until June 23, 1800, after the inauguration of Thomas Jefferson and the Republican-dominated Congress, were these laws allowed to expire. Even some Federalists joined the opposition. Speaking out against the Sedition Law, Hamilton warned, "Let us not establish a tyranny," and John Marshall broke party discipline to cast the deciding vote against the law's extension.

Beyond the assertion of the states' rights theory of the Constitution that provided the legal justification for secession, the resolution identified two features of the Alien Act which made it particularly adaptable for political uses: the resting of discretionary deportation power in the executive branch and the elimination of procedural safeguards. These two aspects of the Alien Act reappeared in other assertions of political power through the use of criminal and quasi-criminal law. Particularly noteworthy was the expressed fear that the restraints of the Alien and Sedition Acts would not long be confined only to "the friendless alien . . . selected as the safest subject of a first experiment."

☆ 70 Resolution of the Kentucky Legislature

J. Madison and T. Jefferson, *Resolutions of Virginia and Kentucky* (Richmond: Shepherd, 1835), 64–69.

[T]wice read and agreed to by the House.

Resolved, That the several States composing the United States of America, are not united on the principle of unlimited submission to their General Government; but that by compact under the style and title of a Constitution for the United States, and of amendments thereto, they constituted a General Government for special purposes, delegated to that Government certain definite powers, reserving each State to itself, the residuary mass of right to their own self-Government; and that whensoever the General Government assumes undelegated powers, its acts are unauthoritative, void, and of no force: That to this compact each State acceded as a State, and is an integral party, its Co-States forming as to itself, the other party: That the Government created by this compact was not made the exclusive or final judge of the extent of the powers delegated to itself; since that would have made its discretion, and not the Constitution, the measure of its powers; but that as in all other cases of compact among parties having no common judge, each party has an equal right to judge for itself, as well of infractions, as of the mode and measure of redress.

2. Resolved, That the Constitution of the United States having delegated to Congress a power to punish treason, counterfeiting the securities and current coin of the United States, piracies and felonies committed on the high seas, and offences against the laws of nations, and no other crimes whatever . . . [the Alien and Sedition Acts are] altogether void and of no force, and that the power to create, define, and punish such other crimes is reserved, and of right, appertains solely and exclusively to the respective States, each within its own territory.

3. Resolved, That it is true as a general principle, and is also expressly declared by one of the amendments to the Constitution, that "the powers not delegated to the United States by the Constitution, nor prohibited by it to the States, are reserved to the States respectively, or to the people;" and that no power over the freedom of religion, freedom of speech, or freedom of the press, being delegated to the United States by the Constitution, nor prohibited by it to the States, all lawful powers respecting the same did of right remain, and were reserved to the States, or to the people. . . .

And that in addition to this general principle and express declaration, another and more special provision has been made by one of the amendments to the Constitution, which expressly declares, that "Congress shall make no law respecting an establishment of religion, or prohibiting the free exercise thereof, or abridging the freedom of speech, or of the press." . . . That therefore the act of the Congress of the United States, passed on the 14th day of July, 1798, entitled "an act, in addition to the act, for the punishment of certain crimes against the United States," which does abridge the freedom of the press, is not law, but is altogether void and of no effect.

4. Resolved, That alien friends are under the jurisdiction and protection of the laws of the State wherein they are; that no power over them has been delegated to the United States, nor prohibited to the individual States distinct from their power over citizens; . . . [accordingly] the act of the Congress of the United States, passed on the 22nd day of June, 1798, entitled "an act concerning aliens," which assumes

power over alien friends not delegated by the Constitution, is not law, but is altogether void and of no force.

*   *   *

6. Resolved, That the imprisonment of a person under the protection of the laws of the Commonwealth on his failure to obey the simple order of the President, to depart out of the United States, as is undertaken by the said act, entitled "an act concerning aliens," is contrary to the Constitution, one amendment to which has provided, that "no person shall be deprived of liberty without due process of law," and that another having provided, "that in all criminal prosecutions, the accused shall enjoy the right to a public trial by an impartial jury, to be informed of the nature and cause of the accusation, to be confronted with the witnesses against him, to have compulsory process for obtaining witnesses in his favour, and to have the assistance of counsel for his defence," the same act undertaking to authorise the President to remove a person out of the United States who is under the protection of the law, on his own suspicion, without accusation, without jury, without public trial, without confrontation of the witnesses against him; without having witnesses in his favour, without defence, without counsel, is contrary to these provisions also of the Constitution, is therefore not law, but utterly void and of no force.

That transferring the power of judging any person who is under the protection of the laws, from the Courts to the President of the United States, as is undertaken by the same act, concerning aliens, is against the article of the Constitution, which provides, that "the judicial power of the United States, shall be vested in Courts, the Judges of which shall hold their offices during good behaviour," and that the said act is void. . . .

7. Resolved, That the construction applied by the General Government, (as is evinced by sundry of their proceedings,) to those parts of the Constitution of the United States which delegates to Congress a power . . . to make all laws which shall be necessary and proper for carrying into execution the powers vested by the Constitution in the Government of the United States, or any department thereof, goes to the destruction of all the limits prescribed to their power by the Constitution — That words meant by that instrument to be subsidiary only to the execution of the limited powers, ought not to be so construed as themselves to give unlimited powers, nor a part so to be taken, as to destroy the whole residue of the instrument. . . .

*   *   *

Resolved, lastly, . . . And that therefore, this Commonwealth is determined, as it doubts not its Co-States are, tamely to submit to undelegated and consequently unlimited powers in no man or body of men on earth: that if the acts before specified should stand, these conclusions would flow from them; that the General Government may place any act they think proper on the list of crimes, and punish it themselves, whether enumerated or not enumerated by the Constitution as cognizable by them; that they may transfer its cognizance to the President or any other person, who may himself be the accuser, counsel, judge and jury, whose suspicions may be the evidence, his order the sentence, his officer, the executioner, and his breast the sole record of the transaction; that . . . the barrier of the Constitution thus swept away from us all, no rampart now remains against the passions and the power of a majority of Congress, to protect from a like exportation or other more grievous punishment the minority of the same body, the Legislatures, Judges, Governors and Counsellors of the States, nor their other peaceable inhabitants who may venture to re-claim the Constitutional rights and liberties of the States and people, or who for other causes, good or bad, may be obnoxious to the views, or marked by the suspicions of the President, or be thought dangerous to his or their elections or other interests public or personal: that the friendless alien has indeed been selected as the safest subject of a first experiment; but the citizen will soon follow, or rather has already followed; for, already has a Sedition Act marked him as its prey: that these successive acts of the same character, unless arrested on the threshold, may tend to drive these States into revolution and blood; . . . free government is founded in jealousy and not in confidence; it is jealousy and not confidence which prescribes limited Constitutions to bind down those whom we are obliged to trust with power. . . . In questions of power, then let no more be heard of confidence in man, but bind him down from mischief, by the chains of the Constitution. That this Commonwealth does therefore call on its Co-States for an expression of their sentiments on the acts concerning aliens, and for the punishment of certain crimes herein-before specified, plainly declaring whether these acts are or are not authorized by the Federal Compact?

*   *   *

EDMUND BULLOCK, S.H.R.
JOHN CAMPBELL, S.S.P.T.
   Passed the House of Representatives, November 10th, 1798. Attest,
THOMAS TODD, C.H.R.
   In Senate, November 13th, 1798, unanimously concurred in. Attest,
B. THRUSTON, Clk. Sen.
   Approved, November 16th, 1798.
JAMES GARRARD, G.K.
   By the Governor.
HARRY TOULMIN, Secretary of State

71 Appeals to the Federal Judiciary — No Suits against One of the States (1798)

Article III, Section 2 of the Constitution provides that "The Judicial Power of the United States shall extend to . . . Controversies . . . between a State and Citizens of another State. . . ." Under the authority of this provision, the United States Supreme Court accepted jurisdiction in *Chisholm v. Georgia*, 2 U.S. (2 Dall.) 419 (1793). The decision prompted an angry reaction in the states, which saw such authority as another step toward the assertion of federal control over the affairs of the sovereign states. The response was swift. Congress met following the decision. It drafted, and the states quickly ratified, the Eleventh Amendment. Although the amendment by its terms speaks only of suits by citizens of other states and foreign subjects, the Supreme Court has construed the amendment to bar suits by citizens against their own states. Citizen applications to the federal judiciary to seek relief against abusive state laws and practices were thus constitutionally forbidden until after adoption of the Fourteenth Amendment. Meanwhile, conflicts between citizens and their states were left to be resolved on the local level.

☆71 United States Constitution, Amendment XI

The Judicial power of the United States shall not be construed to extend to any suit in law or equity, commenced or prosecuted against one of the United States by Citizens of another State, or by Citizens or Subjects of any Foreign State.

72 John Fries's Rebellion (1799-1800)

The first federal excise tax imposed on spirits (1791) led to the Whiskey Rebellion. A different tax imposed within the same decade, to satisfy Hamilton's desire to strengthen the federal government and to finance an expected war with France, gave rise to the similar rebellion of John Fries in 1799. A venue cryer with quickness of wit, Fries became a leader in the opposition. He represented the German-speaking populations of northern and southeastern Pennsylvania by opposing the collection of the new tax "based on the evaluation of lands and dwelling houses and the enumeration of slaves within the United States." When disorderly resistance to the tax led to the mobbing and threatening of the tax collectors, the federal authorities made several arrests. The rebels held local meetings and decided to rescue the prisoners.

Their elected leader, John Fries, proceeded to Bethlehem at the head of an ill-equipped column of about 140 men. Under the threat of arms, the marshall released the prisoners and the irregulars dispersed. But reports of the events reached President John Adams, and although all resistance to the law had ceased, Adams convened his cabinet and issued a proclamation accusing the insurgents of treason and ordering them to lay down their arms. John Fries was arrested, and federal troops proceeded to harass the local inhabitants suspected of opposition to the government. With peace restored, John Adams issued a general pardon.

☆72 Proclamations of President John Adams

☆72a By the President of the United States of America: Proclamation (March 12, 1799)

Reprinted in C. F. Adams, *The Works of John Adams* (New York: AMS Press, 1971), 9:174-75.

WHEREAS, combinations, to defeat the execution of the laws for the valuation of lands and dwelling houses within the United States, have existed within the counties of Northampton, Montgomery and Bucks, in the State of Pennsylvania, have proceeded in a manner subversive of the just authority of the government, by misrepresentations to render the laws odious, by deterring the officers of the United States to forbear the execution of their functions, and by openly threatening their lives. And whereas the endeavors of the well-effected citizens as well as of the executive officers to conciliate compliance with these laws, have failed of success, and certain persons in the county of Northampton, aforesaid, have been hardy enough to perpetrate certain acts, which, I am advised, amount to treason, being overt acts of levying war against the United States, the said persons exceeding one hundred in number, and armed and arrayed in warlike manner, having, on the seventh day of the present month of March, proceeded to the house of Abraham Levering, in the town of Bethlehem, and there compelled William Nichols, Marshal of the United States, for the District of Pennsylvania, to desist from the execution of certain legal processes in his hands to be executed, and having compelled him to discharge and set at liberty, certain persons whom he had arrested by virtue of a criminal process, duly issued for offenses against the United States, and having impeded and prevented the commissioners and assessor, in conformity with the laws aforesaid, by threats of personal injury, from executing the said laws, avowing, as the motive of these illegal and treasonable proceedings, an intention to prevent, by force of arms, the execution of the said laws, and to withstand, by open violence, the lawful authority of the United States. And, whereas, by the Constitution and laws of the United States, I am authorized, whenever the laws of the United States shall be opposed, or the execution thereof obstructed in any State, by combinations too powerful to be suppressed by the ordinary course of judicial proceedings, or by powers, vested in the Marshal, to call forth military force to suppress such combinations, and to cause the laws to be duly executed, and I have accordingly determined so to do, under the solemn conviction that the essential interest of the United States demand it.

Therefore, I, John Adams, President of the United States, do hereby command all persons, being insurgents as aforesaid, and all others whom it may concern, on or before Monday next being the eighteenth day of the present month, to disperse and retire peaceably to their respective abodes: and I do, moreover, warn all persons whomsoever, against aiding, abetting or comforting the perpetrators of the aforesaid treasonable acts, and I do require all officers and others, good and faithful citizens, according to their respective duties and laws of the land, to exert their utmost endeavors to prevent and suppress such dangerous and unlawful proceedings.

*   *   *

☆ 72b Proclamation by John Adams, President of the United States of America (May 21, 1800)

Reprinted in C. F. Adams, *The Works of John Adams* (New York: AMS Press, 1971), 9:178-79.

WHEREAS The late wicked and treasonable insurrection against the just authorities of the United States . . . in the State of Pennsylvania, in the year 1799, having been speedily suppressed without any of the calamities usually attending rebellion, whereupon peace, order, and submission to the laws of the United States were restored in the aforesaid counties, and the ignorant, misguided and misinformed in the counties have returned to a proper sense of their duty; whereby it is become unnecessary for the public good that any future prosecutions should be commenced or carried on against any person or persons, by reason of their being concerned in the said insurrection; wherefore be it known that I, John Adams, President of the United States of America, have granted, and by these presents do grant, a full free and absolute pardon, to all and every person or persons concerned in the said insurrection, excepting as hereinafter excepted, of all felonies, misdemeanors and other crimes by them respectively done or committed against the United States; in either of the said counties, before the 12th day of March, in the year 1799; excepting and excluding therefrom any person who now standeth indicted or convicted of any treason, misprision of treason, or other offence against the United States. . . .

73 The Greatest Crime That Any Man Can Commit (1800)

John Fries, leader of the antitax rebellion, was indicted and tried for treason. Alexander Dallas, a leading Jeffersonian who later would become Madison's secretary of the treasury, defended Fries. His first trial ended in a mistrial, but at the second trial before Justice Samuel Chase and Judge Richard Peters, Fries was convicted and sentenced to death. John Fries's lawyers withdrew from the trial on the grounds that Judge Chase's injudicious conduct made it impossible for them to defend their client. On advice of counsel, Fries rejected substitute counsel and defended himself. Justice Chase's final comment before imposing sentence represents the classic statement on the nonlegitimacy of disobedience to oppressive laws in the United States.

☆ 73 *Case of Fries*

9 F. Cas. 924 (C.C.D. Pa. 1800) (No. 5,127).

CHASE, Circuit Justice (charging jury): — "Gentlemen of the Jury: John Fries, the prisoner at the bar, stands indicted for the crime of treason, of levying war against the United States, contrary to the constitution. . . . It is the opinion of the court, that any insurrection or rising of any body of the people, within the United States, to attain or effect by force or violence any object of a great public nature, or of public and general (or national) concern, is a levying of war against the United States, within the contemplation and construction of the constitution. On this general position the court are of opinion, that any such insurrection or rising to resist, or to prevent by force or violence, the execution of any statute of the United States, . . . under any pretence, as that the statute was unjust, burthensome, oppressive, or unconstitutional, is a levying war against the United States, within the contemplation and construction of the constitution. The reason for this opinion is, that an insurrection to resist or prevent, by force, the execution of any statute of the United States, has a direct tendency to dissolve all the bands of society, to destroy all order and all laws, and also all security for the lives, liberties and property of the citizens of the United States. . . . The legal guilt of levying war may be incurred without the use of military weapons or military array. The court are of opinion that the assembling bodies of men, armed and arrayed in a warlike manner, for purposes only of a private nature, is not treason, although the judges, or other peace officers, should be insulted or resisted. . . .

"The true criterion to determine whether acts committed are treason, or a less offence (as a riot), is the quo animo, or the intention, with which the people did assemble. When the intention is universal or general, as to effect some object of a general public nature, it will be treason, and cannot be considered construed, or reduced to a riot. . . .

*   *   *

"The court are of opinion, that if a body of people conspire and meditate an insurrection to resist or oppose the execution of any statute of the United States by force, that they are only guilty of a high misdemeanour; but if they proceed to carry such intention into execution by force, that they are guilty of the treason of levying war, and the quantum of the force employed neither lessens nor increases the crime—whether by one hundred or one thousand persons, is wholly immaterial. The court are of opinion, that a combination or conspiracy to levy war against the United States is not treason, unless combined with an attempt to carry such combination or conspiracy into execution; some actual force or violence must be used, in pursuance of such design to levy war; but that it is altogether immaterial whether the force used is sufficient to effectuate the object—any force connected with the intention will constitute the crime of levying war. . . ."

*   *   *

The jury retired for the space of two hours, and brought in their verdict, "Guilty."

After the verdict was given, Judge CHASE, with great feeling and sensibility, addressed the prisoner, observing that, as he had no counsel on the trial, if he, or any person for him, could point out any flaw in the indictment, or legal ground for arrest of judgment, ample time would be allowed for that purpose.

*   *   *

The prisoner being set at the bar, Judge CHASE, after observing to the other defendants that what he had to say to Fries would apply generally to them, proceeded:—

"John Fries, you have been already informed, that you stood convicted of the treason, charged upon you by the indictment on which you have been arraigned, of levying war against the United States. You have had a legal, fair, and impartial trial, with every indulgence that the law would permit. Of the whole panel, you peremptorily challenged thirty-four, and with truth I may say, that the jury who tried you were of your own selection and choice. Not one of them before had ever formed and delivered any opinion respecting your guilt or innocence. The verdict of the jury against you was founded on the testimony of many creditable and unexceptionable witnesses. It was apparent from the conduct of the jury, when they delivered their verdict, that if innocent, they would have acquitted you with pleasure; and that they pronounced their verdict against you with great concern and reluctance, from a sense of duty to their country, and a full conviction of your

guilt. The crime of which you have been found guilty is treason; a crime considered, in the most civilized and the most free countries in the world, as the greatest that any man can commit. It is a crime of so deep a dye, and attended with such a train of fatal consequences, that it can receive no aggravation; yet the duty of my station requires that I should explain to you the nature of the crime of which you are convicted; to show the necessity of that justice which is this day to be administered, and to awaken your mind to proper reflections and a due sense of your own condition, which, I imagine, you must have reflected upon during your long confinement. You are a native of this country—you live under a constitution (or form of government) framed by the people themselves; and under laws made by your representatives, faithfully executed by independent and impartial judges. Your government secures to every member of the community equal liberty and equal rights; by which equality of liberty and rights, I mean, that every person, without any regard to wealth, rank, or station, may enjoy an equal share of civil liberty, and equal protection of law, and an equal security for his person and property. You enjoyed, in common with your fellow-citizens, all those rights. If experience should prove that the constitution is defective, it provides a mode to change or amend it, without any danger to public order, or any injury to social rights. If congress, from inattention, error in judgment, or want of information, should pass any law in violation of the constitution, or burdensome or oppressive to the people, a peaceable, safe and ample remedy is provided by the constitution. The people themselves have established the mode by which such grievances are to be redressed; and no other mode can be adopted without a violation of the constitution and of the laws. If congress should pass a law contrary to the constitution, such law would be void, and the courts of the United States possess complete authority, and are the only tribunal to decide, whether any law is contrary to the constitution. If congress should pass burdensome or oppressive laws, the remedy is with their constituents, from whom they derive their existence and authority. If any law is made repugnant to the voice of a majority of their constituents, it is in their power to make choice of persons to repeal it; but until it is repealed, it is the duty of every citizen to submit to it, and to give up his private sentiments to the public will. If a law which is burdensome, or even oppressive in its nature or execution, is to be opposed by force; and obedience cannot be compelled, there must soon be an end to all government in this country. . . .

"The insurrection in 1794, in the four western counties of this state (particularly in Washington), to oppose the execution of the laws of the United

States, which laid duties on stills, and spirits distilled, within the United States, is still fresh in memory: it originated from prejudices and misrepresentations industriously disseminated and diffused against those laws. Either persons disaffected to our government, or wishing to aggrandize themselves, deceived and misled the ignorant and uninformed class of the people. The opposition commenced in meetings of the people, with threats against the officers, which ripened into acts of outrage against them, and were extended to private citizens. Committees were formed to systematize and inflame the spirit of opposition. Violence succeeded to violence, and the collector of Fayette county was compelled to surrender his commission and official books; the dwelling house of the inspector (in the vicinity of Pittsburgh) was attacked and burnt; and the marshal was seized and obtained his liberty on a promise to serve no other process on the west side of the Alleghany mountains. To compel submission to the laws, the government were obliged to march an army against the insurgents, and the expense was above one million one hundred thousand dollars. Of the whole number of insurgents (many hundreds) only a few were brought to trial; and of them only two were sentenced to die (Vigol and Mitchell), and they were pardoned by the late president. Although the insurgents made no resistance to the army sent against them, yet not a few of our troops lost their lives, in consequence of their great fatigue, and exposure to the severity of the season. This great and remarkable clemency of the government had no effect upon you, and the deluded people in your neighbourhood. The rise, progress, and termination of the late insurrection bear a strong and striking analogy to the former; and it may be remembered that it has cost the United States 80,000 dollars. It cannot escape observation, that the ignorant and uninformed are taught to complain of taxes, which are necessary for the support of government, and yet they permit themselves to be seduced into insurrections which have so enormously increased the public burthens, of which their contributions can scarcely be calculated. When citizens combine and assemble with intent to prevent by threats, intimidation and violence, the execution of the laws, and they actually carry such traitorous designs into execution, they reduce the government to the alternative of prostrating the laws before the insurgents, or of taking necessary measures to compel submission. No government can hesitate. The expense, and all the consequences, therefore, are not imputable to the government, but to the insurgents. The mildness and lenity of our government are as striking on the late as on the former insurrection. Of nearly one hundred and thirty persons who might have been put on their trial for treason, only five have been prosecuted and tried for that crime.

"In the late insurrection, you, John Fries, bore a conspicuous and leading part. If you had reflected, you would have seen that your attempt was as weak as it was wicked. It was the height of folly in you to suppose that the great body of our citizens, blessed in enjoyment of a free republican government of their own choice, and of all rights civil and religious; secure in their persons and property; and conscious that the laws are the only security for their preservation from violence, would not rise up as one man to oppose and crush so ill-founded, so unprovoked an attempt to disturb the public peace and tranquillity. If you could see in a proper light your own folly and wickedness, you ought now to bless God that your insurrection was so happily and speedily quelled by the vigilance and energy of our government, aided by the patriotism and activity of your fellow-citizens, who left their homes and business and embodied themselves in the support of its laws. The annual, necessary expenditures for the support of any extensive government like ours must be great; and the sum required can only be obtained by taxes, or loans. In all countries the levying taxes is unpopular, and a subject of complaint. It appears to me that there was not the least pretence of complaint against, much less of opposition and violence to, the law for levying taxes on dwelling-houses; and it becomes you to reflect that the time you chose to rise up in arms to oppose the laws of your country, was when it stood in a very critical situation with regard to France, and on the eve of a rupture with that country. . . . In your serious hours of reflection, you ought to consider the consequences that would have flowed from the insurrection, which you incited, encouraged, and promoted. . . . Violence, oppression and rapine, destruction, waste, and murder, always attend the progress of insurrection and rebellion; the arm of the father would have been raised against the son; that of the son against the father; a brother's hand would have been stained with brother's blood; the sacred bands of friendship would have been broken, and all the ties of natural affection would have been dissolved.

"The end of all punishment is example; and the enormity of your crime requires that a severe example should be made to deter others from the commission of like crimes in future. You have forfeited your life to justice. . . . The judgment of the law is, and this court doth award, "that you be hanged by the neck until dead," and I pray God Almighty to be merciful to your soul!"

74 How Should the Pennsylvania Insurgents Be Treated? (1800)

Fries submitted a petition requesting forgiveness. He raised objections on the grounds that Justice

Chase had tried the case in Philadelphia, in contradiction of the United States' laws requiring a crime to be judged in the county in which it was committed. He also claimed Justice Chase unreasonably limited the arguments of counsel, precipitating their resignation from the case.

The Adams cabinet, taking refuge in the letter of this law, unanimously advised that Fries be hanged. Secretary of the Treasury Wolcott urged that the whole state should be cleansed, since Pennsylvania was "the most villainous compound of heterogeneous matter conceivable." President Adams, however, overruled his cabinet and pardoned John Fries and his followers. Adams's questions provide a glimpse of the broad factors that surround political criminality. He considered not only the penitence and the character of the condemned men, as in any other pardon, but also the public effect of the decision and the degree of danger to the country posed by the crime.

☆74 The Offender, the President, and the Cabinet

Reprinted from C. F. Adams, ed., *The Works of John Adams* (New York: AMS Press, 1971), 9:56–61.

☆74a The Petition of John Fries (Philadelphia Prison, May 1800)

To the President of the United States:

The petition of John Fries respectfully showeth; that your prisoner is one of those deluded and unfortunate men, who, at the Circuit Court of this district, has been convicted of treason against the United States, for which offense he is pressed with a just sense of the crime which he has committed, and with the sincerity of a penitent offender, he entreats mercy and pardon from him on whose determination rests the fate of an unfortunate man. He solicits the interference of the President to save him from an ignominious death, and to rescue a large, and hitherto happy family, from future misery and ruin. If the prayer of his petition should be granted, he will show, by a future course of good conduct, his gratitude to his offended country by a steady and active support of that excellent Constitution and laws, which it has been his misfortune to violate and oppose.

John Fries

*   *   *

☆74b To the Heads of Departments (President's Communication, May 20, 1800)

Philadelphia, 20 May 1800

1. Among the three criminals under sentence of death, is there any discrimination in the essential circumstances of their cases, which would justify a determination to pardon or reprieve one or two, and execute the other?

2. Is the execution of one or more so indispensably demanded by public justice and by the security of the public peace, that mercy cannot be extended to all three, or any two, or one?

3. Will the national Constitution acquire more confidence in the minds of the American people by the execution than by the pardon of one or more of the offenders?

4. Is it clear beyond all reasonable doubt that the crime of which they stand convicted, amounts to a levying of war against the United States, or, in other words, to treason?

5. Is there any evidence of a secret correspondence or combination with other anti-federalists of any denomination in other States in the Union, or in other parts of this State, to rise in force against the execution of the law for taxing houses, &c., or for opposing the commissioners in general in the execution of their offices?

6. *Quo animo* was this insurrection? Was it a design of general resistance to all law, or any particular law? Or was it particular to the place and persons?

7. Was it any thing more than a riot, high-handed, aggravated, daring, and dangerous indeed, for the purpose of a rescue? This is a high crime, but can it strictly amount to treason?

8. Is there not great danger in establishing such a construction of treason, as may be applied to every sudden, ignorant, inconsiderate heat, among a part of the people, wrought up by political disputes, and personal or party animosities?

9. Will not a career of capital executions for treason, once opened, without actual bloodshed or hostility against any military force of government, inflict a deep wound in the minds of the people, inflame their animosities, and make them more desperate in sudden heats, and thoughtless riots in elections, and on other occasions where political disputes run high, and introduce a more sanguinary disposition among them?

10. Is not the tranquillity in the western counties, since the insurrection there, and the subsequent submission to law, a precedent in favor of clemency?

11. Is there any probability that a capital execution will have any tendency to change the political sentiments of the people?

12. Will not clemency have a greater tendency to correct their errors?

13. Are not the fines and imprisonments, imposed and suffered, a sufficient discouragement, for the present, of such crimes?

John Adams

☆ 74c The Heads of the Departments to the President (May 20, 1800)

Philadelphia, 20 May 1800

Having considered the questions proposed by the President for our consideration, we respectfully submit the following opinions.

That the intent of the insurgents in Pennsylvania, in 1798, was to prevent the execution of the law, directing the valuation of houses and lands, and the enumeration of slaves, in the particular district of country where they resided. That we know of no combination in other States, and presume that no combination, pervading the whole State of Pennsylvania, was actually formed. We believe, however, that if the government had not adopted prompt measures, the spirit of insurrection would have rapidly extended.

We are of opinion that the crime committed by Fries, Heyney, and Getman, amounted to treason, and that no danger can arise to the community from the precedents already established by the judges upon this subject. We cannot form a certain judgment of the effect upon public opinion, of suffering the law to have its course, but we think it must be beneficial, by inspiring the well disposed with confidence in the government, and the malevolent and factious with terror.

The Attorney-General and the Secretary of the Navy, however, believe that the execution of one will be enough to show the power of the laws to punish, and may be enough for example, the great end of punishment, and that Fries deserves most to suffer; because though all are guilty, and all have forfeited their lives to the justice of their country, he was the most distinguished in the commission of the crime. The Secretary of the Treasury perceives no good ground for any distinction in the three cases, and he believes that a discrimination, instead of being viewed as an act of mercy, would too much resemble a sentence against an unfortunate individual. He also believes that the mercy of government has been sufficiently manifested by the proceedings of the Attorney of the United States, and that the cause of humanity will be most effectually promoted by impressing an opinion that those who are brought to trial, and convicted of treason, will not be pardoned.

CHARLES LEE
OLIVER WOLCOTT
BEN. STODDERT

75 "lose the respect both of friends and foes" (1800)

President Adams's pardon of Fries and other participants in the rebellion outraged Alexander Hamilton, who had suggested Adams's earlier hard-line position. Hamilton's letter criticized the decision and focused on Adams's previous opinion that Washington's clemency in the Whiskey Rebellion "had been the cause of the second insurrection and that Adams would take care there should not be a third." Hamilton speculated regarding the "novel doctrine" presented by Fries's counsel that treason required more than resistance to and interference with law — it required an act of a military nature.

☆ 75 Letter from Alexander Hamilton Opposing the Fries Pardon

Case of Fries, 9 F. Cas. 924, 944 N. 2 (C.C.D. Pa. 1800) (No. 5,127).

The last material occurrence in the administration of Mr. Adams of which I shall take notice, is the pardon of Fries, and other principals in the late insurrection in Pennsylvania. It is a fact, that a very refractory spirit has long existed in the western counties of that state. Repeatedly, have its own laws been opposed with violence, and as often, according to my information, with impunity. It is also a fact which everybody knows, that the laws of the Union, in the vital article of revenue, have been twice resisted in the same state, by combinations so extensive and under circumstances so violent, as to have called for the employment of military force. . . . Two insurrections in the same state, the one upon the heels of the other, demonstrated a spirit of insubordination or disaffection which required a strong corrective. It is a disagreeable fact, forming a weighty argument in the question, that a large part of the population of Pennsylvania, is of a composition which peculiarly fits it for the intrigues of factious men, who may disturb or overthrow the government. And it is an equally disagreeable fact, that disaffection to the national government is in no other state more general, more deeply rooted, or more envenomed. . . . It ought to be added, that the impunity so often experienced, had made it an article in the creed of those, who were actuated by the insurgent spirit, that neither the general not [*sic*] the state government dared to inflict capital punishment. To destroy this persuasion, to repress this dangerous spirit, it was essential that a salutary rigour should have been exerted, and that those who were under the influence of the one and the other, should be taught that they were the dupes of a fatal illusion. Of this Mr. Adams appeared so sensible [declaring] . . . with no small ostentation, that the mistaken clemency of Washington on the former occasion, had been the cause of the second insurrection, and that he would take care there should not be a third, giving the laws their full course against the convicted offenders. Yet he thought proper, as if distrusting the courts and officers of the United States, to resort, through the attorney general, to the counsel of the culprits, for a statement of their cases; in which was found, besides some objections of form, the novel doctrine, disavowed by every page of our law books, that treason does no [sic] consist of resistance by force to a public law, unless it be an act relative to the militia, or other military force. And upon this, or some other ground not easy to be comprehended, he of a sudden departed from all his former declarations, and against the unanimous advice of his ministers, with the attorney general, came to the resolution, which he executed, of pardoning all those which had received sentence of death. No wonder that the public was thunder-struck at such a result, that the friends of government regarded it as a virtual dereliction; it was impossible to commit a greater error. This particular situation of Pennsylvania, the singular posture of human affairs, in which there is so strong a tendency to the disorganization of the government, the turbulent and malignant humours which exist, and are so industriously nourished throughout the United States; everything loudly demanded that the executive should have acted with exemplary vigour, and should have given a striking demonstration, that condign punishment would be the lot of the violent opposers of the laws. . . . It is by temporizings like these, that men at the head of affairs, lose the respect both of friends and foes; it is by temporizings like these, that in times of fermentation and commotion, governments are prostrated, which might easily have been upheld by an erect and imposing attitude.

*   *   *

76 "to regain the road which alone leads to peace, liberty, and safety" (1801)

In the 1800 elections, the Federalists, in popular disfavor since the Alien and Sedition Acts, lost power in Congress as well as the presidency. Thomas Jefferson, the Republican candidate, won the presidential election. (Aaron Burr, who introduced the machinery of modern American politics in New York, was elected vice-president.) The new dominant party stood for the primacy of state authority in areas of power not explicitly delegated to the central government, and the inaugural address reflected the principles of the Virginia and Kentucky resolutions as well as Jefferson's belief in the importance of tolerating political dissent and opposition.

Although he placed the will of the majority at the pinnacle of our protections of liberty, Jefferson noted, "To be rightful, it must be reasonable." He also rested the liberties of the people on the procedural protections of the Bill of Rights. Jefferson acted on his beliefs by releasing all those convicted under the Alien and Sedition Acts. In his speech, he

nevertheless expressed a hope for, and presumed a unity of loyalty among, the citizens.

☆76 First Inaugural Address by Thomas Jefferson (March 4, 1801)

Reprinted in J. Richardson, ed., *A Compilation of the Messages and Papers of the Presidents* (New York: Bureau of National Literature, 1897), 1:321-24.

FRIENDS AND FELLOW CITIZENS: Called upon to undertake the duties of the first executive office of our country, I avail myself of the presence of that portion of my fellow citizens which is here assembled, to express my grateful thanks for the favor with which they have been pleased to look toward me. . . .

During the contest of opinion through which we have passed, the animation of discussion and of exertions has sometimes worn an aspect which might impose on strangers unused to think freely and to speak and to write what they think; but this being now decided by the voice of the nation, announced according to the rules of the constitution, all will, of course, arrange themselves under the will of the law, and unite in common efforts for the common good. All, too, will bear in mind this sacred principle, that though the will of the majority is in all cases to prevail, that will, to be rightful, must be reasonable; that the minority possess their equal rights, which equal laws must protect, and to violate which would be oppression. Let us, then, fellow citizens, unite with one heart and one mind. Let us restore to social intercourse that harmony and affection without which liberty and even life itself are but dreary things. And let us reflect that having banished from our land that religious intolerance under which mankind so long bled and suffered, we have yet gained little if we countenance a political intolerance as despotic, as wicked, and capable of as bitter and bloody persecutions. . . . But every difference of opinion is not a difference of principle. We have called by different names brethren of the same principle. We are all republicans—we are federalists. If there be any among us who would wish to dissolve this Union or to change its republican form, let them stand undisturbed as monuments of the safety with which error of opinion may be tolerated where reason is left free to combat it. I know, indeed, that some honest men fear that a republican government cannot be strong; that this government is not strong enough. But would the honest patriot, in the full tide of successful experiment, abandon a government which has so far kept us free and firm, on the theoretic and visionary fear that this government, the world's best hope, may by possibility want energy to preserve itself? I trust not. I believe this, on the contrary, the strongest government on earth. I believe it is the only one where every man, at the call of the laws, would fly to the standard of the law, and would meet invasions of the public order as his own personal concern. . . .

... [W]hat more is necessary to make us a happy and prosperous and frugal government, which shall restrain men from injuring one another, which shall leave them otherwise free to regulate their own pursuits of industry and improvement, and shall not take from the mouth of labor the bread it has earned. This is the sum of good government, and this is necessary to close the circle of our felicities.

About to enter, fellow citizens, on the exercise of duties which comprehend everything dear and valuable to you, it is proper that you should understand what I deem the essential principles of our government, and consequently those which ought to shape its administration. I will compress them within the narrowest compass they will bear, stating the general principle, but not all its limitations. Equal and exact justice to all men, of whatever state or persuasion, religious or political; peace, commerce and honest friendship with all nations — entangling alliances with none; the support of the State governments in all their rights, as the most competent administrations for our domestic concerns and the surest bulwarks against anti-republican tendencies; the preservation of the general government in its whole constitutional vigor, as the sheet anchor of our peace at home and safety abroad; a jealous care of the right of election by the people — a mild and safe corrective of abuses of which are lopped by the sword of the revolution where peaceable remedies are unprovided; absolute acquiescence in the decisions of the majority — the vital principle of republics, from which there is no appeal but to force, the vital principle and immediate parent of despotism; ... the diffusion of information and the arraignment of all abuses at the bar of public reason; freedom of religion; freedom of the press; freedom of person under the protection of the habeas corpus; and trial by juries impartially selected — these principles form the bright constellation which has gone before us, and guided our steps through an age of revolution and reformation. The wisdom of our sages and the blood of our heroes have been devoted to their attainment. They should be the creed of our political faith — the text of civil instruction — the touchstone by which to try the services of those we trust; and should we wander from them in moments of error or alarm, let us hasten to retrace our steps and to regain the road which alone leads to peace, liberty, and safety. ...

*   *   *

... I ask so much confidence only as may give firmness and effect to the legal administration of your affairs. I shall often go wrong through defect of judgment. When right, I shall often be thought wrong by those whose positions will not command a view of the whole ground. I ask your indulgence for my own errors, which will never be intentional; and your support against the errors of others, who condemn what they would not if seen in all its parts.

*   *   *

77 Not Acting under the Government's Secret Patronage (1807)

In 1800, the Constitution provided that the person who received the second highest vote in the Electoral College was to serve as vice-president. Although the Jeffersonian Republicans won the elections of 1800, the vote in the Electoral College produced a tie between Jefferson and Aaron Burr of New York — Jefferson's supposed running mate — throwing the election into the House of Representatives. There, the still powerful Federalist faction rallied around Burr as a more acceptable president than their bitter foe, Jefferson. But Federalist Alexander Hamilton's implacable opposition to Burr, stemming from political infighting in New York, finally secured the election for Jefferson. (Burr subsequently killed Hamilton in a duel in 1804.) Although Burr did not campaign actively in the House for the presidency, Jefferson harbored an opinion that Burr had a treacherous streak.

At the conclusion of his term in office as vice-president, this unusually gifted leader found himself politically and financially ruined. President Jefferson used the power of his office to reduce Burr's support among the Republicans in his New York base. Hamilton, the leader of the Federalists, blocked any rapprochement between Burr and that party in New York. These activities frustrated Burr's ambitions, and his duel with Alexander Hamilton, whom he sought to dethrone in order to assume leadership of the Federalists, turned him into a social pariah and a fugitive from justice.

When word reached President Jefferson of Burr's enterprises, he was prepared to believe the worst. On November 27, 1806, Jefferson assembled his cabinet and issued a proclamation charging unidentified "sundry persons" with conspiracy to attack the possessions of the king of Spain and ordering that all men and property engaged in this enterprise be seized and detained. The following message to Congress expounded the government's position with regard to Burr's activities.

☆ 77 Jefferson's Message on the Burr Conspiracy to the Senate and House of Representatives of the United States (January 22, 1807)

Reprinted in J. Richardson, ed., *A Compilation of the Messages and Papers of the Presidents* (New York: Bureau of National Literature, 1897), 195-97.

Agreeably to the request of the House of Representatives communicated in their resolution of the 16th instant, I proceed to state, under the reserve therein expressed, information received touching an illegal combination of private individuals against the peace and safety of the Union, and a military expedition planned by them against the territories of a power in amity with the United States, with the measures I have pursued for suppressing the same....

Some time in the latter part of September I received intimations that designs were in agitation in the Western country unlawful and unfriendly to the peace of the Union, and that the prime mover in these was Aaron Burr, heretofore distinguished by the favor of his country....

*   *   *

... [I]t was known that many boats were under preparation, stores of provisions collecting, and an unusual number of suspicious characters in motion on the Ohio and its waters. Besides dispatching the confidential agent to that quarter, orders were at the time sent to the governors of the Orleans and Mississippi Territories and to the commanders of the land and naval forces there to be on their guard against surprise and in constant readiness to resist any enterprise which might be attempted on the vessels, posts, or other objects under their care; and on the 8th of November instructions were forwarded to General Wilkinson to hasten an accommodation with the Spanish commandant on the Sabine, and as soon as that was effected to fall back with his principal force to the hither bank of the Mississippi for the defense of the interesting points on that river. By a letter received from that officer on the 25th of November, we learnt that a confidential agent of Aaron Burr had been deputed to him with communications, partly written in cipher and partly oral, explaining his designs, exaggerating his resources, and making such offers of emolument and command to engage him and the army in his unlawful enterprise as he had flattered himself would be successful. The General, ... immediately dispatched a trusty officer to me with information of what had passed....

The General's letter ... and some other information received a few days earlier, when brought together developed Burr's general design.... It appeared that he contemplated two distinct objects, which might be carried on either jointly or separately, and either the one or the other first, as circumstances should direct. One of these was the severance of the Union of these States by the Alleghany Mountains; the other an attack on Mexico....

He found at once that the attachment of the Western country to the present Union was not to be shaken; that its dissolution could not be effected with the consent of its inhabitants, and that his re-

sources were inadequate as yet to effect it by force. He took his course then at once, determined to seize on New Orleans, plunder the bank there, possess himself of the military and naval stores, and proceed on his expedition to Mexico, and to this object all his means and preparations were now directed. He collected from all the quarters where himself or his agents possessed influence all the ardent, restless, desperate, and disaffected persons who were ready for any enterprise analogous to their characters. He seduced good and well-meaning citizens, some by assurances that he possessed the confidence of the Government and was acting under its secret patronage, a pretense which procured some credit from the state of our difference with Spain, and others by offers of land in Bastrop's claim on the Washita....

*   *   *

Surmises have been hazarded that this enterprise is to receive aid from certain foreign powers; but these surmises are without proof or probability....

By letters from General Wilkinson ... I received the important affidavit [by which] it will be seen that of three of the principal emissaries of Mr. Burr whom the General had caused to be apprehended, one had been liberated by habeas corpus, and two others ... have been embarked by him for ports in the Atlantic states.... As soon as these persons shall arrive they will be delivered to the custody of the law and left to such course of trial, both as to place and process, as the functionaries of the law may direct....

Tн. Jefferson

78 "conspiracy is not treason" (1807)

Burr instructed Erick Bollman and Samuel Swartwout to carry copies of his own coded letter to General Wilkinson. After their arrest, they were charged with treason and taken to Washington where they filed a petition for a writ of habeas corpus from the United States Supreme Court. After preliminary arguments in which the government contended that the Supreme Court did not have jurisdiction to issue the Great Writ, the following opinion was written. The questions in the cases were difficult for the court to resolve, as only four members were sitting, and there was a two-two split on central evidentiary issues.

☆ 78 *Ex Parte Bollman and Swartwout*

8 U.S. (4 Cranch) 75 (1807).

Marshall, Ch. J., delivered the opinion of the court,—The prisoners having been brought before this court on a writ of *habeas corpus*, ... the question to be determined is, whether the accused shall be discharged or held to trial. . . .

The specific charge brought against the prisoners is treason, in levying war against the United States.

*   *   *

To constitute that specific crime for which the prisoners now before the court have been committed, war must be actually levied against the United States. However flagitious may be the crime of conspiring to subject by force the government of our country, such conspiracy is not treason. To conspire to levy war, and actually to levy war, are distinct offences. The first must be brought into open action, by the assemblage of men for a purpose treasonable itself, or the fact of levying war cannot have been committed. . . .

It is not the intention of the court to say, that no individual can be guilty of this crime, who has not appeared in arms against his country. On the contrary, if war be actually levied, that is, if a body of men be actually assembled, for the purpose of effecting by force a treasonable purpose, all those who perform any part, however minute, or however remote from the scene of action, and who are actually leagued in the general conspiracy, are to be considered as traitors. But there must be an actual assembling of men, for the treasonable purpose, to constitute a levying of war.

*   *   *

To complete the crime of levying war against the United States, there must be an actual assemblage of men for the purpose of executing a treasonable design. In the case now before the court, a design to overturn the government of the United States, in New Orleans, by force, would have been unquestionably a design which, if carried into execution, would have been treason, and the assemblage of a body of men for the purpose of carrying it into execution, would amount to levying of war against the United States; but no conspiracy for this object, no enlisting of men to effect it, would be an actual levying of war.

. . . That the letter from Col. Burr to General Wilkinson relates to a military enterprise meditated by the former, has not been questioned. If this enterprise was against Mexico, it would amount to a high misdemeanor; if against any of the territories of the United States, or if, in its progress, the subversion of the government of the United States, in any of their territories, was a mean, clearly and necessarily, to be employed, if such mean formed a substantive part of the plan, the assemblage of a body of men to effect it, would be levying war against the United States.

*   *   *

The letter is in language which furnishes no distinct view of the design of the writer. The co-opera-

tion, however, which is stated to have been secured, points strongly to some expedition against the territories of Spain. After making these general statements, the writer becomes rather more explicit, and says, "Burr's plan of operations is to move down rapidly from the falls, on the 15th of November, with the first 500 or 1000 men, in light boats now constructing for that purpose, to be at Natchez, between the 5th and 15th of December, there to meet Wilkinson; then to determine whether it will be expedient, in the first instance, to seize on, or to pass by, Baton Rouge. The people of the country to which we are going are prepared to receive us. Their agents, now with Burr, say, that if we will protect their religion, and will not subject them to a foreign power, in three weeks, all will be settled."

There is no expression in these sentences, which would justify a suspicion, that any territory of the United States was the object of the expedition. For what purpose, seize on Baton Rouge? Why engage Spain against this enterprise, if it was designed against the United States?

*   *   *

There certainly is not in the letter delivered to General Wilkinson, so far as the letter is laid before the court, one syllable which has a necessary or a natural reference to an enterprise against any territory of the United States. That the bearer of this letter must be considered as acquainted with its contents, is not to be controverted. The letter and his own declarations evince the fact. . . . [H]e states their object to be, "to carry an expedition to the Mexican provinces." This statement may be considered as explanatory of the letter of Col. Burr, if the expressions of that letter could be thought ambiguous.

But there are other declarations made by Mr. Swartwout, which constitute the difficulty of this case. On an inquiry from General Wilkinson, he said, "this territory would be revolutionized, where the people were ready to join them, and that there would be some seizing, he supposed, at New Orleans." If these words import that the government established by the United States in any of its territories, was to be revolutionized by force, although merely as a step to, or a mean of executing some greater projects, the design was unquestionably treasonable, and any assemblage of men for that purpose would amount to a levying of war. But on the import of the words, a difference of opinion exists. Some of the judges suppose, they refer to the territory against which the expedition was intended; others to that in which the conversation was held. Some consider the words, if even applicable to a territory of the United States, as alluding to a revolution to be effected by the people, rather than by the party conducted by Col. Burr.

But whether this treasonable intention be really imputable to the plan or not, it is admitted, that it must have been carried into execution by an open assemblage of men for that purpose, previous to the arrest of the prisoner, in order to consummate the crime as to him; and a majority of the court is of opinion, that the conversation of Mr. Swartwout affords no sufficient proof of such assembling.

*   *   *

... The mere enlisting of men, without assembling them, is not levying war. The question then, is, whether this evidence proves Col. Burr to have advanced so far in levying an army, as actually to have assembled them.

It is argued, that since it cannot be necessary that the whole 7000 men should have assembled, their commencing their march, by detachments, to the place of rendezvous, must be sufficient to constitute the crime. This position is correct, with some qualification. It cannot be necessary, that the whole army should assemble, and that various parts which are to compose it should have combined. But it is necessary, that there should be an actual assemblage, and therefore, the evidence should make the fact unequivocal. The travelling of individuals to the place of rendezvous would, perhaps, not be sufficient. This would be an equivocal act, and has no warlike appearance. The meeting of particular bodies of men, and their marching from places of partial to a place of general rendezvous, would be such an assemblage.

The particular words used by Mr. Swartwout are, that Col. Burr "was levying an armed body of 7000 men." If the term levying, in this place, imports that they were assembled, then such fact would amount, if the intention be against the United States, to levying war. If it barely imports that he was enlisting or engaging them in his service, the fact would not amount to levying war. It is thought sufficiently apparent, that the latter is the sense in which the term was used. The fact alluded to, if taken in the proper sense, is of a nature so to force itself upon the public view, that if the army had then actually assembled, either together or in detachments, some evidence of such assembling would have been laid before the court.

The words used by the prisoner, in reference to seizing at New Orleans, and borrowing, perhaps by force, from the bank, though indicating a design to rob, and consequently, importing a high offence, do not designate the specific crime of levying war against the United States.

It is, therefore, the opinion of a majority of the court, that in the case of Samuel Swartwout there is not sufficient evidence of his levying war against the United States to justify his commitment on the charge of treason.

Against Erick Bollman, there is still less testimony. Nothing has been said by him, to support the charge that the enterprise in which he was engaged had any other object than stated in the letter of Col. Burr. Against him, therefore, there is no evidence to support a charge of treason.

*   *   *

79 "obviously a military enterprise" (1807)

"The conspiracies of Aaron Burr remain one of the greatest enigmas in American history," wrote historian Nathaniel Weyl. A member of a distinguished family, graduate of Princeton at age sixteen, a leader of New York's Society of Tammany as well as United States Senator from New York, and vice-president in 1800, Burr had little in his history to suggest that he would become the supreme conspirator in American history.

Burr's conspiracy was an act of grandeur as well as desperation. Some historians believe that his aim was to dismember the United States and establish an independent nation, west of the Alleghanies. Talk of secession from the young United States, whether by the mercantile interests of New England or the populists of the West, dominated American political discussion. Others suggest that he was intent on conquering Mexico and making himself its emperor. Holding secret meetings with the British minister to Washington, conspiring with Major General James Wilkinson—governor of the northern part of the newly acquired Louisiana Territory—and building alliances with such western expansionists as Andrew Jackson, Henry Clay, and John C. Calhoun, Burr had one or more enterprises on his mind.

An Irish expatriate supporter of Burr owned Blennerhassett's Island in the Ohio River. It was used as a base of operations for recruitment, and provisions for a military force were established. But on November 25, 1806, General Wilkinson denounced the plan to Jefferson, describing it as an imperial expedition aginst Vera Cruz. Jefferson issued a proclamation warning the citizenry of the Burr conspiracy. On January 17, 1807, Burr surrendered to the acting governor of the Louisiana Territory. In Richmond, Virginia, circuit-riding John Marshall, chief justice of the United States Supreme Court and a bitter opponent of Jefferson, tried Aaron Burr in 1807. The first determination was whether enough evidence existed to require Burr to undergo trial for treason. Marshall, scrupulously adhering to constitutional language, held that Burr could not be indicted for treason, only for the lesser charge of mounting "a military expedition against a nation with whom the United States was at peace."

☆ 79 *United States v. Burr* (April 1807)

25 F. Cas. 2 (C.C.D. Va. 1807) (No. 14,692a).

MARSHALL, Chief Justice. I am required on the part of the attorney for the United States to commit the accused on two charges: (1) For setting on foot and providing the means for an expedition against the territories of a nation at peace with the United States. (2) For committing high treason against the United States.

*   *   *

The first charge stands upon the testimony of General Eaton and General Wilkinson.... To make the testimony of General Wilkinson bear on Colonel Burr, it is necessary to consider as genuine the letter stated by the former to be, as nearly as he can make it, an interpretation of one received in cypher from the latter. Exclude this letter, and nothing remains in the testimony which can in the most remote degree affect Colonel Burr....

*   *   *

... The enterprise described in this letter is obviously a military enterprise, and must have been intended either against the United States, or against the territories of some other power on the continent, with all of whom the United States were at peace. The expressions of this letter must be admitted to furnish at least probable cause for believing that the means for the expedition were provided. In every part of it we find declarations indicating that he was providing the means for the expedition; and as these means might be provided in secret, I do not think that further testimony ought to be required to satisfy me that there is probable cause for committing the prisoner on this charge....

The second charge exhibited against the prisoner is high treason against the United States in levying war against them. As this is the most atrocious offence which can be committed against the political body, so is it the charge which is most capable of being employed as the instrument of those malignant and vindictive passions which may rage in the bosoms of contending parties struggling for power. It is that of which the people of America have been most jealous, and therefore, while other crimes are unnoticed, they have refused to trust the national legislature with the definition of this, but have themselves declared in their constitution that "it shall consist only in levying war against the United States, or in adhering to their enemies, giving them aid and comfort." This high crime consists of overt acts, which must be proved by two witnesses, or by the confession of the party in open court. Under the control of this constitutional regulation, I am to inquire whether the testimony laid before me furnishes probable cause in support of this charge....

That part of [General Eaton's] deposition which bears upon this charge is the plan disclosed by the prisoner for seizing upon New Orleans, and revolutionizing the Western states. That this plan, if consummated by overt acts, would amount to treason, no man will controvert. But it is equally clear that an intention to commit treason is an offence entirely distinct from the actual commission of that crime. War can only be levied by the employment of actual force. Troops must be embodied, men must be assembled, in order to levy war. If Colonel Burr had been apprehended on making these communications to General Eaton, could it have been alleged that he had gone further than to meditate the crime? Could it have been said that he had actually collected forces and had actually levied war? Most certainly it could not. The crime really complete was a conspiracy to commit treason, not an actual commission of treason. If these communications were not treason at the instant they were made, no lapse of time can make them so. They are not in themselves acts. They may serve to explain the intention with which acts were committed, but they cannot supply those acts if they be not proved. The next testimony is the deposition of General Wilkinson, which consists of the letter already noticed, and of the communications made by the bearer of that letter. This letter has already been considered by the supreme court of the United States, and has been declared to import, taken by itself or in connection with Eaton's deposition, rather an expedition against Mexico than the territories of the United States. [Upon the meaning of Mr. Swartwout's testimony] ... it appears that the supreme court was divided. I therefore hold myself at liberty to pursue my own opinion, which was, that the words "this territory must be revolutionized" did not so clearly apply to a foreign territory as to reject that sense which would make them applicable to a territory of the United States, at least so far as to admit of further inquiry into their meaning. And if a territory of the United States was to be revolutionized, though only as a means for an expedition against a foreign power, the act would be treason. This reasoning leads to the conclusion that there is probable cause for the allegation that treasonable designs were entertained by the prisoner so late as July last, when this letter was written.

It remains to inquire whether there is also probable cause to believe that these designs have been ripened into the crime itself, by actually levying war against the United States. It has been already observed that, to constitute this crime, troops must be embodied, men must be actually assembled; and these are facts which cannot remain invisible. Treason may be machinated in secret, but it can be perpetrated only in open day, and in the eye of the world. Testimony of a fact which in its own nature is so notorious ought to be unequivocal. The testimony now offered has been laid before the supreme court of the United States and has been determined in the Cases of Bollman and Swartwout not to furnish probable cause for the opinion that war had been actually levied.... The first piece of testimony relied on to render this fact probable is the declaration of Mr. Swartwout, that "Colonel Burr was levying an armed body of 7,000 men...." The term "levying" has been said, according to the explanation of the lexicons, to mean the embodying of troops, and therefore to prove what is required. Although I do not suppose that Mr. Swartwout had consulted a dictionary, I have looked into Johnson for the term, and find its first signification to be "to raise"; its second, "to bring together." In common parlance, it may signify the one or the other. But its sense is certainly decided by the fact. If when Mr. Swartwout left Colonel Burr, which must be supposed to have been in July, he was actually embodying men from New York to the Western states, what could veil his troops from human sight? An invisible army is not the instrument of war, and had these troops been visible, some testimony relative to them could have been adduced. I take the real sense, then, in which this term was used to be, that Colonel Burr was raising, or in other words engaging or enlisting, men through the country described, for the enterprise he meditated.... I shall readily avow my opinion, that the strength of the presumption arising from this testimony ought to depend greatly on the time at which the application is made. If soon after the period at which the troops were to assemble, when full time had not elapsed to ascertain the fact, these circumstances had been urged as the ground for a commitment on the charge of treason, I should have thought them entitled to great consideration. I will not deny that, in the Cases of Bollman and Swartwout, I was not perfectly satisfied that they did not warrant an inquiry into the fact. But I think every person must admit that the weight of these circumstances daily diminishes....

The fact to be proved in this case is an act of public notoriety. It must exist in the view of the world, or it cannot exist at all. The assembling of forces to levy war is a visible transaction, and numbers must witness it. It is therefore capable of proof; and when time to collect this proof has been given, it ought to be adduced, or suspicion becomes ground too weak to stand upon. Several months have elapsed since this fact did occur, if it ever occurred. More than five weeks have elapsed since the opinion of the supreme court has declared the necessity of proving the fact, if it exists. Why is it not proved? ... I ought not to believe that there has been any remissness on the part of those who prosecute on this important and interesting subject; and consequently, when at this late period no evidence that troops have been actually embodied is given. I must say that the suspicion which in the first instance might have been created ought not to be continued, unless this want of proof can be in some manner accounted for.

*   *   *

...I shall not therefore insert in the commitment the charge of high treason. I repeat, that this is the less important, because it detracts nothing from the right of the attorney to prefer an indictment for high treason, should he be furnished with the necessary testimony.

The CHIEF JUSTICE, having delivered his opinion, observed that ... the case was of course bailable.... The sum was finally fixed at ten thousand dollars....

80 Marshall Meets Burr in the Courtroom a Second Time (1807)

Burr was reindicted on a second and more specific charge of treason by levying of war in moving to seize New Orleans. As he had done previously, Chief Justice Marshall imposed such stringent requirements in his charge to the jury that a conviction was unlikely. In his opinion, Marshall discussed in great detail the highly technical requirements that must be met to satisfy a charge of treason.

After several other lesser trials and acquittals, Aaron Burr went into exile in Europe. His dreams of western conquests continued to haunt him. In 1812, a charitable United States government permitted his return. At age seventy-seven he married again, and three years later his wife divorced him on grounds of adultery. Burr was an adventurer to the end.

☆ 80   *United States v. Burr* (October 1807)

25 F. Cas. 201 (C.C.D. Va. 1807) (No. 14,694a).

[MARSHALL, C. J.]...

The charges against the accused are: 1st, that they have levied war against the United States at the mouth of Cumberland river, in Kentucky; and, 2dly, that they have begun and provided the means for a military expedition against a nation with which the United States were at peace.

*   *   *

Both charges are supported by the same transaction and the same testimony. The assemblage at the mouth of Cumberland is considered as an act of levying war against the United States, and as a military armament collected for the invasion of a neighboring power with whom the United States were at peace. From the evidence which details that transaction, it appears that from sixty to one hundred men, who were collected from the upper parts of the Ohio under the direction of Tyler and Floyd, had descended the river and reached the mouth of Cumberland about the 25th of December, 1806. The next day they went on shore, and formed a line, represented by some somewhat circular, to receive Colonel Burr, who was introduced to them, and who said that he had intended to impart something to them, or that he had intended to communicate his views, but that reasons of his own had induced him to postpone this communication; or, as others say, that there were then too many bystanders to admit of a communication of his objects. The men assembled at the mouth of Cumberland appear to have considered Colonel Burr as their chief. . . . There was no act of disobedience to the civil authority, nor were there any military appearances. There were some arms, and some boxes which might or might not contain arms. There were also some implements of husbandry, but they were purchased at the place. These men assembled under contracts to settle a tract of country on the Red river. No hostile objects were avowed; and, after continuing a day or two on an island in the mouth of the river, the party proceeded down the Ohio. . . . That the men should have been armed with rifles was to be expected, had their single object been to plant themselves in the Wachita; but the musket and bayonet are, perhaps, not the species of arms which are most usually found in our frontier settlements; nor were the individuals who were assembled of that description of persons who would most naturally be employed for such a purpose. The engagement for six months, too, is a stipulation for which it is difficult to account upon the principle that a settlement of lands was the sole or principal object in contemplation. These are circumstances which excite suspicion. How far they may be accounted for by saying that ulterior eventual objects were entertained, and that the event on which those objects depended was believed to be certain or nearly certain, I need not determine; but I can scarcely suppose it possible that it would be contended by any person that the transactions at the mouth of Cumberland do, in themselves, amount to an act of levying war. There was neither an act of hostility committed, nor any intention to commit such act avowed.

Very early in the proceedings which preceded this motion, I declared the opinion that war might be levied without a battle, or the actual application of force to the object on which it was designed to act; that a body of men assembled for the purpose of war, and being in a posture of war, do levy war; and from that opinion I have certainly felt no disposition to recede. But the intention is an indispensable ingredient in the composition of the fact; and if war may be levied without striking the blow, the intention to strike must be plainly proved. To prove this

intention, the prosecutor for the United States offers evidence of conversations held by the accused. . . . That conversations or actions at a different time and place might be given in evidence as corroborative of the overt act of levying war, after that had been proved in such a manner as to be left to a jury, I never doubted for an instant. But that in a case where the intent could not be inferred from the fact, and was not proved by declarations connected with the fact, . . . this defect could be entirely supplied by extrinsic testimony, not applying the intend conclusively to the particular fact, is a point on which I have entertained doubts which are not yet entirely removed. . . .

*   *   *

The first question which arises on the evidence is: With what objects did those men convene who assembled at the mouth of Cumberland? Was it to separate the Western from the Eastern states by seizing and holding New Orleans? Was it to carry on an expedition against Mexico, making the embarkation at New Orleans? Was this expedition to depend on a war with Spain? The conversation held by Colonel Burr with Commodore Decatur stated his object to be an expedition against Mexico, which would be undertaken, as the commodore understood, with the approbation of government in the event of war. To General Eaton, he unfolded, in his various conversations, plans for invading Mexico, and also for severing the Western from the Atlantic states. To Commodore Truxton, he spoke of the invasion and conquest of Mexico in the event of a war, as a plan which he had digested in concert with General Wilkinson, and into which he was extremely desirous to draw the commodore. A circumstance is narrated by this witness. . . . It is the declaration of Colonel Burr that he was about to despatch two couriers with letters to General Wilkinson relative to the expedition. It was at this time that Messrs. Bollman and Swartwout are said to have left Philadelphia, carrying each a copy of the ciphered letter which has constituted so important a document in the various motions that have been made on this occasion. This letter, though expressed in terms of some ambiguity, has been understood by the supreme court, and is understood by me, to relate to a military expedition against the territories of a foreign prince.

*   *   *

. . . The supreme court has said that to revolutionize a territory by force, although merely as a step to or a means of executing some greater projects is treason. But an embarkation of troops against a foreign country may be made without revolutionizing the government of the place, and without subverting the legitimate authority. . . . If the object of the assemblage at the mouth of Cumberland was to embark at New Orleans for the purpose of invading Mexico, the law relative to that assemblage would be essentially different from what it might be if their direct object was to subvert the government of New Orleans by force. If, in prosecuting their purpose at New Orleans, war should be levied, this would be treason at New Orleans when the fact was committed, but it could not, I think, be said to be treason by levying war at the mouth of Cumberland, where the fact was neither committed nor intended. It might be otherwise, if at the mouth of Cumberland the determination to subvert the government of a territory by force had been formed.

*   *   *

. . . The reason why men in a posture of war may be said to levy war before a blow is struck, is that they are ready to strike, and war consists in the various movements of a military force, as well as in actual fighting. But these men were not ready nor willing to strike, nor could their chief be ready to strike without them. He had yet to prevail upon them to come into his measures. This is not a meeting for the purpose of executing a formal design, but a meeting for the purpose of forming a design. It is, therefore, more in the nature of conspiracy than actual war.

*   *   *

Believing, then, the weight of testimony to be in favor of the opinion that the real and direct object of the expedition was Mexico, and inclining, also, to the opinion that, in law, either acts of hostility and resistance to the government, or a hostile intention in the body assembled, is necessary to convert a meeting of men with ordinary appearances into an act of levying war, it would, in my judgement, be improper in me to commit the accused on the charge of treason.

*   *   *

81 Protecting America's Neutrality (1809)

The European wars of the early nineteenth century directly affected the distant American nation. The British and the French, America's largest trading partners, sought to disrupt each other's maritime supply lines. By 1806, the British had seized some 120 American vessels engaged in trade with the French and their colonies. In retaliation for the English interference with neutral commerce, Napoleon responded with his own blockade measures, thus interrupting American trade with Britain.

America's pride, honor, and economy suffered from the interference with its shipping. The growing conflict with England over the freedom of open sea routes resulted in Jefferson's 1807 Embargo

Act, which prohibited any vessel — American or foreign — from leaving domestic ports to engage in international trade. The embargo reportedly struck New England and its ports "like a thunderbolt." When the Embargo Act proved unenforceable, Congress passed the Non-Intercourse Act on March 1, 1809, which closed American harbors to English and French ships and prohibited Americans from engaging in any commercial transactions with the English and the French. Congress expected the shipping interests to comply with this economic burden it imposed on them out of a sense of allegiance to the United States and her interests. The government prescribed sanctions for those who did not obey. For reasons of international politics, the United States had criminalized the act of participating in useful commercial relations between individuals of specified nationalities.

☆ 81 The Non-Intercourse Act

2 Stat. 539 (1809).

Be it enacted, That from and after the passing of this act, the entrance of the harbors and waters of the United States and of the territories thereof, be, and the same is hereby interdicted to all public ships and vessels belonging to Great Britain or France. . . .

SEC. 2. That it shall not be lawful for any citizen or citizens of the United States or the territories thereof, nor for any person or persons residing or being in the same, to have any intercourse with, or to afford any aid or supplies to any public ship or vessel as aforesaid, which shall, contrary to the provisions of this act, have entered any harbor or waters within the jurisdiction of the United States or the territories thereof; and if any person shall, contrary to the provisions of this act, have any intercourse with such ship or vessel, or shall afford any aid to such ship or vessel, either in repairing the said vessel or in furnishing her, her officers and crew with supplies of any kind or in any manner whatever, . . . every person so offending, shall forfeit and pay a sum not less than one hundred dollars, nor exceeding ten thousand dollars; and shall also be imprisoned for a term not less than one month, nor more than one year.

SEC. 3. That from and after the twentieth day of May next, the entrance of the harbors and waters of the United States and the territories thereof be, and the same is hereby interdicted to all ships or vessels sailing under the flag of Great Britain or France, or owned in whole or in part by any citizen or subject of either.

SEC. 4. That from and after the twentieth day of May next, it shall not be lawful to import into the United States or the territories thereof, any goods, wares or merchandise whatever, from any port or place situated in Great Britain or Ireland, or in any of the colonies or dependencies of Great Britain, nor from any port or place situated in France, or in any of her colonies or dependencies, nor from any port or place in the actual possession of either Great Britain or France. Nor shall it be lawful to import into the United States, or the territories thereof, from any foreign port or place whatever, any goods, wares or merchandise whatever, being of the growth, produce or manufacture of France, or of any of her colonies or dependencies, or being of the growth, produce or manufacture of Great Britain or Ireland, or of any of the colonies or dependencies of Great Britain, or being of the growth, produce or manufacture of any place or country in the actual possession of either France or Great Britain. . . .

Approved, March 1, 1809.

82 Winds of Secession (1815)

The War of 1812 put almost unbearable stress on the fledgling Republic. Regional, economic, and political tension reached a peak, and the dissatisfaction of the aristocratic, sophisticated Federalist leaders of New England with the more populist Republican rule in Washington ("government by the worst") led the Federalists to consider the possibility of secession from the Union.

As early as 1808, Jefferson, in a private letter, predicted that "the Federalists may attempt insurrection." When war was declared, furious rioting broke out in various parts of the country—for and against the war. Resistance to the war and its measures was highest in the North. In Massachusetts, recruiting offices were mobbed and an American privateer was sunk. By 1814, the key New England states refused to furnish men or money for the conduct of a war which they considered "iniquitous." The avowed strategy of some of the Federalists, claims historian Nathaniel Weyl, "was to precipitate the military defeat of the United States, thus dissolving the republic and establishing an independent New England Confederacy under English protection."

The fortunes of the national government reached new depths at the end of 1814. On October 17, the Massachusetts legislature issued an invitation of the New England states to convene at Hartford "to lay the foundation for a radical reform in the national compact." Delegates from Massachusetts, Connecticut, Rhode Island, Vermont, and New Hampshire attended the Hartford Convention. But the moderating influence of the chairman, George Cabot of Massachusetts, prevailed, and the resolutions adopted were neither radical nor treasonable.

In early 1815, Andrew Jackson repelled the Brit-

ish naval assault on Louisiana, and the United States signed a favorable peace treaty at Ghent. The secessionist sentiments of New England were forgotten. Regional differences were not to mature into actual conflict until the Civil War.

☆ 82 Report and Resolutions of the Hartford Convention (January 4, 1815)

Reprinted in T. Dwight, *History of the Hartford Convention* (New York: Da Capo Press, 1970), 368.

. . . To investigate and explain the means whereby this fatal reverse has been effected, would require a voluminous discussion. Nothing more can be attempted in this report than a general allusion to the principal outlines of the policy which has produced this vicissitude. Among these may be enumerated—

First. —A deliberate and extensive system for effecting a combination among certain states, by exciting local jealousies and ambition, so as to secure to popular leaders in one section of the Union, the controul of public affairs in perpetual succession. To which primary object most other characteristics of the system may be reconciled.

Secondly. —The political intolerance displayed and avowed in excluding from office men of unexceptionable merit, for want of adherence to the executive creed.

*   *   *

Fourthly. —The abolition of existing taxes, requisite to prepare the country for those changes to which nations are always exposed, with a view of the acquisition of popular favour.

Fifthly. —The influence of patronage in the distribution of offices, which in these states has been almost invariably made among men the least entitled to such distinction. . . .

Sixthly. —The admission of new states into the Union formed at pleasure in the western region, has destroyed the balance of power which existed among the original States, and deeply affected their interest.

Seventhly. —The easy admission of naturalized foreigners, to places of trust, honour or profit, operating as an inducement to the malcontent subjects of the old world to come to these States, in quest of executive patronage, and to repay it by an abject devotion to executive measures.

Eighthly. —Hostility to Great Britain, and partiality to the late government of France, adopted as coincident with popular prejudice, and subservient to the main object, party power. Connected with these must be ranked erroneous and distorted estimates of the power and resources of those nations, of the probable results of their controversies, and of our political relations to them respectively.

Lastly and principally. —A visionary and superficial theory in regard to commerce, accompanied by a real hatred but a feigned regard to its interests, and a ruinous perseverance in efforts to render it an instrument of coercion and war.

But it is not conceivable that the obliquity of any administration could, in so short a period, have so nearly consummated the work of national ruin, unless favoured by defects in the constitution.

To enumerate all the improvements of which that instrument is susceptible, and to propose such amendments as might render it in all respects perfect, would be a task which this convention has not thought proper to assume. They have confined their attention to such as experience has demonstrated to be essential, and even among these, some are considered entitled to a more serious attention than others. . . .

THEREFORE RESOLVED, That it be and hereby is recommended to the legislatures of the several states represented in this Convention, to adopt all such measures as may be necessary effectually to protect the citizens of said states from the operation and effects of all acts which have been or may be passed by the Congress of the United States, which shall contain provisions, subjecting the militia or other citizens to forcible drafts, conscriptions, or impressments, not authorised by the constitution of the United States.

Resolved, That it be and hereby is recommended to the said Legislatures, to authorize an immediate and earnest application to be made to the government of the United States, requesting their consent to some arrangement, whereby the said states may, separately or in concert, be empowered to assume upon themselves the defence of their territory against the enemy; and a reasonable portion of the taxes, collected within said States, may be paid into the respective treasuries thereof. . . .

Resolved, That the following amendments of the constitution of the United States be recommended to the states. . . .

First. Representatives and direct taxes shall be apportioned among the several states which may be included within this Union, according to their respective numbers of free persons, including those bound to serve for a term of years, and excluding Indians not taxed, and all other persons.

Second. No new state shall be admitted into the Union by Congress, in virtue of the power granted by the constitution, without the concurrence of two thirds of both houses.

Third. Congress shall not have power to lay any embargo on the ships or vessels of the citizens of the United States, in the ports or harbours thereof, for more than sixty days.

Fourth. Congress shall not have power, without the concurrence of two thirds of both houses, to interdict the commercial intercourse between the United States and any foreign nation, or the dependencies thereof.

Fifth. Congress shall not make or declare war, or authorize acts of hostility against any foreign nation, without the concurrence of two thirds of both houses, except such acts of hostility be in defence of the territories of the United States when actually invaded.

Sixth. No person who shall hereafter be naturalized, shall be eligible as a member of the senate or house of representatives of the United States, nor capable of holding any civil office under the authority of the United States.

Seventh. The same person shall not be elected president of the United States a second time; nor shall the president be elected from the same state two terms in succession.

Resolved, That if the application of these states to the government of the United States, recommended in a foregoing resolution, should be unsuccessful and peace should not be concluded, and the defence of these states should be neglected, as it has since the commencement of the war, it will, in the opinion of this convention, be expedient for the legislatures of the several states to appoint delegates to another convention, to meet at Boston . . . with such powers and instructions as the exigency of a crisis so momentous may require.

83 I Humbled the Insurgents at a Trifling Expense (1815)

The first quarter-century of the United States was beset by competition and conflict between different political persuasions, feelings of sectional chauvinism, and tension amidst the diverse social and economic elements in the population. Despite almost continual threats of insurrection, secession, and resistance to the national law, America's political leaders readily displayed a spirit of forgiveness against dissidents and rebels once the immediate crises passed. In 1815, former president John Adams, reflecting on his decisions in office, finally spelled out his reasoning behind the pardon of John Fries: national integration was served more by charity than by ruthlessness.

☆ 83 Letter from John Adams to James Lloyd (March 31, 1815)

Reprinted in C. F. Adams, ed., *The Works of John Adams* (New York: AMS Press, 1971), 10:152-55.

*   *   *

I had suppressed an insurrection in Pennsylvania, and effectually humbled and punished the insurgents; not by assembling an army of militia from three or four States, and marching in all the pride, pomp, and circumstance of war, at an expense of millions, but silently, without noise, and at a trifling expense. I pardoned Fries. . . . What good, what example would have been exhibited to the nation by the execution of three or four obscure, miserable Germans, as ignorant of our language as they were of our laws, and the nature and definition of treason? Pitiful puppets danced upon the wires of jugglers behind the scene or under ground. Had the mountebanks been in the place of he puppets, mercy would have had a harder struggle to obtain absolution for them.

The verdict of a jury, and the judgement of the court, would, to be sure, have justified me in the opinion of the nation, and in the judgement of the world, if I had signed the warrant for their execution; but neither, nor both, could have satisfied my conscience, nor tranquillized my feelings. If I had en-

tertained only a doubt of their guilt, notwithstanding verdicts and judgements, it was my duty to pardon them. But my determination did not rest upon so wavering a foundation as a doubt.

My judgement was clear, that their crime did not amount to treason. They had been guilty of a high-handed riot and rescue, attended with circumstances hot, rash, violent, and dangerous, but all these did not amount to treason. And I thought the officers of the law had been injudicious in indicting them for any crime higher than riot, aggravated by rescue. Here I rest my cause on this head, and proceed to another.

CHAPTER 4

*   *   *

Consolidation and Schism

———

Suffrage, Citizenship,
and the Right of Secession
1821-1861

THE regulation of blacks and Native Americans, respectively, forms the main theme of this chapter. The period produced stringent state regulations of slaves as apprehension grew over the danger this population posed to the security of life, property, and the economic system of the South. The documents demonstrate the use of the criminal law to suppress abolitionist and insurrectionist sentiments. Close regulations also were imposed on free blacks and whites who might associate with and assist slaves in their search for revenge or freedom.

The materials relating to Native Americans run almost in counterpoint to those regarding blacks. While the tensions between blacks and whites found expression in the law through tight regulation of the interactions between these populations, the conflict between whites and Native Americans gave rise to the isolation, betrayal, and exile of the Native Americans from their homelands. This chapter documents the resettlement of the Five Civilized Tribes of the southeast in the Indian Territory of what is now Oklahoma. Even in this haven the Native Americans could not maintain long-term refuge, since the government withdrew its promised protection and left them without recourse to the law to safeguard their recognized interests. Martial force finally was utilized to compel their further withdrawal.

These are the bare facts reported by the documents. But there are more subtle messages as well. Although the law treated blacks and Native Americans quite differently, it regulated them for the same reason. These groups constituted identifiable populations whose allegiance to the ruling authority could not be assumed. Blacks were necessary to the economic survival of the South, and their continued presence was essential. The effort was directed instead toward criminalizing the education and organization of blacks, and prohibiting any kind of social intercourse which might kindle a spark of opposition or rebellion.

Native Americans, in contrast, were organized into coherent societies that concededly owed no allegiance to the federal government or to any state. Oppression of individual Native Americans by state law clearly could not operate within the tribal lands. As long as the federal government protected Native American sovereignty over the territory that they inhabited, these societies were immune from disintegration or control by the white society. The direction America's Native American policy took, therefore, was to banish the entire expendable suspect population whose social and political order could not be tolerated within the American Manifest Destiny.

Sprinkled among the documents are items that hint at the major arenas of political criminality in the next few decades. Despite the earlier American articulation of the right of revolution, the prevailing American view no longer justified recourse to political crime or rebellion, since government was considered subject to the will of the people and the ballot box was to be the tool for curbing oppression. This note strikes flat, however, when one observes that vast numbers of people were not only disenfranchised but also held in isolation and bondage. Blacks and Native Americans (not to mention women) were totally excluded from the electoral process, and the working class, likewise, largely was denied political and economic power.

It is difficult to see how, for those on the outside, major reforms could be expected through the conventional political process. Perceived injustice, therefore, was countered through various acts of criminality and violence. Correspondingly, government and its allies utilized the criminal and martial law to suppress and punish those who resisted their assigned roles and conditions.

The documents in this chapter also begin to chart the interaction between federal and state laws with regard to political crime. Electoral dominance throughout the period covered in this chapter gave prominence to Southern and western interests. For the most part the federal law supported the political interests of the Southern states, thereby facilitating the survival of slavery. The Native American-related documents also largely demonstrate a pattern of federal subversion of its treaty obligations in favor of the expanding western populations. Federal failure to prevent the incursions of white settlers into Native American territories placed the Native Americans under continuing duress, which culminated in the Trail of Tears.

Finally, as in earlier periods, the documents of this chapter foreshadow the major arenas of future political criminality: secession, labor, and women's suffrage.

84 Bowing before "the idol of universal suffrage" (1821)

In 1820, the census results showed a total United States population of 9,638,453. Slightly more than half of these Americans lived in the Northern states. The black population, of which nearly 90 percent were slaves, totaled 1,771,656. In most states the circle of political power was narrow, and the right of suffrage was guarded jealously. Slaves, women, and nonpropertied laborers were excluded totally from the political process. State electoral restrictions limited access to the federal ballot as well.

Yet, given the fact that the United States was a federation of democratic republics, any oppressive laws theoretically could be remedied through the political process. Also America's settled frontier reached to the Mississippi River, and the new states exported not only corn and tobacco but also liberal, democratic policies, including the abolition of the property qualification for suffrage. The following excerpt from an address by James Kent, president of the Court of Chancery and a leading American legal scholar, to the New York Constitutional Convention expressed the concerns of the more conservative easterners regarding the widening of the suffrage to include all white males.

☆ 84 Remarks of Chancellor Kent to the New York Constitutional Convention

Reprinted in H. Carter, W. Stone, and M. Gould, eds., *Reports of the Proceedings and Debates of the Convention of 1821* (New York: Da Capo Press, 1970), § 219.

Chancellor Kent.... [W]e are engaged in the bold and hazardous experiment of remodelling the constitution.... [W]e should pause in our career, and reflect well on the immensity of the innovation in contemplation....

The senate has hitherto been elected by the farmers of the state—by the free and independent lords of the soil, worth at least $250 in freehold estate, over and above all debts charged thereon. The governor has been chosen by the same electors, and we have hitherto elected citizens of elevated rank and character. Our assembly has been chosen by freeholders, possessing a freehold of the value of $50, or by persons renting a tenement of the yearly value of $5, and who have been rated and actually paid taxes to the state. By the report before us, we propose to annihilate, at one stroke, all those property distinctions and to bow before the idol of universal suffrage. That extreme democratic principle, when applied to the legislative and executive departments of the government, has been regarded with terror, by the wise men of every age, because

in every European republic, ancient and modern, in which it has been tried, it has terminated disastrously, and been productive of corruption, injustice, violence, and tyranny. And dare we flatter ourselves that we are a peculiar people, who can run the career of history, exempted from the passions which have disturbed and corrupted the rest of mankind? If we are like other races of men, with similar follies and vices, then I greatly fear that our posterity will have reason to deplore in sackcloth and ashes, the delusion of the day....

Now sir, I wish to preserve our senate as the representative of the landed interest.... I wish them to be always enabled to say that their freeholds cannot be taxed without their consent. The men of no property, together with the crowds of dependents connected with great manufacturing and commercial establishments, and the motley and undefinable population of crowded ports, may, perhaps, at some future day, under skilful management predominate in the assembly, and yet we should be perfectly safe if no laws could pass without the free consent of the owners of the soil. That security we at present enjoy; and it is that security which I wish to retain.

... The tendency of universal suffrage, is to jeopardize the rights of property, and the principles of liberty. There is a constant tendency in human society, and the history of every age proves it; there is a tendency in the poor to covet a share in the plunder of the rich; in the debtor to relax or avoid the obligation of contracts; in the majority to tyrannize over the minority, and trample down their rights; in the indolent and profligate, to cast the whole burthens of society upon the industrious and the virtuous; and *there is a tendency in ambitious and wicked men, to inflame these combustible materials*. It requires a vigilant government, and a firm administration of justice, to counteract that tendency. Thou shalt not covet; thou shalt not steal; are divine injunctions induced by this miserable depravity of our nature. Who can undertake to calculate with any precision, how many millions of people, this great state will contain in the course of this and the next century, and who can estimate the future extent and magnitude of our commercial ports? The disproportion between the men of property, and the men of no property, will be in every society in a ratio of its commerce, wealth, and population.

... We are fast becoming a great nation, with great commerce, manufactures, population, wealth, luxuries, and with the vices and miseries that they engender. One seventh of the population of the city of Paris at this day subsists on charity, and one third of the inhabitants of that city die in the hospitals; what would become of such a city with universal suffrage? France has upwards of four, and England upwards of five millions of manufacturing and commercial labourers without property. Could these Kingdoms sustain the weight of universal suffrage? The radicals in England, with the force of that mighty engine, would at once sweep away the property, the laws, and the liberties of that island like a deluge.

The growth of the city of New-York is enough to startle and awaken those who are pursuing the IGNIS FATUUS of universal suffrage. . . .

85 The Crime of Being Black (1823)

An 1820 South Carolina statute required that free blacks aboard vessels entering the harbors of the state be imprisoned on shore for the duration of their ship's stay in port. This assertion of state power to exclude "undesirable" aliens from its territory on racial or other grounds was tested in 1823 before Justice William Johnson, a member of the United States Supreme Court riding circuit. Although the decision primarily rested on the supremacy of the Constitution's commerce clause, it contained other themes. In asserting federal protection for a foreign nation's black seamen, *Elkison* began the process of resorting to federal, as well as international, laws and obligations as the basis for erecting civil and human rights barriers against enforcement of criminal and quasi-criminal laws.

☆ 85 *Elkison v. Deliesseline*

8 F. Cas. 493 (C.C.D.S.C. 1823) (No. 4,366).

JOHNSON, CIRCUIT JUSTICE.

*   *   *

. . . On the unconstitutionality of the law under which this man is confined, it is not too much to say, that it will not bear argument. . . . Neither of the gentlemen has attempted to prove that the power therein assumed by the state can be exercised without clashing with the general powers of the United States to regulate commerce; but they have both strenuously contended, that ex necessitate it was a power which the state must and would exercise, and, indeed, Mr. Holmes concluded his argument with the declaration, that, if a dissolution of the Union must be the alternative, he was ready to meet it. Nor did the argument of Col. Hunt deviate at all from the same course. Giving it in the language of his own summary, it was this: South Carolina was a sovereign state when she adopted the constitution; a sovereign state cannot surrender a right of vital importance; South Carolina, therefore, either did not surrender this right, or still possesses the power to resume it, and whether it is necessary, or when it is necessary, to resume it, she is herself the sovereign judge. But it was not necessary to give this candid exposé of the grounds which this law assumes; for it

is a subject of positive proof, that it is altogether irreconcilable with the powers of the general government; that it necessarily compromits the public peace, and tends to embroil us with, if not separate us from, our sister states; in short, that it leads to a dissolution of the Union, and implies a direct attack upon the sovereignty of the United States.

Let it be observed that the law is, "if any vessel (not even the vessels of the United States excepted) shall come into any port or harbor of this state," etc., bringing in free colored persons, such persons are to become "absolute slaves," and that, without even a form of trial, as I understand the act, they are to be sold. By the next clause the sheriff is vested with absolute power, and expressly enjoined to carry the law into effect, and is to receive the one half of the proceeds of the sale. The object of this law, and it has been so acknowledged in argument, is to prohibit ships coming into this port employing colored seamen, whether citizens or subjects of their own government or not. But if this state can prohibit Great Britain from employing her colored subjects (and she has them of all colors on the globe), or if at liberty to prohibit the employment of her subjects of the African race, why not prohibit her from using those of Irish or of Scottish nativity? If the color of his skin is to preclude the Lascar or the Sierra Leone seaman, why not the color of his eye or his hair exclude from our ports the inhabitants of her other territories? In fact it amounts to the assertion of the power to exclude the seamen of the territories of Great Britain, or any other nation, altogether. With regard to various friendly nations it amounts to an actual exclusion in its present form. . . . [A]nd even the state of Massachusetts might lately, and may perhaps now, expedite to this port a vessel with her officers black, and her crew composed of Nantucket Indians, known to be among the best seamen in our service. These might all become slaves under this act. If this law were enforced upon such vessels, retaliation would follow; and the commerce of this city, feeble and sickly, comparatively, as it already is, might be fatally injured. . . .

Apply the law to the particular case before us, and the incongruity will be glaring. [The] offense, it will be observed, for which this individual is supposed to forfeit his freedom, is that of coming into this port in the ship, Homer, in the capacity of a seaman. . . . The seaman's crime is complete, and the forfeiture incurred by the single act of coming into port; and this even though driven into port by stress of weather, or forced by a power which he cannot control into a port for which he did not ship himself; the law contains no exception to meet such contingencies. The seaman's offense, therefore, is coming into the state in a ship or vessel; that of the captain consists in bringing him in, and not taking him out of the state, and paying all expenses. Now, according to the laws and treaties of the United States, it was both lawful for this seaman to come into this port, in this vessel, and for the captain to bring him in the capacity of a seaman; and yet these are the very acts for which the state law imposes these heavy penalties. Is there no clashing in this? It is in effect a repeal of the laws of the United States, pro tanto, converting a right into a crime.

And here it is proper to notice that part of the argument against the motion, in which it was insisted on that this law was passed by the state in exercise of a concurrent right. "Concurrent" does not mean "paramount," and yet, in order to divest a right conferred by the general government, it is very clear that the state right must be more than concurrent. But the right of the general government to regulate commerce with the sister states and foreign nations is a paramount and exclusive right; and this conclusion we arrive at, whether we examine it with reference to the words of the constitution, or the nature of the grant. . . .

But the case does not rest here. In order to sustain this law, the state must also possess a power paramount to the treaty-making power of the United States, expressly declared to be a part of the supreme legislative power of the land; for the seizure of this man, on board a British ship, is an express violation of the commercial convention with Great Britain of 1815. . . . Such a law as this could not be passed even by the general government, without furnishing a just cause of war.

But to all this the plea of necessity is urged; and of the existence of that necessity we are told the state alone is the judge. Where is this to land us? Is it not asserting the right in each state to throw off the federal constitution at its will and pleasure? If it can be done as to any particular article it may be done as to all; and, like the old confederation, the Union becomes a mere rope of sand. But I deny that the state surrendered a single power necessary to its security, against this species of property. What is to prevent their being confined to their ships, if it is dangerous for them to go abroad? This power may be lawfully exercised. To land their cargoes, take in others, and depart, is all that is necessary to ordinary commerce, and is all that is properly stipulated for in the convention of 1815, so far as relates to seamen. If our fears extend also to the British merchant, the supercargo, or master, being persons of color, I acknowledge that, as to them, the treaty precludes us from abridging their rights to free ingress and egress, and occupying houses and warehouses for the purposes of commerce. As to them, this law is an express infraction of the treaty. No such law can be passed consistently with the treaty, and unless sanctioned by diplomatic arrangement, the

passing of such a law is tantamount to a declaration of war. . . .

*   *   *

Upon the whole, I am decidedly of the opinion that the third section of the state act now under consideration is unconstitutional and void, and that every arrest made under it subjects the parties making it to an action of trespass.

*   *   *

86 "the Indians . . . have retained their savage habits" (1829)

Georgia ultimately compromised its early claims to sovereignty and title over all lands westward to the Mississippi by its cession to the United States of whatever interest it had in the land west of its present borders. Georgia's 1802 cession, nevertheless, included the requirement that the United States "should, at their own expense, extinguish, for the use of Georgia, as early as the same can be peaceably obtained, on reasonable terms, the Indian title to lands within the state of Georgia." The motive behind Georgia's insistence on this provision was the desire for the good farmland which, under the Treaty of Hopewell and subsequent treaties, belonged to the Cherokee and Creek nations.

The United States had taken some measures to remove the Native Americans from Georgia. They did not want to leave, however, and the government could do little to make them move—short of force. Yet settlers continually were intruding upon their lands and establishing themselves in violation of the treaties. The pressures on the Cherokees were not lessened with the discovery of gold in their territory in 1828.

That year, the Georgia legislature passed a series of laws which carved up the Native American-occupied territory and established a system of apportioning land. In addition, the jurisdiction of the laws of the state was extended to include all Native American territory. The administration of President John Quincy Adams intervened on behalf of the Cherokees, much to the anger of the Georgians. The political climate soon changed, however, when Andrew Jackson, who had made a considerable portion of his reputation as a fighter against the Creeks, became President in 1829. In his First Annual Message to Congress, he addressed the need to remove the Native Americans to regions west of the Mississippi. Five months later, Congress passed the Indian Removal Act, which authorized the president to negotiate with the Native Americans for a trade of their lands for lands west of the Mississippi and appropriated $500,000 for that purpose.

Thus began the process whereby an entire people was forced, through operation of law, to choose between self-perpetuation and self-government and their dominion over their homeland. Describing the policies behind the Removal Act, the Comte de Tocqueville commented in 1831: "[The Native Americans] were isolated in their own country, and their race only constituted a little colony of troublesome strangers in the midst of a numerous and dominant people." Their status *as Native Americans* become the grounds for their exile.

☆ 86 First Annual Message from President Jackson to Congress: Indian Removal

Reprinted in J. Richardson, ed., *A Compilation of the Messages and Papers of the Presidents* (New York: Bureau of National Literature, 1897), 2:456-59.

*   *   *

The condition and ulterior destiny of the Indian tribes within the limits of some of our States have become objects of much interest and importance. It has long been the policy of Government to introduce among them the arts of civilization, in the hope of gradually reclaiming them from a wandering life. This policy has, however, been coupled with another wholly incompatible with its success. Professing a desire to civilize and settle them, we have at the same time lost no opportunity to purchase their lands and thrust them farther into the wilderness. By this means they have not only been kept in a wandering state, but been led to look upon us as unjust and indifferent to their fate. Thus, though lavish in its expenditures upon the subject, Government has constantly defeated its own policy, and the Indians in general, receding farther and farther to the west, have retained their savage habits. A portion, however, of the Southern tribes having mingled much with the whites and made some progress in the arts of civilized life, have lately attempted to erect an independent government within the limits of Georgia and Alabama. These States, claiming to be the only sovereigns within their territories, extended their laws over the Indians, which induced the latter to call upon the United States for protection.

Under these circumstances the question presented was whether the General Government had a right to sustain those people in their pretensions. The Constitution declares that "no new State shall be formed or erected within the jurisdiction of any other State" without the consent of its legislature. If the General Government is not permitted to tolerate the erection of a confederate State within the territory of one of the members of this Union against her consent, much less could it allow a foreign and independent government to establish itself there. Georgia became a member of the Confederacy which eventuated in

our Federal Union as a sovereign State, always asserting her claim to certain limits, which, having been originally defined in her colonial charter and subsequently recognized in the treaty of peace, she has ever since continued to enjoy, except as they have been circumscribed by her own voluntary transfer of a portion of her territory to the United States in the articles of cession of 1802. Alabama was admitted into the Union on the same footing with the original States, with boundaries which were prescribed by Congress. There is no constitutional, conventional, or legal provision which allows them less power over the Indians within their borders than is possessed by Maine or New York. Would the people of Maine permit the Penobscot tribe to erect an independent government within their State? And unless they did would it not be the duty of the General Government to support them in resisting such a measure? Would the people of New York permit each remnant of the Six Nations within her borders to declare itself an independent people under the protection of the United States? Could the Indians establish a separate republic on each of their reservations in Ohio? And if they were so disposed would it be the duty of this Government to protect them in the attempt? If the principle involved in the obvious answer to these questions be abandoned, it will follow that the objects of this Government are reversed, and that it has become a part of its duty to aid in destroying the States which it was established to protect.

Actuated by this view of the subject, I informed the Indians inhabiting parts of Georgia and Alabama that their attempt to establish an independent government would not be countenanced by the Executive of the United States, and advised them to emigrate beyond the Mississippi or submit to the laws of those States.

*   *   *

... Surrounded by the whites with their arts of civilization, which by destroying the resources of the savage doom him to weakness and decay, the fate of the Mohegan, the Narragansett, and the Delaware is fast overtaking the Choctaw, the Cherokee, and the Creek. That this fate surely awaits them if they remain within the limits of the States does not admit of a doubt. Humanity and national honor demand that every effort should be made to avert so great a calamity....

As a means of effecting this end I suggest for your consideration the propriety of setting apart an ample district west of the Mississippi, and without the limit of any State or Territory now formed, to be guaranteed to the Indian tribes as long as they shall occupy it, each tribe having a distinct control over the portion designated for its use. There they may be secured in the enjoyment of governments of their own choice, subject to no other control from the United States than such as may be necessary to preserve peace on the frontier and between the several tribes. There the benevolent may endeavor to teach them the arts of civilization, and, by promoting union and harmony among them, to raise up an interesting commonwealth, destined to perpetuate the race and to attest the humanity and justice of this Government.

This emigration should be voluntary, for it would be as cruel as unjust to compel the aborigines to abandon the graves of their fathers and seek a home in a distant land. But they should be distinctly informed that if they remain within the limits of the States they must be subject to their laws. In return for their obedience as individuals they will without doubt be protected in the enjoyment of those possessions which they have improved by their industry. But it seems to me visionary to suppose that in this state of things claims can be allowed on tracts of country on which they have neither dwelt nor made improvements, merely because they have seen them from the mountain or passed them in the chase. Submitting to the laws of the States, and receiving, like other citizens, protection in their persons and property, they will ere long become merged in the mass of our population.

*   *   *

87 School-Houses as Unlawful Assembly (1831)

A growing preoccupation in the Southern states with the management and control of their slave populations began to surface at the end of the first quarter of the nineteenth century. Because of the Southern aristocracy's concern for the protection of its individual rights, the Jeffersonian theories of the primacy of state sovereignty became the rallying point for its effort to insulate the slave system against external influences.

After the plot of Denmark Vesey, a free black, in South Carolina in 1822, state "Slave Codes" became more and more stringent for free blacks and slaves alike. Whites also were regulated more strictly in their relations with blacks. By isolating its members in ignorance, the state sought to neutralize this politically unadhering population.

The Virginia law was passed in April 1831. In August of that year, Nat Turner's rebellion erupted in Southampton County, Virginia.

☆87 An Act Prohibiting Education of Free Negroes and Mulattoes [Virginia]

1831 Va. Acts 107.

*   *   *

4. Be it further enacted, That all meetings of free negroes or mulattoes, at any school-house, church, meeting-house or other place for teaching them reading or writing, either in the day or night, under whatsoever pretext, shall be deemed and considered as an unlawful assembly; and any justice of the county or corporation, wherein such assemblage shall be, either from his own knowledge, or on the information of others, of such unlawful assemblage or meeting, shall issue his warrant, directed to any sworn officer or officers, authorizing him or them, to enter the house or houses where such unlawful assemblage or meting may be, for the purpose of apprehending or dispersing such free negroes or mulattoes, and to inflict corporal punishment on the offender or offenders, at the discretion of any justice of the peace, not exceeding twenty lashes.

5. Be it further enacted, That if any white person or persons assemble with free negroes or mulattoes, at any school-house, church, meeting-house, or other place for the purpose of instructing such free negroes or mulattoes to read or write, such person or persons shall, on conviction thereof, be fined in a sum not exceeding fifty dollars, and moreover may be imprisoned at the discretion of a jury, not exceeding two months.

6. Be it further enacted, That if any white person, for pay or compensation, shall assemble with any slaves for the purpose of teaching, and shall teach any slave to read or write, such person, or any white person or persons contracting with such teacher so to act, who shall offend as aforesaid, shall, for each offence, be fined at the discretion of a jury, in a sum not less than ten, nor exceeding one hundred dollars, to be recovered on an information or indictment.

88 The Motives of the "late insurrection" (1831)

Violence by masters against slaves was a common occurrence in America. Slave revolts and reprisals were relatively infrequent and were usually harshly suppressed. In 1712 when some blacks and Native Americans planned to revolt in New York City and attacked their masters, the governor sent out troops to end the uprising. After trial, eighteen slaves were put to death, some by hanging and others by torture and fire.

A century later more than 150 whites and blacks were killed during a Virginia slave rebellion and subsequent manhunt. Twenty rebels, including leader Nat Turner, a black preacher, were executed after trial.

Thomas Gray claimed to have taken Nat Turner's confession prior to his trial and conviction. Turner, according to Gray, made no attempt to exculpate himself but frankly acknowledged his full participation in the uprising. This observation was consistent with Turner's views on the rightness, or perhaps righteousness, of his course. In answer to the question, "Do you find yourself mistaken now?" he responded without hesitation, "Was not Christ crucified?" Despite the bloodshed of innocents during the insurrection, he remained steadfast in his belief that his cause and actions were morally justified.

☆ 88 Thomas Gray's Introduction and Nat Turner's Confession

Reprinted in Nat Turner, *The Confession, Trial, and Execution of Nat Turner, the Negro Insurrectionist* (New York: AMS Press, 1975), 1-15.

TO THE PUBLIC

The late insurrection in Southampton has greatly excited the public mind, and led to a thousand idle, exaggerated, and mischievous reports. It is the first instance in our history of an open rebellion of the slaves, and attended with such atrocious circumstances of cruelty and destruction, as could not fail to leave a deep impression, not only upon the minds of the community where this fearful tragedy was wrought, but throughout every portion of our country, in which this population is to be found. Public curiosity has been on the stretch to understand the origin and progress of this dreadful conspiracy, and the motives which influence its diabolical actors. The insurgent slaves had all been destroyed, or apprehended, tried, and executed (with the exception of the leader), without revealing anything at all satisfactory as to the motives which governed them, or the means by which they expected to accomplish their object. Every thing connected with the sad affair was wrapt in mystery, until Nat Turner, the leader of this ferocious band, whose name has resounded throughout our widely extended empire, was captured. This "great Bandit" was taken by a single individual, in a cave near the residence of his late owner, on Sunday, the thirtieth of October, without attempting to make the slightest resistance, and on the following day safely lodged in the jail of the County. His captor was Benjamin Phipps, armed with a shotgun well charged. Nat's only weapon was a small light sword which he immediately surrendered, and begged that his life might be spared. Since his confinement, by permission of the Jailor, I have had ready access to him, and finding that he was willing to make a full and free confession of the origin, progress, and consummation of the insurrectory movements of the slaves of which he was the contriver and head, I determined for the gratification of public curiosity to commit his statements to writing, and publish them, with little or no variation, from his own words. That this is a faithful record of his confessions, the annexed certificate of the County Court of Southampton, will attest. They certainly bear one stamp of truth and sincerity. He makes no attempt (as all the other insurgents who were examined did), to exculpate himself, but frankly acknowledges his full participation in all the guilt of the transaction. He was not only the contriver of the conspiracy, but gave the first blow towards its execution....

Believing the following narrative, by removing doubts and conjectures from the public mind which otherwise must have remained, would give general satisfaction, it is respectfully submitted to the public by their ob't serv't,

T. R. GRAY

CONFESSION

Sir, You have asked to me to give a history of the motives which induced me to undertake the late insurrection, as you call it. To do so I must go back to the days of my infancy, and even before I was born. ... In my childhood a circumstance occurred which made an indelible impression on my mind, and laid the groundwork of that enthusiasm which has terminated so fatally to many, both white and black, and for which I am about to atone at the gallows.... Being at play with other children, when three or four years old, I was telling them something, which my mother overhearing, said it had happened before I was born. I stuck to my story, however, and related some things which went, in her opinion, to confirm it. Others being called on were greatly astonished, knowing that these things had happened, and caused them to say in my hearing, I surely would be a prophet, as the Lord had shewn me things that had happened before my birth. And my father and mother strengthened me in this my first impression, saying in my presence, I was intended for some great purpose, which they had always thought from certain marks on my head and breast.... My grandmother, ... my master, ... and other religious persons ... remarked I had too much sense to be raised, and if I was, I would never be of any service to any one as a slave. To a mind like mine, restless, inquisitive, and observant of everything that was passing, ... there was nothing I saw or heard of to which my attention was not directed.... I have no recollection whatever of learning the alphabet; but to the astonishment of the family, one day, when a book was shewn to me to keep me from crying, I began spelling the names of different objects—this was a source of wonder to all in the neighborhood, particularly the blacks—and this learning was constantly improved at all opportunities.... I was not addicted to stealing in my youth, nor have ever been. Yet such was the confidence of the negroes in the neighborhood, even at this early period of my life, in my superior judgment, that they would often carry me with them when they were going on any roguery, to plan for them.

*   *   *

QUESTION: Do you not find yourself mistaken now?

ANSWER: Was not Christ crucified? And by signs in the heavens that it would make known to me when I should commence the great work — and until the first sign appeared, I should conceal if from the knowledge of men. And on the appearance of the sign (the eclipse of the sun last February), I should arise and prepare myself, and slay my enemies with their own weapons. And immediately on the sign appearing in the heavens, the seal was removed from my lips, and I communicated the great work laid out for me to do, to four in whom I had the greatest confidence (Henry, Hark, Nelson, and Sam). It was intended by us to have begun the work of death on the 4th July last. Many were the plans formed and rejected by us, and it affected my mind to such a degree, that I fell sick; and the time passed without our coming to any determination how to commence. Still forming new schemes and rejecting them, when the sign appeared again, which determined me not to wait longer.

... On Saturday evening, the 20th of August, it was agreed between Henry, Hark, and myself to prepare a dinner the next day for the men we expected, and then to concert a plan, as we had not yet determined on any. Hark, on the following morning, brought a pig, and Henry brandy, and being joined by Sam, Nelson, Will, and Jack, they prepared in the woods a dinner, where, about three o'clock, I joined them.

Q. Why were you so backward in joining them?

A. The same reason that had caused me not mix with them for years before.

I saluted them on coming up and asked Will how came he there; he answered, his life was worth no more than others, and his liberty as dear to him. I asked him if he thought to obtain it? He said he would, or lose his life. This was enough to put him in full confidence. Jack, I knew, was only a tool in the hands of Hark; it was quickly agreed we should commence at home (Mr. J. Travis' [Turner's master]) on that night, and until we had armed and equipped ourselves and gathered sufficient force, neither age nor sex was to be spared (which was invariably adhered to). We remained at the feast, until about two hours in the night, when we went to the house and found Austin; they all went to the cider press and drank, except myself. On returning to the house, Hark went to the door with an axe for the purpose of breaking it open, as we knew we were strong enough to murder the family if they were awaked by the noise; but reflecting that it might create an alarm in the neighborhood, we determined to enter the house

secretly, and murder them whilst sleeping. Hark got a ladder and set it against the chimney, on which I ascended, and hoisting a window, entered and came downstairs, unbarred the door, and removed the guns from their places. It was then observed that I must spill the first blood. On which, armed with a hatchet and accompanied by Will, I entered my master's chamber; it being dark, I could not give a deathblow. The hatchet glanced from his head; he sprang from the bed and called his wife. It was his last word. Will laid him dead with a blow of his axe, and Mrs. Travis shared the same fate as she lay in bed. The murder of this family, five in number, was the work of a moment; not one of them awoke. There was a little infant sleeping in a cradle, that was forgotten, until we had left the house and gone some distance, when Henry and Will returned and killed it; we got here four guns that would shoot and several old muskets, with a pound or two of powder. We remained some time at the barn, where we paraded. I formed them in a line as soldiers, and after carrying them through all the manoeuvres I was master of, marched them off to Mr. Salathul Francis', about six hundred yards distant. Sam and Will went to the door and knocked. Mr. Francis asked who was there. Sam replied it was him, and he had a letter for him; on which he got up and came to the door. They immediately seized him, and dragging him out a little from the door, he was dispatched by repeated blows on the head. There was no other white person in the family. We started from there for Mrs. Reese's, maintaining the most perfect silence on our march, where finding the door unlocked, we entered, and murdered Mrs. Reese in her bed, while sleeping; her son awoke, but it was only to sleep the sleep of death. He had only time to say who is that, and was no more.

*   *   *

Our number amounted now to fifty or sixty, all mounted and armed with guns, axes, swords, and clubs. ...

*   *   *

89 "to annihilate the Cherokee as a political society" (1831)

From the beginning of the European colonization of America, the status of the Native American populations caused both philosophical and practical concern. In the early sixteenth century, serious questions arose regarding the capacity of these aboriginal people to be free, to govern themselves, and to own property. By 1539, Spanish theologian Francisco de Vitoria proclaimed the human rights of the native people; and in 1542, Spanish Law of the Indies decreed that Native Americans were free people not to be enslaved nor have their property taken except in fair trade. Other colonizers as well generally accepted these principles.

By their very existence, the English colonies established along the Atlantic seaboard encroached on Native American occupation and sovereignty. Nevertheless, resistance to Europeans, like King Philip's War in 1675, was largely ineffective. From an early date, the colonies sought to reduce tensions by establishing special areas for exclusive Native American use. In these enclaves, the Native American nations were to exist as "distinct, independent, political communities, retaining their original natural rights." In 1827, the Cherokees in northwestern Georgia declared themselves an independent nation and established a government. The Georgia legislature responded by claiming dominion over all Cherokee territory. The Cherokee Nation sued to enjoin the act of Georgia. In his technical decision that the Cherokee Nation was neither a state of the Union nor a foreign state entitled to sue, Chief Justice Marshall withheld the protection of the federal judiciary from the Cherokees, leaving the protection of their rights to the disposition of the executive branch.

☆89 *Cherokee Nation v. Georgia*

29 U.S. (5 Pet.) 1 (1831).

MARSHALL, C. J. This bill is brought by the Cherokee nation, praying an injuction to restrain the state of Georgia from the execution of certain laws of the state, which, as is alleged, go directly to annihilate the Cherokee as a political society, and to seize for the use of Georgia, the lands of the nation which have been assured to them by the United States, in solemn treaties repeatedly made and still in force.

If courts were permitted to indulge their sympathies, a case better calculated to excite them can scarcely be imagined. A people, once numerous, powerful, and truly independent, found by our ancestors in the quiet and uncontrolled possession of an ample domain, gradually sinking beneath our superior policy, our arts and our arms, have yielded their lands by successive treaties, each of which contains a solemn guarantee of the residue, until they retain no more of their formerly extensive territory than is deemed necessary to their comfortable subsistence. To preserve this remnant, the present application is made.

Before we can look into the merits of the case, a preliminary inquiry presents itself. Has this court jurisdiction of the cause? The third article of the constitution . . . closes an enumeration of the cases to which it is extended, with "controversies between a state or citizens thereof, and foreign states, citizens or subjects." A subsequent clause of the same section gives the supreme court original jurisdiction, in all cases in which a state shall be a party. The party

defendant may then unquestionably be sued in this court. May the plaintiff sue in it? Is the Cherokee nation a foreign state, in the sense in which that term is used in the constitution?

. . . So much of the argument as was intended to prove the character of the Cherokees as a state, as a distinct political society, . . . has in the opinion of a majority of the judges, been completely successful. They have been uniformly treated as a state, from the settlement of our country. The numerous treaties made with them by the United States, recognise them as a people capable of maintaining the relations of peace and war, of being responsible in their political character for any violation of their engagements, or for any aggression committed on the citizens of the United States, by any individual of their community. Laws have been enacted in the spirit of these treaties. The acts of our government plainly recognise the Cherokee nation as a state, and the courts are bound by those acts.

A question of much more difficulty remains. Do the Cherokees constitute a foreign state in the sense of the constitution? The counsel have shown conclusively, that they are not a state of the Union, and have insisted that, individually, they are aliens, not owing allegiance to the United States. An aggregate of aliens composing a state must, they say, be a foreign state; each individual being foreign, the whole must be foreign.

This argument is imposing, but we must examine it more closely, before we yield to it. The condition of the Indians in relation to the United States is, perhaps, unlike that of any other two people in existence. . . . The Indian territory is admitted to compose a part of the United States. In all our maps, geographical treaties, histories and laws, it is so considered. In all our intercourse with foreign nations, in our commercial regulations, in any attempt at intercourse between Indians and foreign nations, they are considered as within the jurisdictional limits of the United States, subject to many of those restraints which are imposed upon our own citizens. They acknowledge themselves, in their treaties, to be under the protection of the United States; they admit, that the United States shall have the sole and exclusive right of regulating the trade with them, and managing all their affairs as they think proper; and the Cherokees in particular were allowed by the treaty of Hopewell, which preceded the constitution, "to send a deputy of their choice, whenever they think fit, to congress." . . .

. . . [I]t may well be doubted, whether those tribes which reside within the acknowledged boundaries of the United States can, with accuracy, be denominated foreign nations. They may, more correctly, perhaps, be denominated domestic dependent nations. They occupy a territory to which we assert a title independent of their will, which must take effect in point of possession, when their right of possession ceases. Meanwhile, they are in a state of pupilage; their relation to the United States resembles that of a ward to his guardian. They look to our government for protection: rely upon its kindness and its power; appeal to it for relief to their wants; and address the president as their great father. They and their country are considered by foreign nations, as well as by ourselves, as being so completely under the sovereignty and dominion of the United States, that any attempt to acquire their lands, or to form a political connection with them would be considered by all as an invasion of our territory and an act of hostility. These considerations go far to support the opinion, that the framers of our constitution had not the Indian tribes in view, when they opened the courts of the Union to controversies between a state or the citizens thereof and foreign states.

*   *   *

[T]he eighth section of the third article ... empowers congress to "regulate commerce with foreign nations, and among the several states, and with the Indian tribes." In this clause, they are as clearly contradistinguished, by a name appropriate to themselves, from foreign nations, as from the several states composing the Union. They are designated by a distinct appellation; and as this appellation can be applied to neither of the others, neither can the application distinguishing either of the others be, in fair construction, applied to them. The objects to which the power of regulating commerce might be directed, are divided into three distinct classes—foreign nations, the several states, and Indian tribes. When forming this article, the convention considered them as entirely distinct. We cannot assume that the distinction was lost, in framing a subsequent article, unless there be something in its language to authorize the assumption.

*   *   *

We perceive plainly, that the constitution, in this article, does not comprehend Indian tribes in the general term "foreign nations;" not, we presume, because a tribe may not be a nation, but because it is not foreign to the United States. When, afterwards, the term "foreign state" is introduced, we cannot impute to the convention, the intention to desert its former meaning, and to comprehend Indian tribes within it, unless the context force that construction on us. We find nothing in the context, and nothing in the subject of the article, which leads to it.

The court has bestowed its best attention on this question, and, after mature deliberation, the majority is of opinion, that an Indian tribe or nation within the United States is not a foreign state, in the sense of the constitution, and cannot maintain an action in the courts of the United States.

A serious additional objection exists to the juris-diction of the court. Is the matter of the bill the proper subject for judicial inquiry and decision? It seeks to restrain a state from the forcible exercise of legislative power over a neighboring people, asserting their independence; their right to which the state denies. On several of the matters alleged in the bill, for example, on the laws making it criminal to exercise the usual powers of self-government in their own country, by the Cherokee nation, this court cannot interpose; at least, in the form in which those matters are presented.

That part of the bill which respects the land occupied by the Indians, and prays the aid of the court to protect their possession, may be more doubtful. The mere question of right might, perhaps, be decided by this court, in a proper case, with proper parties. But the court is asked to do more than decide on the title. The bill requires us to control the legislature of Georgia, and to restrain the exertion of its physical force. The propriety of such an interposition by the court may be well questioned; it savors too much of the exercise of political power, to be within the proper province of the judicial department. But the opinion on the point respecting parties makes it unnecessary to decide this question.

If it be true, that the Cherokee nation have rights, this is not the tribunal in which those rights are to be asserted. If it be true, that wrongs have been inflicted, and that still greater are to be apprehended, this is not the tribunal which can redress the past or prevent the future. The motion for an injunction is denied.

90 "I will not retreat a single inch" (1831)

A man of limited formal education, yet skillful in the startling and militant use of language and the press, William Lloyd Garrison began publishing the abolitionist *Liberator* in Boston in 1831. Garrison believed moral persuasion rather than force or the ballot was the most effective means in the campaign for the immediate and complete abolition of slavery. Though its circulation never exceeded two thousand, *The Liberator* became famous nationwide for its inflammatory language and uncompromising call for abolition.

Garrison's bitter attacks on the moderate antislavery movement earned him enemies in both the North and the South. His zeal led him to advocate Northern secession from the Union because the Constitution permitted slavery, and at a public meeting in Framingham, Massachusetts on July 4, 1854, he burned the Constitution. *The Liberator* and other incendiary publications sparked Southern reaction mostly through the passage of laws prohibiting the advocation of abolition, similar to those laws of an earlier generation which punished the expression of sentiments regarding the illegitimacy of the ruling authorities. After Nat Turner's insurrection, an attempt was made to have Garrison extradited as a criminal from his home state of Massachusetts, and Georgia offered five thousand dollars for his apprehension.

☆ 90 The Liberator

Reprinted in W. Garrison and F. Garrison, *William Lloyd Garrison, 1805-1879: The Story of His Life Told by His Children* (New York: Arno Press, 1969), 1:224-26.

To the Public.

* * *

During my recent tour for the purpose of exciting the minds of the people by a series of discourses on the subject of slavery, every place that I visited gave fresh evidence of the fact, that a greater revolution in public sentiment was to be effected in the free states — *and particularly in New England* — than at the south. I found contempt more bitter, opposition more active, detraction more relentless, prejudice more stubborn, and apathy more frozen, than among slave owners themselves. Of course, there were individual exceptions to the contrary. This state of things afflicted, but did not dishearten me. I determined, at every hazard, to lift up the standard of emancipation in the eyes of the nation, *within sight of Bunker Hill and in the birth place of liberty.* That standard is now unfurled; and long may it float, unhurt by the spoliations of time or the missiles of a desperate foe — yea, till every chain be broken, and every bondman set free! Let Southern oppressors tremble — let their secret abettors tremble — let their Northern apologists tremble — let all the enemies of the persecuted blacks tremble.

... I shall not array myself as the political partisan of any man. In defending the great cause of human rights, I wish to derive the assistance of all religions and of all parties.

Assenting to the "self evident truth" maintained in the American Declaration of Independence, "that all men are created equal, and endowed by their Creator with certain inalienable rights — among which are life, liberty and the pursuit of happiness," I shall strenuously contend for the immediate enfranchisement of our slave population. In Park-Street Church, on the Fourth of July, 1829, in an address on slavery, I unreflectingly assented to the popular but pernicious doctrine of *gradual* abolition. I seize this opportunity to make a full and unequivocal recantation, and thus publicly to ask pardon of my God, of my country, and of my brethren the poor slaves, for having uttered a sentiment so full of timidity, injustice and absurdity....

I am aware, that many object to the severity of my language; but is there not cause for severity? I *will be* as harsh as truth, and as uncompromising as justice. On this subject, I do not wish to think, or speak, or write, with moderation. No! No! Tell a man whose house is on fire, to give a moderate alarm; tell him to moderately rescue his wife from the hands of the ravisher; tell the mother to gradually extricate her babe from the fire into which it has fallen; — but urge me not to use moderation in a cause like the present. I am in earnest — I will not equivocate — I will not excuse — I will not retreat a single inch — AND I WILL BE HEARD. The apathy of the people is enough to make every statue leap from its pedestal, and to hasten the resurrection of the dead.

It is pretended, that I am retarding the cause of emancipation by the coarseness of my invective, and the precipitancy of my measures. *The charge is not true.* On this question my influence, — humble as it is, — is felt at this moment to a considerable extent, and shall be felt in coming years — not perniciously, but beneficially — not as a curse, but as a blessing; and posterity will bear testimony that I was right. I desire to thank God, that he enables me to disregard "the fear of man which bringeth a snare," and to speak his truth in its simplicity and power....

William Lloyd Garrison

91 Independent Political Communities (1832)

The Georgia law extending state jurisdiction over Native American country also included a provision exacting a loyalty oath to the state of Georgia from any white person "residing within the limits of the Cherokee nation." For failure to take this oath, Samuel A. Worcester, a missionary from Vermont holding a commission from the United States to proselytize among the Native Americans, was sentenced to four years at hard labor — the maximum penalty under the law.

At issue was the constitutionality of Georgia's enforcement of its law within the territory occupied by Cherokees in the state — sovereignty over the inhabitants of that land. The court rejected all of Georgia's arguments and recognized the Cherokees to be a distinct, sovereign, and self-governing community with the rights to possess a definable tract of land over which they had dominion and authority, except to the extent that they voluntarily ceded it away. The laws of Georgia were ineffective therein, and the citizens of Georgia could not enter the territory without the assent of the Cherokee Nation. The decision was the high-water mark of the legal recognition accorded to the political independence of the Native American nations. There was no language of "pupilage" or "tutelage" as there was in the court's decision in *Cherokee Nation* the term before.

But this legal protection was available only insofar as assaults upon Native American rights were by way of state authority. Native American relations with the United States were not scrutinized in this case, and Justice McLean's concurring opinion, while supportive of the existing rights of the Cherokee Nation, contemplated them as being predicated more upon policy choices of the United States rather than matters of natural right. But these opinions deserve careful reading because they touch upon matters that are at the root of understanding political criminality: the coherence of a people, the exercise of territorial dominion, and the power to demand allegiance. The Cherokees as a people were considered politically independent of Georgia (and the United States), since they were self-governing. Allegiance was not owed by the Cherokee to the United States, and, as Justice McLean pointed out, "We have recognized in them the right to make war. No one has ever supposed that the Indians could commit treason against the United States . . . we have inflicted punishment on them as a nation, and not on individual offenders among them as traitors." Attention also should be directed to his assertion that "the abstract right of every section of the human race to a reasonable portion of the soil, by which to acquire the means of subsistence, cannot be controverted."

☆ 91 *Worcester v. Georgia*

31 U.S. (6 Pet.) 515 (1832).

Mr. Chief Justice MARSHALL delivered the opinion of the Court. The extra-territorial power of every legislature being limited in its action to its own citizens or subjects, the very passage of this act is an assertion of jurisdiction over the Cherokee nation, and of the rights and powers consequent on jurisdiction.

The first step, then, in the inquiry, which the Constitution and laws impose on this Court, is an examination of the rightfulness of this claim.

America, separated from Europe by a wide ocean, was inhabited by a distinct people, divided into separate nations, independent of each other and of the rest of the world, having institutions of their own, and governing themselves by their own laws. It is difficult to comprehend the proposition, that the inhabitants of either quarter of the globe could have rightful original claims of dominion over the inhabitants of the other, or over the lands they occupied; or that the discovery of either by the other should give the discoverer rights in the country discovered, which annulled the pre-existing right of its ancient possessors.

*   *   *

But power, war, conquest, give rights, which, after possession, are conceded by the world; and which can never be controverted by those on whom they descend. . . .

The great maritime powers of Europe discovered and visited different parts of this continent at nearly the same time. The object was too immense for any one of them to grasp the whole; and the claimants were too powerful to submit to the exclusive or unreasonable pretensions of any single potentate. To avoid bloody conflicts, which might terminate disastrously to all, it was necessary for the nations of Europe to establish some principle which all would acknowledge, and which should decide their respective rights as between themselves. This principle, suggested by the actual state of things, was, "that discovery gave title to the government by whose subjects or by whose authority it was made, against all other European governments, which title might be consummated by possession."

This principle, acknowledged by all Europeans, because it was the interest of all to acknowledge it, gave to the nation making the discovery, as its inevitable consequence, the sole right of acquiring the soil and of making settlements on it. It was an exclusive principle which shut out the right of competition among those who had agreed to it; not one which could annul the previous rights of those who had not agreed to it. It regulated the right given by discovery among the European discoverers; but could not affect the rights of those already in possession, either as aboriginal occupants, or as occupants by virtue of a discovery made before the memory of man. It gave the exclusive right to purchase, but did not found that right on a denial of the right of the possessor to sell.

The relation between the Europeans and the natives was determined in each case by the particular government which asserted and could maintain this pre-emptive privilege in the particular place. The United States succeeded to all the claims of Great Britain, both territorial and political; but no attempt, so far as is known, has been made to enlarge them. . . .

Soon after Great Britain determined on planting colonies in America, the king granted charters to companies of his subjects who associated for the purpose of carrying the views of the crown into effect, and of enriching themselves. The first of these charters was made before possession was taken of any part of the country. They purport, generally, to convey the soil, from the Atlantic to the South Sea. This soil was occupied by numerous and warlike nations, equally willing and able to defend their possessions. The extravagant and absurd idea, that the feeble settlements made on the sea-coast, or the companies under whom they were made, acquired legitimate power by them to govern the people, or occupy the lands from sea to sea, did not enter the mind of any man. They were well understood to convey the title which, according to the common law of European sovereigns respecting America, they might rightfully convey, and no more. This was the exclusive right of purchasing such lands as the natives were willing to sell. The crown could not be understood to grant what the crown did not affect to claim; nor was it so understood.

The power of making war is conferred by these charters on the colonies, but defensive war alone seems to have been contemplated. . . .

*   *   *

The charter to Georgia professes to be granted for the charitable purpose of enabling poor subjects to gain a comfortable subsistence by cultivating lands in the American provinces "at present waste and desolate." It recites: "And whereas our provinces in North America have been frequently ravaged by Indian enemies, more especially that of South Carolina, which, in the late war by the neighbouring savages, was laid waste by fire and sword, and great numbers of the English inhabitants miserably massacred; and our loving subjects, who now inhabit there, by reason of the smallness of their numbers, will, in case of any new war, be exposed to the like calamities, inasmuch as their whole southern frontier continueth unsettled, and lieth open to the said savages."

These motives for planting the new colony are incompatible with the lofty ideas of granting the soil and all its inhabitants from sea to sea. They demonstrate the truth, that these grants asserted a title against Europeans only, and were considered as blank paper so far as the rights of the natives were concerned. The power of war is given only for defence, not for conquest.

The charters contain passages showing one of their objects to be the civilization of the Indians, and their conversion to Christianity—objects to be accomplished by conciliatory conduct and good example; not by extermination.

. . . Fierce and warlike in their character, [the Indians] might be formidable enemies, or effective friends. Instead of rousing their resentments, by asserting claims to their lands, or to dominion over their persons, their alliance was sought by flattering professions, and purchased by rich presents. The English, the French, and the Spaniards, were equally competitors for their friendship and their aid. Not well acquainted with the exact meaning of words, nor supposing it to be material whether they were called the subjects, or the children of their father in Europe; lavish in professions of duty and affection, in return for the rich presents they received; so long as their actual independence was untouched, and their right to self-government acknowledged, they were willing to profess dependence on the

power which furnished supplies of which they were in absolute need, and restrained dangerous intruders from entering their country; and this was probably the sense in which the term was understood by them.

Certain it is, that our history furnishes no example, from the first settlement of our country, of any attempt on the part of the crown to interfere with the internal affairs of the Indians, farther than to keep out the agents of foreign powers, who, as traders or otherwise, might seduce them into foreign alliances. The king purchased their lands when they were willing to sell, at a price they were willing to take; but never coerced a surrender of them. He also purchased their alliance and dependence by subsidies; but never intruded into the interior of their affairs, or interfered with their self-government, so far as respected themselves only.

*   *   *

Such was the policy of Great Britain towards the Indian nations inhabiting the territory from which she excluded all other Europeans . . . : she considered them as nations capable of maintaining the relations of peace and war; of governing themselves, under her protection; and she made treaties with them, the obligation of which she acknowledged.

*   *   *

During the war of the revolution, the Cherokees took part with the British. After its termination, the United States, though desirous of peace, did not feel its necessity so strongly as while the war continued. Their political situation being changed, they might very well think it advisable to assume a higher tone, and to impress on the Cherokees the same respect for Congress which was before felt for the King of Great Britain. This may account for the language of the treaty of Hopewell. There is the more reason for supposing that the Cherokee chiefs were not very critical judges of the language, from the fact that every one makes his mark; no chief was capable of signing his name. It is probable the treaty was interpreted to them.

The treaty is introduced with the declaration, that "the commissioners plenipotentiary of the United States give peace to all the Cherokees, and receive them into the favour and protection of the United States of America, on the following conditions."

When the United States gave peace, did they not also receive it? Were not both parties desirous of it? If we consult the history of the day, does it not inform us that the United States were at least as anxious to obtain it as the Cherokees? We may ask, further: did the Cherokees come to the seat of the American government to solicit peace; or, did the American commissioners go to them to obtain it? The treaty was made at Hopewell, not at New York.

The word "give," then, has no real importance attached to it.

*   *   *

The third article acknowledges the Cherokees to be under the protection of the United States of America, and of no other power. . . . The Indians perceived in [an earlier] protection only what was beneficial to themselves—an engagement to punish aggressions on them. It involved, practically, no claim to their lands, no dominion over their persons. It merely bound the nation to the British crown, as a dependent ally, claiming the protection of a powerful friend and neighbour, and receiving the advantages of that protection, without involving a surrender of their national character.

This is the true meaning of the stipulation, and is undoubtedly the sense in which it was made. Neither the British government nor the Cherokees ever understood it otherwise.

The same stipulation entered into with the United States, is undoubtedly to be construed in the same manner. They receive the Cherokee nation into their favour and protection. The Cherokees acknowledge themselves to be under the protection of the United States, and of no other power. Protection does not imply the destruction of the protected. . . .

*   *   *

The ninth article is in these words: "for the benefit and comfort of the Indians, and for the prevention of injuries or oppressions on the part of the citizens or Indians, the United States, in Congress assembled, shall have the sole and exclusive right of regulating the trade with the Indians, and managing all their affairs, as they think proper."

To construe the expression "managing all their affairs," into a surrender of self-government, would be, we think a perversion of their necessary meaning, and a departure from the construction which has been uniformly put on them. The great subject of the article is the Indian trade. . . . Is it credible, that they should have considered themselves as surrendering to the United States the right to dictate their future cessions, and the terms on which they should be made? or to compel their submission to the violence of disorderly and licentious intruders? It is equally inconceivable that they could have supposed themselves, by a phrase thus slipped into an article, on another and most interesting subject, to have divested themselves of the right of self-government on subjects not connected with trade. . . . Such a construction . . . would convert a treaty of peace covertly into an act, annihilating the political existence of one of the parties. Had such a result been intended, it would have been openly avowed.

This treaty . . . treat[s] the Cherokees as a nation capable of maintaining the relations of peace and war; and ascertain[s] the boundaries between them and the United States.

The treaty of Hopewell seems not to have established a solid peace. To accommodate the differences still existing between the state of Georgia and the Cherokee nation, the treaty of Holston was negotiated in July, 1791. . . .

*   *   *

By the fifth article, the Cherokees allow the United States a road through their country, and the navigation of the Tennessee river. The acceptance of these cessions is an acknowledgment of the right of the Cherokees to make or withhold them. . . .

*   *   *

This treaty, thus explicitly recognising the national character of the Cherokees, and their right of self-government; thus guarantying their lands; assuming the duty of protection, and of course pledging the faith of the United States for that protection; has been frequently renewed and is now in full force. . . .

*   *   *

In 1819, Congress passed an act for promoting those humane designs of civilizing the neighbouring Indians, which had long been cherished by the executive. . . .

This act avowedly contemplates the preservation of the Indian nations as an object sought by the United States, and proposes to effect this object by civilizing and converting them from hunters into agriculturists. . . .

*   *   *

The Indian nations had always been considered as distinct, independent political communities, retaining their original natural rights, as the undisputed possessors of the soil, from time immemorial, with the single exception of that imposed by irresistible power, which excluded them from intercourse with any other European potentate than the first discoverer of the coast of the particular region claimed; and this was a restriction which those European potentates imposed on themselves, as well as on the Indians. The very term "nation," so generally applied to them, means "a people distinct from others." The Constitution, by declaring treaties already made, as well as those to be made, to be the supreme law of the land, has adopted and sanctioned the previous treaties with the Indian nations, and consequently admits their rank among those powers who are capable of making treaties. The words "treaty" and "nation" are words of our own language, selected in our diplomatic and legislative proceedings, by ourselves, having each a definite and well understood meaning. We have applied them to Indians, as we have applied them to the other nations of the earth. They are applied to all in the same sense.

*   *   *

In opposition to this original right, possessed by the undisputed occupants of every country; to this recognition of that right, which is evidenced by our history, in every change through which we have passed; is placed the charters granted by the monarch of a distant and distinct region, parcelling out a territory in possession of others whom he could not remove and did not attempt to remove, and the cession made of his claims by the treaty of peace.

The actual state of things at the time, and all history since, explain these charters; and the King of Great Britain, at the treaty of peace, could cede only what belonged to his crown.... [T]he settled doctrine of the law of nations is, that a weaker power does not surrender its independence—its right to self-government, by associating with a stronger, and taking its protection. A weak state, in order to provide for its safety, may place itself under the protection of one more powerful, without stripping itself of the right of government, and ceasing to be a state. Examples of this kind are not wanting in Europe. "Tributary and feudatory states," says Vattel, "do not thereby cease to be sovereign and independent states, so long as self-government and sovereign and independent authority are left in the administration of the state." . . .

The Cherokee nation, then, is a distinct community, occupying its own territory, with boundaries accurately described, in which the laws of Georgia can have no force, and which the citizens of Georgia have no right to enter, but with the assent of the Cherokees themselves, or in conformity with treaties, and with the acts of Congress. The whole intercourse between the United States and this nation, is, by our Constitution and laws, vested in the government of the United States.

*   *   *

[The laws of Georgia] are in direct hostility with treaties, repeated in a succession of years, which mark out the boundary that separates the Cherokee country from Georgia; guaranty to them all the land within their boundary; solemnly pledge the faith of the United States to restrain their citizens from trespassing on it; and recognise the pre-existing power of the nation to govern itself.

They are in equal hostility with the acts of Congress for regulating this intercourse, and giving effect to the treaties.

The forcible seizure and abduction of the plaintiff in error, who was residing in the nation with its permission, and by authority of the President of the United States, is also a violation of the acts which authorize the chief magistrate to exercise this authority.

*   *   *

It is the Opinion of this Court that the judgment of the Superior Court for the county of Gwinnett, in the state of Georgia, condemning Samuel A. Worcester to hard labour in the penitentiary of the state of Georgia, for four years, was pronounced by that Court under colour of a law which is void, as being repugnant to the Constitution, treaties, and laws of the United States, and ought, therefore, to be reversed and annulled.

Mr. Justice McLean. As this case involves principles of the highest importance, and may lead to consequences which shall have an enduring influence on the institutions of this country; and as there are some points in the case on which I wish to state, distinctly, my opinion, I embrace the privilege of doing so.

With the decision just given, I concur.

*   *   *

The abstract right of every section of the human race to a reasonable portion of the soil, by which to acquire the means of subsistence, cannot be controverted. And it is equally clear, that the range of nations or tribes, who exist in the hunter state, may be restricted within reasonable limits. They shall not be permitted to roam, in the pursuit of game, over an extensive and rich country, whilst in other parts, human beings are crowded so closely together as to render the means of subsistence precarious. . . .

In this view, perhaps, our ancestors, when they first migrated to this country, might have taken possession of a limited extent of the domain, had they been sufficiently powerful, without negotiation or purchase from the native Indians. But this course is believed to have been nowhere taken. A more conciliatory mode was preferred, and one which was better calculated to impress the Indians, who were then powerful, with a sense of the justice of their white neighbours. The occupancy of their lands was never assumed, except upon the basis of contract, and on the payment of a valuable consideration.

*   *   *

. . . Some cessions of territory may have been made by the Indians, in compliance with the terms on which peace was offered by the whites; but the soil, thus taken, was taken by the laws of conquest, and always as an indemnity for the expenses of the war, commenced by the Indians.

At no time has the sovereignty of the country been recognised as existing in the Indians, but they have been always admitted to possess many of the attributes of sovereignty. All the rights which belong to self-government have been recognised as vested in them. Their right of occupancy has never been questioned, but the fee in the soil has been considered in the government. This may be called the right to the ultimate domain, but the Indians have a present right of possession.

In some of the old states, Massachusetts, Connecticut, Rhode Island, and others, where small remnants of tribes remain, surrounded by white population, and who, by their reduced numbers, had lost the power of self-government, the laws of the state have been extended over them, for the protection of their persons and property.

*   *   *

It must be admitted, that the Indians sustain a peculiar relation to the United States. They do not constitute, as was decided at the last term, a foreign state, so as to claim the right to sue in the Supreme Court of the United States: and yet, having the right of self-government, they, in some sense, form a state. In the management of their internal concerns, they are dependent on no power. They punish offences under their own laws, and, in doing so, they are responsible to no earthly tribunal. They make war, and form treaties of peace. The exercise of these and other powers, gives to them a distinct character as a people, and constitutes them, in some respects, a state, although they may not be admitted to possess the rights of soil.

*   *   *

Every state is more or less dependent on those which surround it: but, unless this dependence shall extend so far as to merge the political existence of the protected people into that of their protectors, they may still constitute a state. They may exercise the powers not relinquished, and bind themselves as a distinct and separate community.

*   *   *

The question may be asked, is no distinction to be made between a civilized and savage people? Are our Indians to be placed upon a footing with the nations of Europe, with whom we have made treaties?

The inquiry is not, what station shall now be given to the Indian tribes in our country? but what relation have they sustained to us, since the commencement of our government?

We have made treaties with them; and are those treaties to be disregarded on our part, because they were entered into with an uncivilized people? Does this lessen the obligation of such treaties? By entering into them, have we not admitted the power of this people to bind themselves, and to impose obligations on us?

The President and Senate, except under the treaty-making power, cannot enter into compacts with the Indians, or with foreign nations. This power has been uniformly exercised in forming treaties with the Indians.

Nations differ from each other in condition, and that of the same nation may change by the revolu-

tions of time, but the principles of justice are the same. They rest upon a base which will remain beyond the endurance of time.

*   *   *

By numerous treaties with the Indian tribes, we have acquired accessions of territory, of incalculable value to the Union. Except by compact, we have not even claimed a right of way through the Indian lands. We have recognised in them the right to make war. No one has ever supposed that the Indians could commit treason against the United States. We have punished them for their violation of treaties; but we have inflicted the punishment on them as a nation, and not on individual offenders among them as traitors.

*   *   *

It is important, on this part of the case, to ascertain in what light Georgia has considered the Indian title to lands, generally, and particularly, within her own boundaries; and also, as to the right of the Indians to self-government.

*   *   *

In a memorial to the President of the United States, by the legislature of Georgia, in 1819, they say, "it has long been the desire of Georgia, that her settlements should be extended to her ultimate limits." "That the soil within her boundaries should be subjected to her control; and, that her police organization and government should be fixed and permanent." "That the state of Georgia claims a right to the jurisdiction and soil of the territory within her limits." "She admits, however, that the right is inchoate — remaining to be perfected by the United States, in the extinction of the Indian title; the United States pro hac vice as their agents."

*   *   *

Neither Georgia, nor the United States, when the cession was made, contemplated that force should be used in the extinguishment of the Indian title; nor that it should be procured on terms that are not reasonable. . . .

*   *   *

Much has been said against the existence of an independent power within a sovereign state; and the conclusion has been drawn, that the Indians, as a matter of right, cannot enforce their own laws within the territorial limits of a state. The refutation of this argument is found in our past history.

Might not the same objection to this interior independent power, by Georgia, have been urged, with as much force as at present, ever since the adoption of the Constitution? Her chartered limits, to the extent claimed, embraced a great number of different nations of Indians, all of whom were governed by their own laws, and were amenable only to them. Has not this been the condition of the Indians within Tennessee, Ohio, and other states?

The exercise of this independent power surely does not become more objectionable, as it assumes the basis of justice and the forms of civilization. Would it not be a singular argument to admit, that, so long as the Indians govern by the rifle and the tomahawk, their government may be tolerated; but, that it must be suppressed, so soon as it shall be administered upon the enlightened principles of reason and justice?

Are not those nations of Indians who have made some advances in civilization better neighbours than those who are still in a savage state? And is not the principle, as to their self-government, within the jurisdiction of a state, the same?

*　　　*　　　*

The exercise of the power of self-government by the Indians, within a state, is undoubtedly contemplated to be temporary. This is shown by the settled policy of the government, in the extinguishment of their title, and especially by the compact with the state of Georgia. It is a question, not of abstract right, but of public policy. I do not mean to say, that the same moral rule which should regulate the affairs of private life, should not be regarded by communities or nations. But, a sound national policy does require that the Indian tribes within our states should exchange their territories, upon equitable principles, or eventually consent to become amalgamated in our political communities.

At best they can enjoy a very limited independence within the boundaries of a state, and such a residence must always subject them to encroachments from the settlements around them; and their existence within a state, as a separate and independent community, may seriously embarrass or obstruct the operation of the state laws. If, therefore, it would be inconsistent with the political welfare of the states, and the social advance of their citizens, that an independent and permanent power should exist within their limits, this power must give way to the greater power which surrounds it, or seek its exercise beyond the sphere of state authority.

This state of things can only be produced by a co-operation of the state and federal governments. The latter has the exclusive regulation of intercourse with the Indians; and, so long as this power shall be exercised, it cannot be obstructed by the state. It is a power given by the Constitution, and sanctioned by the most solemn acts of both the federal and state governments: consequently, it cannot be abrogated at the will of a state....

*　　　*　　　*

92 The Nullifying Laws of South Carolina (1832)

The Southern states considered Northern opposition to slavery an attack on the vested property rights of Southern citizens. They perceived Northern economic developments and political trends as inimical to Southern interests, and particularly so as these developments found their way into federal legislation. Following earlier patterns of resistance to central authority, Southern legislatures declared certain federal duties and imposts to be invalid under the United States Constitution, making it unlawful for the laws to be enforced and threatening secession. Many of the arguments against the validity of these Northern-inspired economic regulations are reminiscent of the abolitionist denunciations of the South's repressive laws against blacks.

President Andrew Jackson ignored these enactments, endorsing the position that the determination of the constitutionality of United States laws was a judicial function, not state legislative function.

☆ 92 Proclamation by Andrew Jackson, President of the United States (December 10, 1832)

11 Stat. 771 (1832).

WHEREAS, a convention assembled in the State of South Carolina, have passed an ordinance, by which they declare, "That the several acts and parts of acts of the Congress of the United States, purporting to be laws for the imposing of duties and imposts on the importation of foreign commodities, and now having actual operation and effect within the United States ... are unauthorized by the Constitution of the United States, and violate the true meaning and intent thereof, and are null and void, and no law," nor binding on the citizens of that State, or its officers; and by the said ordinance, it is further declared to be unlawful for any of the constituted authorities of the State, or of the United States, to enforce the payment of the duties imposed by the said acts, within the same State, and that it is the duty of the legislature to pass such laws as may be necessary to give full effect to the said ordinance:

*　　　*　　　*

And, finally, the said ordinance declares that the people of South Carolina will maintain the said ordinance at every hazard; and that they will consider the passage of any act, by Congress, abolishing or closing the ports of the said State, or otherwise obstructing the free ingress or egress of vessels to and from the said ports, or any other act of the Federal Government to coerce the State, shut up her ports, destroy or harass her commerce, or to enforce the said acts otherwise than through the civil tribunals of the country, as inconsistent with the longer continuance of South Carolina in the Union; and that the people of the said State will thenceforth hold themselves absolved from all further obligation to maintain or preserve their political connection with the people of the other States, and will forthwith proceed to organize a separate government, and do all other acts and things which sovereign and independent States may of right do:

And whereas the said ordinance prescribes to the people of South Carolina a course of conduct in direct violation of their duty as citizens of the United States, contrary to the laws of their country, subversive of its constitution, and having for its object the destruction of the Union—that Union, which, coeval with our political existence, led our fathers, without any other ties to unite them than those of patriotism and a common cause, through a sanguinary struggle to a glorious independence,—that sacred Union hitherto inviolate, which, perfected by our happy Constitution, has brought us, by the favor of Heaven, to a state of prosperity at home, and high consideration abroad, rarely, if ever, equalled in the history of nations—To preserve this bond of our political existence from destruction, to maintain inviolate this state of national honor and prosperity, and to justify the confidence my fellow-citizens have reposed in me, I, ANDREW JACKSON, President of the United States, have thought proper to issue this my proclamation, stating my views of the Constitution and laws applicable to the measures adopted by the convention of South Carolina, and to the reasons they have put forth to sustain them. . . .

*   *   *

The ordinance is founded, not on the indefeasible right of resisting acts which are plainly unconstitutional, and too oppressive to be endured; but on the strange position that any one State may not only declare an act of Congress void, but prohibit its execution—that they may do this consistently with the Constitution—that the true construction of the instrument permits a State to retain its place in the Union, and yet be bound by no other of its laws than those it may choose to consider as constitutional. It is true, they add, that to justify this abrogation of a law, it must be palpably contrary to the Constitution; but it is evident, that to give the right of resisting laws of the description, coupled with the uncontrolled right to decide what laws deserve that character, is to give the power of resisting all laws. For, as by the theory, there is no appeal, the reasons alleged by the State, good or bad, must prevail. If it should be said that public opinion is a sufficient check against the abuse of this power, it may be asked why it is not deemed a sufficient guard

against the passage of an unconstitutional act by Congress? . . .

If this doctrine had been established at an earlier day, the Union would have been dissolved in its infancy. The excise law in Pennsylvania, the embargo and non-intercourse law in the Eastern States, the carriage tax in Virginia, were all deemed unconstitutional, and were more unequal in their operation than any of the laws now complained of; but fortunately, none of those States discovered that they had the right now claimed by South Carolina. The war [of 1812] . . . might have ended in defeat and disgrace, instead of victory and honor, if the States who supposed it a ruinous and unconstitutional measure, had thought they possessed the right of nullifying the act by which it was declared, and denying supplies for its prosecution. . . . To the statesmen of South Carolina belongs [this] invention, and upon the citizens of that State will unfortunately fall the evils of reducing it to practice.

If the doctrine of a State veto upon the laws of the Union carries with it internal evidence of its impracticable absurdity, our constitutional history will also afford abundant proof that it would have been repudiated with indignation had it been proposed to form a feature in our government.

*   *   *

Under the confederation, no State could legally annul a decision of the Congress, or refuse to submit to its execution; but no provision was made to enforce these decisions. Congress made requisitions, but they were not complied with. The government could not operate on individuals. They had no Judiciary, no means of collecting revenue.

But the defects of the confederation need not be detailed. Under its operation we could scarcely be called a nation. We had neither prosperity at home nor consideration abroad. This state of things could not be endured, and our present happy Constitution was formed, but formed in vain, if this fatal doctrine prevails. . . . [C]an it be conceived, that an instrument made for the purpose of *"forming a more perfect Union,"* than that of the confederation, could be so constructed by the assembled wisdom of our country, as to substitute for that confederation a form of government dependent for its existence on the local interest, the party spirit of a State, or of a prevailing faction in a State? Every man of plain, unsophisticated understanding, who hears the question, will give such an answer as will preserve the Union. Metaphysical subtlety, in pursuit of an impracticable theory could alone have devised one that is calculated to destroy it.

I consider, then, the power to annul a law of the United States, assumed by one State, *incompatible with the existence of the Union, contradicted ex-*

*pressly by the letter of the Constitution, unauthor-
ized by its spirit, inconsistent with every principle
on which it was founded, and destructive of the
great object for which it was formed.*

*   *   *

93 "Slavery is contrary to the principles of natural justice" (1833)

William Lloyd Garrison sought to channel abolitionist sentiments by organizing the Anti-Slavery Society in 1833. A handful of delegates met in Philadelphia for the event. Garrison not only fought in the
United States for abolition but also traveled
throughout the world to foster support for his campaign. Taunted by his fellow citizens who once
raised a gallows for him in front of his Boston home,
Garrison observed in 1851, "The truth is, he who
commences any reform which at last becomes one of
transcendent importance and is crowned with victory is always ill-judged and unfairly estimated. At
the outset he is looked upon with contempt and
treated in the most opprobrious manner as a wild
fanatic or a dangerous organizer. In the clear light of
Reason, it will be seen that he simply stood up to
discharge a duty which he owed to his God, to his
fellow-men, to the land of his nativity."

While these documents call for immediate action,
they eschew physical force as a legitimate means of
accomplishing their ends. Despite the claim they did
only that which was lawful in service of their cause,
many of their actions were illegal under the laws of
the slave states. But of course *those* laws were declared utterly null and void. The document also relates the nature in which the federal government
supported the institution, if not the spread, of
slavery.

☆ 93 Documents of the American Anti-Slavery
Society (December 4, 1833)

Reprinted in W. Garrison and F. Garrison, *William Lloyd
Garrison, 1805-1879: The Story of His Life Told by His Children* (New York: Arno Press, 1969), 1:3-4, 408.

☆ 93a Constitution

Whereas the Most High God "hath made of one
blood all nations of men to dwell on all the face of the
earth," and hath commanded them to love their
neighbors as themselves; and whereas, our National
Existence is based upon this principle, as recognized
in the Declaration of Independence, "that all mankind are created equal, and that they are endowed
by their Creator with certain inalienable rights,
among which are life, liberty, and the pursuit of happiness"; and whereas, after the lapse of nearly sixty

years, since the faith and honor of the American people were pledged to this avowal, before Almighty
God and the World, nearly one-sixth part of the nation are held in bondage by their fellow-citizens; and
whereas, Slavery is contrary to the principles of natural justice, of our republican form of government,
and of the Christian religion, and is destructive of
the prosperity of the country, while it is endangering the peace, union, and liberties of the States; and
whereas, we believe it the duty and interest of the
masters immediately to emancipate their slaves,
and that no scheme of expatriation, either voluntary
or by compulsion, can remove this great and increasing evil; and whereas, we believe that it is practicable, by appeals to the consciences, hearts, and interests of the people, to awaken a public sentiment
throughout the nation that will be opposed to the
continuance of Slavery in any part of the Republic,
and by effecting the speedy abolition of Slavery, prevent a general convulsion; and whereas, we believe
we owe it to the oppressed, to our fellow-citizens
who hold slaves, to our whole country, to posterity,
and to God, to do all that is lawfully in our power to
bring about the extinction of Slavery, we do hereby
agree, with a prayerful reliance on the Divine aid, to
form ourselves into a society, to be governed by the
following Constitution: —

ART. I. — This Society shall be called the AMERI-
CAN ANTI-SLAVERY SOCIETY.

ART. II. — The object of this Society is the entire
abolition of Slavery in the United States. . . .

[I]t shall aim to convince all our fellow-citizens . . .
that Slave-holding is a heinous crime in the sight of
God, and that the duty, safety, and best interests of
all concerned, require its *immediate abandonment*
without expatriation. . . .

ART. III. — This Society shall aim to elevate the
character and condition of the people of color, . . . but
this Society will never, in any way, countenance the
oppressed in vindicating their rights by resorting to
physical force.

*   *   *

☆ 93b Declaration of Sentiments

*   *   *

We have met together for the achievement of an enterprise without which that of our fathers is
incomplete. . . .

Their grievances, great as they were, were trifling in comparison with the wrongs and sufferings
of those for whom we plead. Our fathers were never
slaves — never bought and sold like cattle — never
shut out from the light of knowledge and religion —
never subjected to the lash of brutal taskmasters.

But those, for whose emancipation we are striving — constituting at the present time at least one-

sixth part of our countrymen—are recognized by law, and treated by their fellow-beings, as brute beasts; are plundered daily of the fruits of their toil without redress; really enjoy no constitutional nor legal protection from licentious and murderous outrages upon their persons; and are ruthlessly torn asunder—the tender babe from the arms of its frantic mother—the heartbroken wife from her weeping husband—at the caprice or pleasure of irresponsible tyrants. For the crime of having a dark complexion, they suffer the pangs of hunger, the infliction of stripes, the ignominy of brutal servitude. They are kept in heathenish darkness by laws expressly enacted to make their instruction a criminal offence.

*   *   *

[W]e maintain—that, in view of the civil and religious privileges of this nation, the guilt of its oppression is unequalled by any other on the face of the earth; and, therefore, that it is bound to repent instantly, to undo the heavy burdens, and to let the oppressed go free. . . .

It is piracy to buy or steal an native African, and subject him to servitude. Surely, the sin is as great to enslave an American as an African.

[W]e believe and affirm—that there is no difference, in principle, between the African slave trade and American slavery:

That every American citizen, who detains a human being in involuntary bondage as his property, is, according to Scripture (Ex. xxi, 16), a man-stealer.

That the slaves ought instantly to be set free, and brought under the protection of law:

*   *   *

That if they had lived from the time of Pharaoh down to the present period, and had been entailed through successive generations, their right to be free could never have been alienated, but their claims would have constantly risen in solemnity:

That all those laws which are now in force, admitting the right of slavery, are therefore, before God, utterly null and void; being an audacious usurpation of the Divine prerogative, a daring infringement on the law of nature, a base overthrow of the very foundations of the social compact, a complete extinction of all the relations, endearments and obligations of mankind, and a presumptuous transgression of all the holy commandments; and that therefore they ought instantly to be abrogated.

*   *   *

We maintain that no compensation should be given to the planters emancipating their slaves:

Because it would be a surrender of the great fundamental principle, that man cannot hold property in man:

Because slavery is a crime, and therefore is not an article to be sold:

Because the holders of slaves are not the just proprietors of what they claim; freeing the slave is not depriving them of property, but restoring it to its rightful owner; it is not wronging the master, but righting the slave—restoring him to himself:

*   *   *

Because, if compensation is to be given at all, it should be given to the outraged and guiltless slaves, and not to those who have plundered and abused them.

We regard as delusive, cruel and dangerous, any scheme of expatriation which pretends to aid, either directly or indirectly, in the emancipation of the slaves, or to be a substitute for the immediate and total abolition of slavery.

We fully and unanimously recognise the sovereignty of each State, to legislate exclusively on the subject of the slavery which is tolerated within its limits; we concede that Congress, under the present national compact, has no right to interfere with any of the slave States, in relation to this momentous subject:

But we maintain that Congress has a right, and is solemnly bound, to suppress the domestic slave trade between the several States, and to abolish slavery in those portions of our territory which the Constitution has placed under its exclusive jurisdiction.

We also maintain that there are, at the present time, the highest obligations resting upon the people of the free States to remove slavery by moral and political action, as prescribed in the Constitution of the United States. They are now living under a pledge of their tremendous physical force, to fasten the galling fetters of tyranny upon the limbs of millions in the Southern States; they are liable to be called at any moment to suppress a general insurrection of the slaves; they authorize the slave owner to vote for three-fifths of his slaves as property, and thus enable him to perpetuate his oppression; they support a standing army at the South for its protection; and they seize the slave, who has escaped into their territories, and send him back to be tortured by an enraged master or a brutal driver. This relation to slavery is criminal, and full of danger: IT MUST BE BROKEN UP.

These are our views and principles—these our designs and measures. With entire confidence in the overruling justice of God, we plant ourselves upon the Declaration of our Independence and the truths of Divine Revelation, as upon the Everlasting Rock. . . .

94 Reward for Laying Violent Hands (1835)

Abolitionist newspapers, such as William Lloyd Garrison's *Liberator*, were blamed by many Southerners for Nat Turner's rebellion. Despite bans on the literature, Garrison and his adherents continued to mail newspapers and other antislavery propaganda throughout the nation, particularly to the South. But the supporters of slavery resorted to illegal actions as well. In July 1835 abolitionist literature was taken from post offices in Charleston, South Carolina, and was burned. Northerners, too, were hostile to abolition, seeing it as inimical to the peaceful continuation of the Union. On October 21, Garrison was paraded around Boston in a noose during a riot directed against visiting English abolitionist George Thompson that this poster advertised.

☆ 94 Thompson, the Abolitionist

Reprinted from a poster of October 21, 1835.

THOMPSON,
THE ABOLITIONIST.

That infamous foreign scoundrel THOMPSON, will hold forth *this afternoon*, at the Liberator Office, No. 48, Washington Street. The present is a fair opportunity for the friends of the Union to *snake Thompson out!* It will be a contest between the Abolitionists and the friends of the Union. A purse of $100 has been raised by a number of patriotic citizens to reward the individual who shall first lay violent hands on Thompson, so that he may be brought to the tar kettle before dark. Friends of the Union, be vigilant!

Boston, Wednesday, 12 o'clock.

95 The Removal of the "aboriginal people" (1835)

The Supreme Court decision in *Worcester v. Georgia* was immensely unpopular, and Georgia officials continued to exercise jurisdiction in Cherokee territory. Although Worcester was set free, the case's lofty language went unenforced. The federal executive made every effort to convince the Native Americans they could not be safeguarded and protected under the terms of the federal treaties unless they removed themselves beyond the Mississippi. President Jackson's Seventh Annual Message to Congress reiterated that the Native Americans "cannot live in contact with a civilized community and prosper." Faced with the choice of relinquishing their lands in hostile Georgia but retaining self-government in the West, the Cherokees finally ceded their lands east of the Mississippi. The New Echota Treaty with the Cherokees specified the terms of their removal. The "Trail of Tears" ensued, as virtually the entire Cherokee Nation marched under military "escort" from Georgia to Oklahoma. An estimated twenty-five thousand died in the forced

migrations during the decade of the 1830s. Although they had violated neither federal nor state criminal laws, many Native Americans were treated much like traitors receiving the punishment of exile under martial law. The United States sought to justify this disposition of the Native American "problem" by asserting paternalistic motives.

Not all the Five Civilized Tribes (Choctaw, Chickasaw, Cherokee, Seminole, and Creek) went as peacefully as the Cherokees. Dissatisfied with the land chosen for them west of the Mississippi, the Seminoles, under the leadership of Osceola, refused to migrate. When federal troops were sent to remove them forcibly, a war began that lasted seven years and cost forty million dollars and the lives of two thousand United States troops and an unknown number of Seminoles and their escaped-slave allies. At first the Seminoles were on the offensive, but with the capture of Osceola in 1837 while ostensibly protected by a flag of truce, the Seminoles retreated to the Florida swamps and fought a defensive war for another five years. Osceola died in prison in 1838, and the Seminoles capitulated in 1842, effectively ending the existence of the independent and self-governing Indian nations east of the Mississippi.

☆ 95 A Home in a Country Selected by Their Forefathers

☆ 95a President Jackson's Seventh Annual Message on Indian Removal (December 7, 1835)

Reprinted in J. Richardson, ed., *A Compilation of the Messages and Papers of the Presidents* (New York: Bureau of National Literature, 1897), 3:171.

. . . The plan of removing the aboriginal people who yet remain within the settled portions of the United States to the country west of the Mississippi River approaches its consummation. It was adopted on the most mature consideration of the condition of this race, and ought to be persisted in till the object is accomplished, and prosecuted with as much vigor as a just regard to their circumstances will permit, and as fast as their consent can be obtained. All preceding experiments for the improvement of the Indians have failed. It seems now to be an established fact that they can not live in contact with a civilized community and prosper. Ages of fruitless endeavors have at length brought us to a knowledge of this principle of intercommunication with them. The past we can not recall, but the future we can provide for. Independently of the treaty stipulations into which we have entered with the various tribes for the usufructuary rights they have ceded to us, no one can doubt the moral duty of the Government of the United States to protect and if possible to preserve and perpetuate the scattered remnants of this race which are left within our borders. In the discharge of this duty an extensive region in the West has been assigned for their permanent residence....

The plan ... has been dictated by a spirit of enlarged liberality. A territory exceeding in extent that relinquished has been granted to each tribe. Of its climate, fertility, and capacity to support an Indian population the representations are highly favorable. To these districts the Indians are removed at the expense of the United States, and with certain supplies of clothing, arms, ammunition, and other indispensable articles; they are also furnished gratuitously with provisions for the period of a year after their arrival at their new homes. In that time, from the nature of the country and of the products raised by them, they can subsist themselves by agricultural labor, if they choose to resort to that mode of life; if they do not they are upon the skirts of the great prairies, where countless herds of buffalo roam, and a short time suffices to adapt their own habits to the changes which a change of the animals destined for their food may require. Ample arrangements have also been made for the support of schools; in some instances council houses and churches are to be erected, dwellings constructed for the chiefs, and mills for common use. Funds have been set apart for the maintenance of the poor; the most necessary mechanical arts have been introduced, and blacksmiths, gunsmiths, wheelwrights, millwrights, etc., are supported among them. Steel and iron, and sometimes salt, are purchased for them, and plows and other farming utensils, domestic animals, looms, spinning wheels, cards, etc., are presented to them. ... [A]s a stimulus for exertion, it is now provided by law that "in all cases of the appointment of interpreters or other persons employed for the benefit of the Indians a preference shall be given to persons of Indian descent, if such can be found who are properly qualified for the discharge of the duties."

Such are the arrangements for the physical comfort and for the moral improvement of the Indians. The necessary measures for their political advancement and for their separation from our citizens have not been neglected. The pledge of the United States has been given by Congress that the country destined for the residence of this people shall be forever "secured and guaranteed to them." A country west of Missouri and Arkansas has been assigned to them, into which the white settlements are not to be pushed. No political communities can be formed in that extensive region, except those which are established by the Indians themselves or by the United States for them and with their concurrence. A barrier has thus been raised for their protection against the encroachment of our citizens, and guarding the Indians as far as possible from those evils which have brought them to their present condition.

☆ 95b   Treaty of New Echota with the Cherokees (December 29, 1835)

7 Stat. 478 (1835).

Articles of a treaty concluded at New Echota in the State of Georgia on the 29th day of December 1835 by General William Carroll and John F. Schermerhorn, Commissioners on the part of the United States, and the Chiefs, Head Men and people of the Cherokee tribe of Indians.

WHEREAS THE CHEROKEE are anxious to make some arrangements with the Government of the United States whereby the difficulties they have experienced by a residence within the settled parts of the United States under the jurisdiction and laws of the State Governments may be terminated and adjusted; and with a view to reuniting their people in one body and securing a permanent home for themselves and their posterity in the country selected by their forefathers without the territorial limits of the State sovereignties, and where they can establish and enjoy a government of their choice and perpetuate such a state of society as may be most consonant with their views, habits and condition; and as may tend to their individual comfort and their advancement in civilization.

*   *   *

Therefore the following articles of a treaty are agreed upon and concluded between William Carroll and John F. Schermerhorn commissioners on the part of the United States and the chiefs and head men and people of the Cherokee nation in general council assembled this 29th day of Dec. 1835.

ARTICLE I. The Cherokee nation hereby cede relinquish and convey to the United States all the lands owned claimed or possessed by them east of the Mississippi river, and hereby release all their claims upon the United States for spoliations of every kind for and in consideration of the sum of five millions of dollars to be expended paid and invested in the manner stipulated and agreed upon in the following articles. But as a question has arisen between the commissioners and the Cherokees whether the Senate in their resolution by which they advised "that a sum not exceeding five millions of dollars be paid to the Cherokee Indians for all their lands and possessions east of the Mississippi river" have included and made any allowance or consideration for claims for spoliations it is therefore agreed on the part of the United States that this question shall be again submitted to the Senate for their consideration and decision and if no allowance was made for spoliations that then an additional sum of three hundred thousand dollars be allowed for the same.

*   *   *

ARTICLE V. The United States hereby covenant and agree that the lands ceded to the Cherokee nation in the foregoing article shall, in no future time without their consent, be included within the territorial limits or jurisdiction of any State or Territory. But they shall secure to the Cherokee nation the right by their national councils to make and carry into effect all such laws as they may deem necessary for the government and protection of the persons and property within their own country belonging to their people or such persons as have connected themselves with them: provided always that they shall not be inconsistent with the constitution of the United States and such acts of Congress as have been or may be passed regulating trade and intercourse with the Indians; and also, that they shall not be considered as extending to such citizens and army of the United States as may travel or reside in the Indian country by permission according to the laws and regulations established by the Government of the same.

ARTICLE VI. Perpetual peace and friendship shall exist between the citizens of the United States and the Cherokee Indians. The United States agree to protect the Cherokee nation from domestic strife and foreign enemies and against intestine wars between the several tribes. The Cherokees shall endeavor to preserve and maintain the peace of the country and not make war upon their neighbors they shall also be protected against interruption and intrusion from citizens of the United States, who may attempt to settle in the country without their consent; and all such persons shall be removed from the same by order of the President of the United States. But this is not intended to prevent the residence among them of useful farmers mechanics and teachers for the instruction of Indians according to treaty stipulations.

ARTICLE VII. The Cherokee nation having already made great progress in civilization and deeming it important that every proper and laudable inducement should be offered to their people to improve their condition as well as to guard and secure in the most effectual manner the rights guarantied to them in this treaty, and with a view to illustrate the liberal and enlarged policy of the Government of the United States towards the Indians in their removal beyond the territorial limits of the States, it is stipulated that they shall be entitled to a delegate in the House of Representatives of the United States whenever Congress shall make provision for the same.

*   *   *

ARTICLE XVI. It is hereby stipulated and agreed by the Cherokees that they shall remove to their new homes within two years from the ratification of this treaty and that during such time the United States shall protect and defend them in their possessions and property and free use and occupation of the same and such persons as have been dispossessed of their improvements and houses; and for which no grant has actually issued previously to the enactment of the law of the State of Georgia, of December 1835 to regulate Indian occupancy shall be again put in possession and placed in the same situation and condition, in reference to the laws of the State of Georgia, as the Indians that have not been dispossessed; and if this is not done, and the people are left unprotected, then the United States shall pay the several Cherokees for their losses and damages sustained by them in consequence thereof. . . .

*   *   *

ARTICLE XVIII. Whereas in consequences of the unsettled affairs of the Cherokee people and the early frosts, their crops are insufficient to support their families and great distress is likely to ensue and whereas the nation will not, until after their removal be able advantageously to expend the income of the permanent funds of the nation it is therefore agreed that the annuities of the nation which may accrue under this treaty for two years, the time fixed for their removal shall be expended in provision and clothing for the benefit of the poorer class of the nation; and the United States hereby agree to advance the same for that purpose as soon after the ratification of this treaty as an appropriation for the same shall be made. It is however not intended in this article to interfere with that part of the annuities due the Cherokees west by the treaty of 1819.

ARTICLE XIX. This treaty after the same shall be ratified by the President and Senate of the United States shall be obligatory on the contracting parties.

In testimony whereof the commissioners and the chiefs head men and people whose names are hereunto annexed being duly authorized by the people in general council assembled have affixed their hands and seals for themselves and in behalf of the Cherokee nation.

I have examined the foregoing treaty and although not present when it was made, I approve its provisions generally, and therefore sign it.

WM. CARROLL
J. F. SCHERMERHORN

MAJOR RIDGE
JAMES FOSTER
TESA-TA-ESKY
CHARLES MOORE
GEORGE CHAMBERS
TAH-YESKE
ARCHILLA SMITH
ANDREW ROSS
WILLIAM LASSLEY

CAE-TE-HEE
TE-GAH-E-SKE
ROBERT ROGERS
JOHN GUNTER
JOHN A. BELL
CHARLES F. FOREMAN
WILLIAM ROGERS
GEORGE W. ADAIR
ELIAS BOUDINOT
JAMES STARR
JESSE HALF-BREED

Signed and sealed in presence of

WESTERN B. THOMAS, Secry.
BEN F. CURREY, Special Agent
M. WOLFE BATEMAN, 1st Lt. 6th U.S.A. inf.,
  Disbg. Agent
JNO. L. HOOPER, Lt. 4th inf.
C. M. HITCHCOCK, M.D., Assist. Surg. U.S.A.
G. W. CURREY
WM. H. UNDERWOOD
CORNELIUS D. TERHUNE
JOHN W. H. UNDERWOOD

96 "acts and doings of certain fanatics" (1835-1836)

Southern states met abolitionist propaganda with regulation and repression of the press. Several states asserted the obligation of the Northern members of the Union to suppress, within their boundaries, activities that adversely affected the peace and security of other members of the "common league" and the duty of the federal government to close the mails to "incendiary" literature.

☆96 Opposition to Abolition Societies

☆96a South Carolina Resolutions on Abolition Societies (December 16, 1835)

1835 S.C. Acts 26.

1. *Resolved*, That the formation of the abolition societies, and the acts and doings of certain fanatics, calling themselves abolitionists, in the non-slaveholding states of this confederacy, are in direct violation of the obligations of the compact of the union, dissocial, and incendiary in the extreme.

2. *Resolved*, That no state having a just regard for her own peace and security can acquiesce in a state of things by which such conspiracies are engendered within the limits of a friendly state, united to her by the bonds of a common league of political association, without either surrendering or compromising her most essential rights.

3. *Resolved*, That the Legislature of South Carolina, having every confidence in the justice and friendship of the non-slaveholding states, announces to her co-states her confident expectation, and she earnestly requests that the governments of these states will promptly and effectually suppress all those associations within their respective limits, purporting to be abolition societies, and that they will make it highly penal to print, publish, and distribute newspapers, pamphlets, tracts and pictorial representations calculated and having an obvious tendency to excite the slaves of the southern states to insurrection and revolt.

4. *Resolved*, That, regarding the domestic slavery of the southern states as a subject exclusively within the control of each of the said states, we shall consider every interference, by any other state of the general government, as a direct and unlawful interference, to be resisted at once, and under every possible circumstance.

5. *Resolved*, In order that a salutary negative may be put on the mischievous and unfounded assumption of some of the abolitionists—the non-slaveholding states are requested to disclaim by legislative declaration, all right, either on the part of themselves or the government of the United States, to interfere in any manner with domestic slavery, either in the states, or in the territories where it exists.

                *   *   *

7. *Resolved*, That the legislature of South Carolina, regards with decided approbation, the measures of security adopted by the Post Office Department of the United States, in relation to the transmission of incendiary tracts. But if this highly essential and protective policy, be counteracted by congress, and the United States mail becomes a vehicle for the transmission of the mischievous documents, with which it was recently freighted, we, in this contingency, expect that the Chief Magistrate of our state, will forthwith call the legislature together, that timely measures may be taken to prevent its traversing our territory.

                *   *   *

☆96b An Act to Suppress the Circulation of Incendiary Publications and for Other Purposes (March 23, 1836) [Virginia]

1836 Va. Acts 44.

Whereas attempts have been recently made by certain abolition or anti-slavery societies and evil disposed persons, being and residing in some of the non-slaveholding states, to interfere with the relations existing between master and slave in this state, and to excite in our coloured population a spirit of insubordination, rebellion and insurrection, by distributing among them, through the agency of the United States mail and other means, certain incendiary books, pamphlets, or other writings of an inflammatory and mischievous character and tendency: For remedy whereof, and to provide against the dangers thence arising,

1. *Be it enacted by the general assembly*, That any member of an abolition or anti-slavery society, or agent of an abolition or anti-slavery society, who shall come into this state, and shall here maintain, by speaking or writing, that the owners of slaves have no property in the same, or advocate or advise the abolition of slavery, shall be deemed guilty of a high

misdemeanor, and on conviction thereof shall be fined in a sum of not less than fifty dollars nor more than two hundred dollars, and shall suffer a term of imprisonment of not less than six months nor more than three years, at the discretion of a jury.

2. *And be it further enacted*, That if any person shall hereafter write, print, or cause to be written or printed, any book, pamphlet, or other writing, with intent of advising, enticing, or persuading persons of colour within this commonwealth to make insurrections, or to rebel, or denying the right of masters to property in their slaves, and inculcating the duty of resistance to such right, or shall, with intent to aid the purposes aforesaid of such book, pamphlet, or other writing, knowingly circulate, or cause to be circulated, any such book, pamphlet, or other writing, such person shall, if a slave or other coloured person, be punished by stripes, not exceeding thirty-nine, and transported and sold beyond the limits of the United States, under the orders of the executive of this commonwealth; and if a free white person, shall be deemed guilty of felony, and on conviction thereof be punished by imprisonment in the penitentiary of this commonwealth for a term not less than two years nor more than five years.

3. *Be it further enacted*, That if any post-master or deputy post-master within this commonwealth, shall give notice to any justice of the peace that any book, pamphlet, or other writing, hath been received at his office through the medium of the mail, of the character and description mentioned in the section of this act immediately preceding, it shall be the duty of such justice of the peace to enquire into the circumstances of the case, and to have such book, pamphlet, or other writing, burned in his presence; and if it shall appear to him by satisfactory evidence that the person to whom the same is directed, subscribed for the said book, pamphlet, or other writing, knowing its character and tendency, or agreed to receive it with an intention of circulating it, thereby to aid the purposes of the abolitionists or anti-slavery societies, the said justice shall commit him or her to the jail of his county, to be dealt with according to law.

*   *   *

97 Twenty Journeymen Tailors (1836)

In an 1834 letter to the Workingmen, a radical political party of Massachusetts, American historian George Bancroft wrote: "The Feud between the capitalist and laborer, the House of Have and the House of Want, is as old as the social union and can never be entirely quitted." Toward the middle of the nineteenth century, European immigrants—especially on the eastern seaboard—combined with American craftsmen to create a laboring class sensitive to fair wages and humane working conditions. Their efforts to organize the workers as a prerequisite for exerting the power of collective bargaining nevertheless triggered criminal prosecutions on charges of conspiracy to violate the established law of the land.

The 1836 New York trial of twenty journeymen tailors exemplified the courts' practice of resorting to the common law or statutory crime of conspiracy as a means of interfering with the organization of labor unions. The court in *People v. Faulkner* relied on Supreme Court precedent, as it announced to the jury that such organizations were "a conspiracy and injurious to trade." By 1846, confronted with a similar case, a Massachusetts court reached the opposite conclusion in *Commonwealth v. Hunt.* Justice Shaw acknowledged that the purpose of the organization was neither criminal nor carried out by criminal means.

☆ 97 They Formed Themselves into a Society

☆ 97a *People v. Faulkner* [New York]

Reprinted in J. R. Commons and E. Gillmore, eds., *A Documentary History of American Industrial Society* (New York: Russell & Russell, 1958), 4:315-33.

*   *   *

From the New York *Courier and Enquirer*, May 31, 1836.

The accused, who are journeymen tailors, and members of the Union Society of Journeymen Tailors, were indicted for a conspiracy to injure trade and commerce, and for riot, and assault and battery, &c.

*   *   *

The Court has been occupied several days with the trial of twenty-one [*sic*] journeymen tailors for combination. . . . It will be remembered that some months back there was a strike for wages amongst a large number of journeymen Tailors in this city, and that a certain body called the Trades Union Society, who undertook to make laws and regulations for the trade, made several rules [for the fair distribution of work] which they insisted on being observed by the master tailors, and on their refusing to comply with these rules, a number of journeymen left their employment and had recourse to threats, and promises, and various other modes [picketing] to prevent journeymen tailors from woring for any master tailor who did not conform to the rules, and pay the prices laid down by this association. The charges were fully substantiated by evidence.

The Court charged the jury.

*   *   *

The offence committed by the present defendants, if an offence at all, is against the Statute, which says that if any man enter into a combination injurious to trade or commerce, that constitutes a conspiracy; but at the same time the Act says— "That no agreement, except to commit a felony on the person of another, or to commit arson or burglary, shall be deemed a conspiracy unless some act, besides such agreement, shall be done to effect the object thereof, by one or more of the parties." If then there is a conspiracy against trade or commerce, and any act in furtherance of it, if done by one of the parties it renders them all guilty.

In criminal cases the jury were judges of the law and the facts, this was their constitutional right, but the court trusted that as a discreet jury they would pay proper respect to the opinions of the highest tribunal of the country, which had unanimously concurred as to what was the exposition of the Act, and the Supreme Court had said in a case similar to the present one, that it was a conspiracy and injurious to trade....

*   *   *

Such was the law, and how stood the facts.

The Court then summed up the leading facts of the case.

It was unnecessary for the Court to state more. It would be insulting the understanding of the jury to suppose they could imagine for one moment, that the prisoners had not taken measures to carry their combination into effect; and if they did form a combination and take measures to carry it into effect, and that the law was as the supreme court decided it, then the prisoners were indubitably guilty.

The combination had been of so extensive a character and created so great an excitement that it might possibly have involved some persons for whom the jury might directly or indirectly feel some interest—but the court and jury must raise themselves above all feelings of friendship or sympathy and be true to their oaths, and the well being of the public at large; and it was impossible that the acts of the defendants could escape with impunity unless the court and jury violate their duty in order to take them out of the operation of the law. The Court would again impress upon the minds of the jury that the present question was not to be considered a mere struggle between the masters and journeymen. It was one upon which the harmony of the whole community depended. Let these societies only arise from time to time and they would at last extend to every trade in this city and we should have as many governments as there were societies.

*   *   *

The jury retired for a short time and returned a verdict of guilty against all the defendants. Counsel for the prisoners made a motion for time to put in exceptions to the charge, but the Court stated its determination to sentence the prisoners on Monday next.

*   *   *

From the New York *Evening Post*, June 13, 1836, copied from the *Times*.

COURT OF OYER AND TERMINER. Present—Judge Edwards, Aldermen Banks, Ingraham, Benson and Randall.

SENTENCE OF THE TAILORS.... A large number of persons, who had previously assembled in the passages of the hall, immediately entered, and completely filled the large room. There appeared to be no peculiar excitement however. There was no assembling in the Park as had been predicted....

*   *   *

On enquiring of Mr. Western, one of the counsel, that gentleman informed us that eleven of these were native born citizens; and of the other nine, five were naturalized. Of the native born, he could only call to mind Henry Faulkner, Howell Vail, Livingston, Smith, Gray, Keating, and Delong. Another gentleman stated that Busey and the Douglases were also native born; that eleven of the twenty were born in the United States, two in Ireland, three in Scotland, and four in England.

Mr. Western moved for an arrest of judgment on three grounds. 1st, that no crime was contained in the indictment. 2nd, that even if so, the crime consisted in the men endeavoring to prevent others from working, which had not been proved. And 3d, that the judge took from the jury the decision of the case, by stating what was the law and what the facts.

*   *   *

The Judge then proceeded to pass sentence, which was done in the following words:

You have been convicted of a conspiracy. The bill of indictment charges substantially that you and others, being journeymen tailors, did perniciously form and unite yourselves into an unlawful club or combination to injure trade, and did make certain arbitrary bylaws, rules and orders, intending to govern not only yourselves but other journeymen tailors, and persons engaged in the business of tailors, and to oppress and injure them, and to injure trade and commerce. And also to prevent any journeymen tailors from working for any tailor who would not assent to said by-laws....

*   *   *

Combining to do an act injurious to trade, is declared by a statute of this State, to be a misdemeanor.

That an offence, of the description of the one with which you are charged, is one within the act, has been unanimously decided by the Supreme Court of this State, and for reasons which are deemed by the Court perfectly satisfactory. That such combinations are injurious to trade, has been fully verified in this city. Various trades have from time to time been brought to a stand, and the community extensively inconvenienced and embarrassed by them. . . . [The Legislature has], therefore, re-enacted the common law upon the subject with the additional provision, that some act shall be done to effect the object of it by one or more of the parties, in order to render it a misdemeanor.

The law leaves every individual master of his own individual acts. But it will not suffer him to encroach upon the rights of others. He may work or not, as suits his pleasure, but he shall not enter into a confederacy with a view of controlling others, and take measures to carry it into effect. The reason for the distinction is manifest. So long as individual members of the community do not resort to any acts of violence, their hostility can be guarded against. But who can withstand an extensive combination to injure him in his calling? When such cases, therefore, occur, the law extends its protecting shield.

*   *   *

☆ 97b *Commonwealth v. Hunt* [Massachusetts]

45 Mass. (4 Met.) 45 (1842).

SHAW, C. J. . . . We have no doubt, that by the operation of the constitution of this Commonwealth, the general rules of the common law, making conspiracy an indictable offence, are in force here, and that this is included in the description of laws which had, before the adoption of the constitution, been used and approved in the Province, Colony, or State of Massachusetts Bay, and usually practised in the courts of law. . . . Still it is proper in this connexion to remark, that although the common law in regard to conspiracy in this Commonwealth is in force, yet it will not necessarily follow that every indictment at common law for this offence is a precedent for a similar indictment in this State. The general rule of the common law is, that it is a criminal and indictable offence, for two or more to confederate and combine together, by concerted means, to do that which is unlawful or criminal, to the injury of the public, or portions or classes of the community, or even to the rights of an individual. This rule of law may be equally in force as a rule of the common law, in England and in this Commonwealth; and yet it must depend upon the local laws of each country to determine, whether the purpose to be accomplished by the combination, or the concerted means of accomplishing it, be unlawful or criminal in the respective countries. All those laws of the parent country, whether rules of the common law, or early English statutes, which were made for the purpose of regulating the wages of laborers, the settlement of paupers, and making it penal for anyone to use a trade or handicraft to which he had not served a full apprenticeship—not being adapted to the circumstances of our colonial condition—were not adopted, used or approved, and therefore do not come within the description of the laws adopted and confirmed by the provision of the constitution already cited. . . .

Stripped then of these introductory recitals and alleged injurious consequences, and of the qualifying epithets attached to the facts, the averment is this; that the defendants and others formed themselves into a society, and agreed not to work for any person who should employ any journeyman or other person, not a member of such society, after notice given him to discharge such workman. The manifest intent of the association is, to induce all those engaged in the same occupation to become members of it. Such a purpose is not unlawful. It would give them a power which might be exerted for useful and honorable purposes, or for dangerous and pernicious ones. If the latter were the real and actual object, and susceptible of proof, it should have been specially charged. Such an association might be used to afford each other assistance in times of poverty, sickness and distress; or to raise their intellectual, moral and social condition; or to make improvement in their art; or for other proper purposes. Or the association might be designed for purposes of oppression and injustice. . . .

Nor can we perceive that the objects of this association, whatever they may have been, were to be attained by criminal means. The means which they proposed to employ, as averred in this count, and which, as we are now to presume, were established by the proof, were, that they would not work for a person, who, after due notice, should employ a journeyman not a member of their society. Supposing the object of the association to be laudable and lawful, or at least not unlawful, are these means criminal? The case supposes that these persons are not bound by contract, but free to work for whom they please, or not to work, if they so prefer. In this state of things, we cannot perceive, that it is criminal for men to agree together to exercise their own acknowledged rights, in such a manner as best to subserve their own interests. One way to test this is, to consider the effect of such an agreement, where the object of the association is acknowledged on all hands to be a laudable one. Suppose a class of workmen, impressed with the manifold evils of intemperance, should agree with each other not to work in a shop in which ardent spirit was furnished, or not to work in a shop with any one who used it, or not to work for an employer, who should, after notice, employ a journeyman who habitually used it. The consequences might be the same. A workman, who should still persist in the use of ardent spirit, would find it more difficult to get employment; a master employing such an one might, at times, experience inconvenience in his work, in losing the services of a skilful but intemperate workman. Still it seems to us, that as the object would be lawful, and the means not unlawful, such an agreement could not be pronounced a criminal conspiracy. . . .

We think, therefore, that associations may be entered into, the object of which is to adopt measures that may have a tendency to impoverish another, that is, to diminish his gains and profits, and yet so far from being criminal or unlawful, the object may be highly meritorious and public spirited. The legality of such an association will therefore depend upon the means to be used for its accomplishment. . . .

*   *   *

98 "the encroachments of military despots" (1836)

On June 30, 1835, Texas colonists led by William B. Travis seized the Mexican garrison at Fort Anahuac at the mouth of the Trinity River. Three months later the first major battle of the Texas revolution took place between the American settlers of Gonzales and the Mexican cavalry. A Mexican army of some six thousand under Santa Anna crossed into Texas in early 1836, and the war for independence escalated. On March 1, 1836, at a convention held at Washington, on the Brazos, Texas drew up a declaration of independence. At the same time Travis and his 188 men were preparing to defend the Alamo.

☆98 Texas Declaration of Independence

Reprinted in B. P. Poore, ed., *The Federal and State Constitutions, Colonial Charters, and Other Organic Laws of the United States* (Washington, D.C.: U.S. Government Printing Office, 1877), pt. 2:1752.

WHEREAS, General Antonio Lopez de Santa Anna and other Military Chieftains have, by force of arms, overthrown the Federal Institutions of Mexico, and dissolved the Social Compact which existed between Texas and the other Members of the Mexican Confederacy—Now, the good People of Texas, availing themselves of their natural rights,

SOLEMNLY DECLARE

1st. That they have taken up arms in defence of their Rights and Liberties, which were threatened by the encroachments of military despots, and in defence of the Republican Principles of the Federal Constitution of Mexico of eighteen hundred and twenty-four.

2d. That Texas is no longer, morally or civilly, bounded by the compact of Union; yet, stimulated by the generosity and sympathy common to a free people they offer their support and assistance to such of the Mexicans of the Mexican Confederacy as will take up arms against their military despotism.

3d. That they do not acknowledge, that the present authorities of the nominal Mexican Republic have the right to govern within the limits of Texas.

4th. That they will not cease to carry on war against the said authorities, whilst their troops are within the limits of Texas.

5th. That they hold it to be their right, during the disorganization of the Federal System and the reign of despotism, to withdraw from the Union, to establish an independent Government, or to adopt such measures as they may deem best calculated to protect their rights and liberties; but that they will continue faithful to the Mexican Government so long as that nation is governed by the Constitution and Laws that were formed for the government of the Political Association.

6th. That Texas is responsible for the expenses of their Armies now in the field.

7th. That the public faith of Texas is pledged for the payment of any debts contracted by her Agents.

8th. That she will reward by donations in Land, all who volunteer their services in her present struggle, and receive them as Citizens.

These DECLARATIONS we solemnly avow to the world, and call GOD to witness their truth and sincerity; and invoke defeat and disgrace upon our heads should we prove guilty of duplicity.

RICHARD ELLIS, President

99 "prompted by the pure spirit of christianity" (1837)

The clash between abolitionists and proslavery groups grew violent. In Illinois, newspaper editor Elijah Paris Lovejoy, who held abolitionist views, was shot and killed for his persistence in refurbishing his printing press after mobs twice destroyed it. In Philadelphia, in the summer of 1837, proslavery activities resulted in riots.

The case of *State v. M'Donald* involved an 1812 statute that prohibited aiding in the rebellion of slaves. The judge pointedly remarked, "Even he who professing to be prompted by the pure spirit of christianity shall proclaim to our slaves the doctrine of universal emancipation . . . renders himself a subject for criminal justice." Although the opinion demonstrated the court's attitude toward the defense of moral justification for disobedience to law, it also showed how procedural protections could limit the reach of an overzealous prosecution.

☆99 *State v. M'Donald* [Alabama]

4 Port. 499 (Alabama, 1837).

*   *   *

The prisoner was indicted in the Circuit Court of Lowndes, in an indictment with four counts:

In the first and third it was charged that he "did maliciously, feloniously and traitorously advise, plot and consult with Moses, a slave belonging to one Jesse H. Robertson, for the purpose of encouraging, exciting and aiding an insurrection against the laws and government of the State of Alabama, &c."

In the second and fourth counts, the term "rebellion" was substituted for "insurrection."

The second concluded as the first; and the third and fourth charged the offence to have been committed "against the people," instead of "against the laws and government."

The prisoner plead not guilty, and the case went to the jury. . . .

[From the record:] "The State's counsel introduced witnesses, who gave evidence, that the master of the slave Moses, in consequence of suspicions entertained by him, directed the slave Moses, that if the prisoner should come to him, that he should conduct him to a particular spot, and there hold the conversation with him. That in consequence of this the negro [Moses] did conduct the defendant to that spot, and held the conversation with the defendant, which was detailed in evidence, in the hearing of his master and another. . . . In this conversation the defendant said the negroes ought to rise, and if they would he would head them;—that they had hard masters. That they must raise five hundred men, but he would start with three hundred men. That a negro in the neighborhood, named Frank, was to furnish him with a horse. The defendant promised to give the rifle he had with him to Moses, when they started: he shewed him how to cock it, and snapped it two or three times. The defendant told the slave Moses, that they would go to Mobile, and that if they did not like that, they would then go to Pensacola— that, that was a weaker place. That they could get arms and ammunition there, and could press a ship, with which they could go to Texas. That Texas was a free place, and that they might have their freedom there. That they would be joined by other slaves on their way to Mobile. The defendant urged the slave to go home with him, which the negro declined, but promised to come next evening to his house. . . . [Subsequently] the slave acted under the direction of his master and others, and his questions to the defendant were prompted by instructions from them, and were for the purpose of discovering the defendant. The defendant then told the slave that he must get him one thousand men, but he would start with five hundred. That they would make a forced march to Pensacola, take that, press a ship, and sail to Texas. That it was not safe to stay in Florida, as the United States would reach them:—that he knew how to man a ship:—they could enjoy freedom in Texas. He stated they could get guns from their masters, with ammunition and horses, and escape to Pensacola, and that Moses should have his rifle. The defendant said there was no white men engaged— he would head them, and that Frank should be second in command, and Moses third in command."

* * *

COLLIER, J.—The first inquiry which invites our consideration, in examining this case, is this—What offence does the indictment charge?

. . . [The] statute is as follows: "If any free person shall be aiding and assisting, or in any wise concerned with any slave or slaves, in any actual or mediated rebellion or conspiracy against the laws, government or people of this territory, or shall in any manner advise, plot or consult with any slave or slaves, for the purpose of encouraging, exciting, aiding or assisting any such insurrection or rebellion, or intended insurrection or rebellion, such free person so offending, and being thereof convicted, shall suffer death."

The first branch of the act embraces two distinct descriptions of offence.

1st. For a free person to be aiding and assisting, or in any wise concerned with a slave or slaves, in any actual rebellion or conspiracy.

2d. For a free person to be similarly concerned in any meditated rebellion or conspiracy.

The second branch of the act, is alike comprehensive, and subjects to punishment—

1st. Any free person who shall in any manner advise, plot or consult with any slave or slaves, for the purpose of encouraging, exciting, aiding or assisting any such insurrection or rebellion.

2d. Any free person who shall in any manner advise, plot, &c. an intended insurrection or rebellion.

To make "a free person" guilty of the first offence prescribed by the first branch of the statute, it is necessary that there should be an "actual rebellion." To make out the second offence, it is necessary that the offence should not have developed itself by action . . . [and] it is necessary that a *slave or slaves* should lend to it a favorable ear.

* * *

The terms "rebellion or insurrection," employed in the second branch of the act, are used as synonymous; this is sufficiently indicated by the terms "any such insurrection or rebellion,"—and are referable as the words "any such" prove, to the first branch of the act.

To make a *free person* guilty of *advising, plotting or consulting with any slave or slaves, for the purpose of encouraging, &c. any insurrection or rebellion,* such as the first branch of the act contemplates, it would be necessary to shew that a *slave or slaves* have already assumed a rebellious or insurrectionary attitude, or else, that they *meditate* the assumption of such a position.

It has been already shewn what would constitute a *meditated* rebellion, let us now inquire what is essential to an *actual rebellion or insurrection.* These terms, in their ordinary acceptation, mean a resistance to the established order of things.

However regardless one may be of the dictates of social duty, or reckless of civil order, so long as he locks up, in his own breast, his unpatriotic and wicked feelings, or merely gives vent to them by words, he rebels not against the laws and government of his country. But, when, having indulged these sentiments, for a period sufficiently long to prepare him for active movements, setting at defiance the duties of the man and the citizen, he places himself in hostile array to the quiet and security which society professes to guarantee to its members — he is then, and not sooner, in a state of rebellion to the *laws, government or people of the State.*

In regard to the second offence, denounced by the second branch of the statute, it may be remarked, that a mere intention, undiscovered by any thing said or done, or shewn merely by loose and casual remarks, would not prove an *intended rebellion.*

*   *   *

. . . If a *free person* shall *in any manner advise, &c. with any slave or slaves, for the purpose of encouraging, &c. a rebellion or insurrection intended by him only,* he is guilty of this offence, though the arguments addressed to the slave may not have been such as to command his approbation.

*   *   *

The *free person,* whether white or colored, who seeks to sow in the bosom of our slaves, the seeds of disaffection, and urges them to resist by force, the authority of their legitimate masters, renders himself obnoxious to the penalties of the law. And even he who professing to be prompted by the *pure spirit of christianity,* shall proclaim to our slaves the doctrine of universal emancipation, and denounce slavery as incompatible with the sublime and elevated morality of revelation, and thus scatter broad-cast the seeds of discontent, and estrange the affections of the slave from his master, with the intention of arousing him to the effort to break by force the bonds of servitude, renders himself *a subject* for criminal justice. He whose course is thus characterised, must be supposed *Quixotic indeed,* who, when he had employed the means directly calculated to achieve a result so disastrous, could hope to escape the retribution of justice, by declaring to a jury the purity of his purpose — the integrity of his motive. The intention here, as in every other offence of which it is a constituent, need not be shown by direct and positive proof, where it is inferable from facts and circumstances, in themselves manifest.

*   *   *

Having thus determined the proper interpretation of the statute, let us next inquire whether the evidence warranted the conviction of the prisoner, and whether the charge of the judge was proper, considering the indictment, against him. . . .

The words, "any such," it has been said, refer the terms insurrection or rebellion, to the first branch of the act, and are to be taken to mean an actual or meditated rebellion. . . . There was no proof of an actual rebellion, nor none of a meditated rebellion; but every thing of the kind, is directly disproved, so far as it is possible to shew the non-existence of a fact.

The witnesses all state that there was no insurrection or rebellion, or preparation for it, so far as they could learn — that they had no knowledge of the prisoner tampering with any other slave than Moses. The master of Moses stated that he was faithful and obedient; and that he gave him the earliest information of the advances of the prisoner. — From all this it is clear, that Moses never participated in any criminal design of the prisoner.

*   *   *

. . . [T]here is error; for the indictment before us, charges offences, — to complete which, it is necessary to shew the participation of slaves, as has been sufficiently shewn in considering the different parts of the act.

Had the indictment charged an advising, &c., for the purpose of encouraging, &c., an intended rebellion, &c. — we will not say that the proof would have been sufficient to authorise a conviction. Such an expression by this Court, might prejudice the prisoner, should he be indicted hereafter for that offence; but we cannot forbear the opinion, that such indictment would much better suit the proof than any that could be framed under the statute.

. . . It was argued for the prisoner, that as the advising, plotting or consulting, for the purpose of encouraging, exciting, aiding or assisting an insurrection or rebellion, against the laws, government or people, was treason in other countries, and particularly in England, — these could not be indicted as a distinct and substantive offence here.

*   *   *

Our Legislature . . . exercises all [powers] as are compatible with the social compact, unless restrained by express inhibition or clear implication.

[T]he right of protection belongs to man in a state of nature — and he may exert this right, as a member of society, in cases of emergency, where there is neither time nor opportunity to apply to the government. This right of protection extends itself to communities, and is the foundation of the moral power to punish crimes, or provide against their commission. Society owes to each of its members a security for those rights, which he retains upon entering into it: among these stands first, the right of personal security. If this right is assailed, the assailant is obnoxious to punishment. And the right to punish crime, actually committed, includes the right to prevent it, by punishing him who contemplates it, without waiting for an act of personal aggression. This is preventive justice—the right to exercise which, is unquestionable, at this day.

We do not deem it necessary to enquire, if an actual rebellion or insurrection had taken place, whether the indictment should have been for *treason*; or whether *treason* can be committed against the laws, government or people of a State—as neither of these questions arise in this case: "Sufficient unto the day, is the evil thereof."

*   *   *

Our conclusion is, that the conviction of the prisoner was unauthorised—that the judgment of the Circuit Court must be reversed, and that the prisoner remain in custody, until he be discharged by due course of law.

100 An Incendiary Petition to Congress (1839)

The Virginia law against incendiary publications was applied not only to books, journals, pamphlets, and other circulars but also to citizens' petitions. The court in *Barrett* avoided the question concerning the state's power to restrain a petition to Congress. Nevertheless, the court overturned Barrett's conviction on procedural grounds, thus frustrating law enforcement officials in their attempt to enforce the law.

☆ 100 *Commonwealth v. Barrett* [Virginia]

36 Va. 233 (9 Leigh 655) (1839).

At September term 1839, the attorney prosecuting for the commonwealth in the said court moved for rules against *Lysander Barrett* and ten other persons, to shew cause why criminal informations should not be filed against them respectively, for violations of the "act to suppress the circulation of incendiary publications, and for other purposes," passed March 23, 1836. . . . In support of the motion, the attorney for the commonwealth produced affidavits of several witnesses, proving that the said *Lysander Barrett* had caused to be circulated in the county of *Lewis*, for the purpose of procuring signatures, and that the ten other persons aforesaid had signed, a memorial to congress, which prayed the abolition of slavery in the district of *Columbia*, and contained the following expressions: "In the opinion of your petitioners, slavery and the slave trade, as at present existing in the district of *Columbia*, where congress has sole jurisdiction ought not so to be,—as

a sin against God, a foul stain upon our national character, and contrary to the spirit of our republican institutions." *Lysander Barrett* appeared, and contested the motion for the said rule against him: whereupon, with his consent, the circuit court adjourned to this court, for novelty and difficulty, the following questions: 1. Is circulating the aforesaid memorial to congress, and procuring subscribers thereto, an offence under the provisions of the aforesaid act to suppress the circulation of incendiary publications, and for other purposes, passed March 23, 1836? 2. Is the signing of the said memorial an offence by the signers thereof, under the said statute? 3. Is it necessary, in order to furnish the foundation of a rule for a criminal information against the said *Lysander Barrett* for the causes aforesaid, that there should be proof that he was a member or agent of an abolition or antislavery society?

The response of the general court was as follows:

"This court is unanimously of opinion and doth decide, in answer to the 3d question adjourned, that to sustain a prosecution for the offence created by the first section of the act to suppress the circulation of incendiary publications, and for other purposes, passed March 23, 1836, the person accused must be a member or agent of an abolition or antislavery society.

"This court is also of opinion that the offence created by the 2d section of the aforesaid statute, being a felony, cannot be prosecuted by information; and that consequently the 1st and 2d questions adjourned by the circuit court to this court do not properly arise in this case."

101 "the dreadful acts by which they asserted their liberty" (1841)

Occasionally, the United States courts had to adjudicate the rights of alien blacks. In 1841, the Supreme Court considered a case involving a captured Spanish schooner, *Amistad*, and its cargo of blacks. Taken in Africa, sold in Cuba, and en route to another port, the blacks, under the leadership of Cinque, had seized the vessel and sailed into United States waters. Were they to be treated as slaves to be surrendered to their masters or as liberty-seeking free men? Justice Joseph Story concluded that they were not pirates but "free native Africans" who, unlike slaves, possessed the same rights to use violence to defend or regain liberty as any other kidnapped persons. Although the Supreme Court decision stirred Southern frustration because it seemed to subordinate the property rights of the owners of slaves to a slave's "right to escape," no recourse to abolitionist arguments was made, and the court clearly stated that if these blacks were recognized to be slaves by international and Spanish law, they would be subject to recapture. But such was not the case, since Spanish law prohibited the taking of slaves in Africa. The incident, which caused nationwide attention at the time, was lost to the public until Cinque's namesake in the Symbionese Liberation Army caused a recollection of the incident in the 1970s.

☆ 101 *United States v. Amistad*

40 U.S. (15 Pet.) 518 (1841).

MR. JUSTICE STORY delivered the opinion of the court.

*   *   *

... The vessel, with the negroes and other persons on board, was brought by [Naval] Lieutenant Gedney into the district of Connecticut, and there libelled for salvage [by the United States] in the district court of the United States. A libel for salvage was also filed by Henry Green and Pelatiah Fordham, of Sag Harbor, Long Island. On the 18th of September, Ruiz and Montez filed claims and libels, in which they asserted their ownership of the negroes as their slaves, and of certain parts of the cargo, and prayed that the same might be "delivered to them, or to the representatives of her Catholic Majesty, as might be most proper." ...

On the 7th of January 1840, the negroes ... filed an answer, denying that they were slaves, or the property of Ruiz and Montez, or that the court could, under the constitution or laws of the United States, or under any treaty, exercise any jurisdiction over their persons, by reason of the premises; and praying that they might be dismissed. They specially set forth and insisted in this answer, that they were native-born Africans; born free, and still, of right, ought to be free and not slaves.... The main controversy is, whether these negroes are the property of Ruiz and Montez, and ought to be delivered up.... It has been argued on behalf of the United States, that the court are bound to deliver them up, according to the treaty of 1795, with Spain. The ninth article [of the treaty] provides, "that.... all ships and merchandize, of what nature soever, which shall be rescued out of the hands of any pirates or robbers, on the high seas, shall be brought into some port of either state, and shall be delivered to the custody of the officers of that port, in order to be taken care of and restored, entire, to the true proprietor, as soon as due and sufficient proof shall be made concerning the property thereof." This is the article on which the main reliance is placed on behalf of the United States, for the restitution of these negroes. To bring the case within the article, it is essential to establish: 1st, That these negroes, under all the circumstances, fall within the description of merchandize, in the sense of the treaty. 2d, That there has been a rescue of them on the high seas, out of the hands of the pirates and robbers; which, in the present case, can only be, by showing that they themselves are pirates and robbers: and 3d, That Ruiz and Montez, the asserted proprietors, are the true proprietors, and have established their title by competent proof.

If these negroes were, at the time, lawfully held as slaves, under the laws of Spain, and recognised by those laws as property, capable of being lawfully bought and sold; we see no reason why they may not justly be deemed, within the intent of the treaty, to be included under the denomination of merchandize, and as such ought to be restored to the claimants; for upon that point the laws of Spain would seem to furnish the proper rule of interpretation. But admitting this, it is clear, in our opinion, that neither of the other essential facts and requisites has been established in proof; and the *onus probandi* of both lies upon the claimants to give rise to the *casus foederis*. It is plain, beyond controversy, if we examine the evidence, that these negroes never were the lawful slaves of Ruiz or Montez, or of any other Spanish subjects. They are natives of Africa, and were kidnapped there, and were unlawfully transported to Cuba, in violation of the laws and treaties of Spain, and the most solemn edicts and declarations of that government. By those laws and treaties, and edicts, the African slave-trade is utterly abolished; the dealing in that trade is deemed a heinous crime; and the negroes thereby introduced into the dominions of Spain, are declared to be free.... The supposed proprietary interest of Ruiz and Montez is completely displaced, if we are at liberty to look at the evidence, or the admissions of the district-attorney.

If then, these negroes are not slaves, but are kidnapped Africans, who, by the laws of Spain itself, are entitled to their freedom, and were kidnapped and illegally carried to Cuba, and illegally detained and restrained on board the Amistad; there is no pretence to say, that they are pirates or robbers. We may lament the dreadful acts by which they asserted their liberty, and took possession of the Amistad, and endeavored to regain their native country; but they cannot be deemed pirates or robbers, in the sense of the law of nations, or the treaty with Spain, or the laws of Spain itself; at least, so far as those laws have been brought to our knowledge. Nor do the libels of Ruiz or Montez assert them to be such.

This posture of the facts would seem, of itself, to put an end to the whole inquiry upon the merits. But it is argued, on behalf of the United States that the ship and cargo, and negroes, were duly documented as belonging to Spanish subjects, and this court have no right to look behind these documents; that full faith and credit is to be given to them; and that they are to be held conclusive evidence in this cause, even although it should be established by the most satisfactory proofs, that they have been obtained by the grossest frauds and impositions upon the constituted authorities of Spain. To this argument, we can, in no wise, assent. There is nothing in the treaty which justifies or sustains the argument. . . . [A]lthough public documents of the government, accompanying property found on board of the private ships of a foreign nation, certainly are to be deemed *prima facie* evidence of the facts which they purport to state, yet they are always open to be impugned for fraud; and whether that fraud be in the original obtaining of these documents, or in the subsequent fraudulent and illegal use of them, when once it is satisfactorily established, it overthrows all their sanctity, and destroys them as proof. Fraud will vitiate any, even the most solemn, transactions; and an asserted title to property, founded upon it is utterly void. This is not a mere rule of municipal jurisprudence. Nothing is more clear in the law of nations . . . than the doctrine, that the ship's papers are but prima facie evidence, and that, if they are shown to be fraudulent, they are not to be held proof of any valid title. . . .

It is also a most important consideration, in the present case, which ought not to be lost sight of, that, supposing these African negroes not to be slaves, but kidnapped, and free negroes, the treaty with Spain cannot be obligatory upon them; and the United States are bound to respect their rights as much as those of Spanish subjects. The conflict of rights between the parties, under such circumstances, becomes positive and inevitable, and must be decided upon the eternal principles of justice and international law. If the contest were about any goods on board of this ship, to which American citizens asserted a title, which was denied by the Spanish claimants, there could be no doubt of the right of such American citizens to litigate their claims before any competent American tribunal, notwithstanding the treaty with Spain. A fortiori, the doctrine must apply, where human life and human liberty are in issue, and constitute the very essence of the controversy. The treaty with Spain never could have intended to take away the equal rights of all foreigners, who should contest their claims before any of our courts, to equal justice; or to deprive such foreigners of the protection given them by other treaties, or by the general law of nations. Upon the merits of the case, then, there does not seem to us to be any ground for doubt, that these negroes ought to be deemed free; and that the Spanish treaty interposes no obstacle to the just assertion of their rights.

*   *   *

102 The Recognition of Political Crime (1843)

An 1843 commercial treaty between France and the United States provided the first documented recognition by the United States of a difference between common criminals and those who commit offenses of a "purely political character." Article V stated that the extradition obligations under the treaty were not to apply to the latter class. Although not defined in the treaty, the recognition of such crimes and the propriety of differential treatment for such offenders corresponded with the European jurisprudence of the period. The political offender exception originated in an earlier treaty between France and Belgium (1833) and is attributed to the period of political instability, revolutions, and coups d'état in Europe which the French Revolution inaugurated. The United States, unlike several Continental countries, never extended the political crime differentiation from the treaty to domestic criminal law, but the exception has continued unaffected for extradition purposes to this day.

☆102 Convention for the Surrender of Criminals between the United States of America and His Majesty the King of the French

8 Stat. 585 (1843).

The United States of America and His Majesty the King of the French having judged it expedient, with a view to the better administration of justice, and to the prevention of crime within their respective territories and jurisdictions, that persons charged with the crimes hereinafter enumerated, and being fugitives from justice, should, under certain circumstances, be reciprocally delivered up. . . .

ARTICLE I. It is agreed that the High Contracting Parties shall . . . deliver up to justice persons who, being accused of the crimes enumerated in the next following article, committed within the jurisdiction of the requiring party, shall seek an asylum, or shall be found within the territories of the other: *Provided*, That this shall be done only when the fact of the commission of the crime shall be so established as that the laws of the country in which the fugitive or the person so accused shall be found would justify his or her apprehension and commitment for trial, if the crime had been there committed.

ARTICLE II. Persons shall be so delivered up who shall be charged, according to the provisions of this Convention, with any of the following crimes, to wit: murder, (comprehending the crimes designated in the French Penal Code by the terms, assassination, parricide, infanticide, and poisoning,) or with an attempt to commit murder, or with rape, or with forgery, or with arson, or with embezzlement by public officers, when the same is punishable with infamous punishment.

*   *   *

ARTICLE V. The provisions of the present Convention shall not be applied in any manner to the crimes enumerated in the second article, committed anterior to the date thereof, nor to any crime or offence of a purely political character.

*   *   *

103 "No Union with Slaveholders" (1844)

Garrison and the American Anti-Slavery Society went so far in support of abolitionism as to contend that morally, abolitionists could not vote or hold office under the United States Constitution. Garrison considered the Constitution, which permitted slavery and repression of blacks, a covenant with death and an agreement with hell. Conscientious objection to slavery was so strong among the abolitionists that they viewed it as a justification for their breaking the laws of the states and their repudiation of the authority of the Union and its social compact — the Constitution.

☆ 103 Resolution — Can Abolitionists Vote or Take Office under the United States Constitution? American Anti-Slavery Society Annual Meeting

Reprinted in W. Garrison and F. Garrison, *William Lloyd Garrison: The Story of His Life Told by His Children* (New York: Arno Press, 1969), 3:96-133.

Resolved, That secession from the present United States government is the duty of every abolitionist; since no one can take office, or throw a vote for another to hold office, under the United States Constitution, without violating his anti-slavery principles, and rendering himself an abettor of the slaveholder in his sin.

The passage of this Resolution has caused two charges to be brought against the Society: *First*, that it is a no-government body, and that the whole doctrine of non-resistance is endorsed by this vote; and *secondly*, that the Society transcended its proper sphere and constitutional powers by taking such a step.

The logic which infers that because a man thinks the Federal Government bad, he must necessarily think *all* government so, has at least, the merit and the charm of novelty. There is a spice of arrogance just perceptible, in the conclusion that the Constitution of these United States is so perfect, that one

who dislikes it could never be satisfied with any form of government whatever!

*   *   *

The Society is not opposed to government, but only to *this* Government based upon and acting for slavery.

With regard to the second charge, of exceeding its proper limits and trespassing on the rights of the minority, it is enough to say, that the object of the American Anti-Slavery Society is the "entire abolition of slavery in the United States." Of course it is its duty to find out all the sources of pro-slavery influence in the land. It is its right, it is its duty to try every institution in the land, no matter how venerable, or sacred, by the touch-stone of anti-slavery principle.... It has tried the Constitution, and pronounced it unsound.

... The qualification for membership remains the same, "the belief that slave-holding is a heinous crime." ...

No one who did not vote for the Resolution is responsible for it. No one is asked to quit our platform. We, the majority, only ask him to extend to our opinions the same toleration that we extend to him, and agreeing to differ on this point, work together where we can. We proscribe no man for difference of opinion.

*   *   *

I am aware that we non-voters are rather singular. But history, from the earliest Christians downwards, is full of instances of men who refused all connection with government, and all the influence which office could bestow, rather than deny their principles, or aid in doing wrong. Yet I never heard them called either idiots or over-scrupulous. Sir Thomas More need never have mounted the scaffold, had he only consented to take the oath of supremacy. He had only to tell a lie with solemnity, as we are asked to do, and he might not only have saved his life, but, as the trimmers of his day would have told him, doubled his influence. Pitt resigned his place as Prime Minister of England, rather than break faith with the Catholics of Ireland. Should I not resign a petty ballot rather than break faith with the slave? But I was specially glad to find a distinct recognition of the principle upon which we have acted, applied to a different point, in the life of that Patriarch of the Anti-Slavery enterprise, Granville Sharpe. It is in a late number of the *Edinburgh Review*. While an underclerk in the War Office, he sympathized with our fathers in their struggle for independence. "Orders reached his office to ship munitions of war to the revolted colonies. If his hand had entered the account of such a cargo, it would have contracted in his eyes the stain of innocent blood. To avoid this pollution, he resigned his place and his means of subsistence at a period of life when he could no longer hope to find any other lucrative employment." ...

One friend proposes to vote for men who shall be pledged not to take office unless the oath of the Constitution is dispensed with, and who shall then go on to perform in their offices only such duties as we, their constituents, approve. ... Waiving all other objections, this plan seems to me mere playing at politics, and an entire waste of effort. It loses our high position as moral reformers; it subjects us to all that malignant opposition and suspicion of motives which attend the array of parties; and while thus closing up our access to the national conscience, it wastes in fruitless caucussing and party tactics, the time and the effort which should have been directed to efficient agitation.

The history of our Union is lesson enough, for every candid mind, of the fatal effects of every, the least, compromise with evil. ... The trial of fifty years only proves that it is impossible for free and slave States to unite on any terms, without all becoming partners in the guilt and responsible for the sin of slavery. Why prolong the experiment? Let every honest man join in the outcry of the American Anti-Slavery Society, NO UNION WITH SLAVEHOLDERS.

WENDELL PHILLIPS

104 Franchise for Men of Color (1846)

The Southern states were not alone in passing laws to maintain their social, racial, and political order. The New York Constitution imposed stringent qualifications for the enfranchisement of black citizens despite virtually nonexistent requirements for whites. Additional proof of allegiance was required before free blacks were considered sufficiently adherent to the state to be allowed to participate publicly. Such provisions were common.

☆ 104 New York Constitution of 1846, Article III, Section 1

Reprinted in F. Thorpe, ed., *Federal and State Constitutions* (Washington, D.C.: U.S. Government Printing Office, 1909), 5:2656.

SECTION 1. Every male citizen of the age of twenty-one years, who shall have been a citizen for ten days, and an inhabitant of this State one year next preceding any election, and for the last four months a resident of the county where he may offer his vote, shall be entitled to vote ...; but such citizen shall have been for thirty days next preceding the election, a resident of the district from which the officer is to be chosen for whom he offers his vote. But no man of color, unless he shall have been for three years a citizen of this State, and for one year next preceding

any election shall have been seized and possessed of a freehold estate of the value of two hundred and fifty dollars, over and above all debts and incumbrances charged thereon, and shall have been actually rated and paid a tax thereon, shall be entitled to vote at such election. And no person of color shall be subject to direct taxation unless he shall be seized and possessed of such real estate as aforesaid.

*   *   *

105 Maintaining That "owners have not right of property in their slaves" (1848)

As a result of Nat Turner's insurrection and similar incidents, fear of a widespread black rebellion spread among Southern authorities. Each Southern state embarked on a course of harsh repression of slaves, free blacks, and white sympathizers seeking to ameliorate the black condition. The laws were designed specifically to deter whites and free blacks who felt they had a moral obligation to speak against the status quo. The Slave Codes were perhaps the most extreme example of political and racial suppression in American history and relied on a reward and bounty system for enforcement.

☆ 105 Virginia Slavery Law

1848 Va. Acts 113-21.

*   *   *

24. Any free person who, by speaking or writing, shall maintain that owners have not right of property in their slaves, shall be punished by confinement in the jail not more than twelve months, and by fine not exceeding five hundred dollars; and such person may be arrested by any white person and carried before a judge or justice to be dealt with according to law.

25. Any free person who shall write, print, or cause to be written or printed, any book, pamphlet, or other writing, with intent to advise or incite persons of colour within this commonwealth to rebel or make insurrection, or denying the rights of masters to property in their slaves, and inculcating the duty of resistance to such right, or shall, with intent to aid the purposes aforesaid of such book, pamphlet or other writing, knowingly circulate the same, shall be punished by confinement in the penitentiary for a term not less than one nor more than five years.

26. If any postmaster or deputy postmaster shall know that any such book, pamphlet or other writing mentioned in the preceding section has been received at his office, through the medium of the mail, it shall be his duty to give notice thereof to some justice of the peace, whose duty it shall be to enquire

into the circumstances, and to have such book, pamphlet or other writing burned in his presence; and if it shall appear to him by satisfactory evidence that the person to whom the same is directed, subscribed therefor, knowing its character and tendency, or agreed to receive with intention to circulate it, thereby to aid the purposes of the abolitionists, the said justice shall commit him to the jail to be dealt with according to law. Any postmaster or deputy postmaster who shall knowingly violate the provisions of this section shall be punished by fine not exceeding two hundred dollars.

27. It shall be the duty of any judge, justice of the peace, or mayor, before whom any person may be brought for the offence mentioned in the preceding section, to cause such person to enter into a recognizance, with sufficient security, to appear before the circuit superior court of law and chancery having jurisdiction of the offence, at the next term thereof, to answer for the same; and in default of such recognizance, to commit such offender to jail, there to remain until discharged by order of the said court.

*   *   *

39. Every assemblage of slaves, free negroes or mulattoes, at any meeting house or other place for the purpose of public religious worship, where such worship shall be conducted by a slave, free negro or mulatto, and every such assemblage for the purpose of instruction in reading or writing, by whomsoever conducted, and every such assemblage in the night time under whatsoever pretext, shall be unlawful assembly, and it shall be the duty of all magistrates to suppress all such assemblies which occur within their respective jurisdictions; and as often as any slaves, free negroes or mulattoes shall be unlawfully assembled, it shall be the duty of each magistrate within whose jurisdiction the assemblage may be, forthwith to disperse the same, and to that end he may issue his warrant directed to any sheriff, constable, sergeant, or other person specially designated, commanding him to enter the house or place where such assemblage may be, and seize any slave, free negro or mulatto there found, and it shall be lawful for the magistrate giving such warrant, or any other magistrate before whom the same may be returned, to order any slave, free negro or mulatto so seized to be punished by stripes not exceeding thirty-nine.

40. Any white person who shall assemble with slaves, free negroes or mulattoes for the purpose of instructing them to read or write, or shall associate with slaves, free negroes and mulattoes in an unlawful assembly thereof, shall be punished by confinement in the jail not exceeding six months, and by fine not exceeding one hundred dollars; and it shall be lawful for any magistrate in whose jurisdiction

such assemblage may be, to cause any white person found so associated with slaves, free negroes or mulattoes, to enter into a recognizance with sufficient security to appear before the circuit superior court of law and chancery, or county or corporation court having jurisdiction of the offence, at the next term thereof, to answer for the same, and in the meantime to keep the peace and be of good behaviour; and in default of such recognizance, to commit such person to jail, there to remain until discharged by order of said court.

*   *   *

106 "that all men and women are created equal" (1848)

The first Women's Rights Convention convened in Seneca Falls, New York, in July 1846. Freed slave and political reformer Frederick Douglass described its declaration as "the basis of a grand movement for attaining the civil, social, political, and religious rights of women."

The choice of the Declaration of Independence as a model for the convention's manifesto testifies to the ambitions of the movement. The new declaration, which resorted to natural rights to justify disobedience of unjust manmade laws and deny allegiance to the governments that make them, furnished the theoretical foundation for the illegal actions of suffragist Susan B. Anthony and the modern feminist movement.

☆ 106 Declaration of Sentiments and Resolutions of the First Women's Rights Convention

Reprinted in E. Stanton, S. Anthony, and M. Gage, eds., *History of Woman Suffrage* (New York: Fowler & Wells, 1881), 1:70-73.

When, in the course of human events, it becomes necessary for one portion of the family of man to assume among the people of the earth a position different from that which they have hitherto occupied, but one to which the laws of nature and of nature's God entitle them, a decent respect to the opinions of mankind requires that they should declare the causes that impel them to such a course.

We hold these truths to be self-evident: that all men and women are created equal; that they are endowed by their Creator with certain inalienable rights; that among these are life, liberty, and the pursuit of happiness; that to secure these rights governments are instituted, deriving their just powers from the consent of the governed. Whenever any form of government becomes destructive of these ends, it is the right of those who suffer from it to refuse allegiance to it, and to insist upon the institution of a new government, laying its foundation on such principles, and organizing its powers in such form, as to them shall seem most likely to effect their safety and happiness. Prudence, indeed, will dictate that governments long established should not be changed for light and transient causes; and accordingly all experience hath shown that mankind are more disposed to suffer, while evils are sufferable, than to right themselves by abolishing the forms to which they were accustomed. But when a long train of abuses and usurpations, pursuing invariably the same object evinces a design to reduce them under absolute despotism, it is their duty to throw off such government, and to provide new guards for their future security. Such has been the patient sufferance of the women under this government, and such is now the necessity which constrains them to demand the equal station to which they are entitled.

The history of mankind is a history of repeated injuries and usurpations on the part of man toward woman, having in direct object the establishment of an absolute tyranny over her. To prove this, let facts be submitted to a candid world.

He has never permitted her to exercise her inalienable right to the elective franchise.

He has compelled her to submit to laws, in the formation of which she had no voice.

*   *   *

Now, in view of this entire disfranchisement of one-half the people of this country, their social and religious degradation—in view of ... unjust laws ..., and because women do feel themselves aggrieved, oppressed, and fraudulently deprived of their most sacred rights, we insist that they have immediate admission to all the rights and privileges which belong to them as citizens of the United States.

In entering upon the great work before us, we anticipate no small amount of misconception, misrepresentation, and ridicule; but we shall use every instrumentality within our power to effect our object. We shall employ agents, circulate tracts, petition the State and National legislatures, and endeavor to enlist the pulpit and the press in our behalf. We hope this Convention will be followed by a series of Conventions embracing every part of the country.

RESOLUTIONS

WHEREAS, The great precept of nature is conceded to be, that "man shall pursue his own true and substantial happiness." Blackstone in his Commentaries remarks, that this law of Nature being coeval with mankind, and dictated by God himself, is of course superior in obligation to any other. It is binding over all the globe, in all countries and at all times; no human laws are of any validity if contrary

to this, and such of them as are valid, derive all their force, and all their validity, and all their authority, mediately and immediately, from this original; therefore,

Resolved, That such laws as conflict, in any way, with the true and substantial happiness of woman, are contrary to the great precept of nature and of no validity, for this is "superior in obligation to any other."

Resolved, That all laws which prevent woman from occupying such a station in society as her conscience shall dictate, or which place her in a position inferior to that of man, are contrary to the great precept of nature, and therefore of no force or authority.

Resolved, That woman is man's equal—was intended to be so by the Creator, and the highest good of the race demands that she should be recognized as such.

*   *   *

Resolved, That the same amount of virtue, delicacy, and refinement of behavior that is required of woman in the social state, should also be required of man, and the same transgressions should be visited with equal severity on both man and woman.

Resolved, That the objection of indelicacy and impropriety, which is so often brought against woman when she addresses a public audience, comes with a very ill-grace from those who encourage, by their attendance, her appearance on the stage, in the concert, or in feats of the circus.

*   *   *

Resolved, That it is the duty of the women of this country to secure themselves their sacred right to the elective franchise.

*   *   *

107 Rhode Island's Dorr Rebellion (1849)

The struggle for political power between the established regime and popular forces erupted in Rhode Island in the early 1840s and tested the capacity of America's legal system to resolve revolutionary conflicts. Based on a charter issued by Charles II in 1663, the Rhode Island Constitution enfranchised less than half of the state's male population. As a consequence, the election of the state legislature was within the power of fewer than four thousand voters out of a state population exceeding one hundred thousand.

In 1841, the Rhode Island Peoples' Party, a group organized by Thomas Dorr, convened in Providence and framed a new state constitution, declaring the old charter constitution null and void. The new constitution was ratified in a statewide referendum, and Dorr was elected governor of Rhode Island by the newly franchised voters.

Dorr's supporters unsuccessfully attempted to seize the state's arsenal, and the old charter government declared a state of insurrection and imposed martial law. In the face of the inability of his supporters to gain a military victory, Dorr fled to Connecticut to continue the struggle. Dorr was arrested upon his return a year and a half later, tried for treason, convicted, and sentenced to life imprisonment. The following year the State Assembly ordered his release on the condition that he take an oath of allegiance to the existing state constitution. Stalwartly refusing to do so, Dorr was nevertheless unconditionally released soon thereafter by a more sympathetic legislature.

A new constitution was proposed by the charter legislature and adopted in 1843. The legitimacy of Dorr's regime vis-à-vis the charter government eventually was tested before the United States Supreme Court. Martin Luther, a shoemaker and supporter of the Dorr regime, brought suit for trespass against the defendants who broke into his house without a civil warrant to arrest him under orders from their military commander. Luther contended the charter government was not the lawful government of Rhode Island at the time and therefore had no authority to search and arrest. Further, he argued that the declaration of martial law was improper and that therefore the military had no authority to conduct searches and arrests without warrants. The case reached the Supreme Court in 1849. Chief Justice Roger B. Taney, a supporter of Andrew Jackson and an advocate of state's rights, avoided the issue by writing that the court lacked the authority to pass upon the legitimacy of a state government; that question must be left to the Congress and the president. This approach effectively upheld the charter government. Luther, in his pursuit of wider suffrage, could not shed the cloak of treason.

☆ 107 *Luther v. Borden*

48 U.S. (7 How.) 1 (1849).

Mr. Chief Justice TANEY delivered the opinion of the court:

*   *   *

The charter government ... passed resolutions declaring that all acts done for the purpose of imposing [Dorr's] constitution upon the State to be an assumption of the powers of government, in violation of the rights of the existing government and of the people at large; and that it would maintain its authority and defend the legal and constitutional rights of the people.

But, notwithstanding the determination of the charter government, and of those who adhered to it, to maintain its authority, Thomas W. Dorr, who had been elected governor under the new constitution, prepared to assert the authority of that government by force, and many citizens assembled in arms to support him. The charter government thereupon passed an act declaring the State under martial law, and at the same time proceeded to call out the militia, to repel the threatened attack and to subdue those who were engaged in it. In this state of the contest, the house of the plaintiff, who was engaged in supporting the authority of the new government, was broken and entered in order to arrest him. The defendants were, at the time, in the military service of the old government, and in arms to support its authority.

*   *   *

The Circuit Court ... instructed the jury that the charter government and laws under which the defendants acted were, at the time the trespass is alleged to have been committed, in full force and effect as the form of government and paramount law of the State, and constituted a justification of the acts of the defendants as set forth in their pleas.

It is this opinion of the Circuit Court that we are now called upon to review.

*   *   *

Certainly, the question which the plaintiff proposed to raise by the testimony he offered has not heretofore been recognized as a judicial one in any of the State courts....

In Rhode Island, the question has been directly decided. Prosecutions were there instituted against some of the persons who had been active in the forcible opposition to the old government. And in more than one of the cases evidence was offered on the part of the defense similar to the testimony offered in the Circuit Court, and for the same purpose; that is, for the purpose of showing that the proposed constitution had been adopted by the people of Rhode Island, and had, therefore, become the established government, and consequently that the parties accused were doing nothing more than their duty in endeavoring to support it.

But the courts uniformly held that the inquiry proposed to be made belonged to the political power and not to the judicial; that it rested with the political power to decide whether the charter government had been displaced or not: and when that decision was made, the Judicial Department would be bound to take notice of it as the paramount law of the State, without the aid of oral evidence or the examination of witnesses; that, according to the laws and institutions of Rhode Island, no such change had been recognized by the political power; and that the charter government was the lawful and established government of the State during the period in contest, and that those who were in arms against it were insurgents, and liable to punishment. This doctrine is clearly and forcibly stated in the opinion of the Supreme Court of the State in the trial of Thomas W. Dorr, who was the governor elected under the opposing constitution, and headed the armed force which endeavored to maintain its authority.

*   *   *

It is worthy of remark . . . when we are referring to the authority of State decisions, that the trial of Thomas W. Dorr took place after the constitution of 1843 went into operation. The judges who decided that case held their authority under that constitution; and it is admitted on all hands that it was adopted by the people of the State, and is the lawful and established government. . . .

The point, then raised here has been already decided by the courts of Rhode Island. The question relates, altogether, to the constitution and laws of that State; and the well settled rule in this court is, that the courts of the United States adopt and follow the decisions of the State courts in questions which concern merely the constitution and laws of the State.

Upon what ground could the Circuit Court of the United States which tried this case have departed from this rule, and disregarded and overruled the decisions of the courts of Rhode Island? . . . [T]he power of determining that a State government has been lawfully established, which the courts of the State disown and repudiate, is not one of them. Upon such a question the courts of the United States are bound to follow the decisions of the State tribunals, and must therefore regard the charter government as the lawful and established government during the time of this contest.

*   *   *

Moreover, the Constitution of the United States, as far as it has provided for an emergency of this kind, and authorized the general government to interfere in the domestic concerns of a State, has treated the subject as political in its nature, and placed the power in the hands of that department.

*   *   *

Under . . . the Constitution it rests with Congress to decide what government is the established one in a State. For as the United States guarantee to each State a republican government, Congress must necessarily decide what government is established in the State before it can determine whether it is republican or not. And when the senators and representatives of a State are admitted into the councils of the Union, the authority of the government under which they are appointed, as well as its republican character, is recognized by the proper constitutional

authority. And its decision is binding on every other department of the government, and could not be questioned in a judicial tribunal. . . .

So, too, as relates to the clause in the above mentioned article of the Constitution. . . . Congress . . . provided that, "in case of an insurrection in any State against the government thereof, it shall be lawful for the President of the United States, on application of the Legislature of such State or of the executive (when the Legislature cannot be convened), to call forth such number of the militia of any other State or States, as may be applied for, as he may judge sufficient to suppress such insurrection."

By this act, the power of deciding whether the exigency had arisen upon which the government of the United States is bound to interfere, is given to the President. . . . [H]e must determine what body of men constitute the Legislature, and who is the governor, before he can act. . . . If there is an armed conflict, like the one of which we are speaking, it is a case of domestic violence, and one of the parties must be in insurrection against the lawful government. And the President must, of necessity, decide which is the government, and which party is unlawfully arrayed against it, before he can perform the duty imposed upon him by the act of Congress.

After the President has acted and called out the militia, is a circuit court of the United States authorized to inquire whether his decision was right? Could the court, while the parties were actually contending in arms for the possession of the government, call witnesses before it and inquire which party represented a majority of the people? . . . If the judicial power extends so far, the guarantee contained in the Constitution of the United States is a guarantee of anarchy, and not of order. Yet if this right does not reside in the courts when the conflict is raging, if the judicial power is at that time bound to follow the decision of the political, it must be equally bound when the contest is over. It cannot, when peace is restored, punish as offenses and crimes the acts which it before recognized, and was bound to recognize, as lawful.

It is true that in this case the militia were not called out by the President. But upon the application of the governor under the charter government, the President recognized him as the executive power of the State, and took measures to call out the militia to support his authority if it should be found necessary for the general government to interfere; and it is admitted in the argument, that it was the knowledge of this decision that put an end to the armed opposition to the charter government, and prevented any further efforts to establish by force the proposed constitution. The interference of the President, therefore, by announcing his determination, was as effectual as if the militia had been assembled under his orders. And it should be equally authoritative. For certainly no court of the United States, with a knowledge of this decision, would have been justified in recognizing the opposing party as the lawful government; or in treating as wrong-doers or insurgents the officers of the government which the President had recognized, and was prepared to support by an armed force. In the case of foreign nations, the government acknowledged by the President is always recognized in the courts of justice. And this principle has been applied by the act of Congress to the sovereign States of the Union.

*   *   *

The remaining question is whether the defendants, acting under military orders issued under the authority of the government, were justified in breaking and entering the plaintiff's house.... Unquestionably a military government, established as the permanent government of the State, would not be a republican government and it would be the duty of Congress to overthrow it. But the law of Rhode Island evidently contemplated no such government. It was intended merely for the crisis, and to meet the peril in which the existing government was placed by the armed resistance to its authority. ... And if the government of Rhode Island deemed armed opposition so formidable, and so ramified throughout the State, as to require the use of its military force and the declaration of martial law, we see no ground upon which this court can question its authority. It was a state of war; and the established government resorted to the rights and usages of war to maintain itself, and to overcome the unlawful opposition. And in that state of things the officers engaged in its military service might lawfully arrest anyone, who, from the information before them, they had reasonable grounds to believe was engaged in the insurrection; and might order a house to be forcibly entered and searched, when there were reasonable grounds for supposing he might be there concealed.... No more force, however, can be used than is necessary to accomplish the object. And if the power is exercised for the purposes of oppression, or any injury willfully done to person or property, the party by whom, or by whose order, it is committed would undoubtedly be answerable.

*   *   *

Upon the whole, we see no reason for disturbing the judgment of the Circuit Court. The admission of evidence to prove that the charter government was the established government of the State was an irregularity, but is not material to the judgment....

Much of the argument on the part of the plaintiff turned upon political rights and political questions, upon which the court has been urged to express an opinion. We decline doing so. The high power has been conferred on this court of passing judgment upon the acts of the State sovereignties, and of the legislative and executive branches of the federal government, and of determining whether they are beyond the limits of power marked out for them respectively by the Constitution of the United States. This tribunal, therefore, should be the last to overstep the boundaries which limit its own jurisdiction. And while it should always be ready to meet any question confided to it by the Constitution, it is equally its duty not to pass beyond its appropriate sphere of action, and to take care not to involve itself in discussions which properly belong to other forums. No one, we believe, has ever doubted the proposition, that, according to the institutions of this country, the sovereignty in every State resides in the people of the State, and that they may alter and change their form of government at their own pleasure. But whether they have changed it or not by abolishing an old government, and establishing a new one in its place, is a question to be settled by the political power. And when that power has decided, the courts are bound to take notice of its decision, and to follow it.

The judgment of the Circuit Court must therefore be affirmed.

Mr. Justice WOODBURY, dissenting:

*   *   *

[The] difference ... between me and my brethren extends only to the points in issue concerning martial law.... I concur with the rest of the court in the opinion, that the other leading question, the validity of the old charter at that time, is not within our constitutional jurisdiction.... It must be very obvious, on a little reflection that the last is a mere political question.... For they extend to the power of the people, independent of the Legislature, to make constitutions—to the right of suffrage among different classes of them in doing this—to the authority of naked majorities—and other kindred questions, of such high political interest as during a few years to have agitated much of the Union no less than Rhode Island.

But, fortunately for our freedom from political excitements in judicial duties, this court can never with propriety be called on officially to be the umpire in questions merely political. The adjustment of these questions belongs to the people and their political representatives, either in the State or general government. These questions relate to matters not to be settled on strict legal principles. They are adjusted rather by inclination—or prejudice or compromise, often. Some of them succeed or are defeated even by public policy alone, or mere naked power, rather than intrinsic right.

*   *   *

If it be asked what redress have the people, if wronged in these matters, unless by resorting to the judiciary, the answer is, they have the same as in all other political matters. In those, they go to the ballot boxes, to the Legislature or executive, for the redress of such grievances as are within the jurisdiction of each, and, for such as are not, to conventions and amendments of constitution. And when the former fail, and these last are forbidden by statutes, all that is left in extreme cases, where the suffering is intolerable and the prospect is good of relief by action of the people without the forms of law, is to do as did Hampden and Washington, and venture action without those forms, and abide the consequences. Should strong majorities favor the change, it generally is completed without much violence.

*   *   *

[A]ll which ... is left for us to decide is ... whether the statute establishing martial law over the whole State, and under which the acts done by the defendants are sought to be justified, can be deemed constitutional.

To decide a point like this last is clearly within judicial cognizance, it being a matter of private personal authority and right, set up by the defendants under constitutions and laws, and not of political power, to act in relation to the making of the former.

*   *   *

The Legislature evidently meant to be understood in that sense by using words [martial law] of such well settled construction, without any limit or qualification, and covering the whole State with its influence, under a supposed exigency and justification for such an unusual course. I do not understand this to be directly combated in the opinion just delivered by the Chief Justice. That they could mean no other than the ancient martial law often used before the Petition of Right, and sometimes since, is further manifest from the fact that they not only declared "martial" law to exist over the State, but put their militia into the field to help, by means of them and such a law, to suppress the action of those denominated "insurgents" and this without any subordination to the civil power, or any efforts in conjunction and in co-operation with it.

*   *   *

[I]n every country which makes any claim to political or civil liberty, "martial law," as here attempted and as once practiced in England against her own people, has been expressly forbidden there for near two centuries, as well as by the principles of every other free constitutional government. And it would be not a little extraordinary, if the spirit of our institutions, both State and national, was not much stronger than in England against the unlimited exercise of martial law over a whole people, whether attempted by any chief magistrate or even by a Legislature.

*   *   *

[H]ow under the general principles of American jurisprudence in modern times, [can such a law] properly exist, or be judicially upheld [?]. A brief retrospect of the gradual, but decisive, repudiation of it in England will exhibit many of the reasons why such a law cannot be rightfully tolerated anywhere in this country.

*   *   *

It appears, also, that nobody has dared to exercise it, in war or peace, on the community at large, in England, for the last century and a half, unless specially enacted by Parliament, in some great exigency and under various restrictions, and then under the theory, not that it is consistent with bills of rights and constitutions, but that Parliament is omnipotent, and for sufficient cause may override and trample on them all, temporarily.

After the civil authorities have become prostrated in particular places, and the din of arms has reached the most advanced stages of intestine commotions, a Parliament which alone furnishes the means of war — a Parliament unlimited in its powers — has, *in extremis*, on two or three occasions, ventured on martial law beyond the military; but it has usually confined it to the particular places thus situated, limited it to the continuance of such resistance, and embraced in its scope only those actually in arms.... When speaking of the absence of other and sound precedents to justify such martial law in modern times here, I am aware that something of the kind may have been attempted in some of the doings of the British Colonial governors towards this country at the Revolution.

*   *   *

Having thus seen that "martial law" like this, ranging over a whole people and State, was not by our fathers considered proper at all in peace or during civil strife, and that, in the country from which we derive most of our jurisprudence, the king has long been forbidden to put it in force in war or peace, and that Parliament never, in the most extreme cases of rebellion, allows it, except as being sovereign and unlimited in power, and under peculiar restrictions, the next inquiry is, whether the Legislature of Rhode Island could, looking to her peculiar situation as to a constitution, rightfully establish such a law under the circumstances existing there in 1842. And, to meet this question broadly, whether she could do it, regarding those circumstances, first, as constituting peace, and next, as amounting to war.

*   *   *

All our social usages and political education, as well as our constitutional checks, are the other way. It would be alarming enough to sanction here an unlimited power, exercised either by Legislatures, or the executive, or courts, when all our governments are themselves governments of limitations and checks, and of fixed and known laws, and the people a race above all others jealous of encroachments by those in power. And it is far better that those persons should be without the protection of the ordinary laws of the land who disregard them in an emergency, and should look to a grateful country for indemnity and pardon, than to allow, beforehand, the whole frame of jurisprudence to be overturned, and everything placed at the mercy of the bayonet.

No tribunal or department in our system of governments ever can be lawfully authorized to dispense with the laws, like some of the tyrannical Stuarts, or to repeal, or abolish, or suspend the whole body of them; or, in other words, appoint an unrestrained military dictator at the head of armed men.

*   *   *

In short, then, there was nothing peculiar in the condition of Rhode Island as to a constitution in 1842, which justified her Legislature in peace, more than the Legislature of any other State, to declare martial law over her whole people; but there was much in her ancient charter, as well as in the plainest principles of constitutional liberty, to forbid it. . . . [T]he State Legislature alone possessed no constitutional authority to establish martial law, of this kind and to this extent, over her people generally, whether in peace or civil strife. But some of the members of this court seem to consider the pleadings broad enough to cover the justification, under some rights of war, independent of the act of the Assembly, or, as the opinion just read by the Chief Justice seems to imply, under the supposed authority of the State, in case of domestic insurrection like this, to adopt an act of martial law over its whole people, or any war measure deemed necessary by its Legislature for the public safety.

It looks, certainly, like pretty bold doctrine in a constitutional government, that, even in time of legitimate war, the Legislature can properly suspend or abolish all constitutional restrictions, as martial law does, and lay all the personal and political rights of the people at their feet. But bolder still is it to justify a claim to this tremendous power in any State, or in any of its officers, on the occurrence merely of some domestic violence.

*   *   *

It may not be useless to refresh our minds a tittle on this subject. The Congress [*sic*] expressly provides that "the Congress shall have power to declare war. (Art. 1, sec. 8.) This is not the States, nor the President, and much less the Legislature of a State. Nor is it foreign war alone that Congress is to declare, but "war"—war of any kind existing legitimately or according to the law of nations.

*   *   *

Some mistake has arisen here, probably from not adverting to the circumstance that Congress alone can declare war, and that all other conditions of violence are regarded by the Constitution as but ordinary cases of private outrage, to be punished by prosecutions in the courts; or as insurrections, rebellions, or domestic violence, to be put down by the civil authorities, aided by the militia; or, when these prove incompetent, by the general government, when appealed to by a State for aid, and matters appear to the general government to have reached the extreme stage, requiring more force to sustain the civil tribunals of a State, or requiring a declaration of war, and the exercise of all its extraordinary rights. Of these last, when applied to as here, and the danger has not been so imminent as to prevent an application, the general government must be the judge, and the general government is responsible for the consequences. . . .

Carry these constitutional provisions with us, and the facts which have existed, that there had been no war declared by Congress, no actual invasion of the State by a foreign enemy, no imminent danger of it, no emergency of any kind, which prevented time or delay to apply to the general government, and remember that, in this stage of things, Congress omitted or declined to do anything, and that the President also declined to consider a civil violence or insurrection as existing so as to justify his ordering out troops to suppress it. The State, then, in and of itself, declared martial law, and the defendants attempted to enforce it. In such a condition of things, I am not prepared to say that the authorities of a State alone can exercise the rights of war against their own citizens; persons, too, who, it is to be remembered, were for many purposes at the same time under the laws and protection of the general government. . . .

Under all these circumstances, then, to imply a power like this declaration of martial law over a State as still lawfully existing in its Legislature would be to imply what is forbidden by all constitutional checks, forbidden by all the usages of free governments, forbidden by an exclusive grant of the war power to Congress, forbidden by the fact that there were no exceptions or exigencies existing here which could justify it, and, in short, forbidden by the absence of any necessity in our system for a measure so dangerous and unreasonable, unless in some great extremity, if at all, by the general government, which alone holds the issues of war and the power and means of waging it.

*   *   *

There having been, then, no rights of war on the part of the State when this act of Assembly passed, and certainly none which could justify so extreme a measure as martial law over the whole State as incident to them, and this act being otherwise unconstitutional, the justification set up under it must, in my opinion, fail. If either government, on the 24th of June, possessed authority to pass an act establishing martial law to this extent, it was, of course, that of the United States—the government appointed in our system to carry on war and suppress rebellion or domestic violence when a State is unable to do it by her own powers. But as the general government did not exercise this authority, and probably could not have done it constitutionally in so sweeping a manner, and in such an early stage of resistance, if at all, this furnishes an additional reason why the State alone could not properly do it.

*   *   *

... Under the worst insurrections, and even wars, in our history, so strong a measure as this is believed never to have been ventured on before by the general government, and much less by any one of the States, as within their constitutional capacity, either in peace, insurrection, or war. And if it is to be tolerated, and the more especially in civil feuds like this, it will open the door in future domestic dissensions here to a series of butchery, rapine, confiscation, plunder, conflagration, and cruelty, unparalleled in the worst contests in history between mere dynasties for supreme power. It would go in practice to render the whole country—what Bolivar at one time seemed to consider his—a camp, and the administration of the government a campaign.

It is to be hoped we have some national ambition and pride, under our boasted dominion of law and order, to preserve them by law, by enlightened and constitutional law, and the moderation of superior intelligence and civilization, rather than by appeals to any of the semibarbarous measures of the darker ages, and the unrelenting, lawless persecutions of opponents in civil strife which characterized and disgraced those ages.

Again, when belligerent measures do become authorized by extreme resistance, and a legitimate state of war exists, and civil authority is prostrate, and violence and bloodshed seem the last desperate resort, yet war measures must be kept within certain restraints in all civil contests in all civilized communities.

*   *   *

108 "appeals to passion, and denunciations of the law" (1851)

One outcome of the Compromise of 1850 was the Fugitive Slave Act, which required the return of alleged slaves on the presentation of an affidavit by a person claiming ownership. Northerners severely criticized the act, and its enforcement was uneven.

An incident in eastern Pennsylvania raised suspicions of an organized resistance to enforcement of

the act. Judge Kane's charge to the grand jury, impaneled to investigate and possibly charge the individuals involved, stated the law's position regarding justifications of disobedience based on claims of morality and conscience and gave considerable breadth to the definition of treason.

☆ 108 Charge to the Grand Jury—Treason [Pennsylvania]

30 F. Cas. 1047 (C.C.E.D. Pa. 1851) (No. 18,276).

... Mr. Edward Gorsuch, a citizen of Maryland, who had come to Christiana, in Lancaster county, Pennsylvania, to reclaim his slaves, was met by a body of armed men, assaulted, beaten and murdered.... And it was stated that for some time before this, gatherings of people had been held from time to time at West-Chester, a town near the place of the outbreak, at which denunciations of the law were made as unconstitutional and of no obligation against "the higher law of every man's conscience:" the judges of the United States who would enforce it denounced ..., and exhortations made and pledges given to defy its execution to the last. The murder of Mr. Gorsuch, under such circumstances, caused a deep feeling throughout the whole country; and it being stated to the court that several bills of indictment for treason against the United States would be laid before the grand jury, that body was thus charged on the law of treason, by

KANE, District Judge. Treason against the United States is defined by the constitution (article 3, § 3, cl. 1) to consist in "levying war against them, or in adhering to their enemies, giving them aid and comfort." This definition is borrowed from the ancient law of England (St. 25 Edw. III., St. 5, c. 2), and its terms must be understood of course in the sense which they bore in that law, and which obtained here when the constitution was adopted. The expression "levying war," so regarded, embraces not merely that act of formal or declared war, but any combination forcibly to prevent or oppose the execution or enforcement of a provision of the constitution or of a public statute, if accompanied or followed by an act of forcible opposition in pursuance of such combination....

The definition, as you will observe, includes two particulars, both of them indispensable elements of the offence. There must have been a combination or conspiring together to oppose the law by force, and some actual force must have been exerted; or the crime of treason is not consummated. The highest, or at least the direct proof of the combining may be found in the declared purposes of the individual party before the actual outbreak; or it may be derived from the proceedings of meeting, in which he took part openly, or which he either prompted, or made effective by his countenance or sanction,—commending, counselling or instigating forcible resistance, to the law. I speak, of course, of a conspiring to resist a law, not the more limited purpose to violate it, or to prevent its application and enforcement in a particular case, or against a particular individual. The combination must be directed against the law itself. But such a direct proof of this element of the offence is not legally necessary to establish its existence. The concert of purpose may be deduced from the concerted action itself, or it may be inferred from facts concurring at the time, or afterwards, as well as before. Beside this, there must be some act of violence, as the result or consequence of the combining. But here again, it is not necessary to prove that the individual accused, was a direct, personal actor in the violence.... In treason there are no accessories. There has been, I fear, an erroneous impression on this subject among a portion of our people. If it has been thought safe, to counsel and instigate others to acts of forcible oppugnation to the provisions of a statute,—to inflame the minds of the ignorant, by appeals to passion, and denunciations of the law as oppressive, unjust, revolting to the conscience, and not binding on the actions of men,—to represent the constitution of the land as a compact of iniquity, which it were meritorious to violate or subvert,—the mistake has been a grievous one; and they who have fallen into it may rejoice, if their appeals and their counsels have been hitherto without effect. The supremacy of the constitution, in all its provisions, is at the very basis of our existence as a nation. He, whose conscience, or whose theories of political or individual right forbid him to support and maintain it in its integrity, may relieve himself from the duties of citizenship, by divesting himself of its rights. But while he remains within our borders, he is to remember, that successfully to instigate treason, is to commit it.

It is declared in the article of the constitution which I have already cited, that "no person shall be convicted of treason, unless on the testimony of two witnesses to the same overt act, or on confession in open court." This and the corresponding language in the act of congress of April 30, 1790, seems to refer to the proofs on the trial, and not to the preliminary hearing before the committing magistrate, or the proceeding before the grand inquest. There can be no conviction until after arraignment on bill found. The previous action in the case is not a trial, and cannot convict, whatever be the evidence or the number of witnesses. I understand this to have been the opinion entertained by Chief Justice Marshall, and though it differs from that expressed by Judge Iredell, on the indictment of Fries, I feel authorized to recommend it to you, as within the terms of the constitution, and involving no injustice to the accused.

I have only to add, that treason against the United States may be committed by any one resident or sojourning within its territory and under the protection of its laws, whether he be a citizen or alien.

*   *   *

109 The Treason of Giving Shelter (1851)

The federal grand jury indicated one Castner Hanway for treason for not aiding an officer of the United States in executing a fugitive slave warrant. Hanway told the federal officer trying to enforce the law that "he would not assist—that he did not care for that act of Congress or any other act." The case reflects on the particular character of treason as a manifestation of moral or political protest. In the face of the traditional insistence on strict construction of the elements of the offense of treason, the charge of treason against Hanway, who at most violated the Fugitive Slave Law, was trumped-up.

☆ 109 *United States v. Hanway* [Pennsylvania]

26 F. Cas. 105 (C.C.E.D. Pa. 1851) (No. 15,299).

Hanway was indicted for treason against the United States, the punishment for which is death. A number of other persons also stood indicted at this term for the same offence in which he was said to be engaged. The bill charged Hanway with intending to resist, in a treasonable way, the execution of an act of congress passed September 16, 1850, and commonly called the "Fugitive Slave Law." ...

*   *   *

... On the 9th of September, 1851, Mr. Gorsuch, of Maryland, having procured ... certain warrants to arrest some fugitive slaves of his, went with Kline, an officer, appointed by the commissioner, to Christiana, in Lancaster county, Pennsylvania, to take them. The place was inhabited by people who, in general, were strongly opposed to the fugitive slave law.... The fact that the writs had issued, became known to Williams, a negro in Philadelphia, who ... gave notice that the arrests were to be made, leaving with another person the names of some of Mr. Gorsuch's slaves, on a piece of paper. On the 11th, the officer and the others went over to Parker's, which they reached about daylight. While proceeding along the road, their attention was arrested by the sound of horns and the blowing of a bugle. After watching about Parker's house for a short time, one or two negroes were seen coming out of it. On discovering Kline and his party, they fled back into the house, and on pursuit being made by him, ran up stairs. These negroes were recognized by Mr. Gorsuch as his slaves. Kline entered the house, and almost immediately ascertained that a large number of negroes were concealed in the upper part of it; he nevertheless went to the stairway and called the keeper of the house to come down, stating that he was desirous of speaking to him. The negroes at this time were heard loading their guns. Kline, hearing the noise, said to them that there was no occasion for arming themselves,—that he designed to hurt no one, but meant to arrest two men who were in the house, and for whom he had warrants. Some one replied they would not come down. Mr. Gorsuch then went to the stairway, called his slaves by name, and stated that if they would come down and return home, he would treat them kindly, and forgive the past. Kline then read the warrants three times, and afterwards attempted to go up stairs, when a sharp-pointed instrument was thrust at him, and an axe afterwards thrown down, which struck two of the party below. Mr. Gorsuch then went to the front door of the house, and looking up to the window, again called to his slaves by name, when a shot was fired at him from the window. To show that his party was armed, Kline fired his pistol. At this period a horn was blown in the house, which was answered by other horns from the outside, as if by preconcerted action. The negroes then asked fifteen minutes time for consideration, which was granted to them. At this moment a white man was seen approaching the house on horseback. It turned out to be Hanway.... [Kline] called upon him, in the name of the United States, to assist in making the arrests. Hanway replied "he would not assist—that he did not care for that act of congress or any other act,—that the negroes had rights and could defend themselves, and that he need not come there to make arrests, for he could not do it." By this time another white man had arrived on the ground (Lewis), who walked up to Kline, and asked him for his authority to be there. Kline showed his papers to him also. Lewis then read the warrants, passed them to Hanway, who returned them to the marshal. Lewis, after reading the warrants, said, "the negroes had a right to defend themselves." ... By this time the blacks had gathered in very large numbers around the house, armed with guns, which they commenced pointing towards the marshal. At this juncture, Kline implored Hanway and Lewis to keep the negroes from firing, and he would withdraw his men, leave the ground, and let the negroes go. Hanway instantly replied, "they had a right to defend themselves, and he would not interfere." Kline's answer was, "they were not good citizens, or they never would permit the laws to be set at defiance in this way." One of Mr. Gorsuch's family then remarked, "that all they wanted was their property, and that they did not wish to hurt a hair of any one's head." Lewis replied, "that negroes were not property;" and then walked away. By this time another

gang of negroes had arrived, armed with guns and clubs, and Hanway rode up to them and said something which was not heard. He moved his horse out of the way of the guns; the negroes shouted, and immediately fired from every direction. Hanway rode a short distance down the lane leading from Parker's house, and sat on his horse watching the blacks. Kline then called to Lewis, telling him a man was shot, and begging him to come and assist, which Lewis refused to do.... In the effort to escape, these last of Kline's men rushed towards Hanway, who was on his horse which was yet standing still. They besought him to prevent the negroes from pursuing farther. He said he could not. They then asked for permission to get upon his horse, which would afford the means of making their escape. He refused their request, and putting whip to his horse rode off at full speed.... In connexion with these facts it appeared from Kline's testimony (1) that so soon as Hanway appeared at the bars, the negroes in Parker's house appeared to be encouraged, and gave a shout of satisfaction, when before that they had appeared discouraged, and had asked for time; (2) that before the firing commenced, Kline had given orders to his party to retreat, and they were actually engaged in the retreat when the attack was made; (3) that Mr. Gorsuch, who was killed, had no weapon of any kind in his hands.

*   *   *

For the United States. Levying war against the United States, is a phrase, the meaning of which is settled, both in England and the United States.... The matter is settled by our own decisions. In the Cases of the Western Insurgents, in 1795, Judge Patterson says: "If the object of insurrection was to prevent the execution of an act of congress by force and intimidation, the offence in legal estimation is high treason; it is an usurpation of the authority of the government. It is high treason by levying war." In Fries' Case Judge Iredell, in his charge to the grand jury (A.D. 1799), says: "I am warranted in saying, that if in the case of the insurgents who may come under your consideration, the intention was to prevent by force the execution of any act of the congress of the United States altogether, any forcible opposition calculated to carry that intention into effect, was a levying of war against the United States, and of course an act of treason. But if its intention was merely to defeat its operation in a particular instance, or through the agency of a particular officer, from some private or personal motive, though a high offence may have been committed, it did not amount to the crime of treason. The particular motive, must however, be the sole ingredient in the case, for if committed with a general view to obstruct the execution of the act, the offence must be deemed treason."

*   *   *

For the Prisoner. If the issue were on the fugitive slave law, and the question was, whether Hanway disapproved it? he could not be convicted even of that. There is no certain evidence which shows that he has an opinion about that law. Admitting that he disapproved the law, as he had a right to, there is no evidence which shows what motive brought him to this spot on the morning of the 11th. The sounding of a horn about breakfast time (an usual signal in the country for breakfast) shows nothing; and if it were clearly shown to be a signal for concourse, it follows not that it was a concourse for at treasonable purpose. There is evidence that there was in the neighbourhood a gang of professional kidnappers, who, on recent occasions, without any authority, had seized black men and carried them away, so that they were never heard of again. And that in consequence of this, there was a general alarm and feeling of indignation in the neighbourhood—not against lawful authority, but against man-stealers. Lewis was informed exactly, that there were "kidnappers at Parker's house," and he gave that information and none other to Hanway. And it does not matter, that by the word "kidnappers" slave owners were sometimes called, since there had recently been people in the neighbourhood to whom the word strictly and legally applied. Now who can say on the evidence what took Hanway to this spot? It is the intent which here is every thing. For if Hanway came there with a lawful intent, it is no treason, even though he did afterwards see with composure the laws violated, or even commit a murder.

. . . "Treason against the United States, shall consist only in levying war against them, or in adhering to their enemies, giving them aid and comfort." This definition was framed by men who, in the exercise of the right of revolution, had risked the penalties of treason, and studied the subject on the steps of the scaffold. Indignant at the wrongs that had been perpetrated, and the blood that had been shed for fictitious offences made treason by ingenious construction, they determined to deprive both faction and power of so potent an engine of mischief, long used and abused by demagogues and despots. They cut off at one blow, that once flourishing and fatal branch of interpretative treason. They defined the crime by terms severely strict and rigorously exact. . . . The offence requires the existence of war. Its sole element is war. It cannot be committed in time of peace. To be guilty of the crime, a person must be actually engaged in the war, or giving aid to those that are. To contemplate, or to advise war, or even to conspire to wage it, is not enough. The war must be actually levied. It must not be a mere tumult—a fight—a struggle in arms between individuals or companies, or violence offered to an executive or military officer of the government, in a matter relat-

ing only to individual interest or private right, but it must be national in its scope and object. It must possess that dignity in mischievous design that aims at the life of the government, or at least at the prostration of some branch of its power, by an armed opposition. It must have the impress of universality. . . .

*   *   *

GRIER, Circuit Justice (charging jury).

*   *   *

The bill charges the defendant with "wickedly and traitorously intending to levy war against the United States:" and the jury must find the act or acts to have been committed with such intention. For although the prisoner may have been guilty of riot, robbery, murder, or any other felony, he cannot be found guilty under this bill of indictment, unless you find that he intended to levy war against the United States, or that the acts were committed by himself and others in pursuance of some conspiracy or preconcert for that purpose; and this is a question of fact for the decision of the jury. . . .

. . . [S]ome actual force or violence must be used in pursuance of such design to levy war; but it is altogether immaterial whether the force used is sufficient to effectuate the object; any force, connected with the intention, will constitute the crime of 'levying war.'" . . .

. . . But there must be a conspiracy to resist by force, and an actual resistance by force of arms of intimidation by numbers. The conspiracy and the insurrection connected with it must be to effect something of a public nature, to overthrow the government, or to nullify some law of the United States, and totally to hinder its execution, or compel its repeal. A band of smugglers may be said to set the laws at defiance, and to have conspired together for that purpose, and to resist by armed force, the execution of the revenue laws; they may have battles with the officers of the revenue, in which numbers may be slain on both sides, and yet they will not be guilty of treason, because it is not an insurrection of a public nature, but merely for private lucre or advantage. . . . A number of fugitive slaves may infest a neighbourhood, and may be encouraged by the neighbours in combining to resist the capture of any of their number; they may resist with force and arms, their master or the public officer, who may come to arrest them; they may murder and rob them; they are guilty of felony and liable to punishment, but not as traitors. Their insurrection is for a private object, and connected with no public purpose. It is true that constructively they may be said to resist the execution of the fugitive slave law, but in no other sense than the smugglers resist the revenue laws, and the anti-renters the execution laws. Their insurrection, their violence, however great their numbers may be, so long as it is merely to attain some personal or private end of their own, cannot be called levying war. Alexander the Great may be classed with robbers by moralists, but still the political distinction will remain between war and robbery. One is public and national, the other private and personal.

*   *   *

[The jury found for the defendant.]

110 Teaching Colored Children to Read (1853)

Although Mrs. Margaret Douglas knew that it was against the law to teach slaves, she was unaware that the law forbade the education of free blacks. She and her daughter held school for free black children in a back room in her house in Norfolk, Virginia. City constables searched the house, and she was indicted by the grand jury. Refusing the services of a lawyer, Mrs. Douglas defended herself. She was convicted, but the jury set the penalty at a one-dollar fine. The judge nevertheless disagreed with this leniency, and Mrs. Douglas served a one-month prison sentence.

☆ 110 Remarks by the Judge at the Sentencing of Mrs. Margaret Douglas (January 10, 1854)

State v. Douglas, 7 Am. State Trials 45 (1853).

Judge Baker [remarks at sentencing]. . . . There are persons, I believe, in our community, opposed to the policy of the law in question. They profess to believe that universal intellectual culture is necessary to religious instruction and education, and that such culture is suitable to a state of slavery; and there can be no misapprehension as to your opinions on this subject, judging from the indiscreet freedom with which you spoke of your regard for the colored race in general. Such opinions in the present state of our society I regard as manifestly mischievous. It is not true that our slaves cannot be taught religious and moral duty, without being able to read the Bible and use the pen. . . .

A valuable report or document recently published in the city of New York by the Southern Aid Society sets forth many valuable and important truths upon the condition of the Southern slaves, and the utility of moral and religious instruction, apart from a knowledge of books. I recommend the careful perusal of it to all whose opinions concur with your own. It shows that a system of catechetical instruction, with a clear and simple exposition of Scripture, has been employed with gratifying success; that the slave population of the South are peculiarly susceptible of good religious influences. Their mere residence among a Christian people has

wrought a great and happy change in their condition: they have been raised from the night of heathenism to the light of Christianity, and thousands of them have been brought to a saving knowledge of the Gospel.

Of the one hundred millions of the negro race, there cannot be found another so large a body as the three millions of slaves in the United States, at once so intelligent, so inclined to the Gospel, and so blessed by the elevating influence of civilization and Christianity. Occasional instances of cruelty and oppression, it is true, may sometimes occur, and probably will ever continue to take place under any system of laws: but this is not confined to wrongs committed upon the negro; wrongs are committed and cruelly practiced in a like degree by the lawless white man upon his own color; and while the negroes of our town and State are known to be surrounded by most of the substantial comforts of life, and invited both by precept and example to participate in proper, moral and religious duties, it argues, it seems to me, a sickly sensibility towards them to say their persons, feelings, and interests are not sufficiently respected by our laws, which, in effect, tend to nullify the act of our Legislature passed for the security and protection of their masters.

. . . Bold and open opposition to [this law] is a matter not to be slightly regarded, especially as we have reason to believe that every Southern slave state in our country, as a measure of self-preservation and protection, has deemed it wise and just to adopt laws with similar provisions.

There might have been no occasion for such enactments in Virginia, or elsewhere, on the subject of negro education, but as a matter of self-defense against the schemes of Northern incendiaries, and the outcry against holding our slaves in bondage. Many now living well remember, how, and when, and why the anti-slavery fury began, and by what means its manifestations were made public. Our mails were clogged with abolition pamphlets and inflammatory documents, to be distributed among our Southern negroes to induce them to cut our throats. Sometimes, it may be, these libelous documents were distributed by Northern citizens professing Southern feelings, and at other times by Southern people professing Northern feelings. These, however, were not the only means resorted to by the Northern fanatics to stir up insubordination among our slaves. They scattered far and near pocket handkerchiefs, and other similar articles, with frightful engravings, and printed over with anti-slavery nonsense, with the view to work upon the feeling and ignorance of our negroes, who otherwise would have remained comfortable and happy. Under such circumstances there was but one measure of protection for the South, and that was adopted. . . .

For these reasons, as an example to all others in

like cases disposed to offend, and in vindication of the policy and justness of our laws, which every individual should be taught to respect, the judgment of the Court is, in addition to the proper fine and costs, that you will be imprisoned for the period of one month in the jail of this city.

111 Cutting the Iron Chain or Collar of Any Runaway Slave (1856)

The slavery controversy inspired both words and action from many Americans. Harriet Beecher Stowe's *Uncle Tom's Cabin*, published in 1851, went through 120 United States printings that year alone. In 1854, the Wisconsin Supreme Court released a Wisconsin man convicted of rescuing a runaway slave in violation of the 1850 Fugitive Slave Act and ruled that law unconstitutional. That same year, a mob in Boston attacked the federal courthouse in an attempt to rescue a fugitive slave from return to his Southern owner. In 1856, "Free-Soil" leaders in the territory of Kansas were indicted for treason by their legislature, and raids and lynchings occurred on the Missouri-Kansas border. Slave insurrection and escape to the North became more common.

Louisiana passed its Black Code covering offenses by and against blacks. It established a totally distinct system of criminal justice for slaves and blacks, thereby instituting the first comprehensive system of legal racial apartheid in modern history. The code provided the death penalty for those who wrote, printed, published, or distributed anything "having the tendency to produce discontent among the free colored population or insubordination among the slaves."

☆ 111 Louisiana Black Code

1856 La. Acts 1-105.

CRIMES AND OFFENCES COMMITTED BY SLAVES
AND FREE COLORED PERSONS

Section 1. Any slave who shall commit the crime of wilful murder, on conviction thereof, shall be punished with death.

Sec. 2. Any slave who shall with a dangerous weapon, and with intent to kill, cut or otherwise wound any person, or who shall attempt maliciously to kill by drowning, or strangling, on conviction thereof, shall suffer death.

Sec. 3. Any slave who shall wilfully and maliciously strike his master or mistress, or his master's or mistress' child, or any white overseer appointed by his owner, to superintend said owner's slaves, so as to cause a contusion or shedding of blood, shall be punished with death or imprisonment at hard labor for a term not less than ten years.

Sec. 4. If a slave shall shoot at or stab any person with intent to kill, such slave, on conviction of either of said offences, shall suffer death.

Sec. 5. If any slave or free colored person shall wilfully and maliciously poison or attempt to poison any person, he shall, on conviction thereof, suffer death.

Sec. 6. If any slave or free colored person shall commit a rape, or attempt to do so, upon the body of any white female, he shall, upon conviction thereof, suffer death.

Sec. 7. Any slave who shall encourage or excite any insurrection or revolt in this State, or who shall be in any wise concerned in instigating to the same, on due conviction thereof, shall suffer death.

Sec. 8. If any slave or free colored person shall wilfully and maliciously burn or destroy any building or house, or shall attempt to burn any house or building, he shall on conviction thereof, suffer death.

Sec. 9. If any slave shall strike a white person, for the first and second offence he shall receive such punishment as the jury shall think proper, but for the third offence, the said slave shall suffer death; and whenever any slave shall have grievously and wilfully wounded or mutilated any white person, although it prove to be the first offence, such slave shall suffer death; provided the blow, wound, mutilation or bruises are not made or committed in defence of the person or property of his master, or of some member of his family, or of the person having charge of him, or in whose care he then may be, in which case the said slave shall be excused.

Sec. 10. Any slave who shall feloniously and forcibly take any goods or money from the person of another, by violence or by putting him in fear, shall, upon conviction, be punished with death or otherwise, at the discretion of the court.

*   *   *

Sec. 14. Any slave who shall revolt or rebel against any white overseer, appointed by his owner to superintend the conduct of his slaves, when being punished by him, or another, by his orders, shall, on conviction thereof, be punished at the discretion of the court.

Sec. 15. If a slave, or free person of color, insult or assault and beat any white person, such offender, on conviction of either of said offences, shall be punished at the discretion of the court.

*   *   *

Sec. 18. Whoever shall inflict, or cause to be inflicted, any cruel treatment upon any slave, whether by maltreating, flogging, failing to clothe and feed in a proper manner, by imprisoning, by putting in irons, or by ill treating in any other manner, to be judged of by the court and jury, shall be fined not less than fifty nor more than two hundred dollars. The court and jury shall have power in all cases, whether they convict or not, to decree the sale of the slave at public auction. The owner shall not be allowed to purchase either directly or indirectly, or to have under his control the said slave, under the penalty of one thousand dollars. The price of the slave thus sold, shall be paid over to the owner after deducting all costs. . . .

Sec. 19. Any free person who shall play at any game of chance, or make any bet, or in any manner gamble with any slave, on conviction thereof, be fined not less than one hundred nor more than one thousand dollars, and be imprisoned in the parish jail not less than one month nor more than one year; and on a second or any subsequent conviction for a similar offence, shall be fined one thousand dollars and be imprisoned in the parish jail one year.

Sec. 20. Any master or other person having the charge or government of any slave accused of any capital crime who shall conceal or convey him away, so that he cannot be brought to trial and punishment, shall forfeit the sum of one thousand dollars. But if such slave be accused of a crime not capital, then he shall forfeit the sum of five hundred dollars.

Sec. 21. If any person shall harbor or conceal any runaway slave, knowing him to be such, or shall cut or break any iron chain or collar which any master of slaves may have used, he shall, on conviction thereof, be fined not less than two hundred nor more than one thousand dollars; and in default of payment, he shall be imprisoned not less than three nor more than six months.

*   *   *

Sec. 27. If any person shall, by words, actions, writing, or in any other manner whatsoever, persuade, encourage, or advise any slave to insurrection, against his lawful proprietor, or against the white inhabitants of the State or the government thereof, such person, on conviction, shall suffer death or imprisonment at hard labor at the discretion of the court.

Sec. 28. Whoever shall, with the intent to produce discontent among the free colored population, or insubordination among the slaves, write, print, publish or distribute, anything having a tendency to produce discontent among the free colored population, or insubordination among the slaves therein, shall, on conviction, be sentenced to imprisonment at hard labor or suffer death, at the discretion of the court.

Sec. 29. Whoever, with the intent aforesaid, shall make use of language in any public discourse, from the bar, the bench, the stage, the pulpit, or in any place whatsoever, or whoever shall make use of language in private discourses or conversations, or of signs or actions, having a tendency to produce discontent among the free colored population of this State, or to excite insubordination among the slaves therein; or whosoever shall knowingly be instrumental in bringing into this State any paper, pamphlet or book having such tendency, shall, on conviction thereof, suffer imprisonment at hard labor not less than three nor more than twenty-one years, or death, at the discretion of the court.

Sec. 30. It shall be the duty of Judges in this State to give the two preceding sections in charge to the Grand Jury at each term of their respective courts.

*   *   *

RUNAWAY SLAVES

Sec. 82. It shall be lawful to fire upon runaway negroes who may be armed, when pursued, if they refuse to surrender.

Sec. 83. Every person taking up a runaway slave shall immediately convey him before the nearest Justice of the Peace, who shall either commit the slave to the parish prison or send him to the owner, employer, or overseer, if known, who shall pay the person taking him up the rates herafter specified, to wit:

For taking up a slave in the woods, six dollars.

For taking up on the road or plantation, three dollars.

For mileage in all cases, going and returning, ten cents per mile.

For Magistrates' committing, one dollar.

For Jailer receiving and placing in confinement, one dollar.

For feeding slave while confined, twenty-five cents per day.

For Magistrate, for receiving proof of ownership, one dollar.

For delivery by Jailer to owner, fifty cents.

These fees and no others shall be charged.

Sec. 84. The Jailer shall have every slave by him placed in confinement as a runaway, advertised in the nearest newspaper three times, making the advertisment as brief as possible so as to give a full description of the slave confined, with his name, the name of the owner and place of residence, if known, or as given by the slave; and on the owner's payment of the same the Jailer shall produce the printer's receipt for the payment of the advertisement, or the paper with the advertisement therein contained.

112 "executors of the will of the majority of our citizens" (1856)

In January of 1848 gold was discovered in California. The subsequent mass migration of American settlers (the Forty-Niners) drastically changed the character of the territory, which had expanded greatly through recent acquisitions from Mexico. Upon President Zachary Taylor's urging, the people of California formed a government and adopted a constitution prohibiting slavery. In his 1849 message to Congress, Taylor proposed that California immediately be admitted into the Union, but Southerners opposed the move for fear of upsetting the congressional and electoral college balance between free and slave states. Both the turbulent nature of the settling population and the absence of federal authority hampered the operation of lawful authority in California.

Self-appointed executors of the will of the people, vigilante committees, formed throughout the territory to substitute for civil law enforcement. Despite their pledge to disassociate themselves from all political activities, the vigilantes frequently disregarded the finer details of legal process and exerted great influence upon the political process.

☆112 Constitution of the Committee of Vigilantes of San Francisco (May 15, 1856)

Reprinted in J. D. Lawson, ed., *American State Trials* (St. Louis: Thomas Lawbook Co., 1856), 15:65.

*   *   *

Whereas, it has become apparent to the citizens of San Francisco that there is no security for life and property, either under the regulations of society, as it at present exists, or under the laws as now administered; and that by the association together of bad characters, our ballot boxes have been stolen and others substituted, or stuffed with votes that were not polled, and thereby our elections nullifed, our dearest rights violated, and no other method left by which the will of the people can be manifested; therefore, the citizens whose names are hereunto attached, do unite themselves into an association for maintenance of peace and good order of society — the preservation of our lives and property, and to insure that our ballot boxes shall hereafter express the actual and unforged will of the majority of our citizens . . . we are determined that no thief, burglar, incendiary, assassin, ballot-box stuffer, or other disturbers of the peace, shall escape punishment, either by the quibbles of the law, the insecurity of prisons, the carelessness or corruption of police, or a laxity of those who pretend to administer justice; and to secure the objects of this association, we do hereby agree:

1st. That the name and style of this association shall be the Committee of Vigilance, for the protection of the ballot-box, the lives, liberty and property of the citizens and residents of the City of San Francisco.

2d. That there shall be rooms for the deliberations of the Committee, at which there shall be some one or more members of the Committee appointed for that purpose, in constant attendance . . . and if, in the judgment of the member or members of the Committee present, it be such an act as justifies or demands the interference of this Committee, either in aiding in the execution of the laws, or the prompt and summary punishment of the offender, the Committee shall be at once assembled for the purpose of taking such action as the majority of them, when assembled, shall determine upon.

*   *   *

7th. That the action of this body shall be entirely and vigorously free from all consideration of, or participation in the merits or demerits, or opinion or acts, of any and all sects, political parties, or sectional divisions in the community; and every class of orderly citizens, of whatever sect, party, or nativity, may become members of this body. No discussion of political, sectional, or sectarian subjects shall be allowed in the rooms of the association.

8th. That no persons, accused before this body, shall be punished until after fair and impartial trial and conviction.

9th. That whenever the General Committee have assembled for deliberation, the decision of the majority, upon any question that may be submitted to them by the Executive Committee, shall be binding upon the whole; provided nevertheless, that when the delegates are deliberating upon the punishment to be awarded to any criminals, no vote inflicting the death penalty shall be binding, unless passed by two-thirds of those present and entitled to vote.

10th. That all good citizens shall be eligible for admission to this body, under such regulations as may be prescribed by a committee on qualifications; and if any unworthy persons gain admission, they shall on due proof be expelled; and believing ourselves to be executors of the will of the majority of our citizens, we do pledge our sacred honor, to defend and sustain each other in carrying out the determined action of this committee, at the hazard of our lives and our fortunes.

113 "a subordinate and inferior class of beings" (1857)

Efforts to resolve, through legislation or resort to the courts, some of the public conflicts derived from the institution of slavery usually were not successful. The proslavery forces controlled the Southern state legislatures. In the federal Congress, the Southern delegations likewise exerted great power. The Supreme Court of the United States was unwilling to undertake radical reforms of the original institutions of the country, including the property right in slaves. In the Dred Scott decision the court reiterated that slaves or their descendants, in bondage or liberated, were not United States citizens and therefore were not entitled to access to the federal judicial system.

☆113 *Dred Scott v. Sandford*

60 U.S. (19 How.) 393, 400-54 (1857).

Mr. Chief Justice TANEY....

* * *

The plaintiff ... was, with his wife and children, held as slaves by the defendant, in the State of Missouri, and he brought this action in the Circuit Court of the United States for that district, to assert the title of himself and his family to freedom.

The declaration is ... that he and the defendant are citizens of different States; that is, that he is a citizen of Missouri, and the defendant a citizen of New York.

The defendant pleaded in abatement to the jurisdiction of the court, that the plantiff was not a citizen of the State of Missouri, as alleged in his declaration, being a Negro of African descent whose ancestors were of pure African blood, and who were brought into this country and sold as slaves.

* * *

That plea denies the right of the plaintiff to sue in a court of the United States, for the reasons therein stated.

* * *

The question is simply this: Can a Negro, whose ancestors were imported into this country, and sold as slaves, become a member of the political community formed and brought into existence by the Constitution of the United States, and as such become entitled to all the rights, and privileges, and immunities, guaranteed by that instrument to the citizen? One of which rights is the privilege of suing in a court of the United States in the cases specified in the Constitution.

It will be observed, that the plea applies to that class of persons only whose ancestors were Negroes of the African race, and imported into this country, and sold and held as slaves. The only matter in issue before the court, therefore, is whether the descendants of such slaves, when they shall be emancipated, or who are born of parents who had become free before their birth, are citizens of a State, in the sense in which the word citizen is used in the Constitution of the United States. ...

* * *

The words "people of the United States" and "citizens" are synonymous terms, and mean the same thing. They both describe the political body who, according to our republican institutions, form the sovereignty, and who hold the power and conduct the government through their representatives. They are what we familarily call the "sovereign people,"

and every citizen is one of this people, and a constituent member of this sovereignty. The question before us is, whether the class of persons described in the plea in abatement compose a portion of this people, and are constituent members of this sovereignty? We think they are not, and that they are not included, and were not intended to be included, under the word "citizens" in the Constitution, and can, therefore, claim none of the rights and privileges which that instrument provides for and secures to citizens of the United States. On the contrary, they were at that time considered as a subordinate and inferior class of beings, who had been subjugated by the dominant race, and whether emancipated or not, yet remained subject to their authority, and had no rights or privileges but such as those who held the power and the government might choose to grant them.

* * *

In discussing this question, we must not confound the rights of citizenship which a State may confer within its own limits, and the rights of citizenship as a member of the Union. It does not by any means follow, because he has all the rights and privileges of a citizen of a State, that he must be a citizen of the United States. He may have all of the rights and privileges of the citizen of a State, and yet not be entitled to the rights and privileges of a citizen in any other State. For, previous to the adoption of the Constitution of the United States, every State had the undoubted right to confer on whomsoever it pleased the character of a citizen, and to endow him with all rights. But this character, of course, was confined to the boundaries of the State, and gave him no rights or privileges in other States beyond those secured to him by the laws of nations and the comity of States. Nor have the several States surrendered the power of conferring these rights and privileges by adopting the Constitution of the United States. ...

It is very clear, therefore, that no State can, by any Act or law of its own, passed since the adoption of the Constitution, introduce a new member into the political community created by the Constitution of the United States. It cannot make him a member of this community by making him a member of its own. And for the same reason it cannot introduce any person, or description of persons, who were intended to be embraced in this new political family, which the Constitution brought into existence, but were intended to be excluded from it.

The question then arises, whether the provisions of the Constitution, in relation to the personal rights and privileges to which the citizen of a State should be entitled, embraced the Negro African race, at that time in this country, or who might afterwards be imported, who had then or should afterwards be made free in any State; and to put within the power of a single State to make him a citizen of the United States, and endue him with the full rights of citizenship in every other State without their consent. Does the Constitution of the United States act upon him whenever he shall be made free under the laws of a State, and raised there to the rank of a citizen, and immediately clothe him with all the privileges of a citizen in every other State, and in its own courts?

The court think the affirmative of these propositions cannot be maintained. And if it cannot, the plaintiff in error could not be a citizen of the State of Missouri, within the meaning of the Constitution of the United States, and, consequently, was not entitled to sue in its courts.

It is true, every person, and every class and description of persons, who were at the time of the adoption of the Constitution recognized as citizens in the several States, became also citizens of this new political body; but none other; it was formed by them, and for them and their posterity, but for no one else. And the personal rights and privileges guaranteed to citizens of this new sovereignty were intended to embrace those only who were then members of the several state communities, or who should afterwards, by birthright or otherwise, become members, according to the provisions of the Constitution and the principles on which it was founded. . . .

*   *   *

In the opinion of the court, the legislation and histories of the times, and the language used in the Declaration of Independence show, that neither the class of persons who had been imported as slaves, nor their descendants, whether they had become free or not, were then acknowledged as a part of the people, nor intended to be included in the general words used in that memorable instrument.

*   *   *

They had for more than a century before been regarded as beings of an inferior order and altogether unfit to associate with the white race, either in social or political relations, and so far inferior that they had no rights which the white man was bound to respect; and that the Negro might justly and lawfully be reduced to slavery for his benefit. He was bought and sold and treated as an ordinary article of merchandise and traffic whenever a profit could be made by it. This opinion was at that time fixed and universal in the civilized portion of the white race. It was regarded as an axiom in morals as well as in politics, which no one thought of disputing, or supposed to be open to dispute; and men in every grade and position in society daily and habitually acted upon it in their private pursuits, as well as in matters of public concern, without doubting for a moment the correctness of this opinion.

*   *   *

[T]he men who framed this declaration were great men — high in literary acquirements — high in their sense of honor, and incapable of asserting principles inconsistent with those on which they were acting. They perfectly understood the meaning of the language they used and how it would be understood by others; and they knew that it would not in any part of the civilized world be supposed to embrace the Negro race, which, by common consent, had been excluded from civilized governments and the family of nations and doomed to slavery. They spoke and acted according to the then established doctrine and principles and in the ordinary language of the day, and no one misunderstood them. The unhappy black race were separated from the white by indelible marks, and laws long before established, and were never thought of or spoken of except as property and when the claims of the owner or the profit of the trader were supposed to need protection.

This state of public opinion had undergone no change when the Constitution was adopted, as is equally evident from its provisions and language.

*   *   *

[T]here are two clauses in the Constitution which point directly and specifically to the Negro race as a separate class of persons, and show clearly that they were not regarded as a portion of the people or citizens of the Government then formed.

One of these clauses reserves to each of the thirteen States the right to import slaves until the year 1808, if it thinks it proper. And the importation which it thus sanctions was unquestionably of persons of the race of which we are speaking, as the traffic in slaves in the United States had always been confined to them. And by the other provision the States pledge themselves to each other to maintain the right of property of the master, by delivering up to him any slave who may have escaped from his service, and be found within their respective territories. . . . And these two provisions show, conclusively, that neither the description of persons therein referred to, nor their descendants, were embraced in any of the other provisions of the Constitution; for certainly these two clauses were not intended to confer on them or their posterity the blessings of liberty, or any of the personal rights so carefully provided for the citizen.

*   *   *

. . . Upon a full and careful consideration of the subect, the court is of opinion that, upon the facts stated in the plea in abatement, Dred Scott was not a citizen of Missouri within the meaning of the Constitution of the United States, and not entitled as such to sue in its courts; and, consequently that the Circuit Court had no jurisdiction of the case. . . .

* * *

We proceed, therefore, to inquire whether the facts relied on by the plaintiff entitled him to his freedom.

* * *

The Act of Congress, upon which the plaintiff relies, declares that slavery and involuntary servitude, except as a punishment for crime, shall be forever prohibited in all that part of the territory ceded by France, under the name of Louisiana. . . . [T]his part of the inquiry is, whether Congress was authorized to pass this law under any of the powers granted to it by the Constitution; for if the authority is not given by that instrument, it is the duty of this court to declare it void and inoperative, and incapable of conferring freedom upon any one who is held as slave under the laws of any one of the States.

The counsel for the plaintiff has laid much stress upon that article in the Constitution which confers on Congress the power "to dispose of and make all needful rules and regulations respecting the territory or other property belonging to the United States;" but, in the judgment of the court, that provision has no bearing on the present controversy, and the power there given, whatever it may be, is confined, and was intended to be confined, to the territory which at that time belonged to, or was claimed by, the United States, and was within their boundaries as settled by the treaty with Great Britain, and can have no influence upon a territory afterwards acquired from a foreign Government. . . .

* * *

. . . [A]n Act of Congress which deprives a person of the United States of his liberty or property merely because he came himself or brought his property into a particular Territory of the United States, and who had committed no offense against the laws, could hardly be dignified with the name of due process of law.

* * *

Now . . . the right of property in a slave is distinctly and expressly affirmed in the Constitution. The right to traffic in it, like an ordinary article of merchandise and property, was guaranteed to the citizens of the United States, in every State that might desire it, for twenty years. And the Government in express terms is pledged to protect it in all future time, if the slave escapes from his owner. . . . And no word can be found in the Constitution which gives Congress a greater power over slave property, or which entitles property of that kind to less protection than property of any other description. The only power conferred is the power coupled with the duty of guarding and protecting the owner in his rights.

* * *

114 "threats of assassination" (1858)

Founded by Joseph Smith, the Prophet of Latter-Day Saints, the Mormon church and its members encountered savage persecution wherever they went. Hounded out of Missouri in 1838, Joseph Smith founded the all-Mormon city of Nauvoo on the Mississippi River in Illinois. By 1840, Nauvoo was more populous than Chicago. The murder of Joseph Smith by a mob and the destruction of Nauvoo elevated Brigham Young and resulted in the Mormon move west. In their proposed State of Desert—which would have contained present-day Utah, Nevada, half of California and Arizona, and parts of Oregon, Idaho, Wyoming, Colorado, and New Mexico—the Mormons sought to maintain cultural and religious purity as well as political hegemony.

Assuming the presidency in 1850, Millard Fillmore named Brigham Young territorial governor of Utah. But tensions mounted between the Mormons and the Gentiles in the territory; Brigham Young and his followers were charged by federal officials with establishing an absolute dictatorship in the Utah territory, discrimination against non-Mormons, and disloyalty to Washington. In June of 1857, President Buchanan dispatched an expeditionary force of twenty-six hundred men from Fort Leavenworth to Utah to install non-Mormon officials in the territory. In mid-September Brigham Young ordered his forces to "forbid all armed forces of every description from coming into this territory under any pretense whatever." He further instructed his followers to put the torch to all structures in the line of march of the federal force. Historian Nathaniel Weyl wrote: "The founders of Mormonism in Utah were unquestionably guilty of treason against the United States. They levied an army, declared martial law in Utah Territory, prepared to repel an American expeditionary force, raided its supply depots, attempted to starve its enemy in the desert, and carried out the first scorched earth program in American history."

In 1858 President Buchanan issued a clear and unemotional proclamation in an effort to stop what he thought was "the first rebellion which has existed in our territories."

Although Young planned to burn down Salt Lake City and to retreat into the southern wilderness, the spirit of compromise finally prevailed. Alfred Cumming, the newly appointed territorial governor, counseled negotiations, and in return for Young's recognition of his authority, President Buchanan issued a general amnesty to the rebels of the "Utah War." The decisive action by Washington brought an end to Mormon separatism, yet the costly "Utah War" has continued to be viewed as "Buchanan's Blunder."

☆ 114 President James Buchanan's
Proclamation on the Rebellion in Utah (April 6,
1858)

11 Stat. 796 (1858).

Whereas, the Territory of Utah was settled by certain emigrants from the States, and from foreign countries, who have for several years past manifested a spirit of insubordination to the Constitution and laws of the United States, The great mass of those settlers, acting under the influence of leaders to whom they seem to have surrendered their judgment, refuse to be controlled by any other authority. They have been often advised to obedience, and these friendly counsels have been answered with defiance. Officers of the federal government have been driven from the Territory for no offense but an effort to do their sworn duty. Others have been prevented from going there by threats of assassination. Judges have been violently interrupted in the performance of their functions, and the records of the courts have been seized and either destroyed or concealed. Many other acts of unlawful violence have been perpetrated, and the right to repeat them has been openly claimed by the leading inhabitants, with at least the silent acquiescence of nearly all the others. Their hostility to the lawful government of the country has at length become so violent that no officer bearing a commission from the Chief Magistrate of the Union can enter the Territory or remain there with safety; and all the officers recently appointed have been unable to go to Salt Lake or anywhere else in Utah beyond the immediate power of the army. Indeed, such is believed to be the condition to which a strange system of terrorism has brought the inhabitants of that region, that no one among them could express an opinion favorable to this government, or even propose to obey its laws, without exposing his life and property to peril.

... I accordingly ordered a detachment of the army to march for the City of Salt Lake, or within reach of that place, and to act, in case of need, as a posse for the enforcement of the laws. But, in the meantime, the hatred of that misguided people for the just and legal authority of the government had become so intense that they resolved to measure their military strength with that of the Union. They have organized an armed force far from contemptible in point of numbers, and trained it, if not with skill, at least with great assiduity and perseverance. While the troops of the United States were on their march, a train of baggage wagons, which happened to be unprotected, was attacked and destroyed by a portion of the Mormon forces, and the provisions and stores with which the train was laden were wantonly burnt. In short, their present attitude is one of decided and unreserved enmity to the United States

and to all their loyal citizens. Their determination to oppose the authority of the government by military force has not only been expressed in words, but manifested in overt acts of the most unequivocal character.

Fellow-citizens of Utah! this is rebellion against the government to which you owe allegiance. It is levying war against the United States, and involves you in the guilt to treason. Persistence in it will bring you to condign punishment, to ruin, and to shame; for it is mere madness to suppose that, with your limited resources, you can successfully resist the force of this great and powerful nation.

If you have calculated upon the forbearance of the United States — if you have permitted yourselves to suppose that this government will fail to put forth its strength and bring you to submission — you have fallen into a grave mistake. You have settled upon territory which lies geographically in the heart of the Union. The land you live upon was purchased by the United States and paid for out of their treasury; the proprietary right and title to it is in them, and not in you. Utah is bounded on every side by States and Territories whose people are true to the Union. It is absurd to believe that they will or can permit you to erect in their very midst a government of your own, not only independent of the authority which they all acknowledge, but hostile to them and their interests.

Do not deceive yourselves nor try to mislead others by propagating the idea that this is a crusade against your religion. The Constitution and laws of this country can take no notice of your creed, whether it be true or false. That is a question between your God and yourselves, in which I disclaim all right to interfere. If you obey the laws, keep the peace, and respect the just rights of others, you will be perfectly secure, and may live on in your present faith or change it for another at your pleasure. Every intelligent man among you knows very well that this government has never, directly, or indirectly, sought to molest you in your worship, to control you in your ecclesiastical affairs, or even to influence you in your religious opinions.

This rebellion is not merely a violation of your legal duty; it is without just cause, without reason, without excuse. You never made a complaint that was not listened to with patience. You never exhibited a real grievance that was not redressed as promptly as it could be. The laws and regulations enacted for your government by Congress have been equal and just, and their enforcement was manifestly necessary for your own welfare and happiness. You have never asked their repeal. They are similar in every material respect to the laws which have been passed for the other Territories of the Union, and which everywhere else (with one partial exception) have been cheerfully obeyed. No people ever lived who were freer from unnecessary legal restraints than you. Human wisdom never devised a political system which bestowed more blessings or imposed lighter burdens than the government of the United States in its operation upon the Territories.

But being anxious to save the effusion of blood, and to avoid the indiscriminate punishment of a whole people for crimes of which it is not probable that all are equally guilty, I offer now a free and full pardon to all who will submit themselves to the authority of the federal government. If you refuse to accept it, let the consequences fall upon your own heads. But I conjure you to pause deliberately, and reflect well, before you reject this tender of peace and good will.

Now, therefore, I, James Buchanan, *President of the United States,* have thought proper to issue this, my Proclamation, enjoining upon all public officers in the Territory of Utah to be diligent and faithful, to the full extent of their power, in the execution of the laws; commanding all citizens of the United States in said Territory to aid and assist the officers in the performance of their duties; offering to the inhabitants of Utah, who shall submit to the laws, a free pardon for the seditions and treasons heretofore by them committed; warning those who shall persist, after notice of this proclamation, in the present rebellion against the United States, that they must expect no further lenity, but look to be rigorously dealt with according to their deserts; and declaring that the military forces now in Utah, and hereafter to be sent there, will not be withdrawn until the inhabitants of that Territory shall manifest a proper sense of the duty which they owe to this government.

JAMES BUCHANAN

115 John Brown's Constitution (1858)

In 1857, the Supreme Court decided *Dred Scott v. Sandford,* crushing hopes of moderate abolitionists for the gradual emancipation of slaves through national legislation. The radical wing of the abolitionists had been proven right. A native of Torrington, Connecticut, John Brown attended many antislavery meetings, read William Lloyd Garrison's *Liberator* and other abolitionist literature, and knew several of the antislavery leaders of his day. To him, the failure of peaceful means to liberate slaves was evident. "Brown had learned that slavery was an institution based upon force and terror . . ." wrote historian Louis Ruchames, "[a]nd that against men who never hesitated to use force and violence to keep their slaves . . . the only recourse left to anyone with a sense of justice and compassion for the slave was forceful liberation."

John Brown fought as a guerrilla leader seeking to retain Kansas as a free state. But preparing for a rev-

olution that was designed, ultimately, to overcome slavery in the South, Brown also pressed his adherents to adopt a Provisional Constitution to govern the territories liberated by his forces. The forty-eight-article constitution was adopted at a convention held in Chatham, Canada, on May 8-10, 1858, with participation by forty-six Brown followers of both races. Contrary to the prevailing law of the land, Brown's constitution branded slavery as "perpetual imprisonment" and condemned it to "absolute extermination." As in other movements, these organized resisters to lawful authority presented a document that both enshrined their objective and provided a point of cohesion for the group.

☆ 115 Provisional Constitution and Ordinances for the People of the United States

Reprinted in L. Ruchames, *John Brown: The Making of a Revolutionary* (New York: Grosset & Dunlap, 1969), 119-21.

PREAMBLE

Whereas slavery, throughout its entire existence in the United States, is none other than a most barbarous, unprovoked, and unjustifiable war of one portion of its citizens upon another portion — the only conditions of which are perpetual imprisonment and hopeless servitude or absolute extermination — in utter disregard and violation of those eternal and self-evident truths set forth in our Declaration of Independence:

Therefore we, citizens of the United States, and the oppressed people who, by a recent decision of the Supreme Court, are declared to have no rights which the white man is bound to respect, together with all other people degraded by the laws thereof, do, for the time being, ordain and establish for ourselves the following Provisional Constitution and Ordinances, the better to protect our persons, property, lives, and liberties, and to govern our actions:

ARTICLE I

Qualifications for membership. All persons of mature age . . . who shall agree to sustain and enforce the Provisional Constitution and Ordinances of this organization, together with all minor children of such persons, shall be held to be fully entitled to protection under the same.

*   *   *

ARTICLE III

Legislative. The legislative branch shall be a Congress or House of Representatives, composed of not less than five nor more than ten members, who shall be elected by all citizens of mature age and of sound mind connected with this organization, and who shall remain in office for three years, unless sooner removed for misconduct, inability, or by death. . . .

ARTICLE IV

Executive. The executive branch of this organization shall consist of a President and Vice-President, who shall be chosen by the citizens or members of this organization, and each of whom shall hold his office for three years, unless sooner removed by death or for inability or misconduct.

ARTICLE V

Judicial. The judicial branch of this organization shall consist of one Chief Justice of the Supreme Court and of four associate judges of said court, each constituting a circuit court. They shall each be chosen in the same manner as the President, and shall continue in office until their places have been filled in the same manner by election of the citizens. Said court shall have jurisdiction in all civil or criminal causes arising under this constitution, except breaches of the rules of war.

*   *   *

ARTICLE VII

Commander-in-chief. A Commander-in-chief of the army shall be chosen by the President, Vice-President, a majority of the Provisional Congress, and of the Supreme Court . . . and he shall hold his office for three years, unless removed by death or on proof of incapacity or misbehavior. He shall, unless under arrest, (and until his place is actually filled as provided for by this constitution,) direct all movements of the army and advise with any allies. He shall, however, be tried, removed, or punished, on complaint of the President, by at least three general officers, or a majority of the House of Representatives, or of the Supreme Court; which House of Representatives, (the President presiding,) the Vice-President, and the members of the Supreme Court, shall constitute a court-martial for his trial; with power to remove or punish, as the case may require, and to fill his place, as above provided.

*   *   *

116 "guilty of a great wrong against God and humanity" (1859)

On Sunday night, October 16, 1859, John Brown and twenty-one others set out to attack the United States arsenal at Harper's Ferry, Virginia. Their goal was to seize the armory and to arm the multitudes of slaves expected to flock to his standard. The raid was a military success, but the slave uprising failed to materialize. Brown and his men found themselves surrounded by the Virginia militia. On Tuesday, October 18, the United States Marines, under the command of Colonel Robert E. Lee, stormed the engine house in which the surviving members of Brown's "Army of Liberation" had taken refuge. Ten of Brown's army were killed in the Harper's Ferry raid, five escaped, and seven, including Brown, were captured and later convicted of three crimes: conspiring with slaves to rebel, murder, and treason.

Several Southern leaders interviewed Brown, who was slightly wounded in the battle, the day after his capture.

☆ 116 John Brown's Interview with Southern Leaders (October 19, 1859)

Reprinted in L. Ruchames, *John Brown: The Making of a Revolutionary* (New York: Grosset & Dunlap, 1969), 133-34.

"Old Brown," or "Ossawattomie Brown," as he is often called, the hero of a dozen fights or so with the "border ruffians" of Missouri, in the days of "bleeding Kansas," is the head and front of this offending—the commander of the abolition filibuster army. . . .

Brown is fifty-five years of age, rather small sized, with keen and restless gray eyes, and a grizzly beard and hair. He is a wiry, active man, and should the slightest chance for an escape be afforded, there is no doubt that he will yet give his captors much trouble. His hair is matted and tangled, and his face, hands and clothes all smouched and smeared with blood. Colonel [Robert E.] Lee stated that he would exclude all visiters from the room if the wounded men were annoyed or pained by them, but Brown said he was by no means annoyed; on the contrary he was glad to be able to make himself and his motives clearly understood. He converses freely, fluently and cheerfully, without the slightest manifestation of fear or uneasiness, evidently weighing well his words, and possessing a good command of language. His manner is courteous and affable, and he appears to make a favorable impression upon his auditory, which, during most of the day yesterday, averaged about ten or a dozen men.

When I arrived in the armory . . . Brown was answering questions put to him by Senator [J. M.] Mason [of Virginia], who had just arrived from his residence at Winchester, thirty miles distant; Colonel [Charles James] Faulkner, member of Congress, who lives but a few miles off; Mr. [Clement L.] Vallandigham, member of Congress from Ohio; and several other distinguished gentlemen. The following is a verbatim report of the conversation:—

BROWN'S INTERVIEW WITH MASON,
VALLANDIGHAM, AND OTHERS

SENATOR MASON. Can you tell us who furnished money for your expedition?

JOHN BROWN. I furnished most of it myself; I cannot implicate others. It is by my own folly that I have been taken. I could easily have saved myself from it, had I exercised my own better judgment rather than yielded to my feelings.

MASON. You mean if you had escaped immediately?

BROWN. No. I had the means to make myself secure without any escape; but I allowed myself to be surrounded by a force by being too tardy. I should have gone away; but I had thirty-odd prisoners, whose wives and daughters were in tears for their safety, and I felt for them. Besides, I wanted to allay the fears of those who believed we came here to burn and kill. For this reason I allowed the train to cross the bridge, and gave them full liberty to pass on. I did it only to spare the feelings of those passengers and their families, and to allay the apprehensions that you had got here in your vicinity a band of men who had no regard for life and property, nor any feelings of humanity.

MASON. But you killed some people passing along the streets quietly.

BROWN. Well, sir, if there was anything of that kind done, it was without my knowledge. Your own citizens who were my prisoners will tell you that every possible means was taken to prevent it. I did not allow my men to fire when there was danger of killing those we regarded as innocent persons, if I could help it. They will tell you that we allowed ourselves to be fired at repeatedly, and did not return it.

*   *   *

MASON. If you would tell us who sent you here,—who provided the means,—that would be information of some value.

BROWN. I will answer freely and faithfully about what concerns myself,—I will answer anything I can with honor,—but not about others.

*   *   *

VALLANDIGHAM. How long have you been engaged in this business?

BROWN. From the breaking out of the difficulties in Kansas. Four of my sons had gone there to settle, and they induced me to go. I did not go there to settle, but because of the difficulties.

MASON. How many are there engaged with you in this movement?

BROWN. Any questions that I can honorably answer I will,—not otherwise. So far as I am myself concerned, I have told everything truthfully. I value my word, sir.

MASON. What was your object in coming?

BROWN. We came to free the slaves, and only that.

A VOLUNTEER. How many men, in all, had you?

BROWN. I came to Virginia with eighteen men only, besides myself.

VOLUNTEER. What in the world did you suppose you could do here in Virginia with that amount of men?

*   *   *

MASON. How do you justify your acts?

BROWN. I think, my friend, you are guilty of a great wrong against God and humanity,—I say it without wishing to be offensive,—and it would be perfectly right for any one to interfere with you so far as to free those you wilfully and wickedly hold in bondage. I do not say this insultingly.

MASON. I understand that.

BROWN. I think I did right, and that others will do right who interfere with you at any time and at all times. I hold that the Golden Rule, "Do unto others as ye would that others should do unto you," applies to all who would help others to gain their liberty.

LIEUTENANT [J. E. B.] STUART. But don't you believe in the Bible?

BROWN. Certainly I do.

*   *   *

MASON. Did you consider this a military organization in this Constitution? I have not yet read it.

BROWN. I did, in some sense. I wish you would give that paper close attention.

MASON. You consider yourself the commander-in-chief of these "provisional" military forces?

BROWN. I was chosen, agreeably to the ordinance of a certain document, commander-in-chief of that force.

MASON. What wages did you offer?

BROWN. None.

STUART. "The wages of sin is death."

BROWN. I would not have made such a remark to you if you had been a prisoner, and wounded, in my hands.

*   *   *

VALLANDIGHAM. Have you had correspondence with parties at the North on the subject of this movement?

BROWN. I have had correspondence.

A BYSTANDER. Do you consider this a religious movement?

BROWN. It is, in my opinion, the greatest service man can render to God.

BYSTANDER. Do you consider yourself an instrument in the hands of Providence?

BROWN. I do.

BYSTANDER. Upon what principle do you justify your acts?

BROWN. Upon the Golden Rule. I pity the poor in bondage that have none to help them: that is why I am here; not to gratify any personal animosity, revenge, or vindictive spirit. It is my sympathy with the oppressed and the wronged, that are as good as you and as precious in the sight of God. . . . I want you to understand that I respect the rights of the poorest and weakest of colored people, oppressed by the slave system, just as much as I do those of the most wealthy and powerful. This is the idea that has moved me, and that alone. We expected no reward except the satisfaction of endeavoring to do for those in distress and greatly oppressed as we would be done by. The cry of distress of the oppressed is my reason, and the only thing that prompted me to come here.

BYSTANDER. Why did you do it secretly?

BROWN. Because I thought that necessary to success; no other reason.

* * *

BYSTANDER. The "New York Herald" of yesterday, in speaking of this affair, mentions a letter in this way:—

. . . "[O]ne of Gerrit Smith's letters . . . speaks of the folly of attempting to strike the shackles off the slaves by the force of moral suasion or legal agitation, and predicts that the next movement made in the direction of negro emancipation would be an insurrection in the South."

BROWN. . . . I agree with Mr. Smith that moral suasion is hopeless. I don't think the people of the slave States will ever consider the subject of slavery in its true light till some other argument is resorted to than moral suasion.

VALLANDIGHAM. Did you expect a general rising of the slaves in case of your success?

BROWN. No, sir; nor did I wish it. I expected to gather them up from time to time and set them free.

VALLANDIGHAM. Did you expect to hold possession here till then?

BROWN. Well, probably I had quite a different idea. I do not know that I ought to reveal my plans. I am here a prisoner and wounded, because I foolishly allowed myself to be so. You overrate your strength in supposing I could have been taken if I had not allowed it. I was too tardy after commencing the open attack—in delaying my movements through Monday night, and up to the time I was attacked by the Government troops. It was all occasioned by my desire to spare the feelings of my prisoners and their families and the community at large. . . .

* * *

REPORTER. I do not wish to annoy you; but if you have anything further you would like to say, I will report it.

BROWN. I have nothing to say, only that I claim to be here in carrying out out a measure I believe perfectly justifiable, and not to act the part of an incendiary or ruffian, but to aid those suffering great

wrong. I wish to say, furthermore, that you had better—all you people at the South—prepare yourselves for a settlement of this question, that must come up for settlement sooner than you are prepared for it. The sooner you are prepared the better. You may dispose of me very easily,—I am nearly disposed of now; but this question is still to be settled,—this negro question I mean; the end of that is not yet. These wounds were inflicted upon me—both sabre cuts on my head and bayonet stabs in differents parts of my body—some minutes after I had ceased fighting and had consented to surrender, for the benefit of others, not for my own. I believe the Major would not have been alive; I could have killed him just as easy as a mosquito when he came in, but I supposed he only came in to receive our surrender. There had been loud and long calls of "surrender" from us,—as loud as men could yell; but in the confusion and excitement I suppose we were not heard. I do not think the Major, or any one, meant to butcher us after we had surrendered.

AN OFFICER. Why did you not surrender before the attack?

BROWN. I did not think it was my duty or interest to do so. We assured the prisoners that we did not wish to harm them, and they should be set at liberty. I exercised my best judgment, not believing the people would wantonly sacrifice their own fellow-citizens, when we offered to let them go on condition of being allowed to change our position about a quarter of a mile. The prisoners agreed by a vote among themselves to pass across the bridge with us. We wanted them only as a sort of guarantee of our own safety,—that we should not be fired into. We took them, in the first place, as hostages and to keep them from doing any harm. We did kill some men in defending ourselves, but I saw no one fire except directly in self-defence. Our orders were strict not to harm any one not in arms against us.

Q. Brown, suppose you had every nigger in the United States, what would you do with them? A. Set them free.

Q. Your intention was to carry them off and free them? A. Not at all.

A BYSTANDER. To set them free would sacrifice the life of every man in this community.

BROWN. I do not think so.

BYSTANDER. I know it. I think you are fanatical.

BROWN. And I think you are fanatical. "Whom the gods would destroy they first make mad," and you are mad.

Q. Was it your only object to free the negroes? A. Absolutely our only object.

Q. But you demanded and took Colonel [Lewis] Washington's silver and watch? A. Yes; we intended freely to appropriate the property of slaveholders to carry out our object. It was for that, and only that, and with no design to enrich ourselves with any plunder whatever.

*   *   *

117 "remember them that are in bonds" (1859)

On November 2, 1859, after deliberating for three-quarters of an hour, the jury convicted John Brown of murder, treason, and conspiring with slaves to rebel. Responding to the question of whether he had anything to say or why the sentence of death should not be imposed on him, Brown made his last address.

On December 2, 1859, prior to his execution, John Brown handed a final written statement to the guards:

> Charlestown, Va., 2d December, 1859
>
> I John Brown am now quite *certain* that the crimes of *this guilty* land: will never be purged *away*; but with Blood. I had *as I now think: vainly* flattered myself that without *verry much* bloodshed; it might be done.

☆117 John Brown's Last Speech to the Court (November 2, 1859)

Reprinted in L. Ruchames, *John Brown: The Making of a Revolutionary* (New York: Grosset & Dunlap, 1969), 125-26.

I have, may it please the Court, a few words to say.

In the first place, I deny everything but what I have all along admitted,—the design on my part to free the slaves.... That was all I intended. I never did intend murder, or treason, or the destruction of property, or to excite or incite slaves to rebellion, or to make insurrection.

I have another objection; and that is, it is unjust that I should suffer such a penalty. Had I interfered in the manner which I admit, ... in behalf of the rich, the powerful, the intelligent, the so-called great, or in behalf of any of their friends,—either father, mother, brother, sister, wife, or children, or any of that class,—and suffered and sacrificed what I have in this interference, it would have been all right; and every man in this court would have deemed it an act worthy of reward rather than punishment.

This court acknowledges, as I suppose, the validity of the law of God. I see a book kissed here which I suppose to be the Bible, or at least the New Testament. That teaches me that all things whatsoever I would that men should do to me, I should do even so to them. It teaches me, further, to "remember them that are in bonds, as bound with them." I endeavored to act up to that instruction. I say, I am yet too young to understand that God is any respecter of persons. I believe that to have interfered as I have done—as I have always freely admitted I have done—in behalf of His despised poor, was not wrong, but right. Now, if it is deemed necessary that I should forfeit my life for the furtherance of the ends of justice, and mingle my blood further with the blood of my children and with the blood of millions in this slave country whose rights are disregarded by wicked, cruel, and unjust enactments,—I submit; so let it be done!

Let me say one word further.

I feel entirely satisfied with the treatment I have received on my trial. Considering all the circumstances, it has been more generous than I expected. But I feel no consciousness of guilt. I have stated from the first what was my intention, and what was not. I never have had any design against the life of any person, nor any disposition to commit treason, or excite slaves to rebel, or make any general insurrection. I never encouraged any man to do so, but always discouraged any idea of that kind.

Let me say, also, a word in regard to the statements made by some of those connected with me. I hear it has been stated by some of them that I have induced them to join me. But the contrary is true. I do not say this to injure them, but as regretting their weakness. There is not one of them but joined me of his own accord, and the greater part of them at their own expense. A number of them I never saw, and never had a word of conversation with, till the day they came to me; and that was for the purpose I have stated.

Now I have done.

118 On the Right of Secession (1860)

Abraham Lincoln's election as president in 1860 greatly aggravated the tensions between South and North. With less than 40 percent of the popular vote (compared with nearly 30 percent for Democrat Stephen A. Douglas and 18.2 percent for Southern Democrat John C. Breckenridge), Lincoln carried eighteen free states against Breckenridge's eleven slave states.

On December 3, 1860, President James Buchanan observed in his fourth State of the Union Message that "the different sections of the Union are now arrayed against each other, and the time has arrived, so much dreaded by the Father of his Country, when hostile geographical parties have been formed." Many local and county resolutions on secession preceded the state enactments. The resolution from Floyd County, Georgia, reflected not only the intensity of Southern regionalism but also the fear of a black takeover. Many of these expressions were more eloquently phrased in the state resolutions.

On December 20, 1860, a special state convention

held in Columbia, South Carolina, passed by a unanimous vote an ordinance dissolving the union between South Carolina and the other states of the United States. A few days later the state convention called on the federal government to restore Forts Moultrie and Sumter, the Charleston Arsenal, and Castle Pinckney to state authority. The convention next issued a "Declaration of Immediate Causes" for its decision to secede in legal and political terms. On December 27, 1860, South Carolina troops occupied Fort Moultrie and Castle Pinckney. The *William Aiken*, a federal revenue cutter, was also seized. South Carolina troops occupied the United States arsenal on December 30, thus completing the takeover of all federal facilities in the Charleston area except Fort Sumter. Before Lincoln's inauguration, six states had seceded from the Union: Mississippi, South Carolina, Florida, Alabama, Georgia, and Louisiana.

☆ 118 Resolutions on Secession

☆ 118a Floyd County, Georgia

Reprinted in A. Candler, ed., *The Confederate Records of the State of Georgia* (Atlanta: C. P. Byrd, 1909), 1:115.

Whereas, the abolition sentiment of the *Northern States* first openly manifested in 1820, has for the last forty years, steadily and rapidly increased in volume, and in the intensity of hostility to the form of society, existing in the *Southern States*, and to the rights of these States as equal, independent and sovereign members of the Union; has led to long continued and ever increasing abuse and hatred of the Southern people; to ceaseless war upon their plainest Constitutional rights; to an open and shameless nullification of that provision of the constitution intended to secure the rendition of fugitive slaves, and of the laws of Congress to give it effect; ... has prompted the armed invasion of Southern soil, by stealth ... for the diabolical purpose of inaugurating a ruthless war of the blacks against the whites throughout the Southern States; has prompted large masses of Northern people openly to sympathize with the treacherous and traitorous invaders of our country, and elevate the leader of a band of midnight assassins, and robbers ... to the rank of a hero and a martyr ...; has disrupted the churches, and destroyed all national parties, and has now finally organized a party confined to a *hostile section*, and composed even there of those only who have encouraged, sympathized with, instigated, or perpetuated their long series of insults, outrages and wrongs, for the avowed purpose of making a common government, armed by us with power only for our protection, an instrument, in the hands of enemies of our destruction.

Therefore we, a portion of the people of Floyd County ... do hereby declare:

1st. That Georgia is and of right ought to be a free, sovereign and independent State.

2d. That she came into the union with the other States, as a sovereignty, and by virtue of that sovereignty, has the right to secede whenever, in her sovereign capacity, she shall judge such a step necessary.

3d. That in our opinion, she ought not to submit to the inauguration of Abraham Lincoln and Hannibal Hamlin, as her President and Vice-President; but should leave them to rule over those by whom alone they were elected.

4th. That we request the Legislature to announce this opinion ... and to co-operate with the Governor in calling a Convention of the people to determine on the mode and measures of redress....

*   *   *

6th. That we respectfully suggest to the Legislature to take immediate steps to organize and arm the forces of the State....

☆ 118b South Carolina Declaration of Causes of Secession (December 24, 1860)

Reprinted in F. Moore, ed., *The Rebellion Record* (New York: Putnam, 1861-63), 1:3.

The people of the State of South Carolina in Convention assembled, on the 2d day of April, A.D. 1852, declared that the frequent violations of the Constitution of the United States by the Federal Government, and its encroachments upon the reserved rights of the States, fully justified this State in their withdrawal from the Federal Union; but in deference to the opinions and wishes of the other Slaveholding States, she forbore at that time to exercise this right. Since that time these encroachments have continued to increase, and further forbearance ceases to be a virtue.

And now the State of South Carolina having resumed her separate and equal place among nations, deems it due to herself, to the remaining United States of America, and to the nations of the world, that she should declare the immediate causes which have led to this act.

In 1787, Deputies were appointed by the States to revise the articles of Confederation; and on 17th September, 1787, these Deputies recommended, for the adoption of the States, the Articles of Union, known as the Constitution of the United States.... We hold that the [Federal] Government thus established is subject to the ... law of compact. We maintain that in every compact between two or more parties, the obligation is mutual; that the failure of one of the contracting parties to perform a material part of the agreement, entirely releases the obligation of the other; and that, where no arbiter is provided, each party is remitted to his own judgment to determine the fact of failure, with all its consequences.

In the present case, that fact is established with certainty....

The Constitution of the United States, in its fourth Article, provides as follows:

No person held to service or labor in one State under the laws thereof, escaping into another, shall, in consequence of any law or regulation therein, be discharged from such service or labor, but shall be delivered up, on claim of the party to whom such service or labor may be due.

This stipulation was so material to the compact that without it that compact would not have been made.... The States of Maine, New Hampshire, Vermont, Massachusetts, Connecticut, Rhode Island, New York, Pennsylvania, Illinois, Indiana, Michigan, Wisconsin and Iowa, have enacted laws which either nullify the acts of Congress, or render useless any attempt to execute them.... [I]n none of them has the State Government complied with the stipulation made in the Constitution.... Thus the constitutional compact has been deliberately broken and disregarded by the non-slaveholding States; and the consequence follows that South Carolina is released from her obligation....

We affirm that these ends for which this Government was instituted have been defeated....

... Observing the *forms* of the Constitution, a sectional party has found within that article establishing the Executive Department, the means of subverting the Constitution itself. A geographical line has been drawn across the Union, and all the States north of that line have united in the election of a man to the high office of President of the United States whose opinions and purposes are hostile to Slavery. He is to be intrusted with the administration of the common Government, because he has declared that "Government cannot endure permanently half slave, half free," and that the public mind must rest in the belief that Slavery is in the course of ultimate extinction.

This sectional combination for the subversion of the Constitution has been aided, in some of the States, by elevating to citizenship persons who, by the supreme law of the land, are incapable of becoming citizens; and their votes have been used to inaugurate a new policy, hostile to the South, and destructive of its peace and safety.

*   *   *

Sectional interest and animosity will deepen the irritation; and all hope of remedy is rendered vain, by the fact that the public opinion at the North has invested a great political error with the sanctions of a more erroneous religious belief.

We, therefore, the people of South Carolina, by

our delegates in Convention assembled, appealing to the Supreme Judge of the world for the rectitude of our intentions, have solemnly declared that the Union heretofore existing between this State and the other States of North America is dissolved, and that the State of South Carolina has resumed her position among the nations of the world, as a separate and independent state, with full power to levy war, conclude peace, contract alliances, establish commerce, and to do all other acts and things which independent States may of right do.

119 New York as a Free City (1861)

Opposition to secession was not unanimous in the North, and it was unclear whether the Union would respond with force. Protective of New York City's heavy investments in and trade with the Southern states, Mayor Fernando Wood's sentiments toward "the odious and oppressive connection" with the Union were due also in great part to the fact that his city alone contributed "in revenue two-thirds of the expenses of the United States." He considered the independence of New York City from the state and the Union as a potential benefit of disunion.

☆119 Mayor Wood's Recommendation for the Secession of New York City (January 6, 1861)

Reprinted in E. McPherson, ed., *The Political History of the United States during the Great Rebellion* (Washington, D.C.: Philip and Solomons, 1865), 42.

To the Honorable the Common Council:

Gentlemen: We are entering upon the public duties of the year under circumstances as unprecedented as they are gloomy and painful to contemplate....

It would seem that a dissolution of the Federal Union is inevitable....

*   *   *

... [W]e must rely upon our own resources and assume a position predicated upon the new phase which public affairs will present, and upon the inherent strength which our geographical, commercial, political, and financial preëminence imparts to us.

With our aggrieved brethren of the Slave States, we have friendly relations and a common sympathy. We have not participated in the warfare upon their constitutional rights or their domestic institutions. ... Our ships have penetrated to every clime, and so have New York capital, energy, and enterprise found their way to every State, and, indeed, to almost every county and town of the American Union.... Therefore, New York has a right to expect, and should endeavor to preserve a continuance of uninterrupted intercourse with every section.

It is, however, folly to disguise the fact that, judging from the past, New York may have more cause of apprehension from the aggressive legislation of our own State than from external dangers. We have already suffered largely from this cause. For the past five years, our interests and corporate [municipal] rights have been repeatedly trampled upon....

...[T]he political connection between the people of the city and the State has been used by the latter to our injury. The Legislature, in which the present partizan majority has the power, has become an instrument by which we are plundered to enrich their speculators, lobby agents, and Abolition politicians....

How we shall rid ourselves of this odious and oppressive connection, it is not for me to determine. It is certain that a dissolution cannot be peaceably accomplished, except by the consent of the Legislature itself. Whether this can be obtained or not, is, in my judgement, doubtful....

Much, no doubt, can be said in favor of the justice and policy of a separation.... Why should not New York city, instead of supporting by her contributions in revenue two-thirds of the expenses of the United States, become also equally independent? As a free city, with but nominal duty on imports, her local Government could be supported without taxa-

tion upon her people. Thus we could live free from taxes, and have cheap goods nearly duty free....

*   *   *

When Disunion has become a fixed and certain fact, why may not New York disrupt the bands which bind her to a venal and corrupt master—to a people and a party that have plundered her revenues, attempted to ruin her commerce, taken away the power of self-government, and destroyed the Confederacy of which she was the proud Empire City?...

But I am not prepared to recommend the violence implied in these views. In stating this argument in favor of freedom "peaceably if we can, forcibly if we must," let me not be misunderstood. The redress can be found only in appeals to the magnanimity of the people of the whole State. The events of the past two months have no doubt effected a change in the popular sentiment of the State and National politics. This change may bring us the desired relief, and we may be able to obtain a repeal of the law to which I have referred, and a consequent restoration of our corporate rights.

FERNANDO WOOD, Mayor

CHAPTER 5

The Civil War

—————

1861-1870

The conflagration known as the Civil War or the War between the States provides a unique, concentrated historical laboratory for observing the phenomenon of political criminality in the United States. The very choice of nomenclature reflects the contrasting perspectives on the war: was it to be viewed as a domestic event in which the offenders were engaging in treason and were subject therefore to punishment as criminals, or was it in fact a conflict between sovereign equals with the combatants therefore entitled to be treated as prisoners of war? Beyond the strains of open warfare between contending armies, each swearing allegiance to different sovereigns, the North also had to confront the problem of controlling a population that was not always sympathetic to the goals of the Washington government. In the so-called border states that had not seceded, sentiment ran high in favor of allowing the Southern states to go their own way, if not actually accompanying them in the secession from the Union. Finally, the law had to address not only the combatants during the war but also prisoners, Confederacy officials, and the population of the Southern states—both black and white—after the conflict concluded. The documents in this chapter detail the processes used to deal with these difficult problems.

The core issues of the chapter relate to the legally ambiguous status of the rebel states and their populations. The legislatures of the Confederate states stood in open defiance of the laws and the Constitution of the United States. From the Northern perspective, the act of secession was unlawful and treasonous. By raising armies and seizing United States garrisons, post offices, and arsenals, the leaders of the Southern states and their followers were traitors. But this was not a relatively harmless treasonous insurrection of the type encountered in the early days of the Republic. These actions were undertaken, as in the American Revolution, by the leading political figures of the region. The decisions of secession were enacted into law by fitting forms of legislation, and the new political entity of the Confederate States of America was forged through voluntary adherence.

A government new in form and substance replaced that of the United States throughout the South, but the preexisting governments of the various seceding states went unchanged. Furthermore, the seceding states were not attempting a coup, but rather a partition of the United States of America. Their hostile actions were initially limited to the territory of their newly founded nation, as they sought to divest the federal authority of the United States and to transfer control to the Confederacy. Were the Southern populations who obeyed the laws of their legally constituted state governments implicated as traitors when their legislatures altered their allegiance from the United States to the Confederate States of America? Or should they, instead, have been accorded the status of enemy aliens who under international law remained innocent parties entitled to humane consideration? Should the leaders of the Confederacy then be deemed traitors, or should the high and noble purposes from which they claimed to act—the right of self-government and opposition to the breach of the original compact of the Constitution—immunize them from the ignominy of treason? How should captured rebel combatants be treated—as criminals or as prisoners of war?

At the outbreak of hostilities, President Lincoln engaged in several extraordinary activities intended to secure the lines of defense against the actions of those sympathetic to the Southern cause. The slow and procedurally difficult process of accusing, trying, and convicting people of treason for aiding the South was replaced by military arrest, trial, and execution, facilitated by the suspension of the writ of habeas corpus. These actions were originally accomplished without the approval of Congress, but that body later assented to all of the president's measures undertaken in the face of the perceived threat to the nation's security. The courts, however, were more critical of the unilateral executive supplanting of civilian authority with martial law.

Congress likewise was dissatisfied with the existing law of treason and defined new "treasonous" offenses, which relieved the prosecution of its heavy burden in proving the crime. Congressional authorization of the confiscation of Southern property and Southern sympathizers' property by the military demonstrated confusion over whether these actions constituted criminal penalties for treason or the seizure of the property of innocent enemy aliens under the normal usages of the law of war. Whichever the case, the protections accorded to the suspect individual were far less than either body of law would have provided.

Resort to the law of treason and confiscation also was important in the deliverance of slaves from bondage. This chapter demonstrates that the emancipation of slaves was in response to the political transgressions of their masters in engaging in treasonous activities. Slavery as an institution was not affected in the slave states that remained in the Union. Not until the ratification of the Thirteenth Amendment was slavery abolished throughout the United States.

That abolition, nevertheless, did not put an end to attempts by the remnants of the old Southern political order to assert control over the recently emancipated and therefore increasingly suspect black populations. Special regulation of black activities continued until the imposition of Reconstruction — which was more a program of political and social purging than of economic rebuilding. The quest for political control by the new Reconstruction elites was manifested through the classic techniques: resort to

military rule, the requirement of loyalty oaths, the restriction of the franchise, and the imposition of strict qualifications for officeholding. The response to these controls was similarly classic: the emergence of a resistance underground that attempted to maintain, through illegal activity and terror, the status quo ante.

The ultimate grant of amnesty to those connected with the Confederacy, a common accompaniment to political criminality throughout American history, began the official reassertion of the white power structure in the South. This also was the beginning of the growing tensions emanating from the unfulfilled promises of the Fourteenth Amendment and the Civil Rights Acts. The struggle for the realization of these promises gave rise to new political criminality for the attainment, and at times the containment, of racial justice. Against these major institutional conflicts and transitions flash also the sparks of assassination and anticonscription riots — mere flare-ups of political and sometimes pseudo-political criminality.

---

120 "the inviolability of the sovereign power" (1861)

During late 1860 and early 1861, eleven slaveholding states seceded from the Union. Southern congressmen, politicians, and military officers left the North to stand with their own states. The Southern states seized federal facilities, including forts, arsenals, barracks, ports, custom houses, and mint offices. On April 20, Colonel Robert E. Lee, who had captured John Brown on charges of treason less than two years earlier, resigned his United States commission as the first step toward assuming command of the seceding Virginia troops.

On February 18, 1861, three weeks before Abraham Lincoln's inauguration as the sixteenth president of the United States, Jefferson Davis assumed the provisional presidency of the Confederate States of America. On April 12, the Civil War opened with the attack by four thousand Confederate troops on Fort Sumter, which was defended by a Union force of eighty-five officers and men and forty-three workmen. President Lincoln declared a state of insurrection on April 15, 1861. The onset of the Civil War brought before the courts the question of whether secession was in fact treasonous. This discourse on the law of treason was presented to a grand jury summoned to consider evidence

against persons accused of treason. Despite the consistency of the judicial holding that secession was treasonous, few Confederates were tried and convicted of the charge.

☆ 120 Charge to the Grand Jury — Treason [Massachusetts]

30 F. Cas. 1039 (D.C.D. Ma. 1861) (No. 18,273).

SPRAGUE, District Judge. It is the duty of the court to give you some instructions upon the criminal jurisprudence of the United States.

*   *   *

The highest crime known to our law is treason.

"Treason against the United States shall consist only in levying war against them, or in adhering to their enemies, giving them aid and comfort."

These terms, "levying war," "adhering to enemies," "giving them aid and comfort," were not new. . . .

The question what amounts to levying war, arose soon after the adoption of our constitution. . . .

It is settled that if a body of men be actually assembled for the purpose of effecting a treasonable purpose by force, that is levying war. But it must be an assemblage in force, a military assemblage in a condition to make war. A mere conspiracy to overthrow the government, however atrocious such conspiracy may be, does not of itself amount to the crime of treason. Thus, if a convention, legislature, junto, or other assemblage, entertain the purpose of subverting the government, and to that end pass acts, resolves, ordinances or decrees, even with the view of raising a military force to carry their purpose into effect, this alone does not constitute a levying of war.

What is a treasonable purpose? If the object be to prevent by force the execution of any public law of the United States, generally and in all cases, that is a treasonable purpose, for it is entirely to overthrow the government as to one of its laws. And if there be such an assemblage as I have already described, for the purpose of carrying such an intention into effect by force, it will constitute levying war.

But the sudden outbreak of a mob, or the assembling of men in order, by force, to defeat the execution of the law, in a particular instance, and then to disperse, without the intention to continue together, or to re-assemble for the purpose of defeating the law generally, in all cases, is not levying war.

If the purpose be entirely to overthrow the government at any one place, by force, that is a treasonable purpose.

*   *   *

The constitution has not only defined the crime of treason, but prescribed a rule of evidence: "No person shall be convicted of treason, unless on the testimony of two witnesses to the same overt act, or on confession in open court."

The reason of these extraordinary safeguards is to be found in the nature of the offence, and in the pages of history. An attempt to overthrow the government excites the deepest indignation in great numbers, especially in those who are imbued with a warm and devoted patriotism, the cherished sentiment of a life-time, strengthened by a matured conviction of the vastness of the interests which are wrapped up in the inviolability of the sovereign power, that power which is the guardian of their safety, the daily dispenser of blessings, and the object of their prayers. A traitorous assault arouses the strongest passions, and in the keenness of their resentment, and the eager pursuit of the guilty, they are apt to break down the barriers which are essential to the protection of innocence. Our fathers, therefore, endeavored to render some of these safeguards impregnable, by imbedding them in the fundamental law.

*   *   *

It has been, at a former period, and is now a momentous question, whether, under our complex system, there is any power extrinsic to that of the national government by which its laws can be rightfully resisted, or their obligation impaired. There is no such power.

As I have already said to you, the authority of the United States, within their sphere, is supreme.... And to render this effectual, they provided that the government which they created should be the final judge of the extent of its own powers and the meaning of its own laws. And to this end, they established a judicial department as a co-ordinate branch of the government, to expound and enforce the provisions of the constitution and the acts of congress....

This supremacy has not always been acquiesced in. The legislation of a great country can never meet with universal approbation. And it has sometimes happened that acts of congress have been adverse to the opinions or supposed interests of many persons, sometimes constituting a majority in particular states.

And in such cases, unwilling to submit, they have eagerly sought for some mode of resistance which should wear the semblance of legality, and to this end have invoked state interposition, and the cover of state authority.

Such was nullification. That doctrine did not deny the paramount obligation of laws constitutionally enacted, but it arrogated for a state the right to determine, in the last resort, whether a law was constitutional or not. It sought to overthrow the judicial power by denying its supremacy, and claimed for every state the right to judge of the extent of the powers of the general government, and of the validity of its laws, and to limit, restrain, or annul them, according to the views of each state.

This doctrine, once formidable, has now few adherents.

*   *   *

The disaffected, at different times, and in various sections of the Union, have earnestly sought for some legal mode of resisting legitimate authority. But it has been in vain. There is no such anomalous middle ground between submission and rebellion; and this last extreme has at length been reached. Secession is but another name for revolution; for it is vain to contend for a constitutional right to overthrow the constitution, and a legal right to destroy all law.

*   *   *

121 "affording aid and comfort to rebels" (1861-1864)

The writ of habeas corpus serves to protect individuals from unlawful imprisonment. One form of such imprisonment consists of detention before trial without a judicial officer's determination of the existence of "probable cause" that the individual held had committed a crime.

Article I, Section 9 of the United States Constitution provides that "The Privilege of the Writ of Habeas Corpus shall not be suspended, unless when in Cases of Rebellion or Invasion the public safety may require it." Even though this section is contained in the portion of the Constitution dealing with legislative powers and thus may be considered suspendable only by an act of Congress, President Lincoln unilaterally proclaimed several suspensions of habeas corpus. This action by the president, without congressional approval, was condemned judicially as unconstitutional. The president ignored that decision, but the issue subsequently became moot with congressional authorization and ratification of the suspensions.

President Lincoln's impatience with habeas corpus demonstrated the suspension's utility as a method of suppressing political crime. The initial suspension was limited to parts of Maryland, in order to protect the capital and its lines of communication against the threats of local resistance and Southern invasion. But the president also authorized the writ's selective suspension with regard to particular persons and for those suspected by military authorities of encouraging draft resistance or otherwise obstructing the war effort. In concert with proclamations authorizing military tribunals to try, convict, and sentence war resisters or Southern sympathizers, the suspension of the writ eliminated the difficulties associated with convicting individuals of specific crimes before regularly constituted courts and with attendant procedural protections. The military arrested over ten thousand suspects during the course of the war and denied them the benefit of a habeas corpus hearing. The technique of supplanting civilian authority with military rule is a common response to political criminality.

☆ 121 President Lincoln's Correspondence and Proclamations Suspending Habeas Corpus

Reprinted in J. Richardson, ed., *A Compilation of the Messages and Papers of the Presidents* (Washington, D.C.: U.S. Government Printing Office, 1897), 3:18, 19, 98-99, 170-74, 219-21.

☆ 121a April 27, 1861

THE COMMANDING GENERAL OF THE ARMY OF THE UNITED STATES:

You are engaged in suppressing an insurrection against the laws of the United States. If at any point on or in the vicinity of any military line which is now or which shall be used between the city of Philadelphia and the city of Washington you find resistance which renders it necessary to suspend the writ of *habeas corpus* for the public safety, you personally, or

through the officer in command at the point where resistance occurs, are authorized to suspend that writ.

Given under my hand and the seal of the United States, at the city of Washington, this 27th day of April, 1861, and of the Independence of the United States the eighty-fifth.

ABRAHAM LINCOLN

By the President of the United States:

WILLIAM H. SEWARD, Secretary of State

☆ 121b June 20, 1861

THE LIEUTENANT-GENERAL COMMANDING THE ARMIES OF THE UNITED STATES:

You or any officer you may designate will, in your discretion, suspend the writ of *habeas corpus* so far as may relate to Major Chase, lately of the Engineer Corps of the Army of the United States, now alleged to be guilty of treasonable practices against this Government.

ABRAHAM LINCOLN

By the President:

WILLIAM H. SEWARD

☆ 121c September 24, 1862

BY THE PRESIDENT OF THE UNITED STATES OF AMERICA

A Proclamation

Whereas it has become necessary to call into service not only volunteers, but also portions of the militia of the States by draft in order to suppress the insurrection existing in the United States, and disloyal persons are not adequately restrained by the ordinary processes of law from hindering this measure and from giving aid and comfort in various ways to the insurrection:

Now, therefore, be it ordered, first, that during the existing insurrection, and as a necessary measure for suppressing the same, all rebels and insurgents, their aiders and abettors, within the United States, and all persons discouraging volunteer enlistments, resisting militia drafts, or guilty of any disloyal practice affording aid and comfort to rebels against the authority of the United States, shall be subject to martial law and liable to trial and punishment by courts-martial or military commissions; second, that the writ of *habeas corpus* is suspended in respect to all persons arrested or who are now or hereafter during the rebellion shall be imprisoned in any fort, camp, arsenal, military prison, or other place of confinement by any military authority or by the sentence of any court-martial or military commission.

In witness whereof I have hereunto set my hand and caused the seal of the United States to be affixed.

Done at the city of Washington, this 24th day of September, A.D. 1862, and of the Independence of the United States the eighty-seventh.

ABRAHAM LINCOLN

By the President:

WILLIAM H. SEWARD, Secretary of State

☆ 121d September 15, 1863

BY THE PRESIDENT OF THE UNITED STATES OF AMERICA

A Proclamation

Whereas the Constitution of the United States has ordained that the privilege of the writ of *habeas corpus* shall not be suspended unless when, in cases of rebellion or invasion, the public safety may require it; and

Whereas a rebellion was existing on the 3d day of March, 1863, which rebellion is still existing; and

Whereas by a statute which was approved on that day it was enacted by the Senate and House of Representatives of the United States in Congress assembled that during the present insurrection the President of the United States, whenever in his judgment the public safety may require, is authorized to suspend the privilege of the writ of *habeas corpus* in any case throughout the United States or any part thereof; and

Whereas, in the judgment of the President, the public safety does require that the privilege of the said writ shall now be suspended throughout the United States in the cases where, by the authority of the President of the United States, military, naval, and civil officers of the United States, or any of them, hold persons under their command or in their custody, either as prisoners of war, spies, or aiders or abettors of the enemy, or officers, soldiers, or seamen enrolled or drafted or mustered or enlisted in or belonging to the land or naval forces of the United States, or as deserters therefrom, or otherwise amenable to military law or the rules and articles of war or the rules or regulations prescribed for the military or naval services by authority of the President of the United States, or for resisting a draft, or for any other offense against the military or naval service:

Now, therefore, I, Abraham Lincoln, President of the United States, do hereby proclaim and make known to all whom it may concern that the privilege of the writ of *habeas corpus* is suspended throughout the United States in the several cases before mentioned, and that this suspension will continue throughout the duration of the said rebellion or until this proclamation shall, by a subsequent one to be issued by the President of the United States, be modified or revoked. . . .

In testimony whereof I have hereunto set my hand and caused the seal of the United States to be affixed this 15th day of September, A.D 1863, and of the Independence of the United States of America the eighty-eighth.

ABRAHAM LINCOLN

By the President:

WILLIAM H. SEWARD, Secretary of State

☆ 121e July 5, 1864

BY THE PRESIDENT OF THE UNITED STATES OF AMERICA

A Proclamation

*   *   *

Whereas the said insurrection and rebellion still continue, endangering the existence of the Constitution and Government of the United States; and

Whereas the military forces of the United States are now actively engaged in suppressing the said insurrection and rebellion in various parts of the States where the said rebellion has been successful in obstructing the laws and public authorities, especially in the States of Virginia and Georgia; and

*   *   *

Whereas many citizens of the State of Kentucky have joined the forces of the insurgents, and such insurgents have on several occasions entered the said State of Kentucky in large force, and, not without aid and comfort furnished by disaffected and disloyal citizens of the United States residing therein, have not only greatly disturbed the public peace, but have overborne the civil authorities and made flagrant civil war, destroying property and life in various parts of that State; and

Whereas it has been made known to the President of the United States by the officers commanding the national armies that combinations have been formed in the said State of Kentucky with a purpose of inciting rebel forces to renew the said operations of civil war within the said State and thereby to embarrass the United States armies now operating in the said States of Virginia and Georgia and even to endanger their safety:

Now, therefore, I, Abraham Lincoln, President of the United States, by virtue of the authority vested in me by the Constitution and laws, do hereby declare that in my judgment the public safety especially requires that the suspension of the privilege of the writ of *habeas corpus*, so proclaimed in the said proclamation on the 15th September 1862 be made effectual and be duly enforced in and throughout the said State of Kentucky, and that martial law be for the present established therein. I do therefore hereby require of the military officers in the said State that the privileges of the writ of *habeas corpus* be effectually suspended within the said State, according to the aforesaid proclamation, and that martial law be established therein, to take effect from the date of this proclamation, the said suspension and establishment of martial law to continue until this proclamation shall be revoked or modified, but not beyond the period when the said rebellion shall have been suppressed or come to an end. . . .

The martial law herein proclaimed and the things in that respect herein ordered will not be deemed or taken to interfere with the holding of lawful elections, or with the proceedings of the constitutional legislature of Kentucky, or with the administration of justice in the courts of law existing therein between citizens of the United States in suits or proceedings which do not affect the military operations or the constituted authorities of the Government of the United States.

In testimony whereof I have hereunto set my hand and caused the seal of the United States to be affixed.

Done at the city of Washington, this 5th day of July, A.D. 1864, and of the Independence of the United States the eighty-ninth.

ABRAHAM LINCOLN

By the President:

WILLIAM H. SEWARD, Secretary of State

122 "regal and absolute power" (1861)

Military authorities arrested John Merryman in his home in Baltimore, Maryland, for his participation in antiwar riots and brought him to Fort McHenry. Military officials ignored his requests to have a hearing before a magistrate. They claimed that the president's proclamation suspending the writ of habeas corpus in all offenses against the United States government authorized his detention.

The United States Circuit Court decision in Merryman's case became known as the *Taney Decision* after Chief Justice Taney of the United States Supreme Court, who was sitting as justice for the Maryland circuit. Taney repudiated the authority of the executive to suspend the writ. Both Lincoln and the military, nevertheless, ignored his decision and Merryman remained in Fort McHenry. Congress did not authorize the president to suspend the writ (itself a dubious delegation of authority) until March 3, 1863.

☆122 *Ex Parte Merryman*

17 F. Cas. 144 (C.C.D. Md. 1861) (No. 9,487).

TANEY, Circuit Justice.

* * *

The case, then, is simply this: a military officer, residing in Pennsylvania, issues an order to arrest a citizen of Maryland, upon vague and indefinite charges, without any proof, so far as appears; under this order, his house is entered in the night, he is seized as a prisoner, and conveyed to Fort McHenry, and there kept in close confinement; and when a habeas corpus is served on the commanding officer, requiring him to produce the prisoner before a justice of the supreme court, in order that he may examine into the legality of the imprisonment, the answer of the officer, is that he is authorized by the president to suspend the writ of habeas corpus at his discretion, and in the exercise of that discretion, suspends it in this case, and on that ground refuses obedience to the writ.

As the case comes before me, therefore, I understand that the president not only claims the right to suspend the writ of habeas corpus himself, at his discretion, but to delegate that discretionary power to a military officer, and to leave it to him to determine whether he will or will not obey judicial process that may be served upon him. No official notice has been given to the courts of justice, or to the public, by proclamation or otherwise, that the president claimed this power, and had exercised it in the manner stated in the return. And I certainly listened to it with some surprise, for I had supposed it to be one of those points of constitutional law upon which there was no difference of opinion, and that it was admitted on all hands, that the privilege of the writ could not be suspended, except by act of congress.

* * *

The clause of the constitution, which authorizes the suspension of the privilege of the writ of habeas corpus, is in the 9th section of the first article. This article is devoted to the legislative department of the United States, and has not the slightest reference to the executive department. . . .

* * *

. . . The great importance which the framers of the constitution attached to the privilege of the writ of habeas corpus, to protect the liberty of the citizen, is proved by the fact, that its suspension, except in cases of invasion or rebellion, is first in the list of prohibited [legislative] powers; and even in these cases the power is denied, and its exercise prohibited, unless the public safety shall require it.

It is true, that in the cases mentioned, congress is, of necessity, the judge of whether the public safety does or does not require it; and their judgment is conclusive. But the introduction of these words is a standing admonition to the legislative body of the danger of suspending it, and of the extreme caution they should exercise, before they give the government of the United States such power over the liberty of a citizen.

It is the second article of the constitution that provides for the organization of the executive department, enumerates the powers conferred on it, and prescribes its duties. And if the high power over the liberty of the citizen now claimed, was intended to be conferred on the president, it would undoubtedly be found in plain words in this article; but there is not a word in it that can furnish the slightest ground to justify the exercise of the power.

*   *   *

So too [the President's] powers in relation to the civil duties and authority necessarily conferred on him are carefully restricted.... He is not empowered to arrest any one charged with an offence against the United States, and whom he may, from the evidence before him, believe to be guilty; nor can he authorize any officer, civil or military, to exercise this power, for the fifth article of the amendments to the constitution expressly provides that no person "shall be deprived of life, liberty or property, without due process of law" — that is, judicial process.

Even if the privilege of the writ of habeas corpus were suspended by act of congress, and a party not subject to the rules and articles of war were afterwards arrested and imprisoned by regular judicial process, he could not be detained in prison, or brought to trial before a military tribunal, for the [sixth] article in the amendments to the constitution [would thereby be violated].

*   *   *

The only power, therefore, which the president possesses, where the "life, liberty or property" of a private citizen is concerned, is the power and duty ... which requires "that he shall take care that the laws shall be faithfully executed." He is not authorized to execute them himself, ... but he is to take care that they be faithfully carried into execution, as they are expounded and adjudged by the co-ordinate branch of the government to which that duty is assigned by the constitution. It is thus made his duty to come in aid of the judicial authority, if it shall be resisted by a force too strong to be overcome without the assistance of the executive arm; but in exercising this power he acts in subordination to judicial authority, assisting it to execute its process and enforce its judgments.

... I can see no ground whatever for supposing that the president, in any emergency, or in any state of things, can authorize the suspension of the privileges of the writ of habeas corpus, or the arrest of a citizen, except in aid of the judicial power. He certainly does not faithfully execute the laws, if he takes upon himself legislative power, by suspending the writ of habeas corpus, and the judicial power also, by arresting and imprisoning a person without due process of law.

Nor can any argument be drawn from the nature of sovereignty, or the necessity of government, for self-defence in times of tumult and danger. The government of the United States is one of delegated and limited powers; it derives it existence and authority altogether from the constitution, and neither of its branches, executive, legislative or judicial can exercise any of the powers of government beyond those specified and granted.....

Indeed, the security against imprisonment by executive authority [is like the ancient common law of England]. Blackstone states it in the following words: "To make imprisonment lawful, it must be either by process of law from the courts of judicature, or by warrant from some legal officer having authority to commit to prison."

*   *   *

... [T]he value set upon this writ in England [for protecting rights] has been ... the object of the most jealous care. Accordingly, no power in England short of that of parliament can suspend or authorize the suspension of the writ of habeas corpus.... If the president of the United States may suspend the writ, then the constitution of the United States has conferred upon him more regal and absolute power over the liberty of the citizen, than the people of England have thought it safe to entrust to the crown; a power which the queen of England cannot exercise at this day, and which could not have been lawfully exercised by the sovereign even in the reign of Charles the First.

*   *   *

[T]he Commentaries on the Constitution of the United States of the late Mr. Justice Story, ... and also the clear and authoritative decision of [the supreme] court itself, given more than half a century since, and conclusively establishing the principles I have above stated.

*   *   *

But the documents before me show, that the military authority in this case has gone far beyond the mere suspension of the privilege of the writ of habeas corpus. It has, by force of arms, thrust aside the judicial authorities and officers to whom the constitution has confided the power and duty of interpreting and administering the laws, and substituted a military government in its place, to be administered and executed by military officers. For, at the time these proceedings were had against John Merryman, the district judge of Maryland, the commissioner appointed under the act of congress, the district attorney and the marshal, all resided in the city of Baltimore, a few miles only from the home of the prisoner. Up to that time, there had never been the slightest resistance or obstruction to the process of any court or judicial officer of the United States, in Maryland, except by the military authority.... There was no danger of any obstruction or resistance to the action of the civil authorities, and therefore no reason whatever for the interposition of the military.

Yet, under these circumstances, a military officer, stationed in Pennsylvania, without giving any information to the district attorney, and without any application to the judicial authorities, assumes to himself the judicial power in the district of Maryland; undertakes to decide what constitutes the crime of treason or rebellion; what evidence (if indeed he required any) is sufficient to support the accusation and justify the commitment; and commits the party, without a hearing, even before himself, to close custody, in a strongly garrisoned fort, to be there held, it would seem, during the pleasure of those who committed him.

*　　*　　*

[The Bill of Rights], which congress itself could not suspend, ha[s] been disregarded and suspended, like the writ of habeas corpus, by a military order, supported by force of arms. Such is the case now before me, and I can only say that if the authority which the constitution has confided to the judiciary department and judicial officers, may thus, upon any pretext or under any circumstances, be usurped by the military power, at its discretion, the people of the United States are no longer living under a government of laws, but every citizen holds life, liberty and property at the will and pleasure of the army officer in whose military district he may happen to be found.

In such a case, my duty was too plain to be mistaken. I have exercised all the power which the constitution and laws confer upon me, but that power has been resisted by a force too strong for me to overcome. It is possible that the officer who has incurred this grave responsibility may have misunderstood his instructions, and exceeded the authority intended to be given him; I shall, therefore, order all the proceedings in this case, with my opinion, to be filed and recorded . . . and direct the clerk to transmit a copy, under seal, to the president of the United States. It will then remain for that high officer, in fulfilment of his constitutional obligation to "take care that the laws be faithfully executed," to determine what measures he will take to cause the civil process of the United States to be respected and enforced.

123 "to resist force . . . by force" (1861)

President Lincoln delivered this address to Congress at a special session on July 4, 1861, three months after the attack on Fort Sumter. Lincoln's purpose was threefold: (1) to defend his suspension of habeas corpus, (2) to request money and troops for the preservation of the Union, and (3) to repudiate secession.

Lincoln justified his executive suspension of the writ of habeas corpus on the doctrines of exigency, national security, and lesser evil. "To state the question more directly, 'are all the laws but one to go unexecuted and the government itself go to pieces lest that one be violated?' " he asked. The themes herein had been sounded before and were to be replayed again. But this was the first time that they had been applied directly to the constitutional protection of the Great Writ.

☆ 123 Lincoln's Message to Congress in Special Session (July 4, 1861)

Reprinted in R. P. Basler, ed., *The Collected Works of Abraham Lincoln* (New Brunswick, N.J.: Rutgers University Press, 1959), 1860-61:421-41.

Fellow-citizens of the Senate and House of Representatives: Having been convened on an extraordinary occasion, as authorized by the Constitution, your attention is not called to any ordinary subject of legislation.

At the beginning of the present presidential term, four months ago, the functions of the Federal Government were found to be generally suspended within the several States of South Carolina, Georgia, Alabama, Mississippi, Louisiana, and Florida, excepting only those of the Post-office Department.

*　　*　　*

. . . By the affair at Fort Sumter . . . the assailants of the government began the conflict of arms, without a gun in sight or in expectancy to return their fire. . . . In this act, discarding all else, they have forced upon the country the distinct issue, "immediate dissolution or blood."

And this issue embraces more than the fate of these United States. It presents to the whole family of man the question whether a constitutional republic or democracy—a government of the people by the same people—can or cannot maintain its territorial integrity against its own domestic foes. It presents the question whether discontented individuals, too few in numbers to control administration according to organic law in any case, can always, upon the pretenses made in this case, or on any other pretenses, or arbitrarily without any pretense, break up their government, and thus practically put an end to free government upon the earth. It forces us to ask: "Is there, in all republics, this inherent and fatal weakness?" "Must a government, of necessity, be too strong for the liberties of its own people, or too weak to maintain its own existence?"

So viewing the issue, no choice was left but to call out the war power of the government; and so to resist force employed for its destruction, by force for its preservation.

*   *   *

. . . [C]alls were made for volunteers to serve for three years, unless sooner discharged, and also for large additions to the regular army and navy. These measures, whether strictly legal or not, were ventured upon, under what appeared to be a popular demand and a public necessity; trusting then, as now, that Congress would readily ratify them. It is believed that nothing has been done beyond the constitutional competency of Congress.

Soon after the first call for militia, it was considered a duty to authorize the commanding general in proper cases, according to his discretion, to suspend the privilege of the writ of *habeas corpus*, or, in other words, to arrest and detain, without resort to the ordinary processes and forms of law, such individuals as he might deem dangerous to the public safety. This authority has purposely been exercised but very sparingly. Nevertheless, the legality and propriety of what has been done under it are questioned, and the attention of the country has been called to the proposition that one who has sworn to "take care that the laws be faithfully executed" should not himself violate them. Of course some consideration was given to the questions of power and propriety before this matter was acted upon. The whole of the laws which were required to be faithfully executed were being resisted and failing of execution in nearly one third of the States. Must they be allowed to finally fail of execution, even had it been perfectly clear that by the use of the means necessary to their execution some single law, made in such extreme tenderness of the citizen's liberty that, practically, it relieves more of the guilty than of the innocent, should to a very limited extent be violated? To state the question more directly, are all the laws but one to go unexecuted, and the government itself go to pieces lest that one be violated? Even in such a case, would not the official oath be broken if the government should be overthrown, when it was believed that disregarding the single law would tend to preserve it? But it was not believed that this question was presented. It was not believed that any law was violated. The provision of the Constitution that "the privilege of the writ of *habeas corpus* shall not be suspended, unless when, in cases of rebellion or invasion, the public safety may require it," is equivalent to a provision—is a provision—that such privilege may be suspended when, in case of rebellion or invasion, the public safety does require it. It was decided that we have a case of rebellion, and that the public safety does require the qualified suspension of the privilege of the writ which was authorized to be made. Now it is insisted that Congress, and not the executive, is vested with

this power. But the Constitution itself is silent as to which or who is to exercise the power; and as the provision was plainly made for a dangerous emergency, it cannot be believed the framers of the instrument intended that in every case the danger should run its course until Congress could be called together, the very assembling of which might be prevented, as was intended in this case, by the rebellion.

*   *   *

It might seem, at first thought, to be of little difference whether the present movement at the South be called "secession" or "rebellion." The movers, however, well understand the difference. At the beginning they knew they could never raise their treason to any respectable magnitude by any name which implies violation of law. . . . Accordingly, they commenced by an insidious debauching of the public mind. They invented an ingenious sophism which, if conceded, was followed by perfectly logical steps, through all the incidents, to the complete destruction of the Union. The sophism itself is that any State of the Union may consistently with the National Constitution, and therefore lawfully and peacefully, withdraw from the Union without the consent of the Union or of any other State. The little disguise that the supposed right is to be exercised only for just cause, themselves to be the sole judges of its justice, is too thin to merit any notice.

With rebellion thus sugar-coated they have been drugging the public mind of their section for more than thirty years, and until at length they have brought many good men to a willingness to take up arms against the government the day after some assemblage of men have enacted the farcical pretense of taking their State out of the Union, who could have been brought to no such thing the day before.

This sophism derives much, perhaps the whole, of its currency from the assumption that there is some omnipotent and sacred supremacy pertaining to a State—to each State of our Federal Union. Our States have neither more nor less power than that reserved to them in the Union by the Constitution—no one of them ever having been a State out of the Union. The original ones passed into the Union even before they cast off their British colonial dependence; and the new ones each came into the Union directly from a condition of dependence, excepting Texas. And even Texas, in its temporary independence, was never designated a State. . . . Much is said about the "sovereignty" of the States; but the word even is not in the National Constitution, nor, as is believed, in any of the State constitutions. What is "sovereignty" in the political sense of the term? Would it be far wrong to define it "a political community without a political superior"? Tested by this, no one of our States except Texas ever was a sovereignty. And even Texas gave up the character on coming into the Union; by which act she acknowledged the Constitution of the United States, and the laws and treaties of the United States made in pursuance of the Constitution, to be for her the supreme law of the land. The States have their status in the Union, and they have no other legal status. If they break from this, they can only do so against law and by revolution. The Union, and not themselves separately, procured their independence and their liberty. By conquest or purchase the Union gave each of them whatever of independence or liberty it has. The Union is older than any of the States, and, in fact, it created them as States. . . .

Unquestionably the States have the powers and rights reserved to them in and by the National Constitution; but among these surely are not included all conceivable powers, however mischievous or destructive, but, at most, such only as were known in the world at the time as governmental powers; and certainly a power to destroy the government itself had never been known as a governmental . . . power. . . .

*   *   *

What is now combated is the position that secession is consistent with the Constitution—is lawful and peaceful. It is not contended that there is any express law for it; and nothing should ever be implied as law which leads to unjust or absurd consequences. The nation purchased with money the countries out of which several of these States were formed. Is it just that they shall go off without leave and without refunding? . . .

This is essentially a people's contest. . . .

I am most happy to believe that the plain people understand and appreciate this. It is worthy of note that while in this, the government's hour of trial, large numbers of those in the army and navy who have been favored with the offices have resigned and proved false to the hand which had pampered them, not one common soldier or common sailor is known to have deserted his flag.

Great honor is due to those officers who remained true, despite the example of their treacherous associates; but the greatest honor, and most important fact of all, is the unanimous firmness of the common soldiers and common sailors. To the last man, so far as known, they have successfully resisted the traitorous efforts of those whose commands, but an hour before, they obeyed as absolute law. This is the patriotic instinct of the plain people. They understand, without an argument, that the destroying of the government which was made by Washington means no good to them.

Our popular government has often been called an experiment. Two points in it our people have already settled—the successful establishing and the successful administering of it. One still remains—its successful maintenance against a formidable internal attempt to overthrow it. It is now for them to demonstrate to the world that those who can fairly carry an election can also suppress a rebellion; that ballots are the rightful and peaceful successors of bullets; and that when ballots have fairly and constitutionally decided, there can be no successful appeal back to bullets; that there can be no successful appeal, except to ballots themselves, at succeeding elections. Such will be a great lesson of peace: teaching men that what they cannot take by an election, neither can they take it by a war; teaching all the folly of being the beginners of a war.

*   *   *

And having thus chosen our course, without guile and with pure purpose, let us renew our trust in God, and go forward without fear and with manly hearts.

ABRAHAM LINCOLN
July 4, 1861

124 "a government that thus tramples on all the principles of constitutional liberty" (1861)

Jefferson Davis delivered this message to the Provisional Congress of the Confederate States of America, which met in its new capital of Richmond, Virginia, two weeks after Lincoln's Fourth of July message to Congress. Davis's focus on resolution of the status of prisoners was particularly timely. The Battle of Manassas was fought the day after his address, and the number of captured soldiers on both sides was greatly increased. Although on May 13, 1861, Great Britain had recognized both sides in the Civil War as belligerents, the captives on both sides were not accorded formal prisoner-of-war status until February 14, 1862. Despite this resolution, questions of the status of those enlisted in the Southern cause lingered throughout and after the war.

Ironically, while urging the actual existence of a state of war, which the Confederate Congress had declared on May 6, Davis denounced Lincoln for his imposition of martial law in the border states. The Confederacy, although it too had to confront pockets of population disenchanted with the prosecution of the war, never did suspend habeas corpus.

☆ 124 Jefferson Davis's Message to the Provisional Congress, Third Session (July 20, 1861)

Reprinted in J. Richardson, ed., *A Compilation of Messages and Papers of the Confederacy* (Nashville: United States Publishing Co., 1905), 1:117-22.

To the Congress of the Confederate States of America.

Gentlemen:

*   *   *

[T]he true policy and purposes of the Government of the United States had been previously concealed; their odious features now stand fully revealed; the message of their President and the action of their Congress during the present month confess the intention of subjugating these States by war.... [T]he President of the United States and his advisers succeeded in deceiving the people of those States into the belief that the purpose of this Government was not peace at home, but conquest abroad; not the defense of its own liberties, but the subversion of those of the people of the United States.

*   *   *

Mankind will shudder to hear the tales of outrages committed on defenseless females by soldiers of the United States now invading our homes; yet these outrages are prompted by inflamed passions and the madness of intoxication. But who shall depict the horror with which they will regard the cool and deliberate malignity which, under pretext of suppressing an insurrection, said by themselves to be upheld by a minority only of our people, makes special war on the sick, including the women and the children....

*   *   *

[But] they admit of no retaliation. The humanity of our people would shrink instinctively from the bare idea of waging a like war upon the sick, the women, and the children of the enemy.

But there are other savage practices which have been resorted to by the Government of the United States, which do admit of repression by retaliation. ... The prisoners of war taken by the enemy on board the armed schooner Savannah, sailing under our commission, were, as I was credibly advised, treated like common felons; put in irons; confined in a jail usually appropriated to criminals of the worst dye, and threatened with punishment as such.... I have informed President Lincoln of my resolute purpose to check all barbarities on prisoners of war, by such severity of retaliation on the prisoners held by us as should secure the abandonment of the practice.

... I have directed your attention ... to the peculiar relations which exist between this Government and the States usually termed the border slave States, which cannot properly be withheld from notice.

The hearts of our people are animated by sentiments toward the inhabitants of these States, which found expression in your enactment refusing to consider them as enemies, or to authorize hostilities against them. That a very large portion of the peo-

ple of those States regard us as brethren; that if unrestrained by the actual presence of large armies, the subversion of civil authority and the declaration of martial law, some of them at least would joyfully unite with us; that they are with almost entire unanimity opposed to the prosecution of the war waged against us, are facts of which daily recurring events fully warrant the assertion.

*   *   *

... [A]nother assertion of the message [to Congress is] that the Executive possesses the power of suspending the writ of *habeas corpus*, and of delegating that power to military commanders, at his discretion; and both these propositions claim a respect equal to that which is felt for the additional statement of opinion in the same paper, that it is proper, in order to execute the laws, that "some single law, made in such extreme tenderness of the citizen's liberty, that practically it relieved more of the guilty than the innocent, should, to a very limited extent, be violated."

We may well rejoice that we have forever severed our connection with a government that thus tramples on all the principles of constitutional liberty, and with a people in whose presence such avowals could be hazarded....

*   *   *

JEFFERSON DAVIS
Richmond, July 20, 1961

125 "to overthrow ... by force, the Government of the United States" (1861)

On July 31, 1861, Congress passed "An Act to Define and Punish Certain Conspiracies." Those representatives opposed to the act feared it would nullify the constitutional safeguards regarding treason prosecutions by creating new crimes "kindred to treason" which required lesser evidentiary proof. The act was passed ten days after the first Battle of Bull Run, when defeated Union troops were streaming into Washington—a reminder of the precariousness not only of the nation's capital but also of the Union.

☆ 125 Conspiracies Act

12 Stat. 284 (1861).

Be it enacted by the Senate and House of Representatives of the United States of America in Congress assembled, That if two or more persons within any State or Territory of the United States shall conspire together to overthrow, or to put down, or to destroy by force, the Government of the United States, or to levy war against the United States, or to oppose by force the authority of the Government of the United States; or by force to prevent, hinder, or delay the execution of any law of the United States; or by force to seize, take, or possess any property of the United States against the will or contrary to the authority of the United States; or by force, or intimidation, or threat to prevent any person from accepting or holding any office, or trust, or place of confidence, under the United States; each and every person so offending shall be guilty of a high crime, and upon conviction thereof . . . shall be punished by a fine not more than five thousand dollars; or by imprisonment, with or without hard labor, as the court shall determine, for a period not less than six months nor greater than six years, or by both such fine and imprisonment.

Approved, July 31, 1861.

126 "aiding . . . insurrection or resistance to the laws" (1861)

The first emancipation of slaves by the Union was not the result of abolitionist sentiment but a function of the criminal law. The earliest treason laws mandated forfeiture of property by traitors and rebels, but the treason statute of 1790 did not include forfeiture as a punishment. Relying on tradition, Congress reinstated limited forfeiture of rebels' property by expropriating any "property," including slaves employed in the insurrectionary effort. The institution of slavery itself, therefore, was unaffected in the so-called border states of Delaware, Maryland, Kentucky, and Missouri, and the Fugitive Slave Law continued in force.

☆ 126 An Act to Confiscate Property Used for Insurrectionary Purposes

12 Stat. 319 (1861).

Be it enacted by the Senate and House of Representatives of the United States of America in Congress assembled, That, if, during the present or any future insurrection against the Government of the United States, . . . any person or persons, his, her, or their agent, attorney or employee, shall purchase or acquire, sell or give, any property of whatsoever kind or description, with intent to use or employ the same . . . in aiding, abetting, or promoting such insurrection or resistance to the laws, or . . . shall knowingly use or employ, or consent to the use or employment of the same as aforesaid, all such property is hereby declared to be lawful subject of prize and capture wherever found; and it shall be the duty of the President of the United States to cause the same to be seized, confiscated, and condemned.

*   *   *

SEC. 3. And be it further enacted, That the Attorney-General, or any district attorney of the United States in which said property may at the time be, may institute the proceedings of condemnation, . . . or any person may file an information with such attorney, in which case the proceedings shall be for the use of such informer and the United States in equal parts.

SEC. 4. And be it further enacted, That whenever hereafter, during the present insurrection against the Government of the United States, any person claimed to be held to labor or service under the law of any State shall be required or permitted by the person to whom such labor or service is claimed to be due to take up arms against the United States, or . . . to work or to be employed against the Government and lawful authority of the United States, then and in every such case the person to whom such labor or service is claimed to be due shall forfeit his claim to such labor, any law of the State or of the United States to the contrary notwithstanding. . . .

Approved, August 6, 1861.

127 "furthering the work of disunion" (1862)

On February 14, 1862, President Lincoln granted amnesty to all persons then held by the United States as suspected insurgents. Seized by authority of the president in an unprecedented exercise of power, Lincoln referred to the detainees as "political prisoners."

This document offered an apology for the president's actions based upon the chaos of the early stages of the Civil War. He argued that the Civil War was an insurrection that required resort to "extraordinary powers which the Constitution confides . . . [in the president] in cases of insurrection." There is, however, no mention in the Constitution of the "extraordinary powers" to which Lincoln referred. The Article II powers of the president, although open-ended, make no reference to special events or to conditional authority to meet emergencies.

Lincoln's gesture of amnesty, suggesting the withholding of punishment if the rebels gave up secession, was in vain. The Civil War was to continue until 1865, becoming the bloodiest military conflict in United States history. Despite the general release and grant of amnesty, Lincoln's order did not repudiate the actions previously exercised or forswear their reoccurrence. Rather, it affirmed the claim of the existence of "extraordinary powers."

☆ 127 President Lincoln's Executive Order Number One relating to Political Prisoners (February 14, 1862)

Reprinted in J. Richardson, *A Compilation of the Messages and Papers of the Presidents* (Washington, D.C.: U.S. Government Printing Office, 1897), 6:102-4.

The breaking out of a formidable insurrection based on a conflict of political ideas, being an event without precedent in the United States, was necessarily attended by great confusion and perplexity of the public mind. Disloyalty before unsuspected suddenly became bold, and treason astonished the world by bringing at once into the field military forces superior in number to the standing Army of the United States.

Every department of the Government was paralyzed by treason. Defection appeared in the Senate, in the House of Representatives, in the Cabinet, in the Federal courts; ministers and consuls returned from foreign countries to enter the insurrectionary councils or land or naval forces; commanding and other officers of the Army and in the Navy betrayed our councils or deserted their posts for commands in the insurgent forces. Treason was flagrant in the revenue and in the post-office service, as well as in the Territorial governments and in the Indian reserves.

Not only governors, judges, legislators, and ministerial officers in the States, but even whole States rushed one after another with apparent unanimity into rebellion. The capital was besieged and its connection with all the States cut off.

Even in the portions of the country which were most loyal political combinations and secret societies were formed furthering the work of disunion, while, from motives of disloyalty or cupidity or from excited passions or perverted sympathies, individuals were found furnishing men, money, and materials of war and supplies to the insurgents' military and naval forces. Armies, ships, fortifications, navy-yards, arsenals, military posts, and garrisons one after another were betrayed or abandoned to the insurgents.

Congress had not anticipated, and so had not provided for, the emergency. The municipal authorities were powerless and inactive. The judicial machinery seemed as if it had been designed, not to sustain the Government, but to embarrass and betray it.

*   *   *

In this emergency the President felt it his duty to employ with energy the extraordinary powers which the Constitution confides to him in cases of insurrection. He called into the field such military and naval forces, unauthorized by the existing laws, as seemed necessary. He directed measures to prevent the use of the post-office for treasonable correspondence. He subjected passengers to and from foreign countries to new passport regulations, and he instituted a blockade, suspended the writ of *habeas corpus* in various places, and caused persons who were represented to him as being or about to engage in disloyal and treasonable practices to be arrested by special civil as well as military agencies and detained in military custody when necessary to prevent them and deter others from such practices. Examinations of such cases were instituted, and some of the persons so arrested have been discharged from time to time under circumstances or upon conditions compatible, as was thought, with the public safety.

Meantime a favorable change of public opinion has occurred. The line between loyalty and disloyalty is plainly defined. The whole structure of the Government is firm and stable. Apprehension of public danger and facilities for treasonable practices have diminished with the passions which prompted heedless persons to adopt them. The insurrection is believed to have culminated and to be declining.

The President, in view of these facts, and anxious to favor a return to the normal course of the Administration as far as regard for the public welfare will allow, directs that all political prisoners or state prisoners now held in military custody be released on their subscribing to a parole engaging them to render no aid or comfort to the enemies in hostility to the United States.

The Secretary of War will, however, in his discretion, except from the effect of this order any persons detained as spies in the service of the insurgents, or others whose release at the present moment may be deemed incompatible with the public safety.

To all persons who shall be so released and who shall keep their parole the President grants an amnesty for any past offenses of treason or disloyalty which they may have committed.

Extraordinary arrests will hereafter be made under the direction of the military authorities alone.

By order of the President:

EDWIN M. STANTON, Secretary of War

128 "denying our right to self-government" (1862)

On February 22, 1862, Jefferson Davis was sworn in as the first president under a Confederate Constitution authorizing one six-year presidential term. Detailing the abuses of power and disregard for constitutional rights by Lincoln and his troops and asserting the Confederacy's claim to the true heritage of the Revolution, Davis overlooked slavery's impairment of personal liberty and the Southern curbs on abolitionist sentiment.

☆ 128 Jefferson Davis's Inaugural Address
(February 22, 1862)

Reprinted in J. Richardson, ed., *A Compilation of Messages and Papers of the Confederacy* (Nashville: United States Publishing Co., 1905), 1:184-88.

FELLOW CITIZENS:

... [W]e have assembled to usher into existence the Permanent Government of the Confederate States. Through this instrumentality, under the favor of Divine Providence, we hope to perpetuate the principles of our revolutionary fathers. ...

*   *   *

When a long course of class legislation, directed not to the general welfare, but to the aggrandizement of the Northern section of the Union, culminated in a warfare on the domestic institutions of the Southern States, ... six of those States, withdrawing from the Union, confederated together to exercise the right and perform the duty of instituting a Government which would better secure the liberties for the preservation of which that Union was established.

Whatever of hope [there was of reunion] ... must have been dispelled by the malignity and barbarity of the Northern States in the prosecution of the existing war. The confidence of the most hopeful among us must have been destroyed by the disregard they have recently exhibited for all the time-honored bulwarks of civil and religious liberty. Bastiles filled with prisoners, arrested without civil process or indictment duly found; the writ of *habeas corpus* suspended by Executive mandate; a State Legislature controlled by the imprisonment of members whose avowed principles suggested to the Federal Executive that there might be another added to the list of seceded States; elections held under threats of a military power; civil officers, peaceful citizens, and gentlewomen incarcerated for opinion's sake—proclaimed the incapacity of our late associates to administer a Government as free, liberal, and humane as that established for our common use.

For proof of the sincerity of our purpose to maintain our ancient institutions, we may point to the Constitution of the Confederacy and the laws enacted under it, as well as to the fact that through all the necessities of an unequal struggle there has been no act on our part to impair personal liberty or the freedom of speech, of thought, or of the press. The courts have been open, the judicial functions fully executed, and every right of the peaceful citizen maintained as securely as if a war of invasion had not disturbed the land.

*   *   *

... To save ourselves from a revolution which, in its silent but rapid progress, was about to place us under the despotism of numbers, and to preserve in spirit, as well as in form, a system of government we believed to be peculiarly fitted to our condition, and full of promise for mankind, we determined to make a new association, composed of States homogeneous in interest, in policy, and in feeling.

True to our traditions of peace and our love of justice, we sent commissioners to the United States to propose a fair and amicable settlement of all questions of public debt or property which might be in dispute. But the Government at Washington, denying our right to self-government, refused even to listen to any proposals for a peaceful separation. Nothing was then left to do but to prepare for war.

*   *   *

The period is near at hand when our foes must sink under the immense load of debt which they have incurred, a debt which in their effort to subjugate us has already attained such fearful dimensions as will subject them to burdens which must continue to oppress them for generations to come.

*   *   *

... This great strife has awakened in the people the highest emotions and qualities of the human soul. It is cultivating feelings of patriotism, virtue, and courage. Instances of self-sacrifice and of generous devotion to the noble cause for which we are contending are rife throughout the land. Never has a people evinced a more determined spirit than that now animating men, women, and children in every part of our country. Upon the first call the men flew to arms, and wives and mothers send their husbands and sons to battle without a murmur of regret.

It was, perhaps, in the ordination of Providence that we were to be taught the value of our liberties by the price which we pay for them.

*   *   *

Fellow-citizens, after the struggle of ages had consecrated the right of the Englishman to constitutional representative government, our colonial ancestors were forced to vindicate that birthright by an appeal to arms. Success crowned their efforts, and they provided for their posterity a peaceful remedy against future aggression.

The tyranny of an unbridled majority, the most odious and least responsible form of despotism, has denied us both the right and the remedy. Therefore we are in arms to renew such sacrifices as our fathers made to the holy cause of constitutional liberty. ...

To show ourselves worthy of the inheritance bequeathed to us by the patriots of the Revolution, we must emulate that heroic devotion which made reverse to them but the crucible in which their patriotism was refined.

... With humble gratitude and adoration, acknowledging the Providence which has so visibly protected the Confederacy during its brief but eventful career, to thee, O God, I trustingly commit myself, and prayerfully invoke thy blessing on my country and its cause.

129 Freeing the Slaves of Those Committing Treason (1862)

Economic sanctions were a central feature of the Union strategy in the Civil War. On April 19, 1861, Lincoln proclaimed a blockade of the Confederate states. The first Confiscation Act of August 6, 1861, ordered the freeing of all slaves used by the Confederates either in labor or in arms. On August 16, 1861, Lincoln proclaimed an end to commercial relations with inhabitants of the areas in rebellion. On July 17, 1862, he signed the second Confiscation Act, which recognized the need for a different disposition of "confiscated" slaves than the customary transfer of ownership to the government provided in the law of forfeiture, and authorized the freeing of slaves in areas taken by Union arms.

Congress wanted to maintain the support of pro-slavery elements in the North and continued to be unwilling to address the problem of slavery in general. But two months later, on September 22, 1862, President Lincoln finally issued the Emancipation Proclamation. This proclamation, nevertheless, only declared the freedom of slaves within the rebel states, exempting parts thereof not deemed to be in rebellion. In the four slave states of Delaware, Kentucky, Maryland, and Missouri, the institution of slavery was unaffected. Not until the adoption of the Thirteenth Amendment was the issue resolved.

☆ 129 An Act to Suppress Insurrection, to Punish Treason and Rebellion and Confiscate the Property of Rebels ...

12 Stat. 589 (1862).

Be it enacted by the Senate and House of Representatives of the United States of America in Congress assembled, That every person who shall hereafter commit the crime of treason against the United States, and shall be adjudged guilty thereof, shall suffer death, and all his slaves, if any, shall be declared and made free; or, at the discretion of the court, he shall be imprisoned for not less than five years and fined not less than ten thousand dollars, and all his slaves, if any, shall be declared and made free; said fine shall be levied and collected on any or all of the property, real and personal, excluding slaves, of which the said person so convicted was the owner....

SEC. 2. *And be it further enacted*, That if any person shall hereafter incite, set on foot, assist, or engage in any rebellion or insurrection against the au-

thority of the United States, or the laws thereof, or shall give aid or comfort thereto, or shall engage in, or give aid and comfort to, any such existing rebellion or insurrection, and be convicted thereof, such person shall be punished by imprisonment for a period not exceeding ten years, or by a fine not exceeding ten thousand dollars, and by the liberation of all his slaves, if any he have; or by both of said punishments, at the discretion of the court.

SEC. 3. *And be it further enacted*, That every person guilty of either of the offences described in this act shall be forever incapable and disqualified to hold any office under the United States.

*   *   *

SEC. 5. *And be it further enacted*, That, to insure the speedy termination of the present rebellion, it shall be the duty of the President of the United States to cause the seizure of all the estate and property, money, stocks, credits, and effects of the persons hereinafter named in this section, and to apply and use the same and the proceeds thereof for the support of the army of the United States, that is to say: [army and navy officers, government officials and others giving aid and comfort to the "so called confederate states of America"].

*   *   *

SEC. 9. *And be it further enacted*, That all slaves of persons who shall hereafter be engaged in rebellion against the government of the United States, or who shall in any way give aid or comfort thereto, escaping from such persons and taking refuge within the lines of the army; and all slaves captured from such persons or deserted by them and coming under the control of the government of the United States; and all slaves of such persons found *on* [or] being within any place occupied by rebel forces and afterwards occupied by the forces of the United States, shall be deemed captives of war, and shall be forever free of their servitude, and not again held as slaves.

SEC. 10. *And be it further enacted*, That no slave escaping into any State, Territory, or the District of Columbia, from any other State, shall be delivered up, or in any way impeded or hindered of his liberty, except for crime, or some offence against the laws, unless the person claiming said fugitive shall first make oath that the person to whom the labor or service of such fugitive is alleged to be due is his lawful owner, and has not borne arms against the United States in the present rebellion, nor in any way given aid and comfort thereto; and no person engaged in the military or naval service of the United States shall, under any pretence whatever, assume to decide on the validity of the claim of any person to the service or labor of any other person, or surrender up any such person to the claimant, on pain of being dismissed from the service.

SEC. 11. *And be it further enacted*, That the

President of the United States is authorized to employ as many persons of African descent as he may deem necessary and proper for the suppression of this rebellion, and for this purpose he may organize and use them in such manner as he may judge best for the public welfare.

SEC. 12. *And be it further enacted*, That the President of the United States is hereby authorized to make provision for the transportation, colonization, and settlement, in some tropical country beyond the limits of the United States, of such persons of the African race, made free by the provisions of this act, as may be willing to emigrate, having first obtained the consent of the government of said country to their protection and settlement within the same, with all the rights and privileges of freemen.

* * *

Approved, July 17, 1862.

130 "no service can be more praiseworthy or honorable" (1863)

The combination of enlistments and the impression of the state militias into the Union forces was insufficient to meet the manpower needs of the federal army. On March 3, 1863, Congress passed an act authorizing conscription and punishing speech and conduct resistant to this measure. There was no provision exempting conscientious objectors, although there were exemptions for men who were the sole support of women and children. In addition, men could avoid the service by finding a substitute or paying the government a fee of three hundred dollars.

Opposition to unfair draft laws, combined with race tensions, labor unrest, religious and ethnic conflict, and class antagonism erupted into violence. While the violence was at first directed against the draft offices, the discontent vented itself upon the black population, which was viewed as the cause of the war. In a week of riots in July 1863, as many as one thousand to twelve hundred persons were killed or wounded in New York City alone. Eventually troops were detached from Gettysburg to restore order. Riots occurred also in many other Northern cities, including Newark, Jersey City, Troy, Boston, Toledo, and Evansville. The New York account is from an official army record.

☆130 Resistance to Military Conscription

☆130a An Act for Enrolling and Calling out the National Forces, and for Other Purposes

12 Stat. 731 (1863).

Whereas there now exist in the United States an insurrection and rebellion against the authority thereof, and it is, under the Constitution of the United States, the duty of the government to suppress insurrection and rebellion, to guarantee to each State a republican form of government, and to preserve the public tranquillity; and whereas, for these high purposes, a military force is indispensable, to raise and support which all persons ought willingly to contribute; and whereas no service can be more praiseworthy and honorable than that which is rendered for the maintenance of the Constitution and Union, and the consequent preservation of free government: Therefore —

Be it enacted by the Senate and House of Representatives of the United States of America in Congress assembled, That all able-bodied male citizens of the United States, and persons of foreign birth who shall have declared on oath their intention to become citizens under and in pursuance of the laws thereof, between the ages of twenty and forty-five years, except as hereinafter excepted, are hereby declared to constitute the national forces, and shall be liable to perform military duty in the service of the United States when called out by the President for that purpose.

* * *

SEC. 13. *And be it further enacted*, That any person drafted and notified to appear as aforesaid, may, on or before the day fixed for his appearance, furnish an acceptable substitute to take his place in the draft; or he may pay to such person as the Secretary of War may authorize to receive it, such sum, not exceeding three hundred dollars, as the Secretary may determine, for the procuration of such substitute; which sum shall be fixed at a uniform rate by a general order made at the time of ordering a draft for any state or territory; and thereupon such person so furnishing the substitute, or paying the money, shall be discharged from further liability under that draft. And any person failing to report after due service of notice, as herein prescribed, without furnishing a substitute, or paying the required sum therefor, shall be deemed a deserter, and shall be arrested by the provost-marshal and sent to the nearest military post for trial by court-martial, unless, upon proper showing that he is not liable to do military duty, the board of enrolment shall relieve him from the draft.

* * *

SEC. 24. *And be it further enacted*, That every person not subject to the rules and articles of war who shall procure or entice, or attempt to procure or entice, a soldier in the service of the United States to desert; or who shall harbor, conceal, or give employment to a deserter, or carry him away, or aid in carrying him away, knowing him to be such; or who shall purchase from any soldier his arms, equipments, ammunition, uniform, clothing, or any part thereof; and any captain or commanding officer of any ship or vessel, or any superintendent or conductor of any railroad, or any other public conveyance, carrying away any such soldier as one of his crew or otherwise, knowing him to have deserted, or shall refuse to deliver him up to the orders of his commanding officer, shall, upon legal conviction, be fined, at the discretion of any court having cognizance of the same, in any sum not exceeding five hundred dollars, and he shall be imprisoned not exceeding two years nor less than six months.

SEC. 25. *And be it further enacted*, That if any person shall resist any draft of men enrolled under this act into the service of the United States, or shall counsel or aid any person to resist any such draft; or shall assault or obstruct any officer in making such draft, or in the performance of any service in relation thereto; or shall counsel any person to assault or obstruct any such officer, or shall counsel any drafted men not to appear at the place of rendezvous, or wilfully dissuade them from the performance of military duty as required by law, such person shall be subject to summary arrest by the provost-marshal, and shall be forthwith delivered to the civil authorities, and, upon conviction thereof, be punished by a fine not exceeding five hundred dollars, or by imprisonment not exceeding two years, or by both of said punishments.

*   *   *

Approved, March 3, 1863.

☆ 130b Troops Attacked by Armed Mob

Reprinted in Richard Hofstadter and Michael Wallace, *American Violence: A Documentary History* (New York: Knopf, 1970), 213–14.

. . . About six o'clock P.M., General Dodge and Colonel Mott informed General Brown, that the troops at Grammercy Park had marched down Twenty-second Street, and been attacked by an armed mob; that they had been driven back, leaving their dead in the street. The general ordered me to take my company, and a portion of the Twentieth and Twenty-eighth New York volunteer batteries, about eighty men, armed as infantry, commanded by Lieutenant B. F. Ryer. Lieutenant Ryer had with him Lieutenant Robert F. Joyce and Lieutenant F. M. Chase, Twenty-eighth New York battery. My whole command amounted to one hundred and sixty men.

With this force I marched to the Grammercy Hotel. At a short distance from the hotel, I saw some of the rioters fire from a house on some of Colonel Mott's command. I immediately sent Lieutenant Joyce with a few men to search the house. The search was fruitless, the men having escaped to the rear. I then told the women in the house that the artillery would open on the house, if any more shots

were fired from it. We then marched down Twenty-second Street, between Second and Third Avenues, found the body of a sergeant of Davis' Cavalry, who had been killed two hours before. I ordered a livery-stable keeper to put his horses to a carriage, and accompany me, for the purpose of carrying the dead and wounded. He replied that the mob would kill him if he did, and that he dare not do it. He was informed that he would be protected if he went, but if he refused he would be instantly shot. The horses were speedily harnessed, and the body put into the carriage. The mob at this time commenced firing on us from the houses. We at once commenced searching the houses, while my skirmishers drove the rioters back from every window and from the roofs. The houses were searched from cellar to the roof. The mob made a desperate fight, and evidently seemed to think they could whip us. Every house that was used to conceal these rioters was cleared. A large number was killed, and several prisoners taken. We then marched to Second Avenue, where we found the mob in great force and concealed in houses. They fired on us from house-tops, and from windows, and also from cross streets. We soon cleared the streets, and then commenced searching the houses. We searched thirteen houses, killed those within that resisted, and took the remainder prisoners. Some of them fought like incarnate fiends, and would not surrender. All such were shot on the spot. The soldiers captured a large number of revolvers of large size, which I allowed them to keep. The mob at this place were well armed; nearly every one had some kind of fire-arms, and had one blunderbuss which they fired on us.

If they had been cool and steady, they might have done us great harm. As it was, they fired wildly, running to a window and firing, and then retreating back out of danger.

When my soldiers once got into a house they made short work of it. The fight lasted about forty minutes and was more severe than all the rest in which my company was engaged. There were none of my men killed. Sergeant Cadro, of company F, Twelfth Infantry (my own), was slightly wounded in the hand; private Krouse was also slightly wounded.

The mob being entirely dispersed, we returned to head-quarters.

131 "Treating captured rebels as prisoners of war" (1863)

The exigencies of the American Civil War produced the first attempt to codify the international laws of war, which had by custom been considered to be binding upon all civilized nations. Prepared by Francis Lieber, a professor at Columbia College in New

York, and promulgated by President Lincoln on April 24, 1863, this General Order No. 100 is the forerunner of the Hague Conventions of 1899 and 1907 and the Geneva Convention of 1949.

Although the main part of these instructions pertained to wars between nations, articles 149 to 157 concerned civil wars and insurrections. The instructions did not exempt participants in such domestic armed conflicts from punishment under treason and other domestic criminal laws. But the instructions recognized humanitarian considerations (not to mention the pragmatic impossibility of trying and punishing large numbers of rebels) as a justification for the application of the regular rules of international warfare to domestic insurgents. The Union army thus was given the option of treating Confederate captives as prisoners of war rather than traitors. Yet the instructions hastened to reiterate that such practices were not to constitute a recognition of the rebels as a "sovereign power," nor were they to preclude the trial of the "chief rebels for high treason."

☆ 131 Instructions for the Government of Armies of the United States in the Field (April 24, 1863)

General Order No. 100, Adjutant General's Office, 1863, reprinted in D. Schindler and J. Toman, eds., *The Laws of Armed Conflicts* (Alphen aan den Rijn, The Netherlands: Sijthoff & Noordhoff, 1981), 21-23.

*   *   *

SECTION IX

Assassination

Art. 148. The law of war does not allow proclaiming either an individual belonging to the hostile army, or a citizen, or a subject of the hostile government, an outlaw, who may be slain without trial by any captor, any more than the modern law of peace allows such intentional outlawry; on the contrary, it abhors such outrage. The sternest retaliation should follow the murder committed in consequence of such proclamation, made by whatever authority. Civilized nations look with horror upon offers of rewards for the assassination of enemies as relapses into barbarism.

SECTION X

Insurrection—Civil War—Rebellion

Art. 149. Insurrection is the rising of people in arms against their government, or a portion of it, or against one or more of its laws, or against an officer or officers of the government. It may be confined to mere armed resistance, or it may have greater ends in view.

Art. 150. Civil war is war between two or more portions of a country or state, each contending for the mastery of the whole, and each claiming to be the legitimate government. The term is also sometimes applied to war of rebellion, when the rebellious provinces or portions of the state are contiguous to those containing the seat of government.

Art. 151. The term rebellion is applied to an insurrection of large extent, and is usually a war between the legitimate government of a country and portions of provinces of the same who seek to throw off their allegiance to it and set up a government of their own.

Art. 152. When humanity induces the adoption of the rules of regular war toward rebels, whether the adoption is partial or entire, it does in no way whatever imply a partial or complete acknowledgment of their government, if they have set up one, or of them, as an independent and sovereign power. Neutrals have no right to make the adoption of the rules of war by the assailed government toward rebels the ground of their own acknowledgment of the revolted people as an independent power.

Art. 153. Treating captured rebels as prisoners of war, exchanging them, concluding of cartels, capitulations, or other warlike agreements with them; addressing officers of a rebel army by the rank they may have in the same; accepting flags of truce; or, on the other hand, proclaiming Martial Law in their territory, or levying war-taxes or forced loans, or doing any other act sanctioned or demanded by the law and usages of public war between sovereign belligerents, neither proves nor establishes an acknowledgment of the rebellious people, or of the government which they may have erected, as a public or sovereign power. Nor does the adoption of the rules of war toward rebels imply an engagement with them extending beyond the limits of these rules. It is victory in the field that ends the strife and settles the future relations between the contending parties.

Art. 154. Treating, in the field, the rebellious enemy according to the law and usages of war has never prevented the legitimate government from trying the leaders of the rebellion or chief rebels for high treason, and from treating them accordingly, unless they are included in a general amnesty.

Art. 155. All enemies in regular war are divided into two general classes—that is to say, into combatants and noncombatants, or unarmed citizens of the hostile government.

The military commander of the legitimate government, in a war of rebellion, distinguishes between the loyal citizen in the revolted portion of the country and the disloyal citizen. The disloyal citizens may further be classified into those citizens known to sympathize with the rebellion without positively aiding it, and those who, without taking up arms, give positive aid and comfort to the rebellious enemy without being bodily forced thereto.

Art. 156. Common justice and plain expediency

require that the military commander protect the manifestly loyal citizens, in revolted territories, against the hardships of the war as much as the common misfortune of all war admits.

The commander will throw the burden of the war, as much as lies within his power, on the disloyal citizens, of the revolted portion or province, subjecting them to a stricter police than the noncombatant enemies have to suffer in regular war; and if he deems it appropriate, or if his government demands of him that every citizen shall, by an oath of allegiance, or by some other manifest act, declare his fidelity to the legitimate government, he may expel, transfer, imprison, or fine the revolted citizens who refuse to pledge themselves anew as citizens obedient to the law and loyal to the government.

Whether it is expedient to do so, and whether reliance can be placed upon such oaths, the commander or his government have the right to decide.

Art. 157. Armed or unarmed resistance by citizens of the United States against the lawful movements of their troops is levying war against the United States, and is therefore treason.

132 "that he has never given any aid or comfort to the present rebellion" (1863)

The Abandoned Property Act served two Union objectives: the economic punishment of rebels and the financing of the war through confiscations. The act allowed the government to confiscate property of Southerners without cumbersome legal proceedings and sanctioned the summary collection and sale of property abandoned or captured in any of the rebellious states, with the proceeds going into the United States Treasury. Perhaps in recognition of the Fifth Amendment guarantees against the taking of property without due process of law, the act provided that owners could recover a standardized value of confiscated property two years after the conclusion of the insurrection. But unlike earlier enactments in which the government had the burden of showing some support of the rebellion by the property owner, this act shifted the burden of proof to the claimant to prove he had not supported the rebellion. While Confederate soldiers were accorded prisoner-of-war status, civilians in the South were still held to loyalty to the United States. After the war the United States Supreme Court held the act to be constitutional as a valid exercise of the government's war powers.

☆ 132 An Act to Provide for the Collection of Abandoned Property

12 Stat. 820 (1863).

Be it enacted by the Senate and House of Representatives of the United States of America in Congress assembled, That it shall be lawful for the Secretary of the Treasury ... to receive and collect all abandoned or captured property in any state or territory ... designated as in insurrection against the lawful Government of the United States....

SEC. 2. *And be it further enacted,* That any part of the goods or property received or collected by such agent or agents may be appropriated to public use on due appraisement and certificate thereof, or forwarded to any place of sale within the loyal states, as the public interests may require; and all sales of such property shall be at auction to the highest bidder, and the proceeds thereof shall be paid into the treasury of the United States.

SEC. 3. *And be it further enacted,* That ... any person claiming to have been the owner of any such abandoned or captured property may, at any time within two years after the suppression of the rebellion, prefer his claim to the proceeds thereof in the court of claims; and on proof to the satisfaction of said court of his ownership of said property, of his right to the proceeds thereof, and that he has never given any aid or comfort to the present rebellion, to receive the residue of such proceeds, after the deduction of any purchase-money which may have been paid, together with the expense of transportation and sale of said property, and any other lawful expenses attending the disposition thereof.

SEC. 4. *And be it further enacted,* That all property coming into any of the United States not declared in insurrection as aforesaid, from within any of the states declared in insurrection, through or by any other person than any agent duly appointed under the provisions of this act, or under a lawful clearance by the proper officer of the Treasury Department, shall be confiscated to the use of the Government of the United States....

*   *   *

Approved, March 12, 1863.

133 "too few arrests rather than too many" (1863)

The Albany Democratic Convention voiced complaints that certain military arrests were unconstitutional, particularly the arrest of Congressman Clement L. Vallandigham of Ohio, a famous Copperhead. (This term was first applied to Lincoln's Northern opponents by the *New York Tribune* in 1861.) Lincoln, in defense of his asserted power, wrote to Erastus Corning, a New York political leader. This letter presents a most eloquent defense of the "inherent power" of the executive, in the absence of specific legislative or constitutional authority, to use whatever force necessary to suppress activities deemed inimical to the national security.

Professing a personal distaste for the suspension of the writ of habeas corpus, Lincoln nevertheless asserted its necessity and constitutionality, and the view that it would have no lasting effect on civil liberties. The letter reiterated Lincoln's defiant refusal to accept the court's ruling in *Ex Parte Merryman* that Congress alone had the authority to suspend the writ. Attention should also be given to Lincoln's recitation of the resolution of General Andrew Jackson's brush with civil authorities during an earlier period of martial law.

☆ 133 Letter from Abraham Lincoln to Erastus Corning and Others (June 12, 1863)

Reprinted in J. Nicolay and J. Hay, eds., *Complete Works of Lincoln* (New York: F. D. Tandy, 1905), 8:298-314.

Executive Mansion, June 12, 1863

GENTLEMEN:

Your letter of May 19, inclosing the resolutions of a public meeting held at Albany, New York, on the 16th of the same month, was received several days ago.

*   *   *

... The resolutions promise to support me in every constitutional and lawful measure to suppress the rebellion; and I have not knowingly employed, nor shall knowingly employ, any other. But the meeting, by their resolutions, assert and argue that certain military arrests and proceedings following them, for which I am ultimately responsible are unconstitutional. I think they are not. The resolutions quote from the Constitution the definition of treason, and also the limiting safeguards and guarantees therein provided for the citizen on trials for treason, and on his being held to answer for capital or otherwise infamous crimes, and in criminal prosecutions his right to a speedy and public trial by an impartial jury. They proceed to resolve "that these safeguards of the rights of the citizen against the pretensions of arbitrary power were intended more especially for his protection in times of civil commotion." And, apparently to demonstrate the proposition, the resolutions proceed: "They were secured substantially to the English people after years of protracted civil war, and were adopted into our Constitution at the close of the revolution." Would not the demonstration have been better if it could have been truly said that these safeguards had been adopted and applied during the civil wars and during our revolution, instead of after the one and at the close of the

other? I, too, am devotedly for them after civil war and before civil war, and at all times, "except when, in cases of rebellion or invasion, the public safety may require" their suspension.... But these provisions of the Constitution have no application to the case we have in hand, because the arrests complained of were not made for treason—that is, not for the treason defined in the Constitution, and upon the conviction of which the punishment is death—nor yet were they made to hold persons to answer for any capital or otherwise infamous crimes; nor were the proceedings following, in any constitutional or legal sense, "criminal prosecutions." The arrests were made on totally different grounds, and the proceedings following accorded with the grounds of the arrests.... [The rebel] sympathizers pervaded all departments of the government and nearly all communities of the people. From this material, under cover of "liberty of speech," "liberty of the press," and "*habeas corpus,*" they hoped to keep on foot amongst us a most efficient corps of spies, informers, suppliers and aiders and abettors of their cause in a thousand ways. They knew that in times such as they were inaugurating, by the Constitution itself the "*habeas corpus*" might be suspended; but they also knew they had friends who would make a question as to who was to suspend it; meanwhile their spies and others might remain at large to help on their cause. Or if, as has happened, the Executive should suspend the writ without ruinous waste of time, instances of arresting innocent persons might occur, as are always likely to occur in such cases; and then a clamor could be raised in regard to this.... Yet ... I was slow to adopt the strong measures which [are] ... indispensable to the public safety. Nothing is better known to history than that courts of justice are utterly incompetent to such cases. Civil courts are organized chiefly for trials of individuals, or, at most, a few individuals acting in concert—and this in quiet times, and on charges of crimes well defined in the law. Even in times of peace bands of horse-thieves and robbers frequently grow too numerous and powerful for the ordinary courts of justice. But what comparison, in numbers, have such bands ever borne to the insurgent sympathizers even in many of the loyal States? Again, a jury too frequently has at least one member more ready to hang the panel than to hang the traitor. And yet again, he who dissuades one man from volunteering, or induces one soldier to desert, weakens the Union cause as much as he who kills a Union soldier in battle. Yet this dissuasion or inducement may be so conducted as to be no defined crime of which any civil court would take cognizance.

Ours is a case of rebellion.... [The Suspension Clause] plainly attests the understanding of those who made the Constitution that ordinary courts of justice are inadequate to "cases of rebellion"—attests their purpose that, in such cases, men may be held in custody whom the courts, acting on ordinary rules, would discharge. *Habeas corpus* does not discharge men who are proved to be guilty of defined crime; and its suspension is allowed by the Constitution on purpose that men may be arrested and held who cannot be proved to be guilty of defined crime, "when, in cases of rebellion or invasion, the public safety may require it."

This is precisely our present case—a case of rebellion wherein the public safety does require the suspension.... Arrests in cases of rebellion do not proceed altogether upon the same basis. In the latter case arrests are made not so much for what has been done, as for what probably would be done. The latter is more for the preventive and less for the vindictive than the former. In such cases the purposes of men are much more easily understood than in cases of ordinary crime. The man who stands by and says nothing when the peril of his government is discussed, cannot be misunderstood. If not hindered, he is sure to help the enemy; much more if he talks ambiguously—talks for his country with "buts," and "ifs" and "ands." [Several Confederate leaders] were all within the power of the government since the rebellion began, and were nearly as well known to be traitors then as now. Unquestionably if we had seized and held them, the insurgent cause would be much weaker. But no one of them had then committed any crime defined in the law. Every one of them, if arrested, would have been discharged on *habeas corpus* were the writ allowed to operate. In view of these and similar cases, I think the time not unlikely to come when I shall be blamed for having made too few arrests rather than too many.

By the third resolution the meeting indicate their opinion that military arrests may be constitutional in localities where rebellion actually exists, but that such arrests are unconstitutional in localities where rebellion or insurrection does not actually exist. They insist that such arrests shall not be made "outside of the lines of necessary military occupation and the scenes of insurrection." Inasmuch, however, as the Constitution itself makes no such distinction, I am unable to believe that there is any such constitutional distinction. I concede that the class of arrests complained of can be constitutional only when, in cases of rebellion or invasion, the public safety may require them; and I insist that in such cases they are constitutional wherever the public safety does require them, as well in places to which they may prevent the rebellion extending, as in those where it may be already prevailing; as well where they may restrain mischievous interference with the raising and supplying of armies to suppress the rebellion, as where the rebellion may actually be; as well where they may restrain the enticing men out of the army, as where they would prevent mutiny in the army;

equally constitutional at all places where they will conduce to the public safety, as against the dangers of rebellion or invasion. Take the particular case mentioned by the meeting. It is asserted in substance, that Mr. Vallandigham was, by a military commander, seized and tried "for no other reason than words addressed to a public meeting in criticism of the course of the administration, and in condemnation of the military orders of the general." Now, if there be no mistake about this, if this assertion is the truth and the whole truth, if there was no other reason for the arrest, then I concede that the arrest was wrong. But the arrest, as I understand, was made for a very different reason. Mr. Vallandigham avows his hostility to the war on the part of the Union; and his arrest was made because he was laboring, with some effect, to prevent the raising of troops, to encourage desertions from the army, and to leave the rebellion without an adequate military force to suppress it. He was not arrested because he was damaging the political prospects of the administration or the personal interests of the commanding general but because he was damaging the army, upon the existence and vigor of which the life of the nation depends. He was warring upon the military, and this gave the military constitutional jurisdiction to lay hands upon him.... Long experience has shown that armies cannot be maintained unless desertion shall be punished by the severe penalty of death.... Must I shoot a simple-minded soldier boy who deserts, while I must not touch a hair of a wily agitator who induces him to desert? This is none the less injurious when effected by getting a father, or brother, or friend into a public meeting, and there working upon his feelings till he is persuaded to write the soldier boy that he is fighting in a bad cause, for a wicked administration of a contemptible government, too weak to arrest and punish him if he shall desert. I think that, in such a case, to silence the agitator and save the boy is not only constitutional, but withal a great mercy.

If I be wrong ... my error lies in believing ... that the Constitution is not in its application in all respects the same in cases of rebellion or invasion involving the public safety, as it is in times of profound peace and public security. The Constitution itself makes the distinction, and I can no more be persuaded that the government can constitutionally take no strong measures in times of rebellion, because it can be shown that the same could not be lawfully taken in time of peace, than I can be persuaded that a particular drug is not good medicine for a sick man because it can be shown to not be good food for a well one. Nor am I able to appreciate the danger apprehended by the meeting, that the American people will by means of military arrests during the rebellion lose the right of public discussion, the liberty of speech and the press, the law of evidence, trial by jury, and *habeas corpus* throughout the in-definite peaceful future which I trust lies before them, any more than I am able to believe that a man could contract so strong an appetite for emetics during temporary illness as to persist in feeding upon them during the remainder of his healthful life.

... I cannot overlook the fact that the meeting speak as "Democrats." Nor can I ... suppose that this occurred by accident, or in any way other than that they preferred to designate themselves "Democrats" rather than "American citizens." ... He on whose discretionary judgment Mr. Vallandigham was arrested and tried is a Democrat, having no old party affinity with me, and the judge who rejected the constitutional view expressed in these resolutions, by refusing to discharge Mr. Vallandigham on *habeas corpus*, is a Democrat of better days than these, having received his judicial mantle at the hands of President Jackson. And still more, of all those Democrats who are nobly exposing their lives and shedding their blood on the battle-field, I have learned that many approve the course taken with Mr. Vallandigham, while I have not heard of a single one condemning it. I cannot assert that there are none such. And the name of President Jackson recalls an instance of pertinent history. After the battle of New Orleans, ... General Andrew Jackson still maintained martial or military law.... [A] Mr. Louaillier published a denunciatory newspaper article. General Jackson arrested him. A lawyer by the name of Morel procured the United States Judge Hall to order a writ of *habeas corpus* to release Mr. Louaillier. General Jackson arrested both the lawyer and the judge. A Mr. Hollander ventured to say of some part of the matter that "it was a dirty trick." General Jackson arrested him. When the officer undertook to serve the writ of *habeas corpus*, General Jackson took it from him, and sent him away with a copy.... [When] the ratification of the treaty of peace was regularly announced, ... the judge and others were fully liberated. A few days more, and the judge called General Jackson into court and fined him $1000 for having arrested him and the others named. The general paid the fine, and then the matter rested for nearly thirty years, when Congress refunded principal and interest....

It may be remarked — first, that we had the same Constitution then as now; secondly, that we then had a case of invasion, and now we have a case of rebellion; and, thirdly, that the permanent right of the people to public discussion, the liberty of speech and of the press, the trial by jury, the law of evidence, and the *habeas corpus*, suffered no detriment whatever by that conduct of General Jackson, or its subsequent approval by the American Congress.

*   *   *

I am specifically called on to discharge Mr. Vallandigham.... In response to such appeal I have to

say ... it will afford me great pleasure to discharge him so soon as I can by any means believe the public safety will not suffer by it.

*   *   *

A. LINCOLN

134 Enemies or Traitors (1863)

On March 15, 1863, Union forces seized the schooner *J. M. Chapman* in the harbor of San Francisco. The officers and crew were arrested and indicted for treason on the grounds that they had procured and armed a boat to conduct hostilities under a letter of marque from Jefferson Davis against the United States on the high seas.

In his charge to the jury, Judge Field defined the constitutional meaning of "enemies" and contrasted the judicial conclusion that the rebels were traitors with the ambivalent posture of the executive branch, which accorded prisoner-of-war status to the rebel soldiers. In the courts, civilian supporters of the Southern cause were held to standards expected of citizens of the United States, even though they held a commission from the president of the rebel government.

☆ **134** *United States v. Greathouse*

26 F. Cas. 21 (C.C.N.D. Ca. 1863) (No. 15,254).

FIELD, Circuit Justice (charging jury).... There prevails a very general, but an erroneous opinion, that in all criminal cases the jury are the judges as well of the law as of the fact — that is, that they have a right to disregard the law as laid down by the court, and to follow their own notions on the subject. Such is not the right of the jury. They have the power ... but they have no moral right to adopt their own views of the law. It is their duty to take the law from the court and apply it to the facts of the case....

The defendants are indicted for engaging in, and giving aid and comfort to, the existing rebellion against the government of the United States. The indictment is framed under the second section of the act of congress of July 17, 1862, ... and it charges the commission of acts, which, in the judgment of the court, amount to treason within the meaning of the constitution. "Treason against the United States," is the language adopted, "shall consist only in levying war against them, or adhering to their enemies, giving them aid and comfort." No other acts can be declared to constitute the offense. Congress can neither extend, nor restrict, nor define the crime. Its power over the subject is limited to prescribing the punishment.

*   *   *

The term "enemies" ... applies only to the subjects of a foreign power in a state of open hostility with us. It does not embrace rebels in insurrection against their own government. An enemy is always the subject of a foreign power who owes no allegiance to our government or country. We may, therefore, omit all consideration of this second clause in the constitutional definition of treason. To convict the defendants they must be brought within the first clause of the definition. They must be shown to have committed acts which amount to a levying of war against the United States. To constitute a levying of war there must be an assemblage of persons in force, to overthrow the government, or to coerce its conduct.... The offense is complete, whether the force be directed to the entire overthrow of the government throughout the country, or only in certain portions of the country, or to defeat the execution and compel the repeal of one of its public laws.

It is not, however, necessary that I should go into any close definition of the words "levying war," for it is not sought to apply them to any doubtful case. War has been levied against the United States. War of gigantic proportions is now waged against them, and the government is struggling with it for its life. War being levied, all who aid in its prosecution, whether by open hostilities in the field, or by performing any part in the furtherance of the common object, "however minute or however remote from the scene of action," are equally guilty of treason within the constitutional provision. In treason there are no accessories; all who engage in the rebellion at any stage of its existence, or who designedly give to it any species of aid and comfort, in whatever part of the country they may be, stand on the same platform; they are all principals in the commission of the crime; they are all levying war against the United States.

*   *   *

The indictment in the present case, as I have already stated, is based upon the second section of the act of July 17, 1862. The constitution, although defining treason, leaves to congress the authority to prescribe its punishment. In 1790, congress passed an act fixing to the offense the penalty of death. By the first section of the act of July, 1862, congress gave a discretionary power to the courts to inflict the penalty of death, or fine and imprisonment, providing that in either case the slaves of the party convicted, if any he have, shall be liberated. The second section of the act declares "that if any person shall hereafter incite, set on foot, assist, or engage in any rebellion or insurrection against the authority of the United States, or the laws thereof, or shall give aid or comfort thereto, or shall engage in or give aid and comfort to any such existing rebellion or insurrection, and be convicted thereof, such person shall be pun-

ished by imprisonment for a period not exceeding ten years, or by a fine not exceeding $10,000....

There would seem, upon a first examination, to be an inconsistency between the first and second sections of this act—the first section declaring a particular punishment for treason, and the second declaring, for acts which may constitute treason, a different punishment. It appears from the debate in the senate of the United States, when the second section was under consideration, that it was the opinion of several senators that the commission of the acts which it designates might, under some circumstances, constitute an offense less than treason. ... Rebels not being enemies within the Constitution's meaning, an indictment alleging the giving of aid and comfort to them had been, as it was stated, held defective. But ... not because the giving of aid and comfort to rebels was not treason, but because the parties giving such aid and comfort were equally involved in guilt with those in open hostilities and should have been indicted for levying war; for every species of aid and comfort which, if given to a foreign enemy, would constitute treason within the second clause of the constitutional provision—adhering to the enemies of the United States—would, if given to the rebels in insurrection against the government, constitute a levying of war under the first clause. The second section of the act, however, relieves the subject from any difficulty.... But we are unable to conceive of any act designated in the second section which would not constitute treason, except perhaps as suggested by my associate, that of inciting to a rebellion.... Looking at the act alone, we conclude that congress intended: 1. To preserve the act of 1790, which prescribes the penalty of death, in force for the prosecution and punishment of offenses committed previous to July 17, 1862, unless the parties accused are convicted under the act of the latter date for subsequent offenses; 2. To punish treason thereafter committed with death, or fine and imprisonment in the discretion of the court, unless the treason consist in engaging in or assisting a rebellion or insurrection against the authority of the United States, or the laws thereof, in which event the death penalty is to be abandoned, and a less penalty inflicted. By this construction, the apparent inconsistency in the provisions of the different sections is avoided, and effect given to each clause of the act. The defendants are therefore in fact on trial for treason, and they have had all the protection and privileges allowed to parties accused of treason, without being liable, in case of conviction, to the penalty which all other civilized nations have awarded to this, the highest of crimes known to the law.

*   *   *

[T]he indictment alleges: 1. The existence of a rebellion against the United States, their authority and laws; 2. That the defendants traitorously engaged in and gave aid and comfort to the same; 3. That in the execution of their treasonable and traitorous purposes, they procured, fitted out, and armed a vessel to cruise in the service of the rebellion upon the high seas, and commit hostilities against the citizens, property and vessels of the United States; 4. That they sailed in their vessel from the port of San Francisco upon such cruise in the service of the rebellion.

The existence of the rebellion is a matter of public notoriety, and like matters of general and public concern to the whole country, may be taken notice of by judges and juries without that particular proof which is required of the other matters charged. The public notoriety, the proclamations of the president, and the acts of congress are sufficient proof of the allegation of the indictment in this respect. The same notoriety and public documents are also sufficient proof that the rebellion is organized and carried on under a pretended government, called the Confederate States of America.

As to the treasonable purposes of the defendants there is no conflict in the evidence.... I do not propose to say anything to you upon the much disputed questions whether or not the vessel ever did, in fact, sail from the port of San Francisco, or whether, if she did sail, she started on the hostile expedition. In the judgment of the court they are immaterial, if you find the facts to be what I have said the evidence tends to establish.

When Harpending received the letter of marque, with the intention of using it, ... he became leagued with the insurgents—the conspiracy between him and the chiefs of the rebellion was complete.... The subsequent purchasing of the vessel, and the guns, and the ammunition, and the employment of the men to manage the vessel, if these acts were done in furtherance of the common design, were overt acts of treason. Together, these acts complete the essential charge of the indictment. In doing them, the defendants were performing a part in aid of the great rebellion. They were giving it aid and comfort.

It is not essential to constitute the giving of aid and comfort that the enterprise commenced should be successful and actually render assistance....

Wherever overt acts have been committed which, in their natural consequence, if successful, would encourage and advance the interests of the rebellion, in judgment of law aid and comfort are given. Whether aid and comfort are given—the overt acts of treason being established—is not left to the balancing of probabilities—it is a conclusion of law.

If the defendants obtained a letter of marque from the president of the so-called Confederate States, the fact does not exempt them from prosecution in the tribunals of the country for the acts charged in the indictment. The existence of civil

war, and the application of the rules of war to particular cases, under special circumstances, do not imply the renunciation or waiver by the federal government of any of its municipal rights as sovereign toward the citizens of the seceded states.

As [a] matter of policy and humanity, the government of the United States has treated the citizens of the so-called Confederate States, taken in open hostilities, as prisoners of war, and has thus exempted them from trial for violation of its municipal laws. But the courts have no such dispensing power; they can only enforce the laws as they find them upon the statute-book. They cannot treat any new government as having authority to issue commissions or letters of marque which will afford protection to its citizens until the legislative and executive departments have recognized its existence. The judiciary follows the political department of the government in these particulars. By that department the rules of war have been applied only in special cases; and notwithstanding the application, congress has legislated in numerous instances for the punishment of all parties engaged in or rendering assistance in any way to the existing rebellion. The law under which the defendants are indicted was passed after captives in war had been treated and exchanged as prisoners of war, in numerous instances.

But even if full belligerent rights had been conceded to the Confederate States, such rights could not be invoked for the protection of persons entering within the limits of states which have never seceded, and secretly getting up hostile expeditions against our government and its authority and laws. The local and temporary allegiance, which every one—citizen or alien—owes to the government under which he at the time lives, is sufficient to subject him to the penalties of treason.

These, gentlemen, constitute all the instructions I have to give. My associate, Judge HOFFMAN, will submit some further observations to you....

HOFFMAN, District Judge (charging jury). At the request of the presiding judge, I have prepared some observations which ... [are] to be taken as the expression of my individual opinion. The charge of the presiding judge is to be exclusively received as the opinion and instructions of the court.

*   *   *

In the constitution of the United States it is declared that the crime of treason shall consist only in levying war against the United States, and in adhering to their enemies, giving them aid and comfort. The last branch of this definition has always been admitted to apply only to cases of adhering, and giving aid and comfort to, foreign public enemies. It was therefore held that an indictment charging the defendant with having given aid and comfort to domestic rebels was bad, and that the acts should be charged as "a levying of war against the United

States." It appears, however, to have been considered by congress that some acts might be committed which would constitute an "engaging in the present rebellion, and giving it aid and comfort," which would not amount to a levying of war, or to the crime of treason, within the meaning of the constitution. Under this idea, the act of 1862, in its first section, re-enacts the former statute against treason eo nomine, but modifies, in some respects, the penalty, while the second section denounces, as if it were a different offense, the "engaging in, and giving aid and comfort to, the existing rebellion." We have not been able to concur in the view which congress seems to have taken of the offenses created by these sections.

*   *   *

... As the framers of the constitution restricted the crime of treason to two classes of cases only, the one "adhering to the public enemy, giving him aid and comfort;" the other "levying war against the United States," what motive can be suggested for attaching any less guilt to him who aids and comforts a rebellion, than to him who aids and comforts a public enemy? A moment's consideration of the magnitude and power of the present rebellion, its aim not merely to change the form of government, or to resist the laws, but to dismember the country, and to destroy forever our integrity as a nation, and to inflict a fatal blow on the cause of human progress and civilization, will convince us that the dangers to be apprehended are as great, and the guilt of the actors as deep, when aid and comfort are given to a domestic rebellion, as when given to a public enemy....

*   *   *

It is unnecessary to repeat what has already been said in regard to the letter of marque. The question is not whether the commission, or letter of marque, was in all respects regular or formally executed. Emanating from the rebel government, it could, of course, confer no authority to levy war on the United States, or to destroy or rob the vessels of her citizens....

*   *   *

I have endeavored, gentlemen, to consider the questions involved in this cause in the calm spirit of judicial inquiry, and unaffected by the excitements of the hour or the fierce passions necessarily aroused by the stupendous contest in which the country is engaged. For the accused, personally, I feel a deep regret, and especially for one of them, who appears to have been animated rather by a zeal for the cause which he has unhappily espoused than by the more unworthy motive of enriching himself by the plunder of his fellow-citizens. It is deeply to be regretted that the courage and willingness to sacrifice himself for the benefit of his associates, slight

glimpses of which have been revealed by the evidence, have been wasted on an enterprise which is as indefensible in morals, or even under any political theory ever proclaimed by the advocates of secession, as it is criminal in law.

135 "They were terribly mutilated" (1864)

The North-South hostilities and bloodshed of the Civil War in no way lessened the other tensions between the west-bound white settlers and the native occupants of the western lands. The southern Cheyenne and Arapaho Indians had considered central Kansas and the Rocky Mountains their domain since the early part of the nineteenth century. The increasing number of settlers who came to the territory as part of the Pike's Peak gold rush began encroaching on the Indian lands. Government officials persuaded the Indians, who were located in the very center of the white emigration route, to sell their land to the United States and to move to the arid southeastern sections of the Colorado Territory. Claiming that they were cheated by the transaction, some of the tribes rebelled and attacked the neighboring settlers. The Cheyenne, nevertheless, adhered to a peace policy and were promised federal protection against the revenging Colorado militia.

A contingent of the Colorado militia under Colonel J. M. Chivington, a Methodist preacher in private life, attacked the unsuspecting Cheyenne camp, in spite of the assurance of protection by federal troops. The soldiers ignored the Indians' white flag of surrender, and as many as 450 men, women, and children were slain and mutilated. The soldiers scalped the dead and dying, and the genitals of the women were cut out and stuck on poles or worn on the soldiers' hats. Chivington later remarked that the children had to be killed because "nits make lice." A local newspaper described the attack as "a brilliant feat of arms."

The following document contains the testimony of John S. Smith, an Indian agent.

☆ 135 Massacre of the Cheyenne Indians

Testimony of John S. Smith before the Joint Committee on the Conduct of the War: Massacre of the Cheyenne Indians, 38th Congress, 2d Session, III (1865), reprinted in Richard Hofstadter and Michael Wallace, eds., *American Violence: A Documentary History* (New York: Knopf, 1970), 276-77.

*   *   *

QUESTION. Were the women and children slaughtered indiscriminately, or only so far as they were with the warriors?

ANSWER. Indiscriminately.

QUESTION. Were there any acts of barbarity perpetrated there that came under your own observation?

ANSWER. Yes, sir; I saw the bodies of those lying there cut all to pieces, worse multilated than any I ever saw before; the women cut all to pieces.

By Mr. Buckalew:

QUESTION. How cut?

ANSWER. With knives; scalped; their brains knocked out; children two or three months old; all ages lying there, from sucking infants up to warriors. . . . They were terribly mutilated, lying there in the water and sand; most of them in the bed of the creek, dead and dying, making many struggles. They were so badly mutilated and covered with sand and water that it was very hard for me to tell one from another. . . .

By Mr. Gooch:

QUESTION. Did you see it done?

ANSWER. Yes, sir; I saw them fall.

QUESTION. Fall when they were killed?

ANSWER. Yes, sir.

QUESTION. Did you see them when they were mutilated?

ANSWER. Yes, sir.

QUESTION. By whom were they mutilated?

ANSWER. By the United States troops.

QUESTION. Do you know whether or not it was done by the direction or consent of any of the officers?

ANSWER. I do not; I hardly think it was. . . .

QUESTION. Were there any other barbarities or atrocities committed there other than those you have mentioned, that you saw?

ANSWER. Yes, sir; I had a half-breed son there, who gave himself up. He started at the time the Indians fled; being a half-breed he had but little hope of being spared, and seeing them fire at me, he ran away with the Indians for the distance of about a mile. During the fight up there he walked back to my camp and went into the lodge. It was surrounded by soldiers at the time. He came in quietly and sat down; he remained there that day, that night, and the next day in the afternoon; about four o'clock in the evening, as I was sitting inside the camp, a soldier came up outside of the lodge and called me by name. I got up and went out; he took me by the arm and walked towards Colonel Chivington's camp, which was about sixty yards from my camp. Said he, "I am sorry to tell you, but they are going to kill your son Jack." I knew the feeling towards the whole camp of Indians, and that there was no use to make any resistance. I said, "I can't help it." I then walked on towards where Colonel Chivington was standing by his camp-fire; when I had got within a few feet of him I heard a gun fired, and saw a crowd run to my lodge, and they told me that Jack was dead.

QUESTION. What action did Colonel Chivington take in regard to that matter?

ANSWER. Major Anthony, who was present, told Colonel Chivington that he had heard some remarks made, indicating that they were desirous of killing Jack; and that he (Colonel Chivington) had it in his power to save him, and that by saving him he might make him a very useful man, as he was well acquainted with all the Cheyenne and Arapahoe country, and he could be used as a guide or interpreter. Colonel Chivington replied to Major Anthony, as the Major himself told me, that he had no orders to receive and no advice to give.

136 "[I] have never hated nor wronged any one" (1864-1865)

On April 11, 1865, in his last public address, delivered to an audience gathered in front of the White House, President Lincoln discussed his hopes for the early return of the Southern states to the Union. Two days later, while attending a comedy at Ford's Theater, the president was shot by actor John Wilkes Booth. Secretary of State William H. Seward was stabbed in his bed the same night by an accomplice of Booth. Lincoln died on April 15 of the wound inflicted by the assassin.

Assassination of the head of state is considered by most to be the paradigm political crime and would, of course, be high treason under common law. Although Booth viewed Lincoln as a tyrant set on destroying the country, the excerpts from Booth's letter and diary supply glimpses into the more personal passions and motives of the man who killed Lincoln. After his hasty escape from Washington, Booth was killed in Virginia in an encounter with his pursuers.

☆ 136 Writings of John Wilkes Booth

☆ 136a Letter to the *Philadelphia Enquirer* (1864; published April 19, 1865)

Reprinted in Stanley Kimmel, *The Mad Booths of Maryland* (New York: Dover, 1969), 396.

1864

MY DEAR SIR:

You may use this as you think best. But as *some* may wish to know *when*, who and *why* as I know not *how* to direct, I give it (in the words of your master)—"To whom it may concern."

Right or wrong, God judge me, not man. For be my motives good or bad, of one thing I am sure, the lasting condemnation of the North. . . . All hope for peace is dead. My prayers have proved as idle as my hopes. God's will be done. I go to see and share the bitter end.

*   *   *

The country was formed for the white, not for the black man. And looking upon African slavery from the same standpoint held by the noble framers of our Constitution, I, for one, have ever considered it one of the greatest blessings (both for themselves and us) that God ever bestowed upon a favored nation. Witness heretofore our wealth and power: witness their elevation and enlightenment above their race elsewhere. I have lived among it most of my life, and I have seen *less* harsh treatment from master to man than I have beheld in the North from father to son. Yet, heaven knows, *no one* would be willing to do *more* for the Negro race than I, could I but see the way to *still better their condition.*

But Lincoln's policy is only preparing a way for their total annihilation. The south *are not, nor have they* been fighting for the continuation of slavery. The first battle of Bull Run did away with that idea. Their causes for war have been *as noble and greater far than those that urged our fathers on. Even* should we allow they were wrong at the beginning of this contest, *cruelty and injustice* have made the wrong become the right, and they stand now (before the wonder and admiration of the world) as a noble band of patriotic heroes. Hereafter, reading of their deeds, Thermopylæ will be forgotten.

When I aided in the capture and execution of John Brown (who was a murderer on our Western border and who was fairly tried and convicted before an impartial judge and jury, of treason, and who, by the way, has since been made a god) I was proud of my little share in the transaction, for I deemed it my duty that it was helping our common country to perform an act of justice. But what was a crime in poor John Brown is considered (by themselves) as the greatest and only virtue of the whole Republican party. Strange transmigration. *Vice so* becomes a *virtue*, simply because more indulged in. I thought then as *now* that the Abolitionists were the *only traitors* in the land and that the entire party deserved the fate of poor John Brown, not because they wish to abolish slavery, but on account of the means they have ever used to effect that abolition. If Brown were living I doubt whether he *himself* would set slavery against the Union. Most or many in the North do, and openly curse the Union, if the South are to return and retain a *single right* guaranteed to them by every tie which we once revered as sacred.

The South can make no choice. It is either extermination or slavery for *themselves* (worse than death) to draw from. I know my choice.

I have also studied hard to know upon what grounds the right of a state to secede has been denied, when our very name United States, and the Declaration of Independence *both* provide for secession.

But there is no time for words. I write in haste. I know how foolish I shall be deemed for taking such a step as this. . . .

*   *   *

. . . My love (as things stand to-day) is for the South alone. Nor do I deem it a dishonor in attempting to make for her a prisoner of this man to whom she owes so much misery.

If success attends me, I go penniless to her side. They say she has found that "last ditch" which the North has so long derided and has been endeavoring to force her in, forgetting they are our brothers, and that it's impolitic to force on an enemy to madness. Should I reach her in safety and find it true, I will proudly beg permission to triumph or die in that same "ditch" by her side.

A Confederate doing duty on his own responsibility.

J. WILKES BOOTH

☆ 136b Booth's Diary

Reprinted in L. A. Weichmann, *A True History of the Assassination of Abraham Lincoln and of the Conspiracy of 1865* (New York: Knopf, 1975), 209-38.

April 13, 14, Friday, The Ides [1865]

Until to-day nothing was ever thought of sacrificing to our country's wrongs. For six months we had worked to capture. But, our cause being almost lost, something decisive and great must be done. But its failure was owing to others who did not strike for their country with a heart. I struck boldly, and not as the papers say. I walked with a firm step through a thousand of his friends, was stopped, but pushed on. A colonel was at his side. I shouted "Sic semper" before I fired. In jumping broke my leg. I passed all his pickets, rode sixty miles that night, with the bone of my leg tearing the flesh at every jump.

I can never repent it, though we hated to kill. Our country owed all our [her] troubles to him, and God simply made me the instrument of his punishment.

The country is not what it was. This forced union is not what I have loved. I care not what becomes of me. I have no desire to outlive my country. This night before the deed, I wrote a long article and left it for one of the editors of the *National Intelligencer*, in which I fully set forth our reasons for our proceedings. He or the gov'r—[South].

Friday 21

*   *   *

I am here in despair. And why? For doing what Brutus was honored for—what made Tell a hero. And yet I, for striking down a greater tyrant than they ever knew, am looked [up]on as a common cut-throat. My action [act] was purer than either of theirs. One hoped to be great [himself], the other had not only his country's but his own wrongs to avenge. I hoped for no gain[s]. I knew no private wrong. I struck for my country and that alone. A country groaned beneath this tyranny, and prayed for this end, and yet now behold the cold hand they extend [to] me.

I do not repent the blow I struck, I may before [my] God, but not to man. I think I have done well, though I am abandoned with the curse of Cain upon me, when if the world knew my heart, that one blow would have made me great, thought [*sic*] I did desire no greatness.

To-night I try to escape these blood-hounds once more. Who, who read his fate? God's will be done. "I have too great a soul to die like a criminal. O, may He spare me that, and let me die bravely!"

I bless the entire world. [I] have never hated nor wronged any one. This last was not a wrong, unless God deems it so. And it's with [for] Him to damn or bless me. And for this brave boy with me, who often prays (yes, before and since) with a true and sincere heart,—was it crime in him, if so, why can he pray the same? I do not wish to shed a drop of blood, but "I must fight the course." "T'is all that's left to me."

. . . God cannot pardon me if I have done wrong. Yet I cannot see my [any] wrong, except in serving a degenerate people. The little, the very little, I left behind to clear [bear] my name, the Government will not allow to be printed. So ends all. For my country I have given up all that makes life sweet and holy, brought misery upon my family, and am sure there is no pardon in [the] Heaven for me since man condemns me so. I have only heard of what has been done, (except what I did myself), and it fills me with horror. God!, try and forgive me, and bless my mother. To-night I will once more try the river with [the] intention to cross, though I have a greater desire and almost a mind to return to Washington, and in a measure clear my name, which I feel I can do.

137 "The civil tribunals . . . can not rightfully interfere with the military" (1865)

Under advice from his attorney general, President Andrew Johnson, on May 1, 1865, ordered the trial by a military commission of the eight persons accused of conspiracy in the Lincoln assassination. Since the civil courts in Washington, D.C., were open at the time, public arguments were raised against a military trial for the accused. Attorney General James Speed's opinion recited the legal position supporting a military trial, devoid of the traditional criminal procedure

safeguards, for the civilians accused of the president's murder. On June 30, 1865, the military commission found all eight guilty: Mary E. Surratt and three other coconspirators were sentenced to hang, Samuel A. Mudd and two accomplices were sentenced to life imprisonment, and Edward Spangler was given six years' imprisonment.

☆ 137 Opinion on the Constitutional Power of the Military by Attorney General James Speed

Reprinted in B. Pitman, ed., *The Assassination of President Lincoln and the Trial of the Conspirators* (Cincinnati: Moore, Wilstach & Baldwin, 1865), 403-9.

SIR:

You ask me whether the persons charged with the offense of having assassinated the President can be tried before a military tribunal, or must they be tried before a civil court.

The President was assassinated at a theater in the city of Washington. At the time of the assassination a civil war was flagrant, the city of Washington was defended by fortifications regularly and constantly manned, the principal police of the city was by Federal soldiers, the public offices and property in the city were all guarded by soldiers, and the President's House and person were, or should have been, under the guard of soldiers. Martial law had been declared in the District of Columbia, but the civil courts were open and held their regular sessions, and transacted business as in times of peace.

Such being the facts, the question is one of great importance—important, because it involves the constitutional guarantees thrown about the rights of the citizen, and because the security of the army and the government in time of war is involved; important, as it involves a seeming conflict between the laws of peace and of war.

Having given the question propounded the patient and earnest consideration its magnitude and importance require, I will proceed to give the reasons why I am of the opinion that the conspirators not only may but ought to be tried by a military tribunal.

A civil court of the United States is created by a law of congress, under and according to the Constitution. To the Constitution and the law we must look to ascertain how the court is constituted, the limits of its jurisdiction, and what its mode of procedure.

A military tribunal exists under and according to the Constitution in time of war. Congress may prescribe how all such tribunals are to be constituted, what shall be their jurisdiction and mode of procedure. Should Congress fail to create such tribunals, then, under the Constitution, they must be constituted according to the laws and usages of civilized warfare. They may take cognizance of such offenses as the laws of war permit; they must proceed according to the customary usages of such tribunals in time of war, and inflict such punishments as are sanctioned by the practice of civilized nations in time of war. In time of peace, neither Congress nor the military can create any military tribunals, except such as are made in pursuance of that clause of the Constitution which gives to Congress the power "to make rules for the government of the land and naval forces." I do not think that Congress can, in time of war or peace, under this clause of the Constitution, create military tribunals for the adjudication of offenses committed by persons not engaged in, or belonging to, such forces. This is a proposition too plain for argument. But it does not follow that because such military tribunals can not be created by Congress under this clause, that they can not be created at all. . . . That the law of nations constitutes a part of the laws of the land, must be admitted. . . . But very soon after the organization of the Federal Government, Mr. Randolph, then Attorney General, said: "The law of nations, although not specifically adopted by the Constitution, is essentially a part of the law of the land. Its obligation commences and runs with the existence of a nation, subject to modification on some points of indifference." . . .

. . . The framers of the Constitution knew that a nation could not maintain an honorable place among the nations of the world that does not regard the great and essential principles of the law of nations as a part of the law of the land. Hence Congress may define those laws, but can not abrogate them, or as Mr. Randolph says, may "modify on some points of indifference."

*   *   *

But the laws of war constitute much the greater part of the law of nations. Like the other laws of nations, they exist and are of binding force upon the departments and citizens of the Government, though not defined by any law of Congress. . . .

Congress can declare war. When war is declared, it must be, under the Constitution, carried on according to the known laws and usages of war among civilized nations. . . . The Constitution does not permit this Government to prosecute a war as an uncivilized and barbarous people.

*   *   *

All wars against a domestic enemy or to repel invasions, are prosecuted to preserve the Government. If the invading force can be overcome by the ordinary civil police of a country, it should be done without bringing upon the country the terrible scourge of war; if a commotion or insurrection can be put down by the ordinary process of law, the military should not be called out. A defensive foreign war is declared and carried on because the civil police is inadequate to repel it; a civil war is waged because the laws can not be peacefully enforced by the ordinary tribunals of the country through civil process and by civil officers. . . . Peace is the normal condition of a country, and war abnormal, neither being without law, but each having laws appropriate to the condition of society. The maxim *enter arma silent leges* is never wholly true. The object of war is to bring society out of its abnormal condition; and the laws of war aim to have that done with the least possible injury to persons or property.

*   *   *

. . . Non-combatants are not to be disturbed or interfered with by the armies of either party except in extreme cases. Armies are called out and organized to meet and overcome the active, acting public enemies.

. . . [E]nemies with which an army has to deal are of two classes:

1. Open, active participants in hostilities, as soldiers who wear the uniform, move under the flag, and hold the appropriate commission from their government. Openly assuming to discharge the duties and meet the responsibilities and dangers of soldiers, they are entitled to all belligerent rights, and should receive all the courtesies due to soldiers. The true soldier is proud to acknowledge and respect those rights, and ever cheerfully extends those courtesies.

2. Secret, but active participants, as spies, brigands, bushwhackers, jayhawkers, war rebels and assassins. In all wars, and especially in civil wars, such secret, active enemies rise up to annoy and attack an army, and must be met and put down by the army. When lawless wretches become so impudent and powerful as not to be controlled and governed by the ordinary tribunals of a country, armies are called out, and the laws of war invoked. Wars never have been and never can be conducted upon the principle that an army is but a *posse comitatus* of a civil magistrate.

An army, like all other organized bodies, has a right, and it is its first duty, to protect its own existence and the existence of all its parts, by the means and in the mode usual among civilized nations when at war. Then the question arises, do the laws of war authorize a different mode of proceeding, and the use of different means against secret active enemies from those used against open active enemies?

As has been said, the open enemy or soldier in time of war may be met in battle and killed, wounded or taken prisoner, or so placed by the lawful strategy of war as that he is powerless. Unless the law of self-preservation absolutely demands it, the life of a wounded enemy or a prisoner must be spared. Unless pressed thereto by the extremest necessity, the laws of war condemn and punish with great severity harsh or cruel treatment to a wounded enemy or a prisoner.

Certain stipulations and agreements, tacit or express, betwixt the open belligerent parties, are permitted by the laws of war, and are held to be of very high and sacred character. Such is the tacit understanding, or it may be usage, of war, in regard to flags of truce. Flags of truce are resorted to as a means of saving human life, or alleviating human suffering. When not used with perfidy, the laws of war require that they should be respected. The Romans regarded ambassadors betwixt belligerents as persons to be treated with consideration and respect. Plutarch, in his *Life of Cæsar*, tells us that the barbarians in Gaul having sent some ambassadors to Cæsar, he detained them, charging fraudulent practices, and led his army to battle, obtaining a great victory.

When the Senate decreed festivals and sacrifices for the victory, Cato declared it to be his opinion that Cæsar ought to be given into the hands of the barbarians, that so the guilt which this breach of faith might otherwise bring upon the State might be expiated by transferring the curse on him who was the occasion of it.

Under the Constitution and laws of the United States, should a commander be guilty of such a flagrant breach of law as Cato charged upon Cæsar, he would not be delivered to the enemy, but would be punished after a military trial. The many honorable gentlemen who hold commissions in the army of the United States, and have been deputed to conduct war according to the laws of war, would keenly feel it as an insult to their profession of arms for any one to say that they could not or would not punish a fellow-soldier who was guilty of wanton cruelty to a prisoner, or perfidy toward the bearers of a flag of truce.

The laws of war permit capitulations of surrender and paroles. They are agreements betwixt belligerents, and should be scrupulously observed and performed. They are contracts wholly unknown to civil tribunals. Parties to such contracts must answer any breaches thereof to the customary military tribunals in time of war. If an officer of rank, possessing the pride that becomes a soldier and a gentleman, who should capitulate to surrender the forces and property under his command and control, be charged with a fraudulent breach of the terms of surrender, the laws of war do not permit that he should be punished without a trial, or, if innocent, that he shall have no means of wiping out the foul imputation. If a paroled prisoner is charged with a breach of his parole, he may be punished if guilty, but not without a trial. He should be tried by a military tribunal, constituted and proceeding as the laws and usages of war prescribe.

The law and usage of war contemplate that sol-diers have a high sense of personal honor. The true soldier is proud to feel and know that his enemy possesses personal honor, and will conform and be obedient to the laws of war. In a spirit of justice, and with a wise appreciation of such feelings, the laws of war protect the character and honor of an open enemy. When by the fortunes of war one open enemy is thrown into the hands and power of another, and is charged with dishonorable conduct and a breach of the laws of war, he must be tried according to the usages of war. Justice and fairness say that an open enemy to whom dishonorable conduct is imputed, has a right to demand a trial. If such a demand can be rightfully made, surely it can not be rightfully refused. It is to be hoped that the military authorities of this country will never refuse such a demand, because there is no act of Congress that authorizes it. In time of war the law and usage of war authorize it, and they are a part of the law of the land.

One belligerent may request the other to punish for breaches of the laws of war, and, regularly, such a request should be made before retaliatory measures are taken. Whether the laws of war have been infringed or not, is of necessity a question to be decided by the laws and usages of war, and is cognizable before a military tribunal. When prisoners of war conspire to escape, or are guilty of a breach of appropriate and necessary rules of prison discipline, they may be punished, but not without trial. The commander who should order every prisoner charged with improper conduct to be shot or hung, would be guilty of a high offense against the laws of war, and should be punished therefor, after a regular military trial. If the culprit should be condemned and executed, the commander would be as free from guilt as if the man had been killed in battle.

It is manifest, from what has been said, that military tribunals exist under and according to the laws and usages of war, in the interest of justice and mercy. They are established to save human life, and to prevent cruelty as far as possible. The commander of an army in time of war has the same power to organize military tribunals and execute their judgments that he has to set his squadrons in the field and fight battles. His authority in each case is from the law and usage of war.

Having seen that there must be military tribunals to decide questions arising in time of war betwixt belligerents who are open and active enemies, let us next see whether the laws of war do not authorize such tribunals to determine the fate of those who are active, but secret, participants in the hostilities.

*   *   *

. . . That the laws of war authorized commanders to create and establish military commissions, courts or tribunals, for the trial of offenders against the laws of war, whether they be active or secret participants in the hostilities, can not be denied. That the judgments of such tribunals may have been sometimes harsh, and sometimes even tyrannical, does not prove that they ought not to exist, nor does it prove that they are not constituted in the interest of justice and mercy. Considering the power that the laws of war give over secret participants in hostilities, such as banditti, guerrillas, spies, etc., the position of a commander would be miserable indeed if he could not call to his aid the judgments of such tribunals; he would become a mere butcher of men, without the power to ascertain justice, and there can be no mercy where there is no justice. . . . Impartial history will record the fact that the Bureau of Military Justice, regularly organized during this war, has saved human life and prevented human suffering. The greatest suffering, patiently endured by soldiers, and the hardest battles gallantly fought during this protracted struggle, are not more creditable to the American character than the establishment of this bureau. This people have such an educated and profound respect for law and justice—such a love of mercy—that they have, in the midst of this greatest of civil wars, systematized and brought into regular order, tribunals that before this war existed under the law of war, but without general rule. To condemn the tribunals that have been established under this bureau, is to condemn and denounce the war itself, or justifying the war, to insist that it shall be prosecuted according to the harshest rules, and without the aid of the laws, usages and customary agencies for mitigating those rules. If such tribunals had not existed before, under the laws and usages of war, the American citizen might as proudly point to their establishments as to our inimitable and inestimable constitutions. It must be constantly borne in mind that such tribunals and such a bureau can not exist except in time of war, and can not then take cognizance of offenders or offenses where the civil courts are open, except offenders and offenses against the laws of war.

But it is insisted by some, and doubtless with honesty, and with a zeal commensurate with their honesty, that such military tribunals can have no constitutional existence. The argument against their constitutionality may be shortly, and I think fairly, stated thus:

Congress alone can establish military or civil judicial tribunals. As Congress has not established military tribunals, except such as have been created under the articles of war, and which articles are made in pursuance of that clause in the Constitution which gives to Congress the power to make rules for the government of the army and navy, any other tribunal is and must be plainly unconstitutional, and all its acts void.

This objection thus stated, or stated in any other way, begs the question. It assumes that Congress alone can establish military judicial tribunals. Is that assumption true?

*   *   *

. . . The Constitution was framed by great men—men of learning and large experience, and it is a wonderful monument of their wisdom. Well versed in the history of the world, they knew that the nation for which they were forming a government would, unless all history was false, have wars, foreign and domestic. Hence the government framed by them is clothed with the power to make and carry on war. As has been shown, when war comes, the laws of war come with it. Infractions of the laws of nations are not denominated *crimes*, but *offenses*. Hence the expression in the Constitution that "Congress shall have power to define and punish *offenses* against the law of nations." . . .

There is, then, an apparent but no real conflict in the constitutional provisions. *Offenses* against the laws of war must be dealt with and punished under the Constitution, as the laws of war, they being part of the law of nations direct; *crimes* must be dealt with and punished as the Constitution, and laws made in pursuance thereof, may direct.

*   *   *

That portion of the Constitution which declares that "no person shall be deprived of his life, liberty or property without due process of law," has such direct reference to, and connection with, trials for *crime* or *criminal* prosecutions, that comments upon it would seem to be unnecessary. Trials for offenses against the laws of war are not embraced or intended to be embraced in those provisions. . . .

The fact that the civil courts are open does not affect the right of the military tribunal to hold as a prisoner and to try. The civil courts have no more right to prevent the military, in time of war, from trying an offender against the laws of war than they have a right to interfere with and prevent a battle. A battle may be lawfully fought in the very view and presence of a court; so a spy, a bandit or other offender against the law of war, may be tried, and tried lawfully, when and where the civil courts are open and transacting the usual business.

*   *   *

. . . The civil tribunals of the country can not rightfully interfere with the military in the performance of their high, arduous and perilous, but lawful duties. That Booth and his associates were secret active public enemies, no mind that contemplates the facts can doubt. The exclamation used by him when he escaped from the box onto the stage, after he had fired the fatal shot, *sic semper tyrannis*, and his dying message, "Say to my mother that I died for my country," show that he was not an assassin from private malice, but that he acted as a public foe.

Such a deed is expressly laid down by Vattel, in his work on the law of nations, as an offense against the laws of war, and a great crime. . . .

My conclusion, therefore, is, that if the persons who are charged with the assassination of the President committed the deed as public enemies, as I believe they did, and whether they did or not is a question to be decided by the tribunal before which they are tried, they not only can, but ought to be tried before a military tribunal. If the persons charged have offended against the laws of war, it would be as palpably wrong for the military to hand them over to the civil courts, as it would be wrong in a civil court to convict a man of murder who had, in time of war, killed another in battle.

I am, sir, most respectfully, your obedient servant,

JAMES SPEED, Attorney General

To the President

138 "The relation of husband and wife amongst persons of color" (1865)

The first Emancipation Proclamation, issued on September 22, 1862, allowed slaveholders the opportunity of giving up the war and thereby keeping their human property. The second and better-known Emancipation Proclamation was issued on January 1, 1863. The Thirteenth Amendment, abolishing slavery, was submitted to the states on January 31, 1865, and ratified on December 6 of that year. During the process of ratification, the former slave states were legislating to regulate the status and conduct of blacks under the new regime. The codes related to all aspects of black life from labor and wages to marriage and social intercourse.

Sections of three Black Codes are reproduced here. Although varying in harshness, the purpose of the codes was the same: maintenance of the pre-Civil War social and political order between blacks and whites. Northern reaction to these codes gave rise to the new civil rights acts and the Fourteenth Amendment, which would criminalize the adherence to these state laws.

☆ 138 Southern Black Codes

☆ 138a South Carolina Black Code

1865 S.C. Acts 291-304.

Be it enacted by the Senate and House of Representatives, now met and sitting in General Assembly, and by the authority of the same, as follows:

HUSBAND AND WIFE

I. The relation of husband and wife amongst persons of color is established.

II. Those who now live as such, are declared to be husband and wife.

III. In case of one man having two or more reputed wives, or one woman two or more reputed husbands, the man shall, by the first of April next, select one of his reputed wives, or the woman one of her reputed husbands, and the ceremony of marriage, between this man or woman, and the person so selected, shall be performed.

IV. Every colored child, heretofore born, is declared to be the legitimate child of his mother, and also of his colored father, if he is acknowledged by such a father.

*   *   *

VIII. One who is a pauper, or a charge to the public, shall not be competent to contract marriage. Marriage between a white person and a person of color, shall be illegal and void.

IX. The marriage of an apprentice shall not, without the consent of the master, be lawful.

*   *   *

XVIII. Males of the age of twelve years, and females, of the age of ten years, shall sign the indenture of apprenticeship and be bound thereby.

*   *   *

CONTRACTS FOR SERVICE

XXXV. All persons of color who make contracts for service or labor, shall be known as servants, and those with whom they contract shall be known as masters.

*   *   *

XLV. On farms or in out-door service, the hours of labor, except on Sunday, shall be from sun-rise to sun-set, with a reasonable interval for breakfast and dinner. . . .

*   *   *

XLVII. The master may give to a servant a task at work about the business of the farm which shall be reasonable. If the servant complain of the task, the District Judge, or a Magistrate, shall have power to reduce or increase it. . . .

*   *   *

XLVIII. Visitors or other persons shall not be invited, or allowed by the servant, to come or remain upon the premises of the master, without his express permission.

XLIX. Servants shall not be absent from the premises without the permission of the master.

RIGHTS OF MASTER AS BETWEEN HIMSELF
AND HIS SERVANT

L. . . . The servant shall obey all lawful orders of the master or his agent, and shall be honest, truthful, sober, civil, and diligent in his business. The master may moderately correct servants who have made contracts, and are under eighteen years of age....

*   *   *

MECHANICS, ARTISANS AND SHOP-KEEPERS

LXXII. No person of color shall pursue or practice the art, trade or business of an artisan, mechanic or shop-keeper, or any other trade, employment or business (besides that of husbandry, or that of a servant under a contract for services or labor) on his own account and for his own benefit, or in partnership with a white person, or as agent or servant of any person, until he shall have obtained a license therefor from the Judge of the District Court, which license shall be good for one year only. This license the Judge may grant upon petition of the applicant, and upon being satisfied of his skill and fitness, and of his good moral character, and upon payment, by the applicant, to the Clerk of the District Court of one hundred dollars, if a shop-keeper or pedlar, to be paid annually, and ten dollars if a mechanic artisan, or to engage in any other trade, also to be paid annually: *Provided, however,* That upon complaint being made and proved to the District Judge of an abuse of such license, he shall revoke the same, and: *Provided, also,* That no person of color shall practice any mechanical art or trade, unless he shows that he has served an apprenticeship in such trade or art, or is now practicing such trade or art.

*   *   *

VAGRANCY AND IDLENESS

XCV. These are public grievances, and must be punished as crimes.

XCVI. All persons who have not some fixed and known place of abode, and some lawful and reputable employment; those who have not some visible and known means of a fair, honest and reputable livelihood ... those who, (whether or not they own lands, or are lessees or mechanics,) do not provide a reasonable and proper maintenance for themselves and families....

*   *   *

☆ 138b Black Code of Louisiana

1865 La. Acts 3.

1. AN ACT TO PROVIDE FOR AND REGULATE LABOR CONTRACTS FOR AGRICULTURAL PURSUITS

Sec. 1. Be it enacted ... That all persons employed as laborers in agricultural pursuits shall be required, during the first ten days of the month of January of each year, to make contracts for labor for the then ensuing year, or for the year next ensuing the termination of their present contracts....

Sec. 2. Every laborer shall have full and perfect liberty to choose his employer, but, when once cho-

sen, he shall not be allowed to leave his place of employment until the fulfillment of his contract ... and if they do so leave, without cause or permission, they shall forfeit all wages earned to the time of abandonment....

*   *   *

Sec. 8. Be it further enacted, &c., That in case of sickness of the laborer, wages for the time lost shall be deducted, and where the sickness is feigned for purposes of idleness, and also on refusal to work according to contract, double the amount of wages shall be deducted for the time lost; and also where rations have been furnished; and should the refusal to work continue beyond three days, the offender shall be reported to a Justice of the Peace, and shall be forced to labor on roads, levees, and other public works, without pay, until the offender consents to return to his labor.

Sec. 9. Be it further enacted, &c., That, when in health, the laborer shall work ten hours during the day in summer, and nine hours during the day in winter, unless otherwise stipulated in the labor contract; he shall obey all proper orders of his employer or his agent, ... and employers shall have the right to make a reasonable deduction from the laborer's wages for injuries done to animals or agricultural implements committed to his care, or for bad or negligent work. Bad work shall not be allowed. Failing to obey reasonable orders, neglect of duty, and leaving home without permission will be deemed disobedience.... For all absence from home without leave he will be fined at the rate of two dollars per day. Laborers will not be required to labor on the Sabbath unless by special contract. For all thefts of the laborer from the employer ... or willful destruction of property or injury, the laborer shall pay the employer double the amount of the value of the property stolen, destroyed, or injured.... No live stock shall be allowed to laborers without the permission of the employer. Laborers shall not receive visitors during work-hours. All difficulties arising between the employers and laborers, under this section, shall be settled by the former; if not satisfactory to the laborers, an appeal may be had to the nearest Justice of the Peace and two freeholders, citizens, one of said citizens to be selected by the employer and the other by the laborer....

*   *   *

☆ 138c Black Code of Mississippi

1865 Miss. Laws 82.

1. CIVIL RIGHTS OF FREEDMEN

*   *   *

Sec. 3. ... All freedmen, free negroes, or mulattoes who do now and have herebefore lived and cohabited together as husband and wife shall be taken and held in law as legally married, and the issue shall be taken and held as legitimate for all purposes; that it shall not be lawful for any freedman, free negro, or mulatto to intermarry with any white person; nor for any white person to intermarry with any freedman, free negro, or mulatto; and any person who shall so intermarry, shall be deemed guilty of felony, and on conviction thereof shall be confined in the State penitentiary for life; and those shall be deemed freedmen, free negroes, and mulattoes who are of pure negro blood, and those descended from a negro to the third generation, inclusive, though one ancestor in each generation may have been a white person.

*   *   *

Sec. 7. . . . Every civil officer shall, and every person may, arrest and carry back to his or her legal employer any freedman, free negro, or mulatto who shall have quit the service of his or her employer before the expiration of his or her term of service without good cause, and said officer and person shall be entitled to receive for arresting and carrying back every deserting employe aforesaid the sum of five dollars, and ten cents per mile from the place of arrest to the place of delivery. . . .

*   *   *

Sec. 9. . . . If any person shall persuade or attempt to persuade, entice, or cause any freedman, free negro, or mulatto to desert from the legal employment of any person before the expiration of his or her term of service, or shall knowingly employ any such deserting freedman, free negro, or mulatto, or shall knowingly give or sell to any such deserting freedman, free negro, or mulatto, any food, raiment, or other thing, he or she shall be guilty of a misdemeanor, and, upon conviction, shall be fined not less than twenty-five dollars and not more than two hundred dollars and the costs; and if said fine and costs shall not be immediately paid, the court shall sentence said convict to not exceeding two months' imprisonment in the county jail, and he or she shall moreover be liable to the party injured in damages: *Provided*, if any person shall, or shall attempt to, persuade, entice, or cause any freedman, free negro, or mulatto to desert from any legal employment of any person, with the view to employ said freedman, free negro, or mulatto without the limits of this State, such person, on conviction, shall be fined not less than fifty dollars, and not more than five hundred dollars and costs; and if said fine and costs shall not be immediately paid, the court shall sentence said convict to not exceeding six months imprisonment in the county jail.

*   *   *

2. APPRENTICE LAW

Sec. 1. . . . It shall be the duty of all sheriffs, justices of the peace, and other civil officers . . . to report to the probate courts of their respective counties semi-annually, at the January and July terms of said courts, all freedmen, free negroes, and mulattoes, under the age of eighteen, in their respective counties, beats or districts, who are orphans, or whose parent or parents have not the means or who refuse to provide for and support said minors; and thereupon it shall be the duty of said probate court to order the clerk of said court to apprentice said minors to some competent and suitable person, on such terms as the court may direct, having a particular care to the interest of said minor: *Provided*, that the former owner of said minors shall have the preference when, in the opinion of the court, he or she shall be a suitable person for that purpose.

*   *   *

Sec. 3. . . . In the management and control of said apprentice, said master or mistress shall have the power to inflict such moderate corporate chastisement as a father or guardian is allowed to inflict on his or her child or ward at common law: *Provided*, that in no case shall cruel or inhuman punishment be inflicted.

3. VAGRANT LAW

*   *   *

Sec. 2. . . . All freedmen, free negroes and mulattoes in this State, over the age of eighteen years, found on the second Monday in January, 1866, or thereafter, with no lawful employment or business, or found unlawfully assembling themselves together, either in the day or night time, and all white persons so assembling themselves with freedmen, free negroes or mulattoes, or usually associating with freedmen, free negroes or mulattoes, on terms of equality, or living in adultery or fornication with a freed woman, free negro or mulatto, shall be deemed vagrants, and on conviction thereof shall be fined in a sum not exceeding, in the case of a freedman, free negro or mulatto, fifty dollars, and a white man two hundred dollars, and imprisoned at the discretion of the court, the free negro not exceeding ten days, and the white man not exceeding six months. . . .

*   *   *

4. PENAL LAWS

Sec. 1. *Be it enacted* . . . That no freedman, free negro or mulatto, not in the military service of the United States government, and not licensed so to do by the board of police of his or her county, shall keep or carry fire-arms of any kind, or any ammunition, dirk or bowie knife, and on conviction thereof in the county court shall be punished by fine, not exceeding ten dollars, and pay the costs of such proceedings, and all such arms or ammunition shall be forfeited to the informer. . . .

Sec. 2. . . . Any freedman, free negro, or mulatto committing riots, routs, affrays, trespasses, malicious mischief, cruel treatment to animals, seditious speeches, insulting gestures, language, or acts, or assaults on any person, disturbance of the peace, exercising the function of a minister of the Gospel without a license from some regularly organized church, vending spirituous or intoxicating liquors, or committing any other misdemeanor, the punishment of which is not specifically provided for by law, shall, upon conviction thereof in the county court, be fined not less than ten dollars, and not more than one hundred dollars, and may be imprisoned at the discretion of the court, not exceeding thirty days.

Sec. 3. . . . If any white person shall sell, lend, or give to any freedman, free negro, or mulatto any fire-arms, dirk or bowie knife, or ammunition, or any spirituous or intoxicating liquors, such person or persons so offending, upon conviction thereof in the county court of his or her county, shall be fined not exceeding fifty dollars, and may be imprisoned, at the discretion of the court, not exceeding thirty days.

*   *   *

Sec. 5. . . . If any freedman, free negro, or mulatto, convicted of any of the misdemeanors provided against in this act, shall fail or refuse for the space of five days, after conviction, to pay the fine and costs imposed, such person shall be hired out by the sheriff or other officer, at public outcry, to any white person who will pay said fine and all costs, and take said convict for the shortest time.

139 "the late wicked Rebellion" (1866)

With Lee's surrender to Grant on April 9, 1865, the Civil War hostilities concluded. In August 1866 the new president, Andrew Johnson, declared that the emergency was over. In the same year, the United States Supreme Court asserted its authority by imposing limitations on the power of the executive to resort to martial law and to suspend the writ of habeas corpus safeguards.

Under the authority of Lincoln's proclamations, military authorities arrested Lambden P. Milligan, a civilian, and others in Indiana, a Union state, in October of 1864. A military commission tried Milligan (without the protections of Article III or the Bill of Rights), found him guilty of treason, and sentenced him to hang. After this conviction, a federal grand jury convened to investigate the same charges, but they returned no indictment. Milligan's challenge to the jurisdiction of the military tribunal to try a civil-

ian found its way to the Supreme Court after President Andrew Johnson restored the writ of habeas corpus.

In *Ex Parte Milligan* the court held that the suspension of the writ of habeas corpus permitted the military to arrest and hold persons without charge. The suspension of the writ, nevertheless, did not empower the military commissions to try and to sentence persons so held. The judicial branch alone had jurisdiction to try and to sentence civilians accused of crimes. Only when civil authority had been disrupted and martial law properly declared could military commissions, out of necessity, try and sentence accused persons. Although some justices suggested Congress could suspend civil authority and declare martial law in effect in peaceful zones, they held that the executive could not do so. Only when events precluded the operation of civilian courts could the military authorities unilaterally declare martial law and try civilians. The court concluded that Milligan's trial by military commission was constitutionally invalid.

The case delimits the executive's unilateral supplanting of local civilian authority in the absence of actual hostilities or perhaps a congressional determination of necessity. By so doing, the case acts as a restraint on the use of military authority to combat political crime.

☆ 139 *Ex Parte Milligan*

71 U.S. (4 Wall.) 2 (1866).

December 17, 1866, Mr. Justice DAVIS delivered the opinion of the court: . . .

During the late wicked Rebellion, the temper of the times did not allow that calmness in deliberation and discussion so necessary to a correct conclusion of a purely judicial question. Then, considerations of safety were mingled with the exercise of power; and feelings and interests prevailed which are happily terminated. Now that the public safety is assured, this question, as well as all others, can be discussed and decided without passion or the admixture of any element not required to form a legal judgment. We approach the investigation of this case, fully sensible of the magnitude of the inquiry and the necessity of full and cautious deliberation.

*   *   *

The controlling question in the case is this: Upon the facts stated in Milligan's petition, and the exhibits filed, had the Military Commission mentioned in it jurisdiction, legally, to try and sentence him? Milligan, not a resident of one of the rebellious States, or a prisoner of war, but a citizen of Indiana for twenty years past, and never in the military or naval service, is, while at his home, arrested by the military power of the United States, imprisoned and, on certain criminal charges preferred against him, tried, convicted and sentenced to be hanged by a military commission, organized under the direction of the military commander of the military district of Indiana. Had this tribunal the legal power and authority to try and punish this man?

No graver question was ever considered by this court, nor one which more nearly concerns the rights of the whole people; for it is the birthright of every American citizen when charged with crime, to be tried and punished according to law. The power of punishment is alone through the means which the laws have provided for that purpose, and if they are ineffectual, there is an immunity from punishment, no matter how great an offender the individual may be, or how much his crimes may have shocked the sense of justice of the country, or endangered its safety. By the protection of the law human rights are secured; withdraw that protection, and they are at the mercy of wicked rulers, or the clamor of an excited people. If there was law to justify this military trial, it is not our province to interfere; if there was not, it is our duty to declare the nullity of the whole proceedings. The decision of this question does not depend on argument or judicial precedents, numerous and highly illustrative as they are....

The provisions of [the Constitution] on the administration of criminal justice are too plain and direct to leave room for misconstruction or doubt of their true meaning. Those applicable to this case are found in that clause of the original Constitution which says, "That the trial of all crimes, except in case of impeachment, shall be by jury;" and in the fourth, fifth and sixth articles of the amendments....

Have any of the rights guarantied by the Constitution been violated in the case of Milligan? and if so, what are they?

Every trial involves the exercise of judicial power; and from what source did the Military Commission that tried him derive their authority? Certainly no part of the judicial power of the country was conferred on them; because the Constitution expressly vests it "in one Supreme Court and such inferior courts as the Congress may from time to time ordain and establish," and it is not pretended that the commission was a court ordained and established by Congress. They cannot justify on the mandate of the President; because he is controlled by law, and has his appropriate sphere of duty, which is to execute, not to make, the laws; and there is "no unwritten criminal code to which resort can be had as a source of jurisdiction."

But it is said that the jurisdiction is complete under the "laws and usages of war."

It can serve no useful purpose to inquire what those laws and usages are, whence they orginated, where found, and on whom they operate; they can never be applied to citizens in States which have upheld the authority of the government, and where the courts are open and their process unobstructed. This court has judicial knowledge that in Indiana the federal authority was always unopposed, and its courts always open to hear criminal accusations and redress grievances; and no usage of war could sanction a military trial there for any offense whatever of a citizen in civil life, in nowise connected with the military service. Congress could grant no such power; and to the honor of our National Legislature be it said, it has never been provoked by the state of the country even to attempt its exercise. One of the plainest constitutional provisions was, therefore, infringed when Milligan was tried by a court not ordained and established by Congress, and not composed of judges appointed during good behavior.

It is claimed that martial law covers with its broad mantle the proceedings of this Military Commission. The proposition is this: that in a time of war the commander of an armed force (if in his opinion the exigencies of the country demand it, and of which he is to judge), has the power, within the lines of his military district, to suspend all civil rights and their remedies, and subject citizens as well as soldiers to the rule of his will; and in the exercise of his lawful authority cannot be restrained, except by his superior officer or the President of the United States.

*   *   *

The statement of this proposition shows its importance; for, if true, republican government is a failure, and there is an end of liberty regulated by law. Martial law, established on such a basis, destroys every guaranty of the Constitution, and effectually renders the "military independent of and superior to the civil power." ... Civil liberty and this kind of martial law cannot endure together; the antagonism is irreconcilable and, in the conflict, one or the other must perish.

It is essential to the safety of every government that, in a great crisis, like the one we have just passed through, there should be a power somewhere of suspending the writ of *habeas corpus*. In every war, there are men of previously good character, wicked enough to counsel their fellow citizens to resist the measures deemed necessary by a good government to sustain its just authority and overthrow its enemies; and their influence may lead to dangerous combinations. In the emergency of the times, an immediate public investigation according to law may not be possible; and yet, the peril to the country may be too imminent to suffer such persons to go at large. Unquestionably, there is then an exigency which demands that the government, if it should see fit, in the exercise of a proper discretion, to make arrests, should not be required to produce the person arrested in answer to a writ of *habeas corpus*. The Constitution goes no further. It does not say after a writ of *habeas corpus* is denied a citizen, that he shall be tried otherwise than by the course of common law. If it had intended this result, it was easy by the use of direct words to have accomplished it.

It is difficult to see how the safety of the country required martial law in Indiana. If any of her citizens were plotting treason, the power of arrest could secure them, until the government was prepared for their trial, when the courts were open and ready to try them. . . .

It follows, from what has been said on this subject, that there are occasions when martial rule can be properly applied. If, in foreign invasion or civil war, the courts are actually closed, and it is impossible to administer criminal justice according to law, then, on the theater of active military operations, where war really prevails, there is a necessity to furnish a substitute for the civil authority, thus overthrown, to preserve the safety of the army and society; and as no power is left but the military, it is allowed to govern by martial rule until the laws can have their free course. As necessity creates the rule, so it limits its duration; for, if this government is continued after the courts are reinstated, it is a gross usurpation of power. Martial rule can never exist where the courts are open, and in the proper and unobstructed exercise of their jurisdiction. It is also confined to the locality of actual war. Because, during the late Rebellion it could have been enforced in Virginia, where the national authority was overturned and the courts driven out, it does not follow that it should obtain in Indiana, where that authority was never disputed, and justice was always administered. And so in the case of a foreign invasion, martial rule may become a necessity, in one State, when, in another, it would be "mere lawless violence."

*   *   *

. . . If these averments were true (and their truth is conceded for the purposes of this case), the court was required to liberate him on taking certain oaths prescribed by the law, and entering into recognizance for his good behavior.

But it is insisted that Milligan was a prisoner of war and, therefore, excluded from the privileges of the statute. It is not easy to see how he can be treated as a prisoner of war, when he lived in Indiana for the past twenty years, was arrested there, and had not been, during the late troubles, a resident of any of the States in rebellion. If in Indiana he conspired with bad men to assist the enemy, he is punishable for it in the courts of Indiana; but, when tried for the offense, he cannot plead the rights of war; for he was not engaged in legal acts of hostility against the government, and only such persons, when captured, are prisoners of war. If he cannot enjoy the immunities attaching to the character of a prisoner of war, how can he be subject to their pains and penalties?

*   *   *

140 "any office of honor, trust, or profit" (1867)

Federal and state loyalty oaths were not new, but after the war they became widespread. These all-encompassing oaths were a prerequisite for voting, for holding public office or employment, and for engaging in certain occupations. Those of uncertain political loyalties were to be relegated to second-class citizenship.

Cummings was a Roman Catholic priest convicted of treason and preaching without complying with Missouri's oath requirement. In *Cummings* the Supreme Court struck down the oath as unconstitutional, because it violated Article I, Section 9, which prohibits bills of attainder (legislative acts that inflict punishments without a judicial trial) and ex post facto laws (laws that impose punishment for acts not punishable at the time committed).

In *Garland* the court scrutinized a similar federal oath for the practice of law in federal courts. Protective of the rights of dissenters and private citizens, these decisions also produced adverse side effects. The apparent judicial leniency provided ammunition to the new members of the Radical Republican party in Congress. They argued that the moderate treatment of the postwar South, begun by Lincoln and continued by Johnson—who on June 6, 1865, released the bulk of the Confederate prisoners of war—enabled the South to escape the rebellion without punishment or retribution. Beginning in March 1867 the Congress passed a series of reconstruction acts, which placed portions of the South under martial law, restricted the power of the president, encouraged the reign of the "carpetbaggers," and brought about the impeachment of Andrew Johnson.

☆ 140 The Loyalty Oath Cases

☆ 140a *Cummings v. Missouri*

71 U.S. (4 Wall.) 356 (1867).

. . . The indictment was under the . . . 6th . . . section of the Constitution of Missouri, which [is] as follows:

Sec. 6. "The oath to be taken as aforesaid, shall be known as the oath of loyalty, and shall be in the following terms:

'I, A. B., do solemnly swear that I am well acquainted with the terms of the 3d section of the 2d article of the Constitution of the State of Missouri, adopted in the year 1865, and have carefully considered the same; that I have never, directly or indirectly, done any of the acts in said section specified; that I have always been truly and loyally on the side of the United States against all enemies thereof, foreign and domestic; that I will bear true faith and allegiance to the United States, and will support the Constitution and laws thereof as the supreme law of the land, any law or ordinance of any State to the contrary notwithstanding; that I will, to the best of my ability, protect and defend the Union of the United States, and not allow the same to be broken up and dissolved, or the government thereof to be distroyed or overthrown under any circumstances, if in my power to prevent it; that I will support the Constitution of the State of Missouri; that I make this oath without any mental reservation or evasion, and hold it to be binding on me.' "

*   *   *

Mr. Justice FIELD delivered the opinion of the court:

This case . . . involves a consideration of the test oath imposed by the Constitution of [Missouri]. The plaintiff in error is a priest of the Roman Catholic Church, and was indicted and convicted in one of the circuit courts of the State of the crime of teaching and preaching as a priest and minister of that religious denomination without having first taken the oath, and was sentenced to pay a fine of $500. . . .

The oath prescribed by the [Missouri] Constitution, divided into its separable parts, embraces more than thirty distinct affirmations or tests. . . . It requires the affiant to deny not only that he has ever "been in armed hostility to the United States, or to the lawful authorities thereof," but, among other things, that he has ever, "by act or word," manifested his adherence to the cause of the enemies of the United States, foreign or domestic, or his desire for their triumph over the arms of the United States; or his sympathy with those engaged in rebellion, or has ever harbored or aided any person engaged in guerilla warfare against the loyal inhabitants of the United States; or has ever entered or left the State for the purpose of avoiding enrollment or draft in the military service of the United States; or, to escape the performance of duty in the militia of the United States; has ever indicated, in any terms, his disaffection to the Government of the United States in its contest with the Rebellion.

Every person who is unable to take this oath is declared incapable of holding in the State, "any office of honor, trust or profit under its authority, or of being an officer, councilman, director or trustee, or other manager of any corporation, public or private, now existing or hereafter established by its authority, or of acting as a professor or teacher in any educational institution, or in any common or other school, or of holding any real estate or other prop-

erty in trust for the use of any church, religious society or congregation."

*   *   *

Qualifications relate to the fitness or capacity of the party for a particular pursuit or profession. . . . It is evident from the nature of the pursuits and professions of the parties, placed under disabilities by the Constitution of Missouri, that many of the acts, from the taint of which they must purge themselves, have no possible relation to their fitness for those pursuits and professions. There can be no connection between the fact that Mr. Cummings entered or left the State of Missouri to avoid enrollment or draft in the military service of the United States, and his fitness to teach the doctrines or administer the sacraments of his church. . . . [The oath] was exacted, not from any notion that the several acts designated indicated unfitness for the callings, but because it was thought that the several acts deserved punishment, and that for many of them there was no way to inflict punishment except by depriving the parties who had committed them of some of the rights and privileges of the citizen.

The clauses in the Missouri Constitution . . . were intended especially to operate upon parties who, in some form or manner, by actions or words directly or indirectly, had aided or countenanced the Rebellion, or sympathized with parties engaged in the Rebellion, or had endeavored to escape the proper responsibilities and duties of a citizen in time of war; and they were intended to operate by depriving such persons of the right to hold certain offices and trusts, and to pursue their ordinary and regular avocations. . . . To make the enjoyment of a right dependent upon an impossible condition is equivalent to an absolute denial of the right under any condition, and such denial, enforced for a past act, is nothing less than punishment imposed for that act. It is a misapplication of terms to call it anything else.

Now, some of the acts to which the expurgatory oath is directed were not offenses at the time they were committed. It was no offense against any law to enter or leave the State of Missouri for the purpose of avoiding enrollment or draft in the military service of the United States, however much the evasion of such service might be the subject of moral censure. Clauses which prescribe a penalty for an act of this nature are within the terms of the definition of an *ex post facto* law — "they impose a punishment for an act not punishable at the time it was committed."

*   *   *

And this is not all. The clauses in question subvert the presumptions of innocence, and alter the rules of evidence. . . . They assume that the parties are guilty; they call upon the parties to establish their innocence; and they declare that such innocence can be shown only in one way—by an inquisition, in the form of an expurgatory oath, into the consciences of the parties.

[*Reversed.*]

☆ 140b *Ex Parte Garland*

71 U.S. (4 Wall.) 333 (1867).

FIELD, J.

*   *   *

The petitioner . . . now produces his pardon, and asks permission to continue to practise as an attorney and counsellor of the court without taking the oath required by the act of January 24, 1865, and the rule of the court, which he is unable to take, by reason of the offices he held under the Confederate government. He rests his application principally upon two grounds:

1st. That the act of January 24, 1865, so far as it affects his status in the court, is unconstitutional and void; and,

2. That, if the act be constitutional, he is released from compliance with its provisions by the pardon of the President. . . .

The statute is directed against parties who have offended in any of the particulars embraced by these clauses. And its object is to exclude them from the profession of the law, or at least from its practice in the courts of the United States. As the oath prescribed cannot be taken by these parties, the act, as against them, operates as a legislative decree of perpetual exclusion. And exclusion from any of the professions or any of the ordinary avocations of life for past conduct can be regarded in no other light than as punishment for such conduct. The exaction of the oath is the mode provided for ascertaining the parties upon whom the act is intended to operate, and instead of lessening, increases its objectionable character. All enactments of this kind partake of the nature of bills of pains and penalties, and are subject to the constitutional inhibition against the passage of bills of attainder, under which general designation they are included.

*   *   *

. . . They are officers of the court, admitted as such by its order, upon evidence of their possessing sufficient legal learning and fair private character. . . . They hold their office during good behavior, and can only be deprived of it for misconduct ascertained and declared by the judgment of the court after opportunity to be heard has been afforded. Their admission or their exclusion is not the exercise of a mere ministerial power. It is the exercise of judicial power, and has been so held in numerous cases. . . .

. . . The question, in this case, is not as to the power of Congress to prescribe qualifications, but whether that power has been exercised as a means for the infliction of punishment, against the prohibition of the Constitution. . . .

This view is strengthened by a consideration of the effect of the pardon produced by the petitioner, and the nature of the pardoning power of the President.

The Constitution provides that the President "shall have power to grant reprieves and pardons for offenses against the United States, except in cases of impeachment."

The power thus conferred is unlimited, with the exception stated. It extends to every offense known to the law, and may be exercised at any time after its commission, either before legal proceedings are taken, or during their pendency, or after conviction and judgment. This power of the President is not subject to legislative control. Congress can neither limit the effect of his pardon, nor exclude from its exercise any class of offenders. The benign prerogative of mercy reposed in him cannot be fettered by any legislative restrictions.

. . . A pardon reaches both the punishment prescribed for the offense and the guilt of the offender; and when the pardon is full, it releases the punishment and blots out of existence the guilt, so that in the eye of the law the offender is as innocent as if he had never committed the offense. . . . The pardon produced by the petitioner is a full pardon "for all offenses by him committed, arising from participation, direct or implied, in the Rebellion," and is subject to certain conditions which have been complied with. The effect of this pardon is to relieve the petitioner from all penalties and disabilities attached to the offense of treason, committed by his participation in the Rebellion. So far as that offense is concerned, he is thus placed beyond the reach of punishment of any kind. But to exclude him, by reason of that offense, from continuing in the enjoyment of a previously acquired right, is to enforce a punishment for that offense notwithstanding the pardon. If such exclusion can be effected by the exaction of an expurgatory oath covering the offense, the pardon may be avoided, and that accomplished indirectly which cannot be reached by direct legislation. It is not within the constitutional power of Congress to inflict punishment beyond the reach of executive clemency. From the petitioner, therefore, the oath required by the act of January 24th, 1865, could not be exacted, even if that act were not subject to any other objection than the one thus stated.

It follows, from the views expressed, that the prayer of the petitioner must be granted. . . . And it is so ordered.

141 "until loyal and republican State governments can be legally established" (1867)

Despite the conciliatory actions of presidents Lincoln and Johnson, the Congress of the United States, controlled by the Radical Republicans, undertook to suspend the still-functioning governments of the states that had joined the Confederacy. In addition to establishing military governments in place of state civil authority, these acts provided the terms for the states' "readmission" into the Union. The principal feature of these reconstruction acts was to require the rebellious states to adopt new constitutions drawn up by conventions elected by universal manhood suffrage, excepting those who had supported the rebellion. The conventions, as a result, were loaded with blacks and newly arrived whites from the North—carpetbaggers. Moreover, the states were not to be readmitted until they had ratified the then-proposed Fourteenth Amendment to the United States Constitution.

Once again, the use of military government, loyalty oaths, and restrictions on the franchise provided the mechanisms by which the ascendant political power attempted to insulate and enshrine itself in power over a recalcitrant population.

☆ 141 An Act to Provide for the More Efficient Government of the Rebel States

14 Stat. 428 (1867).

WHEREAS no legal State governments or adequate protection for life or property now exists in the rebel States of Virginia, North Carolina, South Carolina, Georgia, Mississippi, Alabama, Louisiana, Florida, Texas, and Arkansas; and whereas it is necessary that peace and good order should be enforced in said States until loyal and republican State governments can be legally established: Therefore,

Be it enacted by the Senate and House of Representatives of the United States of America in Congress assembled, That said rebel States shall be divided into military districts and made subject to the military authority of the United States as hereinafter prescribed, and for that purpose Virginia shall constitute the first district; North Carolina and South Carolina the second district; Georgia, Alabama, and Florida the third district; Mississippi and Arkansas the fourth district; and Louisiana and Texas the fifth district.

SEC. 2. *And be it further enacted,* That it shall be the duty of the President to assign to the command of each of said districts an officer of the army, not below the rank of brigadier-general, and to detail a sufficient military force to enable such officer to perform his duties and enforce his authority within the district to which he is assigned.

SEC. 3. *And be it further enacted,* That it shall be the duty of each officer assigned as aforesaid, to protect all persons in their rights of person and property, to suppress insurrection, disorder, and violence, and to punish, or cause to be punished, all disturbers of the public peace and criminals; and to this end he may allow local civil tribunals to take jurisdiction of and to try offenders, or, when in his judgment it may be necessary for the trial of offenders, he shall have power to organize military commissions or tribunals for that purpose, and all interference under color of State authority with the exercise of military authority under this act, shall be null and void.

SEC. 4. *And be it further enacted,* That all persons put under military arrest by virtue of this act shall be tried without unnecessary delay, and no cruel or unusual punishment shall be inflicted, and no sentence of any military commission or tribunal hereby authorized, affecting the life or liberty of any person, shall be executed until it is approved by the officer in command of the district, and the laws and regulations for the government of the army shall not be affected by this act, except in so far as they conflict with its provisions: *Provided,* That no sentence of death under the provisions of this act shall be carried into effect without the approval of the President.

*   *   *

142 The Caged Eagle (1867–1871)

After the conclusion of the Civil War, federal troops apprehended Confederate president Jefferson Davis, Mrs. Davis, and several officials of the secessionist government. An editorial in the *New York Times* called for Jefferson Davis's trial on treason charges in order to establish that "the attempted secession was not only a failure but a crime." Lengthy political discussions led to the decision that Davis should be tried for treason in a federal circuit court in Virginia. But Chief Justice Salmon P. Chase refused to hold court in Richmond, which was under martial law. Davis was confined at Fort Monroe for two years before the formal charges were pressed. Although his wife and family accompanied him, and his friends freely visited him (in the European tradition of Festungs arrest—confinement without the usual ardors of prison—accorded to political offenders), he complained of the continuing uncertainty and sought parole, speedy trial, or release on bail. The following excerpt from an argument of Davis's lawyer, Charles O'Conor, urged that the circumstances of the Civil War were such that treason was not a proper charge. Of importance to the distinction between traitor and failed patriot was the assertion of the powers of war by the victorious party.

Davis was released on $100,000 bail on May 13, having been the last of the confined captives. After argument, a motion to quash his indictment was certified to the Supreme Court. The Court rendered no decision on the question. Johnson's proclamation of amnesty in 1868 mooted the possibility of a judicial resolution of the question, and the government took no further action. Davis died in New Orleans twenty-two years later at age eighty-one.

☆ 142 On Behalf of Jefferson Davis — Seeking Bail or Parole

Case of Davis, 7 F. Cas. 63 (C.C.D. Va., 1867-71) (No. 3,621a).

[Argument of Charles O'Conor, Davis's lawyer]

*   *   *

When traitors and rebels oppose their government by open violence, and are summarily put down, those not slain in the combat may fairly be tried for treason in the civil courts and dealt with as ordinary criminals. The transaction constitutes only a species of riot. But far different results ensue when rebellion maintains itself so long and so effectively as to compel between itself, its people and their territory, on the one hand, and the lawful government on the other, an institution and acceptance of the rules and usages which obtain in regular wars between independent nations. Amongst men claiming to have attained a high civilization, war is recognized as a state or condition governed by law. In its conduct or at its close, morality and justice are not lost sight of. If successful, the rebels acquire the power of establishing an independent state, which all men regard as not only legitimate but honorable in its origin; if they fail, the victor may be as indulgent as he will, or as far as he dare may consecrate to his revenge the field of their ruin. Whatever severity can be justified at the bar of public opinion, may be practiced; and certainty no more should be exercised. To the latter proposition every magnanimous spirit will assent. Washington might have failed: Kosciuszko did fail. Trials for treason in the civil courts are not remedies adapted to the close of a great civil war. Honor forbids a resort to them after combatants in open war have recognized each other as soldiers and gentlemen engaged in a legitimate conflict. After they have established truces, exchanged prisoners, and thus made applicable to their hostile intercourse, the laws of chivalry, based upon an acknowledgment of mutual confidence and respect, the rules and usages of war can not in any event be departed from by either. It would be shockingly indecorous for the ultimate victor in such a conflict to send his vanquished opponent before the civil magistrate to be tried as if he were a mere thief or rioter.

*   *   *

. . . After an open territorial war of this kind had existed for four years, it might be thought by some that the rebels were still simply criminal violators of the municipal law; and that they ought to be dealt with as such. By the way of reasoning it might be urged that the extent of their operations merely intensified their guilt, and should not in any way affect the question. But this reasoning, if such it may be called, proves too much. On the fall of a rebellious state, after sustaining a belligerent attitude for one hundred years, its chiefs and leaders might, with equal propriety, be brought to trial as traitors in civil courts, although they and their ancestors had for several generations, been uniformly regarded and treated as public enemies carrying on against the ultimate victor a regular national war. This can not be admitted. The law of nature forbids it; and there are broad and comprehensive doctrines deducible from the universal practice of nations which forbid it. And these doctrines are founded in necessity as well as in reason and justice.

Taking, under positive written law, the narrowest technical view of the subject, one is led to a like result. . . .

*   *   *

. . . Once the lawful government acknowledges the actual existence of public territorial belligerency, and exercises the rights consequent thereon, including the conversion of the opposite party into a public enemy whose acts, as those of a sovereign de facto, are imputable to all within his territory however innocent, thus impressing upon such persons a hostile character, the preliminary action which may have been treason when it occurred, is divested of that character, and is no longer judicially cognizable as such. It is no longer susceptible of a separate consideration and must thenceforth be regarded only as an introductory step which has become part and parcel of the supervening war thus regularly instituted. Technically it is regarded as an incident merged in the principal transaction. A conflict marked by the features alluded to, is to be deemed a regular and formal public war, because it has been clothed with that character by the government itself.

*   *   *

143 "who . . . shall have engaged in insurrection" (1868)

The Fourteenth Amendment not only recognizes the privilege of federal citizenship and affirms the right to equal justice, it also contains punitive features. Section 4 prohibits the United States or any state from assuming or paying any debt or obligation incurred in aid of the Southern war effort. Thus, those who engaged in commercial transactions with the Confederacy and lent money or accepted Confederate specie for payment were penalized economically. Section 3 also exacts a political penalty, which President Andrew Johnson's subsequent full pardon could not lift. The provision stripped the South of most of its mature and proven political leadership.

☆143 United States Constitution, Amendment XIV

Section 1. All persons born or naturalized in the United States and subject to the jurisdiction thereof, are citizens of the United States and of the State wherein they reside. No State shall make or enforce any law which shall abridge the privileges or immunities of citizens of the United States; nor shall any state deprive any person of life, liberty, or property, without due process of law, nor deny to any person within its jurisdiction the equal protection of the laws.

*   *   *

Section 3. No person shall be a Senator or Representative in Congress, or elector of President and Vice President, or hold any office, civil or military, under the United States, or under any State, who, having previously taken an oath, as a member of Congress, or as an officer of the United States, or as a member of any State legislature, or as an executive or judicial officer of any State, to support the Constitution of the United States, shall have engaged in insurrection against the same, or given aid or comfort to the enemies thereof. But Congress may by a vote of two-thirds of each House, remove such disability.

*   *   *

144 "unconditionally, and without reservation, . . . a full pardon" (1868)

On December 8, 1863, in the midst of the Civil War, President Lincoln issued a Proclamation of Amnesty and Reconstruction, a leniency program for pardoning all rebels (except high officials of the Confederacy and military officers who had joined the South) upon their taking a loyalty oath to the federal government. That proclamation also set out to restore self-government in the seceded states when one-tenth of the voting population took the prescribed oath and organized a loyal regime.

President Andrew Johnson followed Lincoln's lenient yet conditional policies in his first amnesty proclamation of May 29, 1865. Johnson announced the final, comprehensive pardon on Christmas Day, 1868. By so doing he reenfranchised those who had

been excluded from the political process by virtue of the reconstruction acts. Their renewed political power would soon assert itself against the federally supported governments of the Southern states.

☆144 President Andrew Johnson's Amnesty Proclamation (December 25, 1868)

15 Stat. 711 (1868).

*   *   *

[W]hereas, the authority of the Federal Government having been re-established in all the States and Territories within the jurisdiction of the United States, . . . and that a universal amnesty and pardon for participation in said rebellion extended to all who have borne any part therein will tend to secure permanent peace, order, and prosperity throughout the land, and to renew and fully restore confidence and fraternal feeling among the whole people, and their respect for and attachment to the National Government, designed by its patriotic founders for the general good:

Now, therefore, be it known that I, ANDREW JOHNSON, . . . hereby proclaim and declare unconditionally, and without reservation, to all and to every person who directly or indirectly participated in the late insurrection or rebellion, a full pardon and amnesty for the offence of treason against the United States, or of adhering to their enemies during the late civil war, with restoration of all rights, privileges, and immunities under the Constitution and the laws which have been made in pursuance thereof.

In testimony whereof, I have signed these presents with my hand, and have caused the seal of the United States to be hereunto affixed.

*   *   *

ANDREW JOHNSON

By the President:

F. W. SEWARD, Acting Secretary of State

145 "are you opposed to negro equality, both social and political?" (1868)

The Ku Klux Klan, founded at Pulaski, Tennessee, in 1865, was one of the largest secret organizations flourishing in the South during Reconstruction. The Order was effective in combating the emergence of black rights in the South and undercutting federal Reconstruction policies. Following reports of lawlessness and violence, the organization formally disbanded in 1869, although its clandestine operations continued.

The Knights of the White Camelia, a lower order of the K.K.K., similarly were dedicated, through violence and intimidation, to preventing blacks from exercising the newly won rights of citizenship. The charge to initiates began by stressing the evidence of white superiority and declaring the objective of "regenerating" the United States "from the humiliating condition to which it has lately been reduced."

These organizing documents are a curious blend of high principle and low purpose—much of it illegal. Nevertheless, these organizations were dedicated to the maintenance of the social and political status quo ante and may be regarded as an underground resistance wing of a broader political movement. They reflect as well the principle of providing a fundamental organizational framework to which allegiance, beyond that owed to the state, may be expected mutually from each member and against which claims of illegality provide an ineffective and illegitimate defense to nonadherence.

☆ 145 The Secret Organizations of the Reconstruction

☆ 145a Organization and Principles of the Ku Klux Klan

Reprinted in W. L. Fleming, ed., *The Ku Klux Klan: Its Origin, Growth, and Disbandment* (New York: Neale, 1905), 154.

CHARACTER AND OBJECTS OF THE ORDER

This is an institution of Chivalry, Humanity, Mercy, and Patriotism; embodying in its genius and its principles all that is chivalric in conduct, noble in sentiment, generous in manhood, and patriotic in purpose; its peculiar objects being

First: To protect the weak, the innocent, and the defenseless, from the indignities, wrongs, and outrages of the lawless, the violent, and the brutal; to relieve the injured and oppressed; to succor the suffering and unfortunate, and especially the widows and orphans of Confederate soldiers.

Second: To protect and defend the Constitution of the United States, and all laws passed in conformity thereto, and to protect the States and the people thereof from all invasion from any source whatever.

Third: To aid and assist in the execution of all constitutional laws, and to protect the people from unlawful seizure, and from trial except by their peers in conformity to the laws of the land.

INTERROGATIONS TO BE ASKED

*   *   *

4th. Did you belong to the Federal army during the late war, and fight against the South during the existence of the same?

5th. Are you opposed to negro equality, both social and political?

6th. Are you in favor of a white man's government in this country?

7th. Are you in favor of Constitutional liberty, and a Government of equitable laws instead of a Government of violence and oppression?

8th. Are you in favor of maintaining the Constitutional rights of the South?

☆ 145b Charge to Initiates of the Knights of the White Camelia

Reprinted in W. L. Fleming, ed., *Documents Relating to Reconstruction* (Morgantown: University of West Virginia, 1904), 22-29.

[QUESTIONS ASKED THE CANDIDATE]

1. Do you belong to the white race? Ans.—I do.

2. Did you ever marry any woman who did not, or does not, belong to the white race? Ans.—No.

3. Do you promise never to marry any woman but one who belongs to the white race? Ans.—I do.

4. Do you believe in the superiority of your race? Ans.—I do.

5. Will you promise never to vote for any one for any office of honor, profit or trust, who does not belong to your race? Ans.—I do.

6. Will you take a solemn oath never to abstain from casting your vote at any election in which a candidate of the negro race shall be opposed to a white man attached to your principles, unless prevented by severe illness or any other physical disability? Ans.—I will.

7. Are you opposed to allowing the control of the political affairs of this country to go in whole or in part, into the hands of the African race, and will you do everything in your power to prevent it? Ans.—Yes.

8. Will you devote your intelligence, energy and influence to a furtherance and propagation of the principles of our Order? A.—I will.

9. Will you, under all circumstances, defend and protect persons of the white race in their lives, rights and property, against all encroachments or invasions from any inferior race, and especially the African? A.—Yes.

10. Are you willing to take an oath forever to cherish these grand principles, and to unite yourself with others who, like you, believing in their truth, have firmly bound themselves to stand by and defend them against all? Ans.—I am.

The C[ommander] shall then say: If you consent to join our Association, raise your right hand and I will administer to you the oath which we have all taken: . . .

[CHARGE TO INITIATES]

Brothers: You have been initiated into one of the most important Orders which have ever been established on this continent: an Order, which, if its principles are faithfully observed and its objects diligently carried out, is destined to regenerate our unfortunate country and to relieve the White Race from the humiliating condition to which it has lately been reduced in this Republic. . . .

As you may have already gathered from the questions which were propounded to you, and which you have answered so satisfactorily, and from the clauses of the Oath which you have taken, our main and fundamental object is the MAINTENANCE OF THE SUPREMACY OF THE WHITE RACE in this Republic. History and physiology teach us that we belong to a race which nature has endowed with an evident superiority over all other races, and that the Maker, in thus elevating us above the common standard of human creation, has intended to give us over inferior races, a dominion from which no human laws can permanently derogate. The experience of ages demonstrates that, from the origin of the world, this dominion has always remained in the hands of the Caucasian Race; whilst all the other races have constantly occupied a subordinate and secondary position; a fact which triumphantly confirms this great law of nature. Powerful nations have succeeded each other on the face of the world, and have marked their passage by glorious and memorable deeds; and among those who have thus left on this globe indelible traces of their splendor and greatness, we find none but descended from the Caucasian stock. We see, on the contrary, that most of the countries inhabited by the other races have remained in a state of complete barbarity; whilst the small number of those who have advanced beyond this savage existence, have, for centuries, stagnated in a semi-barbarous condition of which there can be no progress or improvement. And it is a remarkable fact that as a race of men is more remote from the Caucasian and approaches nearer to the black African, the more fatally that stamp of inferiority is affixed to its sons, and irrevocably dooms them to eternal imperfectibility and degradation.

Convinced that we are of these elements of [white supremacy], we know, besides, that the government of our Republic was established by white men, for white men alone, and that it never was in the contemplation of its founders that it should fall into the hands of an inferior and degraded race. We hold, therefore, that any attempt to wrest from the white race the management of its affairs in order to transfer it to control of the black population, is an invasion of the sacred prerogatives vouchsafed to us by the Constitution, and a violation of the laws established by God himself; that such encroachments are subversive of the established institutions of our Republic, and that no individual of the white race can submit to them without humiliation and shame.

It, then, becomes our solemn duty, as white men, to resist strenuously and persistently those attempts against our natural and constitutional rights, and to do everything in our power in order to maintain, in this Republic, the supremacy of the Caucasian race, and restrain the black or African race to that condition of social and political inferiority for which God has destined it. This is the object for which our Order was instituted; and, in carrying it out, we intend to infringe no laws, to violate no rights, and to resort to no forcible means, except for purposes of legitimate and necessary defense.

As an essential condition of success, this Order proscribes absolutely all social equality between the races. If we were to admit persons of African race on the same level with ourselves, a state of personal relations would follow which would unavoidably lead to political equality; for it would be a virtual recognition of *status*, after which we could not consistently deny them an equal share in the administration of our public affairs. The man who is good enough to be our familiar companion, is good enough also to participate in our political government; and if we were to grant the one, there could be no good reason for us not to concede the other of these two privileges.

. . . [T]herefore, we take the obligation TO OBSERVE A MARKED DISTINCTION BETWEEN THE TWO RACES, not only in the relations of public affairs, but also in the more intimate dealings and intercourse of private life. . . .

[L]et me charge you specially in relation to one of your most important duties as one of its members. Our statutes make us bound to respect sedulously the rights of the colored inhabitants of this Republic, and in every instance, to give to them whatever lawfully belongs to them. It is an act of simple justice not to deny them any of the privileges to which they are legitimately entitled. . . . Besides, it would be ungenerous for us to undertake to restrict them to the narrowest limits as to the exercise of certain rights, without conceding to them, at the same time, the fullest measure of those which we recognize as theirs. . . .

From the brief explanation which I have just given you, you must have satisfied yourselves that our Association is not a political party, and has no connection with any of the organized parties of the day. . . . You may meet here, congregated together, men who belong to all the political organizations which now divide, or may divide, this country; you see some whom embittered feuds and irreconcilable hatred have long and widely separated; they have all cast away these rankling feelings to unite cordially and zealously in the labors of our great undertaking. Let their example be to you a useful lesson of the disinterestedness and devotedness which should characterize our efforts for the success of our cause!

146 "citizens . . . of every race and color" (1866-1875)

Between 1866 and 1875, Congress passed seven acts (including one reenactment) protecting the freed slaves from hostile social and political conditions. Congress would not legislate any further significant civil rights measures until 1957, eighty-two years later.

The first Civil Rights Act, passed on April 9, 1866, in response to the enactment of the Black Codes, declared that all persons born in the United States, whatever their race or color, were citizens thereof and entitled to the same rights in every state as white citizens. Doubts were raised concerning the power of Congress to enact such a law, there being no provision in the Constitution giving Congress the power to define citizenship or to regulate the civil rights of state citizens. Despite the Civil War and the Thirteenth Amendment, the *Dred Scott* case was still the law on the subject of citizenship. Only with the Fourteenth Amendment, which was ratified on July 9, 1868, were the issues of both national and state citizenship resolved and an injunction imposed upon the states to respect the privileges and immunities of United States citizens and not deny any person due process or the equal protection of the laws. Thus *Dred Scott* was overturned, and the great question of primacy of sovereignty—a major cause of political dissension and the Civil War—supposedly was resolved. Conflicts between the commands of state and federal laws governing the social and political relations of whites and blacks nevertheless continued.

☆ 146 The Civil Rights Acts

☆ 146a Civil Rights Act of 1866

14 Stat. 27 (1866).

Be it enacted by the Senate and House of Representatives of the United States of America in Congress assembled, That all persons born in the United States and not subject to any foreign power, excluding Indians not taxed, are hereby declared to be citizens of the United States; and such citizens, of every race and color, without regard to any previous condition of slavery or involuntary servitude, except as a punishment for crime whereof the party shall have been duly convicted, shall have the same right, in every State and Territory in the United States, to make and enforce contracts, to sue, be parties, and give evidence, to inherit, purchase, lease, sell, hold, and convey real and personal property, and to full and equal benefit of all laws and proceedings for the security of person and property, as is enjoyed by white citizens, and shall be subject to like punishment, pains, and penalties, and to none other, any law, statute, ordinance, regulation, or custom, to the contrary notwithstanding.

SEC. 2. *And be it further enacted*, That any person who, under color of any law, statute, ordinance, regulation, or custom, shall subject, or cause to be subjected, any inhabitant of any State or Territory to the deprivation of any right secured or protected by this act, or to different punishment, pains, or penalties on account of such person having at any time been held in a condition of slavery or involuntary servitude, except as a punishment for crime whereof the party shall have been duly convicted, or by reason of his color or race, than is prescribed for the punishment of white persons, shall be deemed guilty of a misdemeanor, and, on conviction, shall be punished by fine not exceeding one thousand dollars, or imprisonment not exceeding one year, or both, in the discretion of the court.

*   *   *

SEC. 6. *And be it further enacted*, That any person who shall knowingly and wilfully obstruct, hinder, or prevent any officer, or other person charged with the execution of any warrant or process issued under the provisions of this act . . . [shall] be subject to a fine not exceeding one thousand dollars, and imprisonment not exceeding six months. . . .

*   *   *

☆ 146b Civil Rights Act of 1870 (The Enforcement Act)

16 Stat. 140 (1870).

Be it enacted by the Senate and House of Representatives of the United States of America in Congress assembled, That all citizens of the United States who are or shall be otherwise qualified by law to vote at any election . . . shall be entitled and allowed to vote at all such elections, without distinction of race, color, or previous condition of servitude. . . .

SEC. 2. *And be it further enacted*, That it shall be the duty of every . . . person and officer to give to all citizens of the United States the same and equal opportunity to perform [any] prerequisite, and to become qualified to vote without distinction of race, color, or previous condition of servitude; and if any . . . person or officer shall refuse or knowingly omit to give full effect to this section, he shall . . . be deemed guilty of a misdemeanor, and shall, on conviction thereof, be fined not less than five hundred dollars, or be imprisoned not less than one month and not more than one year, or both, at the discretion of the court.

*   *   *

SEC. 6. *And be it further enacted*, That if two or more persons shall band or conspire together, or go in disguise upon the public highway, or upon the premises of another, with intent to violate any provision of this act, or to injure, oppress, threaten, or intimidate any citizen with intent to prevent or hinder his free exercise and enjoyment of any right or privilege granted or secured to him by the Constitution or laws of the United States, or because of his having exercised the same, such persons shall be held guilty of felony, and, on conviction thereof, shall be fined or imprisoned, or both, at the discretion of the court, — the fine not to exceed five thousand dollars, and the imprisonment not to exceed ten years, — and shall, moreover, be thereafter ineligible to, and disabled from holding, any office or place of honor, profit, or trust created by the Constitution or laws of the United States.

*   *   *

SEC. 17. *And be it further enacted*, That any person who, under color of any law, statute, ordinance, regulation, or custom, shall subject, or cause to be subjected, any inhabitant of any State or Territory to the deprivation of any right secured or protected by the last preceding section [giving all persons the same rights as white citizens] of this act, or to different punishment, pains, or penalties on account of such person being an alien, or by reason of his color or race, than is prescribed for the punishment of citizens, shall be deemed guilty of a misdemeanor, and, on conviction, shall be punished by fine not exceeding one thousand dollars, or imprisonment not exceeding one year, or both, in the discretion of the court.

☆ 146c Civil Rights Act of 1871

17 Stat. 13 (1871).

*   *   *

SEC. 2. That if two or more persons within any State or Territory of the United States shall conspire together to overthrow, or to put down, or to destroy by force the government of the United States, or to levy war against the United States, or to oppose by force the authority of the government of the United States, or by force, intimidation, or threat to prevent, hinder, or delay the execution of any law of the United States, or by force to seize, take, or possess any property of the United States contrary to the authority thereof, or by force, intimidation, or threat to prevent any person from accepting or holding any office or trust or place of confidence under the United States, or from discharging the duties thereof, or by force, intimidation, or threat to induce any officer of the United States to leave any State, district, or place where his duties as such officer might lawfully be performed, or to injure him in his person or property on account of his lawful discharge of the duties of his office, or to injure his person while engaged in the lawful discharge of the duties of his office, or to injure his property so as to molest, interrupt, hinder, or impede him in the discharge of his official duty, or by force, intimidation, or threat to deter any party or witness in any court of the United States from attending such court, or from testifying in any matter pending in such court fully, freely, and truthfully, or to injure any such party or witness in his person or property on account of his having so attended or testified, or by force, intimidation, or threat to influence the verdict, presentment, or indictment, of any juror or grand juror in any court of the United States, or to injure such juror in his person or property on account of any verdict, presentment, or indictment lawfully assented to by him, or on account of his being or having been such juror, or shall conspire together, or go in disguise upon the public highway or upon the premises of another for the purpose, either directly or indirectly, of depriving any person or any class of persons of the equal protection of the laws, or of equal privileges or immunities under the laws, or for the purpose of preventing or hindering the constituted authorities of any State from giving or securing to all persons within such State the equal protection of the laws, or shall conspire together for the purpose of in any manner impeding, hindering, obstructing, or defeating the due course of justice in any State or Territory, with intent to deny to any citizen of the United States the due and equal protection of the laws, or to injure any person in his person or his property for lawfully enforcing the right of any person or class of persons to the equal protection of the laws, or by force, intimidation, or threat to prevent any citizen of the United States lawfully entitled to vote from giving his support or advocacy in a lawful manner towards or in favor of the election of any lawfully qualified person as an elector of President or Vice-President of the United States, or as a member of the Congress of the United States, or to injure any such citizen in his person or property on account of such support or advocacy, each and every person so offending shall be deemed guilty of a high crime, and, upon conviction thereof in any district or circuit court of the United States or district or supreme court of any Territory of the United States having jurisdiction of similar offences, shall be punished by a fine not less than five hundred nor more than five thousand dollars, or by imprisonment, with or without hard labor, as the court may determine, for a period of not less than six months nor more than six years, as the court may determine, or by both such fine and imprisonment as the court shall determine....

*   *   *

☆ 146d Civil Rights Act of 1875

18 Stat. 335 (1875).

Whereas, it is essential to just government we recognize the equality of all men before the law, and hold that it is the duty of government in its dealings with the people to mete out equal and exact justice to all, of whatever nativity, race, color, or persuasion, religious or political; and it being the appropriate object of legislation to enact great fundamental principles into law: Therefore,

Be it enacted by the Senate and House of Representatives of the United States of America in Congress assembled, That all persons within the jurisdiction of the United States shall be entitled to the full and equal enjoyment of the accommodations, advantages, facilities, and privileges of inns, public conveyances on land or water, theaters, and other places of public amusement; subject only to the conditions and limitations established by law, and applicable alike to citizens of every race and color, regardless of any previous condition of servitude.

SEC. 2. That any person who shall violate the foregoing section by denying to any citizen, except for reasons by law applicable to citizens of every race and color, and regardless of any previous condition of servitude, the full enjoyment of any of the accommodations, advantages, facilities, or privileges in said section enumerated, or by aiding or inciting such denial, shall, for every such offense, forfeit and pay the sum of five hundred dollars to the person aggrieved thereby, to be recovered in an action of debt, with full costs; and shall also, for every such offense, be deemed guilty of a misdemeanor and, upon conviction thereof, shall be fined not less than five hundred nor more than one thousand dollars, or shall be imprisoned not less than thirty days nor more than one year....

*　　　*　　　*

SEC. 4. That no citizen possessing all other qualifications which are or may be prescribed by law shall be disqualified for service as a grand or petit juror in any court of the United States, or of any State, on account of race, color, or previous condition of servitude; and any officer or other person charged with any duty in the selection or summoning of jurors who shall exclude or fail to summon any citizen for the cause aforesaid shall, on conviction thereof, be deemed guilty of a misdemeanor and be fined not more than five thousand dollars.

*　　　*　　　*

147 Rebel Property and Due Process (1870)

In *Miller v. United States*, the Supreme Court upheld the 1861 and 1862 acts providing for the confiscation of the properties of rebels and of their aiders and abettors against complaints that the acts had violated the Fifth and Sixth amendment safeguards of due process of law and fair trial. Miller argued that the confiscation acts were penal laws under the municipal power of Congress and, accordingly, subject to the constitutional limitations on criminal law. The court, nevertheless, found the acts to be exercises of the war powers upon which, it was conceded, the Constitution imposed no restrictions.

Pointing out that the acts were aimed not at external enemies of the United States but at citizens committing acts of treason, the dissenting justices urged that the acts should be considered not under the war powers but as domestic legislation subject to the Fifth and Sixth amendments. While there was no disagreement that the United States could treat the people of the South as *either* enemy aliens or traitors, it was doubtful whether Congress could escape its choice, once made. The confiscation acts did not, as in a foreign war, authorize the appropriation of all property, only that of people engaging in certain acts. Hence the laws were not in aid of the war, but punitive of persons of suspect loyalties. The case demonstrated, again, the ambiguous position of the supporters of the Confederate cause: enemies or traitors?

☆ 147 *Miller v. United States*

78 U.S. (6 Wall.) 268 (1870).

Mr. Justice STRONG delivered the opinion of the court.

*　　　*　　　*

It remains to consider the objection urged on behalf of the plaintiff in error that the acts of Congress under which these proceedings to confiscate the stock have been taken are not warranted by the Constitution, and that they are in conflict with some of its provisions. The objection starts with the assumption that the purpose of the acts was to punish offences against the sovereignty of the United States, and that they are merely statutes against crimes.... But if the assumption of the plaintiff in error is not well made, if the statutes were not enacted under the municipal power of Congress to legislate for the punishment of crimes against the sovereignty of the United States, if, on the contrary, they are an exercise of the war powers of the government, it is clear they are not affected by the restrictions imposed by the fifth and sixth amendments. This we understand to have been conceded in the argument. The question, therefore, is, whether the action of Congress was a legitimate exercise of the war power. The Constitution confers upon Congress expressly power to declare war, grant letters of marque and reprisal, and make rules respecting captures on land and water. Upon the exercise of these powers no restrictions are imposed....

[W]hen the acts of 1861 and 1862 were passed, there was a state of war existing between the

United States and the rebellious portions of the country. . . . War existing, the United States were invested with belligerent rights in addition to the sovereign powers previously held. . . . Mr. Wheaton, in his work on international law, asserts the doctrine to be that "the general usage of nations regards such a war as entitling both the contending parties to all the rights of war as against each other, and even as it respects neutral nations." It would be absurd to hold that, while in a foreign war [the] enemy's property may be captured and confiscated, . . . in a civil war of equal dimensions, . . . the right to confiscate the property . . . does not exist. . . . Every reason for the allowance of a right to confiscate in case of foreign wars exists in full force when the war is domestic or civil. . . .

*   *   *

Mr. Justice FIELD, with whom concurred Mr. Justice CLIFFORD, dissenting.

*   *   *

The authority for the legislation in question must be found in what are termed the war powers of the government; . . . or, in what is termed the municipal power of the government to legislate for the punishment of offences against the United States.

. . . The question is, not as to the right of the United States to adopt either course against the inhabitants of the Confederate States engaged in the rebellion; that is, the right to treat them as public enemies, and to apply to them all the harsh measures justified by the rules of war; or the right to prosecute them in the ordinary modes of criminal procedure for the punishment of treason; but what course has Con-

gress, by its legislation, authorized. For it is evident that legislation founded upon the war powers of the government, and directed against the public enemies of the United States, is subject to different considerations and limitations from those applicable to legislation founded upon the municipal power of the government and directed against criminals. Legislation in the former case is subject to no limitations, except such as are imposed by the law of nations in the conduct of war. Legislation in the latter case is subject to all the limitations prescribed by the Constitution for the protection of the citizen. . . .

*   *   *

If we turn now to the act of July 17th, 1862, we find that its provisions are not directed against enemies at all, but against persons who have committed certain overt acts of treason. . . .

*   *   *

It would seem clear, therefore, that the provisions of the act were not passed in the exercise of the war powers of the government, but in the exercise of the municipal power of the government to legislate for the punishment of offences against the United States. . . .

*   *   *

As the act is highly penal in its nature, it would seem that, according to well-received rules, it should be strictly construed, and a rigid compliance with its provisions exacted. But the very opposite course in the construction of the act appears to have been adopted by the majority of the court.

*   *   *

Top, Doc. 4: The Pilgrims signing the Mayflower Compact on board the ship. Engraving by Gauthier, 1857, after H. Matteson. *Middle, left*, Doc. 17: Nathaniel Bacon, aristocratic Englishman and leader of the Virginia Rebellion (1676). From an original at Lord Viscount Grimston's, at Gorhambury. *Middle, right*, Doc. 5: Indian massacre of early Virginia settlers. Engraving by Theodore DeBry. *Bottom*, Doc. 19: William Penn entering a treaty of mutual respect with the Native Americans upon the founding of the province of Pennsylvania (1681).

Top, Doc. 35: The Boston Massacre. Engraving by Paul Revere. *Middle*, Doc. 45: Ratification of the Declaration of Independence (1776). *Bottom*, Doc. 52: Captured British Major John André, liaison for the Benedict Arnold conspiracy, seeking to bribe a patriotic member of the New York militia to release him (September 23, 1780). From *Harper's Weekly*, September 29, 1860.

Negroes for Sale.

A Cargo of very fine ſtout Men and Women, in good order and fit for immediate ſervice, juſt imported from the Windward Coaſt of Africa, in the Ship Two Brothers.—

Conditions are one half Caſh or Produce, the other half payable the firſt of January next, giving Bond and Security if required.

The Sale to be opened at 10 o'Clock each Day, in Mr. Bourdeaux's Yard, at No. 48, on the Bay.

May 19, 1784.　　JOHN MITCHELL.

Thirty Seaſoned Negroes

To be Sold for Credit, at Private Sale.

AMONGST which is a Carpenter, none of whom are known to be diſhoneſt.

Alſo, to be ſold for Caſh, a regular bred young Negroe Man-Cook, born in this Country, who ſerved ſeveral Years under an exceeding good French Cook abroad, and his Wife a middle aged Waſher-Woman, (both very honeſt) and their two Children. Likewiſe, a young Man a Carpenter.

For Terms apply to the Printer.

Top, Doc. 61: Advertisement for the sale of slaves in America (1784). *Bottom*, Doc. 88: Virginia slaves, under the leadership of Nat Turner, rebel against their masters. Woodcut from an abolitionist tract by S. Warner, 1831.

HORRID MASSACRE IN VIRGINIA.

The Scenes which the above Plate is designed to represent, are—Fig 1. a Mother intreating for the lives of her children.—2. Mr Travis, cruelly murdered by his own Slaves.—3. Mr Barrow, who bravely defended himself until his wife escaped.—4. A comp. of mounted Dragoons in pursuit of the Blacks.

Top, Doc. 95: Native Americans on the "Trail of Tears," prodded along by United States soldiers (1843). Original painting by Robert Lindneux. *Bottom*, Doc. 95: Seminole Chief Osceola, who led a seven-year war in opposition to the federal resettlement of Native Americans west of the Mississippi (1835).

ANTI-TEXAS MEETING
AT FANEUIL HALL!

Friends of Freedom!

A proposition has been made, and will soon come up for consideration in the United States Senate, to annex Texas to the Union. This territory has been wrested from Mexico by violence and fraud. Such is the character of the leaders in this enterprise that the country has been aptly termed "that valley of rascals." It is large enough to make *nine* or *ten* States as large as Massachusetts. It was, under Mexico, a free territory. The freebooters have made it a slave territory. The design is to annex it, with its load of infamy and oppression, to the Union. The immediate result may be a war with Mexico—the ultimate result *will be* some 18 or 20 more slaveholders in the Senate of the United States, a still larger number in the House of Representatives, and the balance of power in the hands of the South! And if, when in a minority in Congress, slaveholders browbeat the North, demand the passage of gag laws, trample on the Right of Petition, and threaten, in defiance of the General Government, to hang every man, caught at the South, who dares to speak against their "domestic institutions," what limits shall be set to their intolerant demands and high handed usurpations, when they are in the majority?

All opposed to this scheme, of whatever sect or party, are invited to attend the meeting at the Old Cradle of Liberty, to-morrow, (Thursday Jan. 25,) at 10 o'clock, A. M., at which time addresses are expected from several able speakers.

Bostonians! Friends of Freedom!! Let your voices be heard in loud remonstrance against this scheme, fraught with such ruin to yourselves and such infamy to your country.

January 24, 1838.

Top, Doc. 98: Appeal to the "Friends of Freedom" to oppose the admission into the Union of Texas, which was "wrested from Mexico by violence and fraud" (1838). *Bottom*, Doc. 116: The trial of John Brown for his rebellion in Harper's Ferry.

Top, Doc. 114: The assassination of Mormon leaders Joseph and Hiram Smith in the Carthage, Illinois, jail (1844). Lithograph by C. G. Crehen (1851). *Bottom*, Doc. 114: The march of the United States Army, across the snowy plains of Utah Territory, against the rebellious Mormons (1858). From *Harper's Weekly*, April 24, 1858.

IN LEXINGTON AVENUE

JEFF DAVIS ON THE RIGHT PLATFORM,
or the last "act of secession".

A PROPER FAMILY RE-UNION.

Top, left, Doc. 130: Antidraft rioters in New York City (1863). Wood engraving in *Leslie's Illustrated News*, July 25, 1863. *Top, right*, Doc. 124: Hostile portrayal of Jefferson Davis, the provisional president of the seceding Confederate States of America (1861). *Bottom*, Doc. 134: Confederate President Jefferson Davis portrayed in a "family reunion" with Benedict Arnold (1865).

TWO MEMBERS OF THE KU-KLUX KLAN IN THEIR DISGUISES.

SATAN TEMPTING BOOTH TO THE MURDER OF THE PRESIDENT.

Top, left, Doc. 145: Two members of the Ku Klux Klan in their disguises (1868). Woodcut from *Harper's Weekly*, December 19, 1868. *Top, right,* Doc. 136: Satan tempting John Wilkes Booth, the assassin of President Lincoln (1865). *Bottom,* Doc. 131: Confederate troops engaging in an indiscriminate massacre of white and black Union troops and followers, including the wounded, children, and women, after the conquest of Fort Pillow, Kentucky (April 12, 1864). From *Harper's Weekly,* April 30, 1864.

CHAPTER 6

Social and Industrial Stress

The Struggles of Native
Americans, Women,
and Labor
1871-1916

The close of the Civil War permitted some longstanding but temporarily dormant social and political movements to come to the fore. The war concluded with a basic restructuring of the state-federal system through the passage of the Fourteenth Amendment, which authorized federal scrutiny of the conduct of the states' legal relations with their citizenry. Other forms of restructuring were now to occupy the nation's sociopolitical agenda after the half-century, as various factions of the population pressed for access to political power — often through illegal and violent means. Southern whites regrasped political control of their states to maintain social and racial hegemony, women sought the franchise and access to public office and the professions, Native Americans fought a losing battle against expatriation and western resettlement, and the labor movement struggled to reform the economic order and to accord workers access to the safeguards, rather than the hostility, of the law.

In all these arenas the existing laws, both criminal and quasi-criminal, shaped the character of the debate and either facilitated or retarded change. This chapter thus focuses on the interactions of the law, particularly the federal law, with these reform and retrenchment movements. To be sure, there was considerable criminal conduct associated with all of the groups included in this chapter: nightriders engaged in acts of terrorism; women sought to cast illegal votes; Native Americans frequently rose in defense of their land and social order; and workers illegally struck, boycotted, and rioted. But this chapter is replete with the richer material of political criminality as well.

The recurring themes of loyalty and allegiance to the social, economic, and political order echoed through these years, but new phenomena came into existence as well. Despite the general amnesty, the confiscation measures of the Civil War continued in effect, and a white man's rights depended on his wartime loyalties. But as franchise restrictions on former Confederate officers and soldiers were lifted, the white Southern political structure asserted itself against the federally supported Reconstruction governments. With the federal presence reduced, many white Southerners undertook terrorist acts to diminish the political power of blacks —

to which neither the new state authorities nor those of federal government effectively responded. The passive attitude of both state and federal criminal law enforcement officials thus permitted the subjugation of blacks through private conspiracies and terrorism.

In contrast to the passive posture of the governments with regard to the enforcement of civil rights stands the active federal role in addressing another resurging social concern — the destiny of the Native American population. The federal government, first through the use of military force to contain and isolate Native Americans on reservations and then through a policy of "assimilation," undertook, through punitive laws and regulations, the ethnocide of a socially and politically distinct people.

Passive and active involvements also marked the federal government's approach to the women's and the labor movements, respectively. A narrow construction of the recently enacted Fourteenth Amendment withheld from women access to federal authority to challenge state restrictions on their political and social rights. Conversely, capital and management often invoked federal power, military and judicial, to neutralize and punish the exercise of economic and political power by organized labor.

In these materials, once again there is a pattern of political criminality arising in and around groups that are excluded from equal participation in the ordinary political processes, yet are held accountable to the demands of the law. The severity of the governmental response to such criminality seems to be related to the perceived loyalty of the offending group. The Native Americans were affected the most directly and heavily by state and federal government policies. They were attacked and held in captivity, and their social cohesion was broken violently. The duplicitous policy of the United States was to recognize the Native Americans as sovereign, and therefore to see them as disloyal to the United States. Before they could be granted politically protected rights they were required to demonstrate their "assimilation" — adherence to the order of the white society.

Workers, especially noncraft laborers, received the next most severe treatment at the hands of government. Many, if not most, of this sector of the working class consisted of immigrants, ineligible to vote, who spoke foreign languages and adhered to foreign customs and ideologies. The government and the general public perceived their organizations as suspiciously foreign and as opposed to the principles of the American Republic, as a threat to the interests of capital.

Women were denied the franchise and could not directly influence policy, but otherwise their deprivation was more evident in economic than in political realms. They were punished when they breached the law to demonstrate their disaffection with the existing order; otherwise their political subjugation was more a matter of exclusion than direct oppression. Blacks were in the most peculiar position of all with regard to governmental authority. Unlike the other groups they were specifically entitled to the special protection of the United States under the Fourteenth Amendment, yet they were victimized through terrorism and state-sanctioned discrimination more than any other group. The United States laws that guaranteed black voting rights proved ineffectual in protecting the

exercise of that right in the face of violent, politically motivated local opposition. The resulting political disenfranchisement, reinforced by blacks' social reisolation, continued at the federal as well as the state level, since federal and state electors were one and the same.

It is the struggle of these groups—Native Americans, women, blacks, and labor—for political and civil rights which constituted a major portion of political criminality in post-Civil War America. None of these groups sought to do anything that was inherently or fundamentally criminal: *malum in se*. Living on one's ancestral property in conformity with traditional cultural values, organizing and collectively asserting economic power and the need for reform, and discharging civic and political responsibilities through the elective process are not usually deemed inimical to the social order. Yet people were for those reasons subjected to punishment, deprivation, and even death, through the use or the nonuse of governmental power.

---

148 "no Indian nation . . . shall be acknowledged or recognized as an independent nation" (1871)

The new federal policies regarding Native Americans were hampered severely by the sovereign status of the Indian nations, entitling them to bilateral and consensual treaty relations. The cumbersome treaty form of managing Native American affairs also was objectionable to the House of Representatives, which was excluded from the treaty ratification process. In 1867, Congress passed a bill (which was plainly unconstitutional and was quickly repealed) that purported to strip the president of treaty negotiating power with the Native Americans. Finally, in 1871 an amendment was tacked on to the appropriations bill terminating this time-honored procedure. The Native American nations, thereafter, were no longer entitled to the procedural trappings of independent nations. Their status had been defined one year earlier when the Supreme Court ruled in the *Cherokee Tobacco Case*, 78 U.S. (11 Wall.) 616 (1870), that an act of Congress could abrogate a treaty obligation.

This loss of treaty-making status provided the foundation for the assertion of federal law-making authority over the heretofore inviolable internal affairs of the various Native American societies. Although often coerced, regulation of internal Native

American affairs had always been based on the consent of the tribal authority. Thereafter this authority existed only at the sufferance of Congress, and the individual Native American, rather than the nation or tribe, became the legitimate object of regulation by Congress. Membership in a Native American society nevertheless precluded individuals from asserting any voice in the enactment of the regulation, even though they were directly subject to penalties.

☆148 An Act Making Appropriation for the Indian Department and for Other Purposes

16 Stat. 544 (1871).

BE IT ENACTED *by the Senate and House of Representatives of the United States of America in Congress assembled,* That the following sums be, and they are hereby, appropriated, out of any money in the treasury not otherwise appropriated, for the purpose of paying the current and contingent expenses of the Indian department, and fulfilling treaty stipulations with the various Indian tribes:—

*   *   *

For insurance and transportation of goods for the Yanktons, one thousand five hundred dollars: *Provided,* That hereafter no Indian nation or tribe within the territory of the United States shall be acknowledged or recognized as an independent nation, tribe, or power with whom the United States may contract by treaty: *Provided further*, That nothing herein contained shall be construed to invalidate or impair the obligation of any treaty heretofore lawfully made and ratified with any such Indian nation or tribe. . . .

*   *   *

149 "grudging obedience to the most reasonable requirements of the Government" (1872)

The final removal of the Seminoles to lands west of the Mississippi temporarily mitigated the tension between Native Americans and whites. But with the westward press of white settlement, the nomadic Native Americans' habit of "straying off the reservation" in pursuit of game engendered more and more friction and brought military intervention. In 1862, Sioux facing semistarvation rose in Minnesota. After the uprising was quelled, thirty-eight Sioux leaders were hanged the day after Christmas in Mankato, Minnesota, by order of President Lincoln. It was clear that the earlier policy of removal could not be repeated. The so-called peace policy finally prevailed, and the reservation system, which segregated the Native American population, was strictly enforced through the use of military.

The implementation of the new federal peace policy—the virtual confinement of the Native Americans—was described starkly in the report of the Commissioner of the Indian Affairs. Pursuit of this policy resulted in several noted events in United States military history, including Custer's Last Stand (1876); the thousand-mile, orderly trek of the Nez Perce under Chief Joseph while pursued by superior United States forces (1877); the guerrilla war of the Chiracawa Apaches and other southwestern tribes, which ended with the capture of Geronimo (1886); and the Ghost Dance Uprising, a combined effort of several tribes, which ended with the massacre at Wounded Knee (1890).

☆ 149 Annual Report of the Commissioner of Indian Affairs

H.R. Exec. Doc. No. 1, 42d Cong., 3d Sess. 391 (1872), reprinted in Francis Paul Prucha, ed., *Documents of United States Indian Policy* (Lincoln: University of Nebraska Press, 1975), 137-41.

THE INDIAN POLICY

The Indian policy, so called, of the Government, is a policy, and it is not a policy, or rather it consists of two policies, entirely distinct, seeming, indeed, to be mutually inconsistent and to reflect each upon the other: the one regulating the treatment of the tribes which are potentially hostile, that is, whose hostility is only repressed just so long as, and so far as, they are supported in idleness by the Government; the other regulating the treatment of those tribes which, from traditional friendship, from numerical weakness, or by the force of their location, are either indisposed toward, or incapable of, resistance to the demands of the Government. . . . It is, of course, hopelessly illogical that the expenditures of the Government should be proportioned not to the good but to the ill desert of the several tribes; that large bodies of Indians should be supported in entire indolence by the bounty of the Government simply because they are audacious and insolent, while well-disposed Indians are only assisted to self-maintenance, since it is known they will not fight. It is hardly less than absurd, on the first view of it, that delegations from tribes that have frequently defied our authority and fought our troops, and have never yielded more than a partial and grudging obedience to the most reasonable requirements of the Government, should be entertained at the national capital, feasted, and loaded with presents. . . . And yet, for all this, the Government is right and its critics wrong; and the "Indian policy" is sound, sensible, and beneficent, because it reduces to the minimum the loss of life and property upon our frontier, and allows the freest development of our settlements and railways possible under the circumstances.

. . . It is not a whit more unreasonable that the Government should do much for hostile Indians and little for friendly Indians than it is that a private citizen should, to save his life, surrender all the contents of his purse to a highwayman; while on another occasion, to a distressed and deserving applicant for charity, he would measure his contribution by his means and disposition at the time. . . . It is not, of course, to be understood that the Government of the United States is at the mercy of Indians; but thousands of its citizens are, even thousands of families. . . . There are innumerable little rifts of agricultural or mining settlements all over the western country which, if unmolested, will in a few years become self-protecting communities, but which, in the event of a general Indian war occurring at the present time, would utterly and instantly disappear, either by abandonment or massacre. . . . It is right that those who criticise the policy of the Government toward the Indians . . . should fairly face the one alternative which is presented. There is no question of national dignity, be it remembered, involved in the treatment of savages by a civilized power. With wild men, as with wild beasts, the question whether in a given situation one shall fight, coax, or run, is a question merely of what is easiest and safest.

THE USE OF THE MILITARY ARM

The system now pursued in dealing with the roving tribes dangerous to our frontier population and obstructing our industrial progress, is entirely consistent with, and, indeed, requires the occasional use of the military arm, in restraining or chastising refractory individuals and bands. Such a use of the military constitutes no abandonment of the "peace policy," and involves no disparagement of it. It was not to be expected—it was not in the nature of things—that the entire body of wild Indians should submit to be restrained in their Ishmaelitish proclivities without a struggle on the part of the more audacious to maintain their traditional freedom. In the first announcement made of the reservation system, it was expressly declared that the Indians should be made as comfortable on, and as uncomfortable off, their reservations as it was in the power of the Government to make them; that such of them as went right should be protected and fed, and such as went wrong should be harassed and scourged without intermission. It was not anticipated that the first proclamation of this policy to the tribes concerned would effect the entire cessation of existing evils; but it was believed that persistence in the course marked out would steadily reduce the number of the refractory, both by the losses sustained in actual conflict and by the desertion of individuals as they should become weary of a profitless and hopeless struggle, until, in the near result, the system adopted should apply without exception to all then roving and hostile tribes. Such a use of the strong arm of the Government is not war, but discipline....

It will be sufficient, perhaps, to mark the distinction, to say that a general Indian war could not be carried on with the present military force of the United States, or anything like it. Regiments would be needed where now are only companies, and long lines of posts would have to be established for the protection of regions which, under the safeguard of the feeding system, are now left wholly uncovered. On the other hand, by the reservation system and the feeding system combined, the occasions for collision are so reduced by lessening the points of contact, and the number of Indians available for hostile expeditions involving exposure, hardship, and danger is so diminished through the appeal made to their indolence and self-indulgence, that the Army in its present force is able to deal effectively with the few marauding bands which refuse to accept the terms of the Government.

THE FORBEARANCE OF THE GOVERNMENT

It is unquestionably true that the Government has seemed somewhat tardy in proceeding under the second half of the reservation policy, and in applying the scourge to individuals and bands leaving their prescribed limits without authority, or for hostile purposes. This has been partly from a legitimate deference to the conviction of the great body of citizens that the Indians have been in the past unjustly and cruelly treated, and that great patience and long forbearance ought to be exercised in bringing them around to submission to the present reasonable requirements of the Government, and partly from the knowledge on the part of the officers of the Government charged with administering Indian affairs, that, from the natural jealousy of these people, their sense of wrongs suffered in the past, and their suspiciousness arising from repeated acts of treachery on the part of the whites; from the great distance of many bands and individuals from points of personal communication with the agents of the Government, and the absence of all means of written communication with them; from the efforts of abandoned and degraded whites, living among the Indians and exerting much influence over them, to misrepresent the policy of the Government, and to keep alive the hostility and suspicion of the savages; and lastly, from the extreme untrustworthiness of many of the interpreters on whom the Government is obliged to rely for bringing its intentions to the knowledge of the Indians: that by the joint effect of all these obstacles, many tribes and bands could come very slowly to hear, comprehend, and trust the professions and promises of the Government....

The patience and forbearance exercised have been fully justified in their fruits. The main body of the roving Indians have, with good grace or with ill grace, submitted to the reservation system. Of those who still remain away from the assigned limits, by far the greater part are careful to do so with as little offense as possible....

THE BEGINNING OF THE END

It belongs not to a sanguine, but to a sober view of the situation, that three years will see the alternative of war eliminated from the Indian question, and the most powerful and hostile bands of to-day thrown in entire helplessness on the mercy of the Government. Indeed, the progress of two years more, if not of another summer, on the Northern Pacific Railroad will of itself completely solve the great Sioux problem, and leave the ninety thousand Indians ranging between the two trans-continental lines as incapable of resisting the Government as are the Indians of New York or Massachusetts.

*   *   *

... The railroads now under construction, or projected with a reasonable assurance of early completion, will multiply fourfold the striking force of the Army in that section; the little rifts of mining settlement, now found all through the mountains of the southern Territories will have become self-protecting communities; the feeble, wavering line of agricultual occupation, now sensitive to the faintest breath of Indian hostility, will then have grown to be the powerful "reserve" to lines still more closely advanced upon the last range of the intractable tribes.

SUBMISSION THE ONLY HOPE OF THE INDIANS

No one certainly will rejoice more heartily than the present Commissioner when the Indians of this country cease to be in a position to dictate, in any form or degree, to the Government; when, in fact, the last hostile tribe becomes reduced to the condition of suppliants for charity. This is, indeed, the only hope of salvation for the aborigines of the continent. If they stand up against the progress of civilization and industry, they must be relentlessly crushed.

THE CLAIMS OF THE INDIAN

The people of the United States can never without dishonor refuse to respect these two considerations: 1st. That this continent was originally owned and occupied by the Indians, who have on this account a claim somewhat larger than the privilege of one hundred and sixty acres of land, and "find himself" in tools and stock, which is granted as a matter of course to any newly-arrived foreigner who declares his intention to become a citizen; that something in the nature of an endowment, either capitalized or in the form of annual expenditures for a series of years for the benefit of the Indians, though at the discretion of the Government as to the specific objects, should be provided for every tribe or band which is deprived of its roaming privilege and confined to a diminished reservation: such an endowment being not in the nature of a gratuity, but in common honesty the right of the Indian on account of his original interest in the soil. 2d. That inasmuch as the progress of our industrial enterprise has cut these people off from modes of livelihood entirely sufficient for their wants, and for which they were qualified, in a degree which has been the wonder of more civilized races, by inherited aptitudes and by long pursuit, and has left them utterly without resource, they have a claim on this account again to temporary support and to such assistance as may be necessary to place them in a position to obtain a livelihood by means which shall be compatible with civilization.

*   *   *

... Surely there is obligation found in considerations like these, requiring us in some way, and in the best way, to make good to these original owners of the soil the loss by which we so greatly gain.

Can any principle of national morality be clearer than that, when the expansion and development of a civilized race involve the rapid destruction of the only means of subsistence possessed by the members of a less fortunate race, the higher is bound as of simple right to provide for the lower some substitute for the means of subsistence which it has destroyed? That substitute is, of course, best realized, not by systematic gratuities of food and clothing continued beyond a present emergency, but by directing these people to new pursuits which shall be consistent with the progress of civilization upon the continent; helping them over the first rough places on "the white man's road," and, meanwhile, supplying such subsistence as is absolutely necessary during the period of initiation and experiment. . . .

150 "The paramount destiny and mission of woman . . . " (1872)

Activist women were a bulwark of the abolitionist movement, even though they maintained a lowered profile. After the Civil War and the emancipation of blacks, many of these American women turned their energies toward improving the professional and political opportunities of their gender. In early 1866, Elizabeth Cady Stanton alerted the American public to the fact that the proposed Fourteenth Amendment to the Constitution, by making reference to the "male inhabitants" and "male citizens," threatened the Women's Movement toward enfranchisement. Two years later, the national convention of the American Equal Rights Association sent a message to Congress that declared "Women and the colored men are loyal, patriotic, property-holding, taxpaying, liberty-loving citizens, and we cannot believe that sex or complexion should be any ground for civil or political degradation . . . [but] one-half of the citizens are disenfranchised by their sex and about one-eighth by the color of their skin."

The privileges and immunities clause of the newly-passed Fourteenth Amendment appeared to be the appropriate vehicle for pressing against state denial of equal rights to women. Overall, the effort was a failure. Myra Colby Bradwell applied for admission to the Illinois bar in 1869 after sitting for and passing the requisite examination. When the Illinois Supreme Court denied her admission on the grounds that she was a woman, Bradwell took her cause to the United States Supreme Court, arguing the right of all citizens to pursue an occupation. The court denied her relief. The concurring opinion by Justice Bradley set the court's approach to feminist issues for nearly a century by declaring that "the paramount destiny and mission of women are to fulfill the noble and benign offices of wife and mother. This is the law of the Creator."

☆ 150 *Bradwell v. Illinois*

83 U.S. (16 Wall.) 130 (1872).

Mr. Justice MILLER delivered the opinion of the court.

The record in this case is not very perfect, but it may be fairly taken that the plaintiff asserted her right to a license [to practice law] on the grounds, among others, that she was a citizen of the United States.

*   *   *

In regard to that [fourteenth] amendment counsel for the plaintiff in this court truly says that there are certain privileges and immunities which belong to a citizen of the United States as such; otherwise it would be nonsense for the fourteenth amendment to prohibit a State from abridging them, and he proceeds to argue that admission to the bar of a State of a person who possesses the requisite learning and character is one of [the privileges and immunities of United States citizenship] which a State may not deny.

In this latter proposition we are not able to concur with counsel. We agree with him that there are privileges and immunities belonging to citizens of the United States. . . . But the right to admission to practice in the courts of a State is not one of them. This right in no sense depends on citizenship of the United States. It has not, as far as we know, ever been made in any State, or in any case, to depend on citizenship at all. . . . [S]o far as it can have any relation to citizenship at all, it would seem that, as to the courts of a State, it would relate to citizenship of the State, and as to Federal courts, it would relate to citizenship of the United States. . . .

. . . [T]he right to control and regulate the granting of license to practice law in the courts of a State is one of those powers which are not transferred for its protection to the Federal government, and its exercise is in no manner governed or controlled by citizenship of the United States in the party seeking such license. . . .

Judgment affirmed.

Mr. Justice BRADLEY:

I concur in the judgment of the court in this case, by which the judgment of the Supreme Court of Illinois is affirmed, but not for the reasons specified in the opinion just read.

The claim of the plaintiff, who is a married woman, to be admitted to practice as an attorney and counsellor-at-law, is based upon the supposed right of every person, man or woman, to engage in any lawful employment for a livelihood. The Supreme Court of Illinois denied the application on the ground that, by the common law, which is the basis of the laws of Illinois, only men were admitted to the bar, and the legislature had not made any change in

this respect. . . . In other respects it was left to the discretion of the court to establish the rules by which admission to the profession should be determined. The court, however, regarded itself as bound by at least two limitations. One was . . . that it should not admit any persons, or class of persons, not intended by the legislature to be admitted, even though not expressly excluded by statute. In view of this latter limitation the court felt compelled to deny the application of females to be admitted as members of the bar. Being contrary to the rules of the common law and the usages of Westminster Hall from time immemorial, it could not be supposed that the legislature had intended to adopt any different rule.

The claim . . . under the fourteenth amendment . . . assumes that [the right to pursue any lawful employment] is one of the privileges and immunities of women as citizens. . . .

It certainly cannot be affirmed, as an historical fact, that this has ever been established as one of the fundamental privileges and immunities of the sex. On the contrary, the civil law, as well as nature herself, has always recognized a wide difference in the respective spheres and destinies of man and woman. Man is, or should be, woman's protector and defender. The natural and proper timidity and delicacy which belongs to the female sex evidently unfits it for many of the occupations of civil life. The constitution of the family organization, which is founded in the divine ordinance, as well as in the nature of things, indicates the domestic sphere as that which properly belongs to the domain and functions of womanhood. The harmony, not to say identity, of interests and views which belong, or should belong, to the family institution is repugnant to the idea of a woman adopting a distinct and independent career from that of her husband. So firmly fixed was this sentiment in the founders of the common law that it became a maxim of that system of jurisprudence that woman had no legal existence separate from her husband, who was regarded as her head and representative in the social state; and, notwithstanding some recent modifications of this civil status, many of the special rules of law flowing from and dependent upon this cardinal principle still exist in full force in most States. One of these is, that a married woman is incapable, without her husband's consent, of making contracts which shall be binding on her or him. This very incapacity was one circumstance which the Supreme Court of Illinois deemed important in rendering a married woman incompetent fully to perform the duties and trusts that belong to the office of an attorney and counsellor.

It is true that many women are unmarried and not affected by any of the duties, complications, and incapacities arising out of the married state, but these are exceptions to the general rule. The paramount destiny and mission of woman are to fulfill the noble and benign offices of wife and mother. This is the law of the Creator. And the rules of civil society must be adapted to the general constitution of things, and cannot be based upon exceptional cases.

The humane movements of modern society, which have for their object the multiplication of avenues for woman's advancement, and of occupations adapted to her condition and sex, have my heartiest concurrence. But I am not prepared to say that it is one of her fundamental rights and privileges to be admitted into every office and position. . . . [I]n my opinion, in view of the peculiar characteristics, destiny, and mission of woman, it is within the province of the legislature to ordain what offices, positions, and callings shall be filled and discharged by men, and shall receive the benefit of those energies and responsibilities, and that decision and firmness which are presumed to predominate in the sterner sex.

For these reasons I think that the laws of Illinois now complained of are not obnoxious to the charge of abridging any of the privileges and immunities of citizens of the United States.

*   *   *

151 Defendant Is Indicted for Having Voted (1873)

Feminists claimed the Fourteenth Amendment's privileges and immunities clause abolished all state restrictions on the franchise. They argued that voting for a United States Congressman was a privilege of United States citizenship and that women were undeniably citizens. Women in several states attempted to vote in 1871 and 1872. Although the state of New York had limited the vote to members of the male sex, Susan B. Anthony and thirteen other women deliberately went to the polls in Rochester and succeeded in either registering or casting their ballots in the congressional elections. Ironically, the women were charged criminally under the 1870 Civil Rights Act for "having voted without the lawful right to vote." This prohibition was designed to prevent white voters from canceling out black votes by repeat voting and was never intended to be used against women suffragists. Anthony unsuccessfully set up the privileges and immunities clause as a defense to the crime, which carried a maximum jail term of three years.

☆151 *United States v. Anthony*

24 F. Cas. 829 (C.C.D. N.Y. 1873) (No. 14,459).

HUNT, Circuit Justice, after argument had been heard on the legal questions involved, ruled as follows:

*   *   *

It is charged that the defendant thus voted, she not having a right to vote, because she is a woman. The defendant insists that she has a right to vote; and that the provision of the constitution of this state, limiting the right to vote to persons of the male sex, is in violation of the fourteenth amendment of the constitution of the United States, and is void.

*   *   *

The right of voting, or the privilege of voting, is a right or privilege arising under the constitution of the state, and not under the constitution of the United States. The qualifications are different in the different states. Citizenship, age, sex, residence, are variously required in the different states, or may be so. If the right belongs to any particular person, it is because such person is entitled to it by the laws of the state where he offers to exercise it, and not because of citizenship of the United States. If the state of New York should provide that no person should vote until he had reached the age of thirty years, or after he had reached the age of fifty, or that no person having gray hair, or who had not the use of all his limbs, should be entitled to vote, I do not see how it could be held to be a violation of any right derived or held under the constitution of the United States. We might say that such regulations were unjust, tyrannical, unfit or the regulation of an intelligent state; but, if rights of a citizen are thereby violated, they are of that fundamental class, derived from his position as a citizen of the state, and not those limited rights belonging to him as a citizen of the United States. . . .

*   *   *

. . . If the fifteenth amendment had contained the word "sex," the argument of the defendant would have been potent. She would have said, that an attempt by a state to deny the right to vote because one is of a particular sex is expressly prohibited by that amendment. The amendment, however, does not contain that word. It is limited to race, color, or previous condition of servitude. The legislature of the state of New York has seen fit to say, that the franchise of voting shall be limited to the male sex. In saying this, there is, in my judgment, no violation of the letter, or of the spirit, of the fourteenth or of the fifteenth amendment.

This view is assumed in the second section of the fourteenth amendment [reducing the representation of a state restricting the male franchise]. Not only does this section assume that the right of male inhabitants to vote was the especial object of its protection, but it assumes and admits the right of a state . . . to deny to classes or portions of the male inhabitants the right to vote which is allowed to other male inhabitants. The regulation of the suffrage is thereby conceded to the states as a state's right.

* * *

If she believed she had a right to vote, and voted in reliance upon that belief, does that relieve her from the penalty?... Two principles apply here: First, ignorance of the law excuses no one; second, every person is presumed to understand and to intend the necessary effects of his own acts. Miss Anthony knew that she was a woman, and that the constitution of this state prohibits her from voting. She intended to violate that provision—intended to test it, perhaps, but certainly intended to violate it. The necessary effect of her act was to violate it, and this she is presumed to have intended. There was no ignorance of any fact, but, all the facts being known, she undertook to settle a principle in her own person. She takes the risk, and she can not escape the consequences.... She voluntarily gave a vote which was illegal, and this is subject to the penalty of the law....

* * *

THE COURT declined to submit the case to the jury, on any question, and directed the jury to find a verdict of guilty. A request, by the defendant's counsel, that that jury be polled, was denied by THE COURT, and a verdict of guilty was recorded....

HUNT, Circuit Justice, in denying the motion [for a new trial] said, in substance:

* * *

... It is the duty of the jury to act upon the facts. It is the duty of the court to decide the law. The facts being specially found by the jury, it is the duty of the court, and not of the jury, to pronounce the judgment of guilty or not guilty. The facts being fully conceded, it is the duty of the court to announce and direct what the verdict shall be, whether guilty or not guilty. Therefore, I cannot doubt the power and the duty of the court to direct a verdict of guilty, whenever the facts constituting guilt are undisputed.

... Every fact in the case was undisputed. There was no inference to be drawn or point made on the facts, that could, by possibility, alter the result. It was, therefore, not only the right, but it seems to me, upon the authorities, the plain duty of the judge to direct a verdict of guilty. The motion for a new trial is denied.

152 "The Court orders the prisoner to sit down" (1873)

Prior to sentencing, Susan B. Anthony articulated the inequities of the judicial process which she had experienced as well as the ultimate justice of the cause for which she had acted. In conformity with her principles, she refused to pay the one-hundred-dollar fine imposed. The judge, in turn, refused to jail Anthony for failure to pay the fine, precluding an appeal to the Supreme Court which she greatly desired.

☆152 Susan B. Anthony's Statement to the Court (1873)

Reprinted in E. C. Stanton, S. B. Anthony, and M. J. Gage, eds., *History of Woman Suffrage* (New York: Fowler & Wells, 1881), 2:687-89.

* * *

[JUDGE HUNT]: The prisoner will stand up. Has the prisoner anything to say why sentence shall not be pronounced?

MISS ANTHONY: Yes, your honor, I have many things to say; for in your ordered verdict of guilty, you have trampled underfoot, every vital principle of our government. My natural rights, my civil rights, my political rights, are all alike ignored. Robbed of the fundamental privilege of citizenship, I am degraded from the status of a citizen to that of a subject; and not only myself individually, but all of my sex, are, by your honor's verdict, doomed to political subjection under this so-called republican government.

JUDGE HUNT: The Court can not listen to a rehearsal of arguments the prisoner's counsel has already consumed three hours in presenting.

MISS ANTHONY: May it please your honor, I am not arguing the question, but simply stating the reasons why sentence can not, in justice, be pronounced against me. Your denial of my citizen's right to vote is the denial of my right of consent as one of the governed, the denial of my right of representation as one of the taxed, the denial of my right to a trial by a jury of my peers as an offender against the law, therefore, the denial of my sacred rights to life, liberty, property, and—

JUDGE HUNT: The Court can not allow the prisoner to go on.

* * *

MISS ANTHONY: Of all my prosecutors, ... not one is my peer, but each and all are my political sovereigns; and had your honor submitted my case to the jury, as was clearly your duty, even then I should have had just cause of protest, for not one of those men was my peer; but, native or foreign, white or black, rich or poor, educated or ignorant, awake or asleep, sober or drunk, each and every man of them was my political superior; hence, in no sense, my peer.... [J]ury, judge, counsel, must all be of the superior class.

JUDGE HUNT: The Court must insist—the prisoner has been tried according to the established forms of law.

MISS ANTHONY: Yes, your honor, but by forms of law all made by men, interpreted by men, administered by men, in favor of men, and against women; and hence, your honor's ordered verdict of guilty, against a United States citizen for the exercise of "that citizen's right to vote," simply because that citizen was a woman and not a man. But, yesterday, the same man-made forms of law declared it a crime punishable with $1,000 fine and six months' imprisonment, for you, or me, or any of us, to give a cup of cold water, a crust of bread, or a night's shelter to a panting fugitive as he was tracking his way to Canada. And every man or woman in whose veins coursed a drop of human sympathy violated that wicked law, reckless of consequences, and was justified in so doing. As then the slaves who got their freedom [had to] take it over, or under, or through the unjust forms of law, precisely so now must women, to get their right to a voice in this Government, take it; and I have taken mine, and mean to take it at every possible opportunity.

JUDGE HUNT: The Court orders the prisoner to sit down. It will not allow another word.

MISS ANTHONY: When I was brought before your honor for trial, I hoped for a broad and liberal interpretation of the Constitution and its recent amendments, that should declare all United States citizens under its protecting aegis—that should declare equality of rights the national guarantee to all persons born or naturalized in the United States. But failing to get this justice—failing, even, to get a trial by a jury *not* of my peers—I ask not leniency at your hands—but rather the full rigors of the law.

JUDGE HUNT: The Court must insist—[Here the prisoner sat down.]

JUDGE HUNT: The prisoner will stand up. [Here Miss Anthony arose again.] The sentence of the Court is that you pay a fine of one hundred dollars and the costs of the prosecution.

MISS ANTHONY: May it please your honor, I shall never pay a dollar of your unjust penalty. All the stock in trade I possess is a $10,000 debt, incurred by publishing my paper—*The Revolution*—four years ago, the sole object of which was to educate all women to do precisely as I have done, rebel against your man-made, unjust, unconstitutional forms of law, that tax, fine, imprison, and hang women, while they deny them the right of representation in the Government; and I shall work on with might and main to pay every dollar of that honest debt, but not a penny shall go to this unjust claim. And I shall earnestly and persistently continue to urge all women to the practical recognition of the old revolutionary maxim, that "Resistance to tyranny is obedience to God."

JUDGE HUNT: Madam, the Court will not order you committed until the fine is paid.

153 "The government of the Confederate States.... had no existence" (1874)

Sprott, a purchaser of cotton from the Confederate government, sought to recover the proceeds of the sale of that cotton after its capture by Union forces. The stridency of the majority opinion, nine years after the cessation of hostilities, demonstrated that the wounds of the war had not healed. Noting that Sprott had given "aid and assistance to the rebellion," and that the Confederacy had no legal status, the court denied the claim.

☆ 153 *Sprott v. United States*

87 U.S. (20 Wall.) 459 (1874).

Mr. Justice MILLER delivered the opinion of the court.... Whether the temporary government of the Confederate States ... is to be recognized as having been a *de facto* government, and if so, what consequences follow in regard to its transactions ... is [of] no necessity in the present case.

*   *   *

... [C]otton was the principal support of the rebellion, so far as pecuniary aid was necessary to its support.... So long as the imperfect blockade of the Southern ports and the unguarded condition of the Mexican frontier enabled them to export this cotton, they were well supplied in return with arms, ammunition, medicine, and the necessaries of life not grown within their lines, as well as with that other great sinew of war, gold. If the rebel government could freely have exchanged the cotton of which it was enabled to possess itself, for the munitions of war or for gold, it seems very doubtful if it could have been suppressed. So when the rigor of the blockade prevented successful export of this cotton, their next resource was to sell it among their own people, or to such persons claiming outwardly to be loyal to the United States, as would buy of them, for the money necessary to support the tottering fabric of rebellion which they called a government.

The cotton which is the subject of this controversy was of this class. It had been in the possession and under the control of the Confederate government, with claim of title. It was captured ... and sold ... and the money deposited in the treasury.

The claimant now asserts a right to this money ... by showing that he purchased it of the Confederate government and paid them for it in money. In doing this he gave aid and assistance to the rebellion in the most efficient manner he possibly could. He could not have aided that cause more acceptably if he had entered its service and become a blockade-runner, or under the guise of a privateer had preyed upon the unoffending commerce of his country. It is asking too much of a court of law sitting under the authority of the government then struggling for existence against a treason respectable only for the numbers and the force by which it was supported, to hold that one of its own citizens, owing and acknowledging to it allegiance, can by the proof of such a transaction establish a title to the property so obtained. . . . A clearer case of turpitude in the consideration of a contract can hardly be imagined unless treason be taken out of the catalogue of crimes.

The case is not relieved of its harsh features by the finding of the court that the claimant did not *intend* to aid the rebellion, but only to make money. It might as well be said that the man who would sell for a sum far beyond its value to a lunatic, a weapon with which he knew the latter would kill himself, only intended to make money and did not intend to aid the lunatic in his fatal purpose. . . .

The recognition of the existence and the validity of the acts of the so called Confederate government, and that of the States which yielded a temporary support to that government, stand on very different grounds, and are governed by very different considerations.

. . . [The laws of the States] were the same, with slight exceptions, whether the authorities of the State acknowledged allegiance to the true or the false Federal power. They . . . must be respected in their administration under whatever temporary dominant authority they may be exercised. It is only when in the use of these powers substantial aid and comfort was given or intended to be given to the rebellion, when the functions necessarily reposed in the State for the maintenance of civil society were perverted to the manifest and intentional aid of treason against the government of the Union, that their acts are void.

The government of the Confederate States can receive no aid from this course of reasoning. It had no existence, except as a conspiracy to overthrow lawful authority. Its foundation was treason against the existing Federal government. . . .

When it was overthrown it perished totally. It left no laws, no statutes, no decrees, no authority which can give support to any contract, or any act done in its service, or in aid of its purpose, or which contributed to protract its existence. So far as the actual exercise of its physical power was brought to bear upon individuals, that may, under some circumstances, constitute a justification or excuse for acts otherwise indefensible, but no validity can be given in the courts of this country to acts voluntarily performed in direct aid and support of its unlawful purpose. . . .

Judgment affirmed.

*   *   *

Mr. Justice FIELD, dissenting.

*   *   *

. . . The question, and the only question, is whether the cotton . . . was at the time the property of the claimant. . . . [W]e are not concerned with the consideration of his loyalty or disloyalty. He was a citizen of Mississippi and resided within the lines of the Confederacy, and the act forbidding intercourse with the enemy does not apply to his case. He was subject to be treated, in common with other citizens of the Confederacy, as a public enemy during the continuance of the war. And if he were disloyal in fact, [he was pardoned] and if by his purchase of the cotton he gave aid and comfort to the rebellion, as this court adjudges, the impediment which such conduct previously interposed to the prosecution of his claim was removed by the proclamation of pardon and amnesty made by the President on the 25th day of December, 1868. . . . In legal contemplation the executive pardon not merely releases an offender from the punishment prescribed for his offence, but it obliterates the offence itself.

*   *   *

Now, . . . the confiscation of private property of persons engaged in the rebellion require[s] legal proceedings resulting in a judicial decree of condemnation before the title of the owner can be divested. . . . No proceedings for the condemnation and forfeiture of the cotton seized, or of its proceeds, have ever been instituted by the government. The title of the claimant remains, therefore, at this day, as perfect as it did on the day the cotton was seized.

*   *   *

154 "all citizens . . . were not invested with the right of suffrage" (1874)

Despite the inability of Susan B. Anthony to appeal her conviction to the Supreme Court, the issue of women's suffrage was presented to the court in 1874. Virginia L. Minor and her husband, Francis, instituted legal action against Reese Happersett, a Missouri registering officer, for refusal to register the wife as a lawful voter. When the case, which relied on the Fourteenth Amendment to press Mrs. Minor's claim, reached the Supreme Court, the court construed the amendment narrowly, denying that it had any impact on the status of women. Significantly, the court made no reference to the equal protection requirement that had figured so prominently in Anthony's case.

☆154 *Minor v. Happersett*

88 U.S. (21 Wall.) 162 (1874).

The CHIEF JUSTICE delivered the opinion of the court.

The question is presented in this case, whether, since the adoption of the fourteenth amendment, a woman, who is a citizen of the United States and of the State of Missouri, is a voter in that State, notwithstanding the provision of the constitution and laws of the State, which confine the right of suffrage to men alone. We might, perhaps, decide the case upon other grounds, but this question is fairly made. From the opinion we find that it was the only one decided in the court below, and it is the only one which has been argued here. The case was undoubtedly brought to this court for the sole purpose of having that question decided by us, and in view of the evident propriety there is of having it settled, so far as it can be by such a decision, we have concluded to waive all other considerations and proceed at once to its determination.

It is contended that the provisions of the constitution and laws of the State of Missouri which confine the right of suffrage and registration therefor to men, are in violation of the Constitution of the United States, and therefore void. The argument is, that as a woman, born or naturalized in the United States and subject to the jurisdiction thereof, is a citizen of the United States and of the State in which she resides, she has the right of suffrage as one of the privileges and immunities of her citizenship, which the State cannot by its laws or constitution abridge.

There is no doubt that women may be citizens. They are persons, and by the fourteenth amendment "all persons born or naturalized in the United States and subject to the jurisdiction thereof" are expressly declared to be "citizens of the United States and of the State wherein they reside." But, in our opinion, it did not need this amendment to give them that position. Before its adoption the Constitution of the United States did not in terms prescribe who should be citizens of the United States or of the several States, yet there were necessarily such citizens without such provision. There cannot be a nation without a people. The very idea of a political community, such as a nation is, implies an association of persons for the promotion of their general welfare. Each one of the persons associated becomes a member of the nation formed by the association. He owes it allegiance and is entitled to its protection. Allegiance and protection are, in this connection, reciprocal obligations. The one is a compensation for the other; allegiance for protection and protection for allegiance.

For convenience it has been found necessary to give a name to this membership. The object is to designate by a title the person and the relation he bears to the nation. For this purpose the words "subject," "inhabitant," and "citizen" have been used, and the choice between them is sometimes made to depend upon the form of the government. Citizen is now more commonly employed, however, and as it has been considered better suited to the description of one living under a republican government, it was adopted by nearly all of the States upon their separation from Great Britain and was afterwards adopted in the Articles of Confederation and in the Constitution of the United States. When used in this sense it is understood as conveying the idea of membership of a nation, and nothing more.

To determine, then, who were citizens of the United States before the adoption of the amendment it is necessary to ascertain what persons originally associated themselves together to form the nation, and what were afterwards admitted to membership.

*   *   *

... [S]ex has never been made one of the elements of citizenship in the United States. In this respect men have never had an advantage over women. The same laws precisely apply to both. The fourteenth amendment did not affect the citizenship of women any more than it did of men. In this particular, therefore, the rights of Mrs. Minor do not depend upon the amendment. She has always been a citizen from her birth, and entitled to all the privileges and immunities of citizenship. The amendment prohibited the State, of which she is a citizen, from abridging any of her privileges and immunities as a citizen of the United States; but it did not confer citizenship on her. That she had before its adoption.

If the right of suffrage is one of the necessary privileges of a citizen of the United States, then the constitution and laws of Missouri confining it to men are in violation of the Constitution of the United States, as amended, and consequently void. The direct question is, therefore, presented whether all citizens are necessarily voters.

The Constitution does not define the privileges and immunities of citizens. For that definition we must look elsewhere. In this case we need not determine what they are, but only whether suffrage is necessarily one of them.

It certainly is nowhere made so in express terms. ...

*   *   *

The [fourteenth] amendment did not add to the privileges and immunities of a citizen. It simply furnished an additional guaranty for the protection of such as he already had. No new voters were necessarily made by it. Indirectly it may have had that effect, because it may have increased the number of citizens entitled to suffrage under the constitution and laws of the States, but it operates for this purpose, if at all, through the States and the State laws, and not directly upon the citizen.

It is clear, therefore, we think, that the Constitution has not added the right of suffrage to the privileges and immunities of citizenship as they existed at the time it was adopted. This makes it proper to inquire whether suffrage was coextensive with the citizenship of the States at the time of its adoption.

*   *   *

... [A]ll the citizens of the States were not invested with the right of suffrage. In all, save perhaps New Jersey, this right was only bestowed upon men and not upon all of them.... Women were excluded from suffrage in nearly all the States by the express provision of their constitutions and laws.

*   *   *

Certainly, if the courts can consider any question settled, this is one. For nearly ninety years the people have acted upon the idea that the Constitution, when it conferred citizenship, did not necessarily confer the right of suffrage. If uniform practice long continued can settle the construction of so important an instrument as the Constitution of the United States confessedly is, most certainly it has been done here. Our province is to decide what the law is, not to declare what it should be.

We have given this case the careful consideration its importance demands. If the law is wrong, it ought to be changed; but the power for that is not with us. The arguments addressed to us bearing upon such a view of the subject may perhaps be sufficient to induce those having the power, to make the alteration but they ought not to be permitted to influence our judgment in determining the present rights of the parties now litigating before us. No argument as to woman's need of suffrage can be considered. We can only act upon her rights as they exist. It is not for us to look at the hardship of withholding. Our duty is at an end if we find it is within the power of a State to withhold.

Being unanimously of the opinion that the Constitution of the United States does not confer the right of suffrage upon any one, and that the constitutions and laws of the several States which commit that important trust to men alone are not necessarily void, we

Affirm the judgment.

155 "the rights of one citizen as against another" (1876)

In *United States v. Cruikshank* the United States Supreme Court had before it the convictions of three whites who were among a mob that had broken up a meeting of blacks, killing two participants. The meeting had been called to discuss local Louisiana elections. The fundamental question was whether newly enfranchised blacks would be able to rely on the power of the federal government to protect their exercise of political rights or whether that protection would be withdrawn.

The defendants were convicted in federal court for their politically motivated act of terrorism under Section 6 of the 1866 Civil Rights Act. The Supreme Court reversed the convictions. In its decision, the court relied on the State Action Doctrine, that is, that the Fourteenth Amendment guaranteed the rights of citizens only against encroachment by the state or its agents, not against actions by private individuals. While the language of Section 6 was left intact, its protective application was limited to safeguarding federally- rather than state-derived rights. The State Action Doctrine subsequently was used to invalidate major provisions of the 1875 Civil Rights Act which imposed penalties on private individuals who discriminated against blacks. The grounds for invalidation were that Congress did not intend such a broad grant of legislative power in the Fourteenth Amendment, which was only to be restrictive of the states. Thus, the judicial branch eliminated the authority of the federal law to protect racial minorities from resurgent white domination as Reconstruction ended and the franchise was extended to former rebels. Blacks could resort only to unsympathetic state officials to remedy terrorist violations of their rights by private parties.

☆ 155   *United States v. Cruikshank*

92 U.S. 542 (1876).

MR. CHIEF JUSTICE WAITE delivered the opinion of the court.

*   *   *

The general charge in the first eight counts is that of "banding," and in the second eight, that of "conspiring" together to injure, oppress, threaten, and intimidate Levi Nelson and Alexander Tillman, citizens of the United States, of African descent and persons of color, with the intent thereby to hinder and prevent them in their free exercise and enjoyment of rights and privileges "granted and secured" to them "in common with all other good citizens of the United States by the constitution and laws of the United States."

*   *   *

We have in our political system a government of the United States and a government of each of the several States. Each one of these governments is distinct from the others, and each has citizens of its own who owe it allegiance, and whose rights, within its jurisdiction, it must protect. The same person may be at the same time a citizen of the United States and a citizen of a State, but his rights of citizenship under one of these governments will be different from those he has under the other.

*   *   *

The first and ninth counts state the intent of the defendants to have been to hinder and prevent the citizens named in the free exercise and enjoyment of their "lawful right and privilege to peaceably assemble together with each other and with other citizens of the United States for a peaceful and lawful purpose."...

*   *   *

The particular amendment [the first] now under consideration assumes the existence of the right of the people to assemble for lawful purposes, and protects it against encroachment by Congress. The right was not created by the amendment; neither was its continuance guaranteed, except as against congressional interference. For their protection in its enjoyment, therefore, the people must look to the States. The power for that purpose was originally placed there, and it has never been surrendered to the United States.

The right of the people peaceably to assemble for the purpose of petitioning Congress for a redress of grievances, or for any thing else connected with the powers of the duties of the national government, is an attribute of national citizenship, and, as such, under the protection of, and guaranteed by, the United States. . . . If it had been alleged in these counts that the object of the defendants was to prevent a meeting for such a purpose, the case would have been within the statute, and within the scope of the sovereignty of the United States. Such, however, is not the case. The offence, as stated in the indictment, will be made out, if it be shown that the object of the conspiracy was to prevent a meeting for any lawful purpose whatever.

*   *   *

The fourteenth amendment prohibits a State from depriving any person of life, or property, without due process of law; but this adds nothing to the rights of one citizen as against another. . . .

. . . When stripped of its verbiage, the case as presented amounts to nothing more than that the defendants conspired to prevent certain citizens of the United States, being within the State of Louisiana, from enjoying the equal protection of the laws of the State and of the United States.

[B]ut [the equal protection clause] does not . . . add any thing to the rights which one citizen has . . . against another.

*   *   *

The seventh and fifteenth counts are no better than the sixth and fourteenth. The intent here charged is to put the parties named in great fear of bodily harm, and to injure and oppress them, because, being and having been in all things qualified, they had voted. . . . There is nothing to show that the elections voted at were any other than State elections, or that the conspiracy was formed on account of the race of the parties against whom the conspirators were to act. The charge as made is re-

ally of nothing more than a conspiracy to commit a breach of the peace within a State. Certainly it will not be claimed that the United States have the power or are required to do mere police duty in the States. If a State cannot protect itself against domestic violence, the United States may, upon the call of the executive, when the legislature cannot be convened, lend their assistance for that purpose. This is a guaranty of the Constitution (art. 4, sect. 4); but it applies to no case like this.

*   *   *

The order of the Circuit Court arresting the judgment upon the verdict is, therefore, affirmed; and the cause remanded, with instructions to discharge the defendants.

156 Rifle Clubs (1876)

With the post-Civil War disenfranchisement of nearly all the native white populations of the Southern states, political power rested in the hands of blacks and whites sympathetic to the Radical Republican powers in Washington. President Grant's administration was not known for its integrity, and the corruption of the national party infected the "occupation" administrations in the former Confederate states. One by one, as civil disabilities were gradually removed from Confederate soldiers and officers, and as the growth of the Ku Klux Klan and other terrorist organizations increasingly intimidated the black population, states were returning to native white rule. By 1876, the remaining strictly Republican Southern states were Florida, Louisiana, and South Carolina. In South Carolina the Republican officeholders were severely challenged both in the community and at the polls by the Democratic "Red Shirts" led by General Wade Hampton. Ostensibly a faction of the Democratic party, the "Red Shirts" (named for their "uniform") were an irregular militia whose purpose was to protect Democratic whites and blacks from official militias and unofficial mobs controlled by the Republicans. In the face of the armed clashes between blacks and whites—some political and some racial—and the growing tensions of the impending political campaign, Governor Chamberlain appealed to President Grant to permit the use of the federal troops stationed in South Carolina. Grant obliged, and martial law was declared in several counties shortly before the election.

☆156 Grant's Proclamation of Insurrection in South Carolina

Reprinted in J. Richardson, ed., *A Compilation of the Messages and Papers of the Presidents* (New York: Bureau of National Literature, 1917), 396.

Whereas it has been satisfactorily shown to me that insurrection and domestic violence exist in several counties of the State of South Carolina, and that certain combinations of men against law exist in many counties of said State known as "rifle clubs," who ride up and down by day and night in arms, murdering some peaceable citizens and intimidating others, which combinations, though forbidden by the laws of the State, can not be controlled or suppressed by the ordinary course of justice; and

Whereas it is provided in the Constitution of the United States that the United States shall protect every State in this Union, on application of the legislature, or of the executive (when the legislature can not be convened), against domestic violence; and

Whereas by laws in pursuance of the above it is provided (in the laws of the United States) that in all cases of insurrection in any State or of obstruction to the laws thereof it shall be lawful for the President of the United States, on application of the legislature of such State, or of the executive (when the legislature can not be convened), to call forth the militia of any other State or States, or to employ such part of the land and naval forces as shall be judged necessary, for the purpose of suppressing such insurrection or causing the laws to be duly executed; and

Whereas the legislature of said State is not now in session and can not be convened in time to meet the present emergency, and the executive of said State, under section 4 of Article IV of the Constitution of the United States and the laws passed in pursuance thereof, has therefore made due application to me in the premises for such part of the military force of the United States as may be necessary and adequate to protect said State and the citizens thereof against domestic violence and to enforce the due execution of the laws; and

Whereas it is required that whenever it may be necessary, in the judgment of the President, to use the military force for the purpose aforesaid, he shall forthwith, by proclamation, command such insurgents to disperse and retire peaceably to their respective homes within a limited time:

Now, therefore, I, Ulysses S. Grant, President of the United States, do hereby make proclamation and command all persons engaged in said unlawful and insurrectionary proceedings to disperse and retire peaceably to their respective abodes within three days from this date, and hereafter abandon said combinations and submit themselves to the laws and constituted authorities of said State.

And I invoke the aid and cooperation of all good citizens thereof to uphold the laws and preserve the public peace.

*   *   *

U. S. GRANT

By the President:

JOHN L. CADWALADER, Acting Secretary of State

157 "insurrectionary forces too powerful to be resisted" (1877)

1876 witnessed not only the hotly contested Hayes-Tilden presidential election but also a virtual coup d' état in South Carolina. Disputed election returns from South Carolina counties previously declared by President Grant to be in a state of rebellion caused the division of the state legislature into two factions. Each side met separately, claimed to be the legitimate authority of the state, and installed its own governor in December of 1876. For over three months there were two rival governments in the state, each promulgating the illegality of the other. The federal troops, on the orders of Grant, supported the administration of Republican D. H. Chamberlain against the claims of Democrat Wade Hampton. Congress implicitly seconded this acknowledgment of Chamberlain as the governor of South Carolina by its recognition of the Republican delegates to the Electoral College.

Although Chamberlain thus had been recognized by the United States as the legitimate governor of South Carolina, President Hayes's administration (in exchange, for congressional Democratic acquiescence to his election) decided to withdraw the federal troops from South Carolina as of April 10, 1877. Without federal support, Chamberlain's administration fell, and he retired to self-imposed exile in his native Massachusetts. Wade Hampton acceded to the undisputed governorship of the state on April 11. The resignation of Republican legislators gave the Democrats full control of the legislature. Several indictments were issued against Chamberlain and officeholders under his administration for fraud, graft, and corruption, but since they had fled, they were never tried. Subsequently, the actions and obligations of the "unlawful" Chamberlain regime were repudiated by the new government. The following documents relate to the transfer of lawful authority from "Governor" Chamberlain to "Governor" Hampton. Even while graciously abdicating, Chamberlain's parting message excoriated the federal government for failing to support his "lawful" administration against "insurrectionary forces."

☆ 157 Abdication of Governor
D. H. Chamberlain

Reprinted in W. Allen, *Governor Chamberlain's Administration in South Carolina* (New York: Negro Universities
Press, 1969), 480.

☆ 157a Letter from the Heads of Departments

Executive Department
Office of Attorney General
Columbia, S. C., April 10, 1877

To His Excellency, D. H. Chamberlain, Governor
of South Carolina, Columbia, S. C.:

DEAR SIR— . . .

Whilst we are no less inspired with admiration for
the dignified and resolute manner in which you have
consistently maintained your claims to the guberna-
torial chair, by virtue of the election held in November last, than we are solemnly impressed with the
validity of your title to the office, we are unanimous
in the belief that to prolong the contest, in the absence of that moral aid to which we feel ourselves
and our party justly entitled at the hands of a National Administration installed, in large measure,
through the same agencies which are now held to be
insufficient for our maintenance, will be to incur the
responsibility of keeping alive partisan prejudices
which are in the last degree detrimental to the best
interests of the people of the State; and perhaps of
precipitating a physical conflict that could have but
one result to our defenceless constituency. We cannot afford to contribute, however indirectly, to such
a catastrophe, even in the advocacy of what we
know to be our right.

We are agreed, therefore, in counselling you to
discontinue the struggle for the occupancy of the gu-
bernatorial chair, convinced as we are that, in view
of the disastrous odds to which its maintenance has
been subjected by the action of the National Administration, your retirement will involve no surrender
of principle, nor its motive be misapprehended by
the great body of that political party to which, in
common with ourselves, you are attached, and
whose success in the past in this State has been en-
nobled by your intelligent and unselfish services.

We have the honor to be, very respectfully,
yours,

ROBERT B. ELLIOTT, Attorney General
JOHN R. TOLBERT, Superintendent of Education
JAMES KENNEDY, Adjutant and Inspector General
THOMAS C. DUNN, Comptroller General
F. L. CARDOZO, Treasurer
H. E. HAYNES, Secretary of State

☆ 157b Correspondence between the Governors

State of South Carolina
Executive Chamber
Columbia, S. C., April 10, 1877

SIR—

Having learned that you now purpose to turn over
to me the Executive Chamber, with the records and
papers belonging to the Executive Office, now in
your possession, I beg to inform you that I will send
a proper officer to receive the same at any hour you
may indicate as most convenient to yourself.

I am, very respectfully, your obedient servant,

WADE HAMPTON, Governor

State of South Carolina
Executive Chamber
Columbia, S. C., April 10, 1877

SIR—

Replying to your note of this date, I have to say that
my Private Secretary will meet such officer as you
may designate, at twelve meridian to-morrow, at the
Executive Chamber, for the purpose indicated in
your note.

Very respectfully,

D. H. CHAMBERLAIN, Governor S. C.

☆ 157c Chamberlain's Abdication Address

TO THE REPUBLICANS OF SOUTH CAROLINA:

By your choice I was made Governor of this State in
1874. At the election on the 7th of November last, I
was again, by your votes, elected to the same office.
My title to the office, upon every legal and moral
ground, is to-day clear and perfect. By the recent decision and action of the President of the United
States, I find myself unable longer to maintain my
official rights, and I hereby announce to you that I
am unwilling to prolong a struggle which can only
bring further suffering upon those who engage in it.

In announcing this conclusion, it is my duty to say
for you, that the Republicans of South Carolina entered upon their recent political struggle for the
maintenance of their political and civil rights. Constituting, beyond question, a large majority of the
lawful voters of the State, you allied yourselves with
that political party whose central and inspiring principle has hitherto been the civil and political freedom of all men under the Constitution and laws of
our country. By heroic efforts and sacrifices which
the just verdict history will rescue from the cowardly scorn now cast upon them by political place-
men and traders, you secured the electoral vote of
South Carolina for Hayes and Wheeler. In accomplishing this result, you became the victims of every
form of persecution and injury. From authentic evidence it is shown that not less than one hundred of
your number were murdered because they were
faithful to their principles and exercised rights solemnly guaranteed to them by the nation. You were
denied employment, driven from your homes,

robbed of the earnings of years of honest industry, hunted for your lives like wild beasts, your families outraged and scattered, for no offence except your peaceful and firm determination to exercise your political rights. You trusted, as you had a right to trust, that if by such efforts you established the lawful supremacy of your political party in the nation, the Government of the United States, in the discharge of its constitutional duty, would protect the lawful Government of the State from overthrow at the hands of your political enemies. From causes patent to all men, and questioned by none who regard truth, you have been unable to overcome the unlawful combinations and obstacles which have opposed the practical supremacy of the Government which your votes have established.

... To-day—April 10, 1877—by the order of the President whom your votes alone rescued from overwhelming defeat, the Government of the United States abandons you, deliberately withdraws from you its support, with the full knowledge that the lawful Government of the State will be speedily overthrown. By a new interpretation of the Constitution of the United States at variance alike with the previous practice of the Government and with the decisions of the Supreme Court, the Executive of the United States evades the duty of ascertaining which of two rival State Governments is the lawful one, and by the withdrawal of troops now protecting the State from domestic violence, abandons the lawful State Government to a struggle with insurrectionary forces too powerful to be resisted....

No effective means of resistance to the consummation of the wrong are left. The struggle can be prolonged. My strict legal rights are, of course, wholly unaffected by the action of the President. No Court of the State has jurisdiction to pass upon the title of my office. No lawful Legislature can be convened except at my call. If the use of these powers promised ultimate success to our cause, I should not shrink from any sacrifices which might confront me. It is a cause in which by the light of reason and conscience a man might well lay down his life.

But, to my mind, my present responsibility involves the consideration of the effect of my action upon those whose representative I am. I have hitherto been willing to ask you, Republicans, to risk all dangers and endure all hardships until relief should come from the Government of the United States. That relief will never come. I cannot ask you to follow me further. In my best judgment I can no longer serve you by further resistance to the impending calamity.

With gratitude to God for the measure of endurance with which He has hitherto inspired me, with gratitude to you for your boundless confidence in me, with profound admiration for your matchless fidelity to the cause in which we have struggled, I now announce to you and to the people of the State that I shall no longer actively assert my right to the office of Governor of South Carolina.

The motives and purposes of the President of the United States in the policy which compels me to my present course are unquestionably honorable and patriotic. I devoutly pray that events may vindicate the wisdom of his action, and that peace, justice, freedom, and prosperity may hereafter be the portion of every citizen of South Carolina.

D. H. CHAMBERLAIN, Governor of South Carolina

158 To Secure to the Toilers a Proper Share of the Wealth (1878)

American labor's dissatisfaction with the economic conditions of the working men and women gave rise, from time to time, to concerted economic and political action. In 1860, Massachusetts shoemakers in Lynn and Natick struck for higher wages, and the strike spread to some twenty thousand New England workers.

The labor movement in the United States underwent a marked transition during the decade of the 1870s. During the economic depression of 1873-74, employer opposition to trade unions became bitter. Union workers suffered lockouts and blacklists. Concerted activity and strikes by workers often were prosecuted under criminal conspiracy laws. Since open unions could not survive, labor leaders met secretly and formed "nonpublic" labor societies. The leading organization of this type in the 1870s was the Noble Order of the Knights of Labor, formed in Philadelphia by Uriah Smith in 1869. At the society's convention at Reading in January of 1878, the Knights of Labor organized as a national labor union, which, at its height in the mid-1880s, claimed membership of over 700,000 workers. In the organization's constitution, which proclaimed adherence to democratic and egalitarian doctrines, the Knights focused their attention on the manner in which the law gave unfair advantage to the forces of capital in its resistance to the social and economic agenda of labor. The perceived injustice of these laws provided the foundation for common and honorable disobedience to them and their enforcers.

☆158 Constitution of the Knights of Labor: Preamble (January 1, 1878)

Reprinted in T. V. Powderly, *Thirty Years of Labor* (Columbus, Ohio: Excelsior, 1980), 243.

The alarming development and aggressiveness of the power of money and corporations under the present industrial and political systems will inevitably lead to the hopeless degradation of the people. It is imperative, if we desire to enjoy the full blessings of life, that unjust accumulation and this power for evil of aggregated wealth shall be prevented. This much-desired object can be accomplished only by the united efforts of those who obey the divine injunction: "In the sweat of thy face shalt thou eat bread." Therefore we have formed the order of the Knights of Labor for the purpose of organizing, educating, and directing the power of the industrial masses.

It is not a political party; it is more, for in it are crystallized sentiments and measures for the benefit of the whole people; but it should be borne in mind, when exercising the right of suffrage, that most of the objects herein set forth can only be obtained through legislation, and that it is the duty, regardless of party, of all to assist in nominating and supporting with their votes such candidates as will support these measures. No one shall, however, be compelled to vote with the majority.

Calling upon all who believe in securing "the greatest good to the greatest number" to join and assist us, we declare to the world that our aims are:

I. To make industrial and moral worth, not wealth, the true standard of individual and national greatness.

II. To secure to the workers the full enjoyment of the wealth they create; sufficient leisure in which to develop their intellectual, moral, and social faculties; all of the benefits, recreations, and pleasures of association; in a word, to enable them to share in the gains and honor of advancing civilization.

In order to secure these results, we demand at the hands of the law-making power of municipality, State, and nation:

III. The establishment of the referendum in the making of all laws.

IV. The establishment of bureaus of labor statistics, that we may arrive at a correct knowledge of the educational, moral, and financial condition of the laboring masses, and the establishment of free State labor bureaus.

V. The land, including all the natural sources of wealth, is the heritage of all the people, and should not be subject to speculative traffic. Occupancy and use should be the only title to the possession of land. The taxes upon land should be levied upon its full value for use, exclusive of improvements, and should be sufficient to take for the community all unearned increment.

VI. The abrogation of all laws that do not bear equally upon capitalists and laborers, and the removal of unjust technicalities, delays, and discriminations in the administration of justice.

VII. The adoption of measures providing for the health and safety of those engaged in mining, manufacturing, and building industries, and for indemnification to those engaged therein for injuries received through lack of necessary safeguards.

VIII. The recognition, by incorporation, of orders and other associations organized by the workers to improve their condition and to protect their rights.

IX. The enactment of laws to compel corporations to pay their employees weekly, in lawful money, for the labor of the preceding week, and giving mechanics and laborers a first lien upon the product of their labor to the extent of their full wages.

X. The abolition of the contract system on national, State, and municipal works.

XI. The enactment of laws providing for arbitration between employers and employed, and to enforce the decision of the arbitrators.

XII. The prohibition by law of the employment of children under fifteen years of age; the compulsory attendance at school for at least ten months in the year of all children between the ages of seven and fifteen years; and the furnishing at the expense of the State of free text-books.

XIII. That a graduated tax on incomes and inheritances be levied.

XIV. To prohibit the hiring out of convict labor.

*   *   *

159 "a removal and not an assassination" (1881)

Charles Jules Guiteau resided for a considerable time in the utopian Oneida Community. Upon departing he engaged in successive careers in law, bill collecting, theological writing, public lecturing, and politics. Guiteau joined the Stalwart faction of the Republican party and supported Garfield's election effort. He subsequently moved to Washington, slept on park benches, and petitioned the State Department for a post either in Vienna or in Paris. Disappointed in the lack of official response, Guiteau's criticism of Garfield's policies grew. In 1881 he decided Garfield's alignment with the Half-Breed faction of the Republican party, the enemies of the Stalwarts, called for Garfield's elimination from the political scene. After considerable planning, Guiteau finally shot Garfield on July 2 in the Washington railroad station. The President died on September 19. Guiteau was tried, pleaded the then still novel defense of insanity, but was found guilty and was executed on July 30, 1882.

The accompanying document provides Guiteau's own account of the assassination.

☆ 159 The Account of Garfield's Assassin

H. H. Alexander, "The Life of Guiteau and the Official History of the Most Exciting Case on Record" (1882), reprinted in Richard Hofstadter and Michael Wallace, eds., *American Violence: A Documentary History* (New York: Knopf, 1970), 413.

I have not ... used the words "assassination" or "assassin" in this work. These words grate on the mind and produce a bad feeling. I think of General Garfield's condition as a removal and not as an assassination. My idea simply stated was to remove as easily as possible Mr. James A. Garfield, a quiet and good-natured citizen of Ohio, who temporarily occupied the position of President of the United States, and substitute in his place Mr. Chester A. Arthur, of New York, a distinguished and highly estimable gentleman. . . .

Two weeks after I conceived the idea my mind was thoroughly settled on the intention to remove the President. I then prepared myself. I sent to Boston for a copy of my book, "The Truth," and I spent a week in preparing that. I cut out a paragraph and a line and a word here and there and added one or two new chapters, put some new ideas in it and I greatly improved it. I knew that it would probably have a large sale on account of the notoriety that the act of removing the President would give me, and I wished the book to go out to the public in proper shape. That was one preparation for it.

Another preparation was to think the matter all out in detail and to buy a revolver and to prepare myself for executing the idea. This required some two or three weeks, and I gave my entire time and mind in preparing myself to execute the conception of removing the President. . . . My mind was perfectly clear in regard to removing the President; I had not the slightest doubt about my duty to the Lord and to the American people in trying to remove the President, and I want to say here, as emphatically as words can make it, that, from the moment when I fully decided to remove the President, I have never had the slightest shadow on my mind; my purpose had been just as clear and just as determined as anything could be. I believed that I was acting under a special Divine authority to remove him, and this Divine pressure was upon me from the time when I fully resolved to remove him until I actually shot him. It was only by nerving myself to the utmost that I did it at all, and I never had the slightest doubt as the Divine inspiration of the act, and that it was for the best interest of the American people.

160 "to solve the Indian problem" (1881)

The "Indian problem," somewhat submerged during the Civil War and Reconstruction, was a central concern to President Chester A. Arthur in his first State of the Union Message. The earlier "peace policy," a separatist approach that sought to contain Native American tribes within assigned territories, had not eliminated the tensions within the Native American communities or the conflicts with the expanding white populations. The assimilationist measures suggested by Arthur were directed toward reforming the internal structures of Native American life. Seeking to vest ownership of land in individual members of the tribes, these measures were, in part, a benevolent gesture motivated by humanitarian concerns for providing individual Native Americans with the means for their self-support. But the thrust of the recommendations was to render the tribes and nations superfluous units and to subject Native Americans to local and state law.

Quite clearly, the ultimate goal of this policy was the elimination of a people, not through genocide, but rather by destroying the identity and cohesion of the ethnic or racial group and rendering them politically ineffectual. It was a policy of ethnocide.

☆ 160 President Arthur's First Annual Message (December 6, 1881)

Reprinted in J. Richardson, *A Compilation of the Messages and Papers of the Presidents* (New York: Bureau of National Literature, 1897), 8:54.

*   *   *

. . . Prominent among the matters which challenge the attention of Congress at its present session is the management of our Indian affairs. While this question has been a cause of trouble and embarrassment from the infancy of the Government, it is but recently that any effort has been made for its solution at once serious, determined, consistent, and promising success.

*   *   *

It was natural, at a time when the national territory seemed almost illimitable and contained many millions of acres far outside the bounds of civilized settlements, that a policy should have been initiated which more than aught else has been the fruitful source of our Indian complications.

I refer, of course, to the policy of dealing with the various Indian tribes as separate nationalities, of relegating them by treaty stipulations to the occupancy of immense reservations in the West, and of encouraging them to live a savage life, undisturbed by any earnest and well-directed efforts to bring them under the influences of civilization.

*   *   *

As the white settlements have crowded the borders of the reservations, the Indians, sometimes contentedly and sometimes against their will, have been transferred to other hunting grounds, from which they have again been dislodged whenever their new-found homes have been desired by the adventurous settlers.

These removals and the frontier collisions by which they have often been preceded have led to frequent and disastrous conflicts between the races.

    *   *   *

We have to deal with the appalling fact that though thousands of lives have been sacrificed and hundreds of millions of dollars expended in the attempt to solve the Indian problem, it has until within the past few years seemed scarcely nearer a solution than it was half a century ago. . . .

For the success of the efforts now making to introduce among the Indians the customs and pursuits of civilized life and gradually to absorb them into the mass of our citizens, sharing their rights and holden to their responsibilities, there is imperative need for legislative action.

My suggestions in that regard will be chiefly such as have been already called to the attention of Congress and have received to some extent its consideration.

First. I recommend the passage of an act making the laws of the various States and Territories applicable to the Indian reservations within their borders and extending the laws of the State of Arkansas to the portion of the Indian Territory not occupied by the Five Civilized Tribes.

The Indian should receive the protection of the law. He should be allowed to maintain in court his rights of person and property. He has repeatedly begged for this privilege. Its exercise would be very valuable to him in his progress toward civilization.

Second. Of even greater importance is a measure which has been frequently recommended by my predecessors in office, and in furtherance of which several bills have been from time to time introduced in both Houses of Congress. The enactment of a general law permitting the allotment in severalty, to such Indians, at least, as desire it, of a reasonable quantity of land secured to them by patent, and for their own protection made inalienable for twenty or twenty-five years, is demanded for their present welfare and their permanent advancement.

In return for such considerate action on the part of the Government, there is reason to believe that the Indians in large numbers would be persuaded to sever their tribal relations and to engage at once in agricultural pursuits. Many of them realize the fact that their hunting days are over and that it is now for their best interests to conform their manner of life to the new order of things. By no greater inducement than the assurance of permanent title to the soil can they be led to engage in the occupation of tilling it.

The well-attested reports of their increasing interest in husbandry justify the hope and belief that the enactment of such a statute as I recommend would be at once attended with gratifying results. A resort to the allotment system would have a direct and powerful influence in dissolving the tribal bond, which is so prominent a feature of savage life, and which tends so strongly to perpetuate it.

Third. I advise a liberal appropriation for the support of Indian schools, because of my confident belief that such a course is consistent with the wisest economy.

    *   *   *

161 The Fire of the Mob (1884)

Opposition to authority and acts of violence against the police or courts were not always triggered by, nor were they in response to, outright manifestations of public policy and power. At times the object of hostility was a private individual or group, and the assault on public authority was merely a means for voicing general dissatisfaction with the system of law and justice. Various activities of the vigilante organizations fell into this category.

When on March 28, 1884, William Berner, a confessed murderer, was sentenced to twenty years in prison instead of the customary death penalty, ten thousand indignant citizens held a mass protest in Cincinnati against the "disgraceful verdict." Unaware that Berner had been transferred to the state penitentiary, the mob broke into the jail and the next day burned down the courthouse. General rioting followed. At least fifty people were killed in the course of the three days of disturbances, which necessitated the calling up of the militia. At the end the mayor of Cincinnati called on the city's "leading two hundred businessmen" and the officers of the Grand Army of the Republic to help extinguish the riot.

☆ 161 The Cincinnati Riot

J. S. Tunison, "The Cincinnati Riot: Its Causes and Results" (1886), reprinted in Richard Hofstadter and Michael Wallace, eds., *American Violence: A Documentary History* (New York: Knopf, 1970), 467-69.

The crowd had been dense all day, and it gathered numbers and confidence as dark fell. The barricades looked ugly, and the crowd gathered chiefly in front of the Court-house. The riot began with the throwing of bowlders and brick-bats at the Court-house, while some fired pistols and shot-guns at the windows. Gaining confidence, a storming party was formed, and the iron doors in the Court-house front were battered down in a few minutes. About the same time a crowd of boys began breaking in the County Treasurer's office, which was in the northwest corner of the basement. The idea of firing the Court-house began with this crowd of boys and half-grown men, who are said to have been led by men and boys from Kentucky. The furniture and broken counters were piled up in the middle of the room, and coal-oil was poured upon them. The match was applied, and a small flame shot forth. It leaped from one article to another, gathered head, and roared with increasing strength. The crowd cheered and yelled. One office after another was fired, and soon the flames were dancing in every apartment of the front basement. When the crowd reached South Court Street it rushed along the side of the Court-house, intending to fire the offices on that side. It was met by a volley of musketry which made it stagger and rush around the corner again. Soon after a white handkerchief tied to a stick was waved, and then a number of the rioters cautiously appeared and carried off the dead and wounded. In a few minutes afterward the sheriff's red auction flag, through which the crowd had been firing bullets, was waved and again the mob surged around the corner, emptying its fire-arms at the barricade. "Fire!" Another crash made every wall in the narrow street tremble, and the multitude rushed back, some reeling and falling, others tripping over them, then picking themselves up and continuing the flight. Again the white flag was waved. "Make way, gentlemen, make way for the wounded," called out several surgeons, whom a sense of professional duty had called to the scene. "Make way," and the crowd opened lanes through which was carried many a poor fellow who had rushed around the corner but a minute before. Soon the tables of the Debolt Exchange were covered with mangled bodies, some from which life had fled, others which were gasping with feeble and perishing breath. The surgeons busied themselves with these while the battle went on without. After this the militia kept up a dropping fire on the crowd whenever it showed itself, and continually the number of the wounded grew. The Debolt could not hold them all. Burdsal's drug-store, below Canal, and a saloon on Ninth Street were turned into temporary hospitals. This sort of skirmishing continued for hours, and amid it all the Court-house burned slowly. Slowly the flames crept from room to room through a building alleged to be fire-proof. Anon the flames pierced the roof, dense volumes of smoke roared through the ventilator over the rotunda, iron shutters bent in the heat, iron girders sprang from their seats on iron pillars with loud explosions, records which were eloquent with human joys and sorrows turned into bright flame and vanished, while passions as hot as the fire raged around the devoted pile. Nothing could be done to stay the flames — the mob would not allow it.

But another turning point had been reached, and the insulted majesty of law and order began to assert itself with greater force. Soldiers began to arrive from other parts of the State who a few hours before had been plying the peaceful arts of the citizen. First came the Fourth Regiment, but only to teach Dayton how little reliance she might place in her citizen-soldiery. Appalled by the hostility of the crowd, which would have made respectful room before a gleaming line of bayonets, this regiment halted within sight almost of the building, which was only beginning to burn then, and ingloriously returned to the depot from which it came. Captain Frank Brown, of Company A, after trying vainly to rally the command, returned with several members of his Dayton company to the lines the next day and did good service. The remainder of that company left for their homes in Dayton. Companies of the regiment from Springfield and other points retrieved their fame by assisting in quelling the following day, and some of the Daytonians were forced to return by the scorn of their wives and fellow-townsmen. But most of them would not risk their precious lives.

*   *   *

... Occasionally some section of the mob, with reckless daring, sprang from behind a sheltering corner to fire on the troops. The troops returned the fire, not in volley, now, for the discharge of two or three guns was enough to disperse the crowd, and almost every such episode added to the list of the dead and wounded. Thus the night wore away, and with the gray dawn the firing gradually ceased.

162 To Be "let out of the state of pupilage" (1884)

More than a year before his application to register as a voter, John Elk had severed all relations with the tribe into which he had been born, relinquished the privileges based on his Native American ancestry, become a bona fide resident of the state of Nebraska, and submitted himself to the full jurisdiction of the laws of Nebraska and the United States. His application was rejected. Elk sued, claiming the denial of registration violated the Fourteenth and Fifteenth amendments.

Although the avowed policy of the United States toward the Native Americans involved "civilizing them so they would disestablish their tribal relations and join the mass of the population," the law deemed them unacceptable for admission to citizenship, withholding from them access to the political process that decided their fate.

☆ 162 *Elk v. Wilkins*

112 U.S. 94 (1884).

MR. JUSTICE GRAY delivered the opinion of the court.

*   *   *

The petition, while it does not show of what Indian tribe the plaintiff was a member, yet, by the allegations that he "is an Indian, and was born within the United States," and that "he had severed his tribal relation to the Indian tribes," clearly implies that he was born a member of one of the Indian tribes within the limits of the United States, which still exists and is recognized as a tribe by the government of the United States. Though the plaintiff alleges that he "had fully and completely surrendered himself to the jurisdiction of the United States," he does not allege that the United States accepted his surrender, or that he has ever been naturalized, or taxed, or in any way recognized or treated as a citizen, by the State or by the United States. Nor is it contended by his counsel that there is any statute or treaty that makes him a citizen.

The question then is, whether an Indian, born a member of one of the Indian tribes within the United States, is, merely by reason of his birth within the United States, and of his afterwards voluntarily separating himself from his tribe and taking up his residence among white citizens, a citizen of the United States, within the meaning of the first section of the Fourteenth Amendment of the Constitution.

Under the Constitution of the United States, as originally established, "Indians not taxed" were excluded from the persons according to whose numbers representatives and direct taxes were apportioned among the several States; and Congress had and exercised the power to regulate commerce with the Indian tribes, and the members thereof, whether within or without the boundaries of one of the States of the Union. The Indian tribes, being within the territorial limits of the United States, were not, strictly speaking, foreign States; but they were alien nations, distinct political communities, with whom the United States might and habitually did deal, as they thought fit, either through treaties made by the President and Senate, or through acts of Congress in the ordinary forms of legislation. The members of those tribes owed immediate allegiance to their several tribes, and were not part of the people of the United States. They were in a dependent condition, a state of pupilage, resembling that of a ward to his guardian. Indians and their property, exempt from taxation by treaty or statute of the United States, could not be taxed by any State. General acts of Congress did not apply to Indians, unless so expressed as to clearly manifest an intention to include them.

The alien and dependent condition of the members of the Indian tribes could not be put off at their own will, without the action or assent of the United States. They were never deemed citizens of the United States, except under explicit provisions of treaty or statute to that effect, either declaring a certain tribe, or such members of it as chose to remain behind on the removal of the tribe westward,

to be citizens, or authorizing individuals of particular tribes to become citizens on application to a court of the United States for naturalization, and satisfactory proof of fitness for civilized life. . . .

. . . The main object of the opening sentence of the Fourteenth Amendment was to settle the question, upon which there had been a difference of opinion throughout the country and in this court, as to the citizenship of free negroes (*Scott v. Sandford*); and to put it beyond doubt that all persons, white or black, and whether formerly slaves or not, born or naturalized in the United States, and owing no allegiance to any alien power, should be citizens of the United States and of the State in which they reside. . . .

This section contemplates two sources of citizenship, and two sources only: birth and naturalization. The persons declared to be citizens are "all persons born or naturalized in the United States, and subject to the jurisdiction thereof." The evident meaning of these last words is, not merely subject in some respect or degree to the jurisdiction of the United States, but completely subject to their political jurisdiction, and owing them direct and immediate allegiance. And the words relate to the time of birth in the one case, as they do to the time of naturalization in the other. Persons not thus subject to the jurisdiction of the United States at the time of birth cannot become so afterwards, except by being naturalized, either individually, as by proceedings under the naturalization acts, or collectively, as by the force of a treaty by which foreign territory is acquired.

Indians born within the territorial limits of the United States, members of, and owing immediate allegiance to, one of the Indian tribes (an alien, though dependent, power), although in a geographical sense born in the United States, are no more "born in the United States and subject to the jurisdiction thereof," within the meaning of the first section of the Fourteenth Amendment, than the children of subjects of any foreign government born within the domain of that government, or the children born within the United States, of ambassadors or other public ministers of foreign nations.

*   *   *

Such Indians, then, not being citizens by birth, can only become citizens in the second way mentioned in the Fourteenth Amendment, by being "naturalized in the United States," by or under some treaty or statute.

*   *   *

Since the ratification of the Fourteenth Amendment, Congress has passed several acts for naturalizing Indians of certain tribes, which would have been superfluous if they were, or might become, without any action of the government, citizens of the United States.

*   *   *

The national legislation has tended more and more towards the education and civilization of the Indians, and fitting them to be citizens. But the question whether any Indian tribes, or any members thereof, have become so far advanced in civilization, that they should be let out of the state of pupilage, and admitted to the privileges and responsibilities of citizenship, is a question to be decided by the nation whose wards they are and whose citizens they seek to become, and not by each Indian for himself.

*   *   *

The condition of the tribe from which he derived his origin, so far as any fragments of it remained within the State of New York, resembled the condition of those Indian nations of which Mr. Justice Johnson said in *Fletcher v. Peck* that they "have totally extinguished their national fire, and submitted themselves to the laws of the States;" and which Mr. Justice McLean had in view, when he observed in *Worcester v. Georgia* that in some of the old States, "where small remnants of tribes remain, surrounded by white population, and who, by their reduced numbers, had lost the power of self-government, the laws of the State have been extended over them, for the protection of their persons and property." See also, as to the condition of Indians in Massachusetts, remnants of tribes never recognized by the treaties or legislative or executive acts of the United States as distinct political communities. . . .

*   *   *

The law upon the question before us has been well stated by Judge Deady in the District Court of the United States for the District of Oregon. . . . [H]e said: "But an Indian cannot make himself a citizen of the United States without the consent and co-operation of the government. The fact that he has abandoned his nomadic life or tribal relations, and adopted the habits and manners of civilized people, may be a good reason why he should be made a citizen of the United States, but does not of itself make him one. To be a citizen of the United States is a political privilege which no one, not born to, can assume without its consent in some form. The Indians in Oregon, not being born subject to the jurisdiction of the United States, were not born citizens thereof, and I am not aware of any law or treaty by which any of them have been made so since."

The plaintiff, not being a citizen of the United States under the Fourteenth Amendment of the Constitution, has been deprived of no right secured by the Fifteenth Amendment, and cannot maintain this action.

Judgment affirmed.

Mr. Justice Harlan, with whom concurred Mr. Justice Woods, dissenting.

*   *   *

. . . Is it conceivable that the statesmen who framed, the Congress which submitted, and the people who adopted that amendment, intended to confer citizenship, national and State, upon the entire population in this country of African descent (the larger part of which was shortly before held in slavery), and by the same constitutional provision to exclude from such citizenship Indians who had never been in slavery, and who, by becoming *bona fide* residents of States and Territories within the complete jurisdiction of the United States, had evinced a purpose to abandon their former mode of life and become a part of the People of the United States? If this question be answered in the negative, as we think it must be, then we are justified in withholding our assent to the doctrine which excludes the plaintiff from the body of citizens of the United States, upon the ground that his parents were, when he was born, members of an Indian tribe. . . .

Our brethren, it seems to us, construe the Fourteenth Amendment as if it read: "All persons *born subject* to the jurisdiction of, or naturalized in, the United States, are citizens of the United States and of the State in which they reside;" whereas the amendment, as it is, implies in respect of persons born in this country, that they may claim the rights of national citizenship from and after the moment they become subject to the complete jurisdiction of the United States. This would not include the children, born in this country, of a foreign minister, for the reason that, under the fiction of extra-territoriality as recognized by international law, such minister, "though actually in a foreign country, is considered still to remain within the territory of his own State," and, consequently, he continues "subject to the laws of his own country, both with respect to his personal status, and his rights of property; and his children, though born in a foreign country, are considered as natives." Halleck's International Law, ch. 10, § 12.

*   *   *

163 "Revenge! Workingmen! To Arms!" (1886)

During an 1886 strike at the McCormick Harvesting Machine Company, the Chicago police fired into a crowd of strikers. Angered, anarchist August Spies composed the circular reproduced below, with the exception of the heading "Revenge," and circulated it that night. The flyer heaped particular calumny upon the police as the enforcers of the capitalist will. At a protest meeting the following day in Haymarket Square, a bomb thrown at the closing of the demonstration killed seven policemen and four other persons. Eight anarchists, including August

Spies, were arrested, tried, and convicted despite the absence of any direct evidence that they had made or thrown the bomb. The theory of the prosecution, adopted by the court, was codified subsequently in Illinois' extremely broad Merritt Conspiracy Act. Four of the convicts, including Spies, were hanged, and one committed suicide. After the passage of five years, the Merritt Act was repealed; and after seven years' imprisonment the surviving three convicts were pardoned by Illinois' governor, John Peter Altgeld.

☆ 163 The Haymarket Conspiracy

Reprinted in H. David, *The History of the Haymarket Affair* (New York: Farrar & Rinehart, 1936), 191-92.

*   *   *

☆ 163a The Spies Circular

REVENGE! WORKINGMEN! TO ARMS!

Your masters sent out their bloodhounds—the police—they killed six of your brothers at McCormick's this afternoon. They killed the poor wretches, because they, like you, had courage to disobey the supreme will of your bosses. They killed them because they dared ask for the shortening of the hours of toil. They killed them to show you "free American citizens" that you must be satisfied and contented with whatever your bosses condescend to allow you, or you will get killed!

You have for years endured the most abject humiliations; you have for years suffered immeasurable iniquities; you have worked yourselves to death; you have endured the pangs of want and hunger; your children you have sacrificed to the factory lords—in short, you have been miserable and obedient slaves all these years. Why? To satisfy the insatiable greed and fill the coffers of your lazy thieving masters! When you ask him now to lessen your burden, he sends his bloodhounds out to shoot you, to kill you!

If you are men, if you are the sons of your grandsires, who have shed their blood to free you, then you will rise in your might, Hercules, and destroy the hideous monster that seeks to destroy you.

To arms, we call you, to arms!

YOUR BROTHERS

☆ 163b Merritt Conspiracy Act

1887 Ill. Laws 168, *repealed*, May 28, 1891.

*   *   *

Sec. 2. If any person shall, by speaking to any public or private assemblage of people or in any public place, or shall, by writing, printing or publishing or by causing to be written, printed, published or circu-

lated any written or printed matter, advise, encourage, aid, abet, or incite a local revolution, or the overthrowing or destruction of the existing order of society by force or violence, or the resistance to, and destruction of, the lawful power and authority of the legal authorities of this State, . . . or advise, abet, encourage, or incite the disturbance of the public peace, and by such disturbance an attempt at revolution or destruction of public order, or resistance to such authorities shall therefore ensue, and human life is taken, or any person injured or property destroyed, every person so aiding, etc., shall be deemed as having conspired with the person or persons who actually commit the crime, and shall be deemed a principal in the perpetration of the same, and shall be punished accordingly, and it shall not be necessary for the prosecution to show that the speaking was heard or the written or printed matter was read or communicated to the person or persons actually committing the crime, if such speaking, writing, etc., is shown to have been done in a public manner.

*   *   *

164 "even though you erect a gibbet on every street corner" (1886)

Michael Schwab, in addition to August Spies, was one of the anarchists tried, convicted, and sentenced to death for his part in the Haymarket Affair. Schwab's sentence was commuted to life imprisonment, and in 1893 he was granted a pardon.

The Spies and Schwab views on anarchism and violence were set forth before the court. In particular, they equated anarchism with a higher and more peaceful human condition and eschewed the use of violence except in defense against the violence inherent in the capitalist system.

☆ 164 Speeches of Michael Schwab and August Spies before the Court

Reprinted in *The Chicago Martyrs: The Famous Speeches of Eight Anarchists in Judge Gary's Court* (San Francisco: Free Society, 1899), 14, 19-20.

*   *   *

SCHWAB. "Anarchy" is Greek, and means, verbatim, without rulership; not being ruled. According to our vocabulary, anarchy is a state of society in which the only government is reason; a state of society in which all human beings do right for the simple reason that it is right, and hate wrong because it is wrong. In such a society, no laws, no compulsion will be necessary. The attorney of the State was wrong when he said: "Anarchy is dead." Anarchy, up to the present day, has existed only as a doctrine, and Mr. Grinnell has not the power to kill any doctrine whatever. You may call anarchy, as defined by us, an idle dream, but that dream was dreamed by Gotthold Ephraim Lessing, one of the three great German poets and the most celebrated German critic of the last century. If anarchy were the thing the State's attorney makes it out to be, how could it be that such eminent scholars as Prince Kropotkine and the greatest living geographer, Elisee Reclus, were avowed anarchists, even editors of anarchistic newspapers? Anarchy is a dream, but only in the present. It will be realized. Reason will grow in spite of all obstacles. Who is the man that has the cheek to tell us that human development has already reached its culminating point? I know that our ideal will not be accomplished this or next year, but I know that it will be accomplished as near as possible, some day, in the future. It is entirely wrong to use the word anarchy as synonymous with violence. Violence is one thing and anarchy another. In the present state of society violence is used on all sides, and, therefore, we advocated the use of violence against violence, but against violence only, as a necessary means of defence.

SPIES. Society will reclaim its own, even though you erect a gibbet on every street corner. And anarchism, this terrible "ism," deduces that under a cooperative organization of society, under economic equality and individual independence, the "state"—the political state—will pass into barbaric antiquity. And we will be where all are free, where there are no longer masters and servants, where intellect stands for brute force; there will no longer be any use for the policemen and militia to preserve the so-called "peace and order"—the order that the Russian general speaks of when he telegraphed to the Czar after he had massacred half of Warsaw, "Peace reigns in Warsaw." Anarchism does not mean bloodshed; does not mean, robbery, arson, etc. These monstrosities are, on the contrary, the characteristic features of capitalism. Anarchism means peace and tranquillity to all. Anarchism means the reorganization of society upon scientific principles and the abolition of causes which produce vice and crime.

165 The Indian Soil Is under United States Political Control (1886)

Prior to 1885, Native American offenses against Native Americans within Native American territory were tried and punished under tribal law. Treaties always had recognized this authority. In that year, Congress passed the Major Crimes Act, which explicitly extended federal court jurisdiction over seven crimes when both the victim and the alleged perpetrator were Native Americans and the crime was committed on a Native American reservation. Despite the abolition in 1871 of the treaty-making status of Native American tribes, this was the first time Congress actually had regulated the internal affairs of Native Americans without the consent, through treaty, of the tribe or nation affected. In 1886, the Supreme Court considered the constitutionality of the legislation. Initially determining the act was not based on the commerce clause or the apportionment clauses of Article I and the Fourteenth Amendment, the court nevertheless upheld Congress's power to regulate Native Americans directly and without their consent through either organized tribal negotiation or individual participation in the electoral process. In the final analysis, the political and civil rights of Native Americans rested within the unilateral power of Congress.

☆ 165 *United States v. Kagama*

118 U.S. 375 (1886).

MILLER, J. . . .

*   *   *

. . . [W]e are not able to see, in either of these clauses of the Constitution and its amendments, any delegation of power to enact a code of criminal law for the punishment of the worst class of crimes known to civilized life when committed by Indians. . . .

But these Indians are within the geographical limits of the United States. The soil and the people within these limits are under the political control of the Government of the United States, or of the States of the Union. There exist within the broad domain of sovereignty but these two. There may be cities, counties, and other organized bodies with limited legislative functions, but they are all derived from, or exist in, subordination to one or the other of these. The territorial governments owe all their powers to the statutes of the United States conferring on them the powers which they exercise, and which are liable to be withdrawn, modified, or repealed at any time by Congress. . . . But this power of Congress to organize territorial governments, and make laws for their inhabitants, arises not so much from the clause in the Constitution in regard to disposing of and making rules and regulations concerning the Territory and other property of the United States, as from the ownership of the country in which the Territories are, and the right of exclusive sovereignty which must exist in the National Government, and can be found nowhere else.

*   *   *

The Indian reservation in the case before us is land bought by the United States from Mexico by the treaty of Guadaloupe Hidalgo, and the whole of

California, with the allegiance of its inhabitants, many of whom were Indians, was transferred by that treaty to the United States.

The relation of the Indian tribes living within the borders of the United States, both before and since the Revolution, to the people of the United States has always been an anomalous one and of a complex character.

... They were, and always have been, regarded as having a semi-independent position when they preserved their tribal relations; not as States, not as nations, not as possessed of the full attributes of sovereignty, but as a separate people, with the power of regulating their internal and social relations, and thus far not brought under the laws of the Union or of the State within whose limits they resided.

Perhaps the best statement of their position is found in the two opinions of this court by Chief Justice Marshall in the case of the *Cherokee Nation v. Georgia* and in the case of *Worcester v. State of Georgia.* These opinions are exhaustive; and in the separate opinion of Mr. Justice Baldwin, in the former, is a very valuable résumé of the treaties and statutes concerning the Indian tribes previous to and during the confederation.

In the first of the above cases it was held that these tribes were neither States nor nations, had only some of the attributes of sovereignty, and could not be so far recognized in that capacity as to sustain a suit in the Supreme Court of the United States. In the second case it was said that they were not subject to the jurisdiction asserted over them by the State of Georgia, which, because they were within its limits, where they had been for ages, had attempted to extend her laws and the jurisdiction of her courts over them.

In the opinions in these cases they are spoken of as "wards of the nation," "pupils," as local dependent communities. In this spirit the United States has conducted its relations to them from its organization to this time. But, after an experience of a hundred years of the treaty-making system of government, Congress has determined upon a new departure—to govern them by acts of Congress. This is seen in the act of March 3, 1871, embodied in § 2079 of the Revised Statutes:

"No Indian nation or tribe, within the territory of the United States shall be acknowledged or recognized as an independent nation, tribe, or power, with whom the United States may contract by treaty; but no obligation of any treaty lawfully made and ratified with any such Indian nation or tribe prior to March third, eighteen hundred and seventy one, shall be hereby invalidated or impaired."

... The decision in [*Ex Parte Crow Dog*] admits that if the intention of Congress had been to punish, by the United States courts, the murder of one In-

dian by another, the law would have been valid.... The passage of the act now under consideration was designed to remove that objection, and to go further by including such crimes on reservations lying within a State.

Is this latter fact a fatal objection to the law? ...

... It does not interfere with the process of the State courts within the reservation, nor with the operation of State laws upon white people found there. Its effect is confined to the acts of an Indian of some tribe, of a criminal character, committed within the limits of the reservation.

It seems to us that this is within the competency of Congress. These Indian tribes *are* the wards of the nation. They are communities *dependent* on the United States. Dependent largely for their daily food. Dependent for their political rights. They owe no allegiance to the States, and receive from them no protection. Because of the local ill feeling, the people of the States where they are found are often their deadliest enemies. From their very weakness and helplessness, so largely due to the course of dealing of the Federal Government with them and the treaties in which it has been promised, there arises the duty of protection, and with it the power. This has always been recognized by the Executive and by Congress, and by this court, whenever the question has arisen.

*   *   *

The power of the General Government over these remnants of a race once powerful, now weak and diminished in numbers, is necessary to their protection, as well as to the safety of those among whom they dwell. It must exist in that government, because it never has existed anywhere else, because the theatre of its exercise is within the geographical limits of the United States, because it has never been denied, and because it alone can enforce its laws on all the tribes.

We answer the questions propounded to us, that the 9th section of the act of March, 1885, is a valid law in both its branches, and that the Circuit Court of the United States for the District of California has jurisdiction of the offence charged in the indictment in this case.

166 "rights, privileges, and immunities" (1887)

Native Americans were unalterably opposed to the idea of individual allocation of lands, recognizing that loss of the tribal lands would, as intended, undermine and diminish tribal authority and culture. But lingering doubts concerning the authority of the United States directly to affect internal tribal affairs had been dispelled by *United States v. Kagama*, and the Dawes Act, allotting Native American lands to be held in severalty, was passed the following year.

The Dawes Act was not self-executing, and the allotment program was gradual. Under the act, 118 reservations were broken up, and because of the terms of Section 5, some eighty-six million acres of Native American-held lands (62 percent of the total) were opened to white settlement and homesteading. Subsequent amendments extended the allotment policy to the Five Civilized Tribes, delayed acquisition of citizenship, and extended the trust periods. The policies behind the act led to the adoption of other ethnocidal measures by the Bureau of Indian Affairs, including the prohibition of certain religious practices and the refusal to teach Native American children their own language.

☆ 166 An Act to Provide for the Allotment of Lands in Severalty to Indians (Dawes Act)

24 Stat. 388 (1887).

BE IT ENACTED *by the Senate and House of Representatives of the United States of America in Congress assembled*, That in all cases where any tribe or band of Indians has been, or shall hereafter be, located upon any reservation created for their use, either by treaty stipulation or by virtue of an act of Congress or executive order setting apart the same for their use, the President of the United States be, and he hereby is, authorized, whenever in his opinion any reservation or any part thereof of such Indians is advantageous for agricultural and grazing purposes, to cause said reservation, or any part thereof, to be surveyed, or resurveyed if necessary, and to allot the lands in said reservation in severalty to any Indian located thereon in quantities as follows: . . .

*   *   *

SEC. 2. That all allotments set apart under the provisions of this act shall be selected by the Indians, heads of families selecting for their minor children, and the agents shall select for each orphan child, and in such manner as to embrace the improvements of the Indians making the selection. Where the improvements of two or more Indians have been made on the same legal subdivision of land, unless they shall otherwise agree, a provisional line may be run dividing said lands between them, and the amount to which each is entitled shall be equalized in the assignment of the remainder of the land to which they are entitled under this act: *Provided*, That if any one entitled to an allotment shall fail to make a selection within four years after the President shall direct that allotments may be made on a particular reservation, the Secretary of the Interior may direct the agent of such tribe or band, if

such there be, and if there be no agent, then a special agent appointed for that purpose, to make a selection for such Indian, which election shall be allotted as in cases where selections are made by the Indians, and patents shall issue in like manner.

*   *   *

SEC. 4. That where any Indian not residing upon a reservation, or for whose tribe no reservation has been provided by treaty, act of Congress, or executive order, shall make settlement upon any surveyed or unsurveyed lands of the United States not otherwise apropriated, he or she shall be entitled, upon application to the local land-office for the district in which the lands are located, to have the same allotted to him or her, and to his or her children, in quantities and manner as provided in this act for Indians residing upon reservations. . . .

SEC. 5. That upon the approval of the allotments provided for in this act by the Secretary of the Interior, he shall cause patents to issue therefor in the name of the allottees, which patents shall be of the legal effect, and declare that the United States does and will hold the land thus allotted, for the period of twenty-five years, in trust for the sole use and benefit of the Indian to whom such allotment shall have been made, or, in case of his decease, of his heirs according to the laws of the State or Territory where such land is located, and that at the expiration of said period the United States will convey the same by patent to said Indian, or his heirs as aforesaid, in fee, discharged of said trust and free of all charge or incumbrance whatsoever: *Provided*, That the President of the United States may in any case in his discretion extend the period. . . . *And provided further*, That at any time after lands have been allotted to all the Indians of any tribe as herein provided, or sooner if in the opinion of the President it shall be for the best interests of said tribe, it shall be lawful for the Secretary of the Interior to negotiate with such Indian tribe for the purchase and release by said tribe, in conformity with the treaty or statute under which such reservation is held, of such portions of its reservation not allotted as such tribe shall, from time to time, consent to sell, on such terms and conditions as shall be considered just and equitable between the United States and said tribe of Indians, which purchase shall not be complete until ratified by Congress, and the form and manner of executing such release shall also be prescribed by Congress: *Provided however*, That all lands adapted to agriculture, with or without irrigation so sold or released to the United States by any Indian tribe shall be held by the United States for the sole purpose of securing homes to actual settlers and shall be disposed of by the United States to actual and bona fide settlers only in tracts not exceeding one hundred and sixty acres to any one person, on such terms as Congress shall prescribe, subject to grants which Congress may make in aid of education: ... And the sums agreed to be paid by the United States as purchase money for any portion of any such reservation shall be held in the Treasury of the United States for the sole use of the tribe or tribes of Indians; to whom such reservations belonged; and the same, with interest thereon at three per cent per annum, shall be at all times subject to appropriation by Congress for the education and civilization of such tribe or tribes of Indians or the members thereof. . . .

SEC. 6. That upon the completion of said allotments and the patenting of the lands to said allottees, each and every member of the respective bands or tribes of Indians to whom allotments have been made shall have the benefit of and be subject to the laws, both civil and criminal, of the State or Territory in which they may reside; and no Territory shall pass or enforce any law denying any such Indian within its jurisdiction the equal protection of the law. And every Indian born within the territorial limits of the United States to whom allotments shall have been made under the provisions of this act, or under any law or treaty, and every Indian born within the territorial limits of the United States who has voluntarily taken up, within said limits, his residence separate and apart from any tribe of Indians therein, and has adopted the habits of civilized life, is hereby declared to be a citizen of the United States, and is entitled to all the rights, privileges, and immunities of such citizens, whether said Indian has been or not, by birth or otherwise, a member of any tribe of Indians within the territorial limits of the United States without in any manner impairing or otherwise affecting the right of any such Indian to tribal or other property.

*   *   *

SEC. 8. That the provision of this act shall not extend to the territory occupied by the Cherokees, Creeks, Choctaws, Chickasaws, Seminoles, and Osage, Miamies and Peorias, and Sacs and Foxes, in the Indian Territory, nor to any of the reservations of the Seneca Nation of New York Indians in the State of New York, nor to that strip of territory in the State of Nebraska adjoining the Sioux Nation on the south added by executive order.

167 "combination . . . in restraint of trade" (1890)

Enacted for the purpose of combating commercial monopolistic practices, the Sherman Antitrust Act and the remedies provided therein served as a major "union-busting" device. Management was able to invoke the sanctions of the act against union-di-rected strikes and boycotts. While the sanctions were civil in form, they had a highly punitive and quasi-criminal flavor. In 1902 the courts held that union effort to boycott Loewe Hats violated the Sherman Act and assessed triple damages in the amount of $240,000 against the union. In *Gompers v. Buck's Stove and Range Co.*, management succeeded in obtaining a sweeping injunction forbidding a boycott by the American Federation of Labor, and when AFL officials defied the order, they were jailed for contempt of court. To labor, these applications of the Sherman Act were another example of the law unjustly siding with capital on the economic battleground. Disobedience of the labor injunction became union policy.

☆ 167 Sherman Antitrust Act

26 Stat. 209 (1890).

Be it enacted by the Senate and House of Representatives of the United States of America in Congress assembled,

SEC. 1. Every contract, combination in the form of trust or otherwise, or conspiracy, in restraint of trade or commerce among the several States, or with foreign nations, is hereby declared to be illegal. Every person who shall make any such contract or engage in any such combination or conspiracy, shall be deemed guilty of a misdemeanor, and, on conviction thereof, shall be punished by fine not exceeding five thousand dollars, or by imprisonment not exceeding one year, or by both said punishments, in the discretion of the court.

SEC. 2. Every person who shall monopolize, or attempt to monopolize, or combine or conspire with any other person or persons, to monopolize any part of the trade or commerce among the several States, or with foreign nations, shall be deemed guilty of a misdemeanor, and, on conviction thereof, shall be punished by fine not exceeding five thousand dollars, or by imprisonment not exceeding one year, or by both said punishments, in the discretion of the court.

SEC. 3. Every contract, combination in form of trust or otherwise, or conspiracy, in restraint of trade or commerce in any Territory of the United States or of the District of Columbia, or in restraint of trade or commerce between any such Territory and another, or between any such Territory or Territories and any State or States or the District of Columbia, or with foreign nations, or between the District of Columbia and any State or States or foreign nations, is hereby declared illegal. Every person who shall make any such contract or engage in any such combination or conspiracy, shall be deemed guilty of a misdemeanor, and, on conviction thereof, shall be punished by fine not exceeding five thousand dollars, or by imprisonment not exceeding one year, or by both said punishments, in the discretion of the court.

SEC. 4. The several circuit courts of the United States are hereby invested with jurisdiction to prevent and restrain violations of this act.... Such proceedings may be by way of petition setting forth the case and praying that such violation shall be enjoined or otherwise prohibited....

*   *   *

SEC. 7. Any person who shall be injured in his business or property by any other person or corporation by reason of anything forbidden or declared to be unlawful by this act, may sue therefor ... and shall recover three fold the damages by him sustained, and the costs of suit, including a reasonable attorney's fee.

*   *   *

168 "The President of the United States of America to Eugene V. Debs" (1894)

In 1893, the United States had three million unemployed workers and more than six hundred bank failures. After years of bustling economic growth with rampant speculation in the stock market and overextended industrial production, corporate profits fell rapidly and wages dropped drastically. Labor, acknowledging the depressed economic conditions, submitted to management's stringent measures. The economy showed some improvement the following year, but it failed to make a substantial recovery. Restless, labor responded with an explosion of strikes and disturbances. In 1894, the nation was confronted with the Pullman strike, or "Debs's Rebellion," in which George Mortimer Pullman and the railroads were pitted against labor leader Eugene Victor Debs and the American Railway Union.

The strike paralyzed transportation from Chicago to the Pacific Coast, and the railroad operators beseeched President Grover Cleveland to intervene. He did, sending two thousand troops to keep the trains moving. The power of the United States was enlisted further in aid of management, which sought and obtained injunctions under the Sherman Antitrust Act to restrain Debs and his union from their activities. When Debs defied the law, which he viewed as being favorable to management, the court cited him for criminal contempt and ordered him jailed for six months as punishment.

☆ 168 Debs's Rebellion

☆ 168a *In re Debs Injunction*

S. Ex. Doc. No. 7, 53d Cong., 3d Sess. 179-80 (1894).

UNITED STATES CIRCUIT COURT,
DISTRICT OF INDIANA

The President of the United States of America to Eugene V. Debs ... [et al.] and the American Railway Union. And all other persons combining and conspiring with them, and to all other persons whomsoever:

You are hereby restrained, commanded, and enjoined absolutely to desist and refrain from in any way or manner interfering with, hindering, obstructing, or stopping any of the business of any of the following-named railroads: [23 named] As common carriers of passengers and freight between or among any States of the United States, and from in any way interfering with, hindering, obstructing, or stopping any mail trains, express trains, whether freight or passenger, engaged in interstate commerce, or carrying passengers or freight between or among the States; ... and from compelling or inducing, or attempting to compel or induce, by threats, intimidation, persuasion, force, or violence, any of the employees of any of said railroads to refuse or fail to perform any of their duties as employees of any of said railroads in connection with the interstate business or commerce of such railroads, or the carriage of the United States mail by such railroads, or the transportation of passengers or property between or among the States; ... and from doing any act whatever in furtherance of any conspiracy or combination to restrain either of said railroad companies in the free and unhindered control and handling of interstate commerce over the lines of said railroads, and of transportation of persons and freight between and among the States; and from ordering, directing, aiding, assisting, or abetting, in any manner whatever, any person or persons to commit any or either of the acts aforesaid.

And Eugene V. Debs and all other persons are hereby enjoined and restrained from sending out any letters, messages, or communications directing, inciting, encouraging, or instructing any person whatsoever to interfere with the business or affairs, directly or indirectly, of any of the railway companies hereinabove named, or from persuading any of the employees of said railway companies while in the employment of their respective companies to fail or refuse to perform the duties of their employment....

*   *   *

☆ 168b *United States v. Debs*

64 F. 724 (C.C.N.D. Ill. 1894).

WOODS, Circuit Judge....

*   *   *

[T]he question now to be considered [is] whether or not the injunction was authorized by the [Sherman Antitrust A]ct of July 2, 1890.... [I]t has been seriously questioned in this proceeding, as well as by an eminent judge and by lawyers elsewhere, whether the statute is by its terms applicable. . . .

*   *   *

. . . The position of the defendants in respect to this statute, as stated in one of the briefs, is that it "is directed at capital", "at dangers very generally supposed to result from vast aggregations of capital", that "the evil aimed at is one of a contractual character, and not of force and violence." . . .

. . . [T]he original measure, as proposed in the senate, "was directed wholly against trusts, and not at organizations of labor in any form". But . . . it is worthy of note that a proviso to the effect that the act should not be construed to apply "to any arrangements, agreements or combinations made between laborers with a view of lessening hours of labor or of increasing their wages, nor to any arrangements, agreements or combinations among persons engaged in agriculture made with the view of enhancing the price of agricultural . . . products" was not adopted. . . . [T]he offering of the proposition shows that the possible application of the statute to cases not in the nature of trusts or monopolies, and in which workmen or farmers should be concerned, was not overlooked. But it is more significant that, upon the introduction of the bill into the house, the chairman of the judiciary committee . . . made the following statement: "Now just what contracts, what combinations in the form of trusts, or what conspiracies will be in restraint of trade or commerce, mentioned in the bill, will not be known until the courts have construed and interpreted this provision."

It is therefore the privilege and duty of the court, uncontrolled by considerations drawn from other sources, to find the meaning of the statute in the terms of its provisions, interpreted by the settled rules of construction. That the original design to suppress trusts and monopolies created by contract or combination in the form of trust, which of course would be of a "contractual character" was adhered to, is clear; but it is equally clear that a further and more comprehensive purpose came to be entertained, and was embodied in the final form of the enactment. Combinations are condemned, not only when they take the form of trusts, but in whatever form found, if they be in restraint of trade. That is the effect of the words "or otherwise." . . . Any proposed restraint of trade, though it be in itself innocent, if it is to be accomplished by conspiracy, is unlawful. . . .

*   *   *

I have not failed, I think, to appreciate the just force of the argument to the contrary, of my opinion,—it has sometimes entangled me in doubt,—but my conclusion is clear, that under the act of 1890, the court had jurisdiction of the case presented in the application, and that the injunction granted was not without authority of law, nor for any reason invalid.

*   *   *

169 "keeping those highways of interstate commerce free from obstruction" (1894)

Eugene V. Debs sought a writ of habeas corpus from the United States Supreme Court to review the lawfulness of his imprisonment for violating the injunction against participation in the railroad strike. Clarence Darrow, Debs's lawyer, argued that the United States had no power to intervene in matters of local peacekeeping, that the Sherman Act was not intended to cover labor activities, and that the imprisonment of Debs without a jury trial (suits for injunctions, as well as all equity proceedings, are conducted without a jury) violated the Sixth Amendment. Darrow also made an impassioned plea for the justice of the labor cause. The plea fell on deaf ears. Despite the fact that no law of the United States was defied, the court concluded that the government's interest in the movement of the mails was sufficient cause to uphold Debs's imprisonment through the invocation of the quasi-criminal law. Of particular note is the court's reiteration of the dogma that all social wrongs were to be addressed through the ballot box or the courts—not through mob violence.

☆ 169 *In re Debs*

158 U.S. 564 (1894).

MR. JUSTICE BREWER, after stating the case, delivered the opinion of the court.

The case presented by the bill is this: The United States, finding that the interstate transportation of persons and property, as well as the carriage of the mails, is forcibly obstructed, and that a combination and conspiracy exists to subject the control of such transportation to the will of the conspirators, applied to one of their courts, sitting as a court of equity, for an injunction to restrain such obstruction and prevent carrying into effect such conspiracy. Two questions of importance are presented: First. Are the relations of the general government to interstate commerce and the transportation of the mails such as authorize a direct interference to prevent a forcible obstruction thereof? Second. If authority exists, as authority in governmental affairs implies both power and duty, has a court of equity jurisdiction to issue an injunction in aid of the performance of such duty[?]

First. What are the relations of the general government to interstate commerce and the transportation of the mails? They are those of direct supervision, control, and management.

*   *   *

As, under the Constitution, power over interstate commerce and the transportation of the mails is vested in the national government, and Congress by virtue of such grant has assumed actual and direct control, it follows that the national government may prevent any unlawful and forcible interference therewith. But how shall this be accomplished? Doubtless, it is within the competency of Congress to prescribe by legislation that any interference with these matters shall be offences against the United States, and prosecuted and punished by indictment in the proper courts. But is that the only remedy? Have the vast interests of the nation in interstate commerce, and in the transportation of the mails, no other protection than lies in the possible punishment of those who interfere with it? To ask the question is to answer it. . . .

. . . The entire strength of the nation may be used to enforce in any part of the land the full and free exercise of all national powers and the security of all rights entrusted by the Constitution to its care. The strong arm of the national government may be put forth to brush away all obstructions to the freedom of interstate commerce or the transportation of the mails. If the emergency arises, the army of the Nation, and all its militia, are at the service of the Nation to compel obedience to its laws.

But passing to the second question, is there no other alternative than the use of force on the part of the executive authorities whenever obstructions arise to the freedom of interstate commerce or the transportation of the mails? . . . [T]he existence of this right of forcible abatement is not inconsistent with nor does it destroy the right of appeal in an orderly way to the courts for a judicial determination, and an exercise of their powers by writ of injunction and otherwise to accomplish the same result. . . .

So, in the case before us, the right to use force does not exclude the right of appeal to the courts for a judicial determination and for the exercise of all their powers of prevention. . . .

Neither can it be doubted that the government has such an interest in the subject-matter as enables it to appear as party plaintiff in this suit. . . . [T]he United States have a property in the mails, the protection of which was one of the purposes of this bill. . . .

We do not care to place our decision upon this ground alone. Every government, entrusted, by the very terms of its being, with powers and duties to be exercised and discharged for the general welfare, has a right to apply to its own courts for any proper assistance in the exercise of the one and the discharge of the other, and it is no sufficient answer to

its appeal to one of those courts that it has no pecuniary interest in the matter. The obligations which it is under to promote the interest of all, and to prevent the wrongdoing of one resulting in injury to the general welfare, is often of itself sufficient to give it a standing in court. . . .

*   *   *

The national government, given by the Constitution power to regulate interstate commerce, has by express statute assumed jurisdiction over such commerce when carried upon railroads. It is charged, therefore, with the duty of keeping those highways of interstate commerce free from obstruction, for it has always been recognized as one of the powers and duties of a government to remove obstructions from the highways under its control.

*   *   *

It is said that seldom have the courts assumed jurisdiction to restrain by injunction in suits brought by the government, either state or national, obstructions to highways, either artificial or natural. This is undoubtedly true, but the reason is that the necessity for such interference has only been occasional. Ordinarily the local authorities have taken full control over the matter, and by indictment for misdemeanor, or in some kindred way, have secured the removal of the obstruction and the cessation of the nuisance. . . .

That the bill filed in this case alleged special facts calling for the exercise of all the powers of the court is not open to question. The picture drawn in it of the vast interests involved, not merely of the city of Chicago and the State of Illinois, but of all the States, and the general confusion into which the interstate commerce of the country was thrown; the forcible interference with that commerce; the attempted exercise by individuals of powers belonging only to government, and the threatened continuance of such invasions of public right, presented a condition of affairs which called for the fullest exercise of all the powers of the courts. If ever there was a special exigency, one which demanded that the court should do all that courts can do, it was disclosed by this bill. . . .

The difference between a public nuisance and a private nuisance is that the one affects the people at large and the other simply the individual. The quality of the wrong is the same, and the jurisdiction of the courts over them rests upon the same principles and goes to the same extent. . . .

. . . Of course, circumstances may exist in one case, which do not in another, to induce the court to interfere or to refuse to interfere by injunction, but the jurisdiction, the power to interfere, exists in all cases of nuisance. True, many more suits are brought by individuals than by the public to enjoin nuisances, but there are two reasons for this. First, the instances are more numerous of private than of public nuisances; and, second, often that which is in fact a public nuisance is restrained at the suit of a private individual, whose right to relief arises because of a special injury resulting therefrom.

Again, it is objected that it is outside of the jurisdiction of a court of equity to enjoin the commission of crimes. This, as a general proposition, is unquestioned. A chancellor has no criminal jurisdiction. Something more than the threatened commission of an offence against the laws of the land is necessary to call into exercise the injunctive powers of the court. There must be some interferences, actual or threatened, with property or rights of a pecuniary nature, but when such interferences appear the jurisdiction of a court of equity arises, and is not destroyed by the fact that they are accompanied by or are themselves violations of the criminal law. . . .

. . . [T]he acts of the defendants may or may not have been violations of the criminal law. If they were, that matter is for inquiry in other proceedings. The complaint made against them in this is of disobedience to an order of a civil court, made for the protection of property and the security of rights. If any criminal prosecution be brought against them for the criminal offences . . . it will be no defence to such prosecution that they disobeyed the orders of injunction served upon them and have been punished for such disobedience.

Nor is there in this any invasion of the constitutional right of trial by jury. We fully agree with counsel that "it matters not what form the attempt to deny constitutional right may take. It is vain and ineffectual, and must be so declared by the courts." . . . But the power of a court to make an order carries with it the equal power to punish for a disobedience of that order, and the inquiry as to the question of disobedience has been, from time immemorial, the special function of the court.

*   *   *

A most earnest and eloquent appeal was made to us in eulogy of the heroic spirit of those who threw up their employment, and gave up their means of earning a livelihood, not in defence of their own rights, but in sympathy for and to assist others whom they believed to be wronged. We yield to none in our admiration of any act of heroism or self-sacrifice, but we may be permitted to add that it is a lesson which cannot be learned too soon or too thoroughly that under this government of and by the people the means of redress of all wrongs are through the courts and at the ballot-box, and that no wrong, real or fancied, carries with it legal warrant to invite as a means of redress the coöperation of a mob, with its accompanying acts of violence.

We have given to this case the most careful and anxious attention, for we realize that it touches closely questions of supreme importance to the people of this country. Summing up our conclusions, we hold that . . . the Circuit Court had power to issue its process of injunction; that it having been issued and served on these defendants, the Circuit Court had authority to inquire whether its orders had been disobeyed, and when it found that they had been, to proceed under section 725, Revised Statutes, which grants power "to punish, by fine or imprisonment, . . . disobedience, . . . by any party . . . or other person, to any lawful writ, process, order, rule, decree or command," and enter the order of punishment complained of; and, finally, that, the Circuit Court, having full jurisdiction in the premises, its finding of the fact of disobedience is not open to review on *habeas corpus* in this or any other court. . . .

We enter into no examination of the [Sherman Antitrust Act], upon which the Circuit Court relied mainly to sustain its jurisdiction. It must not be understood from this that we dissent from the conclusions of that court in reference to the scope of the act, but simply that we prefer to rest our judgment on the broader ground which has been discussed in this opinion, believing it of importance that the principles underlying it should be fully stated and affirmed.

The petition for a writ of habeas corpus is denied.

170 "this raid was part of 'a political movement'" (1896)

A band of over 130 armed men raided the village of San Ygnacio in Mexico, then returned to Texas. The Mexican government sought the extradition of the alleged bandits. Warrants for their arrest were issued by a United States commissioner, and they were confined to await the decision of the executive branch on whether they were extraditable under the treaty between Mexico and the United States. The treaty contained the usual provisions making extradition inapplicable to any crime or offense of a purely political character. The detainees applied to the district court for release under a writ of habeas corpus. The writ was granted. The Mexican government, through its counsel, Ornelas, appealed. The Supreme Court upheld the commissioner's arrest warrant and reversed the district court. Although the outcome hinged on procedural considerations, the Supreme Court's decision reflected the judiciary's reluctance to entertain claims based on the political offense exception to the law of extradition.

☆170 *Ornelas v. Ruiz*

161 U.S. 502 (1896).

*   *   *

The release of petitioners was ordered on the sole ground that, as appears from the portion of the opinion of the learned District Judge contained in the record, this raid was part of "a political movement, having for its purpose the overthrow of the existing government in Mexico, and that the offences committed by the petitioners and their associates in their vain and visionary attempt to accomplish their purpose were purely political offences within the meaning of the sixth article of the treaty of extradition." The evidence before the commissioner, from which this conclusion was deduced, tended to show that on December 10, 1892, a band of armed men to the number of one hundred and thirty or forty, under the leadership of one Francisco Benevides, passed over the Rio Grande from Texas into Mexico, and attacked about forty Mexican soldiers stationed at the village of San Ygnacio; killing and wounding some of them, and capturing others, who were afterwards released; burning their barracks and taking away their horses and equipments; that private citizens were also violently assaulted; horses belonging to them taken; houses burned; small sums of money extorted from women; clothes, provisions, and goods appropriated; and three citizens kidnapped and carried over the river to the Texas side, finally escaping; that these men were bandits, without uniforms or flag, but with a red band on their hats; and that Garza was not there and had nothing to do with the expedition. The band remained on the Mexican side of the river about six hours and recrossed at the village ford. Petitioners were members of the band, and citizens of Mexico, as appeared from the complaints and testimony, though one of them at least had resided a large part of the time, for many years, in Texas. Evidence on behalf of petitioners was adduced indicating that there had been a revolutionary movement on that border under one Garza in 1891; that indictments had been found against the participants for violation of the neutrality laws; and that the aim, object and purpose of Benevides' men was the same as Garza's, "to cross over the river and fight against the government."

In the course of his opinion the District Judge referred to the views of the State Department as to the transaction at San Ygnacio. . . . The Secretary [of State] concluded his résumé with these words: "The idea that these acts were perpetrated with *bona fide* political or revolutionary designs is negatived by the fact that immediately after this occurrence, though no superior armed force of the Mexican government was in the vicinity to hinder their advance into the country, the bandits withdrew with their booty across the river into Texas." . . .

The District Judge entertained different views from those of the Secretary, and arrived at a different result from that reached by the commissioner on the evidence on which the latter proceeded, and so

was induced to substitute his judgment for that of the commissioner, in whom was reposed the authority of decision. . . .

Can it be said that the commissioner had no choice on the evidence but to hold, in view of the character of the foray, the mode of attack, the persons killed or captured, and the kind of property taken or destroyed, that this was a movement in aid of a political revolt, an insurrection or a civil war, and that acts which contained all the characteristics of crimes under the ordinary law were exempt from extradition because of the political intentions of those who committed them? In our opinion this inquiry must be answered in the negative.

. . . [I]f it appear that there was legal evidence on which the commissioner might properly conclude that the accused had committed offences within the treaty as charged, [he is] justified in exercising his power to commit them to await the action of the Executive Department. The rule as to probable cause was thus laid down by Mr. Chief Justice Marshall, sitting as a committing magistrate, in *Burr's case.* . . .

We are of opinion that it cannot be held that there was substantially no evidence calling for the judgment of the commissioner. . . .

The final order of the District Court is therefore reversed and the case remanded for further proceedings in conformity to law.

171 "an invention of the devil" (1898)

In Oshkosh, Wisconsin, in 1898, the woodworkers at the Paine Lumber Company, the country's largest manufacturer of sashes, doors, and blinds, walked off their jobs and demanded higher wages, the abolition of child and woman labor, the recognition of the union, and a weekly paycheck. A warrant was issued against Thomas I. Kidd, general secretary of the union, whose headquarters were in Chicago. He, along with others, was accused of "criminal conspiracy" to injure the business of the Paine Lumber Company.

After a three-week trial, defense attorney Clarence Darrow's argument to the jury lasted two entire days and detailed the grievances of the workers against Paine Lumber Company, the history of trade unionism, and the justification for fighting oppression. Darrow delivered his argument without notes. Stating, "Whenever a king wanted to get rid of somebody, whenever a political disturber was in someone's way, then they brought a charge of conspiracy," Darrow urged that personal rights should take precedence over property rights. The jury took fifty minutes to return a verdict of "not guilty."

☆171 Clarence Darrow's Argument to the Jury in the *Kidd Case*

Reprinted in A. Weinberg, ed., *Attorney for the Damned* (New York: Simon & Schuster, 1957), 267-326.

*   *   *

GENTLEMEN OF THE JURY: The defendants in this case, Thomas I. Kidd, George Zentner and Michael Troiber, are on trial charged with a conspiracy to injure the business of the Paine Lumber Company, by means of a strike, and the incidents arising therefrom. . . . [I]t is impossible to present the case to you without a broad survey of the great questions that are agitating the world today. For whatever its form, this is really not a criminal case. It is but an episode in the great battle for human liberty, a battle which was commenced when the tyranny and oppression of man first caused him to impose upon his fellows and which will not end so long as the children of one father shall be compelled to toil to support the children of another in luxury and ease.

*   *   *

Ordinarily men are brought into a criminal court for the reason that they are bad. Thomas I. Kidd is brought into this court because he is good, and they understand it well. If Thomas I. Kidd had been mean and selfish and designing, if he had held out his hand to take the paltry bribes that these men pass out wherever they find one so poor and weak as to take their dirty gold, this case would not be here today. Kidd is a defendant in these criminal proceedings because he loves his fellow-men. This is not the first case of its kind in the history of the world, and I am afraid it will not be the last. It is not the first time that evil men, men who are themselves criminals, have used the law for the purpose of bringing righteous ones to death or to jail. . . .

Let us understand exactly who are the parties to this case. Counsel for the prosecution will stand before this jury with hypocritical voice and false words, and say it is the great state of Wisconsin on the one hand and these three defendants upon the other. I say that this is not true, and every person in the hearing of my voice knows that it is not true.

Who is the state of Wisconsin, and how does the state of Wisconsin act? It moves only through its officers, ordinary men, strong in some ways, weak in others, subject to all those influences that move you and me and every other man that lives. Mr. Quartermass, the District Attorney, represents the state of Wisconsin. He comes into court, moved and influenced by the people of the community where he lives, by some more, by some less. He is persuaded to file an information charging a crime or offense against his fellow-citizens, and he haltingly complies with the request. He is simply the tool that is used, nothing more and nothing less; and the seal of the state of Wisconsin is not broad enough and heavy enough to cover up the infamy which caused this information to be filed branding these three men as criminals before the law.

*   *   *

Gentlemen, George M. Paine is not supporting these men. These men and women and little children are supporting him. It is through their labor and their toil that he has grown rich and prosperous and great. Here are some of the things that are expected of a man who goes to work for Paine:

"The following rules are made in the interest of good order and strict attention to business [recitation of restraints upon workers]:

*   *   *

Why, gentlemen, the only difference that I can see between the state's prison and George M. Paine's factory is that Paine's men are not allowed to sleep on the premises. American citizens do not exactly relish the idea of being locked up even in a factory; they have inherited certain foolish traditions of liberty that make them object, but they doubtless get over these prejudices in time. Don't be in such a hurry, gentlemen — give them a little time, a little time.

And because these men dared to go to Paine and ask for higher wages, because they had the effrontery to ask for a few more pennies of that wealth that they are grinding out at his machines, because they asked a little more of that money which comes from the sashes and the doors and the blinds which he sends to fourteen states of this great union, he wants to send them to jail.

Gentlemen of the jury, it is the theory of the State in this case, so far as they have a theory, that Mr. Kidd was responsible for this strike. Now, there is one beauty about a conspiracy case; there is one thing that made it valuable to ancient tyrants, and that makes it equally valuable to modern tyrants, and that is that you do not need much of any theory to carry it on. . . . [I]f there happens to be someone you are after, then you make a charge of conspiracy, and you are allowed to prove what the defendant said and did, and what everybody else said and did over any length of time that you see fit to carry it, and there you get your conspiracy. Conspiracy is the child of the Star Chamber [secret] Court of England, and it has come down to us, like most bad things and many good ones, from the remote past, without much modification. Whenever a king wanted to get rid of somebody, whenever a political disturber was in someone's way, then they brought a charge of conspiracy, and they not only proved everything he said, but everything everyone else said and everyone else did.

*   *   *

When these manufacturers set out to get rid of Kidd they started for injunctions. Now, an injunction is a sort of an invention of the devil. But they evidently could not find a judge in Oshkosh that could be used for that purpose. Not one. George M. Paine, when he was on the stand, admitted, although his memory is very faulty—excepting in matters that he wishes to tell—but he admitted that he did try to get these men enjoined, but he could not do it. The judges would not do it; and then he sought to have them arrested, and he went to Quartermass, and he hired lawyers. . . . They could not prosecute him for vagrancy, and so they unearthed this old Star Chamber proceeding, the same proceedings that in every age of the world have been used to condemn patriots and heretics and the great and the humane of the earth because miserable tyrants desired their blood. . . .

*   *   *

Now, gentlemen, I want to say a few words in relation to the labor question, which is really the controversy involved in this case, because that is all there is of it. Back of all this prosecution is the effort on the part of George M. Paine to wipe these labor organizations out of existence, and you know it. That's all there is of it.

You have heard a great deal of evidence as to whether Thomas I. Kidd provoked this strike. I do not care whether he did or did not. Gentlemen, if it was in my power tomorrow to provoke another strike in this city that would succeed, I would do it, even though the jail opened to receive me. I would do it for the duty I owe to my fellow-men. I do not care whether Kidd provoked this strike or not. I know, gentlemen, that he did what he could in his poor way, with his poor strength, to fight those great monopolies in the interest of the men and women and little children that he loves; and for that you are asked to send him to jail.

*   *   *

Let me tell you something of labor organizations. I have studied this question because I believe in it, because I love it as I do my very life; because it has been the strongest passion of my years; because in this great battle between the powerful and the weak I have ever been and will ever be with the weak so long as the breath is left in my body to speak. I have read it—not, gentlemen, for this case, not for the dirty gold of Paine—but I have read it because I loved it, and because in my own way I wished to do what I could for the thousands—aye, the millions of people who are yet poorer than myself. I know the history of the labor movement; I know what it has come through. I know the difficulties it is in today.

*   *   *

The first step in the conspiracy was forming this organization; the next step was making this request for wages. The letter containing the request was courteous, it was kind; it was not altogether true because it was too kind; but if any man ever received a courteous letter from a body of his employees, then George M. Paine received such a letter from his men. They respectfully asked him to do four things. First, to raise wages—a terrible crime. Next, to have a weekly pay day. Mr. Houghton [Paine's lawyer] had told them that they had a right to do this. Of course, when he said that he did not get a retainer, so perhaps the advice was not good. You cannot trust a lawyer unless you pay him, and you had better watch him even then. The next request was that he should not employ women, and I think that was right. And then they asked that the union be recognized, although they did not make that as a demand; and I think that was right. But it is not what I think. It is not what you think. These men were employees: they had as much at stake in the running of this factory as George M. Paine. They at least had the right to make these respectful requests in a respectful way; and were they not courteous and decent?

*   *   *

This organization addressed a respectful letter to George M. Paine, and he received it. . . . And they gave him two days to answer their respectful letter; and he received the letter and put it in the wastebasket. He is a nice man, is he not?

*   *   *

These workmen struck, and this was another conspiracy. . . .

*   *   *

But now let us see what took place. We have heard a great deal about riot and bloodshed and violation of the law. Let me talk with you and reason with you for a moment about that. How much disorder was there in the city of Oshkosh? First, let me call your attention to the fact that sixteen hundred men, honest workingmen of your town, were on a strike; that this strike lasted for fourteen weeks. Of course there was excitement; it could not have been otherwise. Men were taking the places of some of the workers; men were idle on the streets; the matter was the chief topic of thought and discussion. The militia was called out, and of course the tension was extreme during those long fourteen weeks. And yet, gentlemen, aside from these riots . . . there was but one single act of violence in the whole fourteen weeks.

*   *   *

Thomas I. Kidd is to be made responsible upon two theories. First, that he knew of and had to do with these unlawful acts, although no human being has yet brought that home to him; not one. Next, because he advised and counseled them.

*   *   *

But did Kidd advise riot?

*   *   *

Gentlemen, the overwhelming evidence in this case shows that from the beginning to the end Kidd counseled peace and order and quiet, and told the men that only in this way could they gain their ends. . . .

*   *   *

Men do not build for today; they do not build for tomorrow. They build for the centuries, for the ages; and when we look back it is the despised criminal and outlaw, the man perhaps without home or country or friend, who has lifted the world upward and onward toward the blessed brotherhood which one day will come. Here is Thomas I. Kidd. He draws a salary of twenty dollars a week. This is more than the Oshkosh woodworkers are paid. It is not a munificent salary, gentlemen. It is not too large for a man who goes up and down the land to help his fellowmen. . . . Gentlemen, it is not a bed of roses in which the agitator sleeps. He may hear himself make speeches, but he often feels that the crowd draws back and shuns him as they would a leper's touch. He may hear himself speak and may receive applause, but it means social ostracism. Aye, gentlemen, it means more. The man who undertakes to serve humanity consecrates his life and he must endure all things, and risk all things, for the cause he serves.

*   *   *

Gentlemen, the world is dark; but it is not hopeless. Here and there through the past some man has ever risen, some man like Kidd, willing to give the devotion of his great soul to humanity's holy cause. Here and there all through the past these men have come, and through the future they will come again. They will come to move the world onward and upward; they will come beckoning their fellow-men to follow in their lead; they will point to a sunrise far away, so distant that the ordinary mortal cannot see, but which is clear to their prophetic eye.

*   *   *

172 To Establish "White Supremacy" (1898)

Toward the end of the century, political activity among North Carolina blacks increased. A fusion of Populists and Republicans elected a Republican governor in 1896, and growing numbers of blacks were appointed to federal and state offices. Ousted from power, the Democrats grew hostile, resorting to inflammatory propaganda and violence against black voters. A vigilante group, the Red Shirts, was particularly instrumental in the terrorist campaign that resulted in a Democratic electoral victory in 1898. Emboldened by the victory, the white population of Wilmington on November 8 burned down the office of a black newspaper, then proceeded to riot and attack local blacks. The number of those killed is estimated between twenty and one hundred. The rioters deposed the mayor and forced all black officials to resign, thereby forcing the formation of a new government. Resort to the poll tax and a grandfather clause by the state assembly completed the process of divesting blacks of political power.

The document records the reminiscences of Gunner Jessie Blake, a participant in the riot.

☆ 172 The Wilmington Rebellion

Account by Gunner Jessie Blake in Harry Hayden, *The Wilmington Rebellion* (1938), reprinted in Richard Hofstadter and Michael Wallace, *American Violence: A Documentary History* (New York: Knopf, 1970), 231-34.

"You boys were too young to remember much about the Wilmington Rebellion, November 10, 1898," began Mr. Blake, an unreconstructed Rebel who to this day *holds that the South fought for Independence, not Slavery*, and who continues to use the ante- and post-bellum by-word, damnedyank, as a single word without even dignifying the appellation with a capital "D."

"So, I am going to give you the inside story of this insurrection," he proceeded, "wherein the white people of Wilmington overthrew the constituted municipal authority overnight and substituted a reform rule, doing all this legally and with some needless bloodshed, to be sure, but at the same time they eliminated the Negroes from the political life of the city and the state. This Rebellion was the very beginning of Negro disfranchisement in the South and an important step in the establishment of 'White Supremacy' in the Southland. . . .

"The Rebellion was an organized resistance," Mr. Blake said, "on the part of the white citizens of this community to the established government, which had long irked them because it was dominated by 'Carpet Baggers' and Negroes, and also because the better element here wished to establish 'White Supremacy' in the city, the state and throughout the South, and thereby remove the then stupid and ignorant Negroes from their numerically dominating position in the government. . . .

"The older generation of Southern born men were at their wits' end. They had passed through the rigors of the North-South war and through the tyrannies of Reconstruction when Confiscation (the latter the most hated word in the conquered Confederacy next to damnedyankee) of properties without due process of law, was the rule rather than the exception. They had seen 'Forty Acres and a Mule' buy many a Negro's vote.

"Black rapists were attacking Southern girls and women, those pure and lovely creatures who graced the homes in Dixie Land, and the brutes were committing this dastardly crime with more frequency while the majority of them were escaping punishment through the influence of the powers that be.

*   *   *

"A group of nine citizens met at the home of Mr. Hugh MacRae and there decided that the attitude and actions of the Negroes made it necessary for them to take some steps towards protecting their families and homes in their immediate neighborhood, Seventh and Market Streets. . . .

"This group of citizens, who will hereafter be referred to as the 'Secret Nine,' divided the city into sections, placing a responsible citizen as captain in charge of each area, and they named Messrs. Lathrop and Manning as their contact men, who were the only ones of the 'Secret Nine' known to the divisional captains. . . .

"The better element planned to gain relief from Negro impudence and domination, from grafting and from immoral conditions; the 'Secret Nine' and the white leaders marked time, hoping something would happen to arouse the citizenry to concerted action.

"But the 'watch-and-wait policy' of the 'Secret Nine' did not obtain for long, as during the latter part of October (1898) there appeared in the columns of The Wilmington (Negro) Daily Record an editorial, written by the Negro editor, Alex Manly, which aroused a state-wide revulsion to the city and state administrations then in the hands of the Republicans and Fusionists. The editorial attempted to justify the Negro rape fiends at the expense of the virtue of Southern womanhood."

Mr. Blake walked over to the library table, stooped and picked up an old scrap book that was reposing on the table's shelf, and then he read the following obnoxious editorial from The Wilmington Record:

Poor whites are careless in the matter of protecting their women, especially on the farm. They are careless of their conduct towards them, and our experience among the poor white people in the county teaches us that women of that race are not more particular in the matter of clandestine meetings with colored men, than are the white man and colored women.

Meetings of this kind go on for some time until the woman's infatuation, or the man's boldness, bring attention to them, and the man is lynched for rape.

Every Negro lynched is called a "big, burly, black brute," when in fact, many of those who have been thus dealt with had white men for their fathers, and were not only not "black" and "burly," but were sufficiently attractive for white girls of culture and refinement to fall in love with them, as is very well known to all.

"That editorial," Mr. Blake declared with some vehemence as he banged the closed scrap book with his fist, "is the straw that broke Mister Nigger's political back in the Southland." . . .

"A thousand or more white citizens, representative of all walks of life from the minister to the merchant, the mariner to the mendicant, attended the mass meeting in the New Hanover county court house the next morning, November 10, at 11 o'clock.

"Colonel Alfred Moore Waddell, a mild mannered Southern gentleman, noted for his extremely conservative tendencies, was called upon to preside over the gathering. In addressing this meeting, Colonel Waddell said: . . . 'We will not live under these intolerable conditions. No society can stand it. We intend to change it, if we have to choke the current of Cape Fear River with (Negro) carcasses!'

"*That* declaration," Mr. Blake said, "brought forth tremendous applause from the large gathering of white men at the mass meeting. His speech, other than the two paragraphs I have just quoted, was largely a statement of facts, but he was a silver tongued orator and the crowd cheered this distinguished white haired and bearded Southern gentleman throughout the course of his address." (He was as much respected by the Negroes as he was admired by the whites; his character was unimpeachable.)

"Colonel Waddel [*sic*], in concluding his address, announced that he heartily approved the set of resolutions which had been prepared by Mr. Hugh MacRae and which included the latter's 'Declaration of White Independence.'

"These resolutions were unanimously approved by the meeting, followed by a wonderful demonstration, the assemblage rising to its feet and cheering: 'Right! Right! Right!' and there were cries of 'Fumigate' the city with 'The Record' and 'Lynch Manly.' "

Mr. Blake then read the resolutions from the scrap book, as follows:

Believing that the Constitution of the United States contemplated a government to be carried on by an enlightened people; believing that its framers did not anticipate the enfranchisement of an ignorant population of African origin, and believing that those men of the state of North Carolina, who joined in framing the union, did not contemplate for their descendants subjection to an inferior race.

We, the undersigned citizens of the city of Wilmington and county of New Hanover, do hereby declare that we will no longer be ruled and will never again be ruled, by men of African origin.

This condition we have in part endured because we felt that the consequences of the war of secession were such as to deprive us of the fair consideration of many of our countrymen. . . .

173 "a lifetime in the handling of dynamite" (1899-1900)

Dissatisfied with the available relief from their grievances against management, and seeing the law enlisted against them, workers sometimes resorted to violence. An important western mining center, Shoshone County, Idaho, had been in a state of unrest since 1892. In 1899, following the events reported below, the governor of Idaho declared martial law and called for federal assistance in suppressing the insurrection. The local populace and officials allegedly were sympathetic to the miners. President McKinley dispatched two hundred troops, who were accused of active brutality and unconstitutional activity. Pursuant to a resolution of the House of Representatives, the Committee on Military Affairs investigated these charges and exonerated the military force of wrongdoing. Nevertheless, both the propriety of the use of federal military force in connection with this essentially local violent act against management and Congress's conclusion concerning the interaction of martial and civil law remain questionable.

☆173 Coeur D'Alene Labor Troubles Report

H.R. Rep. No. 1999, 56th Cong., 1st Sess. (1900).

[SYLLABUS]

*   *   *

Under the circumstances the governor of Idaho was warranted in making application to the President for troops to aid the civil authorities in executing the laws of the State.

It is conceded on all sides that the President of the United States was justified in sending troops to Shoshone County, Idaho, in response to the application of the governor.

Since October, 1899, the troops, not over 200 in number, have performed no duty in enforcing martial law or guarding prisoners, and the prison has been torn down. The troops are now in garrison in Osborne, 8 miles from the scene of the riot. They are there at the official request of the governor of Idaho, supported by a petition signed by 1,500 citizens of that community.

Under the conditions prevailing in Shoshone County in May, 1899, it was not necessary for the President to proclaim martial law under section 5300, Revised Statutes of the United States, and he did not declare martial law.

None of the charges preferred against the United States Army and its officers in Idaho, as set forth in the various paragraphs of the resolution, have been sustained by the testimony.

The military force in Shoshone County, under command of General Merriam, was used strictly in aid of the civil authorities. The sheriff and other county officials were in collusion with the rioters, and therefore civil authority could not be enforced. Some of the county officials were afterwards duly removed from office by judicial process because of said collusion and malfeasance in office.

The United States Army and its officers acted strictly within their instructions and the law.

President McKinley and the War Department exercised every precaution that the military act solely within the Constitution and not encroach in the distinct sphere of the civil authorities. The President exhibited his deep interest and solicitude in the cause of labor by his instruction "that the military must have nothing whatever to do with enforcing rules for the government of miners or miners' unions."

The writ of habeas corpus was not suspended in Shoshone County by the governor in 1899. The supreme court of Idaho refused to issue the writ on the facts presented, and the finding of the highest court of the State on this point, not having been reversed, is binding on this committee.

The proof is positive that the "right of free speech, free press, and peaceable assemblages" were not denied to the peaceable citizens of that community by the use of military power.

The so-called "permit system" is an extreme measure, devised and administered by the State authorities alone, and which they justify by the necessities of martial law. It was not directed against organized labor, but against the criminal members of certain organizations masquerading under the cloak of organized labor, who have for years conducted a reign of terror and lawlessness in the Cœur d'Alene mining district of that county.

The prisoners confined in the temporary prison in Shoshone County were civil prisoners under guard of the military forces. The military commander was authorized to enforce prison discipline against prisoners violating prison rules. The punishments inflicted were not excessive, and the treatment of the prisoners by the soldiers was humane and considerate.

As to all other charges in the resolution not hereinbefore referred to, reference is made to the statement hereinafter set forth.

Martial law and the administration of justice by civil courts can proceed side by side in a community which is in a state of insurrection and riot when the courts can not perform their proper functions without military protection.

Martial law ceases when the necessity for it ceases. It ceases when the civil authorities resume their unobstructed functions, although the military may be present to aid them if the need of such aid should arise.

When the United States Army is called upon to

protect the State against "domestic violence," the military forces act in aid of the State authorities to the extent that the purpose is to reestablish the civil authorities; but the military forces of the United States are not under the command of the State authorities, but of the military officers, under the President. To this extent it is an independent force, operating under the order of the President to perform the guaranty imposed upon the United States by the Constitution.

*   *   *

On the 8th day of December, 1899, Mr. Lentz introduced House resolution No. 31, to provide a committee to investigate the conduct of the United States Army and its officers in Idaho, which, as amended, was adopted January 8, 1900. Said resolution reads as follows:

> Whereas it is a matter of general information given out by the public press and charged by the industrial organization known as the Western Federation of Miners that United States troops have been sent into the State of Idaho in defiance of and contrary to the provisions of Article IV, section 4, of the Constitution of the United States, in that it was done at the individual request of the governor of Idaho, without the authority of the legislature, and at a time when there was no condition of insurrection or riot, and when the legislature could have been called together without danger or delay from any source whatever; and, further, without even consultation by the governor with the sheriff of Shoshone County, where it was desired that the troops should be, and actually were, sent; and
>
> Whereas, in defiance of section 9, Article I, of the Constitution, martial law was declared and the writ of habeas corpus suspended in said county in a time of profound peace, when there was no condition of rebellion or invasion or any menace to the public safety; and
>
> Whereas it is charged that Brig. Gen. H. C. Merriam [acted in violation of the sixth and fourth amendments]; and
>
> Whereas it is charged that the said military commander arbitrarily and in defiance of the civil law ordered the arrest of the sheriff of the county and the board of county commissioners, and subsequently deposed them from office on the unproved pretext of neglect of duty; and
>
> Whereas it is charged that the said Brigadier-General Merriam, immediately upon the arrival of the troops, ordered the arrest of every man who was a member of the miners' union, and also of all citizens who were supposed to sympathize with the cause of organized labor; and
>
> Whereas it is charged that those citizens were imprisoned in what was known as the "bull pen," a place unfit for human habitation . . . ; and
>
> Whereas the imprisoned citizens . . . were held in this vile and inhuman imprisonment for several months without charge or indictment

against them, although two sessions of the grand jury were held in the meantime . . . ; and

> Whereas it is charged that by the use of the military power the writ of habeas corpus was suspended for months in Shoshone County, and the right of free speech, free press, and peaceable assemblages were denied to the peaceable citizens of that community without any excuse or justification whatever; and
>
> Whereas when the Industrial Commission sat in Wallace all union men who had been long residents of the county were in the "bull pen" and had no opportunity to appear before the commission; others were arrested while on their way to Wallace to appear before the commission, and thrown into the "bull pen" until after the commission adjourned. . . .

*   *   *

The population of the county of Shoshone is about 10,000, the greater portion of which is engaged in mining.

The towns and mining camps involved in the crimes of April 29, 1899, are Burke, Gem, Mullan, Kellogg, and Wardner. Out of 1,500 miners living in these camps, 1,000 were implicated, directly or indirectly, in the riot. The following extract from the Idaho State Tribune, published at Wallace, May 3, 1899, was written by James R. Sovereign, its editor, who was an eyewitness to the affair. It gives a graphic account of the occurrences of April 29, 1899, which were the immediate cause of the declaration of martial law [by the Governor of Idaho] and the call for United States troops:

> Saturday last witnessed what might properly be considered the close of a seven years' war. . . . About 10.30 a man on horseback came galloping down Bank street from Canyon Creek, and . . . said, "They are coming." . . . Five minutes later the whistle on the Northern Pacific engine pulling the train from Burke and Gem resounded with its usual regularity. . . . On its 9 freight and ore cars were packed 1,000 men, half of whom were masked and armed with Winchester rifles. After a short halt the train proceeded . . . toward Wardner.
>
> [B]efore the train proceeded to Wardner with its human freight on its mission of destruction, armed men walked the streets in quest of an abundant supply of ammunition. It was evident to all that some of the scenes of 1892 were to be repeated, and this time the Bunker Hill and Sullivan Mining Company at Wardner, 12 miles below Wallace, was to be the victim of a forceful demonstration on the part of the organized miners of the Cœur d'Alenes. . . .
>
> The train reached Wardner at 1 o'clock, and the work of clearing the country of all opposition was begun. A detachment of union miners armed with Winchester rifles was dispatched to the mountain side beyond the mill, and the work of placing under the mill 3,000 pounds of dynamite,

taken from the magazine of the Frisco mine at Gem, was commenced. At no time did the demonstration assume the appearance or the attitude of a disorganized mob. All the details were managed with the discipline and precision of a perfectly trained military organization. Each miner participating in the affair either wore a strip of white handkerchief in the buttonhole of his coat or a strip of white cloth tied on his right arm. Sixty armed scabs in the employ of the Bunker Hill company offered the only resistance, and they only gave expression to the most pitiable and lamentable cowardice. Only a few desultory shots from the miners were necessary to send them fleeing over the mountains. At the same time Mr. Burbidge, manager of the mine, might have been seen running [away] toward Kingston, skulking behind every conceivable object and wringing his hands in the desperation of fear. Probably a more humiliating spectacle has not presented itself to the world since the capture of King Charles, nor a more striking evidence of supreme cowardice than was shown by Mr. Burbidge, who heretofore has displayed the defiant air of a tyrant equaled only by Sir Henry Morgan, the leader of the buccaneers of the Spanish Main.

At 2.30 the arrangements were complete, the dynamite was placed under the mill in three departments, the fuse attached, and all was in readiness for the destruction of one of the largest concentrators in the world, costing the company the enormous sum of $250,000. All miners and friends of the miners were warned to take a safe distance from the work of destruction about to begin. The fuses were lighted, and at 2.26 there was an awful crash, and broken machinery and fragments of the building were hurled high into the air. Fifteen seconds later another followed, and in about the same time a third. From the force of the third shot débris was hurled in every direction, and a huge canopy was formed in the heavens. Fragments of machinery and broken timbers rained down upon the ruins for several seconds. The shock of each explosion was terrific and was heard 20 miles away. The work of destruction was complete. The great concentrator was as completely demolished as it could have been if months had been spent in preparing the giant explosives for that purpose. The work was planned and executed by men who have received the training of a lifetime in the handling of dynamite.

*   *   *

The explosion was indeed an awe-inspiring scene, and to the eyewitness, were it not for the horrors of destruction, presented a pyrotechnical display which would satisfy the most expert critic of Fourth of July fireworks.

. . . [An] ominous stillness of a few minutes followed. Winchesters and revolvers were everywhere in evidence. The silence was broken by a single shot from a Winchester from some person on top of one of the cars, followed by a deafening fusillade. For five minutes the rattle of musketry

was incessant. It was evident, however, from the beginning of the firing that no harm was intended; that the men were simply celebrating the victory they had secured in the destruction of the Bunker Hill concentrator. In the midst of the firing the enemies gave the starting signal and the train moved slowly toward Wallace. . . .

. . . Ranchers and laboring people living in the valley congregated along the track and cheered the men lustily as they passed along. The train reached Wallace about 4 o'clock, and about a hundred of the people of the city were congregated at the depot to witness its arrival. Mayor Smith had taken the precaution to temporarily close the saloons. . . .

During the desultory firing at Wardner, shortly after the train from Wallace arrived, Jack Smythe, a miner at the Frisco mine, was shot and instantly killed. How it happened or by whom he was shot is not definitely known. Some say he was shot by scabs in the employ of the Bunker Hill company, others that he was shot by the striking miners through mistake. James Cheyne, a vanner man at the Bunker Hill mill, was shot through the hip and died at the Sacred Heart Hospital in Spokane yesterday morning. R. R. Rogers, the stenographer of the Bunker Hill company, was slightly wounded in the upper lip. So far as known, this constitutes all the casualties of the day's doings in connection with the Bunker Hill explosion.

174 "that organized government should be overthrown" (1902)

Toward the end of the nineteenth century, violence at the hands of anarchists spread throughout Europe. America was not immune from this terror. A Polish-born anarchist, Leon Czolgosz, assassinated President McKinley on September 6, 1901. In that same year, the United Mine Workers staged a five-month strike, which crippled the nation. Public confusion existed over the difference between militant unionism and anarchism, particularly since the joint strike by anarchists and unionists which had resulted in the Haymarket Riot of 1886. Reacting to fears of anarchism, the New York law set out to suppress not only violent conduct but also the doctrine itself and all political activity connected with it.

☆ 174 New York Criminal Anarchy Law

New York Penal Code 1881, § 468(a), (b), (c), (d), (e), added L. 1902, c. 371, § 1.

CHAP. 371

AN ACT to amend the penal code by inserting therein five additional sections. . . .

Became a law, April 3, 1902, with the approval of the Governor. . . .

                                        *   *   *

§ 468-a. *Criminal anarchy defined.* — Criminal anarchy is the doctrine that organized government
should be overthrown by force or violence, or by assassination of the executive head or of any of the executive officials of government, or by any unlawful
means. The advocacy of such doctrine either by
word of mouth or writing is a felony.

§ 468-b. *Advocacy of criminal anarchy.* — Any
person who:

1. By word of mouth or writing advocates,
advises or teaches the duty, necessity or propriety
of overthrowing or overturning organized government by force or violence, or by assassination of
the executive head or of any of the executive officials of government, or by any unlawful means; or

2. Prints, publishes, edits, issues or knowingly circulates, sells, distributes or publicly displays any book, paper, document, or written or
printed matter in any form, containing or advocating, advising or teaching the doctrine that organized government should be overthrown by force,
violence or any unlawful means; or,

3. Openly, willfully and deliberately justifies by word of mouth or writing the assassination
or unlawful killing or assaulting of any executive
or other officer of the United States or of any state
or of any civilized nation having an organized government because of his official character, or any
other crime, with intent to teach, spread or advocate the propriety of the doctrines of criminal anarchy; or

4. Organizes or helps to organize or becomes a member of or voluntarily assembles with
any society, group or assembly of persons formed
to teach or advocate such doctrine;
is guilty of a felony and punishable by imprisonment
for not more than ten years, or by a fine of not more
than five thousand dollars, or both.

§ 468-c. *Liability of editors and others.* — Every
editor or proprietor of a book, newspaper or serial
and every manager of a partnership or incorporated
association by which a book, newspaper or serial is
issued, is chargeable with the publication of any
matter contained in such book, newspaper or serial.
But in every prosecution therefor, the defendant
may show in his defense that the matter complained
of was published without his knowledge or fault and
against his wishes, by another who had no authority
from him to make the publication and whose act was
disavowed by him so soon as known.

§ 468-d. *Assemblages of anarchists.* — Whenever
two or more persons assemble for the purpose of advocating or teaching the doctrines of criminal anarchy, . . . such an assembly is unlawful, and every person voluntarily participating therein by his
presence, aid or instigation, is guilty of a felony and
punishable by imprisonment for not more than ten

years, or by a fine of more than five thousand dollars, or both.

§ 468-e. *Permitting premises to be used for assemblages of anarchists.* — The owner, agent, superintendent, janitor, caretaker or occupant of any
place, building or room, who willfully and knowingly
permits therein any assemblage of persons prohibited . . . is guilty of a misdemeanor, and punishable
by imprisonment for not more than two years, or by
a fine of not more than two thousand dollars, or both.

175 "person[s] . . . opposed to all organized government" (1903)

After McKinley died from the bullet of Leon
Czolgosz, President Theodore Roosevelt directed
his attention to tightening America's immigration
laws. In an address to the Fifty-seventh Congress,
he called for excluding all anarchists or members of
anarchistic societies. He also called for excluding
persons who were of "low moral tendency" or "unsa-
vory reputation." Representative Shattuc of Ohio introduced the new immigration act, which contained
several of Roosevelt's suggestions, in addition to exclusion of the mentally impaired, epileptics, paupers,
beggars, and the contagiously diseased. While exempting "purely political" offenders from exclusion,
it nevertheless provided for the debarment of the
advocates of anarchy and provided criminal penalties for those who aided an anarchist's entry into the
country.

☆ 175 Immigration Act of 1903

32 Stat. 1213 (1903).

                    *   *   *

SEC. 2. That the following classes of aliens shall be
excluded from admission into the United States: All
. . . persons who have been convicted of a felony or
other crime or misdemeanor involving moral
turpitude. . . .

Provided, That nothing in this Act shall exclude
persons convicted of an offense purely political, not
involving moral turpitude. . . .

                    *   *   *

SEC. 38. That no person who disbelieves in or
who is opposed to all organized government, or who
is a member of or affiliated with any organization en-
tertaining and teaching such disbelief in or opposition to all organized government, or who advocates
or teaches the duty, necessity, or propriety of the
unlawful assaulting or killing of any officer or officers, either of specific individuals or of officers generally, of the Government of the United States or of
any other organized government, because of his or

their official character, shall be permitted to enter the United States....

That any person who knowingly aids or assists any such person to enter the United States ... or who connives or conspires with any person or persons to allow, procure, or permit any such person to enter therein ... shall be fined not more than five thousand dollars, or imprisoned for not less than one nor more than five years, or both.

176 "undesirable additions to our population" (1904)

John Turner, an Englishman alleging to be a paid labor organizer, entered the United States in order to deliver a series of lectures on the "Essentials of Anarchism," the "General Strike," and the "Legal Murder of 1887" (the Haymarket trials). Arrested within ten days of his arrival on a warrant charging him with being an anarchist, Turner was sent to and detained at Ellis Island. Turner challenged his detention by means of a writ of habeas corpus, arguing that the immigration law of 1903 was unconstitutional.

In upholding Turner's arrest and deportation, Chief Justice Fuller noted that "the deportation of an alien who is found to be here in violation of law is not a deprivation of liberty without due process of law, and that the provisions of the Constitution securing the right of trial by jury have no application."

☆ 176 *Turner v. Williams*

194 U.S. 279 (1904).

Statement by Mr. Chief Justice FULLER: John Turner filed in the United States circuit court for the southern district of New York, October 26, 1903, a petition alleging—

"First. That on October 23, in the city of New York, your relator was arrested by divers persons claiming to be acting by authority of the government of the United States, and was by said persons conveyed to the United States immigration station at Ellis island, in the harbor of New York, and is now there imprisoned by the commissioner of immigration of the port of New York.

"Second. Your relator is so imprisoned by virtue of a warrant sworn out by the Secretary of the Department of Commerce and Labor, which warrant charges your relator with being an anarchist, and being unlawfully within the United States, in violation of § 2 and § 20 of the immigration laws of the United States....

*　　　*　　　*

"Fourth. Your relator denies that he is an anarchist within the meaning of the immigration laws of the United States, and states to the court that about six years ago he took out his first papers of application for citizenship in this country, and that he has at no times been engaged as a propagandist of doctrines inciting to, or advising, violent overthrow of government, but for about six years last past he has been the paid organizer of the retail clerks of Great Britain, and his business in this country is solely to promote the interests of organized labor, and that he has at all times conducted himself as a peaceful and law-abiding citizen."

*　　　*　　　*

... Turner testified that he was an Englishman; that he had been in the United States ten days, and that he did not come through New York, but declined to either affirm or deny that he arrived via Canada; that he would not undertake to deny that he had, in the lecture delivered in New York, October 23, declared himself to be an anarchist, which, he said, was a statement that he would make; and that the testimony of the inspectors was about correct. That evidence gave extracts from the address referred to, including these: "Just imagine what a universal tie-up would mean. What would it mean in New York city alone if this idea of solidarity were spread through the city? If no work was being done, if it were Sunday for a week or a fortnight, life in New York would be impossible, and the workers, gaining audacity, would refuse to recognize the authority of their employer, and eventually take to themselves the handling of the industries.... All over Europe they are preparing for a general strike, which will spread over the entire industrial world. Everywhere the employers are organizing, and to me, at any rate, as an anarchist, as one who believes that the people should emancipate themselves, I look forward to this struggle as an opportunity for the workers to assert the power that is really theirs."

Certain papers were found on Turner, one of them being a list of his proposed series of lectures (which, when the warrant was in execution, he rolled up and threw away), the subjects including: "The Legal Murder of 1887," and "The Essentials of Anarchism;" notices of meetings, one of a mass meeting November 9, at which "speeches will be delivered by John Turner in English, John Most in German, and several other speakers. Don't miss this opportunity to hear the truth expressed about the great Chicago tragedy on the eleventh of November, 1887;" and another, stating: "It may be interesting to all that Turner has recently refused to accept a candidacy to Parliament because of his anarchistic principles."

*　　　*　　　*

Mr. Chief Justice FULLER delivered the opinion of the court:

*　　　*　　　*

It is contended that the act of March 3, 1903, is unconstitutional because in contravention of the 1st, 5th, and 6th articles of amendment of the Constitution, and of § 1 of article 3 of that instrument; and because no power "is delegated by the Constitution to the general government over alien friends with reference to their admission into the United States or otherwise, or over the beliefs of citizens, denizens, sojourners, or aliens, or over the freedom of speech or of the press."

Repeated decisions of this court have determined that Congress has the power to exclude aliens from the United States; to prescribe the terms and conditions on which they may come in; to establish regulations for sending out of the country such aliens as have entered in violation of law, and to commit the enforcement of such conditions and regulations to executive officers; that the deportation of an alien who is found to be here in violation of law is not a deprivation of liberty without due process of law, and that the provisions of the Constitution securing the right of trial by jury have no application.

*   *   *

Whether rested on the accepted principle of international law, that every sovereign nation has the power, as inherent in sovereignty and essential to self-preservation, to forbid the entrance of foreigners within its dominions, or to admit them only in such cases and upon such conditions as it may see fit to prescribe; or on the power to regulate commerce with foreign nations, which includes the entrance of ships, the importation of goods, and the bringing of persons into the ports of the United States, the act before us is not open to constitutional objection. . . .

*   *   *

. . . [I]t is said that the act violates the 1st Amendment, which prohibits the passage of any law "respecting an establishment of religion, or prohibiting the free exercise thereof; or abridging the freedom of speech, or of the press; or the right of the people peaceably to assemble, and to petition the government for a redress of grievances."

We are at a loss to understand in what way the act is obnoxious to this objection. It has no reference to an establishment of religion, nor does it prohibit the free exercise thereof; nor abridge the freedom of speech or of the press; nor the right of the people to assemble and petition the government for a redress of grievances. It is, of course, true, that if an alien is not permitted to enter this country, or, having entered contrary to law, is expelled, he is in fact cut off from worshiping or speaking or publishing or petitioning in the country; but that is merely because of his exclusion therefrom. He does not become one of the people to whom these things are secured by our Constitution by an attempt to enter, forbidden by law. . . .

Appellant's contention really comes to this: that the act is unconstitutional so far as it provides for the exclusion of an alien because he is an anarchist.

The argument seems to be that, conceding that Congress has the power to shut out any alien, the power, nevertheless, does not extend to some aliens, and that if the act includes all alien anarchists, it is unconstitutional, because some anarchists are merely political philosophers, whose teachings are beneficial rather than otherwise.

*   *   *

If the word "anarchists" should be interpreted as including aliens whose anarchistic views are professed as those of political philosophers, innocent of evil intent, it would follow that Congress was of opinion that the tendency of the general exploitation of such views is so dangerous to the public weal that aliens who hold and advocate them would be undesirable additions to our population, whether permanently or temporarily, whether many or few; and, in the light of previous decisions; the act, even in this aspect, would not be unconstitutional, as applicable to any alien who is opposed to all organized government.

*   *   *

Order affirmed.

177 The Assassination of Governor Steunenberg (1905)

On December 30, 1905, Governor Frank Steunenberg of Idaho was killed by a bomb. Steunenberg was the carrier of a union card and was elected governor in 1896 and again in 1898 with heavy labor support, but he later became instrumental in the crushing of the Coeur d'Alene strike. It was a common belief that the Western Federation of Miners, which viewed Steunenberg as a betrayer of labor, was responsible for his murder.

While the W.F.M. denied the accusation, the apprehended assassin, Harry Orchard, confessed to a police informant that the leaders of the union instigated the crime. The three named by Orchard, including William D. Haywood, the secretary-treasurer of the union, were arrested in Colorado and were brought to Idaho without legal extradition. The events touched off an uproar in labor and radical circles. Public protests were held in Boston, New York, and San Francisco. Clarence Darrow served as defense counsel at Haywood's trial. After eighteen months in jail and eleven weeks of trial, Haywood was found not guilty. The second union leader also was acquitted, and the third was never tried.

Orchard was sentenced to death, but the sentence was commuted by the Pardons Board. He died in jail in 1954, at age eighty-eight, having spent nearly fifty years in prison.

Portions of Clarence Darrow's summation before the Boise jury in the Haywood trial are contained in the accompanying document.

☆ 177 The Defense Summation in the Trial of William D. "Big Bill" Haywood

Reprinted in A. Weinberg, ed., *Attorney for the Damned* (New York: Simon & Schuster, 1957), 483-86.

I don't claim that this man is an angel. The Western Federation of Miners could not afford to put an angel at their head. Do you want to hire an angel to fight the Mine Owners' Association and the Pinkerton detectives, and the power of wealth? Oh, no, gentlemen; you better get a first-class fighting man who has physical courage, who has mental courage, who has strong devotion, who loves the poor, who loves the weak, who hates iniquity and hates it more when it is with the powerful and the great; and you cannot win without it, and I believe that down in your hearts there is not one of you would wish him to be an angel. You know an angel would not be fitted for that place, and I make no claim of that; but he is not a demon. If he were a demon or a bad man he would never be working in this cause, for the prizes of the world are somewhere else. The man who enters the labor movement, either as an organizer, a member, or a lawyer, and who enters it in the hope of reward, is a foolish man indeed. The rewards are on the other side—unless you look for your reward to your conscience and to your consciousness of a duty well done. I presume that this big, strong man is a man, a man that has strength and has power, and has weakness; a man of love and affection, a man of strong nature, of strong purposes—I don't know about that, and I don't care about it; I don't look for anything else in man; I want the man of courage and brains and devotion and strength.

*   *   *

I have known Haywood—I have known him well and I believe in him. God knows it would be a sore day to me if he should go upon the scaffold. The sun would not shine or the birds would not sing on that day—for me. It would be a sad day, indeed, if any such calamity would come to him. I would think of him, I would think of his wife, of his mother, I would think of his children, I would think of the great cause that he represents. It would be a sore day for me, but, gentlemen, he and his mother, and his wife and his children, are not my chief concern in this great case. If you should decree that he must die, ten thousand men will work in the mines and send a portion of the proceeds of their labor to take care of that widow and these orphan children, and a million people throughout the length and breadth of the civilized world will send their messages of kindness and good cheer to comfort them in their bereavement and to heal their wounds. It is not for them I plead. Other men have died before. Other men have died in the same cause in which Bill Haywood has risked his life. Men strong with devotion, men who loved liberty, men who loved their fellow-men, patriots who have raised their voices in defense of the poor, in defense of right, have made their good fight and have met death on the scaffold, on the rack, in the flame, and they will meet it again and again until the world grows old and gray. William Haywood is no better than the rest. He can die if die he must. He can die if this jury decrees it; but, oh, gentlemen, do not think for a moment that if you hang him you will crucify the labor movement of the world; do not think that you will kill the hopes and the aspirations and the desires of the weak and poor. You men of wealth and power, you people anxious for his blood, are you so blind as to believe that liberty will die when he is dead? Think you there are no other brave hearts, no other strong arms, no other devoted souls who will risk all in that great cause which has demanded martyrs in every land and age?

178 *Mother Earth* (1906)

Emma Goldman (1869-1940), born in Russia, moved to St. Petersburg at age thirteen, one year after the assassination of Czar Alexander II. After arriving in the United States in 1886, she worked in clothing factories in Rochester, New York. Goldman became active in the anarchist movement after 1889, and her speeches received widespread attention. In 1892, she helped Alexander Berkman in his assassination attempt on Henry Clay Frick of United States Steel during the Homestead Strike in Pittsburgh. She was imprisoned for inciting to riot in 1893. She and Berkman published the anarchist paper *Mother Earth*.

Arrested in June 1917 for obstructing the draft and sedition, she was deported to Russia two years later. Goldman left Russia in 1921 because of her disagreement with the Bolshevik government. Although an advocate of political change through violence in her early years, she eventually came to condemn it. In 1928, she wrote to Berkman that she wished she could adopt the nonviolent attitude of Gandhi and Tolstoy: "I feel that violence in whatever form never had and probably never will bring constructive results." Nevertheless, in this essay Goldman distinguished the general political philosophy of anarchism from the ultimate resort to terrorism in the face of tyranny, suggesting that terrorist acts are the natural response of normal people to stresses of intolerable oppressions.

☆178 The Psychology of Political Violence
(Emma Goldman)

Reprinted in E. Goldman, *Anarchism and Other Essays*
(Port Washington, N.Y.: Kennikat Press, 1969), 85-114.

*   *   *

The ignorant mass looks upon the man who makes a
violent protest against our social and economic iniquities as upon a wild beast, a cruel, heartless monster, whose joy it is to destroy life and bathe in
blood; or at best, as upon an irresponsible lunatic.
Yet nothing is further from the truth. As a matter of
fact, those who have studied the character and personality of these men, or who have come in close contact with them, are agreed that it is their supersensi-
tiveness to the wrong and injustice surrounding
them which compels them to pay the toll of our social crimes. The most noted writers and poets, discussing the psychology of political offenders, have
paid them the highest tribute. . . .

[I]t is among the Anarchists that we must look for
the modern martyrs who pay for their faith with
their blood, and who welcome death with a smile, because they believe, as truly as Christ did, that their
martyrdom will redeem humanity.

*   *   *

[The] indisputable fact is that homicidal outrages
have, from time immemorial, been the reply of
goaded and desperate classes, and goaded and desperate individuals, to wrongs from their fellowmen,
which they felt to be intolerable. Such acts are the
violent recoil from violence, whether aggressive or
repressive; they are the last desperate struggle of
outraged and exasperated human nature for breath-
ing space and life. And their cause lies not in any
special conviction, but in the depths of that human
nature itself. The whole course of history, political
and social, is strewn with evidence of this fact. To go
no further, take the three most notorious examples
of political parties goaded into violence during the
last fifty years: the Mazzinians in Italy, the Fenians
in Ireland, and the Terrorists in Russia. Were these
people Anarchists? No. Did they all three even hold
the same political opinions? No. The Mazzinians
were Republicans, the Fenians political separatists,
the Russians Social Democrats or Constitutionalists.
But all were driven by desperate circumstances into
this terrible form of revolt. And when we turn from
parties to individuals who have acted in like manner,
we stand appalled by the number of human beings
goaded and driven by sheer desperation into conduct obviously violently opposed to their social
instincts.

*   *   *

That every act of political violence should nowa-
days be attributed to Anarchists is not at all surprising. Yet it is a fact known to almost everyone familiar with the Anarchist movement that a great
number of acts, for which Anarchists had to suffer,
either originated with the capitalist press or were
instigated, if not directly perpetrated, by the police.

*   *   *

Can one doubt the logic, the justice of these
words:

Repression, tyranny, and indiscriminate punishment of innocent men have been the watchwords
of the government of the alien domination in India ever since we began the commercial boycott
of English goods. The tiger qualities of the British are much in evidence now in India. They think
that by the strength of the sword they will keep
down India! It is this arrogance that has brought
about the bomb, and the more they tyrannize
over a helpless and unarmed people, the more
terrorism will grow. We may deprecate terrorism as outlandish and foreign to our culture, but
it is inevitable as long as this tyranny continues,
for it is not the terrorists that are to be blamed,
but the tyrants who are responsible for it. It is
the only resource for a helpless and unarmed people when brought to the verge of despair. It is
never criminal on their part. The crime lies with
the tyrant.

*   *   *

Anarchism, more than any other social theory,
values human life above things. All Anarchists
agree with Tolstoy in this fundamental truth: if the
production of any commodity necessitates the sacrifice of human life, society should do without that
commodity, but it can not do without that life. That,
however, nowise indicates that Anarchism teaches
submission. How can it, when it knows that all suffering, all misery, all ills, result from the evil of
submission?

Has not some American ancestor said, many
years ago, that resistance to tyranny is obedience to
God? And he was not an Anarchist even. I would say
that resistance to tyranny is man's highest ideal. So
long as tyranny exists, in whatever form, man's
deepest aspiration must resist it as inevitably as
man must breathe.

Compared with the wholesale violence of capital
and government, political acts of violence are but a
drop in the ocean. That so few resist is the strongest
proof how terrible must be the conflict between
their souls and unbearable social iniquities.

High strung, like a violin string, they weep and
moan for life, so relentless, so cruel, so terribly inhuman. In a desperate moment the string breaks.

Untuned ears hear nothing but discord. But those
who feel the agonized cry understand its harmony,
they hear in it the fulfillment of the most compelling
moment of human nature.

Such is the psychology of political violence.

179 "desperate men are now securing dynamite" (1907)

The United States experienced serious financial panic in 1907. In the West, unrest in the mines of Nevada gave rise once more to calls for federal military action in suppression of labor militancy. The telegraphic communications between Governor Sparks of Nevada and President Roosevelt reflected state efforts to obtain unlawfully the presence of federal military authority as a preventive police measure in order to maintain the peace between the rival economic forces—labor and management. It was perhaps not totally coincidental that the federal presence would chill the use of violence by labor and therefore maintain the status quo favorable to management. Nevertheless, after initially acceding to Nevada's alarm, Washington insisted on strict adherence to the constitutional standards for federal intervention and removed the troops.

☆ 179 Telegraphic Correspondence between Nevada Governor John Sparks and President Theodore Roosevelt

Reprinted in Report on Labor Troubles at Goldfield, Nevada, H.R. Doc. No. 607, 60th Cong., 1st Sess. 2 (1908), Ser. 5374.

Carson City, Nev.
December 3-4, 1907

Hon. Theodore Roosevelt
President of the United States

MR. PRESIDENT:

It now seems apparent that in the near future Nevada may expect serious labor troubles in the district of Goldfield and adjoining camps, which may result in violence and great destruction of both life and property. The State has no enrolled militia and if it had I doubt very much whether it would be effective in maintaining law and order. I am this day in communication with our Congressional representatives urging them to consult with you concerning conditions above stated, and as we now see them, it appears to me as governor of Nevada that it is my duty to ask if you can consistently give us assurance that we may depend upon immediate relief from the Presidio Barracks. I assure you Mr. President I am aware of the fact and consider it an extraordinary request to be made by any governor of the United States, but the existence of the case seems to require it at this time. I am informed that desperate men are now securing dynamite and arms to destroy property and human life. The sheriff of the county seems to be absolutely unable to cope with the situation. A committee of mine owners, mine operators and mill operators from the Goldfield district is now in consultation with me and I assure you, Mr. President, that they are well satisfied that we need relief. We have no military garrison in the State of Nevada and a small detachment of Federal troops stationed at Goldfield would certainly relieve the situation.

Very respectfully,

JOHN SPARKS, Governor of Nevada
R. C. STODDARD, Attorney General

The White House, Washington
December 4, 1907

Hon. John Sparks, Governor
Carson City, Nev.

Telegram received 3.05 o'clock this afternoon. The Federal Government is prepared to send detachment of troops at any moment subject of course to your making call under conditions prescribed by the United States Constitution. . . . I have ordered not to exceed two companies to be ready to move immediately if you make such request, as two companies would, I suppose, amount to the small detachment of which you speak.

THEODORE ROOSEVELT

Carson City, Nev.
December 5, 1907

His Excellency Theodore Roosevelt
President of the United States
Washington, D.C.

At Goldfield, Esmeralda County, State of Nevada, there does now exist domestic violence and unlawful combinations and conspiracies which do now so obstruct . . . the laws of the State of Nevada and now deprive and continue to deprive the people of said section of the State of the rights, privileges, immunities, and protection named in the Constitution of the United States and of the State of Nevada. . . .

The lawfully constituted authorities of this State are unable to apprehend and punish the perpetrators of . . . crimes and to prevent the commission of other threatened crimes and unless the relief hereinafter requested is granted this State and the lives and property of large numbers of its people will be irreparably affected and damaged, contrary to the peace and dignity of the United States and of the State of Nevada.

Therefore, pursuant to Article IV, section 4 of the Constitution of the United States, . . . I, John Sparks, governor, do hereby respectfully request that Your Excellency Theodore Roosevelt, President, do immediately sent to Goldfield, Esmeralda County, Nev., two companies of the troops of the Army of the United States to suppress unlawful disorder and violence, to protect life and property, to restore peace, and to insure protection of law to the people of the State of Nevada.

*   *   *

JOHN SPARKS, Governor

Attest

W. G. DOUGLASS, Secretary of State

The White House, Washington
December 5, 1907

Hon. John Sparks, Governor
Carson City, Nev.

I have received your request for troops made in accordance with the Constitution and laws of the United States and will accordingly immediately direct that a sufficient number of troops be sent to Nevada. The number must be determined by the military authorities.

THEODORE ROOSEVELT

December 14, 1907

Hon. John Sparks, Governor
Carson City, Nev.

... The President has instructed me to advise you officially that he has caused several companies of the Regular Army to proceed to the locality in which such disturbances exist or are anticipated, to the end that they may be available in case the occasion contemplated by the Constitution and the laws of the United States for their interposition shall arise.

The calls upon the President on the part of the government of Nevada for the interposition of troops do not at present satisfy the requirements of the Constitution and the laws so as to justify orders that the military force now at Goldfield shall take any affirmative action. If such action should be desired under the Constitution ... to suppress an insurrection a call must be made by the legislature of the State unless circumstances are such that the legislature can not be convened, and no statement or intimation has been made that the legislature of Nevada can not be convened....

A mere statement of domestic disturbance would not seem to be sufficient.

The facts thus far stated in the telegraphic communications from the governor of Nevada, high and unimpeachable as is the source, do not seem sufficient....

It therefore appears that the communications thus far received from the government of Nevada do not constitute or furnish the basis for authority on the part of the President to direct the use of the armed forces of the United States in the maintenance of public order at Goldfield.

I respectfully suggest that if in your judgment such interposition is needed you furnish further evidence of facts justifying action by the President to enforce the laws of the United States, or cause the legislature of Nevada to be convened and to make the necessary call in accordance with the Constitution....

ELIHU ROOT

Goldfield, Nev.
December 15, 1907
(Received December 16 — 9.20 A.M.)

The President, Washington, D.C.

Fourteenth from Secretary of State. Submit that conditions in Goldfield necessitates presence but does not warrant active intervention of United States troops. However, am prepared to submit affidavits of more than one hundred representative citizens that they have been deprived of their rights as citizens of the United States and of State of Nevada. Arrival of troops in Goldfield undoubtedly prevented rioting and other disorder, as is shown by statements of same people, including sheriff. Although active intervention of United States troops not now necessary, withdrawal at present would unquestionably precipitate disorder which local and State authorities would be unable to control. In the event of rioting and other disorder justifying military intervention will make requisition in accordance with statutes.

*   *   *

JOHN SPARKS, Governor

The White House, Washington
December 17, 1907

Hon. John Sparks, Governor of Nevada
Goldfield, Nev.

I sent the troops at your request because from the tenor of your telegrams and from the representations made me by the two Senators from Nevada it appeared that an insurrection was imminent against which the State authorities would be powerless. The troops have now been in Goldfield ten days and no insurrection has occurred, and seemingly no circumstances exist to justify your now calling on me for action by the troops under the provision of the Constitution. The troops were sent to Goldfield to be ready to meet a grave emergency which seemed likely at once to arise and to provide a substitute for the exercise by the State of its police function. I do not feel at liberty to leave them indefinitely under such circumstances that they will in effect be performing on the part of the United States those ordinary duties of maintaining public order in the State of Nevada which rest upon the State government. As the legislature of Nevada has not been convened, I am bound to assume that the powers already vested in the peace officers of the State are adequate, and that if they choose to do so they can maintain order themselves. Under these circumstances, unless there be forthwith further cause shown to justify keeping the troops at Goldfield, I shall direct that they return to their former station.

THEODORE ROOSEVELT

Goldfield, Nev.
December 20, 1907

The President, Washington, D.C.

We do find no warrant for statement that there has been or is a complete collapse of civil authority here. All the machinery of civil government has been in operation, but has been ineffective in dealing with certain forms of crime because local sentiment has nullified its action. . . . Our investigation so far completely has failed to sustain the general and sweeping allegations in the governor calling for troops, and the impression as to conditions here given in that call is misleading and without warrant. We do find no evidence that any condition then existed not easily controlled by the local authorities. Neither immediately preceding nor since the arrival of troops has there been any particular disorder, but immediately after arrival of troops mine owners announced reduction of wages from $5 to $4, and positively refused employment to all men who do not agree to renounce in writing the local union, although a law of Nevada prohibits such requirement. Large majority of our witnesses assert very earnestly that if troops should be withdrawn now and owners insist upon above requirements there will result serious violence directed against life and property. Rifles in considerable numbers brought in by both sides sometime ago are still believed to be in their possession. Many say they will leave as soon as possible if troops should be withdrawn, and we believe that many of them are sincere in these assertions. . . .

So far as can be learned no county officer was consulted by governor previous to calling for troops. All still resent his action and consider it was unnecessary. They do not believe there has been any need for troops here up to date, but they all further agree and have given us signed statement to the effect that the new element brought into situation since arrival of troops create a dangerous condition, and they recommend troops be left here until present difficulties are adjusted. . . . These men are trying to secure the benefit of Federal assistance to more easily maintain the public order for which they are responsible and at the same time place the responsibility on the President. The governor states to us in writing that he will not convene the legislature to consider call for troops nor will he take the necessary steps to form a State military, as is legally provided for, and that if the [troops] should be withdrawn he will do substantially nothing. In other words, the State authorities propose to do nothing but wholly rely on the Federal authorities. There has been substantial agreement by everybody who

appeared before us that the number of violent or [criminal] men in the organization here is certainly less than 200. With a population of about 14,000 people there would seem to be no good reason why the civil authorities here can not take care of their own city. . . .

MURRAY, NEILL, SMITH

Carson City, Nev.
December 26, 1907

The President, Washington

As chief magistrate of the State of Nevada, I have been of the opinion for the past year that a condition bordering on domestic violence and insurrection has existed in the Goldfield mining district. There has been an almost constant state of war between the miners' union and the mine owners, who employ the members of the union. . . . [T]he entire district became divided into two hostile camps—on the one hand the miners with their adherents and sympathizers, and on the other hand the mine owners with their adherents and sympathizers. The union alone claimed a membership of 3,000, and fully one-half of the membership were constantly armed. Arms and ammunition were purchased and kept by the union as a body. On the other hand the mine owners had in their employ a large number of watchmen and guards who were constantly armed and on duty. In addition to these forces were an unusually large number of the criminal element attracted to the new and booming mining camp. Under such conditions the civil authorities were practically powerless. They could attend to the ordinary petty offenders from day to day, but at the first conflict between the real armies of labor and capital they would have been swept away.

. . . A state of domestic violence and insurrection arises, in my judgment, when armed bodies are in existence with sufficient power to overcome the civil authorities, and continual threats were made of the destruction of life and property. This condition has existed in the Goldfield mining districts the past year and exists there now. It calls for the presence of the troops to keep the peace. As this condition has been of slow growth it will take time to remove it. . . . The communist and anarchist must seek new fields; the laboring man be convinced that arbitration and peaceful methods are more certain and lasting methods of improving his condition than by dynamite and the shotgun. This can only come about with time, and for the present and sometime in the future the strong arm of the military must be in evidence to convince all that no other method will be tolerated. . . . I called for the opinions of different representatives and individual citizens of the State generally as to the advisability of convening a special session to act upon a then existing emergency, which, however, did not relate to the present situation. The expressions received at that time indicated that 95 percent of the people were opposed to such an extra session. For geographical reasons and on account of the customary ten days' notice to members it would be impossible to convene and organize a special session of the legislature in less than three weeks, presuming on the most expeditious action on the part of the members. For these reasons I deem it impossible to convene the legislature in special session to meet the present emergency and still think it highly inadvisable.

JOHN SPARKS, Governor

_____

The White House
December 28, 1907

Hon. John Sparks, Governor
Carson City, Nev.

Your telegram December 26 received. It in effect declares that you have failed to call the legislature together because, in your judgment, the legislature would not call upon the Government of the United States for the use of troops, although in your opinion it ought to do so. The Constitution of the United States imposes, not upon you, but upon the legislature, if it can be convened, the duty of calling upon the Government of the United States to protect the State of Nevada against domestic violence. You now request me to use the armed forces of the United States in violation of the Constitution because in your judgment the legislature would fail to perform its duty under the Constitution. The State government certainly does not appear to have made any serious effort to do its duty by the effective enforcement of its police functions. I repeat again what I have already said to you several times, that under the circumstances now existing in the State of Nevada as made known to me, an application from the legislature of the State is an essential condition to the indefinite continuance of the troops at Goldfield. Circumstances may change, and if they do I will take whatever action the needs of the situation require so far as my constitutional powers permit. But the first need is that the State authorities should do their duty, and the first step toward this is the assembling of the legislature. It is apparent from your telegram that the legislature of Nevada can readily be convened. You have fixed the period of three weeks as the time necessary to convene and organize a special session. If within five days from the receipt of this telegram you shall have issued the necessary notice to convene the legislature of Nevada, I shall continue the station of the troops at Goldfield during such period of three weeks. If within the term of five days such notice has not been issued, the troops will be immediately returned to their former stations.

THEODORE ROOSEVELT

180 Triple Damages and the Danbury Hatters Union (1908)

Although no one denied the right of labor to organize in local and in nationwide trade unions, concerted labor action in the form of strikes and boycotts frequently came under attack. Management and government resorted to both the common law of conspiracy and the Sherman Anti-Trust Act in efforts to curtail labor activism. In 1908, The Supreme Court approved the applicability of the antitrust laws to the activities of the hatters union of Danbury, Connecticut. The court rendered a verdict of seventy-four thousand dollars in damages against the union, which had attempted to boycott the products of a local hat manufacturer.

Later, in the case of *Gompers v. Buck's Stove and Range Co.*, Samuel Gompers, president of the American Federation of Labor, was held to have been properly cited for contempt of court under the Sherman Act for disobeying a court injunction to abandon the listing of the company as "unfair to labor" in union publications.

☆ 180 *Loewe v. Lawlor*

208 U.S. 274 (1908).

Mr. Chief Justice FULLER delivered the opinion of the Court:

*   *   *

The question is whether [a treble damage action against a union for its boycott] can be maintained under the Anti-Trust Act.

*   *   *

In our opinion, the combination described in the [complaint] is a combination "in restraint of trade or commerce among the several States," in the sense in which whose words are used in the act, and the action can be maintained accordingly.

And that conclusion rests on many judgments of this court, to the effect that the act prohibits any combination whatever to secure action which essentially obstructs the free flow of commerce between the States, or restricts, in that regard, the liberty of a trader to engage in business.

The combination charged falls within the class of restraints of trade aimed at compelling third parties and strangers involuntarily not to engage in the course of trade except on conditions that the combination imposes; and there is no doubt that (to quote from the well-known work of Chief Justice Erle on Trade Unions) "at common law every person has individually, and the public also has collectively, a right to require that the course of trade should be kept free from unreasonable obstruction. . . ."

*   *   *

The averments here are that there was an existing interstate traffic between plaintiffs and citizens of other States, and that for the direct purpose of destroying such interstate traffic defendants combined not merely to prevent plaintiffs from manufacturing articles then and there intended for transportation beyond the State, but also to prevent the vendees from reselling the hats which they had imported from Connecticut, or from further negotiating with plaintiffs for the purchase and intertransportation of such hats from Connecticut to the various places of destination. So that, although some of the means whereby the interstate traffic was to be destroyed were acts within a State, and some of them were in themselves as a part of their obvious purpose and effect beyond the scope of Federal authority, still, as we have seen, the acts must be considered as a whole, and the plan is open to condemnation, notwithstanding a negligible amount of intrastate business might be affected in carrying it out. If the purposes of the combination were, as alleged, to prevent any interstate transportation at all, the fact that the means operated at one end before physical transportation commenced and at the other end after the physical transportation ended was immaterial.

Nor can the act in question be held inapplicable because defendants were not themselves engaged in interstate commerce. The act made no distinction between classes. It provided that "every" contract, combination or conspiracy in restraint of trade was illegal. The records of Congress show that several efforts were made to exempt, by legislation, organizations of farmers and laborers from the operation of the act and that all these efforts failed, so that the act remained as we have it before us.

* * *

[The complaint alleges] that defendants were members of a vast combination called The United Hatters of North America, comprising about 9,000 members and including a large number of subordinate unions, and that they were combined with some 1,400,000 others into another association known as The American Federation of Labor, of which they were members, whose members resided in all the places in the several States where the wholesale dealers in hats and their customers resided and did business; that defendants were "engaged in a combined scheme and effort to force all manufacturers of fur hats in the United States, including the plaintiffs, against their will and their previous policy of carrying on their business, to organize their workmen in the departments of making and finishing, in each of their factories, into an organization, to be part and parcel of the said combination known as The United Hatters of North America, or as the defendants and their confederates term it, to unionize

their shops, with the intent thereby to control the employment of labor in and the operation of said factories, and to subject the same to the direction and control of persons, other than the owners of the same, in a manner extremely onerous and distasteful to such owners, and to carry out such scheme, effort and purpose, by restraining and destroying the interstate trade and commerce of such manufacturers, by means of intimidation of and threats made to such manufacturers and their customers in the several States, of boycotting them, their product and their customers, using therefor all the powerful means at their command, as aforesaid, until such time as, from the damage and loss of business resulting therefrom, the said manufacturers should yield to the said demand to unionize their factories."

* * *

We think a case within the statute was set up and that the demurrer should have been overruled.

Judgment reversed and cause remanded with a direction to proceed accordingly.

181 Liability for Imposing Martial Law (1909)

The power of state officials, in cases of labor disputes, to declare a state of insurrection and to order imprisonments by the military was challenged in *Moyer v. Peabody*. Invoking a provision of the Civil Rights Act of 1871 (the Ku Klux Klan Act), a member of the Western Federation of Miners claimed damages from the governor of Colorado and officers of the National Guard of Colorado for having deprived him of his constitutional rights while acting under color of state law. Writing for the Supreme Court, Justice Holmes denied relief: "When it comes to a decision by the head of the state upon a matter involving its life, the ordinary rights of individuals must yield to what he deems the necessities of the moment." While management had ready access to the courts and the law to protect its interests, individuals were abandoned by the judiciary when asserting that their civil rights had been violated by government forces suppressing labor unrest.

☆ 181 *Moyer v. Peabody*

212 U.S. 78 (1909).

MR. JUSTICE HOLMES delivered the opinion of the court.

This is an action for damages, brought by the plaintiff in error against the former Governor of the State of Colorado et al. for an imprisonment of the plaintiff by them while in office....

The complaint alleges that the imprisonment was continued from the morning of March 30, 1904, to

the afternoon of June 15, and . . . was without probable cause, that no complaint was filed against the
plaintiff, and that (in that sense) he was prevented
from having access to the courts of the State, although they were open during the whole time; but it
sets out proceedings on *habeas corpus*, instituted by
him before the Supreme Court of the State, in which
that court refused to admit him to bail and ultimately discharged the writ. *In re Moyer*, 35 Colorado, 154 and 159. In those proceedings it appeared
that the Governor had declared a county to be in a
state of insurrection, had called out troops to put
down the trouble, and had ordered that the plaintiff
should be arrested as a leader of the outbreak, and
should be detained until he could be discharged with
safety, and that then he should be delivered to the
civil authorities to be dealt with according to law.

*   *   *

The plaintiff's position, stated in a few words, is
that the action of the Governor, sanctioned to the extent that it was by the decision of the Supreme
Court, was the action of the State and therefore
within the Fourteenth Amendment; but that if that
action was unconstitutional the Governor got no protection from personal liability for his unconstitutional interference with the plaintiff's rights. It is
admitted, as it must be, that the Governor's declaration that a state of insurrection existed is conclusive
of that fact. It seems to be admitted also that the
arrest alone would not necessarily have given a
right to bring this suit. But it is said that a detention
for so many days, alleged to be without probable
cause, at a time when the courts were open, without
an attempt to bring the plaintiff before them, makes
a case on which he has a right to have a jury pass.

. . . Of course the plaintiff's position is that he has
been deprived of his liberty without due process of
law. But it is familiar that what is due process of law
depends on circumstances. . . . What, then, are the
circumstances of this case? . . . The facts that we are
to assume are that a state of insurrection existed
and that the Governor, without sufficient reason but
in good faith, in the course of putting the insurrection down held the plaintiff until he thought that he
safely could release him.

. . . In such a situation we must assume that he
had a right under the state constitution and laws to
call out troops, as was held by the Supreme Court of
the State. . . . That means that he shall make the ordinary use of the soldiers to that end; that he may
kill persons who resist and, of course, that he may
use the milder measure of seizing the bodies of those
whom he considers to stand in the way of restoring
peace. Such arrests are not necessarily for punishment, but are by way of precaution to prevent the
exercise of hostile power. So long as such arrests are
made in good faith and in the honest belief that they

are needed in order to head the insurrection off, the
Governor is the final judge and cannot be subjected
to an action after he is out of office on the ground
that he had not reasonable ground for his belief. If
we suppose a Governor with a very long term of office, it may be that a case could be imagined in which
the length of the imprisonment would raise a different question. But there is nothing in the duration of
the plaintiff's detention or in the allegations of the
complaint that would warrant submitting the judgment of the Governor to revision by a jury. It is not
alleged that his judgment was not honest, if that be
material, or that the plaintiff was detained after
fears of the insurrection were at an end.

. . . When it comes to a decision by the head of the
State upon a matter involving its life, the ordinary
rights of individuals must yield to what he deems
the necessities of the moment. Public danger warrants the substitution of executive process for judicial process. . . . As no one would deny that there
was immunity for ordering a company to fire upon a
mob in insurrection, and that a state law authorizing
the Governor to deprive citizens of life under such
circumstances was consistent with the Fourteenth
Amendment, we are of opinion that the same is true
of a law authorizing by implication what was done in
this case. . . .

Judgment affirmed.

182 "an instrument of tyranny" (1909)

In its struggle for greater social and economic justice, the American labor movement was limited to
strikes and boycotts. Management could invoke the
forces of government through prosecutions, damage
actions, and proceedings in equity, but organized labor had no comparable mechanism to air its grievances before the courts. Labor viewed the judicial
intervention in the economic conflict as favoring capital and management, and sought legislative measures to redress the perceived imbalance.

Before being elected president, William Howard
Taft had been the nation's solicitor general and a circuit court judge. His judicial decisions had aroused
the unions' wrath. He predicated his extreme position on injunctions in labor disputes and his hostility
to the secondary boycott outlined in his inaugural
address upon a view of the labor movement as
threatening to governmental authority.

☆ 182 President Taft's Inaugural Address:
The Use of Injunctions in Labor Disputes
(March 4, 1909)

Reprinted in J. Richardson, *Supplement to the Messages
and Papers of the Presidents Covering the Administration
of W. H. Taft* (New York: Bureau of National Literature,
1912), 17:7378.

      *   *   *

... Another labor question has arisen which has awakened the most excited discussion. That is in respect to the power of the federal courts to issue injunctions in industrial disputes. As to that, my convictions are fixed. Take away from the courts, if it could be taken away, the power to issue injunctions in labor disputes, and it would create a privileged class among the laborers and save the lawless among their number from a most needful remedy available to all men for the protection of their business against lawless invasion. The proposition that business is not a property or pecuniary right which can be protected by equitable injunction is utterly without foundation in precedent or reason. The proposition is usually linked with one to make the secondary boycott lawful. Such a proposition is at variance with the American instinct, and will find no support, in my judgment, when submitted to the American people. The secondary boycott is an instrument of tyranny, and ought not to be made legitimate.

      *   *   *

183 "unlawful obstructions" (1914)

On November 5, 1912, Woodrow Wilson, having compiled impressive academic credentials as a professor and president of Princeton University, and a liberal record as governor of New Jersey, was elected president of the United States. He defeated incumbent president William Howard Taft and former president Theodore Roosevelt, running again as the Bull Moose party candidate. Despite his mild manner, Wilson did not hesitate to use the military arm of the government. When General Victoriano Huerta overthrew the moderate government of Mexico in 1913, Wilson refused to recognize Huerta's military regime and announced instead United States support for the revolutionary regime under Venustiano Carranza. A year later, when Mexico failed to make the demanded apologies for the temporary arrest of nine American sailors in Tampico, President Wilson ordered a United States naval force to Tampico Bay. He also ordered the taking of Vera Cruz, where German infiltration was suspected.

The same week the Marines were taking Vera Cruz with a loss of fifteen men, a smoldering miners' strike in Colorado erupted into a pitched battle between striking miners and the combined forces of the state militia and John D. Rockefeller's mine guards. In ten days of fighting, before federal troops restored order sixty-six people died, including some women and children of the striking miners who perished when the strikers' tent city at Ludlow was set on fire. The delay in the arrival of the federal troops was due to troop shortages caused by the Mexican

intervention. Six months later, Wilson acted more swiftly in responding to a call for military aid when a federal judge sought help to enforce a labor injunction against a miners' strike in Arkansas.

Despite Wilson's decisiveness both domestically and internationally, he issued a proclamation of neutrality and later called on Americans to be neutral "in thought as well as action" when war broke out in Europe on August 4, 1914. The United States did not enter World War I until 1917.

☆ 183 President Wilson and the Labor Wars

☆ 183a Suppressing Insurrection in Colorado

38 Stat. 1994 (1914).

BY THE PRESIDENT OF THE UNITED STATES OF AMERICA

A Proclamation

Whereas it is provided by the Constitution of the United States that the United States shall protect every State in this Union, on application of the legislature, or of the executive (when the legislature can not be convened), against domestic violence; and

Whereas the Governor of the State of Colorado has represented that domestic violence exists in said State which the authorities of said State are unable to suppress; and has represented that it is impossible to convene the legislature of the State in time to meet the present emergency; and

Whereas the laws of the United States require that in all cases of insurrection in any State or of obstruction to the laws thereof, whenever in the judgment of the President it becomes necessary to use the military forces to suppress such insurrection or obstruction to the laws, he shall forthwith by proclamation command such insurgents to disperse and retire peaceably to their respective abodes within a limited time:

Now, therefore, I, Woodrow Wilson, President of the United States, do hereby admonish all good citizens of the United States and all persons within the territory and jurisdiction of the United States against aiding, countenancing, abetting, or taking part in such unlawful proceedings; and I do hereby warn all persons engaged in or connected with said domestic violence and obstruction of the laws to disperse and retire peaceably to their respective abodes on or before the thirtieth day of April, instant.

In testimony whereof I have hereunto set my hand and caused the seal of the United States to be affixed.

      *   *   *

WOODROW WILSON

By the President:

W. J. BRYAN, Secretary of State

☆ 183b Dispersion of Unlawful
Assemblages in Arkansas

38 Stat. 2035 (1914).

BY THE PRESIDENT OF THE UNITED STATES OF
AMERICA

A Proclamation

Whereas by reason of unlawful obstructions, combinations, and assemblages of persons, it has become impracticable in the judgment of the President to enforce by the ordinary course of judicial proceedings the laws of the United States within the State of Arkansas and especially within the western Federal district and in the neighborhood of the towns of Hartford, Midland, and Fort Smith in said district; and whereas for the purpose of enforcing the faithful execution of the laws of the United States and protecting property in the charge of the courts of the United States, the President deems it necessary to employ a part of the military forces of the United States, in pursuance of the statute in that case made and provided:

Now, therefore, I, Woodrow Wilson, President of the United States, do hereby admonish all persons who may be or come within the State, district, or towns aforesaid against doing, countenancing, encouraging, or taking any part in such unlawful obstructions, combinations, and assemblages, and I hereby warn all persons in any manner connected therewith to disperse and retire peaceably to their respective abodes on or before 12 o'clock noon of the 6th day of November instant.

Those who disregard this warning and persist in taking part with a riotous mob in forcibly resisting and obstructing the execution of the laws of the United States or interfering with the functions of the Government or destroying or attempting to destroy property in the custody of the courts of the United States or under its direction can not be regarded otherwise than as public enemies.

Troops employed against such combinations and assemblages of persons will act with all the moderation and forbearance consistent with the accomplishment of their duty in the premises; but all citizens must realize that, if they mingle with or become a part of such riotous assemblages, there will be no opportunity for discrimination in the methods employed in dealing with such assemblages. The only safe course, therefore, for those not intentionally participating in such unlawful procedure is to abide at their homes or, at least, not to go or remain in the neighborhood of such riotous assemblages.

In testimony whereof I have hereunto set my hand and caused the seal of the United States to be affixed.

*   *   *

WOODROW WILSON

By the President:

ROBERT LANSING, Acting Secretary of State

184 "the labor of a human being is not a commodity" (1914)

The Clayton Antitrust Act reflected in large part President Wilson's 1912 campaign ideology, originally advanced by future Supreme Court justice Louis D. Brandeis, which called for the tightening of federal policy toward capital and management and a liberalization of attitudes toward labor. The Act's exemption of labor organizations from the prohibitions of the Sherman Act, its recognition of union strikes, boycotts, and picketing, and the limitations it placed upon the use of federal injunctions against strikes and boycotts helped to neutralize federal law as an instrument of management and resulted in a major legislative victory for labor. By the time the Clayton Act passed, President Wilson had moved closer to the antitrust approach embodied in the Federal Trade Commission Act of 1914 and articulated by Theodore Roosevelt during the 1912 campaign.

☆ 184 Clayton Antitrust Act

38 Stat. 730 (1914).

*   *   *

SEC. 6. That the labor of a human being is not a commodity or article of commerce. Nothing contained in the anti-trust laws shall be construed to forbid the existence and operation of labor, agricultural, or horticultural organizations, instituted for the purposes of mutual help, and not having capital stock or conduced for profit, or to forbid or restrain individual members of such organizations from lawfully carrying out the legitimate objects thereof; nor shall such organizations, or the members thereof, be held or construed to be illegal combinations or conspiracies in restraint of trade, under the anti-trust laws.

*   *   *

SEC. 20. That no restraining order or injunction shall be granted by any order of the United States, or a judge or the judges thereof, in any case between an employer and employees or between employers and employees, or between employees, or between persons employed and persons seeking employment, involving, or growing out of, a dispute concerning terms or conditions of employment, unless necessary to prevent irreparable injury to property, or to a property right, of the party making the application, for which injury there is no adequate remedy at law, and such property or property right must be described with a particularity in the application, which must be in writing and sworn to by the applicant or by his agent or attorney.

And no such restraining order or injunction shall prohibit any person or persons, whether singly or in concert, from terminating any relation of employment, or from ceasing to perform any work of labor, or from recommending, advising, or persuading others by peaceful means so to do; or from attending at any place where any such person or persons may lawfully be, for the purpose of peacefully obtaining or communicating information, or from peacefully persuading any person to work or to abstain from working; or from ceasing to patronize or to employ any party to such dispute, or from recommending, advising, or persuading others by peaceful and lawful means so to do; or from paying or giving to, or withholding from, any person engaged in such dispute, any strike benefits or other moneys or things of value; or from peaceably assembling in a lawful manner, and for lawful purposes; or from doing any act or thing which might lawfully be done in the absence of such dispute by any party thereto; nor shall any of the acts specified in this paragraph be considered or held to be violations of any law of the United States.

185 The Execution of Joe Hill (1915)

"Murdered by the Authorities of the State of Utah." So read the banner over Joe Hill's coffin during his funeral in Chicago.

It has been alleged that Joe Hill was killed by a firing squad of Salt Lake County for political reasons because he was a member of the "fighting section of the American working class, the I.W.W." Whether Hill received a fair trial for the first-degree murder of a grocery store owner (wounded in a similar attack long before Hill came to Utah) will continue to be debated by labor sympathizers and legal scholars. The Supreme Court of Utah's opinion makes little reference to his leadership in the Industrial Workers of the World. Although the IWW never developed into a major rival of the AFL, its organizers brought the plight of the migrant worker of the western United States and the immigrant factory worker of the East to the attention of the craft-dominated union movement. The IWW demonstrated that unskilled workers, speaking in many tongues, could combine to form a militant labor organization.

The careful review of the evidence by the Utah Supreme Court was unconvincing to Hill's followers. They could easily believe Joe Hill was framed, considering their inherent mistrust of the law and courts, which had so often acted to frustrate their goals. Joe Hill's body received a hero's funeral in Chicago, and a judge detailed the legal errors of the

Utah courts during the funeral oration. In his life, as well as his songs, Joe Hill, born Joseph Hillstrom, greatly enriched American folklore.

☆ 185 *State v. Hillstrom*

46 Utah 341, 150 P. 935 (1915).

STRAUP, C. J. . . . The claim made is that there is not sufficient evidence to identify the defendant, to connect him with the commission of the offense, nor to show motive.

In the information it is charged that he with a revolver shot and killed J. G. Morrison. . . . As the deceased and his two sons [Arling, 17; Merlin, 13] were preparing to close the store, two men with red bandana handkerchiefs over their faces as masks, and with revolvers in their hands, suddenly entered the store. . . . Merlin, the only living witness to the shooting, testified that as the two assailants entered the store and approached his father they said, "We have got you now," and immediately shot. He gave it as his best judgment that about seven shots in all were fired, when the assailants fled, without attempting to take anything from the cash register or elsewhere. The father and Arling were both killed. . . . Two bullet marks were found in shelving or the counter where the deceased was killed, another on the inside of the ice chest, where the deceased kept his revolver, and two or three where lay the body of Arling, behind the counter, and one bullet hole through his body and straight down through the floor. Merlin testified he did not see the first shot fired, which hit his father, but saw the second, which was shot by the taller of the two assailants, who then directed his attention towards the ice chest. Merlin retreated into a little storeroom, where he no longer saw Arling nor the assailants, but heard shots. After the assailants had fled, Merlin first went to his father, and then to Arling. He found the latter dead behind the south counter, and but a short distance from the ice chest. Near [Arling's] outstretched hand lay the revolver which was kept in the ice chest, with one chamber discharged. . . . From this it is quite evident that at some period during the shooting Arling went to the ice chest, got the gun, and discharged it at the assailants.

Another witness . . . saw the taller of the two assailants come out of the store in a rather stooped position, with his hands drawn over his chest, and heard him exclaim as if in great pain, "Oh, Bob!" Another witness saw the taller of the two assailants run from the store . . . and heard him in a clear voice say, "I am shot." . . . The blood [on the sidewalk] had the appearance, as described by the witnesses, as coughed up and spat on the sidewalk. . . .

The defendant and Applequist [a friend] . . . left [the Eselius house in Murray] that evening some time between 6 and 9; the exact time is not made to appear. Applequist did not return, and has not been seen nor heard of since. That night between 11:30 and 12 o'clock the defendant called at a Dr. McHugh's office on Fourteenth South and State streets, about 2-1/2 miles south of the place of the homicide, and about midway between the place of the homicide and Murray. . . . [T]he defendant [said] that he was shot, and stated: "I wish this kept private." The doctor removed the defendant's clothes, and found him suffering from a gunshot wound through the chest and lungs. . . . From the appearance of the wound the doctors [a Dr. Bird had arrived] gave it as their opinion that the bullet causing the wound was shot from a 38 caliber gun. They further testified that such a wound would cause internal hemorrhages, coughing, and spitting of blood. After the wound was attended the doctors assisted the defendant in dressing. In doing that a revolver in a holster with shoulder straps fell from the defendant's clothes to the floor. . . . The doctors saw but the handle of the gun sticking out of the holster. From the appearance of the handle they gave it as their opinion that the gun was a 38 caliber automatic gun, and that the handle was similar to a Colt's automatic 38 gun exhibited to them. While the defendant was there at the office he told the doctors that "he had had a quarrel with some one over a woman, and that in the quarrel he was shot, and that he was as much to blame as the other fellow, and wanted it kept quiet, kept private." That was all that was said by him concerning the manner in which he received the wound. . . . [Dr. Bird offered the defendant a ride.] As Dr. Bird and the defendant approached the Eselius place the defendant requested the doctor to turn down the lights of the automobile. Dr. Bird did so. As they neared the house the defendant, "with a combination of the teeth, tongue, and lips, gave two shrill, penetrating whistles." Dr. Bird assisted the defendant to the kitchen or back door. As the defendant and Dr. Bird entered "a number of men seemed to have just gone from the back room that we first entered into the next room, and all were standing or walking in that direction as we entered the door, and turned and recognized the defendant, and, seeing him with me, expressed surprise, and asked if he was hurt." . . . Two or three days after that the defendant was arrested. In his room on a table was found a red bandana handkerchief similar to that worn by the assailants. The defendant's coat and clothing worn by him on the night of the homicide were seized and put in evidence. They were similar in appearance to those worn by the taller assailant. One of the officers asked the defendant where his gun was. He told him that Dr. Bird, on the way from Dr. McHugh's office to the Eseliuses [*sic*], had trouble with his automobile, and as Dr. Bird got out to crank it the defendant threw the gun away. No gun was found. The defendant was not a witness in the

case, and at no time explained or offered to explain the place where, nor the circumstances under which he received his wound, except as stated by him to the doctors, that he received it in a quarrel over a woman; nor did he offer any evidence whatever to show his whereabouts or movements on the night of the homicide.

A Mrs. Seeley . . . testified that she met two men with red bandana handkerchiefs tied around their necks. One of the men was tall and slender. In passing they crowded her off the sidewalk. She turned and looked at them. The taller turned and looked at her. She gave this description of him. . . .

*   *   *

When the defendant stood erect with his coat on and his arms down the bullet hole where the bullet entered the coat was four inches lower than the wound where the bullet entered his body. From this it is argued by defendant's counsel that the defendant received the shot causing his wound when his hand and arm were raised above his head drawing his coat up, and that the arms of the assailant in the store were at no time in such a position, and therefore the defendant's wound was not received in the store. Such argument does not demonstrate that the defendant was not the man who was shot in the store by Arling. At most, it is but an inference of fact, which, and the weight of it, were for the jury. That Arling shot one of the assailants in the store is sufficiently shown; indeed, that fact is not seriously controverted. But no one at that moment saw either the assailant or Arling. In what position Arling was when he shot or the assailant when he received the shot is not disclosed. . . . [C]ounsel base a positive conclusion upon nonexisting premises, at least upon premises wholly conjectural and speculative—the position the assailant or Arling was in at the time the former was shot. The argument that the defendant, if he was one of the assailants, must, when he was shot, have been in the middle of the room with his hands raised above his head, is not the only deducible inference. . . . It also can be inferred that Arling may have shot the assailant as the latter was leaning and reaching over the counter, which position would account for the upraised arm and coat of the defendant and the course the bullet took through his coat and body. That, of course, is but an inference, but it is as probable as the argument of counsel that the defendant, when he was shot, must have had his hands in the air above his head. . . . But all this is mere matter of inference and argument, and was for the jury.

It further is claimed that no bullet shot from the deceased's gun was found in the store . . . from which, and from the further fact that the bullet which produced the defendant's wound went clear through his body, it is argued that it was not the defendant, but another, who was shot in the store by

Arling. . . . These also are positive conclusions based on but conjectural or speculative premises. . . . Such argument is proper enough addressed to a jury; but it has no foundation when addressed to a court. . . .

Evidence also was given to show that the red bandana handkerchief . . . was given him by Mrs. Eselius the next morning after the defendant was shot. . . . The credibility and weight of her testimony were for the jury, not for us.

*   *   *

But the claim of insufficiency of the evidence is chiefly based on the fact that none of the witnesses who saw the assailant at or about the store on the night of the homicide testified positively that the defendant was one of them; and for that reason it is argued that the case is no stronger than the case of *State v. Hill*, where the evidence was held insufficient to connect the accused with the commission of that offense. We think the cases on the facts dissimilar. The testimony of Merlin . . . is alone not sufficient. But there is the testimony of the witnesses who saw the taller of the two assailants . . . heard his voice, and that the voice, size, and appearance of that man were similar to those of the defendant. Though it be conceded that that also was insufficient, still there is the further testimony of the witness who but a few minutes prior to the homicide, close to one of the assailants, in a bright light nearly as light as day, looked him directly in the face. . . . That man and the defendant, as testified to by her, were similar in size and features, had the same slim face, sharp nose, and large nostrils, and the same "defection" or scar on the side of the face and neck. True, that witness would not testify positively that the defendant was that man; but the facts testified to by her as to the description of that man pointed most strikingly to the defendant. . . . In addition to all this was the fresh bullet wound on the defendant. That wound, unexplained, or unsatisfactorily explained by him, was, in connection with other evidence that one of the perpetrators of the crime answering the defendant's description was shot in the store, a relevant mark of identification, especially in light of the defendant's effort to have the fact of his wound concealed, and in view of his statement that he threw his gun away, of his request that the lights of the automobile be turned down, and of no apparent good reason for his giving two sharp penetrating whistles before he entered the Eselius house with Dr. Bird. Gunshot wounds such as had the defendant are unusual and extraordinary. Under all the circumstances the defendant's wound, unexplained, was quite as much a distinguishing mark as though one of the assailants in the assault had one of his ears chopped off. The only explanation the defendant gave of his wound was that he received it at some undisclosed place in a quarrel with some undescribed man over some undescribed woman, in

which he "was to blame as much as the other fellow." . . . One suffering from such a wound as did the defendant—a wound of such serious and oft-fatal consequences—ordinarily does not walk around the country seeking surgical aid until, from loss of blood, he is about to collapse. Generally such aid is promptly summoned and brought to such a sufferer. . . . [An] officer after the defendant's arrest stated to him that, if the defendant would tell him the place where and the circumstances under which he received his wound, . . . and if true that the defendant received his wound in a quarrel over a woman, he would be given his liberty. The defendant declined to give the officer any information. . . . The defendant, of course, was not required to make any statement to the officer. His refusal to make any or to answer any question cannot, though the fact was brought out by the defendant, be considered as an admission of guilt. He had a right to remain silent. Nor can his neglect or refusal to be a witness in any manner prejudice him or be used against him. The state, as in all other criminal cases, was required to prove the defendant's guilt beyond a reasonable doubt. But the defendant, without some proof tending to rebut them, may not avoid the natural and reasonable inferences deducible from proven facts by merely declining to stay off the stand or remaining silent. . . . While the proven facts and inferences against him are neither strengthened nor weakened by his mere silence or failure to take the stand, yet when he, with peculiar knowledge of facts remains silent, or has evidence in his power by which he may repel or rebut such proven facts and inferences, and chooses not to avail himself of it, he must suffer the consequences of whatever the facts and inferences adduced against him tend fairly and reasonably to prove.

We think the evidence sufficient to justify a finding that the defendant was one of the perpetrators of the crime. To hold otherwise is to hold that the accused must be identified or connected with the commission of the offense by direct testimony of eyewitnesses who unerringly are able to testify positively and unequivocally that he was the perpetrator. . . . To . . . place ourselves in the jury box . . . is to ignore the law and to usurp a function not possessed by us. And yet the import of their argument . . . is on mere weight and worthiness of testimony, arguments such as the witnesses had not positively identified the defendant and had not sufficient means or opportunity of observing and giving a reliable description of the assailants; that of discrepancies as to the description of the hat and clothes worn by one of them; that the defendant was not shot in the store, because the bullet hole in his coat was four inches lower than the wound on his body, and because no bullet shot from the gun near the outstretched hand of Arling's body was found; . . . that the handkerchief found in defendant's room was given him the day after he was shot; and that no motive was shown for the defendant to mask himself and with gun in hand to enter the store and shoot to death his victim, with whom it was not shown he had any acquaintance. All this, it is contended, when properly considered and weighed, so clearly repelled whatever testimony there may be to point to the defendant's guilt as to leave no evidence to connect him with the commission of the offense. It is apparent all this was for the jury.

With this conclusion it is unnecessary to inquire into the question of motive. . . . Since the evidence is sufficient to show that the defendant was one of the perpetrators who, with his face masked and gun in hand, entered the store and deliberately shot his victim to death, it is immaterial to inquire whether the motive was assassination or robbery. Nothing but a wicked motive emanating from a depraved and malignant heart is attributable to the commission of such a crime as is here indisputably shown.

*   *   *

186 This Struggle Will Go On (1915)

William ("Big Bill") Haywood (1869-1928) was born in Salt Lake City, Utah, and lost an eye at the age of nine in a mining accident. Haywood was a leader of the Western Federation of Miners during a series of violent strikes and also helped organize the Industrial Workers of the World in 1905. He ran as a socialist candidate for governor of Colorado while imprisoned on the charge of assassinating the former governor of Idaho. Haywood opposed America's entry into World War I and in 1917 was arrested for sedition. He jumped bail and went to the Soviet Union in 1921. Like Emma Goldman before him, he became disillusioned with Russia's revolution.

Haywood and the IWW envisioned a future society in which workers would control the means of production and their own destinies. This goal was to be achieved through the direct action of a general strike. In his testimony before the Industrial Relations Commission Haywood also called for "filling the jails" as an antiestablishment tactic.

☆ 186 William Haywood: Testimony before the Industrial Relations Commission

Reprinted in S. Lynd, ed., *Nonviolence in America: A Documentary History* (New York: Bobbs-Merrill, 1966), 217-40.

CHAIRMAN WALSH: Are you familiar with the formation of the Western Federation of Miners?

MR. HAYWOOD: Yes; being a miner, of course I kept acquainted with what the miners were doing and remember when that federation of miners was organized, and have since become acquainted with all of the circumstances that brought about the federation of miners.

CHAIRMAN WALSH: Will you please describe the conditions that led to the formation of the Western Federation of Miners?

MR. HAYWOOD: It was organized as the result of a strike that occurred in the Coeur d'Alene.

*   *   *

. . . In 1902 and 1903 came the strike that is so well known as the Cripple Creek strike, and that strike was in the nature of a sympathetic strike. The men who were working in the mills in Colorado City, although entitled to the benefits of the 8-hour law which had been passed in Colorado at that time, were working 12 hours a day 11 hours on the day shift and 13 hours on the night shift.

This condition prevails in the smelting plants of Colorado at the present time, and in some of the milling plants. They went out on strike in September, I think, 1902.

CHAIRMAN WALSH: Was the attention of the authorities called to the condition—that is, that the law was being violated with reference to the hours of labor?

MR. HAYWOOD: Oh, yes, indeed.

CHAIRMAN WALSH: Was the law inoperative, or why didn't they prosecute the officials?

MR. HAYWOOD: The smelter officials, or mine owners, do you mean?

CHAIRMAN WALSH: Yes.

MR. HAYWOOD: Did you ever hear of a mine owner or of a manufacturer being prosecuted for violation of a law? Well, they were not, anyway. The courts don't work that way.

*   *   *

They were striking as they struck ten years before, for the enforcement of a state law. The laws at that time were inoperative at Cripple Creek. The militia ran the district. They threw the officers out of office. Sheriff Robinson, I remember, had a rope thrown at his feet and was told to resign or they would hang him. . . . Habeas corpus was denied. I recall Judge Seed's court, where he had three men brought in that were being held by the militia. While his court was in session it was surrounded by soldiers who had their gatling guns and rifles trained on the door. He ordered those three prisoners released, and the soldiers went after them and they were taken back to trial. That strike was not won. . . .

*   *   *

. . . The authorities of the city took up the side of the employment sharks, and between 500 and 600 men and women, members of the organization, were thrown into prison.

*   *   *

... [E]verywhere, I might say, that I have seen courts in action; they took the side of the capitalists.

*   *   *

... [T]here is a class struggle in society, with workers on one side of that struggle and the capitalists on the other; that the workers have nothing but their labor power and the capitalists have the control of and the influence of all branches of government—legislative, executive, and judicial; that they have on their side of the question all of the forces of law; they can hire detectives, they can have the police force for the asking or the militia, or the Regular Army.

There are workers who have come to the conclusion that there is only one way to win this battle. We don't agree at all with the statement that you heard reiterated here day after day—that there is an identity of interests between capital and labor. We say to you frankly that there can be no identity of interests between labor, who produces all by their own labor power and their brains, and such men as John D. Rockefeller, Morgan, and their stockholders, who neither by brain or muscle or by any other effort contribute to the productivity of the industries that they own.

*   *   *

COMMISSIONER WEINSTOCK: Well then, summing up, we find that I.W.W.'ism teaches the following: ...

MR. HAYWOOD: Read me that over again.

COMMISSIONER WEINSTOCK: "(a) that the workers are to use any and all tactics that will get the results sought with the least possible expenditure of time and energy."

MR. HAYWOOD: Yes; I believe in the worker using any kind of tactics that will get results. . . .

COMMISSIONER WEINSTOCK: "(b) The question of right or wrong is not to be considered."

MR. HAYWOOD: What is right and wrong? What I think is right in my mind or what you think is right in your mind?

COMMISSIONER WEINSTOCK: "(c) The avenging sword is to be unsheathed, with all hearts resolved on victory or death."

MR. HAYWOOD: What that means is a general strike.

COMMISSIONER WEINSTOCK: "(d) The workman is to help himself when the proper time comes."

MR. HAYWOOD: When the proper time comes, when he needs it let him go and get it.

COMMISSIONER WEINSTOCK: "(e) No agreement with an employer of labor is to be considered by the worker as sacred or inviolable."

*   *   *

MR. HAYWOOD: ... You can let that about contract and agreement stand.

COMMISSIONER WEINSTOCK: "(f) The worker is to produce inferior goods and kill time"—we will cut that out, that which relates to the production of inferior goods and killing time; that is out of the subject.

MR. HAYWOOD: Yes.

COMMISSIONER WEINSTOCK: "(g) The worker is to look forward to the day when he will confiscate the factories and drive out the owners."

MR. HAYWOOD: I would drive them in instead of out.

*   *   *

COMMISSIONER WEINSTOCK: And the last is, "(i) Strikers are to disobey and treat with contempt all judicial injunctions."

MR. HAYWOOD: Well, I have been plastered up with injunctions until I do not need a suit of clothes, and I have treated them with contempt.

COMMISSIONER WEINSTOCK: And you advocate that?

MR. HAYWOOD: I do not believe in that kind of law at all. I think that is a usurpation on the part of the courts of a function that was never vested in the courts by the Constitution.

*   *   *

COMMISSIONER WEINSTOCK: ... As I understand it, I.W.W.'ism is socialism, with this difference—

MR. HAYWOOD (interrupting): With its working clothes on.

COMMISSIONER WEINSTOCK: As an I.W.W., are you a believer in free speech?

MR. HAYWOOD: Yes, sir.

COMMISSIONER WEINSTOCK: Are you a believer in free press?

MR. HAYWOOD: Yes, sir.

COMMISSIONER WEINSTOCK: Now, if your idea prevails and you went to bed tonight under the capitalistic system and woke up tomorrow morning under your system, the machinery of production and distribution would belong to all the people.

MR. HAYWOOD: Under our system it would be under the management of the working class.

*   *   *

COMMISSIONER WEINSTOCK: ... [W]ill you briefly outline to us, Mr. Haywood, how would you govern and direct the affairs under your proposed system of 100,000,000 of people, as we are in this country today?

MR. HAYWOOD: Well, how are the affairs of the hundred million people conducted at the present time? The workers have no interest, have no voice in anything except the shops. Many of the workers are children. They certainly have no interest and no voice in the franchise. They are employed in the shops, and of course my idea is that children who work should have a voice in the way they work—in the hours they work, in the wages that they should receive—that is, children who labor. The same is true of women. The political state, the Government, says that women are not entitled to vote—that is, except in the 10 free States of the West; but they are industrial units; they are productive units.... My idea is that they should have a voice in the control or disposition of their labor power, and the only place where they can express themselves to the fullest as citizens of industry, if you will, as to the purpose of their work and the conditions under which they will labor. Now, you recognize that in conjunction with women and children.

The black men of the South are on the same footing. They are all citizens of this country, but they have no voice in its government. Millions of black men are disfranchised, who if organized would have a voice in saying how they should work and how the conditions of labor should be regulated. But unorganized they are as helpless and in the same condition of slavery as they were before the [Civil W]ar. This is not only true of women and children and black men, but it extends to the foreigner who comes to this country and is certainly a useful member of society. Most of them at once go into industries, but for five years they are not citizens. They plod along at their work and have no voice in the control or use of their labor power. And as you have learned through this commission there are corporations who direct the manner in which these foreigners shall vote. Certainly you have heard something of that in connection with the Rockefeller interests in the Southern part of Colorado. You know that the elections there were never carried on straight, and these foreigners were directed as to how their ballot should be placed.

They are not the only ones who are disfranchised, but there is also the workingman who is born in this country, who is shifted about from place to place by industrial depressions; their homes are broken up and they are compelled to go from one city to another, and each State requires a certain period of residence before a man has the right to vote. Some States say he must be a resident 1 year, others say 2 years; he must live for a certain length of time in the county; he must live for 30 days or such a matter in the precinct before he has any voice in the conduct of government. Now, if a man was not a subject of a State or Nation, but a citizen of industry, moving from place to place, belonging to his union, wherever he went he would step in the union hall, show his card, register, and he at once has a voice in the conduct of the affairs pertaining to his welfare. That is the form of society I want to see, where the men who do the work, and who are the only people who are worth while—understand me, Mr. Weinstock, I think that the workingman, even doing the meanest

kind of work, is a more important member of society than any judge on the Supreme Bench and other useless members of society. I am speaking for the working class, and I am a partisan to the workers....

COMMISSIONER HARRIMAN: Mr. Haywood, I understand that you do not believe in war. Now, if you don't believe in war, why do you believe in violence in labor disputes? One is war between nations, and the other is war between—

MR. HAYWOOD (interrupting): You say I believe in violence?

*   *   *

COMMISSIONER HARRIMAN: I thought you did.

MR. HAYWOOD: Probably I do; but I don't want it to be taken for granted without giving me an opportunity to explain what violence means. I think you will agree that there is nothing more violent that you can do to the capitalist than to drain his pocketbook. In that sort of violence I believe, and we are trying to make it impossible for the growth of more capitalists and to make useful citizens out of the existing capitalists.

*   *   *

187 "use a little direct action" (1916, 1918, 1927-1930)

On Saturday afternoon, July 22, 1916, a bomb was thrown into a San Francisco crowd during a Preparedness Day parade, designed to stimulate popular support for the national and state war effort. Nine spectators were killed by the explosion, which was viewed as the work of left-wing, antimilitary anarchists. Five local labor leaders, some with radical reputations, were arrested and indicted for murder. Of the four who were tried, two were convicted: Warren Billings, sentenced to life imprisonment; and Tom Mooney, a self-proclaimed Marxist and labor organizer, sentenced to death. Rena Mooney, Tom's wife, was found not guilty. Celebrated as a labor martyr and victim of militarist capitalism, Tom Mooney gained national and international prominence. Anarchist and labor organizations demonstrated on his behalf in Russia and England and on the Continent. His sentence was commuted to life imprisonment a year later, two weeks before the scheduled execution. After twenty-one years in prison, Tom Mooney and Warren Billings were released and pardoned in 1939 by California governor Culbert L. Olsen.

☆ 187 The San Francisco Preparedness Day Bombing and the Mooney Case

☆ 187a An Anonymous Warning Received by San Francisco Newspapers (July 21, 1916)

Reprinted in R. Frost, *The Mooney Case* (Stanford: Stanford University Press, 1968), 82-83.

Our protests have been in vain in regards to this preparedness proppoganda, so we are going to use a little direct action on the 22nd which will echo around the earth and show that Frisco really knows how, and that militarism cant be forced on us and our children without a violent protest. Things are going to happen to show that we will go to any extreme, the same as the controlling class, to preserve what little democracy we still have, Dont take this as a joke or you will be rudely awaken, *We have sworn to do our duty to the masses*, and only send this warning to those who are wise but are forced to march to hold their jobs, as we want to give only *the hypocritical patriots who shout for war but never go*, a real taste of w[ar.] Kindly ask the Chamber of Commerce to march [in] a solid body, *if they want to prove they [are] not cowards*. Our duty has been done so far, Thank Mr Older for his great work of the past in enlightening the masses and ho[pe] he will never allow himself to become the intellectual prostitute as the other dailys....

TH[E] DETERMINED EXILES FROM MILITARISTIC GOVERNMENT
U.S.
Holland
Italy
Russia
Italy
Germany

☆ 187b Excerpts from the Police Interrogation of Tom Mooney (July 28, 1916)

Reprinted in R. Frost, *The Mooney Case* (Stanford: Stanford University Press, 1968), 106-8.

Q. [Prosecutor JAMES F. BRENNAN] How long have you known Billings?

A. [MOONEY] *I insist that I have the right to counsel.* There is [no] fair minded, honest, liberty loving men that can deny me that right.

MR. FICKERT: We thought you wanted to make a statement.

*   *   *

MR. BRENNAN: There are some circumstances can be cleared up. How long do you know Billings?

A. Listen Mr. Brennan,—Well, you don't intend to give us our rights?

Q. You sent a telegram for the purpose of making the people believe you are an innocent man.

A. To let you and Mr. Fickert and Chief of Police White know where I was.

Q. You knew we were right on your tail with five or six officers, right after you all the time. You knew you couldn't step ten feet without an officer being on top of you.

A. Why did you put in the paper a state wide search—a nation wide search—

*   *   *

Q. [BRENNAN] (Int'g) Let me tell you something. One of the most dastardly crimes that has been committed in this country has been committed in the last ten days.

A. *I know that. The most fiendish crime, the most heinous crime.*

Q. *Yes, and you are guilty of that crime.*

A. *Is that so!* [At this point Mooney rushed Brennan, calling him a "S.O.B." Police hauled him off and quieted him down.]

*   *   *

A. ... I am only a working man and there are many tricks in this game and I want my rights all safe guarded and I realize they cannot be safe guarded under these circumstances. I realize the seriousness of this charge that has been lodged against me. There is no provocation or justification for it, absolutely none, and you know it.

Q. Then if there is absolutely none your conscience is clear.

A. Absolutely.

Q. There is no reason why you should fear— have any fear of being contradicted.

A. I saw what was in the Examiner [local paper] today.

Q. Then you are fore-warned of what might be asked of you?

A. I saw what was in the Examiner. I know why it was there and who put it there. *I am going to have counsel.*

MR. BRENNAN: Q. What was in the Examiner that came to your notice?

A. The whole paper.

Q. Give us just one idea of it, just one thing or suggestion.

A. All of it. All of my past. My trials at Martinez in connection with strikes and being tried for dynamite, which was not true, and all that stuff. It was to prejudice the minds of the people and inflame them, to make them believe I actually committed this dirty, dastardly crime. That is what it was done for.

*   *   *

Q. [BRENNAN] In this case, of course, nobody claims you, well known as you are, actually placed the bomb, ... but if you are responsible for this crime at all it is because of the fact [that] you aided and abetted in its perpetration, and therefore, the only way to connect you up is to connect you with certain people who are claimed to be perpetrators. . . . As soon as we touch on any dangerous ground, that is, your connection with any of the parties who are responsible for this outrage, why, you immediately refuse to answer.

☆ 187c Reports of President Wilson's Mediation Commission (January 28, 1918)

Reprinted in R. Frost, *The Mooney Case* (Stanford: Stanford University Press, 1968), 293-94.

. . . We conceived it to be our duty merely to determine whether a solid basis exists for a feeling that an injustice was done . . . and that an irreparable injustice would be committed to allow such conviction to proceed to execution. . . .

*   *   *

. . . It is now well known that the attention to the situation in the East was first aroused through meetings of protest against the Mooney conviction in Russia. From Russia and the Western States protest spread to the entire country until it has gathered momentum from many sources, sources whose opposition to violence is unquestioned, whose devotion to our cause in the war is unstinted. The liberal sentiment of Russia was aroused, the liberal sentiment of the United States was aroused, because the circumstances of Mooney's prosecution, in the light of his history, led to the belief that the terrible and sacred instruments of criminal justice were consciously or unconsciously made use of against labor by its enemies in an industrial conflict.

However strange or however unexpected it may be, the just disposition of the Mooney case thus affects influences far beyond the confines of California, and California can be depended upon to see the wider implications of the case. With the mere local aspects, with the political and journalistic conflicts which the case has occasioned, neither the commission nor the country at large is concerned. But the feeling of disquietude aroused by the case must be heeded, for if unchecked, it impairs the faith that our democracy protects the lowliest and even the unworthy against false accusations. War is fought with moral as well as material resources. We are in this war to vindicate the moral claims of unstained processes of law, however slow at times, such processes may be. These claims must be tempered by the fire of our own devotion to them at home.

Your Commission, therefore respectfully recommends in case the Supreme Court of California should find it necessary (confined as it is by jurisdictional limitations) to sustain the conviction of Mooney on the record of the trial, that the President use his good offices to invoke action by the governor of California and the cooperation of its prosecuting officers to the end that a new trial may be had for Mooney whereby guilt or innocence may be put to the test of unquestionable justice. This result can easily be accomplished by postponing the execution of the sentence of Mooney to await the outcome of a new trial, based upon prosecution under one of the untried indictments against him.

☆ 187d Excerpts of Letters to Governor Clement C. Young of California Opposing Proposed Pardon for Tom Mooney (1927-1930)

Reprinted in R. Frost, *The Mooney Case* (Stanford: Stanford University Press, 1968), 383-84.

"MY DEAR GOVERNOR:" "HONORABLE SIR:" "MY DEAR GOVERNOR YOUNG:"

"Stand firm, Mr. Governor." "Too many criminals in the whole United States are having leniency extended to them." "I remember, and so do you, the agitation that was gotten up on behalf of the McNamara brothers who destroyed the Times Building in Los Angeles. It was claimed that they were the innocent victims of capitalistic conspiracy under the direction of Harrison Gray Otis. The agitators knew nothing more about the facts of that affair than do the present excitable friends of Mr. Mooney." "[Mooney] was caught out in Suisun Bay with a boatload of dynamite." "If Mooney was not a strong union radical there wouldn't be all this fuss made over him to liberate him."

"Pardoning Mooney would mean that the preparedness parade [was] unpatriotic and wrong and should not have been held." "One of my childhood friends was killed in that frightful affair." "Emma Goldman was in the city at the same time, and I regard them all as accessories to crime." "The Department of Labor during the Wilson administration seems never to have missed a single opportunity for unwarranted interference with due process of state law where agitators were involved." "We hope you will be courageous enough to hold your own ground (as Calvin Coolidge did when the Police and Firemen of Boston wanted to unionize) and not be politically influenced by the murderers and rough necks of the country." "None of these petitioners have suggested who might have been guilty of this crime, and some doubtless have inside information. In my judgment his sentence should be relentlessly carried out."

"These men are not Savanarolas. The class to which they belong is entitled to the same consideration we give mad dogs, hydrophobia skunks, and rattlesnakes." "Sympathy should not thwart the purpose of our people in meting out appropriate punishment to a misguided Russian, posing under an Irish name." "If Tom Mooney ever be Pardoned or released, He should by all means be deported because every body knows, he has been working against our flag. Tom and his Brother has allways been an I.W.W." "Mrs. Mooney was also as vicious as her husband." "Many of the anarchist-Communist-American Civil Liberties Union crowd would like to see them released." "The Communists wish to get these prisoners out of jail to advance the cause of communism, which is exactly what their pardon would do." "I commend you for not allowing the Hearst mud slinging machine to rail Road you into making a decision on the Mooney Billings cases." "I have just been talking to a few spies and if the Mooney methods of political threats are successful the whole state will soon be worse than Chicago."

"Have you noticed since Mooney and Billings have been locked up that there has been no dynamiting of buildings?" "Do you believe for one moment that money in great sums has not been used to bring about their release?" "Dont be a 'jellyfish' again by liberating this convicted assassin. You were fooled as to the Whitney female but dont repeat that mistake in the Mooney case." "The idea of such notariety hunters such as Sinclair Lewis going out and retrying the case and playing Judge and Jury and declaring him innocent." "They cry for his release like those of old cried for Barabas's release."

"Stick to your guns like the good soldier that the people of this great State believe you to be." "If I have helped just a little to stiffen your backbone I'll feel repaid." "This republic would crumble to pieces if it wasnt for the courageous fellows like you." "It is unfortunate that the matter came up now, but I am sure you have the approbation of our best people."

World War I
and the
Rise of Totalitarianism

———

1917-1940

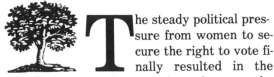

The steady political pressure from women to secure the right to vote finally resulted in the adoption of the Nineteenth Amendment to the United States Constitution. Success did not come without dramatic confrontations between suffragists and the forces of law and order, which resulted in the arrest, conviction, and imprisonment of women activists for the zealous pursuit of their cause.

The second and more central focus of this chapter is on America's response to World War I, a war in which the Old World nations had a vested interest. Pacifists, socialists, partisans of the various European camps, and America Firsters strongly opposed the New World's involvement in this conflagration. The resistance to America's involvement gave rise to a new class of political offenders—antiwar activists.

The wartime and postwar fears and anxieties also gave rise to a movement for the purification of the American melting pot by eliminating "un-American" influences. United States entry into World War I and the success of the Russian Revolution had a dramatic effect upon the American public. Socialism and communism were not mere idle notions expounded by foreign philosophers but could provide a stimulus for conspiracies on American soil. In addition, the call to arms, which previously had been resisted in instances of domestic conflict, was likely to encounter even greater opposition in cases of foreign wars. In short, the suspicion grew that the nation's pluralistic population was not as committed to the American Way as had been assumed and could be manipulated by foreign agitators.

The criminal law was invoked directly to punish war and draft resisters, as well as those who advocated the forceful overthrow of government. Other quasi-criminal methods for purging the country of the disloyal, such as the exclusion and deportation of politically suspect aliens—often associated with the labor movement—were also utilized. Ideological dissidents were subject to punishment for political associations, and several documents reflect less a concern with the enforcement of traditional justice than the desire of the authorities to convey a symbolic message to left-leaning aliens to watch their step.

This chapter documents as well the first resorts to the Constitution, particularly the First Amendment, as a judicially enforceable protection against the criminalizing of unorthodox political belief and advocacy.

Although it was at the height of World War I and shortly thereafter that the movement toward enforcing American homogeneity reached its peak, its legacies lingered on for several decades and are still evident today.

The labor movement continued to be a focus for much of the material in this chapter. In its quest for legitimacy, labor finally achieved its long-sought goal of preventing federal power, in the form of the labor injunction, from playing a partisan role in the contest between labor and capital. It ultimately succeeded in having the federal government cast as an impartial referee of labor disputes, and several long-standing management techniques for curbing labor's power were determined to be illegal. The changing relations between capital and labor are reflected further in the increased sophistication of labor tactics, including the sit-down strike, which led to many violent confrontations with local police.

Greatly diminished from the labor scene, federal force was evident, nevertheless, in Washington, D.C., during the Depression, as the encampment of the Bonus Marchers was dispersed by military force. But tensions continued between state and federal authorities in several other arenas of political and civil rights. The power of the state to resort to martial law in order to avoid the command of a federal injunction was tested and denied. But federal involvement in protecting blacks in the South from terrorist attacks was as passive as before. Also, the failure of the assimilationist policies toward Native Americans accounted in large part for the new grant of limited powers of self-determination to them.

At the close of this chapter, with the blowing winds of World War II, one can observe the beginning of the government's renewed attempts to curb political and related activities motivated by sympathy to various foreign causes. With mounting tensions overseas, the authorities set out once again, as they had done a quarter-century earlier, to enforce the American Way.

188 How Long Must Women Wait for Liberty? (1917)

The suffragist movement contributed to Woodrow Wilson's continuing political education. Before he secured reelection in 1916, Wilson had decided that women's right to vote could be denied no longer. Yet he was reluctant to assume an active role in securing suffrage for them.

The militant suffragists were convinced that only a strong exercise of presidential power could overcome congressional resistance, and they set out to spur Wilson into action. They picketed the White House throughout 1917. After the United States declared war on Germany, banners continued to point out to "Kaiser Wilson!" that "20,000,000 American women are not self-governed."

After six months of picketing, the authorities stepped in to suppress the embarrassing demonstrations. The following contemporaneous account of the events reported the escalation of government response from toleration to arrest and release to the filing of charges, fines, and imprisonment. Those arrested received sentences of up to sixty days. The prosecutions only served to stiffen the resolve of the suffragists. They engaged in more alarming tactics: hunger strikes, public burnings of Wilson's lofty speeches on democracy, and the burning of the president in effigy.

It was not until September 1918 that Wilson directly urged Congress to pass the National Suffrage Amendment. Though gravely ill, Wilson worked hard to ensure that women could vote in the presidental election of 1920.

☆ 188 Militant Suffragists Picket President Wilson

Reprinted in D. Stevens, *Jailed for Freedom* (New York: Boni and Liveright, 1920), 93-111.

. . . The Chief of Police, Major Pullman, was detailed to "request" us to stop "picketing" and to tell us that if we continued to picket, we would be arrested.

"We have picketed for six months without interference," said Miss Paul. "*Has the law been changed?*"

"No," was the reply, "but you must stop it."

"But, Major Pullman, we have consulted our lawyers and know we have a legal right to picket."

"I warn you, you will be arrested if you attempt to picket again."

The following day Miss Lucy Burns and Miss Katherine Morey of Boston carried to the White House gates "We shall fight for the things we have always held nearest our hearts, for democracy, for the right of those who submit to authority to have a voice in their own government," and were arrested.

News had spread through the city that the pickets were to be arrested. A moderately large crowd had gathered to see the "fun." One has only to come into conflict with prevailing authority, whether rightly or wrongly, to find friendly hosts vanishing with lightning speed. To know that we were no longer wanted at the gates of the White House and that the police were no longer our "friends" was enough for the mob mind.

Some members of the crowd made sport of the women. Others hurled cheap and childish epithets at them. Small boys were allowed to capture souvenirs, shreds of the banners torn from non-resistant women, as trophies of the sport.

Thinking they had been mistaken in believing the pickets were to be arrested, and having grown weary of their strenuous sport, the crowd moved on its way. Two solitary figures remained, standing on the sidewalk, flanked by the vast Pennsylvania Avenue, looking quite abandoned and alone, when suddenly without any warrant in law, they were arrested on a completely deserted avenue.

Miss Burns and Miss Morey upon arriving at the police station, insisted to the great surprise of all the officials, upon knowing the charge against them. Major Pullman and his entire staff were utterly at a loss to know what to answer. . . .

. . . Hours passed. Finally the two prisoners were pompously told that they had "obstructed the traffic" on Pennsylvania Avenue, were dismissed on their own recognizance, and never brought to trial.

The following day, June 23rd, more arrests were made; two women at the White House, two at the Capitol. All carried banners with the same words of the President. There was no hesitation this time. They were promptly arrested for "obstructing the traffic." They, too, were dismissed and their cases never tried. It seemed clear that the Administration hoped to suppress picketing merely by arrests. When, however, women continued to picket in the face of arrest, the Administration quickened its advance into the venture of suppression. It decided to bring the offenders to trial.

On June 26, six American women were tried, judged guilty on the technical charge of "obstructing the traffic," warned by the court of their "unpatriotic, almost treasonable behavior," and sentenced to pay a fine of twenty-five dollars or serve three days in jail.

"Not a dollar of your fine will we pay," was the answer of the women. "To pay a fine would be an admission of guilt. We are innocent."

Independence Day, July 4, 1917, is the occasion for two demonstrations in the name of liberty. Champ Clark, late Democratic speaker of the House, is declaiming to a cheering crowd behind the White House, "Governments derive their just powers from the consent of the governed." In front of the White

House thirteen silent sentinels with banners bearing the same words, are arrested. It would have been exceedingly droll if it had not been so tragic. Champ Clark and his throng were not molested. The women with practically a deserted street were arrested and served jail terms for "obstructing traffic."

It is Bastille Day, July fourteenth. . . .

The proud banner is scarcely at the gates when the leader is placed under arrest. Her place is taken by another. She is taken. Another, and still another steps into the breach and is arrested.

Meanwhile, the crowd grows, attracted to the spot by the presence of the police and the patrol wagon. Applause is heard. There are cries of "shame" for the police, who, I must say, did not always act as if they relished carrying out what they termed "orders from higher up." An occasional hoot from a small boy served to make the mood of the hostile ones a bit gayer. But for the most part an intense silence fell upon the watchers, as they saw not only younger women, but white-haired grandmothers hoisted before the public gaze into the crowded patrol, their heads erect, their eyes a little moist and their frail hands holding tightly to the banner until wrested from them by superior brute force. . . .

The stuffy court room is packed to overflowing. . . . The prosecuting attorney now elaborately proves that we walked, that we carried banners, that we were arrested by the aforesaid officers while attempting to hold banners at the White House gates.

Each woman speaks briefly in her own defense. She denounces the government's policy with hot defiance. The blame is placed squarely at the door of the Administration, and in unmistakable terms. Miss Anne Martin opens for the defense:

"This is what we are doing with our banners before the White House, petitioning the most powerful representative of the government, the President of the United States, for a redress of grievances; we are asking him to use his great power to secure the passage of the national suffrage amendment.

"As long as the government and the representatives of the government prefer to send women to jail on petty and technical charges, we will go to jail. Persecution has always advanced the cause of justice. The right of American women to work for democracy must be maintained. . . . We would hinder, not help, the whole cause of freedom for women, if we weakly submitted to persecution now. Our work for the passage of the amendment must go on. It *will* go on."

Mrs. John Rogers, Jr., descendant of Roger Sherman, one of signers of the Declaration of Independence, speaks: "We are not guilty of any offence, not even of infringing a police regulation. We know full well that we stand here because the President of the United States refuses to give liberty to American women. We believe, your Honor, that the wrong persons are before the bar in this Court. . . ."

"I object, your Honor, to this woman making such a statement here in Court," says the District Attorney.

"We believe the President is the guilty one and that we are innocent."

Mrs. Florence Bayard Hilles speaks in her own defense: . . . "I am a Democrat, and to a Democratic President I went with my appeal. . . . What a spectacle it must be to the thinking people of this country to see us urged to go to war for democracy in a foreign land, and to see women thrown into prison who plead for that same cause at home.

*　　　*　　　*

"My services as an American woman are being conscripted by order of the President of the United States to help win the world war for democracy, . . . 'for the right of those who submit to authority to have a voice in their own government.' I shall continue to plead for the political liberty of American women — and especially do I plead to the President, since he is the one person who . . . can end the struggles of American women to take their proper places in a true democracy."

There is a continuous objection from the prosecutor, eager advice from the judge, "you had better keep to the charge of obstructing traffic." . . . And how utterly puny the "charge" is! If it were true that the prisoners actually obstructed the traffic, how grotesque that would be. The importance of their demand, the purity of their reasoning, the nobility and gentle quality of the prisoners at the bar; all conspire to make the charge against them, and the attorney who makes it, and the judge who hears it, petty and ridiculous.

But justice must proceed.

Mrs. Gilson Gardner of Washington, D.C., a member of the Executive Committee of the National Woman's party, and the wife of Gilson Gardner, a well-known Liberal and journalist, speaks:

"It is impossible for me to believe that we were arrested because we were obstructing traffic or blocking the public highway.

"We have been carrying on activities of a distinctly political nature, and these political activities have seemingly disturbed certain powerful influences. Arrest followed. I submit that these arrests are purely political and that the charge of an unlawful assemblage and of obstructing traffic is a political subterfuge. Even should I be sent to jail which, I could not, your Honor, anticipate, I would be in jail, not because I obstructed traffic, but because I have offended politically, because I have demanded of this government freedom for women."

189 Suffragists as Political Prisoners (1917)

The country's preoccupation with winning World War I did not deter the suffragists. Arrested for their persistent picketing, the suffragists carried their struggle to the jails. Although segregated from each other, they collectively managed to frame and sign the earliest known claim in the United States for special treatment, in the European tradition, as political prisoners. Refusal of the authorities to accede to the demands led to hunger strikes and forced feeding.

☆ 189 Suffragists, Letters from Prison

Reprinted in D. Stevens, *Jailed for Freedom* (New York: Boni & Liveright, 1920), 175.

TO THE COMMISSIONERS OF THE DISTRICT OF CO-LUMBIA:

As political prisoners, we, the undersigned, refuse to work while in prison. We have taken this stand as a matter of principle after careful consideration, and from it we shall not recede.

This action is a necessary protest against an unjust sentence. In reminding President Wilson of his pre-election promises toward woman suffrage we were exercising the right of peaceful petition, guaranteed by the Constitution. . . .

Conscious, therefore, of having acted in accordance with the highest standards of citizenship, we ask the Commissioners of the District to grant us the rights due political prisoners. We ask that we no longer be segregated and confined under locks and bars in small groups, but permitted to see each other, and that Miss Lucy Burns, who is in full sympathy with this letter, be released from solitary confinement in another building and given back to us.

We ask exemption from prison work, that our legal right to consult counsel be recognized, to have food sent to us from outside, to supply ourselves with writing material for as much correspondence as we may need, to receive books, letters, newspapers, our relatives and friends.

Our united demand for political treatment has been delayed, because on entering the workhouse we found conditions so very bad that before we could ask that the suffragists be treated as political prisoners, it was necessary to make a stand for the ordinary rights of human beings for all the inmates. Although this has not been accomplished we now wish to bring the important question of the status of political prisoners to the attention of the commissioners, who, we are informed, have full authority to make what regulations they please for the District prison and workhouse.

The Commissioners are requested to send us a written reply so that we may be sure this protest has reached them.

Signed by,

MARY WINSOR
LUCY BRANHAM
ERNESTINE HARA
HILDA BLUMBERG
MAUD MALONE
PAULINE F. ADAMS
ELEANOR A. CALNAN
EDITH AINGE
ANNIE ARNEIL
DOROTHY J. BARTLETT
MARGARET FOTHERINGHAM

*   *   *

The Commissioners' only answer to this was a hasty transfer of the signers and the leader, Miss Burns, to the District Jail, where they were put in solitary confinement. The women were not only refused the privileges asked but were denied some of the usual privileges allowed to ordinary criminals.

190 "war is wrong" (1917)

John Haynes Holmes served as minister of the Community Church of New York from 1907 to 1949. An outspoken pacifist, he reaffirmed his unwavering opposition to all wars in the immediate aftermath of Pearl Harbor in 1941. In his 1917 "Statement to My People," he unequivocally condemned America's imminent entry into World War I and affirmed his support for draft resistance. Recognizing that "statements of this kind, made on the eve of War, seem to many persons to be treasonable," Holmes insisted, nevertheless, that the "whole fabric of democracy is threatened" by war, conscription, the national war fever, and the "orgy of bigotry, intolerance, and persecutions for opinions' sake as America has not seen since the days of the Salem witches." The trustees of Holmes's church were nearly unanimous in disavowing his antiwar positions, but they also defended his right to speak freely from the pulpit. The Secret Service placed agents in the congregation to monitor his sermons. The federal government subsequently imposed criminal sanctions on individuals who refused to be inducted because of their adherence to the principles of conscientious objection as summarized in the following document.

☆ 190 A Statement to My People on the Eve of War (John Haynes Holmes)

The Messiah Pulpit, May 1917, 4-5, 6, 8-9, 10-12, 15-16 (The Community Church of New York), reprinted in David R. Weber, ed., *Civil Disobedience in America* (Ithaca: Cornell University Press, 1978), 234-39.

... You have a right to know what I shall say and do in the event of war, upon what road of doctrine I shall set my feet, into what hazards of pain and peril I shall lead this church. The pew is always entitled to the full confession of the pulpit, but never so urgently as at the time when such confession touches the deep issues of life and death. If there be any here who is tempted to question the wisdom or the sincerity of what I am now doing, let him think for a moment of how easy it would have been for me to keep silent, avoid the questions which are to-day setting the son "at variance against his father, the daughter against her mother, the daughter-in-law against her mother-in-law," ... before the bugles sing and the flags are lifted high, I ask you to hear me. ...

... War is in open and utter violation of Christianity. If war is right, then Christianity is wrong, false, a lie. If Christianity is right, then war is wrong, false, a lie. The God revealed by Jesus, and by every great spiritual leader of the race, is no God of battles. He lifts no sword—he asks no sacrifice of blood. He is the Father of all men, Jew and Gentile, bond and free. His spirit is love, his rule is peace, his method of persuasion is forgiveness. His law, as interpreted and promulgated by the Nazarene, is "love one another," "resist not evil with evil," "forgive seventy times seven," "overcome evil with good," "love your enemies, bless them that curse you, do good to them that hate you, pray for them which despitefully use you and persecute you." Such a God and such a law, others may reconcile with war, if they can. I cannot—and what I cannot do, I will not profess to do.

But I must go farther—I must speak not only of war in general, but of this war in particular. Most persons are quite ready to agree, especially in the piping times of peace, that war is wrong. But let a war cloud no bigger than a man's hand, appear on the horizon of the nation's life, and they straightway begin to qualify their judgment, and if the war cloud grow until it covers all the heavens, they finally reverse it. This brings the curious situation of all war being wrong in general, and each war being right in particular. ...

In its ultimate causes, this war is the natural product and expression of our unchristian civilization. Its armed men are grown from the dragon's teeth of secret diplomacy, imperialistic ambitions, dynastic pride, greedy commercialism, economic exploitation at home and abroad. In the sowing of these teeth, America had had her part; and it is therefore only proper, perhaps, that she should have her part also in the reaping of the dreadful harvest. ... Any honor, dignity, or beauty which there may be in our impending action, is to be found in the impulses, pure and undefiled, which are actuating many patriotic hearts to-day, and not at all in the real facts of the situation. The war itself is wrong.

Its prosecution will be a crime. There is not a question raised, an issue involved, a cause at stake, which is worth the life of one blue-jacket on the sea or one khaki-coat in the trenches. ... I say to you that when, years hence, the whole of this story has been told, it will be found that we have been tragically deceived, and all our sacrifices been made in vain.

... Nothing that America can do, can quench my passion for her beauty, or divert my loyalty from her service. She is the only country I have, or shall ever have, and I propose that she shall be mine forever, in war or peace, in storm or calm, in evil or good. In this impending crisis with Germany, I believe that she is wrong. She seems to me to be faithless to her own supreme calling among the nations of the earth, disloyal to high interests of humanity long since committed to her care, guilty for a selfish motive of a grievous fault. But her infidelity shall not shake my faith, her disloyalty shall not change my loyalty, her guilt shall not discharge my obligation. I shall decline to become, or to be made, "a man without a country." America has committed wrongs in the past, and she will undoubtedly commit other wrongs in the future. But she is mine. ...

And how shall I, a pacifist, serve my country in time of war?

When hostilities begin, it is universally assumed that there is but a single service which a loyal citizen can render to the state—that of bearing arms and killing the enemy. Will you understand me if I say, humbly and regretfully, that this I cannot, and will not, do. If any man or boy in this church answers the call to arms, I shall bless him as he marches to the front. When he lies in the trenches, or watches on the lonely sentinel post, or fights in the charge, I shall follow him with my prayers. If he is brought back dead from hospital or battlefield, I shall bury him with all the honors not of war but of religion. He will have obeyed his conscience and thus performed his whole duty as a man. But I also have a conscience, and that conscience I also must obey. When, therefore, there comes a call for volunteers, I shall have to refuse to heed. When, or if, the system of conscription is adopted, I shall have to decline to serve. If this means a fine, I will pay my fine. If this means imprisonment, I will serve my term. If this means persecution, I will carry my cross. No order of president or governor, no law of nation or state, no loss of reputation, freedom or life, will persuade me or force me to this business of killing. On this issue, for me at least, there is "no compromise." Mistaken, foolish, fanatical, I may be; I will not deny the charge. But false to my own soul I will not be. [S]o long as I am your minister, the Church of the Messiah will answer no military summons. Other pulpits may preach recruiting sermons; mine will not. Other parish houses may be turned into drill halls and rifle ranges; ours will not. Other clergymen may pray to God for victory for our arms; I will not. In this church, if nowhere else in all America, the Germans will still be included in the family of God's children. No word of hatred shall be spoken against them — no evil fate shall be desired upon them. . . . [I]t remains for us who cannot take up arms at her behest, to keep it in her stead. How better can we serve our country than by restoring to her, or fulfilling for her, that high mission of peace-making, which is so uniquely and divinely hers! . . .

No nation is worthy the allegiance of even the meanest of her citizenry, which is not dedicated to the establishment of that larger and more inclusive life of universal association, which is the glad promise of mankind. America, for more than a hundred years, has been first among the countries of the world, in recognition and service of this ideal. She has been a gathering place of all the tribes of earth — a melting-pot into which the ingredients of every race, religion and nationality have been poured. And out of it has come not so much a new nation as a new idea — the idea of brotherhood. This idea has stamped our people a chosen people. It has set our land apart as a holy land. It has exalted our destiny as a divine destiny. And now, with the plunge into the welter of contending European nationalities, all this is gone. Gone, at least, if those of us who see not today's quarrel but tomorrow's prophecy, do not dedicate ourselves unfalteringly to the forgotten vision! This I am resolved to do. . . .

191 " 'Extreme Penalty for Traitors' " (1917)

Ammon Hennacy opposed World War I as being contrary to his socialist political beliefs. He refused to register for the draft and was imprisoned in Atlanta for speaking out in opposition to war. He entered prison "an atheist and not a pacifist. I would fight in a revolution but not in a capitalist war." His religious conversion while in prison turned him from violence — but not from militancy.

This account of Hennacy's prison experience portrays many of the difficulties which the correctional system faces when dealing with political offenders and the manner in which traditional penal techniques of appealing to an inmate's self-interest (either to avoid punishment or to obtain reward) have little impact upon the "politicals." Resistance and obstinance yield harsher punishment but also greater respect from officials. The superintendent of federal prisons wanted to co-opt this stiff-necked man and make him a Secret Service agent. Hennacy turned down the job and was paroled nevertheless. He eventually became a leader of the Catholic Worker movement, founded in 1933, which encouraged non-payment of taxes and civil disobedience in opposition to war.

☆ 191 Atlanta Prison (Ammon Hennacy)

A. Hennacy, ed., *Two Agitators: Peter Maurin — Ammon Hennacy* (New York: Catholic Worker, 1959), 6-19.

I was arrested when I spoke against the coming war at Broad and High in Columbus, Ohio before about 10,000 people on the evening of April 5, 1917. The next day war was declared and I was released for trial May 30. Meanwhile I distributed leaflets over Ohio for the Socialist Party, advising young men to refuse to register for the draft. When I was picked up again I asked to see a lawyer but was told I could not see one. Detective Wilson said that unless I registered for the draft by June 5th, which was registration day, I was to be shot on orders from Washington. I was shown a copy of the local paper with headlines "Extreme Penalty for Traitors." I only saw it through the bars and was not allowed to read it. . . . Spike Moore, . . . from Pittsburgh who was in Columbus, sneaked me a note and a clipping from the paper in which a reporter asked my mother if she was not frightened because I was to be shot soon. Her reply was that the only thing she was afraid of was that they might scare me to give in. This gave me added courage. June 5th passed and no move was made to shoot me. . . . My partner and I each got 2 years in Atlanta. After this term was served I was to do 9 months in Delaware, Ohio, County Jail nearby for refusal to register.

*   *   *

The conscientious objectors were scattered in different gangs and cell houses over the prison. The warden told me that the orders from Washington were to put us all in one place, but he knew better and scattered us out, for if we were in one place we would plot. This reminded me of the farmer who caught the ground-mole and said, "Hanging's too good; burning's too good; I'll bury you alive." So we conscientious objectors were scattered around where we could do propaganda instead of being segregated where we would argue among ourselves.

*   *   *

. . . A white man and a Negro had been killed by guards and I was incensed about it. My cell mates laughed and said I should worry about the living, for the dead were dead and no one could do anything about it. That if I wanted anything to do I should raise a fuss about the poor fish served on Fridays by the new mess guard, who was accused of making his rake by charging for good food and giving us junk. Accordingly I got cardboard from John Dunn and painted signs which I put up in all of the toilets around the place telling the prisoners to work on Fridays, but to stay in their cells and refuse to go to dinner or to eat the rotten fish. The guards and stoolpigeons tore the signs down, but I made others and put them up. The last Friday 20 of us stayed in our cells. The guards came around and asked us if we were sick. We said we were sick of that damn fish. The next Friday 200 stayed in their cells; and the next Friday 600. That was too many people thinking alike, as on the next Thursday the warden came to the second mess and said that those who did not come to dinner the next day would be put in the hole. Some kid squeaked out in a shrill voice: "You can't do it warden; there's only 40 solitary cells and there's a thousand of us." The next day 900 out of the 1,100 who ate at this shift stayed in their cells.

The next Monday I was called to the office and was told that I had been seen plotting to blow up the prison with dynamite, and was promptly sent to the dark hole.

*   *   *

Once when I was going to get a shave I saw Popoff entering his cell with his head bandaged. This must have been the result of the blows which I had heard faintly the day before. He was mistreated for a year or more until he went insane. Selma and I visited him in 1921 at St. Elizabeth's Hospital in Washington, D.C. He did not recognize me until I said "Johnson, the guard." I sent notes to my sister Lola for the newspapers about the treatment of Popoff. I heard the chains fall which bound him to the bars and then the thump of his body to the floor. I was told that papers in Atlanta printed something about it but no official investigation was ever made....

It was now nearly three months that I had been in solitary. Fred Zerbst, the warden, came in and asked me to sign a paper. It was registration for the second war draft. I told him that I had not changed my mind about the war. He said I wouldn't get anything around here acting that way. I told him that I wasn't asking for anything around here: I was just doing time. He said that I would get another year back in the hole for this second refusal to register. I told him that was o.k. It was September 21, 1918. The warden came in again and said this was all the longer they kept prisoners in solitary and that he would let me out in the regular prison the next day, if I would not plot to blow up any more prisons.

"You know I didn't do that," I said.

"I know you didn't," he replied, "but what do you suppose I am warden for? If I had told the prisoners that you were put in solitary for leading in that food sit-down, all of them would be your friends. When you are accused of plotting to blow up the prison they are all afraid to know you. Why didn't you come and tell me about the food?"

"Why didn't you come in the kitchen and find out? No one but stoolies go to your office," I answered. He left hurriedly.

In about five minutes he returned, saying, "I forgot to ask you something, Hennacy. I'll leave you out tomorrow just the same."

"What's on your mind?" I asked.

"Have you been sneaking any letters out of this prison?" he asked in an angry tone.

"Sure," I replied, smiling.

"Who is doing it for you?" he demanded.

"A friend of mine," I answered.

"What is his name?" was the query.

"That is for you and your guards and stool pigeons to find out."

He stormed around my cell, somewhat taken back by the fact that I had not lied or given in.

"You'll stay in here all your good time and get another year, you stubborn fool," he said as he left.

*   *   *

... I could not see anywhere except across the hall to the solid door of another cell, but I could hear Popoff in the next cell groaning and calling for water. He was still hanging from his hands for the eight hours a day as he had been for months. As the guard came down the hall he opened Popoff's door, dipping his tin cup in the toilet and threw the dirty water in Popoff's face. ...

Two months later I heard the whistles blow and shouts resound throughout the prison. The war was over. The Armistice had been signed. It was not until then that I was informed in a [secret] note from [fellow prisoner and anarchist Alexander] Berkman that November 11 was also an anarchist anniversary: the date of the hanging of the Chicago anarchists of the Haymarket in 1887. ...

[I decided that] the remainder of my two years in solitary must result in a clear-cut plan whereby I could go forth and be a force in the world. I could not take any half-way measures. If assassination, violence and revolution was the better way, then military tactics must be studied and a group of fearless rebels organized. ... I also remembered what Berkman had said about being firm, but quiet. He had tried violence but did not believe in it as a wholesale method. I read of the wars and hatred in the Old Testament. I also read of the courage of Daniel and the Hebrew children who would not worship the golden image; of Peter who chose to obey God rather than the properly constituted authorities who placed him in jail; and of the victory of these men by courage and peaceful methods. I read of Jesus, who was confronted with a whole world empire of tyranny and chose not to overturn the tyrant and make Himself King, but to change the hatred in the hearts of men to love and understanding—to overcome evil with goodwill.

I had called loudly for the sword and mentally listed those whom I desired to kill when I was free. Was this really the universal method which should be used? ... Gradually I came to gain a glimpse of what

Jesus meant when He said, "The Kingdom of God is within you." In my heart now after six months I could love everybody in the world but the warden, but if I did not love him then the Sermon on the Mount meant nothing at all. I really saw this and felt it in my heart but I was too stubborn to admit it in my mind. One day ... the thought came to me: "Here I am locked up in a cell. The warden was never locked up in any cell and he never had a chance to know what Jesus meant. Neither did I until yesterday. So I must not blame him. I must love him." ... The warden had said that he did not understand political prisoners. He and the deputy, in plain words, did not know any better; they had put on the false face of sternness and tyranny because this was the only method which they knew. It was my job to teach them another method: that of goodwill overcoming their evil intentions, or rather habits. The opposite of the Sermon on the Mount was what the whole world had been practicing, in prison and out of prison; and hate piled on hate had brought hate and revenge. It was plain that this system did not work. ...

I fancied what my radical friends in and out of prison would say when I spoke of the above teachings of Jesus. I knew that I would have to bear their displeasure, just as I had born the hysteria of the patriots and the silence of my friends when I was sent to prison. This did not mean that I was going to "squeal" and give in to the officials, but in my heart I would try to see the good in them and not hate them. Jesus did not give in to His persecutors. He used strong words against the evil doers of His time, but He had mercy for the sinner. I now was not alone fighting the world for I had Him as my helper. I saw that if I held this philosophy for myself I could not engage in violence for a revolution—a good war, as some might call it—but would have to renounce violence even in my thought. Would I be ready to go the whole way? At that time I had not heard of Tolstoy and his application of Christ's teachings to society. Berkman had just mentioned his name along with other anarchists and he might have told me more if I had had a lengthy conversation with him; but I never saw him again. ...

*   *   *

It was now in February of 1919 and I had been in solitary for 7½ months. Mr. Duehay, Superintendent of Federal Prisons from Washington, and his secretary, and Warden Zerbst came to my cell. Duehay wanted to know why I was being held so long here. I told him I was telling the world of evil conditions in the prison and would not divulge the source of my outlet for contraband mail. ...

*   *   *

The next morning a runner came down from the office to measure me for an outgoing suit, saying: "The warden told us 'that damn Hennacy wouldn't

tell anything in 7½ months; he won't tell anything in 7½ years. Get him the hell out of hole give him back his good time and let him go to his other jail. He is too much of a nuisance.' "

The next month went very quickly. It was now March 19, 1919, and I was to be released the next day. That night the deputy came in and said:

"Going out tomorrow, Hennacy?"

"That's what they say; sure a fine feeling," I replied.

"We give; we take. You tell who is getting out your contraband mail or you'll stay here another 5½ months and lose your good time and then another year for refusing to register. You don't think we will allow anyone to get on by bucking us, do you?"

Tears came to my eyes as I chokingly replied, "I can do it. Go away and don't bother me any more." After he left I wept, but I was at the stage where I felt strong enough to take it.

The next morning after breakfast I wrote on the wall that I was beginning to do the "good time" that I had lost, when the door opened suddenly and old Johnson smiled for once, saying, "Going out of this jail, Hennacy." I did not believe him; and even while the barber was shaving me I thought it was some trick to bedevil me. I was given my out-going suit and an overcoat. It is customary for the warden to shake hands with those who leave and to admonish them to live a good life out in the world. A guard gave me my $10 outgoing money and a bundle of letters that had come to me while I was in solitary, but the warden never appeared.

When I walked out of prison a plain clothes man met me saying that I was being arrested for refusing to register for the draft in August 1918 and would be taken to the county tower to await trial. ...

*   *   *

... Sam Castelton, who was to be Debs' lawyer in Atlanta, was also my lawyer. My case came up for trial after seven weeks. Castleton told me that if I was not too radical he might get me off with six months. I was asked if I had really refused to register for the first and second drafts and if I had not changed my mind and would I be ready to register for the third draft if and when it came along. I replied that I had entered prison an atheist and not a pacifist. I would fight in a revolution but not in a capitalist war. I had got locked up with the Bible in solitary and read it and become a Christian and a pacifist. ... [M]y study of the Bible had made me see that Christ was the greatest Revolutionist. And a few weeks ago I had read Tolstoy [while awaiting trial] and had become an anarchist.

"What's an anarchist?" asked the judge. My lawyer shook his head and put his finger to his lips as a warning for me not to be too radical.

"An anarchist is one who doesn't have to have a

cop to make him behave. It is the individual, the family, or the small co-operative group as a unit rather than the State." And, I continued for about ten minutes to quote Tolstoy to the effect that one had to obey God rather than man. The District Attorney, Hooper Alexander, an old fashioned looking southerner, came up to the judge and whispered, and the judge said, "case dismissed." I looked around to see whose case it was and it was mine. My lawyer seemed bewildered and so was I. I had approached the court this time with love for my enemy and had never thought I would get my freedom, for he allowed me to go 10 days on my own before I reported to the court in Columbus, Ohio, to do my 9 months in Delaware County jail for my first refusal to register.

192 "false reports or false statements" (1917)

On June 15, 1917, Congress passed the Espionage Act giving the United States broad powers to punish acts of gathering, transmitting, or negligently handling information that would be injurious to the defense of the United States if in the hands of a foreign nation or enemy. The act also imposed penalties for certain antiwar commentary and opinions. Congress enacted the law in large part to check enemy sympathizers residing in the United States. A widespread propaganda campaign had stirred up Germanophobia, and German immigrants throughout the country were accused of supporting the kaiser and spying for him.

President Woodrow Wilson, apparently recognizing the potential for abuse, approved the Espionage Act with the statement that "I shall not permit . . . any part of this law to apply to me . . . as a shield against criticism."

☆ 192 The Espionage Act

40 Stat. 217 (1917).

CHAP. 30—An Act to punish acts of interference with the foreign relations, the neutrality, and the foreign commerce of the United States, to punish espionage, and better to enforce the criminal laws of the United States, and for other purposes.

Be it enacted by the Senate and House of Representatives of the United States of America in Congress assembled:

TITLE I. ESPIONAGE

*   *   *

SEC. 3. Whoever, when the United States is at war, shall willfully make or convey false reports or false statements with intent to interfere with the operation or success of the military or naval forces of the United States or to promote the success of its enemies and whoever, when the United States is at war, shall willfully cause or attempt to cause insubordination, disloyalty, mutiny, or refusal of duty, in the military or naval forces of the United States, or shall willfully obstruct the recruiting or enlistment service of the United States, to the injury of the service or of the United States, shall be punished by a fine of not more than $10,000 or imprisonment for not more than twenty years, or both.

SEC. 4. If two or more persons conspire to violate the provisions of sections two or three of this title, and one or more of such persons does any act to effect the object of the consipiracy, each of the parties to such conspiracy shall be punished as in said sections. . . .

SEC. 5. Whoever harbors or conceals any person who he knows, or has reasonable grounds to believe or suspect, has committed, or is about to commit, an offense under this title shall be punished by a fine of not more than $10,000 or by imprisonment for not more than two years, or both.

*   *   *

193 "I do not believe that I am seeking martyrdom" (1917-1918)

Some conscientious objectors declined to register for the draft and were prosecuted in regular civilian courts. But in 1917 and 1918 the army inducted more than twenty thousand men who previously had filed claims to be classified as objectors. Of these, some four thousand declined to perform military service. The conscription bill made liberal provisions for members of recognized religious sects to choose a noncombatant corps. In addition, conscientious objectors whom a presidential board of inquiry deemed to be "sincere" were eligible for noncombatant service or for agricultural furloughs. But some men refused all forms of alternative service. The military court-martialed several hundred such men, together with the "insincere" objectors who professed no religious or moral antipathy to war.

The statements of three objectors illustrate the variety of motives for refusing conscription. Carl Haessler, a Rhodes Scholar and a professor of philosophy, objected on political grounds. Maurice Hess, voicing religious objections, also later became a college professor. Roger Baldwin, who founded the American Civil Liberties Union, articulated moral grounds. These men and the others were punished for refusing to accommodate their political, religious, or moral beliefs to the duties of allegiance owed to their government. Their criminality lay not in any affirmative deed against the government but rather in refusing to act in accordance with the demands of the authorities.

☆ 193 Statements of Conscientious Objection

Reprinted in N. Thomas, *The Conscientious Objector in America* (New York: B. W. Heubsch, 1923), 23-28.

☆ 193a Carl Haessler

I, Carl Haessler, Recruit, Machine Gun Company, 46th Infantry, respectfully submit the following statement in extenuation in connection with my proposed plea of guilty to the charge of violation of the 64th Article of War, the offense having been committed June 22, 1918, in Camp Sheridan, Ala.

The offense was not committed from private, secret, personal, impulsive, religious, pacifist or pro-German grounds.

The willful disobedience of my Captain's and of my Lieutenant-Colonel's orders to report in military uniform arose from a conviction ... that America's participation in the World War was unnecessary, of doubtful benefit (if any) to the country and to humanity, and accomplished largely, though not exclusively, through the pressure of the Allied and American commercial imperialists.

Holding this conviction, I conceived my part as a citizen to be opposition to the war before it was declared, active efforts for a peace without victory after the declaration, and a determination so far as possible to do nothing in aid of the war while its character seemed to remain what I thought it was. I hoped in this way to help bring the war to an earlier close and to help make similar future wars less probable in this country.

I further believe that I shall be rendering the country a service by helping to set an example for other citizens to follow in the matter of fearlessly acting on unpopular convictions instead of forgetting them in time of stress....

... I regret that I have been forced to make myself a nuisance.... Although officers have on three occasions offered me noncombatant service if I would put on the uniform, I have regretfully refused each time on the ground that "bomb-proof" service on my part would give the lie to my sincerity.... If I am to render any war services, I shall not ask for special privileges.

I wish to conclude this long statement by reiterating that I am not a pacifist or pro-German, not a religious or private objector, but regard myself as a patriotic political objector, acting largely from public and social grounds.

I regret that, while my present view of this war continues, I cannot freely render any service in aid of the war. I shall not complain about the punishment that the court may see fit to mete out to me.

☆ 193b Maurice Hess

I do not believe that I am seeking martyrdom. As a young man, life and its hopes and freedom and opportunities for service are sweet to me....

But I know that I dare not purchase these things at the price of eternal condemnation. I know the teaching of Christ, my Savior. He taught us to resist not evil, to love our enemies, to bless them that curse us, and do good to them that hate us. Not only did he teach this, but he also practiced it....

... We know that obedience to Christ will gain for us the glorious prize of eternal life. We cannot yield, we cannot compromise, we must suffer.

Two centuries ago our people were driven out of Germany by religious persecution, and they accepted the invitation of William Penn to come to his colony where they might enjoy the blessing of religious liberty which he promised them. This religious liberty was later confirmed by the Constitution of Pennsylvania, and the Constitution of the United States.

If the authorities now see fit to change those fundamental documents and take away our privilege of living in accordance with the teaching of the scriptures of God, then we have no course but to endure persecution as true soldiers of Christ.

If I have committed anything worthy of bonds or death, I do not refuse to suffer or to die.

I pray God for strength to remain faithful.

☆ 193c Roger N. Baldwin

The compelling motive for refusing to comply with the draft act is my uncompromising opposition to the principle of conscription of life by the state for any purpose whatever, in time of war or peace. I not only refuse to obey the present conscription law, but I would in future refuse to obey any similar statute which attempts to direct my choice of service and ideals. I regard the principle of conscription of life as a flat contradiction of all our cherished ideals of individual freedom, democratic liberty, and Christian teaching.

I am the more opposed to the present act, because it is for the purpose of conducting war. I am opposed to this and all other wars. I do not believe in the use of physical force as a method of achieving any end, however good....

But, I believe most of us are prepared even to die for our faith, just as our brothers in France are dying for theirs. To them we are comrades in spirit — we understand one another's motive, though our methods are wide apart. We both share deeply the common experience of living up to the truth as we see it, whatever the price.

Though at the moment I am of a tiny minority, I feel myself just one protest in a great revolt surging up from among the people — the struggle of the masses against the rule of the world by the few — profoundly intensified by the war. It is a struggle against the political state itself, against exploitation, militarism, imperialism, authority in all forms....

Having arrived at the state of mind in which

those views mean the dearest things in life to me, I cannot consistently, with self-respect, do other than I have, namely, to deliberately violate an act which seems to me to be a denial of everything which ideally and in practice I hold sacred.

194 "any profane, scurrilous, or abusive language about the form of government" (1918)

The Espionage Act of 1917 proved unable to curtail all criticism of the war effort. Attorney General Gregory requested amendments prohibiting attempts to obstruct recruitment and efforts to discredit war loans. The Senate Judiciary Committee responded by revamping Section Three provisions in order to eliminate all disloyal utterances. There were nearly two thousand prosecutions and nine hundred convictions under the combined espionage acts, including that of motion picture producer Robert Goldstein, sentenced to ten years in prison for his unbecoming portrayal of the British, now United States allies, in a film about the American Revolution. Socialist leader Eugene V. Debs was convicted as the result of a speech at a Socialist party state convention in which he criticized former president Theodore Roosevelt's support of the war and praised the moral courage of our revolutionary forefathers who "opposed the social system of their time."

☆ 194 The Espionage Act (as Amended)†

40 Stat. 555 (1918).

*   *   *

Sec. 3. Whoever, when the United States is at war, shall willfully make or convey false reports or false statements with intent to interfere with the operation or success of the military or naval forces of the United States, or to promote the success of its enemies, or shall willfully make or convey false reports or false statements, *or say or do anything except by way of bona fide and not disloyal advice to an investor or investors, with intent to obstruct the sale by the United States of bonds or other securities of the United States or the making of loans by or to the United States,* and whoever, when the United States is at war, shall willfully cause or attempt to cause, *or incite or attempt to incite,* insubordination, disloyalty, mutiny, or refusal of duty, in the military or naval forces of the United States, or shall willfully obstruct *or attempt to obstruct* the recruiting or enlistment service of the United States [to the injury of the service or of the United States], *and whoever, when the United States is at war, shall willfully utter, print, write, or publish any disloyal, profane, scurrilous, or abusive language about the form of government of the*

United States, or the Constitution of the United States or the military or naval forces of the United States, or the flag of the United States, or the uniform of the Army or Navy of the United States, or any language intended to bring the form of government of the United States, or the Constitution of the United States, or the military or naval forces of the United States, or the flag of the United States, or the uniform of the Army or Navy of the United States into contempt, scorn, contumely, or disrepute, or shall willfully utter, print, write or publish any language intended to incite, provoke, or encourage resistance to the United States, or to promote the cause of its enemies, or shall willfully display the flag of any foreign enemy, or shall willfully by utterance, writing, printing, publication, or language spoken, urge, incite, or advocate any curtailment of production in this country of any thing or things, product or products, necessary or essential to the prosecution of the war in which the United States may be engaged, with intent by such curtailment to cripple or hinder the United States in the prosecution of the war, and whoever shall willfully advocate, teach, defend, or suggest the doing of any of the acts or things in this section enumerated, and whoever shall by word or act support or favor the cause of any country with which the United States is at war or by word or act oppose the cause of the United States therein, shall be punished by a fine of not more than $10,000 or imprisonment for not more than twenty years, or both: *Provided, That any employee or official of the United States Government who commits any disloyal act or utters any unpatriotic or disloyal language, or who, in an abusive and violent manner criticizes the Army or Navy or the flag of the United States shall be at once dismissed by the head of the department in which the employee may be engaged, and any such official shall be dismissed by the authority having power to appoint a successor to the dismissed official.*

*   *   *

———

† Language added to the 1917 Espionage Act is in italics; language deleted is in brackets. In 1920 the amendments were repealed, leaving the original 1917 act in effect.

195 "any unlawful method of terrorism" (1919)

In essence, California's antisedition law, similar to laws passed by some two-thirds of the states, was directed not against overt acts but against seditious doctrines and their advocacy. The law was enacted against the background of the Red Scare. Communists had succeeded in Russia, and Germany and other industrialized countries seemed in danger.

The California law defined criminal syndicalism as a doctrine that advocated resort to force and violence for effectuating changes in the political arena or in industrial ownership. Syndicalism, an anticapitalist, working class ideology, held that any form of the state was an instrument of oppression. In a syndicalist society, a universal union, in which membership would entitle one to vote regardless of age, sex, race, property, or residence, would make all social and political decisions. Until its demise in the 1920s, the Industrial Workers of the World (IWW) was the chief syndicalist-oriented organization in the United States.

The sense of urgency regarding communist and syndicalist infiltration and power led to the anti-Red "Palmer Raids" (named after U.S. Attorney General A. Mitchell Palmer, assisted by a twenty-four-year-old lawyer, J. Edgar Hoover) against political and labor activists. Arrested aliens, including Emma Goldman and Alexander Berkman, were deported summarily. On January 2, 1920, twenty-seven hundred people in thirty-three cities were seized. The raids, which ceased in May 1920, were a major impetus for the organization of the American Civil Liberties Union.

☆ 195 California Criminal Syndicalism Law

1919 Cal. Stat. 281-82.

CHAPTER 188

An act defining criminal syndicalism and sabotage, proscribing certain acts and methods in connection therewith and in pursuance thereof and providing penalties and punishments therefor.

[*Approved, April 30, 1919.*]

The people of the State of California do enact as follows:

SECTION 1. The term "criminal syndicalism" as used in this act is hereby defined as any doctrine or precept advocating, teaching or aiding and abetting the commission of crime, sabotage (which word is hereby defined as meaning wilful and malicious physical damage or injury to physical property), or unlawful acts of force and violence or unlawful methods of terrorism as a means of accomplishing a change in industrial ownership or control, or effecting any political change.

SECTION 2. Any person who:

1. By spoken or written words or personal conduct advocates, teaches or aids and abets criminal syndicalism or the duty, necessity or propriety of committing crime, sabotage, ... violence or any unlawful method of terrorism as a means of accomplishing a change in industrial ownership or control, or effecting any political change; or

2. Wilfully and deliberately by spoken or written words justifies or attempts to justify criminal syndicalism or the commission or attempt to commit crime, sabotage, violence or unlawful methods of terrorism with intent to approve, advocate or further the doctrine of criminal syndicalism; or

3. Prints, publishes, edits, issues or circulates or publicly displays any book, paper, pamphlet, document, poster or written or printed matter in any other form, containing or carrying written or printed advocacy, teaching, or aid and abetment of, or advising, criminal syndicalism; or

4. Organizes or assists in organizing, or is or knowingly becomes a member of, any organization, society, group or assemblage of persons organized or assembled to advocate, teach or aid and abet criminal syndicalism; or

5. Wilfully by personal act or conduct, practices or commits any act advised, advocated, taught or aided and abetted by the doctrine or precept of criminal syndicalism, with intent to accomplish a change in industrial ownership or control, or effecting any political change;

is guilty of a felony and punishable by imprisonment in the state prison not less than one nor more than fourteen years.

*   *   *

SECTION 4. Inasmuch as this act concerns and is necessary to the immediate preservation of the public peace and safety, for the reason that at the present time large numbers of persons are going from place to place in this state advocating, teaching and practicing criminal syndicalism, this act shall take effect upon approval by the governor.

*   *   *

196 "an aid to propaganda" (1919)

Between 1917 and 1921, thirty-three states supplemented their syndicalism or antisedition legislation with prohibitions against the display of red flags or other symbols of forceful or violent opposition to organized government. The laws manifested the authorities' fear of the communist propaganda threat. In 1931, the Supreme Court, in *Stromberg v. California*, declared California's Red Flag Law unconstitutional.

☆ 196 California Red Flag Law

Cal. Penal Code § 403a (1919).

An act to add a new section to the Penal Code ... prohibiting the use of a red flag in aid of anarchistic or seditious activities.

[*Approved, April 30, 1919. In effect, July 22, 1919.*]

The people of the State of California do enact as follows: ...

403a. Any person who displays a red flag, banner or badge or any flag, badge, banner, or device of any color or form whatever in any public place or in any meeting place or public assembly, or from or on any house, building or window as a sign, symbol or emblem of opposition to organized government or as an invitation or stimulus to anarchistic action or as an aid to propaganda that is of a seditious character is guilty of a felony.

197 "falsely shouting fire" (1919)

In *Schenck v. United States*, a convicted draft resistance organizer attacked the constitutionality of the 1917 Espionage Act on First Amendment grounds. The Supreme Court reviewed this wartime law in an opinion by Justice Oliver Wendell Holmes, Jr., in which he enunciated the famous "clear and present danger" doctrine. Justice Holmes pronounced, "The question in every case is whether the words used are used in such circumstances and are of such a nature as to create a clear and present danger that they will bring about the substantive evils that Congress has a right to prevent." The Supreme Court upheld Schenck's conviction.

☆ 197 *Schenck v. United States*

249 U.S. 47 (1919).

Mr. Justice HOLMES delivered the opinion of the Court.

This . . . indictment . . . charges a conspiracy to violate the Espionage Act of June 15, 1917 by causing and attempting to cause insubordination . . . in the military and naval forces of the United States, and to obstruct the recruiting and enlistment service of the United States, when the United States was at war with the German Empire, to-wit, that the defendant wilfully conspired to have printed and circulated to men who had been called and accepted for military service . . . a document set forth and alleged to be calculated to cause such insubordination and obstruction. The count alleges overt acts in pursuance of the conspiracy, ending in the distribution of the document set forth. . . . They set up the First Amendment to the Constitution forbidding Congress to make any law abridging the freedom of speech, or of the press. . . .

*　　　*　　　*

The document in question upon its first printed side recited the first section of the Thirteenth Amendment, said that the idea embodied in it was violated by the conscription act and that a conscript is little better than a convict. In impassioned language it intimated that conscription was despotism in its worst form and a monstrous wrong against humanity in the interest of Wall Street's chosen few. It said, "Do not submit to intimidation," but in form at least confined itself to peaceful measures such as a petition for the repeal of the act. The other and later printed side of the sheet was headed "Assert Your Rights." It stated reasons for alleging that any one violated the Constitution when he refused to recognize "your right to assert your opposition to the draft," and went on, "If you do not assert and support your rights, you are helping to deny or disparage rights which it is the solemn duty of all citizens and residents of the United States to retain." It described the arguments on the other side as coming from cunning politicians and a mercenary capitalist press, and even silent consent to the conscription law as helping to support an infamous conspiracy. It denied the power to send our citizens away to foreign shores to shoot up the people of other lands, and added that words could not express the condemnation such cold-blooded ruthlessness deserves, &c., &c., winding up, "You must do your share to maintain, support and uphold the rights of the people of this country." Of course the document would not have been sent unless it had been intended to have some effect, and we do not see what effect it could be expected to have upon persons subject to the draft except to influence them to obstruct the carrying of it out. The defendants do not deny that the jury might find against them on this point.

But it is said, suppose that that was the tendency of this circular, it is protected by the First Amendment to the Constitution. . . . We admit that in many places and in ordinary times the defendants in saying all that was said in the circular would have been within their constitutional rights. But the character of every act depends upon the circumstances in which it is done. The most stringent protection of free speech would not protect a man in falsely shouting fire in a theatre and causing a panic. It does not even protect a man from an injunction against uttering words that may have all the effect of force. The question in every case is whether the words used are used in such circumstances and are of such a nature as to create a clear and present danger that they will bring about the substantive evils that Congress has a right to prevent. It is a question of proximity and degree. When a nation is at war many things that might be said in time of peace are such a hindrance to its effort that their utterance will not be endured so long as men fight and that no Court could regard them as protected by any constitutional right. It seems to be admitted that if an actual obstruction of the recruiting service were proved, liability for words that produced that effect might be enforced. The statute of 1917 punishes conspiracies to obstruct as well as actual obstruction. If the act, (speaking, or circulating a paper) its tendency and the intent with which it is done are the same, we perceive no ground for saying that success alone warrants making the act a crime.

*　　　*　　　*

Judgments affirmed.

198 "There can be no peace" (1919)

In 1905, the Industrial Workers of the World organized in Chicago as an industrial union uniting
skilled and unskilled workers for the purpose of
overthrowing capitalism and building a socialist society. Committed to total class warfare, the IWW
opposed arbitration and collective bargaining. IWW
members, nicknamed "Wobblies," were vocally antimilitaristic during World War I, and their union's
uncompromising rhetoric led to zealous federal and
state suppression during the postwar era. The IWW
led a total of 150 strikes, including the 1919 general
strike in Seattle, before internal rifts and a loss of
members to the Communist Party accounted for its
demise.

☆ 198 Preamble of the Industrial Workers of the World

Reprinted in S. Lynd, ed., *Nonviolence in America: A Documentary History* (New York: Bobbs-Merrill, 1966), 240-41.

The working class and the employing class have
nothing in common.

There can be no peace so long as hunger and
want are found among millions of the working people, and the few who make up the employing class
have all the good things of life.

Between these two classes a struggle must go on
until the workers of the world organize as a class,
take possession of the earth, and the machinery of
production, and abolish the wage system.

We find that the centering of the management of
industries into fewer and fewer hands makes the
trade-unions unable to cope with the ever-growing
power of the employing class.

The trade-unions foster a state of affairs which
allows one set of workers to be pitted against another set of workers in the same industry, thereby
helping to defeat one another in wage wars.

Moreover the trade-unions aid the employing
class to mislead the workers into the belief that the
working class have interests in common with their
employers.

These conditions can be changed and the interests of the working class upheld only by an organization formed in such a way that all its members in any
one industry, or in all industries, if necessary, cease
work whenever a strike or lockout is on in any department thereof, thus making an injury to one an
injury to all.

Instead of the conservative motto, "A fair day's
wage for a fair day's work," we must inscribe on our
banner the revolutionary watchword, "Abolition of
the wage system."

It is the historic mission of the working class to
do away with capitalism.

The army of production must be organized, not
only for the everyday struggle with the capitalists,
but also to carry on production when capitalism shall
have been overthrown.

By organizing industrially we are forming the
structure of a new society within the shell of the old.

199 The "cowardly silence about the intervention in Russia" (1919)

In March 1918, Russia signed a peace treaty with
Germany and withdrew from the "capitalist war."
Internal warfare soon was raging in Russia between
the Red Army under Lenin and Trotsky and the
White Army led by General Anton Denikin, which
had Allied support. A seven-thousand-man American army contingent occupied the Russan Pacific
port of Vladivostok, ostensibly as a watch over the
Japanese threat to the shipping lanes, but also as a
possible spearhead for an armed suppression of the
Bolshevik revolution. The British likewise occupied
the ports of Murmansk and Archangel on Russia's
northern Barents Sea and White Sea coasts.

To the revolutionaries around the world, it was
reasonable that the capitalist countries would unite
to suppress the new hope of the workers. Anarchists, socialists, and workers generally strongly
protested. The protest resulted in prosecutions under the 1918 amendments to the Espionage Act.
Abrams v. United States reached the Supreme
Court.

☆ 199 *Abrams v. United States*

250 U.S. 616 (1919).

MR. JUSTICE CLARKE delivered the opinion of the
court.

*   *   *

It was charged in each count of the indictment
that it was a part of the conspiracy that the defendants would attempt to accomplish their unlawful
purpose by printing, writing and distributing in the
City of New York many copies of a leaflet or circular, printed in the English language, and of another
printed in the Yiddish language, copies of which,
properly identified, were attached to the indictment.

All of the five defendants were born in Russia.
They were intelligent, had considerable schooling,
and at the time they were arrested they had lived in
the United States terms varying from five to ten
years, but none of them had applied for naturalization. Four of them testified as witnesses in their own
behalf and of these, three frankly avowed that they
were "rebels," "revolutionists," "anarchists," that
they did not believe in government in any form, and
they declared that they had no interest whatever in
the Government of the United States. The fourth defendant testified that he was a "socialist" and be-

lieved in "a proper kind of government, not capitalistic," but in his classification the Government of the United States was "capitalistic."

It was admitted on the trial that the defendants had united to print and distribute the described circulars and that five thousand of them had been printed and distributed. . . .

*   *   *

Thus the conspiracy and the doing of the overt acts charged were largely admitted and were fully established.

On the record thus described it is argued, somewhat faintly, that the acts charged against the defendants were not unlawful because within the protection of that freedom of speech and of the press which is guaranteed by the First Amendment to the Constitution of the United States, and that the entire Espionage Act is unconstitutional because in conflict with that Amendment.

This contention is sufficiently discussed and is definitely negatived in *Schenck v. United States*. . . .

The first of the two articles attached to the indictment is conspicuously headed, "The Hypocrisy of the United States and her Allies." After denouncing President Wilson as a hypocrite and a coward because troops were sent into Russia, it proceeds to assail our Government in general, saying:

"His [the President's] shameful, cowardly silence about the intervention in Russia reveals the hypocrisy of the plutocratic gang in Washington and vicinity."

It continues:

"He [the President] is too much of a coward to come out openly and say: 'We capitalist nations cannot afford to have a proletarian republic in Russia.' "

Among the capitalistic nations Abrams testified the United States was included.

Growing more inflammatory as it proceeds, the circular culminates in:

"The Russian Revolution cries: Workers of the World! Awake! Rise! Put down your enemy and mine!

"Yes! friends, there is only one enemy of the workers of the world and that is CAPITALISM."

This is clearly an appeal to the "workers" of this country to arise and put down by force the Government of the United States which they characterize as their "hypocritical," "cowardly" and "capitalistic" enemy.

It concludes:

"Awake! Awake, you Workers of the World! "REVOLUTIONISTS."

The second of the articles was printed in the Yiddish language and in the translation is headed, "Workers—Wake up." After referring to "his Majesty, Mr. Wilson, and the rest of the gang; dogs of all colors!", it continues:

"Workers, Russian emigrants, you who had the least belief in the honesty of *our* Government," which defendants admitted referred to the United States Government, "must now throw away all confidence, must spit in the face the false, hypocritic, military propaganda which has fooled you so relentlessly, calling forth your sympathy, your help, to the prosecution of the war."

Ths purpose of this obviously was to persuade the persons to whom it was addressed to turn a deaf ear to patriotic appeals in behalf of the Government of the United States, and to cease to render it assistance in the prosecution of the war.

It goes on:

"With the money which you have loaned, or are going to loan them, they will make bullets not only for the Germans, but also for the Workers Soviets of Russia. *Workers in the ammunition, factories, you are producing bullets, bayonets, cannon, to murder not only the Germans, but also your dearest, best, who are in Russia and are fighting for freedom.*"

It will not do to say, as is now argued, that the only intent of these defendants was to prevent injury to the Russian cause. . . . [T]he obvious effect of this appeal, if it should become effective, as they hoped it might, would be to persuade persons of character such as those whom they regarded themselves as addressing, not to aid government loans and not to work in ammunition factories, where their work would produce "bullets, bayonets, cannon" and other munitions of war, the use of which would cause the "murder" of Germans and Russians.

Again, the spirit becomes more bitter as it proceeds to declare that—

"America and her Allies have betrayed (the Workers). Their robberish aims are clear to all men. The destruction of the Russian Revolution, that is the politics of the march to Russia.

"*Workers, our reply to the barbaric intervention has to be a general strike! An open challenge* only will let the Government know that not only the Russian Worker fights for freedom, but also *here in America lives the spirit of Revolution.*"

. . . [T]he manifest purpose of such a publication was to create an attempt to defeat the war plans of the Government of the United States, by bringing upon the country the paralysis of a general strike, thereby arresting the production of all munitions and other things essential to the conduct of the war.

This purpose is emphasized in the next paragraph, which reads:

"Do not let the Government scare you with their wild punishment in prisons, hanging and shooting. We must not and will not betray the splendid fighters of Russia. *Workers, up to fight.*"

After more of the same kind, the circular concludes:

"Woe unto those who will be in the way of progress. Let solidarity live!"

It is signed, "The Rebels."

... [T]he additional writings found in the meeting place of the defendant group and on the person of one of them [support our interpretation]. One of these circulars is headed: "Revolutionists! Unite for Action!"

After denouncing the President as "Our Kaiser" and the hypocrisy of the United States and her Allies, this article concludes:

"Socialists, Anarchists, Industrial Workers of the World, Socialists, Labor party men and other revolutionary organizations *Unite for action* and let us save the Workers' Republic of Russia!

"Know you lovers of freedom that in order to save the Russian revolution, we must keep the armies of the allied countries busy at home."

Thus was again avowed the purpose to throw the country into a state of revolution if possible and to thereby frustrate the military program of the Government.

The remaining article, after denouncing the President for what is characterized as hostility to the Russian revolution, continues:

"We, the toilers of America, who believe in real liberty, shall *pledge ourselves*, in case the United States will participate in that bloody conspiracy against Russia, *to create so great a disturbance that the autocrats of America shall be compelled to keep their armies at home, and not be able to spare any for Russia.*"

It concludes with this definite threat of armed rebellion:

"If they will use arms against the Russian people to enforce their standard of order, *so will we use arms*, and they shall never see the ruin of the Russian Revolution." ... A technical distinction may perhaps be taken between disloyal and abusive language applied to the *form* of our government or language intended to bring the *form* of our government into contempt and disrepute, and language of like character and intended to produce like results directed against the President and Congress, the agencies through which that form of government must function in time of war. But it is not necessary to a decision of this case to consider whether such distinction is vital or merely formal, for the language of these circulars was obviously intended to provoke and to encourage resistance to the United States in the war, ... and, the defendants, in terms, plainly urged and advocated a resort to a general strike of workers in ammunition factories for the purpose of curtailing the production of ordnance and munitions necessary and essential to the prosecution of the war....

Affirmed.

MR. JUSTICE HOLMES dissenting.

This indictment is founded wholly upon the publication of two leaflets....

*   *   *

No argument seems to me necessary to show that these pronunciamentos in no way attack the form of government of the United States.... [T]he suggestion to workers in the ammunition factories that they are producing bullets to murder their dearest, and the further advocacy of a general strike, both in the second leaflet, do urge curtailment of production of things necessary to the prosecution of the war within the meaning of the Act. But to make the conduct criminal that statute requires that it should be "with intent by such curtailment to cripple or hinder the United States in the prosecution of the war." It seems to me that no such intent is proved.

I am aware of course that the word intent as vaguely used in ordinary legal discussion means no more than knowledge at the time of the act that the consequences said to be intended will ensue.... But, when words are used exactly, a deed is not done with intent to produce a consequence unless that consequence is the aim of the deed....

It seems to me that this statute must be taken to use its words in a strict and accurate sense. They would be absurd in any other. A patriot might think that we were wasting money on aeroplanes, or making more cannon of a certain kind than we needed, and might advocate curtailment with success, yet even if it turned out that the curtailment hindered and was thought by other minds to have been obviously likely to hinder the United States in the prosecution of the war, no one would hold such conduct a crime. I admit that my illustration does not answer all that might be said but it is enough to show what I think and to let me pass to a more important aspect of the case. I refer to the First Amendment to the Constitution that Congress shall make no law abridging the freedom of speech.

I never have seen any reason to doubt that the questions of law that alone were before this Court in the cases of *Schenck*, *Frohwerk* and *Debs* were rightly decided. I do not doubt for a moment that by the same reasoning that would justify punishing persuasion to murder, the United States constitutionally may punish speech that produces or is intended to produce a clear and imminent danger that it will bring about forthwith certain substantive evils that the United States constitutionally may seek to prevent. The power undoubtedly is greater in time of war than in time of peace because war opens dangers that do not exist at other times.

But as against dangers peculiar to war, as against others, the principle of the right to free speech is always the same. It is only the present danger of immediate evil or an intent to bring it about that warrants Congress in setting a limit to the expression of opinion where private rights are not concerned. Congress certainly cannot forbid all effort to change the mind of the country.... Publishing those opinions for the very purpose of obstructing however, might indicate a greater danger and at any rate would have the quality of an attempt.... [But] an actual intent in the sense that I have explained is necessary to constitute an attempt where a further act of the same individual is required to complete the substantive crime.... An intent to prevent interference with the revolution in Russia might have been satisfied without any hindrance to carrying on the war in which we were engaged.

I do not see how anyone can find the intent required by the statute in any of the defendants' words.... [T]he only object of the paper is to help Russia and stop American intervention there against the popular government—not to impede the United States in the war that it was carrying on....

*   *   *

In this case sentences of twenty years imprisonment have been imposed for the publishing of two leaflets that I believe the defendants had as much right to publish as the Government has to publish the Constitution of the United States now vainly invoked by them....

Persecution for the expression of opinions seems to me perfectly logical.... [T]he best test of truth is the power of the thought to get itself accepted in the competition of the market, and that truth is the only ground upon which their wishes safely can be carried out. That at any rate is the theory of our Constitution. It is an experiment, as all life is an experiment. Every year if not every day we have to wager our salvation upon some prophecy based upon imperfect knowledge. While that experiment is part of our system I think that we should be eternally vigilant against attempts to check the expression of opinions that we loathe and believe to be fraught with death, unless they so imminently threaten immediate interference with the lawful and pressing purposes of the law that an immediate check is required to save the country. I wholly disagree with the argument of the Government that the First Amendment left the common law as to seditious libel in force. History seems to me against the notion. I had conceived that the United States through many years had shown its repentance for the Sedition Act of 1798, by repaying fines that it imposed. Only the emergency that makes it immediately dangerous to leave the correction of evil counsels to time warrants making any exception to the sweeping command, "Congress shall make no law ... abridging the freedom of speech." Of course I am speaking only of expressions of opinion and exhortations, which were all that were uttered here, but I regret that I cannot put into more impressive words my belief that in their conviction upon this indictment the defendants were deprived of their rights under the Constitution of the United States.

MR. JUSTICE BRANDEIS concurs with the foregoing opinion.

200 "using the bullet, the assassin's dagger, the torch, or the bomb" (1919)

On November 10, 1919, the same day that the Supreme Court upheld the convictions in *Abrams v. United States*, the United States House of Representatives voted to exclude Socialist Victor L. Berger from its membership. Berger had been active in the Socialist party and in Milwaukee politics. He had been an alderman in Milwaukee and had served as a member of the United States House of Representatives from Wisconsin in the Sixty-second Congress (1911-13).

When the United States declared war upon Germany in 1917, America's Socialist party called a convention in St. Louis to consider the posture of the party toward the war. Although the Socialists opposed the United States' entry into the war, some believed they should support the country in its efforts now that war had been declared. Berger led the extreme antiwar faction, which controlled the convention. The extremists expelled the nationalist socialists from the party, claiming that the government's declaration of war was a crime against the people of the United States and against the nations of the world and arguing for "continuous, active, and public opposition to the war through demonstrations, mass petitions and all other means within our power."

For editing war-resistant editorials published in the *Milwaukee Leader* (the postmaster general of the United States banned the paper from the mails), Berger and four others were convicted under the Espionage Act of 1917. Prior to his conviction, Berger had won election to the Sixty-sixth Congress from the Fifth District of Wisconsin (Milwaukee). On May 19, 1919, House members objected to the seating of Berger on the grounds that the third section of the Fourteenth Amendment prevented him from serving. Six months later, after a special committee recommended his exclusion, the matter reached the floor of the House. The following excerpt is from the five-and-one-half-hour debate on the motion to exclude Berger. Only one member spoke for three minutes against the motion, defending Berger's right to make such statements on First Amendment grounds. The motion carried 319 to 1.

☆ 200 Remarks of Representative Monahan on the Seating of Victor L. Berger

58 Cong. Rec. 8257 (Nov. 10, 1919).

Mr. MONAHAN of Wisconsin. Mr. Speaker, shall Victor L. Berger be given the seat in the House to which he was elected in 1918 or shall he, because of his own words and deeds, be denied the right to sit as a Member in this Congress? Stripped of all legal verbiage that is really the issue before the House.

No question is raised by the Government concerning the regularity of his election nor of the correctness of the election returns, and Berger practically admits the acts and deeds charged against him by the United States, but holds they were in no sense treasonable and that he was strictly within his rights in saying and doing what he did; that the Constitution and laws of the United States gave him that unqualified right.

Victor L. Berger is a living example of that old saying, "A leopard can not change his spots nor the Ethiopian his skin," and of the further fact that we are largely the creatures of heredity and environment.

Sixty years ago he was born in autocratic Austria, where for 18 years, during the time when the heart was young and the mind plastic, he drank deeply from the poisoned waters of autocracy. But seeing no opportunity for himself to become an autocrat in the land of the Hapsburg he came to America, landing at Bridgeport, Conn., in 1878, and in 1881 he, to the everlasting misfortune of Wisconsin, made Milwaukee his home. He had found a way and a place to become an autocrat that gave promise of enabling him to wield a power undreamed of by king, prince, or potentate of ancient or modern times.

To appreciate fully the foregoing sentence, one must know Mr. Berger as we in Wisconsin know him. He is large, well proportioned, has ideal Teutonic features, a mentality above the average, and in many ways is a natural leader of men. Had these great gifts been used in safe and sane methods for the uplifting of the race, Berger would have lived in history as a great and good man, but never as an autocrat or one striving for autocracy.

But all these great qualities are lost in the immensity of his colossal egoism. The gibes leveled at the late Kaiser as being called "the all highest" and the senior member of the firm of "Me und Gott" would have in no sense been pleasing to Berger, who, had he possessed the power, would probably have dissolved the firm and hung out a new sign reading, "Me und Victor."

The foregoing is, I believe, a fair and honest description of the man as the world knows him.

Berger early in life became a Marxian disciple, and continued to be until his ego told him he was a far wiser, much greater man than Marx ever was. When he discovered that Marx was only a man, while he was a really-truly superman, he sought for a land as boundless in resources as his own ego was measureless and all prevailing.

Hence, he came to America, took the oath of allegiance to this Government, swore fealty to the flag and support to the Constitution, and, having done

this, adopted the red flag of socialism, communism, anarchy, the I.W.W., and Bolshevism, and began the spreading of a propaganda which he hoped would ultimately lead to the undermining of the Constitution, the destruction of the Government, the breaking down of all commercial and social laws and customs, the tearing down of Old Glory from her place in the skies, and the raising of the red flag in its stead.

All students of history know that socialism and all attending schools of political economy invariably lead to autocracy, and thus Berger intended to become an autocrat who could sit in his office and by pushing a button call a strike in certain industries (as has been done recently in the coal fields) unless their demands were immediately complied with.

Here Berger and his codestructionists met with an unlooked-for obstruction. They found the task much more difficult than they anticipated. They found that the Civil War was ended and the country rapidly recovering from its horrors and devastation. They found the men behind the industrial guns were largely made up of soldiers of the late war, and whether they wore the blue or the gray each carried a loyal American heart, whether he had been born here or across the sea.

So strong was Americanism in those days that Bergerism was a foul weed of slow growth.

Then the soldier began to grow old with increasing years. The foreigner, who had grown up in the blighting atmosphere of autocracy, came to this country in ever increasing numbers and gradually took the jobs formerly held by the Americans.

They could not speak our language, neither did they understand our institutions. They were oftimes despondent and homesick, and too often fell an easy prey to the propaganda of the Bergers, who, like hookworms, worked in the dark to weaken and destroy this Government.

These people were not naturally vicious, but they were ignorant of our laws, language, and customs, and blindly followed when and where the Bergers led. For how could they reason when they did not know? . . .

Many of the socialists never intended to become anarchists, nor the anarchists I.W.W.'s nor Bolshevists, and Mr. Berger in his latest pamphlet, which reached my desk on Saturday, says in effect that there are differences and distinctions in the aims, objects, and methods of these various camps, and that they have in fact no common grounds of union, yet it is also in the record of the trial that when an I.W.W. was indicted for crime Berger sent him $10 to aid in his defense and addressed him as "My dear comrade."

The innocent socialist, having in view only the betterment of his material conditions, away from the land of his birth, unable to read or speak our language, falls an easy prey to the harpings of these ravens of discontent. Beautiful Eutopian dreams are painted for them. The harshness of their physical conditions is magnified and harped upon, until they honestly believe that they have a grievance, whether it be true or not. When they reach this condition of mind it is easy to lead them from socialism to anarchy and to I.W.W.'ism and finally to Bolshevism.

*　　　*　　　*

The transition has been easy. First, from socialism—the wet nurse of anarchy—then to anarchy, then to I.W.W.'ism, then to Bolshevism, which means the destruction of all civilization, all laws, all liberties, with the establishment of an autocracy, headed by the Bergers of these various movements, and all bound together by an underlying, overlapping, intertwining system of signals and sympathies, with the trial of the serpent of destruction over all.

Let me plead with you here and now to get away from these false ideas and false teachings. Get back to the teachings of Washington and the founders of the Constitution and become in heart what you really profess to be—American citizens, standing for American ideals.

The laws, customs, and usages that are in force to-day are not here by accident. They are an evolution of all the best the past has given us—a survival of the fittest—the sole hope of the race. Whenever these laws and customs become obsolete, caused by changing conditions and higher ideals, let such laws be changed or modified to meet present conditions, but make those changes by peaceful and constitutional methods and not attempt it by using the bullet, the assassin's dagger, the torch, or the bomb.

Mr. Speaker, we to-day stand at the parting of the ways. One road leads to the land of justice, hope, constitutional law, progress, and enlightenment; the other to the fetid slough of dishonor, where, fed by the foul streams of autocracy, treason, and disloyalty, the reign of Bolshevism becomes a horrible reality, where civilization will be crucified and human hopes destroyed. Are we going to stand for Americanism or Bergerism?

You can not serve two masters. You can not be for the Stars and Stripes, which represents the greatest democracy on the globe, and for the red flag of the Bergers. "Ye can not serve God and mammon," says Holy Writ.

*　　　*　　　*

Victor L. Berger once occupied a seat in this House as a Member of Congress from Milwaukee. Before taking his seat he raised his right hand and took a solemn oath to support the laws and Constitution of this country. Yet when the hour came and the existence of this Nation and the liberties of the world were at stake he wretchedly failed in every test of loyalty to the country of his adoption.

*　　　*　　　*

He opposed enlistments; he opposed conscriptions; he opposed, wherever and whenever he could with safety, the buying of Liberty bonds, and all efforts of the Government to carry on the war.

His paper, the Milwaukee Leader, was so virulent in its attacks upon the Government that the Postmaster General took away from him the right of using the United States mails, and finally he was indicted under the espionage act, tried for treason in the city of Chicago by a jury of his peers, found guilty, and sentenced by Judge Landis to 20 years in the Federal penitentiary, and has several other indictments for these or similar offenses now pending against him. Yet, in the face of all this, he comes to this Congress, glorifying in his past record, offering no apologies for his past misdeeds, and asks to be seated as a Member of this House, the greatest lawmaking body of the Nation, to take the same oath which he took eight years ago, only to violate, and to become an active lawmaker for the Nation which for years he has sought to destroy.

*　　　*　　　*

The proper place for Berger is a cell in the Federal penitentiary—not a seat in Congress. Neither have I any patience or sympathy with these anemic patriots who prattle about: "Now that the war is over, all war prisoners should be released." Why? Are they not just as guilty now as the day they were convicted? Were not their offenses of the blackest of crimes? Were they not rounded up and convicted by our Government at great expense and at an hour when all the man power of the Nation was needed to save the civilization of the globe?

A man steals a horse and is arrested; after several days the horse is found and returned to the owner. Would any of you advocate that, now the horse has been recovered, the thief should be given his liberty? Not one of you. When a man commits as heinous a crime as treason to his country the spirit of the law says: "He shall be punished."

*　　　*　　　*

Wisconsin is to-day eagerly awaiting the result of our deliberations on the question now before the House. Shall we by our vote send a message to the heroic men of the Badger State . . . ; to the mothers who gave their boys for human liberty, that liberty might live; to that innumerable army of Red Cross workers and trained nurses who suffered and worked, and with tearful eyes, on bended knees, prayed to God while our Armies fought; and to our invincible soldiers, who maintained the highest traditions of American Armies in the past, a message of appreciation for their valor and soldierly deeds which aided in crushing the Hun and rolling back the waves of gray seeking world dominion, and who tonight will stand in groups with uncovered heads and say, "God bless the House of Representatives! Our comrades who made the supreme sacrifice have not died in vain"?

Or shall we say by our vote, "Now that the war is ended, give this traitor to our country a seat among America's most loyal and patriotic"?

If the former, it will mean that Old Glory will continue to wave o'er the land, beloved, honored, and respected.

If the latter, that Berger's red flag, which to him is greater and dearer than the Stars and Stripes, shall become not only the emblem of this country and perhaps the world, but that the civilization of the ages will be lost in chaos and ruin.

The foregoing is the only issue in this case. Mr. Berger pretends to believe that he is to be kept out of Congress because he is a Socialist. This is the sheerest nonsense. Mr. Berger was not kept out of Congress before when he was elected, nor has any Socialist been denied a seat because of his political belief. It is not because he is a Socialist but because he, as an individual, working through the Socialist Party, in which organization he held a commanding position, was recognized as one of the leaders, and as such proved disloyal to his country in time of war. This is the reason.

*   *   *

. . . It can not be that the people of the fifth congressional district of Wisconsin will ever again elect Berger to any office; but if they do, now that he stands convicted by a jury, sentenced by a judge, and his case thoroughly gone into by a committee of this Congress, it will only show that a majority of the voters of the fifth congressional district are just as disloyal as Berger himself. That is unbelievable.

But if they should send Berger back he will come bearing the same burden of disloyalty and treason that he does to-day, and in my opinion no Congress would ever seat him, for while he might be the choice of the fifth congressional district of Wisconsin and that district sends him back I believe that the Members of this House will reach out their hands to the struggling loyalists of that district and say: "If you are unable to clean house within we will assist you by giving your district a dry cleaning from without."

Mr. Speaker, to-day the powers of the evil, the emissaries of darkness, the foes of constitutional law and the civilization of the Nazarene, are knocking at the door of the House of Representatives, demanding admission for their representative, Victor L. Berger. Let us answer that challenge by hurling back the answer of heroic France at Verdun, and say to him, "You shall not pass." [Applause.]

Let us here to-day figuratively engrave those words over the door, so that the Bergers of to-day, to-morrow, a hundred or a thousand years hence,

when they with traitorous hands knock at that door demanding admission, will be met with that sign, ablaze with patriotic justice: "You shall not pass. You shall not pass." [Great applause.]

201 " 'Let our people go' " (1920)

The ruling of the district court judge in *United States v. Steene* demonstrated the reach of the 1918 Amended Espionage Act (generally known as the 1918 Sedition Act), even for events occurring after the Armistice of November 11, 1918. The court held the distribution of handbills (containing pictures of torture), which called a mass meeting to protest the imprisonment of conscientious objectors, was calculated "to inflame and arouse the ignorant and vicious," and resistance to the United States therefore could have been expected.

☆ 201 *United States v. Steene*

263 F. 130 (D.C.N.Y. 1920).

GARVIN, District Judge. Defendants have been indicted for conspiracy to violate and for a violation of section 3 of title 1 of the Espionage Act approved June 15, 1917, and amended May 16, 1918. The indictment is in three counts and charges briefly:

First, a conspiracy to utter, publish, and distribute disloyal, profane, scurrilous, and abusive language about the form of government of the United States and the Constitution. . . .

The second count alleges a violation of said section 3 in the manner above mentioned, by the distribution of said handbills.

The third count sets forth that the defendants did utter, print, write, and publish language intending to incite and promote resistance to the United States and to promote the success of its enemies by distributing the aforesaid handbills.

The defendants pleaded not guilty, and later by permission of the court withdrew that plea, and have filed a demurrer setting forth numerous grounds of objection to the indictment, which may be summarized thus:

*   *   *

(2) No offense was committed, because the United States was not at the time at war with the Imperial German government and the Austrian-Hungarian government.

This contention cannot be sustained. The Supreme Court of the United States has recently held otherwise in the war-time prohibition cases.

*   *   *

(4) The circulation of the handbill complained of by the government is not a violation of law.

This is the real question involved. The handbills

contain four pictures: One representing a man suspended by his wrists, apparently in a cell, under which appears "Hung by the wrists from ceiling for 8 Hours a Day. McNeil's Island, Washington." A second, the picture of a man whose appearance gives the impression of one being brutally struck with a club; under this appears "Political Prisoners Beaten with a Baseball Bat at Leavenworth Penitentiary." The third is that of a man chained to prison bars, under which is "Chained to the Bars 8 Hours a Day for Two Weeks on Bread and Water." The last is a representation of a man, barefoot, stripped to the waist, being lifted off his feet by a rope around his neck, which runs up over a beam and back into the hands of a man who stands near him, who is pulling it. This man who holds the rope, wears the style of hat common in the army. Near by is another man, with pistol in belt and wearing a similar hat, who is kicking the hapless victim. This is described as "Punishment of a Conscientious Objector in Disciplinary Barracks." These pictures appear in the four corners. The handbill is as follows:

> Attend the Mass Meeting, Moose Hall 235 East Genesse Street Friday, November 21 8:00 P.M. To Protest Against These Atrocities and Voice the Following Demand: Mr President—Let our people go. American Citizens, charged with no crime against persons or property and guilty only of expressing their political, industrial and religious beliefs, are subjected to these tortures in your prisons. These people were convicted in violation of the spirit of the Declaration of Independence and the Constitution of the United States. Their conviction was made possible only by the war hysteria prevailing at that time. Whatever justification those conditions gave no longer exists. The war is over. No justification exists, or ever did exist, for these brutal and inhuman tortures inflicted on defenseless victims by your agents and representatives. In the name of Liberty and Justice we demand the release of all prisoners whose alleged crimes consisted in the peaceable expression and maintenance of their political opinions, industrial activities or religious beliefs. Come to the meeting. Everybody Invited to Join in the above Demand. George R. Kirkpatrick will lecture on Political Prisoners in America. Under the Auspices of the Socialist Party. Admission 25 cents.

The Espionage Act—so called—... provides in part that—

> Whoever, when the United States is at war, shall willfully utter, print, write, or publish any disloyal, profane, scurrilous, or abusive language about the form of government of the United States, or the Constitution of the United States, or the military or naval forces of the United States, or the flag of the United States, or the uniform of the army or navy of the United States,

or any language intended to bring the form of government of the United States, or the Constitution of the United States, or the military or naval forces of the United States, or the flag of the United States, or the uniform of the army or navy of the United States, into contempt, scorn, contumely, or disrepute, or shall willfully utter, print, write, or publish any language intended to incite, provoke, or encourage resistance to the United States, or to promote the cause of its enemies, ... shall be punished by a fine of not more than $10,000 or imprisonment for not more than twenty years, or both.

It will be observed that these provisions go much further than the preceding portion of the section, which is designed to prevent any act openly directed against the successful conduct of the war by the United States. The provisions here involved are obviously for the purpose of preventing the sort of abuse of the form of government which, harmless in itself, though usually not the utterance of those who believe in our national institutions, is calculated to inflame and arouse the ignorant and vicious to an actual attempt to bring about open disloyalty. The constitutional guaranty of free speech is unaffected by the conclusion that the pamphlet or handbill involved, rendered conspicuous by the pictures described (which are entirely unnecessary to announce a mass meeting), must be taken to mean that the form of government of the United States and the Constitution upon which it rests have proved inadequate to secure justice for American citizens, who have been not only unjustly convicted (the insinuation is clear that they have been convicted of no offense whatever), but during incarceration have been subjected to most inhuman tortures. Such an allegation, made during a period of war, when loyalty is to a great extent predicated upon belief that the form of government of the United States rests upon liberty and justice, is calculated to bring into disrepute the form of government and its Constitution, under which such conditions could exist, and likewise its military forces, whose members are responsible for the brutalities portrayed in the last-described picture.

When a mass meeting is assembled as a result of an invitation of this character, we may expect that resistance to the United States itself will follow, if the meeting is addressed in the manner outlined by the call, and that the demand upon the President to "Let our people go" will be followed by such action during and after the meeting as indicates a contempt for the Constitution and for the form of government which will not grant the demand so made. That the utterance be an open attack on the form of government or Constitution is not necessary. Indeed, the care with which the pamphlet seems to have been written suggests the desire to accomplish the result forbidden by the act without incurring the penalty involved in a violation. But, even if this was meant as a mere announcement of a public meeting, its form was well calculated to have the effect of arousing the contempt, scorn, contumely, and disrepute which Congress sought to prevent, and under the well-settled principle that one is presumed to intend the natural consequences of his act the indictment charges a crime.

Demurrer overruled.

202 "There was no disorder save that of the raiders" (1920)

In 1918 and 1919, employers' agents, federal agents, and uniformed soldiers raided several meetings of the Butte Union of the Industrial Workers of the World and obtained certain IWW pamphlets without a warrant. The literature formed the basis or deportation proceedings against Jackson on the grounds that he advocated the unlawful destruction of property. In *Ex Parte Jackson*, the federal district court in Montana demonstrated the value of the provisions of the Bill of Rights and the writ of habeas corpus, which are available to aliens and citizens alike. The court stated that "[n]o emergency in war or peace warrants the violation of the rights of personal security and safety and order and due process of law." The court also held that the defendant had the right to confront all witnesses at the deportation proceeding—a right the lower court had denied him.

Banishment and transportation (to a penal colony) are classic penal sanctions that generally are not utilized today. Exile is also a convenient way of eliminating political adversaries. In the United States these sanctions have only rarely been imposed (including the banishment of Anne Hutchinson and Roger Williams from Massachusetts during the colonial period and Clement Vallandigham's expulsion to the Confederacy during the Civil War). Nevertheless, aliens are subject to deportation for certain violations of the law. Technically not exile, such deportations have the same effect; and in 1920, the nation was actively engaged in purging the country of undesirable, especially politically undesirable, aliens.

☆ 202 *Ex Parte Jackson*

263 F. 110 (D. Mont. 1920).

BOURQUIN, District Judge. Petitioner, held for deportation as an alien "found advocating or teaching the unlawful destruction of property," . . . seeks habeas corpus, for that evidence against him in the deportation proceedings was unlawfully secured, the proceedings were unfair, and the findings quoted

without support. Respondent returns the record of said proceedings. Therefrom it appears that from August, 1918, to February, 1919, the Butte Union of the Industrial Workers of the World was dissatisfied with working places, conditions, and wages in the mining industry, and to remedy them was discussing ways and means, including strike if necessary. In consequence, its hall and orderly meetings were several times raided and mobbed by employers' agents, and federal agents and soldiers duly officered, acting by federal authority and without warrant or process. The union members, men and women, many of them citizens, limited themselves to oral protests, though in the circumstances the inalienable right and law of self-defense justified resistance to the last dread extremity. There was no disorder save that of the raiders. These, mainly uniformed and armed, overawed, intimidated, and forcibly entered, broke, and destroyed property, searched persons, effects, and papers, arrested persons, seized papers and documents, cursed, insulted, beat, dispersed, and bayoneted union members by order of the commanding officer. They likewise entered petitioner's adjacent living apartment, insulted his wife, searched his person and effects, arrested him, and seized his papers and documents, and in general, in a populous and orderly city, perpetrated a reign of terror, violence, and crime against citizen and alien alike, and whose only offense seems to have been peaceable insistence upon and exercise of a clear legal right.

The raid of February, 1919, three months after practical end of the war, was upon a union meeting in discussion of the condition created by a reduction of $1 per day made in miners' wages. Petitioner, arrested, for several days was imprisoned and denied bail and counsel. He was then taken before immigration inspector, flanked by a policeman and a soldier, and, these four alone present, was interrogated. He objected generally, but finally answered, and also in respect to pamphlets seized as aforesaid and introduced in evidence against him. At later appearances before the inspector, petitioner was permitted to have counsel. At these, statements made by raiders, without petitioner's presence, identifying papers and pamphlets so seized, and somewhat in respect to petitioner's conduct of a union meeting, were introduced in evidence against him. . . . Objections by petitioner throughout the proceedings are excluded from the record and are now forgotten.

The facts in respect to the condition and objections aforesaid appear ex necessitate by oral testimony in the instant proceeding. The record further discloses that petitioner . . . was assistant secretary of the Butte union, and also janitor of the hall for a Finnish society, its owner. He disclaims advocacy, teaching, or belief in unlawful destruction of property, admits having seen some of the pamphlets in the hall and for sale, admits having sold any thereof asked for and on hand for sale, admits having read some thereof, but, disremembering contents, cannot say he indorses them. These pamphlets are assumed to advocate and teach sabotage, and because thereof, and of petitioner's status and relation to them as aforesaid, in the deportation proceedings it is inferred and found that he advocated and taught unlawful destruction of property. Without these pamphlets, and brought home to petitioner, there is no evidence against him.

[I]t is believed the deportation proceedings are unfair and invalid, in that they are based upon evidence and procedure that violate the search and seizure and due process clauses of the Constitution. . . . The law and courts no more sanction such evidence than such methods, and no more approve either than the thumbscrew and the rack. Otherwise the vicious circle of age-old tyranny — to subject to and convict by unlawful means because guilty, and to condemn as guilty because subjected to and convicted by unlawful means, to which both alien and citizen fall victim. The Declaration of Independence, the writings of the fathers, the Revolution, the Constitution, and the Union, all were inspired to overthrow and prevent like governmental despotism. They are yet living, vital, and potential forces to those ends, to safeguard all domiciled in the country, alien as well as citizen.

For the inalienable rights of personal security and safety, orderly and due process of law, are the fundamentals of the social compact, the basis of organized society, the essence and justification of government, the foundation, key, and capstones of the Constitution. They are limited to no man, race, or nation, to no time, place, or occasion, but belong to man, always, everywhere, and in all circumstances. Every nation demands them for its people from all other nations. No emergency in war or peace warrants their violation, for in emergency, real or assumed, tyrants in all ages have found excuse for their destruction. Without them, democracy perishes, autocracy reigns, and the innocent suffer with the guilty. . . .

Assuming petitioner is of the so-called "Reds" and of the evil practice charged against him, he and his kind are less a danger to America than are those who indorse or use the methods that brought him to deportation. These latter are the mob and the spirit of violence and intolerance incarnate, the most alarming manifestation in America today. Far worse than the immediate wrongs to individuals that they do, they undermine the morale of the people, excite the latter's fears, distrust of our institutions, doubts of the sufficiency of law and authority; they incline the people toward arbitrary power, which for protection cowards too often seek, and knaves too readily grant, and subject to which the people cease to be

courageous and free, and become timid and enslaved. They advocate and teach, not only unlawful destruction of property, but in addition unlawful destruction of persons, and they engage in the practice of both. They lay the ax to the root of all government. Doubtless some of those, of some variety of prestige, who horrify the thoughtful lovers of America by their loose suggestion and advocacy of stone walls, shootings at sunrise, and other lynch law, are animated by sincere, but mistaken, concern for national welfare; but equally doubtless many of them are incited by unholy desire for personal advantage — money profit, popular approval, or political preferment. They are breeders of suspicion, fear, anger, revenge, riot, crime, class hatred, "Reds," despotism, threatening, if aught can, civil anarchy and revolution, and they and the government by hysteria that they stimulate are more to be feared than all the miserable, baited, bedeviled "Reds" that are their ostensible occasion and whose sins they exaggerate.

The application of the principle that convicted the Haymarket anarchists may hold guilty these advocates of lynch law, if their recommendations be followed, unless, indeed, there are distinctions in administration of criminal law. They are no new thing, these present excesses. They are the reactions of all great wars, and in due time run their course. In his Constitutional History of England, Freeman describes much the same following the Napoleonic wars, viz. that in England those who ventured to raise their voice to reform corrupt politics and oppressive government, or to improve conditions for the working class, were bitterly denounced as pro-French, charged and tried for treason, popular clamor and violence directed against them, and the bar intimidated from defending them. How history doth repeat itself! . . . And yet confidence in the Constitution and national sanity is justified. All extremists will fail to overthrow them. Even as the "Reds," the advocates of arbitrary power, whether within or without law, will in due time pass away. It is for the courts to restrain both, when brought within jurisdiction.

. . . Whether fair or not in ordinary cases, in a case wherein the alien's rights have been infringed to the extent here, the court will take note of it, . . . and hold the proceedings unfair. . . .

The writ is granted.

203 "make America safe for democracy first" (1920)

Dissent against World War I, much like the opposition to earlier and later wars, came from many and diverse sources: the faint at heart and confirmed pacifists; supporters of foreign interests and America Firsters. The pursuit of the war effort was made not only a federal task but a state undertaking as well. In the *Gilbert* case, which reached the United States Supreme Court after the war's conclusion, a citizen of Minnesota was convicted under state law for speaking in public against the war with Germany. The right of free speech, the nation's highest judicial tribunal ruled, did not protect Gilbert, because "every word that he uttered in denunciation of the war was false, was deliberate misrepresentation of the motives which impelled it, and the objects for which it was prosecuted."

☆ 203 *Gilbert v. Minnesota*

254 U.S. 325 (1920).

MR. JUSTICE MCKENNA delivered the opinion of the court.

A statute of Minnesota makes it unlawful "to interfere with or discourage the enlistment of men in the military or naval forces of the United States or of the State of Minnesota."

Its second and third sections are as follows:

"Sec. 2. Speaking by word of mouth against enlistment unlawful. — It shall be unlawful for any person in any public place, or at any meeting where more than five persons are assembled, to advocate or teach by word of mouth or otherwise that men should not enlist in the military or naval forces of the United States or the state of Minnesota.

"Sec. 3. Teaching or advocating by written or printed matters against enlistment unlawful. — It shall be unlawful for any person to teach or advocate by any written or printed matter whatsoever, or by oral speech, that the citizens of this state should not aid or assist the United States in prosecuting or carrying on war with the public enemies of the United States."

Section 4 defines a citizen to be "any person within the confines of the state," and § 5 declares violations of the act to be gross misdemeanors and punishable by fine and imprisonment.

The indictment charged that Gilbert at a time and place designated in the State, and under the conditions prohibited by § 2, the United States being then and there at war with the Kingdom and Imperial Government of Germany, used the following language:

"We are going over to Europe to make the world safe for democracy, but I tell you we had better make America safe for democracy first. You say, what is the matter with our democracy. I tell you what is the matter with it: Have you had anything to say as to who should be president? Have you had anything to say as to who should be Governor of this state? Have you had anything to say as to whether we would go into this war? You know you have not.

If this is such a great democracy, for Heaven's sake why should we not vote on conscription of men. We were stampeded into this war by newspaper rot to pull England's chestnuts out of the fire for her. I tell you if they conscripted wealth like they have conscripted men, this war would not last over forty-eight hours. . . ."

A demurrer to the indictment was overruled, and Gilbert was tried and convicted. The judgment was that he pay a fine of $500 and be imprisoned in the county jail of the County of Goodhue for one year, and pay the costs of the prosecution. The judgment was affirmed by the Supreme Court of the State.

*   *   *

The . . . contention is, that the statute is violative of the right of free speech, and therefore void. . . . In *Schaefer v. United States*, . . . it was said that the curious spectacle was presented of the Constitution of the United States being invoked to justify the activities of anarchy or of the enemies of the United States, and by a strange perversion of its precepts it was adduced against itself. And we did more than reject the contention, we forestalled all repetitions of it, and the contention in the case at bar is a repetition of it. It is a direct assault upon the statute of Minnesota, and a direct assertion in spite of the prohibition of the statute that one can by speech, teach or advocate that the citizens of the State should not aid or assist "the United States in prosecuting or carrying on war with the public enemies of the United States," and be protected by the Constitution of the United States.

[A] condition of war and its emergency existed, and there was explicit limitation to § 3 in the charge of the trial court to the jury. The court read §§ 2 and 3 of the statute to the jury and said, "I take it from the reading of the whole indictment that it is prosecuted under Section 3, which I have just read to you."

Gilbert's speech had the purpose they denounce. The Nation was at war with Germany, armies were recruiting, and the speech was the discouragement of that — its purpose was necessarily the discouragement of that. It was not an advocacy of policies or a censure of actions that a citizen had the right to make. The war was flagrant; it had been declared by the power constituted by the Constitution to declare it, and in the manner provided for by the Constitution. It was not declared in aggression, but in defense, in defense of our national honor, in vindication of the "most sacred rights of our Nation and our people."

This was known to Gilbert for he was informed in affairs and the operations of the Government, and every word that he uttered in denunciation of the war was false, was deliberate misrepresentation of the motives which impelled it, and the objects for which it was prosecuted. He could have had no purpose other than that of which he was charged. It would be a travesty on the constitutional privilege he invokes to assign him its protection.

Judgment affirmed.

204 "a so-called political conscience" (1921)

In the early 1920s pleas arose for the extension of a general amnesty to the conscientious objectors and the other political offenders of the war and Red Scare eras. President Harding appointed Harry Daugherty attorney general for leading Harding's successful 1920 Republican nomination campaign. Harry Daugherty's address to the American Bar Association demonstrated the government's official position on the subject. The speech articulated a policy of law and order and warned against the lenient treatment of those asserting defenses of conscience. Daugherty later was implicated in the Teapot Dome Scandal (the secret leasing of naval oil reserves to private companies), and in 1924 President Coolidge forced his resignation. Daugherty's prosecution for alleged conspiracy to defraud the United States government ended in two hung juries, and the case eventually was dismissed.

☆ 204 Respect for Law

Attorney General H. M. Daugherty's Address to the Joint Session of the American Bar Association and the Ohio State Bar Association, Cincinnati

7 A.B.A. J. 505 (1921).

*   *   *

[I]t seems fitting to speak to you on the general subject of *respect for law*, or rather, to enumerate to you, for your consideration, some of the things that tend to *undermine respect for law*.

. . . My purpose will be mainly to call attention to certain theories of political philosophy advanced by those who either violate the law or sympathize with law violators as a defense and justification of their course. Some of these theories are as old as constitutional government and have been advanced from time to time by those who have sought to evade the penalties of the law.

*   *   *

Respect for law is the one essential fact of our civilization. Without it life, liberty and property are insecure. Without it civilization falls back to the chaos and anarchy of primitive times. . . .

The history of civilization has been a continuous struggle for law and order. Through all the centuries men have striven for that protection of life, liberty and property that comes through well-ordered government. Mankind has paid allegiance to lords and overlords who were able to give this protection.

*   *   *

. . . [T]he supremacy of the law, though challenged, is not undermined by the ordinary criminal who commits murder, robbery, larceny, etc. To the contrary, every occurrence of crimes of this sort tends to impress upon society the profound importance of the supremacy of the law and its vigorous enforcement. The supremacy of the law is and has been challenged mainly in that class of legislation where there exists a difference of opinion as to governmental policy in enacting the legislation in question.

. . . At the present time among the forces that are undermining respect for law are the following: The doctrine of so-called political offenses, erroneous conceptions of personal liberty, and false doctrines as to the rights of individuals and minorities. These may not be the only sources of disrespect for law, but they are deserving of attention at this time because their proponents have been especially active in asserting them since the world war.

*   *   *

Political offenses is a term, as you know, of international law used to denote certain classes of offenses which are excepted from the operation of treaties of extradition between States. The offenses comprehended under this term for which extradition will not be granted are usually those involving matters pertaining to civil, religious or political liberty. The state in which the fugitive has found asylum frequently reserves to itself the right to refuse to surrender such fugitive on the ground that it is one of the excepted cases under the extradition treaty. . . .

*   *   *

The term is unknown in the domestic law of this country. However, in the debates in Congress, in the few years subsequent to the Civil War, the term is found in the discussions pertaining to the status of persons in the Southern Confederacy who gave allegiance to their particular state as against the Union. Here, again, the term has an international rather than a domestic character.

*   *   *

From the history of the origin of the doctrine of political offenses, it will be seen that there can be no recognition of that doctrine in the municipal law of this country. Why? Because when the sovereign will of the state expresses itself through duly enacted law it is repugnant to the very nature of the supremacy of the law and its uniform application to recognize the doctrine of political offenses. Again, the reason for this doctrine is not present under municipal law—that is, the domestic law of a State.... It would destroy the sovereignty of the state to permit two standards, one repugnant to the other, to exist side by side—the standard of the law and the standard of some individual, or group acting as individuals to set up a so-called political conscience at variance therewith. Such a doctrine has never been recognized in the municipal law of this country. It is one of the most dangerous cloaks that has yet been devised by the enemies of our constitutional system of government to cover lawlessness and disrespect for law. It is dangerous because it is a term incapable of definition. If sought to be applied, it would be as omnibus in meaning as the various shades of elasticity of the political conscience of those who sought to apply it. By the propaganda before us, we can readily imagine how elastic this political conscience would be when we are asked to apply it to the idealists such as anarchists, I.W.W.'s and socialists.

There might have been some excuse, or even justification, for the recognition of such a doctrine in the schisms and controversies, rebellions, revolts, and revolutions of the old world, whose history has been in some states one continuous struggle between the arbitrary exercise of tyrannical power on the one hand, and the just fight for civil, political or religious liberty on the other. Again, no organ of government existed in many of these states for the sovereign will of the people to express itself. Hence, revolution, rebellion, revolt, and feud within the state were the agencies that necessity compelled them to invoke in order that the spirit of liberty and democracy might express itself. In view of this, the various factions within the state frequently had the *de facto* status of belligerents. Hence, the development of the doctrine after the analogy of international law within the government of these countries. No such justification for the doctrine can exist in this country. Our constitutional system is so organized that at the ballot box the sovereign elector expresses his will. Changes are to be wrought through the constitutional organs of government and by the orderly processes of law. The constitution by the rights, privileges and immunities granted therein amply protects any citizen in his religious or political liberty. The limitations of the powers of legislation in the Constitution under its Bill of Rights, together with the judiciary system as the agency for protecting the individual against the invasion of these rights by government, furnish ample security for even the most conscientious. In addition thereto, our government during the late war, as it always has in other wars, adopted a considerate and liberal policy toward conscientious objectors. Hence, there is no occasion to engraft this so-called doctrine of political offenses, the child of the struggles against arbitrary power in the old world, upon our American political philosophy.

One word more upon this subject.... A man may have a certain religious or political opinion, but one who not only violates the laws his country imposes, but uses his full power to induce others to violate law, to break down peace and order in society, is going too far to excuse himself on the ground that he obeyed his political conscience and thereby committed only a political offense for which he should not be punished. Such a plea offered as a defense or justification, or even extenuation of his conduct, is not consistent with the uniform application and enforcement of law. This subject could not be more forcibly or tersely expressed than by the present President of the United States in a speech delivered at Omaha, Nebraska, October 7, 1920, in which he said:

No true American will argue that our laws should not be enforced. I refer to laws, no matter of what nature, whether they be those which deal with ordinary crimes and misdemeanors, or those which deal with acts of treason to the United States, threatening to the Constitution and the fabric of our social organization.

I wish no one to misunderstand me, and, therefore, I will say as plainly as I can that for my part I can see no essential difference between ordinary crimes on the one hand and political crimes and political prisoners on the other hand. If there is a distinction, surely it is not a distinction which favors political crimes or political prisoners. The thief, or any ordinary criminal, is surely less a menace to those things which we hold dear than the man or woman who conspires to destroy our American institutions.

*   *   *

Those who do not believe in our government and the enforcement of our laws should go to a country which gives them their *peculiar liberty.*

To those who come to our shores to take advantage of American opportunities it is becoming to wave the hands of welcome. But it is our duty to warn them to stay away unless they intend to observe our customs and obey our laws.

My duty is clear. As long as I am the responsible head of the Department of Justice the law will be enforced with all the power possessed by the Government which I am at liberty to call to my command.

205 "The civil functions and processes ... will not be interfered with" (1921)

President Warren G. Harding dispatched federal troops in 1921 to pacify a festering labor dispute in the coal mines of West Virginia. During the previous decade the disagreements between the union miners and the operators of coal mines had produced disorders requiring intervention by the state's National Guard. The President's ordering of the guard into federal service in 1917 had left West Virginia without a military force. At the governor's request federal troops were sent to the state, both in 1920 and in 1921. In the 1921 disorder, authorities estimated the insurgents to number at least five thousand. The United States government dispatched a total of two thousand federal troops to the region, and they met no resistance. Some fourteen hundred insurgents who surrendered to the troops were returned to their homes. The troops disarmed some three hundred who bore arms and turned their weapons over to the state.

States have the authority to maintain law and quell domestic violence within their borders. Nevertheless, when the disruption goes beyond the control of the state police and National Guard, a state may resort to federal assistance under Title 10, Section 331 of the U.S. Code. Enacted to implement Article IV, Section 4 of the United States Constitution, in which the federal government assumes protection of every state against "invasion" and "domestic violence," the statute provides:

> Whenever there is an insurrection in any State against its government, the President may, upon the request of its legislature or of its governor if the legislature cannot be convened, call into Federal service such of the militia of the other States, in the number requested by that State, and use such of the armed forces as he considers necessary to suppress the insurrection.

In recent history, President Johnson invoked his authority on the request of the governor of Michigan during the 1967 Detroit riots; and in April 1968, the statute justified the deployment of troops to Washington, D.C., Baltimore, and Chicago.

☆ 205 Protection against Domestic Violence in West Virginia

☆ 205a President Harding's Proclamation

42 Stat. 2247 (1921).

Whereas the Governor of the State of West Virginia has represented that domestic violence exists in said State which the authorities of said State are unable to suppress; and

Whereas it is provided in the Constitution of the United States that the United States shall protect each State in this Union, on application of the legislature, or of the executive when the legislature cannot be convened, against domestic violence; and

Whereas by the law of the United States in pursuance of the above it is provided that in all cases of insurrection in any State or of obstruction to the laws thereof it shall be lawful for the President of the United States on application of the legislature of such State, or of the executive when the legislature

cannot be convened, to call forth the militia of any other State or States or to employ such part of the land and naval forces of the United States as shall be judged necessary for the purpose of suppressing such insurrection and causing the laws to be duly executed; and

Whereas the Legislature of the State of West Virginia is not now in session and can not be convened in time to meet the present emergency, and the executive of said State, under Section 4 of Article IV of the Constitution of the United States and the laws passed in pursuance thereof, has made due application to me in the premises for such part of the military forces of the United States as may be necessary and adequate to protect the State of West Virginia and the citizens thereof against domestic violence and to enforce the due execution of the laws; and

Whereas it is required that whenever it may be necessary, in the judgment of the President, to use the military forces of the United States for the purposes aforesaid he shall forthwith by proclamation command such insurgents to disperse and retire peaceably to their respective homes within a limited time;

Now, therefore, I, Warren G. Harding, President of the United States, do hereby make proclamation and I do hereby command all persons engaged in said unlawful and insurrectionary proceedings to disperse and retire peaceably to their respective abodes on or before 12 o'clock noon of the 1st day of September, 1921, and hereafter abandon said combinations and submit themselves to the laws and constituted authorities of said State;

And I invoke the aid and cooperation of all good citizens thereof to uphold the laws and preserve the public peace.

In witness whereof I have hereunto set my hand and caused the seal of the United States to be affixed.

Done at the City of Washington, this thirtieth day of August, in the year of our Lord one thousand nine hundred and twenty-one, and of the Independence of the United States the one hundred and forty-sixth.

WARREN G. HARDING

CHARLES E. HUGHES, Secretary of State

☆ 205b Instructions to General H. H. Bandholtz

Office of the Chief of Staff
Washington, August 31, 1921

FROM: THE DEPUTY CHIEF OF STAFF
TO: BRIG. GEN. H. H. BANDHOLTZ, UNITED STATES ARMY
SUBJECT: INSTRUCTIONS

Copies of the President's proclamation and orders covering your movements have been sent to you.

Your primary object is to suppress domestic violence and to establish and maintain order in the disturbed areas. You will cause to be obeyed the command of the proclamation that all persons engaged in unlawful and insurrectionary proceedings disperse and retire to their abodes, and thereafter submit to the laws and constituted authorities of the State. You will make such dispensations as shall appear proper with respect to those who commit or may be about to commit physical violence. Any conduct on the part of any person, group, or association whatever which in your judgment is contributory to or likely to be productive of domestic violence or the continuance of disorder, where such conduct is apparently lawful and would not be interfered with under normal conditions, will be immediately communicated to the War Department and you will await specific instructions, unless the emergency is so grave as to necessitate a departure from that course. In achieving your object necessity is the measure of your authority. You will always countenance and support the civil officers in executing their laws, and if necessary you will protect and support and aid them in the execution of their duties. The civil functions and processes of the State will not be interfered with, nor superseded, if exercised effectually in the suppression of violence and the restoration of order. Persons arrested should either be admonished and sent home, or if detained they should be delivered to the State authorities as soon as practicable. Where that course results in the release and return to scenes of disorder of persons whose presence there impedes the accomplishment of your purpose, such persons may be retained in military custody so long as the necessity exists. Persons in military custody will be held by authority of the United States and with respect to writs of habeas corpus the directions of section 477, 478, and 479, court-martial manual, will be followed, reporting each such case by telegraph direct to the Adjutant General of the Army.

By order of the Secretary of War:

J. G. HARBORD, Major General

206 "to foster a homogeneous people" (1923)

During World War I, the United States' efforts to consolidate the home front behind the martial campaign created widespread prejudice not only against the German nation but also against German immigrants and their culture. At the time, many immigrant families still spoke their mother tongue at home and wished that it be taught to their children.

In 1919, Nebraska, like many states, passed an "emergency measure" making it a crime to teach a language other than English in any school, public or private, to students who had not completed the eighth grade. Meyer was convicted of teaching German to a ten-year-old boy enrolled in a parochial school. The Supreme Court overturned the conviction on the grounds that the law invaded the right of the teacher to pursue a useful occupation—a right protected by the due process clause—and that limits existed on the exercise of the state's power to foster a patriotic population.

☆ 206 *Meyer v. Nebraska*

262 U.S. 390 (1923).

MR. JUSTICE MCREYNOLDS delivered the opinion of the Court.

*   *   *

The Supreme Court of the State affirmed the judgment of conviction. It declared the offense charged and established was "the direct and intentional teaching of the German language as a distinct subject to a child who had not passed the eighth grade," in the parochial school maintained by Zion Evangelical Lutheran Congregation, a collection of Biblical stories being used therefor. And it held that the statute forbidding this did not conflict with the Fourteenth Amendment, but was a valid exercise of the police power. The following excerpts from the opinion sufficiently indicate the reasons advanced to support the conclusion.

"The salutary purpose of the statute is clear. The legislature had seen the baneful effects of permitting foreigners, who had taken residence in this country, to rear and educate their children in the language of their native land. The result of that condition was found to be inimical to our own safety. To allow the children of foreigners, who had emigrated here, to be taught from early childhood the language of the country of their parents was to rear them with that language as their mother tongue. It was to educate them so that they must always think in that language, and, as a consequence, naturally inculcate in them the ideas and sentiments foreign to the best interests of this country. The statute, therefore, was intended not only to require that the education of all children be conducted in the English language, but that, until they had grown into that language and until it had become a part of them, they should not in the schools be taught any other language. The obvious purpose of this statute was that the English language should be and become the mother tongue of all children reared in this state. The enactment of such a statute comes reasonably within the police power of the state."

*   *   *

The problem for our determination is whether the statute as construed and applied unreasonably infringes the liberty guaranteed to the plaintiff in error by the Fourteenth Amendment. "No State shall ... derive any person of life, liberty, or property, without due process of law."

*   *   *

The American people have always regarded education and acquisition of knowledge as matters of supreme importance which should be diligently promoted. . . .

Practically, education of the young is only possible in schools conducted by especially qualified persons who devote themselves thereto. The calling always has been regarded as useful and honorable, essential, indeed, to the public welfare. Mere knowledge of the German language cannot reasonably be regarded as harmful. Heretofore it has been commonly looked upon as helpful and desirable. Plaintiff in error taught this language in school as part of his occupation. His right thus to teach and the right of parents to engage him so to instruct their children, we think, are within the liberty of the Amendment.

*   *   *

It is said the purpose of the legislation was to promote civil development by inhibiting training and education of the immature in foreign tongues and ideals before they could learn English and acquire American ideals; and "that the English language should be and become the mother tongue of all children reared in this State." It is also affirmed that the foreign born population is very large, that certain communities commonly use foreign words, follow foreign leaders, move in a foreign atmosphere, and that the children are thereby hindered from becoming citizens of the most useful type and the public safety is imperiled.

That the State may do much, go very far, indeed, in order to improve the quality of its citizens, physically, mentally and morally, is clear; but the individual has certain fundamental rights which must be respected. The protection of the Constitution extends to all, to those who speak other languages as well as to those born with English on the tongue. Perhaps it would be highly advantageous if all had ready understanding of our ordinary speech, but this cannot be coerced by methods which conflict with the Constitution—a desirable end cannot be promoted by prohibited means.

*   *   *

. . . In order to submerge the individual and develop ideal citizens, Sparta assembled the males at seven into barracks and intrusted their subsequent education and training to official guardians. Although such measures have been deliberately approved by men of great genius, their ideas touching the relation between individual and State were wholly different from those upon which our institutions rest; and it hardly will be affirmed that any legislature could impose such restrictions upon the people of a State without doing violence to both letter and spirit of the Constitution.

The desire of the legislature to foster a homogeneous people with American ideals prepared readily to understand current discussions of civil matters is easy to appreciate. Unfortunate experiences during the late war and aversion toward every characteristic of truculent adversaries were certainly enough to quicken that aspiration. But the means adopted, we think, exceed the limitations upon the power of the State and conflict with rights assured to plaintiff in error. The interference is plain enough and no adequate reason therefor in time of peace and domestic tranquility has been shown.

The power of the State to compel attendance at some school and to make reasonable regulations for all schools, including a requirement that they shall give instructions in English, is not questioned. . . . No emergency has arisen which renders knowledge by a child of some language other than English so clearly harmful as to justify its inhibition with the consequent infringement of rights long freely enjoyed. We are constrained to conclude that the statute as applied is arbitrary and without reasonable relation to any end within the competency of the State.

*   *   *

Reversed.

207 "The Left Wing Manifesto" (1925)

Published and distributed in New York, "The Left Wing Manifesto" advocated militant revolution and urged "the proletariat of the world to the final struggle!" Against the background of the Red Scare in America and the post-Lenin power struggle between Stalin and Trotsky in Russia, the Supreme Court agreed that "[s]uch utterances by their very nature involve danger to the public peace and to the security of the State."

Gitlow v. New York marked the first time the First Amendment principles of free speech and press were assumed to circumscribe state legislation through the Fourteenth Amendment. Although the court upheld the convictions under the 1902 New York Criminal Anarchy Law, state laws and prosecutions, henceforth, were subject to review by federal authority when they involved claims that the rights of expression or assembly had been abridged.

☆ 207 *Gitlow v. New York*

268 U.S. 652 (1925).

MR. JUSTICE SANFORD delivered the opinion of the Court.

                                    *   *   *

The contention here is that the statute, by its terms and as applied in this case, is repugnant to the due process clause of the Fourteenth Amendment. Its material provisions are:

                                    *   *   *

"§ 161. *Advocacy of criminal anarchy.* Any person who:

"1. By word of mouth or writing advocates, advises or teaches the duty, necessity or propriety of overthrowing or overturning organized government by force or violence, or by assassination of the executive head or of any of the executive officials of government, or by any unlawful means; or,

"2. Prints, publishes, edits, issues or knowingly circulates, sells, distributes or publicly displays any book, paper, document, or written or printed matter in any form, containing or advocating, advising or teaching the doctrine that organized government should be overthrown by force, violence or any unlawful means . . . ,

"Is guilty of a felony and punishable" by imprisonment or fine, or both.

The indictment was in two counts. The first charged that the defendant had advocated, advised and taught the duty, necessity and propriety of overthrowing and overturning organized government by force, violence and unlawful means, by certain writings therein set forth entitled "The Left Wing Manifesto"; the second that he had printed, published and knowingly circulated and distributed a certain paper called "The Revolutionary Age," containing the writings set forth in the first count advocating, advising and teaching the doctrine that organized government should be overthrown by force, violence and unlawful means.

[There was no dispute that the defendant had published the material.]

The following facts were established on the trial by undisputed evidence and admissions: The defendant is a member of the Left Wing Section of the Socialist Party, a dissenting branch or faction of that party formed in opposition to its dominant policy of "moderate Socialism." Membership in both is open to aliens as well as citizens. The Left Wing Section was organized nationally at a conference in New York City in June, 1919, attended by ninety delegates from twenty different States. The conference elected a National Council, of which the defendant was a member, and left to it the adoption of a "Manifesto." This was published in The Revolutionary Age, the official organ of the Left Wing. . . .

                                    *   *   *

. . . The sole contention here is, essentially, that as there was no evidence of any concrete result flowing from the publication of the Manifesto or of circumstances showing the likelihood of such result, the statute as construed and applied by the trial court penalizes the mere utterance, as such, of "doctrine" having no quality of incitement, without regard either to the circumstances of its utterance or to the likelihood of unlawful sequences; and that, as the exercise of the right of free expression with relation to government is only punishable "in circumstances involving likelihood of substantive evil," the statute contravenes the due process clause of the Fourteenth Amendment. . . .

The precise question presented, and the only question which we can consider under this writ of error, then is, whether the statute, as construed and applied in this case by the state courts, deprived the defendant of his liberty of expression in violation of the due process clause of the Fourteenth Amendment.

The statute does not penalize the utterance or publication of abstract "doctrine" or academic discussion having no quality of incitement to any concrete action. It is not aimed against mere historical or philosophical essays. It does not restrain the advocacy of changes in the form of government by constitutional and lawful means. What it prohibits is language advocating, advising or teaching the overthrow of organized government by unlawful means. . . .

The Manifesto, plainly, is neither the statement of abstract doctrine nor, as suggested by counsel, mere prediction that industrial disturbances and revolutionary mass strikes will result spontaneously in an inevitable process of evolution in the economic system. It advocates and urges in fervent language mass action which shall progressively foment industrial disturbances and through political mass strikes and revolutionary mass action overthrow and destroy organized parliamentary government. It concludes with a call to action in these words: "The proletariat revolution and the Communist reconstruction of society — *the struggle for these* — is now indispensable. . . . The Communist International calls the proletariat of the world to the final struggle!" This is not the expression of philosophical abstraction, the mere prediction of future events; it is the language of direct incitement.

                                    *   *   *

That a State in the exercise of its police power may punish those who abuse this freedom by utterances inimical to the public welfare, tending to corrupt public morals, incite to crime, or disturb the public peace, is not open to question. . . .

                                    *   *   *

By enacting the present statute the State has determined, through its legislative body, that utterances advocating the overthrow of organized government by force, violence and unlawful means, are so inimical to the general welfare and involve such danger of substantive evil that they may be penalized in the exercise of its police power. That determination must be given great weight. . . . That utterances inciting to the overthrow of organized government by unlawful means, present a sufficient danger of substantive evil to bring their punishment within the range of legislative discretion, is clear. Such utterances, by their very nature, involve danger to the public peace and to the security of the State. They threaten breaches of the peace and ultimate revolution. And the immediate danger is none the less real and substantial, because the effect of a given utterance cannot be accurately foreseen. The State cannot reasonably be required to measure the danger from every such utterance in the nice balance of a jeweler's scale. A single revolutionary spark may kindle a fire that, smouldering for a time, may burst into a sweeping and destructive conflagration. It cannot be said that the State is acting arbitrarily or unreasonably when in the exercise of its judgment as to the measures necessary to protect the public peace and safety, it seeks to extinguish the spark without waiting until it has enkindled the flame or blazed into the conflagration. . . .

* * *

And finding, for the reasons stated, that the statute is not in itself unconstitutional, and that it has not been applied in the present case in derogation of any constitutional right, the judgment of the Court of Appeals is

Affirmed.

MR. JUSTICE HOLMES [with BRANDEIS, J.], dissenting.

. . . If I am right, then I think that the criterion sanctioned by the full Court in *Schenck v. United States* applies. "The question in every case is whether the words used are used in such circumstances and are of such a nature as to create a clear and present danger that they will bring about the substantive evils that [the State] has a right to prevent." . . . If what I think the correct test is applied, it is manifest that there was no present danger of an attempt to overthrow the government by force on the part of the admittedly small minority who shared the defendant's views. It is said that this manifesto was more than a theory, that it was an incitement. Every idea is an incitement. It offers itself for belief and if believed it is acted on unless some other belief outweighs it or some failure of energy stifles the movement at its birth. The only difference between the expression of an opinion and an incitement in the narrower sense is the speaker's enthusiasm for the result. Eloquence may set fire to reason. But whatever may be thought of the redundant discourse before us it had no chance of starting a present conflagration. If in the long run the beliefs expressed in proletarian dictatorship are destined to be accepted by the dominant forces of the commu-

nity, the only meaning of free speech is that they should be given their chance and have their way.

If the publication of this document had been laid as an attempt to induce an uprising against government at once and not at some indefinite time in the future it would have presented a different question. The object would have been one with which the law might deal, subject to the doubt whether there was any danger that the publication could produce any result, or in other words, whether it was not futile and too remote from possible consequences. But the indictment alleges the publication and nothing more.

208 Conduct of a Nature to Bring Discredit upon the Military Service (1925)

Colonel William Mitchell accumulated a distinguished record during World War I. He foresaw the potential for the effective use of air power and urged the buildup of the nation's armed forces and the creation of an independent air service. He was highly critical of the Navy and War Departments' reliance on battleships to secure the national defense and believed this policy was based on personal and venal motives of high military and government officials. He also charged that belittlement of the prowess of well-developed air power—especially Japanese—was fostering a false sense of security in the public. For earlier criticism he had been relieved of his post as assistant chief of the Air Service and its temporary rank of brigadier general. After two unrelated concurrent aircraft disasters in 1925, Billy Mitchell issued the following statement: "These accidents are the result of the incompetency, the criminal negligence, and the almost treasonable negligence of our national defense by the Navy and War Departments.

Mitchell was court-martialed and convicted for this and other critical assessments of his superiors. He was charged with "conduct prejudicial to good order and military discipline and of a nature to bring discredit upon the military service by uttering insubordinate and highly contemptuous and disrespectful statements intended to discredit the Navy and War Departments." The sentence of five years' suspension of rank and forfeiture of all pay and allowances was approved by President Coolidge. Mitchell resigned his commission within the week. "Had he lived through World War II he would have seen the fulfillment of many of his prophecies," one of his judges, Douglas MacArthur, wrote later.

☆ 208 Excerpts from the Billy Mitchell Trial Transcript

Reprinted in D. Davis, *The Billy Mitchell Affair* (New York: Random House, 1967), 249-51, 291-92.

[Opening statement of defense counsel Frank R. Reid, explaining the reasons for Mitchell's San Antonio statements after the Shenandoah disaster:]

* * *

"His heart was sad due to the distresses of his brave brethren and the thought of his companions who had passed one by one into the Great Beyond, and feeling it his overwhelming duty to do so he issued the statements of September 5, in the hope that it would arouse the conscience of the American people, and that they would . . . through their representatives, cause the evils to be corrected. . . .

. . . Colonel Mitchell, after exhausting every usual means to safeguard the aerial defense of the United States, without result, took the only way possible that would cause a study of the conditions of the national defense to be made."

* * *

One of the first defense witnesses was Major Carl ("Tooey") Spaatz, the thirty-five-year-old tactical chief of the Air Service, who wore the Distinguished Service Cross, had shot down three German planes and commanded a training school in France. In World War II he was to become commander of the U.S. Strategic Air Forces in Europe and the Pacific. Spaatz told the court of a pathetically small air force, short of men and planes and almost at a standstill in training.

All told, there were 1820 planes, but 1300 of these were obsolete—and only 400 were "standard." Of these 400, more than half were left over from the war. Only 26 bombers and 39 observation planes were rated as standard, and Spaatz insisted that only 59 planes in the United States were modern and fit for duty. As for properly equipped pursuit planes, with oxygen tanks, synchronized guns, radios and bomb racks, there were none.

By dragging all administrative officers from their desks at his post, Spaatz said, he could put 15 pursuit planes into the air: "It is very disheartening to attempt to train or do work under such circumstances."

Reid asked him if he thought aviation was being retarded by the War Department. The prosecution objected, since that called for a conclusion by the witness, but Spaatz managed to shout: "I do!" The crowd applauded.

* * *

[Cross-examination of William Mitchell by assistant prosecutor Allen W. Gullion:]

* * *

". . . Now, Colonel Mitchell, in one of your statements you speak of 'we in the air fraternity'—do you recall the expression?"

"Yes."

"Is this 'we in the air fraternity' an incorporated organization?"

"Unquestionably, it is not."

"What does this air fraternity consist of?"

"It means the people who fly in the air."

"Is there an organized air fraternity?"

"No. Just a community of spirit and a community of interest."

"Has this community of spirit and community of interest been recognized by anybody as an official organization?"

"No."

"Who are the leaders of this air fraternity?"

"Everybody that flies has an equal voice in it."

". . . How are the funds raised to support this air fraternity?"

"There are no funds raised."

"Who is this 'we' you refer to in the air fraternity that 'then and there decided to put the issue squarely up to Congress and the people'?"

"We talked it over and discussed what had gone on and decided we would stand that sort of stuff no longer."

* * *

[Gullion read from Mitchell's charges on the *Shenandoah:*] " 'Her survivors are muzzled by the Navy Department, pending a whitewash board. Are these things so, or are they not? I'm down here in Texas and have not all the data at hand, but I'm sure the facts are practically as stated.' "

"Are you still sure the facts are practically as stated?"

"More so than ever. I know they are now."

The examination turned to the Army's "propaganda service": "Did you ever give any information to the press, while Assistant Chief of the Air Service?"

"Often. There was no other way of getting the truth out, I found."

* * *

209 No Right to Strike (1926)

Despite the Clayton Act's withdrawal of federal judicial power to penalize labor for exercising economic sanctions against employers, state laws continued to deny labor's right to resort to strikes to gain concessions from management. *Dorchy v. Kansas* involved the criminal conviction of a United Mine Workers vice-president under the Kansas Industrial Relations Act, which made it an unlawful conspiracy to induce others to quit their employment for the purpose of hindering mining operations. The Supreme Court unequivocally upheld the states' authority to maintain a balance between the competing interests of labor and management, continuing the latter's access to the force of law to support its interests.

272 U.S. 306 (1926).

MR. JUSTICE BRANDEIS delivered the opinion of the Court.

Section 17 of the Court of Industrial Relations Act, while reserving to the individual employee the right to quit his employment at any time, makes it unlawful to conspire "to induce others to quit their employment for the purpose and with the intent to hinder, delay, limit or suspend the operation of" mining. Section 19 makes it a felony for an officer of a labor union wilfully to use the power or influence incident to his office to induce another person to violate any provision of the act. Dorchy was prosecuted criminally for violating § 19. The jury found him guilty through inducing a violation of § 17.... Dorchy duly claimed ... that § 19 as applied was void because it prohibits strikes; and that to do so is a denial of the liberty guaranteed by the Fourteenth Amendment....

*   *   *

... The question requiring decision is not, however, the broad one whether the legislature has power to prohibit strikes. It is whether the prohibition of § 19 is unconstitutional as here applied. The special facts out of which the strike arose must, therefore, be considered.

... So far as appears, there was no trade dispute. ... The ... strike was called to compel the company to pay a claim of one Mishmash for $180. The men were told this; and they were instructed not to return to work until they should be duly advised that the claim had been paid.... The claim was disputed. It had been pending nearly two years. So far as appears, Mishmash was not in the company's employ at the time of the strike order. The men went out in obedience to the strike order.... While the men were out on strike this criminal proceeding was begun.

*   *   *

The right to carry on business—be it called liberty or property—has value. To interfere with this right without just cause is unlawful. The fact that the injury was inflicted by a strike is sometimes a justification. But a strike may be illegal because of its purpose, however orderly the manner in which it is conducted. To collect a stale claim due to a fellow member of the union who was formerly employed in the business is not a permissible purpose.... To enforce payment by a strike is clearly coercion. The legislature may make such action punishable criminally, as extortion or otherwise. And it may subject to punishment him who uses the power or influence

incident to his office in a union to order the strike. Neither the common law, nor the Fourteenth Amendment, confers the absolute right to strike.

Affirmed.

210 "fight ... for your rights" (1926)

In September of 1925, Dr. Ossian H. Sweet, a black gynecologist with an M.D. from Howard University, moved into a newly purchased home in a lower-middle-class white neighborhood in Detroit. The black population of Detroit had grown dramatically from about six thousand in 1910 to some seventy thousand at the time of the Sweets' arrival. It was the World War I boom in the automobile industry which accounted for the influx of black workers from the South into the city. Black housing was limited, and the city's white population violently opposed black expansion into their neighborhoods.

On the first night after the Sweets' arrival, an intimidating white crowd gathered in front of the house. A larger crowd—estimated at several hundred—gathered on the third night, and eight policemen were placed on duty to prevent disorder. Dr. Sweet, his wife, two brothers, and seven friends were in the house at the time. Suddenly, several shots were fired from the Sweet house, and a white man, Leon Breiner, sitting nearby, was killed. The eleven blacks in the house were charged with first-degree murder. Clarence Darrow served as defense counsel. After forty-six hours of deliberation, the jury could not reach a verdict. Five months later, Dr. Sweet's younger brother, Henry Sweet, was tried again. On May 19, 1926, the jury returned a verdict of not guilty. Portions of the Darrow summation in the trial of Henry Sweet appear in the document.

Reprinted in A. Weinberg, ed., *Attorney for the Damned* (New York: Simon & Schuster, 1957), 241-42.

*   *   *

Gentlemen, lawyers are very intemperate in their statements. My friend, Moll, said that my client here was a coward. A coward, gentlemen. Here, he says, were a gang of gunmen, and cowards—shot Breiner through the back. Nobody saw Breiner, of course. If he had his face turned toward the house, while he was smoking there, waiting for the shooting to begin, it wasn't our fault. It wouldn't make any difference which way he turned. I suppose the bullet would have killed him just the same, if he had been in the way of it. If he had been at home, it would not have happened. Who are the cowards in this case? Cowards, gentlemen! Eleven people with black skins, eleven people, gentlemen, whose ancestors did not come to America because they wanted to, but were brought here in slave ships, to toil for nothing, for the whites — whose lives have been taken in nearly every state in the Union — they have been victims of riots all over this land of the free. They have had to take what is left after everybody else had grabbed what he wanted. The only place where he has been put in front is on the battlefield. When we are fighting we give him a chance to die, and the best chance. But, everywhere else, he has been food for the flames, and the ropes, and the knives, and the guns and hate of the white, regardless of law and liberty, and the common sentiments of justice that should move men. Were they cowards?

No, gentlemen, they may have been gunmen. They may have tried to murder. But they were not cowards. Eleven people, knowing what it meant, with the history of the race behind them, with the knowledge of shootings and killings and insult and injury without end, eleven of them go into a house, gentlemen, with no police protection, in the face of a mob, and the hatred of a community, and take guns and ammunition and fight for their rights, and for your rights and for mine, and for the rights of every being that lives. They went in and faced a mob seeking to tear them to bits. Call them something besides cowards. The cowardly curs were in the mob gathered there with the backing of the law. A lot of children went in front and threw the stones. They stayed for two days and two nights in front of this home, and by their threats and assault were trying to drive the Negroes out. Those were the cowardly curs, and you know it. I suppose there isn't any ten of them that would come out in the open daylight against those ten. Oh no, gentlemen, their blood is too pure for that. They can only act like a band of coyotes baying some victim who has no chance. And then my clients are called cowards.

All right, gentlemen, call them something else. These blacks have been called many names along down through the ages, but there have been those through the sad years who believed in justice and mercy and charity and love and kindliness, and there have been those who believed that a black man should have some rights, even in a country where he was brought in chains. There are those even crazy enough to hope and to dream that sometime he will come from under this cloud and take his place amongst the people of the world. If he does, it will be through his courage and his culture. It will be by his intelligence and his scholarship and his effort, and I say, gentlemen of the jury, no honest, right-feeling man, whether on a jury or anywhere else, would place anything in his way in this great struggle behind him and before him.

*   *   *

211 Revolutionary Class Struggle (1927)

Whitney v. California was the most notable case prosecuted under the 1919 California Criminal Syndicalism Law. The defendant, Anita Whitney, was a niece of the late United States Supreme Court justice Stephen J. Field. A member of the Oakland branch of the Socialist party, she attended a 1919 party convention in Chicago at which a schism developed between party factions. The more militant faction formed the Communist Labor party, which called for "a revolutionary class struggle." Whitney joined the new party and participated in its meetings but actively opposed the adoption of a call for revolutionary tactics. At her trial, she testified that she did not favor the use of terrorism or violence by the Communist Labor party of California. She claimed in the Supreme Court the syndicalism law violated her rights under the Fourteenth Amendment. Nevertheless, the court upheld her conviction.

Most Americans in 1927 were enjoying the economic boom of the postwar decade, and talk of class struggle seemed anomalous. The Crash of 1929 and the ensuing depression gave these ideas more importance within the large numbers of the unemployed.

☆ 211 *Whitney v. California*

274 U.S. 357 (1927).

Mr. Justice SANFORD delivered the opinion of the Court.

*   *   *

The pertinent provisions of the Criminal Syndicalism Act are:

"Section 1. The Term 'criminal syndicalism' as used in this act is hereby defined as any doctrine or precept advocating, teaching or aiding and abetting the commission of crime, sabotage (which word is hereby defined as meaning willful and malicious physical damage or injury to physical property), or unlawful acts of force and violence or unlawful methods of terrorism as a means of accomplishing a change in industrial ownership or control, or effecting any political change.

"Sec. 2. Any person who: . . . 4. Organizes or assists in organizing, or is or knowingly becomes a member of, any organization, society, group or assemblage of persons organized or assembled to advocate, teach or aid and abet criminal syndicalism; . . .

"Is guilty of a felony and punishable by imprisonment."

*   *   *

The Act, plainly, meets the essential requirement of due process that a penal statute be "sufficiently explicit to inform those who are subject to it what conduct on their part will render them liable to its penalties," and be couched in terms that are not "so vague that men of common intelligence must necessarily guess at its meaning and differ as to its application." . . .

* * *

Neither is the Syndicalism Act repugnant to the equal protection clause, on the ground that as its penalties are confined to those who advocate a resort to violent and unlawful methods as a means of changing industrial and political conditions, it arbitrarily discriminates between such persons and those who may advocate a resort to these methods as a means of maintaining such conditions.

* * *

The Syndicalism Act is not class legislation; it affects all alike, no matter what their business associations or callings, who come within its terms and do the things prohibited. . . .

Nor is the Syndicalism Act as applied in this case repugnant to the due process clause as a restraint of the rights of free speech, assembly, and association.

That the freedom of speech which is secured by the Constitution does not confer an absolute right to speak, without responsibility, whatever one may choose, . . . and that a State in the exercise of its police power may punish those who abuse this freedom . . . is not open to question.

By enacting the provisions of the Syndicalism Act the State has declared, through its legislative body, that to knowingly be or become a member of or assist in organizing an association to advocate, teach or aid and abet the commission of crimes or unlawful acts of force, violence or terrorism as a means of accomplishing industrial or political changes, involves such danger to the public peace and the security of the State, that these acts should be penalized in the exercise of its police power. That determination must be given great weight. . . .

The essence of offense denounced by the Act is the combining with others in an association for the accomplishment of the desired ends through the advocacy and use of criminal and unlawful methods. It partakes of the nature of a criminal conspiracy. That such united and joint action involves even greater danger to the public peace and security than the isolated utterances and acts of individuals is clear. We cannot hold that, as here applied, the Act is an unreasonable or arbitrary exercise of the police power of the State, unwarrantably infringing any right of free speech, assembly or association. . . .

* * *

Affirmed.

Mr. Justice BRANDEIS, concurring.

* * *

Those who won our independence . . . knew that order cannot be secured merely through fear of punishment for its infraction; that it is hazardous to discourage thought, hope and imagination; that fear breeds repression; that repression breeds hate; that hate menaces stable government; that the path of safety lies in the opportunity to discuss freely supposed grievances and proposed remedies; and that the fitting remedy for evil counsels is good ones. Believing in the power of reason as applied through public discussion, they eschewed silence coerced by law—the argument of force in its worst form. Recognizing the occasional tyrannies of governing majorities, they amended the Constitution so that free speech and assembly should be guaranteed.

Fear of serious injury cannot alone justify suppression of free speech and assembly. Men feared witches and burnt women. It is the function of speech to free men from the bondage of irrational fears. To justify suppression of free speech there must be reasonable ground to fear that serious evil will result if free speech is practiced. There must be reasonable ground to believe that the danger apprehended is imminent. There must be reasonable ground to believe that the evil to be prevented is a serious one. . . . The wide difference between advocacy and incitement, between preparation and attempt, between assembling and conspiracy, must be borne in mind. In order to support a finding of clear and present danger it must be shown either that immediate serious violence was to be expected or was advocated, or that the past conduct furnished reason to believe that such advocacy was then contemplated.

* * *

. . . Whenever the fundamental rights of free speech and assembly are alleged to have been invaded, it must remain open to a defendant to present the issue whether there actually did exist at the time a clear danger, whether the danger, if any, was imminent, and whether the evil apprehended was one so substantial as to justify the stringent restriction interposed by the Legislature. The legislative declaration, like the fact that the statute was passed and was sustained by the highest court of the State, created merely a rebuttable presumption that these conditions have been satisfied.

Whether in 1919, when Miss Whitney did the things complained of, there was in California such clear and present danger of serious evil, might have been made the important issue in the case. She might have required that the issue be determined either by the court or the jury. She claimed below that the statute as applied to her violated the federal Constitution; but she did not claim that it was void because there was no clear and present danger of serious evil, nor did she request that the existence of these conditions of a valid measure thus restrict-

ing the rights of free speech and assembly be passed
upon by the court or a jury. On the other hand, there
was evidence on which the court or jury might have
found that such danger existed. I am unable to assent to the suggestion in the opinion of the court
that assembling with a political party, formed to advocate the desirability of a proletarian revolution by
mass action at some date necessarily far in the future, is not a right within the protection of the Fourteenth Amendment. In the present case, however,
there was other testimony which tended to establish
the existence of a conspiracy, on the part of members of the International Workers of the World, to
commit present serious crimes, and likewise to show
that such a conspiracy would be furthered by the activity of the society of which Miss Whitney was a
member. Under these circumstances the judgment
of the State court cannot be disturbed.

*   *   *

Mr. Justice HOLMES joins in this opinion.

212 "violence . . . impelled by persecution and self-defense" (1923-1927)

The 1920s were a period of widespread anti-alien
and anti-radical hysteria. Nicola Sacco, a shoemaker,
and Bartolomeo Vanzetti, a fish peddler, were tried
and convicted in connection with the murders of
Alessandro Berardelli, a guard, and F. A. Parmen-
ter, paymaster of a shoe factory, in South Braintree,
Massachusetts. Sacco and Vanzetti were Italian-
born members of the Galleani anarchist group. The
alleged motive for the crime was the robbery of the
shoe factory payroll. To distribute some radical literature, they had borrowed a car identified as the vehicle used in the earlier hold-up and murder. The
worldwide popular interest in the case stemmed
from a belief that the men were denied a fair trial
because of their political and social views. Many petitions were filed for clemency after Judge Webster
Thayer imposed the death sentence on April 9, 1927.
Governor Alvan T. Fuller appointed a committee to
investigate charges of prejudice against the defendants. The committee characterized the judge's hostile private statements as "a grave breach of deco-
rum" but decided they had not affected his conduct
or influenced the jury. The defendants were executed on August 23, 1927.

Vanzetti's letters and his last statement in court
reflect the political overtones of the case.

☆212 Bartolomeo Vanzetti's Ideology

☆212a Vanzetti's Letters

Reprinted in M. D. Frankfurter and G. Jackson, eds., *The
Letters of Sacco and Vanzetti* (New York: Viking Press,
1928), 96.

May 26, 1923
Charlestown Prison

DEAR COMRADE [MRS. ELSIE] HILLSMITH:

*   *   *

. . . I decided not to enter into a discussion [of politics
with you] before . . . the answer to the following
questions: Are you contrary or in favor of the Anarchistic view and aim? — of a real physical equality in
ownership, in rights and duties among the human
beings? Did you mean to possess relatively and hu-
manly speaking, the whole truth and reason? If it
were that humans should be compelled to the violence either for justice or for injustice, then would
you approve those who would use the violence
against the violence that compel them to be unjust
and violent? Did you ever study Kropotkin, Reclus,
Bakunin, Proudhon, or Tolstoy and compare their
doctrines with those of liberals or authority Socialists? [Unfinished]

Reprinted in Louis Joughin and E. M. Morgan, *The Legacy
of Sacco and Vanzetti* (New York: Harcourt, Brace, 1948),
493-94.

May 23, 1926
Charlestown Prison

[TO THE INTERNATIONAL LABOR DEFENSE:]

*   *   *

. . . I repeat, I will repeat to the last, only the people,
our comrades, our friends, the world revolutionary
proletariat can save us from the powers of the capitalist reactionary hyenas, or vindicate our names
and our blood before history. . . .

There are some who think that our case is a trial
for a common crime; that our friends should contest
our innocence but not turn the case into a political
issue, because it would only damage us. Well, I could
answer to them all that our case is more than a political case, is a case of class war in which our enemies
are personally interested to lose us — not only for
class purposes but for personal passions, resentments, and fear. . . .

*   *   *

Joughin and Morgan, 490.

May 4, 1927
Dedham Jail

[PETITION FOR CLEMENCY TO GOVERNOR ALVAN
T. FULLER:]

*   *   *

. . . We cannot deny that acts of violence have been
committed by men calling themselves anarchists,
and sometimes by men who had a right to call themselves that. But they were impelled by persecution
and self-defence, or provoked by violence, oppression and intolerance on the part of persons in power.

*   *   *

Frankfurter and Jackson, 306-7.

July 22, 1927
Charlestown Prison

DEAR COMRADE [HARRY] DRAGAN:

*   *   *

As long as the several schools of socialism will look
for power to themselves, be fatalist and authoritar-
ian, and the workers follow their leaders, there will
always be brotherly strife and hatred among them,
instead of brothers and harmony. This was clearly
seen at the beginning of the Socialist movement, by
men who had eyes to see.

Power and abuse of power are synonyms. The
working class shall smash all the powers against it,
not create a power for itself, except for self defense.

. . . From what I can understand, we are doomed.
Maybe I am wrong; I would be wrong, but things
look like that.

. . . Anyhow, even if they will kill us, they cannot
kill all of us; all the good men and women, and still
less, kill ideas, rights, necessities, aspirations and
ideals. So the cause of freedom and justice, of class
and of human emancipation will not be destroyed
not stopped by the bodies, burnt, of two more victims of our foes.

So have heart, be cheerful, victory is ahead, and
do your share with a glad heart.

BARTOLOMEO VANZETTI

☆ 212b Vanzetti's Last Statement in Court

Reprinted in O. K. Fraenkel, *The Sacco-Vanzetti Case* (New
York: Knopf, 1931), 138.

Yes. What I say is that I am innocent. . . . [I]n all my
life I have never stole and I have never killed and I
have never spilled blood. . . . I have struggled all my
life, since I began to reason, to eliminate crime from
the earth.

*   *   *

. . . [N]ot only have I not been in Braintree to steal
and kill and have never steal or kill or spilt blood in

all my life, not only have I struggled hard against
crimes, but I have refused myself the commodity or
glory of life, the pride of life of a good position because in my consideration it is not right to exploit
man. . . .

Now, I should say that I am not only innocent of
all these things, not only have I never committed a
real crime in my life to eliminate crimes that the official law and the official moral condemns, but also the
crime that the official moral and the official law sanctions and sanctifies, — the exploitation and the oppression of the man by the man, and if there is a reason why I am here as a guilty man, if there is a
reason why you in a few minutes can doom me, it is
this reason and none else.

*   *   *

We have proved that there could not have been
another Judge on the face of the earth more preju-
diced and more cruel than you have been against us.
We have proved that. Still they refuse the new trial.
We know, and you know in your heart, that you have
been against us from the very beginning, before you
see us. Before you see us you already know that we
were radicals, that we were underdogs, that we
were the enemy of the institution that you can believe in good faith in their goodness — I don't want to
condemn that — and that it was easy on the time of
the first trial to get a verdict of guiltiness.

We know that you have spoke yourself and have
spoke your hostility against us, and your despise-
ment against us with friends of yours on the train, at
the University Club, of Boston, on the Golf Club of
Worcester, Massachusetts. I am sure that if the people who know all what you say against us would
have the civil courage to take the stand, maybe your
Honor — I am sorry to say this because you are an
old man, and I have an old father — but maybe you
would be beside us in good justice at this time.

*   *   *

We were tried during a time that has now passed
into history. I mean by that, a time when there was
hysteria of resentment and hate against the people
of our principles, against the foreigner, against
slackers, and it seems to me — rather, I am positive,
that both you and Mr. Katzmann has done all what it
were in your power in order to work out, in order to
agitate still more the passion of the juror, the prejudice of the juror, against us. . . .

Well, I have already say that I not only am not
guilty of these crimes, but I never commit a crime in
my life, — I have never steal and I have never kill
and I have never spilt blood, and I have fought and I
have sacrificed myself even to eliminate the crimes
that the law and the church legitimate and sanctify.

*   *   *

But my conviction is that I have suffered for
things that I am guilty of. I am suffering because I

am a radical and indeed I am a radical; I have suffered because I was an Italian, and indeed I am an
Italian; I have suffered more for my family and for
my beloved than for myself; but I am so convinced to
be right that if you could execute me two times, I
would live again to do what I have done already. I
have finished. Thank you.

213 " 'peaceful and orderly opposition to government' " (1931)

By 1931, political hysteria, which had subsided somewhat, once more was reawakened as a result of De-
pression-connected hunger marches by the unemployed and the resultant violent police responses.
Nevertheless, many of the measures for controlling
dissent fell into desuetude, and when they were invoked, the courts viewed them with a more skeptical eye. *Stromberg v. California* was the first Supreme Court case to uphold a challenge, based on
the First Amendment, to political prosecution and is
noteworthy for its tacit recognition of "symbolic
speech" and its application of what has come to be
called the "overbreadth doctrine." The court opinion
contained no general condemnation of the legislation
in question, only the requirement that it be sufficiently explicit so as not to be construed to apply to
peaceful opposition to government.

☆ 213 *Stromberg v. California*

283 U.S. 359 (1931).

MR. CHIEF JUSTICE HUGHES delivered the opinion
of the Court.

*   *   *

The information . . . charged [in the statutory lan-
guage] that the appellant and other defendants, at
the time and place set forth, "did wilfully, unlawfully
and feloniously display a red flag and banner in a
public place and in a meeting place as a sign, symbol
and emblem of opposition to organized government
and as an invitation and stimulus to anarchistic
action and as an aid to propaganda that is and was of
a seditious character."

*   *   *

. . . It appears that the appellant, a young woman
of nineteen, a citizen of the United States by birth,
was one of the supervisors of a summer camp for
children, between ten and fifteen years of age, in the
foothills of the San Bernardino mountains. Appellant led the children in their daily study, teaching
them history and economics. "Among other things,
the children were taught class consciousness, the
solidarity of the workers, and the theory that the
workers of the world are of one blood and brothers
all." Appellant was a member of the Young Commu-

nist League, an international organization affiliated
with the Communist Party. The charge against her
concerned a daily ceremony at the camp, in which
the appellant supervised and directed the children
in raising a red flag, "a camp-made reproduction of
the flag of Soviet Russia, which was also the flag of
the Communist Party in the United States." In connection with the flag-raising, there was a ritual at
which the children stood at salute and recited a
pledge of allegiance "to the worker's red flag, and to
the cause for which it stands; one aim throughout
our lives, freedom for the working class." The stipulation further shows that "a library was maintained
at the camp containing a large number of books, papers and pamphlets, including much radical communist propaganda, specimens of which are quoted in
the opinion of the state court." These quotations
abundantly demonstrated that the books and pamphlets contained incitements to violence and to
"armed uprisings," teaching "the indispensability of
a desperate, bloody, destructive war as the immediate task of the coming action." Appellant admitted
ownership of a number of the books, some of which
bore her name. It appears from the stipulation that
none of these books or pamphlets were used in the
teaching at the camp.

*   *   *

. . . [D]oubting the constitutionality of the first
clause, the state court rested its decision upon the remaining clauses. The basis of the decision, as more
fully stated in the opinion of the two concurring justices, was this: "The constitutionality of the phrase of
this section, 'of opposition to organized government'
is questionable. This phrase can be eliminated from
the section without materially changing its purposes,
. . ." Accordingly, disregarding the first clause of the
statute, and upholding the other clauses, the conviction of the appellant was sustained.

We are unable to agree with this disposition of
the case. The verdict against the appellant was a
general one. It did not specify the ground upon
which it rested. . . . If any one of these clauses, which
the state court has held to be separable, was invalid,
it cannot be determined upon this record that the appellant was not convicted under that clause. . . .

*   *   *

. . . We have no reason to doubt the validity of the
second and third clauses of the statute as construed
by the state court to relate to such incitements to
violence.

The question is thus narrowed to that of the validity of the first clause, that is, with respect to the
display of the flag "as a sign, symbol or emblem of
opposition to organized government," and the construction which the state court has placed upon this
clause removes every element of doubt. The state
court recognized the indefiniteness and ambiguity of
the clause. The court considered that it might be

construed as embracing conduct which the State could not constitutionally prohibit. Thus it was said that the clause "might be construed to include the peaceful and orderly opposition to a government as organized and controlled by one political party by those of another political party equally high minded and patriotic, which did not agree with the one in power. It might also be construed to include peaceful and orderly opposition to government by legal means and within constitutional limitations." The maintenance of the opportunity for free political discussion to the end that government may be responsive to the will of the people and that changes may be obtained by lawful means, an opportunity essential to the security of the Republic, is a fundamental principle of our constitutional system. A statute which upon its face, and as authoritatively construed, is so vague and indefinite as to permit the punishment of the fair use of this opportunity is repugnant to the guaranty of liberty contained in the Fourteenth Amendment. The first clause of the statute being invalid upon its face, the conviction of the appellant, which so far as the record discloses may have rested upon that clause exclusively, must be set aside.

*   *   *

Judgment reversed.

MR. JUSTICE BUTLER, dissenting.

*   *   *

. . . It seems to me that on this record the Court is not called on to decide whether the mere display of a flag as the emblem of a purpose, whatever its sort, is speech within the meaning of the constitutional protection of speech and press or to decide whether such freedom is a part of the liberty protected by the Fourteenth Amendment or whether the anarchy that is certain to follow a successful "opposition to organized goverment" is not a sufficient reason to hold that all activities to that end are outside the "liberty" so protected. . . .

*   *   *

214 "jurisdiction to issue a restraining order" (1932)

Industry and business management's ability to secure (through the labor injunction) the power and authority of the law to combat strikes, collective bargaining, and other techniques that the modern labor movement used to gain its demands gave rise to labor's argument that the government was partial to capital, and hence unjust. The Norris-La Guardia Act was the climax of the movement toward stricter limitations on the use of the labor injunction, which began when the earlier attempt in the Clayton Act proved ineffective. The declaration of public policy

in section two of the Norris-La Guardia Act showed a marked shift from earlier pronouncements in positioning the federal government as a more neutral player in the labor-management bouts of the future, thus reducing the inclination of labor to view government authority as the co-opted tool of capital. The goal was a concomitant reduction in the frequency and degree of organized violence surrounding labor disputes.

By its terms, the act prohibited the issuance of an injunction against certain conduct; most notably, striking, picketing and/or publicizing, advocating, and advising or agreeing to engage in collective activity in a labor dispute "without fraud or violence." In addition, management forces had to overcome stricter procedural requirements, including an adversary hearing, before they could obtain an injunction. Finally, courts could impose punishments for contempt (committed outside the presence of the court) only after a speedy trial by jury. The 1947 Taft-Hartley Act modified the Norris-La Guardia Act by again broadening the availability of the labor injunction.

☆ 214 The Norris-La Guardia Act

47 Stat. 70 (1932).

An Act to amend the Judicial Code and to define and limit the jurisdiction of courts sitting in equity, and for other purposes.

Be it enacted by the Senate and House of Representatives of the United States of America in Congress assembled, That no court of the United States, as herein defined, shall have jurisdiction to issue any restraining order or temporary or permanent injunction in a case involving or growing out of a labor dispute, except in a strict conformity with the provisions of this Act; nor shall any such restraining order or temporary or permanent injunction be issued contrary to the public policy declared in this Act.

SEC. 2. In the interpretation of this Act and in determining the jurisdiction and authority of the courts of the United States, as such jurisdiction and authority are herein defined and limited, the public policy of the United States is hereby declared as follows:

Whereas under prevailing economic conditions, developed with the aid of governmental authority for owners of property to organize in the corporate and other forms of ownership association, the individual unorganized worker is commonly helpless to exercise actual liberty of contract and to protect his freedom of labor, and thereby to obtain acceptable terms and conditions of employment, wherefore, though he should be free to decline to associate with his fellows, it is necessary that he have full freedom of association, self-organization, and designation of representatives of his own choosing, to negotiate the terms and conditions of his employment, and that he shall be free from the interference, restraint, or coercion of employers of labor, or their agents, in the designation of such representatives or in self-organization or in other concerted activities for the purpose of collective bargaining or other mutual aid or protection; therefore, the following definitions of, and limitations upon, the jurisdiction and authority of the courts of the United States are hereby enacted.

SEC. 3. Any undertaking or promise, such as is described in this section, or any other undertaking or promise in conflict with the public policy declared in section 2 of this Act, is hereby declared to be contrary to the public policy of the United States, shall not be enforceable in any court of the United States and shall not afford any basis for the granting of legal or equitable relief by any such court, including specifically the following:

Every undertaking or promise hereafter made, whether written or oral, express or implied, constituting or contained in any contract or agreement of hiring or employment between any individual, firm, company, association, or corporation, and any employee or prospective employee of the same, whereby

(a) Either party to such contract or agreement undertakes or promises not to join, become, or remain a member of any labor organization or of any employer organization; or

(b) Either party to such contract or agreement undertakes or promises that he will withdraw from an employment relation in the event that he joins, becomes, or remains a member of any labor organization or of any employer organization.

SEC. 4. No court of the United States shall have jurisdiction to issue any restraining order or temporary or permanent injunction in any case involving or growing out of any labor dispute to prohibit any person or persons participating or interested in such dispute (as these terms are herein defined) from doing, whether singly or in concert, any of the following acts:

(a) Ceasing or refusing to perform any work or to remain in any relation of employment;

(b) Becoming or remaining a member of any labor organization or of any employer organization, regardless of any such undertaking or promise as is described in section 3 of this Act;

(c) Paying or giving to, or withholding from, any person participating or interested in such labor dispute, any strike or unemployment benefits or insurance, or other moneys or things of value;

(d) By all lawful means aiding any person participating or interested in any labor dispute who is being proceeded against in, or is prosecuting, any action or suit in any court of the United States or of any State;

(e) Giving publicity to the existence of, or the facts involved in, any labor dispute, whether by advertising, speaking, patrolling, or by any other method not involving fraud or violence;

(f) Assembling peaceably to act or to organize to act in promotion of their interests in a labor dispute;

(g) Advising or notifying any person of an intention to do any of the acts heretofore specified;

(h) Agreeing with other persons to do or not to do any of the acts heretofore specified; and

(i) Advising, urging, or otherwise causing or inducing without fraud or violence the acts heretofore specified, regardless of any such undertaking or promise as is described in section 3 of this Act.

SEC. 5. No court of the United States shall have jurisdiction to issue a restraining order or temporary or permanent injunction upon the ground that any of the persons participating or interested in a labor dispute constitute or are engaged in an unlawful combination or conspiracy because of the doing in concert of the acts enumerated in section 4 of this Act.

SEC. 6. No officer or member of any association or organization, and no association or organization participating or interested in a labor dispute, shall be held responsible or liable in any court of the United States for the unlawful acts of individual officers, members, or agents, except upon clear proof of actual participation in, or actual authorization of, such acts, or of ratification of such acts after actual knowledge thereof.

SEC. 7. No court of the United States shall have jurisdiction to issue a temporary or permanent injunction in any case involving or growing out of a labor dispute, as herein defined, except after hearing the testimony of witnesses in open court (with opportunity for cross-examination) in support of the allegations of a complaint made under oath, and testimony in opposition thereto, if offered, and except after findings of fact by the court, to the effect—

(a) That unlawful acts have been threatened and will be committed unless restrained or have been committed and will be continued unless restrained, but no injunction or temporary restraining order shall be issued on account of any threat or unlawful act excepting against the person or persons, association, or organization making the threat or committing the unlawful act or actually authorizing or ratifying the same after actual knowledge thereof;

(b) That substantial and irreparable injury to complainant's property will follow;

(c) That as to each item of relief granted greater injury will be inflicted upon complainant by the denial of relief than will be inflicted upon defendants by the granting of relief;

(d) That complainant has no adequate remedy at law; and

(e) That the public officers charged with the duty

to protect complainant's property are unable or unwilling to furnish adequate protection.

*   *   *

Approved, March 23, 1932.

215 "Government cannot be coerced by mob rule" (1932)

At the end of World War I, each veteran of military service received sixty dollars as a special gratuity. The veterans lobbied and demanded an additional bonus for the difference between military and civilian salaries during their service time. On May 19, 1924, President Coolidge signed the "adjusted compensation" bill under which each veteran received a certificate that would entitle him and his family to about five hundred dollars in 1945. In May 1932, somewhere between fifteen thousand and twenty-five thousand unemployed veterans formed the "Bonus Expeditionary Force," which encamped in Washington, D.C., demanding that Congress immediately honor the certificates. In mid-June, Congress failed to pass the necessary appropriation but authorized transportation funds for the men. About two-thirds left the city. On July 28 an uneasy President Hoover, fearing a communist-led insurrection, ordered federal troops to remove the remaining bonus marchers from federal property after the District of Columbia police failed in their attempt to do so. Chief of Staff Douglas MacArthur ordered an attack, led by Majors Dwight D. Eisenhower and George S. Patton and employing tanks, tear gas, machine guns, cavalry, and fixed bayonets. The demonstrators were routed; two veterans and two policemen were left dead. On January 24, 1936, Congress, over President Franklin D. Roosevelt's veto, passed a law providing for the exchange of the bonus certificates for cashable bonds.

☆ 215 The Bonus Army March on Washington

Reprinted in W. Myles, ed., *The State Papers and Other Public Writings of Herbert Hoover* (Garden City, N.Y.: Doubleday, Doran, 1934), 2:244-45.

☆ 215a President Hoover's Letter to Commissioner Reichelderfer

The White House, Washington
July 29, 1932

Honorable Luther H. Reichelderfer
Commissioner, District of Columbia
Washington, D.C.

MY DEAR MR. COMMISSIONER:

In response to your information that the police of the District were overwhelmed by an organized attack by several thousand men, and were unable to maintain law and order, I complied with your request for aid from the Army to the police. It is a matter of satisfaction that, after the arrival of this assistance, the mobs which were defying the municipal government were dissolved without the firing of a shot or the loss of a life.

I wish to call attention of the District Commissioners to the fact that martial law has not been declared; that responsibility for order still rests upon your commission and the police. The civil government of Washington must function uninterrupted. The Commissioners, through their own powers, should now deal with this question decisively.

It is the duty of the authorities of the District to at once find the instigators of this attack on the police and bring them to justice. It is obvious that, after the departure of the majority of the veterans, subversive influences obtained control of the men remaining in the District, a large part of whom were not veterans, secured repudiation of their elected leaders and inaugurated and organized this attack.

They were undoubtedly led to believe that the civil authorities could be intimidated with impunity because of attempts to conciliate by lax enforcement of city ordinances and laws in many directions. I shall expect the police to strictly enforce every ordinance of the District in every part of the city. I wish every violator of the law to be instantly arrested and prosecuted under due process of law.

I have requested the law enforcement agencies of the Federal Government to coöperate with the District authorities to this end.

There is no group, no matter what its origins, that can be allowed either to violate the laws of this city or to intimidate the Goverment.

Yours faithfully,

HERBERT HOOVER

☆ 215b President Hoover's Press Conference (July 20, 1932)

The President said:

A challenge to the authority of the United States Government has been met, swiftly and firmly.

After months of patient indulgence, the Government met overt lawlessness as it always must be met if the cherished processes of self-government are to be preserved. We cannot tolerate the abuse of Constitutional rights by those who would destroy all government, no matter who they may be. Government cannot be coerced by mob rule.

The Department of Justice is pressing its investigation into the violence which forced the call for Army detachments, and it is my sincere hope that those agitators who inspired yesterday's attack upon the Federal authority may be brought speedily to trial in the civil courts. There can be no safe harbor in the United States of America for violence.

Order and civil tranquillity are the first requisites in the great task of economic reconstruction to which our whole people now are devoting their heroic and noble energies. This national effort must not be retarded in even the slightest degree by organized lawlessness. The first obligation of my office is to uphold and defend the Constitution and the authority of the law. This I propose always to do.

216 "oil and gas producers . . . in a state of insurrection" (1932)

The power of the United States president or a state governor to declare martial law in response to public disorder has not been subject to much judicial review. In 1932, the governor of Texas proclaimed martial law over several oil-producing counties to stop wasteful production. Without denying that a state governor had the power to declare martial law, the Supreme Court held that the propriety of the exercise of that power was subject to judicial scrutiny when private rights were in jeopardy. This judicial review could address the question of whether the facts justified an exertion of a military power. Another thread of political criminality running through this document is the attempt by the lawfully constituted state officials, Governor Sterling and General Wolters, to defy the orders of the federal district court.

☆ 216 *Sterling v. Constantin*

287 U.S. 378 (1932).

MR. CHIEF JUSTICE HUGHES delivered the opinion of the Court.

*   *   *

In August, 1931, the Legislature of Texas passed an amended oil and conservation act. The Governor in issuing his proclamation of August 16th recited the provisions of the constitution and statutes of Texas for the conservation of oil and gas and the existence in the East Texas oil field, the territory in question, of an organized group of oil and gas producers who were said to be in a state of insurrection against the conservation laws; that the civil officers did not have a sufficient force to compel them to obey; that by reason of their reckless production enormous physical waste was being created; that this condition had brought about such a state of public feeling that if the state government could not protect the public's interest they would take the law into their own hands; that this condition had caused threats of acts of violence; that it was necessary to give the Railroad Commission time to have hearings and promulgate proper orders to put the law into force; that a state of "insurrection, tumult, riot and breach of the

peace existed in the defined area" and that there was "serious danger threatening to citizens and property, not only there, but in other oil producing areas of the State"; and that it was necessary "that the reckless and illegal exploitation" should be stopped until such time as the said resources might be properly conserved and developed under the protection of the civil authorities. The troops were then called out and the oil wells were shut down. In September, after the Commission had made its order limiting production, while the proclamation of martial law was not rescinded nor the troops entirely withdrawn, the military occupation in force ended. The wells were opened and continued to produce daily under the order of the Railroad Commission. General Wolters, with the assistance of the "Rangers," the civil officers of the community, and "the few military still remaining in the field," and in aid of the Commission, patrolled the territory to see that its orders were complied with; that from time to time the Commission, sometimes with the approval, and sometimes with the disapproval, of the Governor made its orders further limiting production, and these orders were obeyed.

[Complainants filed suit against the Railroad Commission and secured a temporary restraining order against the production limits. The Commission obeyed the order.]

[A]fter the restraining order against the Commission had been issued in this suit, the defendants, Governor Sterling and General Wolters, "determined not to brook court interference with the program of restricted production which they determined to continue." . . . [T]hey "ousted the Commission from the fixing of and superintendence over the daily production allowed, and have since controlled production by purported military orders."

As to the actual conditions in the area affected by these orders the District Court made the following finding:

"It was conceded that at no time has there been any actual uprising in the territory. At no time has any military force been exerted to put riots or mobs down. At no time, except in the refusal of defendant Wolters to observe the injunction in this case, have the civil authorities or courts been interfered with or their processes made impotent. Though it was testified to by defendants that from reports which came to them they believed that, if plaintiff's wells were not shut in, there would be dynamiting of property in the oil fields, and efforts to close them and any others which opened by violence, and that, if that occurred, there would be general trouble in the field, no evidence of any dynamite having been used, or show of violence practiced or actually attempted, or even threatened against any specific property in the field, was offered. We find, therefore, that not only was there never any actual riot, tumult, or insurrection, which would create a state of war existing in the field, but that, if all of the conditions had come to pass, they would have resulted merely in breaches of the peace to be suppressed by the militia as a civil force, and not at all in a condition constituting, or even remotely resembling, a state of war."

* * *

... As the State has no more important interest than the maintenance of law and order, the power it confers upon its Governor as Chief Executive and Commander in Chief of its military forces to suppress insurrection and to preserve the peace is of the highest consequence. The determinations that the Governor makes within the range of that authority have all the weight which can be attributed to state action, and they must be viewed in the light of the object to which they may properly be addressed and with full recognition of its importance. It is with appreciation of the gravity of such an issue that the governing principles have been declared.

By virtue of his duty to "cause the laws to be faithfully executed," the Executive is appropriately vested with the discretion to determine whether an exigency requiring military aid for that purpose has arisen. His decision to that effect is conclusive. That construction, this Court has said, in speaking of the power constitutionally conferred by the Congress upon the President to call the militia into actual service, "necessarily results from the nature of the power itself, and from the manifest object contemplated." The power "is to be exercised upon sudden emergencies, upon great occasions of state, and under circumstances which may be vital to the existence of the Union." Similar effect, for corresponding reasons, is ascribed to the exercise by the Governor of a State of his discretion in calling out its military forces to suppress insurrection and disorder. The nature of the power also necessarily implies that there is a permitted range of honest judgment as to the measures to be taken in meeting force with force, in suppressing violence and restoring order, for without such liberty to make immediate decisions, the power itself would be useless. Such measures, conceived in good faith, in the face of the emergency and directly related to the quelling of the disorder or the prevention of its continuance, fall within the discretion of the Executive in the exercise of his authority to maintain peace....

It does not follow from the fact that the Executive has this range of discretion, deemed to be a necessary incident of his power to suppress disorder, that every sort of action the Governor may take, no matter how unjustified by the exigency or subversive of private right and the jurisdiction of the courts, otherwise available, is conclusively supported by mere executive fiat. The contrary is well established. What are the allowable limits of military discretion, and whether or not they have been overstepped in a particular case, are judicial questions....

We need not undertake to determine the intended significance of the expression "martial law," and all its possible connotations, as it was employed in the Governor's proclamation.... The question before us is simply with respect to the Governor's attempt to regulate by executive order the lawful use of complainant's properties in the production of oil. ... The assertion that such action can be taken as conclusive proof of its own necessity and must be accepted as in itself due process of law has no support in the decisions of this Court.

Appellant's contentions find their appropriate answer in what was said by this Court in *Ex Parte Milligan*, a statement as applicable to the military authority of the State in the case of insurrection as to the military authority of the Nation in time of war:

"... Martial law established [at the discretion of executive authority] destroys every guarantee of the Constitution, and effectually renders the military independent of and superior to the civil power. ... Civil liberty and this kind of martial law cannot endure together; the antagonism is irreconcilable; and, in the conflict, one or the other must perish."

* * *

In the present case, the findings of fact made by the District Court are fully supported by the evidence. They leave no room for doubt that there was no military necessity which, from any point of view, could be taken to justify the action of the Governor in attempting to limit complainants' oil production, otherwise lawful. Complainants had a constitutional right to resort to the federal court to have the validity of the Commission's orders judicially determined. There was no exigency which justified the Governor in attempting to enforce by executive or military order the restriction which the District Judge had restrained pending proper judicial inquiry. If it be assumed that the Governor was entitled to declare a state of insurrection and to bring military force to the aid of civil authority, the proper use of that power in this instance was to maintain the federal court in the exercise of its jurisdiction and not to attempt to override it; to aid in making its process effective and not to nullify it; to remove, and not to create, obstructions to the exercise by the complainants of their rights as judicially declared....

The judgment of the District Court is affirmed.

217 "The San Francisco *débacle*" (1934)

In 1934, a general strike failed to materialize in San Francisco. The general strike was practically unknown in the United States, although it had been a powerful weapon in the hands of European labor. General strikes were instrumental in winning universal manhood suffrage in Belgium, in stopping the use of troops to break up strikes in Italy, and in the issuance of the liberal Czarist October Manifesto (1905) in Russia. In more recent times the general strike, as a tool of political protest, spread particularly to the Middle East and Latin America.

In this article, "The Revolutionary Logic of the General Strike," Wilfred H. Crook argued that whether economic, political, or revolutionary, the general strike tended to overthrow constituted political authority and supplant it with *de facto* government by the workers. It was perhaps this feature of labor power which caused the instruments of government to concern themselves with labor's revolutionary rather than economic potential.

☆ 217 The Revolutionary Logic of the General Strike

Wilfred H. Crook, *American Political Science Review* 28 (1934): 655-63.

THE REVOLUTIONARY LOGIC OF THE GENERAL STRIKE

Spanish and Cuban events during the past three years, and the recent labor disputes on the Pacific coast, have once again brought the general strike into the limelight. The abdication of King Alphonso and the flight of President Machado showed the potentialities of a successful general strike when labor faces the revolutionary logic of that weapon. The San Francisco *débacle* proved the futility of that method when labor refuses to admit its revolutionary implications.

. . . The writer is concerned in this article with exposing the implicit revolutionary logic contained in even the most peaceable general strike.

In every general strike, organized labor sets up a dual or rival government, by the purposeful and general cessation of its normal functions. When workers in a single trade or industry go on strike, this revolutionary logic is seldom involved, unless a vital public service is affected, such as the police force or hospital and medical service. It is when a strike takes on the gravity of a general cessation of work that it contains a tacit challenge to the continued functioning of social life and thereby brings in against it the forces of the existing government. It is then that an incipient rival government can be found, no matter

how orderly the strike may be, nor how fervently its leaders proclaim their non-political aims.

*   *   *

For purposes of discussion, the writer has classified general strikes, so defined, into three types, (1) economic, (2) political, and (3) revolutionary. . . . The economic general strike is, in its inception, a protest against some real or imagined economic injustice to fellow workers. . . . [A] real distinction is made by strike leaders themselves between the *political* general strike, which "directs its efforts against the State," yet "does not seek to transform society, but rather to make the political masters yield," and the *revolutionary* general strike, in which the leaders aim from the outset to introduce confusion into the life of the State and overthrow the existing order. . . .

It would be superfluous, by the very definitions used above, to argue the existence of a rival government where a revolutionary general strike is concerned. . . . It is not so simple a matter to prove the implicit revolutionary logic behind the political general strike. . . .

. . . Despite the careful limitation . . . set to the use of the general strike as a political weapon, in many, if not in all, such strikes there can be found an undercurrent of criticism of the existing form of government, with the implication that stronger, perhaps even more revolutionary, methods would be used if the more orderly political strike should fail.

*   *   *

It is far more difficult to prove the economic general strike revolutionary in its basic logic. . . . The economic general strike grows out of a smaller dispute, where it is possible to make very clear to vast numbers of workers in other industries the economic injustice involved in the original struggle. A sympathy strike of this type calls for more undiluted sacrifice by all workers not concerned in the original dispute, for in this type of general strike the vast majority stand to lose a great deal in wages and insecurity of employment, but to gain nothing for themselves, not even the right to vote. The issue, therefore, must so clearly appeal to all wage-workers as to approach closely to the issue of the class struggle.

The purpose underlying an economic general strike . . . [is] to force the general public, who are not taking part in the strike, to become umpires between the ranks of striking workers on the one side and the massed forces of capital and the government on the other. . . .

The leaders of an economic general strike do not have to act as if they felt themselves to be a rival government. It is enough that the strike orders, given by them to the labor ranks, should in effect select the essential public services that shall continue to function. To discover the rival government in action, it is therefore necessary to turn to the interpretation of the general strike orders by the ranks of labor. Evidence will be found most abundantly in the granting or withholding of permits to work issued by the various strike committees, and in the conception of their own function held by those committees.

Four outstanding examples of a strictly economic general strike provide ample data for the discussion in hand, occurring in Sweden in 1909, in Seattle and Winnipeg in 1919, and in Great Britain in 1926....

*   *   *

In Seattle, a startling editorial appeared in the daily labor paper, the *Union Record*, shortly before the strike broke out: "Labor will feed the people! Twelve great kitchens have been offered, and from them food will be distributed by the provision trades at low cost to all. Labor will care for the babies and the sick!... Not the withdrawal of labor, but the power of the strikers to manage, will win this strike. Labor will not only shut down the industries, but labor will reopen, under the management of the appropriate trades, such activities as are needed to preserve public health and public peace. If the strike continues, labor may feel led to avoid public suffering by reopening more and more activities, under its own management."

City firemen were instructed to stay at their posts, garbage-wagon drivers were told to collect garbage, but to leave ashes and paper. Auto drivers might drive the mail and answer emergency calls for funerals and hospitals, if those calls were made through the office of their trade union. A police force of unarmed war veterans was organized to aid the strike committee in the preservation of order.

Popular recognition of the de facto government of the strike committee was evident, the *Nation* reported: "Before the committee appeared a long succession of business men, city officials, and the mayor himself, not to threaten or bully, but to discuss the situation and ask the approval of the committee for this or that step...."

During a speaking tour in the East, Mayor Ole Hanson declared of the struggle in his city: "The general strike, as practised in Seattle, is of itself the weapon of revolution, all the more dangerous because quiet. To succeed, it must suspend everything; stop the entire life stream of a community. That is to say, it puts the government out of operation. And that is all there is revolt, no matter how achieve."

*   *   *

The greatest economic general strike in labor history occurred in Great Britain in May, 1926, the result of long-standing troubles in the coal-mining industry. Responsible leaders of the general council of the Trades Union Congress emphatically denied that they were attacking either the government or the general public. Constantly the strike sheet, the *Daily Worker*, emphasized the purely industrial aspect of the dispute. Nevertheless, the same evidence of the existence of a rival government can be found in the acts of the various strike committees .

The Rt. Hon. Winston Churchill declared that British labor was prepared with a scheme for paralyzing the nation. Nothing was farther from the truth. The government itself was thoroughly prepared and at least two strong citizens' groups had been organized to meet the general strike peril many weeks before it occurred. Labor alone was appallingly unready to face the logic of its action. Its plans were in chaos until two days before the strike actually commenced. Even then, a further forty-eight hours were required to untangle the maze of orders and counter-orders issued from the London headquarters of the strike.

The London labor leaders offered to run enough trains and road transportation to feed the nation, a sample of their refusal to face the problems of a really effective general strike, and yet in itself a significant instance of their tacit assumption of authority. Churchill's reply indicated that the government, of which he was an important part, had no illusions as to such an offer. "What government in the world," he asked, "could enter into a partnership with a rival government, against which it is endeavoring to defend itself and society, and allow that rival government to sit in judgment on every train that runs and on every lorry on the road?

*   *   *

The common attitude of the strike committees toward their own function during the strike can best be seen in a naïve comment of a strike-leader in one of Arnold Bennett's *Five Towns*. Referring to the employers who were coming to the strike committee "cap in hand" to ask for permits to move their goods, he said: "Most of them turned empty away after a most humiliating experience, for one and all were put through a stern questioning, just to make them realize that we and not they were the salt of the earth."

The British government and the press promptly raised the issue of "civil war," and the government organ, the *British Gazette*, spoke glibly of the strikers as "the enemy." Yet no impartial student of the British national strike can question that the vast majority of the strike leaders had not the slightest desire to overthrow the existing form of government, A. J. Cook, the radical leader of the miners, notwithstanding. At the same time no student can doubt that the orders of the the strike leaders, as interpreted and practised by the local strike committees and the ranks of the strikers, did logically constitute an attempt to set up a rival authority to that of the legitimate local and national governing bodies. If that contention be granted in the case of so peaceable an economic general strike, it would seem that the revolutionary logic of all three types of the general strike has been proved.

*   *   *

It seems, therefore, that in these days a successful general strike in Western civilization is likely to occur only where the labor forces have faced the full revolutionary logic of that weapon, and where the ruling class or the government has at the same time remained so blind to progress and so unjust to the masses of the people that anything, even revolution, is preferable. Even at that, success in the use of the weapon demands that the cause be so clear that most of the citizens outside the ranks of labor, and the majority of the military and naval forces, express strong sympathy with the strikers. This was evidently the situation in the recent Spanish and Cuban general strikes, where the revolutionary aim of the method was successfully achieved.

218 "the right to organize for its common welfare" (1934)

Both the individual and the communal political rights of the Native Americans finally stabilized during the post-World War I era as the earlier policies of ethnocide through assimilation proved ineffective in eliminating their culture. In 1924, Congress granted United States citizenship to all Native Americans in the United States, whether they wanted it or not. Congress had long wavered between policies encouraging tribalism and those supporting assimilation. In 1934 the Indian Reorganization Act reestablished the Native Americans' right to limited self-determination, permitting the tribes to reorganize as corporate entities for their collective benefit.

☆ 218 The Indian Reorganization Act

48 Stat. 984 (1934).

Be it enacted by the Senate and House of Representatives of the United States of America in Congress assembled, That hereafter no land of any Indian reservation, created or set apart by treaty or agreement with the Indians, Act of Congress, Executive order, purchase, or otherwise, shall be allotted in severalty to any Indian.

*   *   *

SEC. 15. Nothing in this Act shall be construed to impair or prejudice any claim or suit or any Indian tribe against the United States. It is hereby declared to be the intent of Congress that no expenditures for the benefit of Indians made out of appropriations authorized by this Act shall be considered as offsets in any suit brought to recover upon any claim of such Indians against the United States.

SEC. 16. Any Indian tribe, or tribes, residing on the same reservation, shall have the right to organize for its common welfare, and may adopt an appropriate constitution and bylaws, which shall become effective when ratified by a majority vote of the adult members of the tribe, or of the adult Indians residing on such reservation, as the case may be, at a special election authorized and called by the Secretary of the Interior under such rules and regulations as he may prescribe. Such constitution and bylaws when ratified as aforesaid and approved by the Secretary of the Interior shall be revocable by an election open to the same voters and conducted in the same manner as hereinabove provided. Amendments to the constitution and bylaws may be ratified and approved by the Secretary in the same manner as the original constitution and bylaws.

In addition to all powers vested in any Indian tribe or tribal council by existing law, the constitution adopted by said tribe shall also vest in such tribe or its tribal council the following rights and powers: To employ legal counsel, the choice of counsel and fixing fees to be subject to the approval of the Secretary of the Interior; to prevent the sale, disposition, lease, or encumbrance of tribal lands, interests in lands, or other tribal assets without the consent of the tribe; and to negotiate with the Federal, State, and local Governments. The Secretary of the Interior shall advise such tribe or its tribal counsel of all appropriation estimates or Federal projects for the benefit of the tribe prior to the submission of such estimates to the Bureau of the Budget and the Congress.

SEC. 17. The Secretary of the Interior may, upon petition by at least one-third of the adult Indians, issue a charter of incorporation to such tribe: *Provided*, That such charter shall not become operative until ratified at a special election by a majority vote of the adult Indians living on the reservation. Such charter may convey to the incorporated tribe the power to purchase, take by gift, or bequest, or otherwise, own, hold, manage, operate, and dispose of property of every description, real and personal, including the power to purchase restricted Indian lands and to issue in exchange therefor interests in corporate property, and such further powers as may be incidental to the conduct of corporate business, not inconsistent with law, but no authority shall be granted to sell, mortgage, or lease for a period exceeding ten years any of the land included in the limits of the reservation. Any charter so issued shall not be revoked or surrendered except by Act of Congress.

SEC. 18. This Act shall not apply to any reservation wherein a majority of the adult Indians, voting at a special election duly called by the Secretary of the Interior, shall vote against its application. It shall be the duty of the Secretary of the Interior, within one year after passage and approval of this Act, to call such an election, which election shall be held by secret ballot upon thirty days' notice.

SEC. 19. The term "Indian" as used in this Act shall include all persons of Indian descent who are members of any recognized Indian tribe now under Federal jurisdiction, and all persons who are descendants of such members who were, on June 1, 1934, residing within the present boundaries of any Indian reservation, and shall further include all other persons of one-half or more Indian blood. For the purpose of this Act, Eskimos and other aboriginal peoples of Alaska shall be considered Indians. The term "tribe" wherever used in this Act shall be construed to refer to any Indian tribe, organized band, pueblo, or the Indians residing on one reservation. The words "adult Indians" wherever used in this Act shall be construed to refer to Indians who have attained the age of twenty-one years.

*   *   *

Approved, June 18, 1934.

219 "strikes and other forms of industrial strife" (1935)

With the passage of the National Industrial Recovery Act (NIRA) which, among other things, legalized union organization and collective bargaining, labor disputes increased dramatically. The Bureau of Labor Statistics reported a fivefold increase from 1932 to 1933. The 1933-34 New Deal strikers were concerned primarily with union recognition rather than disputes over wages, hours, and working conditions. The wave of unrest which began in 1933 continued into 1935. That year the NIRA was held unconstitutional. Congress reacted by passing the National Labor Relations Act (NLRA), popularly known as the Wagner Act after its chief sponsor. The NLRA was designed to guarantee workers' rights to associate, organize, and choose representatives to negotiate with management. To this end, it defined employer actions hindering organization as unfair labor practices and created an independent agency, the National Labor Relations Board, to conduct secret ballot elections by employees, settle controversies regarding union representation, oversee collective bargaining, investigate unfair labor practices, and issue cease and desist orders to restrain them. The selected sections of the act convey the flavor of the legislation placing governmental authority behind the rights of workers. The Supreme Court upheld the NLRA as constitutional in *NLRB v. Jones & Laughlin Steel Corp.*, 301 U.S. 1 (1937).

Whereas previously only the acts of workers were subject to government sanction, this act positions the federal government as an overseer of management tactics as well. Importantly, these new declarations of public authority were placed largely outside the reach of a judiciary that was still perceived by many as promanagement. Altogether, the government was now viewed as a referee rather than a participant in labor-management conflicts.

☆ 219 The National Labor Relations Act (The Wagner Act)

49 Stat. 449 (1935).

Be it enacted by the Senate and House of Representatives of the United States of American in Congress assembled,

FINDINGS AND POLICY

SECTION 1. The denial by employers of the right of employees to organize and the refusal by employers to accept the procedure of collective bargaining lead to strikes and other forms of industrial strife, or unrest, which have the intent or the necessary effect of burdening or obstructing [interstate] commerce....

The inequality of bargaining power between employees who do not possess full freedom of association or actual liberty of contract, and employers who are organized in the corporate or other forms of ownership association substantially burdens and affects the flow of [interstate] commerce, and tends to aggravate recurrent business depressions, by depressing wage rates and the purchasing power of wage earners in industry and by preventing the stabilization of competitive wage rates and working conditions within and between industries.

Experience has proved that protection by law of the right of employees to organize and bargain collectively safeguards commerce from injury, impairment, or interruption, and promotes the flow of [interstate] commerce by removing certain recognized sources of industrial strife and unrest, by encouraging practices fundamental to the friendly adjustment of industrial disputes arising out of differences as to wages, hours, or other working conditions, and by restoring equality of bargaining power between employers and employees.

It is hereby declared to be the policy of the United States to eliminate the causes of certain substantial obstructions to the free flow of [interstate] commerce and to mitigate and eliminate these obstructions when they have occurred by encouraging the practice and procedure of collective bargaining and by protecting the exercise by workers of full freedom of association, self-organization, and designation of representatives of their own choosing, for the purpose of negotiating the terms and conditions of their employment or other mutual aid or protection.

*   *   *

RIGHTS OF EMPLOYEES

SEC. 7. Employees shall have the right to self-organization, to form, join, or assist labor organizations, to bargain collectively through representatives of their own choosing, and to engage in concerted activities, for the purpose of collective bargaining or other mutual aid or protection.

SEC. 8. It shall be an unfair labor practice for an employer—

(1) To interfere with, restrain, or coerce employees in the exercise of the rights guaranteed in section 7.

(2) To dominate or interfere with formation or administration of any labor organization or contribute financial or other support to it: *Provided,* That subject to rules and regulations made and published by the Board . . . , an employer shall not be prohibited from permitting employees to confer with him during working hours without loss of time or pay.

(3) By discrimination in regard to hire or tenure of employment or any term or condition of employment to encourage or discourage membership in any labor organization: *Provided,* That nothing in this Act, or in the National Industrial Recovery Act . . . or in any other statute of the United States, shall preclude an employer from making an agreement with a labor organization . . . to require as a condition of employment membership therein, if such labor organization is the representative of the employees as provided in section 9 (a), in the appropriate collective bargaining unit covered by such agreement when made.

(4) To discharge or otherwise discriminate against an employee because he has filed charges or given testimony under this Act.

(5) To refuse to bargain collectively with the representatives of his employees. . . .

*   *   *

LIMITATIONS

SEC. 13. Nothing in this Act shall be construed so as to interfere with or impede or diminish in any way the right to strike.

*   *   *

Approved, July 5, 1935.

220 "combined resistance to the lawful authority of the State" (1936)

The 1930s reflected a renewed concern with the spread of alien doctrines and political activities in the United States. While the initial attention was directed towards communism, other forms of totalitarianism—fascism and nazism—later gave rise to governmental concern. Efforts to organize whites and blacks in Georgia in the name of the Communist party resulted in Angelo Herndon's indictment and conviction in the state courts. His sentence was eighteen to twenty years' imprisonment. On appeal, the United States Supreme Court reversed the conviction and held the Georgia insurrection statute violated protections of the Fourteenth Amendment.

☆ 220 *Herndon v. Lowry*

301 U.S. 242 (1936).

MR. JUSTICE ROBERTS delivered the opinion of the Court.

*   *   *

. . . The charge was founded on § 56 of the Penal Code, one of four related sections. Section 55 defines insurrection, § 56 defines an attempt to incite insurrection, § 57 prescribes the death penalty for conviction of the offenses described in the two preceding sections unless the jury shall recommend mercy, and § 58 penalizes, by imprisonment, the introduction and circulation of printed matter for the purpose of inciting insurrection, riot, conspiracy, etc. The sections are copied in the margin.[1]

The appellant was brought to trial and convicted. He appealed on the ground that, under the statute as construed by the trial court in its instructions to the jury, there was no evidence to sustain a verdict of guilty.

*   *   *

The evidence on which the judgment rests consists of appellant's admissions and certain documents found in his possession. The appellant told the state's officers that some time prior to his arrest he joined the Communist Party in Kentucky and later came to Atlanta as a paid organizer for the party, his duties being to call meetings, to educate and disseminate information respecting the party, to distribute literature, to secure members, and to work up an organization of the party in Atlanta; and that he had held or attended three meetings called by him. He made no further admission as to what he did as an organizer, or what he said or did at the meetings. When arrested he carried a box containing documents. After he was arrested he conducted the officers to his room where additional documents and bundles of newspapers and periodicals were found, which he stated were sent him from the headquarters of the Communist Party in New York. He gave the names of persons who were members of the organization in Atlanta, and stated he had only five or six actual members at the time of his apprehension. The stubs of membership books found in the box indicated he had enrolled more members than he stated. There was no evidence that he had distributed any of the material carried on his person and found in his room, or had taken any of it to meetings, save two circulars or appeals respecting county relief which are confessedly innocuous.

... Certain documents in his possession when he was arrested were placed in evidence. They fall into five classes: first, receipt books showing receipts of small sums of money, pads containing certificates of contributions to the Communist Party's Presidental Election Campaign Fund, receipts for rent of a post office box, and Communist Party membership books; secondly, printed matter consisting of magazines, pamphlets, and copies of the "Daily Worker," styled the "Central Organ of the Communist Party," and the "Southern Worker," also, apparently, an official newspaper of the party; thirdly, two books, one "Life and Struggles of Negro Toilers," by George Padmore, and the other "Communism and Christianism Analyzed and Contrasted from the Marxian and Darwinian Points of View" by Rt. Rev. William Montgomery Brown, D. D.; fourthly, transcripts of minutes of meetings apparently held in Atlanta; fifthly, two circulars, one of which was prepared by the appellant and both of which had been circulated by him in Fulton County. All of these may be dismissed as irrelevant except those falling within the first and second groups. No inference can be drawn from the possession of the books mentioned, either that they embodied the doctrines of the Communist Party or that they represented views advocated by the appellant. The minutes of meetings contain nothing indicating the purposes of the organization or any intent to overthrow organized government; on the contrary, they indicate merely discussion of relief for the unemployed. The two circulars, admittedly distributed by the appellant, had nothing to do with the Communist Party, its aims or purposes, and were not appeals to join the party but were concerned with unemployment relief in the county and included appeals to the white and negro unemployed to organize and represent the need for further county aid. They were characterized by the Supreme Court of Georgia as "more or less harmless."

*   *   *

The matter appearing upon the membership blanks is innocent upon its face however foolish and pernicious the aims it suggests. Under the heading "What is the Communist Party?" this appears:

"The Party is the vanguard of the working class and consists of the best, most class conscious, most active, the most courageous members of that class. It incorporates the whole body of experience of the proletarian struggle, basing itself upon the revolutionary theory of Marxism and representing the general and lasting interests of the whole of the working class, the Party personifies the unity of proletarian principles, of proletarian will and of proletarian revolutionary action.

"We are the Party of the working class. Consequently, nearly the whole of that class (in time of war and civil war, the whole of that class) should work under the guidance of our Party, should create the closest contacts with our Party."

This vague declaration falls short of an attempt to bring about insurrection either immediately or within a reasonable time but amounts merely to a statement of ultimate ideals. The blanks, however, indicate more specific aims for which members of the Communist Party are to vote. They are to vote Communist for

"1. Unemployment and Social Insurance at the expense of the State and employers.

"2. Against Hoover's wage-cutting policy.

"3. Emergency relief for the poor farmers without restrictions by the government and banks; exemption of poor farmers from taxes and from forced collection of rents or debts.

"4. Equal rights for the Negroes and self-determination for the Black Belt.

"5. Against capitalistic terror: against all forms of suppression of the political rights of the workers.

"6. Against imperialist war; for the defense of the Chinese people and of the Soviet Union."

None of these aims is criminal upon its face....

*   *   *

Section 56, under which the indictment is laid, makes no reference to force or violence except by the phrase "combined resistance to the lawful authority of the State."...

To ascertain how the Act is held to apply to the appellant's conduct we turn to the rulings of the state courts in his case. The trial court instructed the jury: "In order to convict the defendant, ... it must appear clearly by the evidence that immediate serious violence against the State of Georgia was to be expected or advocated." The jury rendered a verdict of guilty....

*   *   *

The appellant had a constitutional right to address meetings and organize parties unless in so doing he violated some prohibition of a valid statute. The only prohibition he is said to have violated is that of § 56 forbidding incitement or attempted incitement to insurrection by violence. If the evidence fails to show that he did so incite, then, as applied to him, the statute unreasonably limits freedom of speech and freedom of assembly and violates the Fourteenth Amendment. We are of opinion that requisite proof is lacking. From what has been said above with respect to the evidence offered at the trial it is apparent that the documents found upon the appellant's person were certainly, as to some of the aims stated therein, innocent and consistent with peaceful action for a change in the laws or the constitution. The proof wholly fails to show that the appellant had read these documents; that he had distributed any of them; that he believed and advocated any or all of the principles and aims set forth in them, or that those he had procured to become members of the party knew or approved of any of these documents.

* * *

Reversed.

[1.] Insurrection shall consist in any combined resistance to the lawful authority of the State, with intent to the denial thereof, when the same is manifested or intended to be manifested by acts of violence. . . .

221 " 'mob or riotous assemblage' " (1937)

The atrocious murder of two blacks by a mob at Duck Hill, Mississippi, on April 13, 1937, rekindled national concern for the quality of justice for blacks in the South. A sheriff was transporting two black prisoners accused of the murder of a country merchant to the county jail when a mob forced him to surrender them. They took the two prisoners to the scene of the murder, lashed them, tied them to trees, tortured them with blow torches, riddled them with bullets, and burned them.

The antilynching bill introduced by New York congressman Joseph Gavagan passed the House but failed in the Senate owing to a Southern filibuster founded on states' rights arguments. The proposed law would have imposed penalties upon the political subdivision in which a lynching occurred as well as upon delinquent peace officers. Later antilynching bills sought direct punitive action against members of the mob.

☆ 221 The Gavagan Antilynching Bill

H.R. 1507, 75th Cong., 1st Sess. (1973).

An Act. To assure to persons within the jurisdiction of every State the equal protection of the laws, and to punish the crime of lynching.

Be it enacted by the Senate and House of Representatives of the United States of America in Congress assembled, That, for the purposes of this Act, the phrase "mob or riotous assemblage," when used in this Act, shall mean an assemblage composed of three or more persons acting on concert, without authority of law, to kill or injure any person in the custody of any peace officer, with the purpose or consequence of depriving such person of due process of law or the equal protection of the laws.

SEC. 2. If any State or governmental subdivision thereof fails, neglects, or refuses to provide and maintain protection to the life or person of any individual within its jurisdiction against a mob or riotous assemblage, whether by way of preventing or punishing the acts thereof, such State shall by reason of such failure, neglect, or refusal be deemed to have denied to such person due process of law and the equal protection of the laws of the State, and to the end that the protection guaranteed to persons within the jurisdiction of the several States, or to citizens of the United States, by the Constitution of the United States, may be secured, the provisions of this Act are enacted.

SEC. 3. (a) Any officer or employee of any State or governmental subdivision thereof who is charged with the duty or who possesses the power or authority as such officer or employee to protect the life or person of any individual injured or put to death by any mob or riotous assemblage or any officer or employee of any State or governmental subdivision thereof having any such individual in his custody, who fails, neglects, or refuses to make all diligent efforts to protect such individual from being so injured or being put to death, or any officer or employee or any State or governmental subdivision thereof charged with the duty of apprehending, keeping in custody, or prosecuting any person participating in such mob or riotous assemblage who fails, neglects, or refuses to make all diligent efforts to perform his duty in apprehending, keeping in custody, or prosecuting to final judgment under the, laws of such State all persons so participating, shall be guilty of a felony, and upon conviction thereof shall be punished by a fine not exceeding $5,000 or by imprisonment not exceeding five years, or by both such fine and imprisonment.

* * *

SEC. 4. The District Court of the United States judicial district wherein the person is injured or put to death by a mob or riotous assemblage shall have jurisdiction to try and to punish, in accordance with the laws of the State where the injury is inflicted or the homicide is committed, any and all persons who participate therein: *Provided*, that it is first made to appear to such court (1) that the officers of the State charged with the duty of apprehending, prosecuting, and punishing such offenders under the laws of the State shall have failed, neglected, or refused to apprehend, prosecute, or punish such offenders; or (2) that the jurors obtainable for service in the State court having jurisdiction of the offense are so strongly opposed to such punishment that there is probability that those guilty of the offense will not be punished in such State court. A failure for more than thirty days after commission of such an offense to apprehend or to indict the persons guilty thereof, or a failure diligently to prosecute such persons, shall be sufficient to constitute prima face evidence of the failure, neglect, or refusal described in the above proviso.

SEC. 5. Any county in which a person is seriously injured or put to death by a mob or riotous assemblage shall be liable to the injured person or the legal representatives of such person for a sum not less than $2,000 nor more than $10,000 as liquidated damages, which sum may be recovered in a civil action against such county in the United States District Court of the judicial district wherein such person is put to the injury or death. . . .

SEC. 6. In the event that any person so put to death shall have been transported by such mob or riotous assemblage from one county to another county during the time intervening between his seizure and putting to death, the country in which he is seized and the county in which he is put to death shall be jointly and severally liable to pay the forfeiture herein provided. . . .

Passed the House of Representatives, April 15, 1937.

222 "Obeying the Rules" (1937)

The Congress of Industrial Organizations (CIO) adopted the sit-down strike as a technique to organize workers in mass production industries. The label "sit-down" derived from the method employed—strikers quit working and "sat" at their work stations until management met their demands. Between September 1936 and May 1937, sit-down strikes proliferated, and as many as 485,000 male and female workers remained in plants, eating food supplied by outside friends and relatives and sleeping in makeshift quarters. Charged with trespassing, the strikers asserted that human rights came first. The following account was printed in a publication of the socialist-oriented League for Industrial Democracy.

☆ 222 Sit Down (1937)

Joel Seidman, *Sit Down* (New York: League for Industrial Democracy, 1937), 3, 5-19, 22-31.

*   *   *

When they tie the can to a union man,
    Sit down! Sit down!
When they give him the sack, they'll take him back,
    Sit down! Sit down!
            Chorus
Sit down, just take a seat,
Sit down, and rest your feet,
Sit down, you've got 'em beat.
    Sit down! Sit down!

A new strike technique has swept the country, arousing enthusiasm among workers, and bewilderment among employers. In industry after industry, in state after state, the workers remain at their posts but refuse to work. No longer is it possible to introduce strikebreakers, for the workers are in possession. Nor are the workers readily dispersed, for they can barricade themselves in a strong defensive position. If strikebreakers or police storm the factory gate, they are clearly responsible in the eyes of the public for whatever violence may occur. The employer cannot too easily afford to alienate public opinion, nor risk damage to his machinery. And so the workers remain in possession of the plant, in much more comfort and security than on the picket line. . . .

*   *   *

EARLY USES OF THE SIT-DOWN IN AMERICA

It is impossible to determine accurately when and where the sit-down strike was first used. It seems such a logical tactic for workers to employ that there are probably many unrecorded instances, each one short in duration, going back almost as far as our modern industrial civilization. The wonder is that its use did not become widespread much earlier.

*   *   *

KEEPING COMFORTABLE

Sit-downers have had a host of new problems to solve, not the least of which have been living in factory buildings. Food, sleeping quarters, and sanitation are matters that must be properly attended to if morale is to be kept up and health maintained for long. The necessary work must be done, and facilities for recreation provided. In all of these respects our experience with sit-downs, brief though it has been, is illuminating.

With hundreds or perhaps several thousands of sit-downers in a plant, the problem of food becomes urgent. The union must assume responsibility for seeing that the workers receive three meals a day. This is a severe strain on the union treasury, but thus far adequate meals have been furnished. Indeed, in some strikes most of the sit-downers have gained weight. One of the most important committees in many sit-down strikes is the chiseling committee, which seeks donations from food merchants. It calls for resourcefulness when the committee is unable to obtain the food for the menu as planned, and the cook must prepare whatever is brought back. The Midland Steel Products Company sit-downers in Detroit were aided by a daily donation of 30 gallons of milk by the milk drivers' union. Often the means furnished by the union are supplemented by food brought to individual strikers by their families or friends.

Usually the food is cooked in a nearby hall or restaurant, and brought in milk cans, kettles, or other large containers to the plant. In the case of the Wahl-Eversharp Pen Company of Chicago, police refused to allow friends of the strikers to bring food into the plant. The sit-downers then lowered a rope from an upper window to the roof of an adjoining bakery, and obtained food in this fashion. The menu of sit-downers is usually simple, but adequate. Barrels, kegs, and whatever else is suitable are used for chairs, and tables are likewise improvised. Newspapers sometimes serve as tablecloths. Liquor is strictly forbidden.

Usually the cooking is done by a committee of the strikers' wives. In large strikes, however, a professional cook may be obtained. The cook in the Flint strike, for example, was sent there to help by the Cooks' Union of Detroit. He had previously cooked for four other sit-down strikes. For the Flint strike the union installed new kitchen equipment worth more than $1,000.

"The food goes into the factories in twenty kettles of various sizes," the cook reported. "The amount of food the strikers use is immense. Five hundred pounds of meat, one thousand pounds of potatoes, three hundred loaves of bread, one hundred pounds of coffee, two hundred pounds of sugar, thirty gallons of fresh milk, four cases of evaporated milk!"

In Detroit a cooperative kitchen was established to feed 800 sit-down strikers in the Bohn Aluminum, Cadillac, and Fleetwood plants:

> The kitchen runs on efficient lines, not speed-up, in two shifts. About 50 men and women comprise the working crew; the first shift working from 7:00 until 2:00 in the afternoon, the second from 11:00 in the morning until 6:00 in the afternoon. Everyone attends the meetings held at 2:00 o'clock daily at I.A.S. Hall where the various committees make their reports. There is the kitchen committee, which takes care of preparing the food, with a chef from the Cooks' Union, Local No. 234, to supervise the preparation of it. Then there is a finance committee, with two treasurers, working in shifts, one from the Cadillac plant and one from the Bohn Aluminum plant.

Other important committees were the drivers' committee, which delivered the food, and the chiseling committee, which covered the city for donations of food or money. About two-thirds of the supplies were obtained in this fashion.

*   *   *

Most visitors to sit-down strikes have been impressed by the neatness of the men and the tidy appearance of the plants. One of the important jobs is to see that the factories are kept clean. The machinery is kept in good order, for the sit-downers wish to return to work as soon as possible after the strike ends. Often a former barber is found among the strikers, and he is made to resume his old trade. In the Kelsey-Hayes plant a wheelbarrow on a platform served as a barber chair. In one sit-down strike where there were women employees, a beauty parlor was opened for them by a former worker in such an establishment. Washing is often a problem, however, for in most plants only ordinary washbowls are available. One sit-down, in the Detroit plant of the Aluminum Company of America, had to be transformed into a walk-out because a number of the men became ill and lack of sufficient sanitary facilities made further stay in the plant hazardous to health.

OBEYING THE RULES

A certain amount of work is required, for meals must be served, the place kept clean, a watch kept, and discipline maintained....

*   *   *

Discipline and morale are of vital importance. Those who do not conform to the rules may be sentenced to extra clean-up duty for minor offenses, and ejected for serious violations. In the General Motors strike in Flint, court was held each morning, with bringing in liquor and circulating rumors the most frequent offenses. Elsewhere it may be overstaying leaves that is most frequently punished. In the Standard Cotton Products Company strike in Flint the judge himself was twice convicted of breaking the rules, and had to do extra dish washing as the penalty. Sometimes foremen and other company officials are allowed to converse only with union officers, for fear that they may adversely affect the strikers' morale. In some instances subterfuges have been employed by strikers or their wives in order to get out of the plant. Serious illness has been reported at home, or a birth in the family. Where too many such cases seemed to be reported a check was made, and the member immediately dropped. In some cases foremen have visited wives of sit-downers, making false reports of illness or hardships within the plant, in order to break down morale.

Except when trouble is feared, sit-downers are usually permitted to leave the plant for short intervals, under rules that they decide upon. In most cases they are required to return by a specified hour, and a check is made as they go and come. If an outside picket line is maintained as well, the strikers take turns staying within the plant. In one case a sit-downer who belonged to the National Guard was released for strike duty with the Guard.

Visitors are admitted only after a careful check of their credentials. Usually a pass signed by a responsible union officer is required. In many plants everyone who enters must submit to a search for weapons, and a similar search is made of all who leave. A communications system calls to the gate those who have visitors. A post office is sometimes set up to handle the mail, which may be censored. Gates and doors are often barricaded against a surprise attack, with guards on duty at all times. In Flint, sentries, in six-hour watches, were on duty twenty-four hours a day, with an alarm system to warn quickly of impending danger. Sometimes metal strips are welded across doorways and windows, to make police entry more difficult, and to provide protection from gas bombs and bullets. In some plants pickets assigned to make the rounds have had to punch the time clock as they went on or off duty.

*   *   *

Race relations may be another problem faced by sit-downers. In the Midland plant in Detroit both whites and negroes were employed. Workers of both races occupied the plant, and worked together in harmony throughout the strike.

*   *   *

A TYPICAL SET OF RULES

Sit-downers must govern their community, and solve each problem as it arises. Fundamentally these problems are similar, though new situations will arise in each plant. The rules adopted by the sit-down strikers in the Standard Cotton Products Company in Flint, Michigan, may be taken as fairly typical. With fewer than a hundred strikers, they were able to transact business in a full meeting held at 10 o'clock each morning, without the more complex and elaborate organization that a large plant would require. A strike committee of five members was placed in charge. Other officers included a chairman, a secretary, a judge, a press agent, and three clerks. There was a patrol committee of two, a food committee of two, a clean-up committee of three, and an entertainment committee of one.

Posted on the wall of the mess hall were the following rules, which were added to from time to time by majority vote:

Rules and Regulations

Rule No. 1. Any man who disturbes anyone while sleeping without good reason will have to wash the dishes and mop floor for one day.

Rule No. 2. Any man found drinking or looking for arguments will wash dishes and mop floor for one day — 1st offense.

Rule No. 3. Every man who leaves must get a pass from the committee and check with the clerk. Passes must be shown to the doorman when going in and out, and on returning must check with the clerk. The doorman must obey these rules very strictly.

Rule No. 4. Doormen answer the phone and if the call is important he calls a committee man. No long-distance calls shall be made. All local calls are allowed. No profane language used over phone.

Rule No. 5. When photographers or outsiders come in no one speaks to them but a committee man.

Rule No. 6. Everyone must line up single file before meals are served. Dishwashers will be appointed before each meal by the clean-up committee. Every man must serve his turn.

Rule No. 7. Anyone eating between meals must wash his own dishes.

Rule No. 8. Every man must attend meetings.

Rule No. 9. No standing on tables.

Rule No. 10. No passes will be issued after 12:00 P.M. — except emergency calls.

Rule No. 11. Judge's decision on all broken rules will be regarded as final.

Rule No. 12. No conversation about the strike to the management. Any information concerning the strike will be furnished by the committee.

Rule No. 13. No more than a two-hour grace period allowed on passes. No grace period on a 20-minute leave.

Rule No. 14. No women allowed in the plant at any time.

Rule No. 15. No passes issued during meals and not until the dishes are done unless it is business.

Rule No. 16. All committees must attend meetings and report their activities.

Rule No. 17. No card playing or walking around or any disturbance during meetings.

WHAT OF THE LAW?

Unquestionably most judges will hold the sit-down strike illegal, under the law of trespass. The fact that the law of trespass was developed in a different social situation will be of no avail. Yet labor need not be unduly disturbed, for most weapons used by it were first held illegal. That was true both of the strike and the boycott....

Attacks upon the sit-down strike have already begun, and many more may be expected. Governor Hoffman of New Jersey, for example, has warned that the entire resources of the state, if necessary, would be used to eject sit-downers. In his view, workers have no more right to take possession of a factory than gangsters have to take possession of a bank. Early in 1937, legislation to outlaw the sit-down strike was being considered in Alabama and Vermont....

Wyndham Mortimer, vice-president of the United Automobile Workers, has thus stated the case for the sit-down strike:

Is it wrong for a worker to stay at his job? The laws of the state and nation recognize, in a hundred ways, that the worker has a definite claim upon his job; more fundamentally, it is recognized that every workman has a moral right to continue on his job unless some definite misconduct justifies his discharge. These sit-down strikers are staying at their work-places; no one has a better right to be there than have these men themselves. No one else, certainly, has any right to those positions. But the sit-down strikers have performed valuable services in those factories; General Motors and the public alike have profited by those services. To call them trespassers now, and to deny their right as human beings to remain with their jobs, is logically unsound and is manifestly unjust.

The union asserts that the workers have a property right in their jobs which is superior to the company's right to the use of the property. . . .

The sit-down strike has served notice on society that mere ownership does not carry with it all possible rights with reference to a factory. Those who work in it, who make it produce with their labor and who depend upon it for their livelihood, should likewise have a voice in its control. Those who invest their lives in an industry have at least as much at stake as those who merely invest their money. The sit-down strike brings these facts forcibly to public attention. It is interesting to note that, in the sit-down strike, workers are re-establishing the control over the tools of production that they lost with the Industrial Revolution.

The ethical case for the sit-down strike has well been presented by Rabbi Edward L. Israel, former chairman of the Social Justice Commission of the Central Conference of American Rabbis. The problem involved, Rabbi Israel asserts, is one of the comparative emphasis of human rights over against property rights. The entire struggle of the human race from bondage toward freedom, he points out, has been a constant battling against vested interests.

*   *   *

The argument that a worker has a property right in his job has thus been stated by Homer Martin, president of the automobile workers union:

> What more sacred property right is there in the world than the right of a man in his job? This property right involves the right to support his family, feed his children and keep starvation away from the door. This property right is the very foundation stone of American homes. It is the most sacred, most fundamental property right in America. It means more to the stabilization of American life, morally, socially and economically, than any other property right.

*   *   *

223 Peaceful Assembly Cannot Be Made a Crime (1937)

In 1937 President Franklin Delano Roosevelt revealed his plan to "pack" the Supreme Court, which had been holding unconstitutional the New Deal social welfare and economic recovery programs enacted by Congress. Roosevelt proposed to increase the court's membership from nine to a maximum of fifteen by adding one new justice for each member past age seventy who failed to retire. It was the conservative court, nevertheless, that denied to Oregon the right to interfere with the legitimate rights of syndicalist militants. The repudiation of Oregon's criminal syndicalism statute, which made it a crime to assist in conducting a meeting of an organization that advocated the overthrow of the government by unlawful means, illustrated the technique whereby the Supreme Court applied the safeguards of the Bill of Rights to the states via the Fourteenth Amendment.

☆ 223 *De Jonge v. Oregon*

299 U.S. 353 (1937).

MR. CHIEF JUSTICE HUGHES delivered the opinion of the Court.

Appellant, Dirk De Jonge, was indicted in Multnomah County, Oregon, for violation of the Criminal Syndicalism Law of that State. The Act . . . defines "criminal syndicalism" as "the doctrine which advocates crime, physical violence, sabotage or any unlawful acts or methods as a means of accomplishing or effecting industrial or political change or revolution." . . .

. . . The charge is that appellant assisted in the conduct of a meeting which was called under the auspices of the Communist Party, an organization advocating criminal syndicalism. . . .

*   *   *

The stipulation [of facts] set forth various extracts from the literature of the Communist Party to show its advocacy of criminal syndicalism. The stipulation does not disclose any activity by the defendant as a basis for his prosecution other than his participation in the meeting in question. Nor does the stipulation show that the Communist literature distributed at the meeting contained any advocacy of criminal syndicalism or of any unlawful conduct. . . .

*   *   *

The broad reach of the statute as thus applied is plain. While defendant was a member of the Communist Party, that membership was not necessary to conviction on such a charge. A like fate might have attended any speaker, although not a member, who "assisted in the conduct" of the meeting. However innocuous the object of the meeting, however lawful the subjects and tenor of the addresses, however reasonable and timely the discussion, all those assisting in the conduct of the meeting would be subject to imprisonment as felons if the meeting were held by the Communist Party.... Thus if the Communist Party had called a public meeting in Portland to discuss the tariff, or the foreign policy of the Government, or taxation, or relief, or candidacies for the offices of President, members of Congress, Governor, or State legislators, every speaker who assisted in the conduct of the meeting would be equally guilty with the defendant in this case, upon the charge as here defined and sustained. The list of illustrations might be indefinitely extended to every variety of meetings under the auspices of the Communist Party although held for the discussion of political issues or to adopt protests and pass resolutions of an entirely innocent and proper character.

While the States are entitled to protect themselves from the abuse of the privileges of our institutions through an attempted substitution of force and violence in the place of peaceful political action in order to effect revolutionary changes in government, none of our decisions go to the length of sustaining such a curtailment of the right of free speech and assembly as the Oregon statute demands in its present application....

Freedom of speech and of the press are fundamental rights which are safeguarded by the due process clause of the Fourteenth Amendment of the Federal Constitution.... The right of peaceable assembly is a right cognate to those of free speech and free press and is equally fundamental. As this Court said in *United States v. Cruikshank*, "The very idea of a government, republican in form, implies a right on the part of its citizens to meet peaceably for consultation in respect to public affairs and to petition for a redress of grievances." The First Amendment of the Federal Constitution expressly guarantees that right against abridgment by Congress. But explicit mention there does not argue exclusion elsewhere. For the right is one that cannot be denied without violating those fundamental principles of liberty and justice which lie at the base of all civil and political institutions—principles which the Fourteenth Amendment embodies in the general terms of its due process clause.

These rights may be abused by using speech or press or assembly in order to incite to violence and crime. The people through their legislatures may protect themselves against that abuse. But the legislative intervention can find constitutional justification only by dealing with the abuse. The rights themselves must not be curtailed. The greater the importance of safeguarding the community from incitements to the overthrow of our institutions by force and violence, the more imperative is the need to preserve inviolate the constitutional rights of free speech, free press and free assembly in order to maintain the opportunity for free political discussion, to the end that government may be responsive to the will of the people and that changes, if desired, may be obtained by peaceful means. Therein lies the security of the Republic, the very foundation of constitutional government.

It follows from these considerations that, consistently with the Federal Constitution, peaceable assembly for lawful discussion cannot be made a crime. The holding of meetings for peaceable political action cannot be proscribed. Those who assist in the conduct of such meetings cannot be branded as criminals on that score. The question, if the rights of free speech and peaceable assembly are to be preserved, is not as to the auspices under which the meeting is held but as to its purpose; not as to the relations of the speakers, but whether their utterances transcend the bounds of the freedom of speech which the Constitution protects. If the persons assembling have committed crimes elsewhere, if they have formed or are engaged in a conspiracy against the public peace and order, they may be prosecuted for their conspiracy or other violation of valid laws. But it is a different matter when the State, instead of prosecuting them for such offenses, seizes upon mere participation in a peaceable assembly and a lawful public discussion as the basis for a criminal charge.

*   *   *

We hold that the Oregon statute as applied to the particular charge as defined by the State court is repugnant to the due process clause of the Fourteenth Amendment....

224 "the prohibition of the export of arms" (1937)

The belief of many Americans that the United States' involvement in World War I was a mistake led to several legislative enactments designed to keep the country uninvolved in the brewing European conflicts. The Neutrality Act of 1935 banned shipments of war materials to belligerents at the discretion of the president. The Neutrality Act of 1936 prohibited sending arms to nations at war but did not apply to civil wars. In 1936 a civil war erupted in Spain, and the following year the United States placed an embargo on all arms shipments to Spain.

The push for neutrality culminated in the Neutrality Act of 1937. Motivated by the spectacle of American volunteers fighting for the Spanish Republic in the Abraham Lincoln Brigade, Congress extended the act to cover all civil wars, granted broader discretion to the president, excised the distinction between aggressor and victim nations, and imposed severe restrictions on citizens engaging in commercial activity in foreign countries at war. Although the act did not prohibit Americans from participating personally in foreign wars, those who sought to assist a foreign nation through arms, commerce, or financial aid were subject to criminal penalties, regardless of their motivations.

☆ 224 The Neutrality Act

50 Stat. 121 (1937).

Resolved by the Senate and House of Representatives of the United States of America in Congress assembled, That the joint resolution entitled "Joint resolution providing for the prohibition of the export of arms, ammunition, and implements of war to belligerent countries; the prohibition of the transportation of arms, ammunition, and implements of war by vessels of the United States for the use of belligerent states; for the registration and licensing of persons engaged in the business of manufacturing, exporting, or importing arms, ammunition, or implements of war; and restricting travel by American citizens on belligerent ships during war," approved August 31, 1935, as amended, is amended to read as follows:

"EXPORT OF ARMS, AMMUNITION, AND IMPLEMENTS OF WAR

"SECTION 1. (a) Whenever the President shall find that there exists a state of war between, or among, two or more foreign states, the President shall proclaim such fact, and it shall thereafter be unlawful to export, or attempt to export, or cause to be exported, arms, ammunition, or implements of war from any place in the United States to any belligerent state named in such proclamation, or to any neutral state for transshipment to, or for the use of, any such belligerent state.

"(b) The President shall, from time to time, by proclamation, extend such embargo upon the export of arms, ammunition, or implements of war to other states as and when they may become involved in such war.

"(c) Whenever the President shall find that a state of civil strife exists in a foreign state and that such civil strife is of a magnitude or is being conducted under such conditions that the export of arms, ammunition, or implements of war from the United States to such foreign state would threaten or endanger the peace of the United States, the President shall proclaim such fact, and it shall thereafter be unlawful to export, or attempt to export, or cause to be exported, arms, ammunition, or implements of war from any place in the United States to

such foreign state, or to any neutral state for transshipment to, or for the use of, such foreign state.

*   *   *

"(e) Whoever, in violation of any of the provisions of this Act, shall export, or attempt to export, or cause to be exported, arms, ammunition, or implements of war from the United States shall be fined not more than $10,000, or imprisoned not more than five years, or both, and the property vessel, or vehicle containing the same shall be [seized and forfeited].

*   *   *

"EXPORT OF OTHER ARTICLES AND MATERIALS

"SEC. 2. (a) Whenever the President shall have issued a proclamation under the authority of section 1 of this Act and he shall thereafter find that the placing of restrictions on the shipment of certain articles or materials in addition to arms, ammunition, and implements of war from the United States to belligerent states, or to a state wherein civil strife exists, is necessary to promote the security or preserve the peace of the United States or to protect the lives of citizens of the United States, he shall so proclaim, and it shall thereafter be unlawful, except under such limitations and exceptions as the President may prescribe ... for any American vessel to carry such articles or materials to any belligerent state, or to any state wherein civil strife exists, named in such proclamation issued under the authority of section 1 of this Act, or to any neutral state for transshipment to, or for the use of, any such belligerent state or any such state wherein civil strife exists. The President shall by proclamation from time to time definitely enumerate the articles and materials which it shall be unlawful for American vessels to so transport.

*   *   *

"FINANCIAL TRANSACTIONS

"SEC. 3. (a) Whenever the President shall have issued a proclamation under the authority of section 1 of this Act, it shall thereafter be unlawful for any person within the United States to purchase, sell, or exchange bonds, securities, or other obligations of the government of any belligerent state or of any state wherein civil strife exists, named in such proclamation, or of any political subdivision of any such state, or of any person acting for or on behalf of the government of any such state, or of any faction or asserted government within any such state wherein civil strife exists, or of any person acting for or on behalf of any faction or asserted government within any such state wherein civil strife exists, issued after the date of such proclamation, or to make any loan or extend any credit to any such government, political subdivision, faction, asserted government, or person, or to solicit or receive any contribution for any such government, political subdivision, faction, asserted government, or person: *Provided*, That if the President shall find that such action will serve to protect the commercial or other interests of the United States or its citizens, he may, in his discretion, and to such extent and under such regulations as he may prescribe, except from the operation of this section ordinary commercial credits and short-time obligations in aid of legal transactions and of a character customarily used in normal peacetime commercial transactions. Nothing in this subsection shall be construed to prohibit the solicitation or collection of funds to be used for medical aid and assistance, or for food and clothing to relieve human suffering, when such solicitation or collection of funds is made on behalf of and for use by any person or organization which is not acting for or on behalf of any such government, political subdivision, faction, or asserted government, but all such solicitations and collections of funds shall be subject to the approval of the President and shall be made under such rules and regulations as he shall prescribe.

*   *   *

"EXCEPTIONS—AMERICAN REPUBLICS

"SEC. 4. This Act shall not apply to an American republic or republics engaged in war against a non-American state or states, provided the American republic is not cooperating with a non-American state or states in such war.

"NATIONAL MUNITIONS CONTROL BOARD

"SEC. 5. (a) There is hereby established a National Munitions Control Board (hereinafter referred to as the 'Board')....

"(b) Every person who engages in the business of manufacturing, exporting, or importing any of the arms, ammunition, or implements of war referred to in this Act, whether as an exporter, importer, manufacturer, or dealer, shall register with the Secretary of State his name, or business name, principal place of business, and places of business in the United States, and a list of the arms, ammunition, and implements of war which he manufactures, imports, or exports.

*   *   *

"(d) It shall be unlawful for any person to export, or attempt to export, from the United States to any other state, any of the arms, ammunition, or implements of war referred to in this Act, or to import, or attempt to import, to the United States from any other state, any of the arms, ammunition, or implements of war referred to in this Act, without first having obtained a license [from the Secretary of State] therefor.

"(e) All persons required to register under this section shall maintain, subject to the inspection of the Secretary of State, or any person or persons designated by him, such permanent records of manufacture for export, importation, and exportation of arms, ammunition, and implements of war as the Secretary of State shall prescribe.

*   *   *

"(g) Whenever the President shall have issued a proclamation under the authority of section 1 of this Act, all licenses theretofore issued under this Act shall ipso facto and immediately upon the issuance of such proclamation, cease to grant authority to export arms, ammunition, or implements of war from any place in the United States to any belligerent state, or to any state wherein civil strife exists, named in such proclamation, or to any neutral state for transshipment to, or for the use of, any such belligerent state or any such state wherein civil strife exists; and said licenses, insofar as the grant of authority to export to the state or states named in such proclamation is concerned, shall be null and void.

*   *   *

"AMERICAN VESSELS PROHIBITED FROM CARRYING ARMS TO BELLIGERENT STATES

"SEC. 6. (a) Whenever the President shall have issued a proclamation under the authority of section 1 of this Act, it shall thereafter be unlawful, until such proclamation is revoked, for any American vessel to carry any arms, ammunition, or implements of war to any belligerent state, or to any state wherein civil strife exists, named in such proclamation, or to any neutral state for transshipment to, or for the use of, any such belligerent state or any such state wherein civil strife exists.

"(b) Whoever, in violation of the provisions of this section, shall take, or attempt to take, or shall authorize, hire, or solicit another to take, any American vessel carrying such cargo out of port or from the jurisdiction of the United States shall be fined not more than $10,000, or imprisoned not more than five years, or both; and, in addition, such vessel, and her tackle, apparel, furniture, and equipment, and the arms, ammunition, and implements of war on board, shall be forfeited to the United States.

"USE OF AMERICAN PORTS AS BASE OF SUPPLY

"SEC. 7. (a) Whenever, during any war in which the United States is neutral, the President, or any person thereunto authorized by him, shall have cause to believe that any vessel, domestic or foreign, whether requiring clearance or not, is about to carry out of a port of the United States, fuel, men, arms, ammunition, implements of war, or other supplies to any warship, tender, or supply ship of a belligerent state, but the evidence is not deemed sufficient to justify forbidding the departure of the vessel, . . . and if, in the President's judgment, such action will serve to maintain peace between the United States and foreign states, or to protect the commercial interests of the United States and its citizens, or to promote the security or neutrality of the United States, he shall have the power and it shall be his duty to require the owner, master, or person in command thereof, before departing from a port of the United States, to give a bond to the United States, with sufficient sureties, in such amount as he shall deem proper, conditioned that the vessel will not deliver the men, or any part of the cargo, to any warship, tender, or supply ship of a belligerent state.

"(b) If the President, or any person thereunto authorized by him, shall find that a vessel, domestic or foreign, in a port of the United States, has previously cleared from a port of the United States during such war and delivered its cargo or any part thereof to a warship, tender, or supply ship of a belligerent state, he may prohibit the departure of such vessel during the duration of the war.

*   *   *

"TRAVEL ON VESSELS OF BELLIGERENT STATES

"SEC. 9. Whenever the President shall have issued a proclamation under the authority of section 1 of this Act it shall thereafter be unlawful for any citizen of the United States to travel on any vessel of the state or states named in such proclamation, except in accordance with such rules and regulations as the President shall prescribe: *Provided, however,* That the provisions of this section shall not apply to a citizen of the United States traveling on a vessel whose voyage was begun in advance of the date of the President's proclamation, and who had no opportunity to discontinue his voyage after that date: *And provided further,* That they shall not apply under ninety days after the date of the President's proclamation to a citizen of the United States returning from a foreign state to the United States. Whenever, in the President's judgment, the conditions which have caused him to issue his proclamation have ceased to exist, he shall revoke his proclamation and the provisions of this section shall thereupon cease to apply with respect to the state or states named in such proclamation, except with respect to offenses committed prior to such revocation.

"ARMING OF AMERICAN MERCHANT VESSELS PROHIBITED

"SEC. 10. Whenever the President shall have issued a proclamation under the authority of section 1, it shall thereafter be unlawful, until such proclamation is revoked, for any American vessel engaged in

commerce with any belligerent state, or any state wherein civil strife exists, named in such proclamation, to be armed or to carry any armament, arms, ammunition, or implements of war, except small arms and ammunition therefor which the President may deem necessary and shall publicly designate for the preservation of discipline aboard such vessels."

*   *   *

Approved, May 1, 1937, 6:30 p.m. Central Standard Time.

225 "smashing . . . strike demonstrators" (1937)

The growing determination of the labor unions, aided by the new legislation and government policies under the New Deal, increased the zeal of the drive to organize industrial workers. Although by 1937 such employers as General Motors and United States Steel had come to accept unions, many others strongly continued to oppose labor organizers. When the Steel Workers Organizing Committee called a strike against its opposition, Republic Steel decided to continue its operations by relying on non-strikers. In response, some two thousand to three thousand strikers decided to march on the Republic plant in south Chicago and picket it. When the labor column, singing labor songs and chanting "CIO," neared the mill, they were stopped by the police. Violence erupted. The police opened fire on the crowd—five people were killed instantly and five others later died of their wounds. Six of the dead were shot in the back. Fifty-eight strikers and sixteen policemen were injured.

The police claimed they had fired in self-defense against a bloodthirsty armed mob of agitators and communists. None of the marchers was charged with possession of guns. The march was filmed by Paramount Pictures and was given a congressional screening by order of Senator Robert La Follette, who then was investigating violations of free speech and the rights of labor. The following document contains an account of the screening by a reporter for the *St. Louis Post-Dispatch* on June 16, 1937.

☆ 225 Memorial Day Massacre

St. Louis Post-Dispatch, reprinted in Richard Hofstadter and Michael Wallace, eds., *American Violence: A Documentary History* (New York: Knopf, 1970), 180-81.

WASHINGTON, June 16—Five agents of the La Follette Civil Liberties Committee, headed by Robert Wohlforth, the committee's secretary, arrived in Chicago yesterday to begin an investigation of the tragic events of Memorial Day, when nine persons were killed or fatally wounded by city police in smashing an attempt by steel strike demonstrators to march past the Republic Steel Co. plant in South Chicago.

Appearance of the committee's agents on the scene coincided with the death of the ninth victim, a 17-year-old boy reported to have joined the pickets in the hope of getting a job in the mill after settlement of the strike.

It was learned today that the committee's decision to proceed with the inquiry was hastened by the private showing here last week of a suppressed newsreel, in which the police attack on the demonstrators is graphically recorded. The committee obtained possession of the film in New York, after its maker, the Paramount Co., had announced that it would not be exhibited publicly, for fear of inciting riots throughout the country.

Senators Shocked by Scenes. The showing of the film here was conducted with the utmost secrecy. The audience was almost limited to Senators La Follette (Prog.), Wisconsin, and Thomas (Dem.), Utah, who compose the committee, and members of the staff. Those who saw it were shocked and amazed by scenes showing scores of uniformed policemen firing their revolvers pointblank into a dense crowd of men, women, and children, and then pursuing and clubbing the survivors unmercifully as they made frantic efforts to escape.

The impression produced by these fearful scenes was heightened by the sound record which accompanies the picture, reproducing the roar of police fire and the screams of the victims. It was run off several times for the scrutiny of the investigators, and at each showing they detected additional instances of "frightfulness." It is expected to be of extraordinary value in identifying individual policemen and their victims. The film itself evidently is an outstanding example of camera reporting under difficult conditions.

226 "cruel and inhuman punishment" (1938)

Despite occasional anti-alien sentiments and the Chinese Exclusion Acts, for most of its history the United States had adhered to a generous immigration policy. The country's total open door policy ended, however, with the Immigration and Naturalization Act of 1917 and the imposition of quotas on aliens in 1921. Thereafter, an alien had to meet strict criteria and qualify under the quota or face exclusion or deportation. Many political refugees who could not qualify were to be turned away, often with nowhere to go except back to face confinement or death.

In the late 1920s and 1930s, a series of cases challenging Immigration and Naturalization Service de-portation orders on the grounds of a right to political asylum reached the courts. The courts invariably denied the existence of such a right under American law. Despite pleas by refugees for protection from the oppression of fascism, courts upheld the deportation orders. But in a case that was strongly condemned (yet never reversed or overruled), District Judge Philip L. Sullivan recognized the existence of political repression and found a constitutional justification for granting relief from deportation.

☆ 226 *United States ex rel. Weinberg v. Scholtfeldt*

26 F. Supp. 283 (N.D. Ill. 1938).

SULLIVAN, District Judge.

*   *   *

The record discloses that the relator is a jew, thirty-one years of age, having been born in that part of Austria Hungary which is now Czechoslovakia; ... He (the relator) was married to a United States citizen, but after their marriage they separated when he learned that his wife had formerly given birth to an illegitimate child. The record further discloses that he has never been on relief but has always worked and supported himself; that he has never been arrested except that he was once fined for a traffic violation; and that he has never been guilty of a crime involving moral turpitude.

It is a matter of common knowledge that at the present time in Central Europe the jews are being persecuted, their property confiscated and that they are obliged to seek sanctuary in other countries.

Under conditions as they now exist it would be cruel and inhuman punishment to deport this petitioner to Czechoslovakia, belonging as he does to the race which is thus being persecuted and exiled, especially when the charge against him is that at the time of his entry into the United States he was not in possession of an unexpired immigration visa. I do not believe that the immigration laws contemplate any such strict compliance with the letter thereof, as would oblige the court to return at this time a jew to a country where his property would be confiscated, where his life might be in jeopardy, and from which, if he were permitted to enter it at all, he would be forced immediately to flee.

The prayer of the petition for habeas corpus is granted, the petition is sustained, and petitioner discharged from custody.

227 Those Inherent and Fundamental Rights That Distinguish This Country from All Foreign Nations (1938-1940)

The economic recovery promised to America by the New Deal was not a speedy process. In 1934, over a year after Franklin D. Roosevelt's inauguration, more than eleven million Americans were still out of work and between sixteen and eighteen million were on the relief rolls. By the end of 1937, the unemployed continued to number nine million, and the economy's new downswing gave rise to the term "recession."

By 1938 tensions in Europe mounted as Hitler's Germany annexed Austria and occupied the Sudetenland in Czechoslovakia. The spread of racism in Europe and the organization of domestic fascist organizations seemingly adherent to their overseas counterparts caused growing concern in the late 1930s. Several congressional committees had investigated these organizations, but in 1938 a new special committee formed. Popularly known as the Dies Committee after its chairman, Martin Dies of Texas, its activities and tactics received much criticism. Dies seemed more interested in the exposure of communist and socialist activities than fascist ones and complained that the federal government contained "hundreds of left-wingers and radicals who do not believe in our system of private enterprise" and that there were "two thousand outright Communists and Partyliners ... in the government in Washington."

Although the Dies Committee had the duty to investigate "the extent, character, and objects of un-American propaganda activities in the United States," the congressional debate reflected the difficulty of defining the meaning of "un-American." In 1945, the Dies Committee became the standing House Committee on Un-American Activities.

☆ 227 The Dies Committee on Un-American Activities

☆ 227a Debate on H.R. Res. No. 282, 75th Cong., 3d Sess., 83 Cong. Rec. 7568 (May 26, 1938)

The Clerk read the resolution, as follows:

HOUSE RESOLUTION 282

Resolved, That the Speaker of the House of Representatives be, and he is hereby, authorized to appoint a special committee to be composed of seven members for the purpose of conducting an investigation of (1) the extent, character, and objects of un-American propaganda activities in the United States, (2) the diffusion within the United States of subversive and un-American propaganda that is instigated from foreign countries or of a domestic origin and attacks the principle of the form of govern-

ment as guaranteed by our Constitution, and (3) all other questions in relation thereto that would aid Congress in any necessary remedial legislation.

*   *   *

Mr. DIES. ... I have often believed that the distinction between the American form of government and the forms of government which prevail in many European countries is the conception we have in America that we derive fundamental and inherent rights not from society, not from governments, but from Almighty God, and having derived those fundamental rights from God, no man or no majority of men can deprive us of the inherent right to worship God according to the dictates of our conscience or to speak our opinions and our convictions as we feel them. I can assure the House here and now that if I have anything to do with this investigation it will in no sense be an effort to abridge the undisputed right of every citizen in the United States to express his honest convictions and enjoy freedom of speech.

*   *   *

Now, I know the argument will be used, What is the value of an investigation? I have a mass of information that has been supplied to me that is shocking, information which shows the extent of the Nazi and Communist movements in the United States. I am not one of those who are inclined to be alarmists. I am not inclined to look under every bed for a Communist, but I can say to this House that there is in my possession a mass of information showing the establishment and operation of some 32 Nazi camps in the United States, that all of these camps have been paid for, that they claim a total membership of 480,000, that they assemble in these camps, and I have seen photographs that have been furnished from various sources showing the fact that in these camps men are marching and saluting the swastika, if that is the proper word for it. Not only is this true, but I have information in my possession that certain individuals and groups in America have contributed funds for the purpose of encouraging the Fascist or Nazi movement in this country, and may I say in that connection that so far as I am concerned I regard communism and nazi-ism and fascism as having one underlying principle—dictatorship—the theory that government should have the right to control the lives, the fortunes, the happiness, the beliefs, and every detail of the life of the human being, and that man is a pawn of the government, rather than the American conception that government is created for the benefit of mankind.

*   *   *

Mr. TAYLOR of Tennessee.

*   *   *

When we investigated Nazi and other propaganda pursuant to House resolution 198, Seventy-third Congress, the Nazi organization in this country was known as "the friends of New Germany." While at that time their activities were a gross prostitution of the privileges which they were accorded in this country, nevertheless there were few signs of militarism in their maneuvers. But ... under the new designation—German-American Bund—they [Nazis] have vastly increased their number, have acquired by purchase some 30 camp sites where they carry on military training schools attired in a foreign uniform and under a foreign flag. I understand that in these camps they assemble the youths on the holy Sabbath and teach them to goose-step and heil Hitler. I understand that as a feeble pretense they sometimes have an American flag inconspicuously displayed, but it is so deluged with drapery bearing the swastika insignia that our flag dwindles into comparative insignificance.

Mr. Speaker, we have no place in our scheme of government for dual citizenship. We must be either American or alien. There can be no qualification or reservation when it comes to allegiance to our flag and to our country. No man can maintain allegiance to the United States and at the same time bear allegiance to some foreign king, potentate, or dictator no more than he can serve both God and mammon. Such a performance is a sheer mockery "of the purest ray serene," and it is the purpose of this investigation to develop the facts to the end that the necessary legislation may be enacted to put a stop to this sort of skullduggery. [Applause.]

Think of it, Mr. Speaker, American soil, purchased undoubtedly with foreign money, dedicated and used as camps in which to assemble, and clad in a foreign uniform, under a foreign flag, and to the music of foreign military airs, hail a foreign ruler, and drill and parade in the honor, and at least constructively, in the service of a foreign government.

*   *   *

Mr. Speaker, it is nigh unto inconceivable that such a travesty could happen here in this proud, intelligent, and patriotic country. It is a menace to good citizenship. It is a national scandal and must be eradicated in the name of national decency, if nothing more.

Aside from the military aspects of the bund, it preaches intolerance, bigotry, and race and religious persecution. This conduct violates the sacred tenets upon which our Government was founded—race, color, and creed are made inviolable under the terms of the Bill of Rights, which is our ark of the covenant.

*   *   *

Mr. Speaker, a few days ago, in the Madison Square Roof Garden in New York City, 18,000 militant Communists assembled, denounced and advocated the overthrow of this Republic, and sang the Communist anthem, the Internationale, with red flags flying and Old Glory only conspicuous by absence. Communist radicals recently for the second time had the unmitigated audacity and depravity to desecrate that hallowed shrine sacred to every red-blooded American—Plymouth Rock—by enveloping it in red paint. The miserable wretches who committed this dastardly deed ought to be hunted down like rattlesnakes and kicked out of the country. [Applause.]

One thing is certain, Mr. Speaker, unless we arrest this insidious un-American influence, it is only a question of a short time until a revolution will ensue and the soil of our great country will be soaked in blood. Incendiary and un-American propaganda is being smuggled into this country by truckloads. Members of the American Legion and other patriotic organizations who are trying to suppress this deadly menace single-handed are being clubbed and sent to the hospital by these alien racketeers. It is up to Congress to do something. Why sit we here idle and supine, so to speak, when the very soul of this Republic is being violated and debauched. It is not only our responsibility, but it is our duty to ourselves, to our flag, and to our country to act now before it is too late.

*   *   *

One of the chief reasons which inspired my ambition to come to Congress was to help stop the indiscriminate flow of immigration to this country. Mr. Speaker, we have hundreds of thousands of good citizens in this country who were born abroad.... They availed themselves of the first opportunity to renounce foreign political ties and become naturalized American citizens. But, on the contrary, Mr. Speaker, we have millions of others who came over imbued with an entirely different spirit and different viewpoint. They care nothing about America or American institutions and traditions. They wanted to exploit America for their own selfish benefit and gratification. They never tried to become assimilated. They did not want to be absorbed; and that is one of our problems today. They have never become citizens, and hundreds of thousands of them are a burden to our society—inmates of jails, asylums, and other public institutions. They have jammed our relief rolls at the expense and to the exclusion of worthy native-born and naturalized citizens.

*   *   *

... [D]uring the last years of the Hoover administration more aliens were deported when added to the number who voluntarily departed than the total number admitted for the same period. For instance, in 1932 there were 19,426 deportations of aliens, whereas in 1934, under Mme. Perkins, Secretary of Labor, the number had dwindled to 8,879; and yet there are nearly a million—some estimates say more than 3,000,000—aliens in this country illegally, from whose ranks the Communist Party draws a considerable part of its following. There is in this country a large alien-minded element which wants to break down the quota barriers against restricted immigration and open the gates wide to the riff-raff of Europe. . . .

*   *   *

Mr. COFFEE of Washington.

*   *   *

I want to know who is going to define "un-American." What are its economic and political connotations? What infallible instrument or high tribunal of justice will lay down a definition which will be accepted by the American people? "Un-American" is a relative term. What was American 75 years ago is un-American today and vice versa. This country was founded upon the recognition of the doctrine of free speech and its preservation against all hazards.

*   *   *

Who is un-American now? Oh, I recall we had the Fish committee a few years ago, which was a witch-pursuing expedition designed to hold up to public obloquy and condemnation every liberal political organization in the United States. Then we had another, a Democratic committee, the McCormack committee. Are we going to repeat now? My God, the whole Nation is crying out for succor in its [financial] distress, . . . and you spend the solemn time of the House of Representatives, in the ninth year of the depression, in trying to investigate what you characterize as un-American activities. To what a low degree have we sunk in the legislative chambers of the Congress of the United States.

*   *   *

The last sentence on the first page of the Dies resolution states that "All other questions in relation thereto shall be investigated by the committee." Where are we going to stop on this snooping, punitive expedition? Are we going to open up the whole field of political and economic endeavor in the United States? . . .

*   *   *

. . . [M]y distrust of this legislation gravitates from my fear that it is aimed at progressive movements, parties, ideas. Inveighing at communism per se is a puerile pastime. Attempting to eliminate the social injustices which breed discontent is a laudable objective. Let us engage in that pursuit. Let us decline to temporize and refuse to embark upon running after will-o'-the-wisps when there are mountains of ice and apathy around us to melt.

*   *   *

Mr. MCCORMACK. . . . One of the speakers has talked about the Fish committee as a "red baiting" committee. I caution that distinguished gentleman that the use of names is a dangerous field to enter

into and is also a sign of weakness. Mr. FISH is not a "red baiter." You know when one calls a man a "red baiter" he can call someone else a "red lover." I simply refer to this so that some of our friends who have a tendency to enter into the field of personalities may realize in the future that when they open the issue the other fellow has a chance to say something in return.

*   *   *

What is un-American in the political field is entirely different from that is un-American so far as the basic fundamentals of our country are concerned.

*   *   *

Mr. O'MALLEY. Can the gentleman assure us that if this committee is created we will have a membership of gentlemen who would be able to distinguish, like the gentleman does, between what is un-American or otherwise?

Mr. MCCORMACK. . . . [O]f course, I cannot answer the gentleman's question.

*   *   *

Mr. BOILEAU. Does the gentleman agree with me that about the only thing that is un-American is the advocacy of the overthrow of our form of government by force and violence?

Mr. MCCORMACK. I think the gentleman made a very fine contribution to this debate, but there is just one further field I might suggest to my friend. . . . [T]here should be included the activities of foreign agencies in the United States seeking to mold public opinion or to form group action, not for the purpose of the overthrow of the Government but for the purpose of influencing the domestic or the external policies of our Government. Such activities are equally subversive of our institutions. . . .

☆ 227b Report of the Dies Committee: H.R. Rep. No. 1476, 76th Cong., 3d Sess. (1940)

INTRODUCTION

There is at present taking place in the world a struggle between democracy on the one hand and dictatorship on the other, upon the outcome of which the future of human liberties in the next few centuries may well depend.

. . . It is of primary importance to prevent the growth or spread of influence of . . . dictatorship of whatever sort. . . . But it is at least equally important that . . . nothing be done which would undermine the fundamental structure of constitutional liberty itself.

One method which can and should from time to time be used is the method of investigation to inform the American people of the activities of [subversive] organizations in their nation. This is the real purpose of the House Committee to Investigate un-

American Activities. By un-American activities we mean organizations or groups existing in the United States which are directed, controlled or subsidized by foreign governments or agencies and which seek to change the policies and form of government of the United States in accordance with the wishes of such foreign governments.

*   *   *

... The committee finds that the danger to American democracy lies not only in the rather remote possibility that Communists, Nazis, or Fascists will succeed in a frontal attack on our Constitutional government and overthrow it, but also in the much greater chance that each extreme totalitarian group seeking by deception to advance its own cause and pad its ranks will succeed in convincing a really substantial number of people that their only defense against violence from the opposite extreme is to accept the violence of the one they find least objectionable.

*   *   *

The committee's work should result in freeing the progressive and labor movements from Communist control or domination and in preventing sincere conservatives from temporizing with essentially Fascist or Nazi groups or philosophies.... The committee wishes to state emphatically that the only proper and democratic method whereby un-American activities can be effectively combatted is by the duly constituted law-enforcing bodies of America operating under our Constitution and with the support of an informed public opinion.

THE PROBLEM OF THE LABOR MOVEMENT

... In [1934] ... the attempt was made by Communists to bore from within the American Federation of Labor. On the whole this effort met with but slight success.

With the formation of the C.I.O. the principal efforts of the Communists were turned in the direction of that organization. It is unmistakably clear that the overwhelming majority of the members of the C.I.O. as well as its president are not Communists or Communist sympathizers.... The evidence before the committee indicates, however, that the leadership of some 10 or 12 of the constituent unions of the C.I.O. out of a total of some 48 unions is more than tinged with communism. The evidence shows that some of their leaders are either card-holding members of the Communist Party or subservient followers of that party's "line." In the rank and file membership of these unions, on the contrary, the

proportion of Communists and Communist sympathizers is very small indeed. There is encouraging evidence of an attempt on the part of the C.I.O. leadership to remove this Communist influence and it is a matter of record that most of its largest organizations are free of any Communist control, domination, or even serious influence....

*   *   *

... [T]he Communist Party is interested in trade-unions primarily for the purpose of attempting to utilize those labor organizations for the benefit of the Russian dictatorship and its foreign policies.

NAZI-FASCIST ORGANIZATIONS

*   *   *

... These groups and organizations make their chief appeal to the basest forms of religious and racial hatred. They promise to deliver this country from the menace of communism; they heap scorn upon the institutions of democracy; and they urge the short cuts of force and violence.

THE GERMAN-AMERICAN BUND

.. [T]he German-American Bund receives its inspiration, program, and direction from the Nazi Government of Germany through the various propaganda organizations which have been set up by that Government and which function under the control and supervision of the Nazi Ministry of Propaganda and Enlightenment.

... Fritz Kuhn ["fuehrer" of the Bund] testified that the bund has a membership of approximately 20,000 to 25,000. (A Department of Justice investigation made of the bund in 1937 placed the membership at 6,500.) In addition to the regular membership, it has what is known as the sympathizer or "fellow traveler" group, consisting of those who are sympathetic to the bund but do not actively participate in its proceedings. He testified that the sympathizer group is composed of approximately 80,000 to 100,000 individuals.

*   *   *

It was established ... that the bund had worked sympathetically with other organizations throughout the United States and cooperates with them. Kuhn testified that some of these groups are the Christian Front, the Christian Mobilizers, the Christian Crusaders, the Social Justice Society, the Silver Shirt Legion of America, the Knights of the White Camelia and various Italian Fascist, White Russian and Ukrainian organizations.

*   *   *

Top, Doc. 151: Feminist leaders Susan B. Anthony (*right*) and Elizabeth Cady Stanton (1873). *Bottom*, Doc. 188: The National Anti-Suffrage Association. Harris & Ewing Photos.

Top, Doc. 158: Rioting workingmen, demanding the right to unionize during the economic depression of 1873-1874, driven from Tompkins Square. Wood engraving by Matt Morgan (1874). *Middle*, Doc. 159: Charles Jules Guiteau, a one-time resident of the utopian Oneida Community and a disappointed office-seeker, shooting President James A. Garfield at the Washington railroad station (1881). *Bottom*, Doc. 163: Anarchist protest at Haymarket Square, a dynamite bomb exploding among the police (1886). Wood engraving by T. de Thulstrup in *Harper's Weekly*, May 15, 1886.

Top, left, Doc. 177: IWW leader "Big Bill" Haywood (1907). *Top, right*, Doc. 178: Anarchist Emma Goldman before entering the penitentiary (1918). *Bottom*, Doc. 185: The body of Joe Hill, poet laureate of the IWW movement, carried through the streets of Chicago after his execution by a five-man firing squad at the Utah State Penitentiary (1915).

Top, Doc. 194: Socialist leader Eugene V. Debs pardoned by President Harding and released from prison after his conviction for criticizing the government's war policy (1921). *Bottom, left*, Doc. 215: General Douglas MacArthur, Army Chief of Staff, personally directing the advance against the "Bonus Army" (1932). *Bottom, right*, Doc. 212: Radical press portrayal of the execution and martyrdom of Sacco and Vanzetti (1927). From *Labor Age*, April 1931.

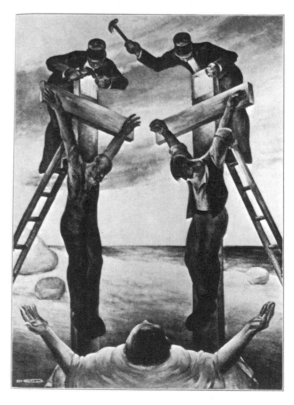

Top, Doc. 231: Japanese and Japanese-Americans, under United States Army supervision, waiting for registration at the Santa Anita Reception Center (1942). *Bottom*, *left*, Doc. 251: Senator Joseph McCarthy conducting public hearings into alleged Communist subversion (1950). *Bottom*, *right*, Doc. 244: American poet Ezra Pound, indicted for treason for broadcasting Fascist propaganda to the United States during World War II (1946).

Top, Doc. 297: Antisegregation demonstrators picket the St. Louis School Board (1963). From the *St. Louis Dispatch*. *Bottom*, Doc. 339: Wounded Knee revisited: the 1890 massacre at Wounded Knee, after which the bodies were buried in a large pit, gave rise to the modern (1974) Native American protest on the same site.

CHAPTER 8

The World War II Era

1939-1946

As war approached, Congress enacted legislation to secure the loyalties of federal employees and to prevent interference with the military and war objectives. Ironically, the laws were enforced more often against those of communist or other leftist leanings than those of rightist persuasion, who in the minds of most people appeared to be the potential wartime enemies. At the onset of war the loyalties of the citizenry similarly were subjected to scrutiny at the state level. Those who routinely declined either to swear or to discuss their allegiance to the country and its Constitution, or who refused their services to the war effort, were subjected to quasi-criminal pains and penalties.

In the Supreme Court, the success of the government's measures against politically suspect activities was mixed. The main record of the challenges to these restrictive laws is contained in the following chapter. But the major focus of this chapter is the use of executive and military power to supplement or supplant the common course of civilian law in order to avoid the constitutional strictures upon the exercise of governmental power. This phenomenon is documented best in the materials on the Japanese evacuation and internment, as military law and authority were utilized to uproot and confine thousands of American citizens and residents on an unspecified suspicion of their political loyalty. While the government acted in a more circumspect manner against enemy aliens, many of those interned for their Japanese ancestry were citizens of the United States.

The government's proclivity for avoiding the constraints of the ordinary civil law when dealing with political offenders is illustrated further by other documents. Some of these contrast the difficulties of sustaining a conviction for treason in the civilian system with the relative ease of accomplishing the same result through invocation of martial law or the law of war in military tribunals. Alternative methods of imposing sanctions on politically suspect individuals are suggested by the psychiatric solution in the Ezra Pound case. One should note the growing number of judicial opinions among the documents, as the courts increasingly began considering constitutional challenges to the use of governmental power against political offenders.

228 "the overthrow of our constitutional form of government" (1939)

President Roosevelt's January 4, 1939, message to Congress emphasized the threat that the growing strength of the totalitarian nations posed to world peace. In March 1939, the Spanish Republic fell to the Fascist forces, and Germany moved into Czechoslovakia, claiming disorder in that country threatened German nationals. After concluding a non-aggression treaty with the Soviet Union, Adolf Hitler, on September 1, commenced a blitzkrieg against Poland.

On August 2, 1939, Congress passed the Hatch Act, sponsored by Senator Carl Hatch of New Mexico, forbidding federal civil servants from taking an active part in political parties and campaigns. But the first prohibition of federal employment based on party membership was written also into this civil service reform. The Civil Service Commission, responsible for administering the Hatch act, interpreted Section 9A, which prohibited federal employees from being members of a party that advocated "the overthrow of our constitutional form of government," to preclude federal employment of members of "the Communist Party, the German Bund, or any other Communist, Nazi or Fascist organization." By 1942, the Civil Service Commission concluded that being a "follower" of Communism raised a "strong presumption" against one's loyalty to the government of the United States.

☆228 An Act to Prevent Pernicious Political Activities (The Hatch Act)

53 Stat. 1147 (1939).

Be it enacted by the Senate and House of Representatives of the United States of America in Congress assembled, That....

*   *   *

SEC. 8. Any person who violates any of the foregoing provisions of this Act upon conviction thereof shall be fined not more than $1,000 or imprisoned for not more than one year, or both.

SEC. 9. (a) It shall be unlawful for any person employed in the executive branch of the Federal Government, or any agency or department thereof, to use his official authority or influence for the purpose of interfering with an election or affecting the result thereof. No officer or employee in the executive branch of the Federal Government, or any agency or department thereof, shall take any active part in political management or in political campaigns. All such persons shall retain the right to vote as they may choose and to express their opinions on all political subjects. For the purposes of this section the term "officer" or "employee" shall not be construed to include (1) the President and Vice President of the United States; (2) persons whose compensation is paid from the appropriation for the office of the President; (3) heads and assistant heads of executive departments; (4) officers who are appointed by the President, by and with the advice and consent of the Senate, and who determine policies to be pursued by the United States in its relations with foreign powers or in the Nation-wide administration of Federal laws.

(b) Any person violating the provisions of this section shall be immediately removed from the position or office held by him, and thereafter no part of the funds appropriated by any Act of Congress for such position or office shall be used to pay the compensation of such person.

SEC. 9A. (1) It shall be unlawful for any person employed in any capacity by any agency of the Federal Government, whose compensation, or any part thereof, is paid from funds authorized or appropriated by any Act of Congress, to have membership in any political party or organization which advocates the overthrow of our constitutional form of government in the United States.

(2) Any person violating the provisions of this section shall be immediately removed from the position or office held by him, and thereafter no part of the funds appropriated by any Act of Congress for such position or office shall be used to pay the compensation of such person.

*   *   *

Approved, August 2, 1939, 11:50 a.m., E.S.T.

229 To "teach the ... propriety of overthrowing or destroying any government in the United States by force" (1940)

Congressional concern over foreign influences in the United States also manifested itself through passage of the Alien Registration Act of 1940, requiring all aliens to be fingerprinted and register annually. Nevertheless, Title I of this enactment, the so-called Smith Act, was not restricted to aliens. This act, named after Congressman Howard W. Smith of Virginia, was the first peacetime federal sedition law since the Alien and Sedition Acts of 1798. Congress modeled the act after the New York Criminal Anarchy Act of 1902 and prohibited speech or publications that advocated or taught the "duty, necessity, desirability, or propriety" of overthrowing any level of government "by force or violence." Enacted in the year in which Hitler occupied Paris, the Smith Act, reminiscent also of the 1917 Espionage Act, was one of many steps which began to make Americans expect that war was virtually at hand.

☆ 229 An Act to Prohibit Certain Subversive Activities (The Smith Act)

54 Stat. 670 (1940).

Be it enacted by the Senate and House of Representatives of the United States of America in Congress assembled,

TITLE I

SECTION 1. (a) It shall be unlawful for any person, with intent to interfere with, impair, or influence the loyalty, morale, or discipline of the military or naval forces of the United States—

(1) to advise, counsel, urge, or in any manner cause insubordination, disloyalty, mutiny, or refusal of duty by any member of the military or naval forces of the United States; or

(2) to distribute any written or printed matter which advises, counsels, or urges insubordination, disloyalty, mutiny, or refusal of duty by any member of the military or naval forces of the United States.

*   *   *

SEC. 2. (a) It shall be unlawful for any person—

(1) to knowingly or willfully advocate, abet, advise, or teach the duty, necessity, desirability, or propriety of overthrowing or destroying any government in the United States by force or violence, or by the assassination of any officer of any such government;

(2) with the intent to cause the overthrow or destruction of any government in the United States, to print, publish, edit, issue, circulate, sell, distribute, or publicly display any written or printed matter advocating, advising, or teaching the duty, necessity, desirability, or propriety of overthrowing or destroying any government in the United States by force or violence;

(3) to organize or help to organize any society, group, or assembly of persons who teach, advocate, or encourage the overthrow or destruction of any government in the United States by force or violence; or to be or become a member of, or affiliate with, any such society, group, or assembly of persons, knowing the purposes thereof.

(b) For the purposes of this section, the term "government in the United States" means the Government of the United States, the government of any State, Territory, or possession of the United States, the government of the District of Columbia, or the government of any political subdivision of any of them.

SEC. 3. It shall be unlawful for any person to attempt to commit, or to conspire to commit, any of the acts prohibited by the provisions of this title.

*   *   *

SEC. 5. (a) Any person who violates any of the provisions of this title shall, upon conviction thereof, be fined not more than $10,000 or imprisoned for not more than ten years, or both.

(b) No person convicted of violating any of the provisions of this title shall, during the five years next following his conviction, be eligible for employment by the United States, or by any department or agency thereof (including any corporation the stock of which is wholly owned by the United States).

*   *   *

Approved, June 28, 1940.

230 "All alien enemies are enjoined to preserve the peace" (1941)

On December 7, 1941, Japanese naval and air forces attacked Pearl Harbor, bringing to an end the peaceful but strained American-Japanese relations that had existed since the 1937 Japanese drive into China. The United States declared war on Japan the following day. President Franklin D. Roosevelt issued Proclamation Number 2525 restricting the travel and other movements of Japanese aliens in the United States and authorizing civil and military authorities to detain all suspicious aliens. Subsequent proclamations affected German and Italian aliens at the commencement of war with their countries. The United States authorities initially directed security measures against all alien enemies. But as the War Department gradually assumed control over this program, it directed more resources toward the Japanese.

During the first year of the United States' entry into World War II, 12,071 alien enemies were arrested. Of this number, government attorneys released 3,567 after a preliminary investigation. On the recommendation of the hearing boards, the attorney general placed 2,933 on parole, released 1,048 outright, and ordered 3,646 interned for the duration of the war. Of those interned pursuant to this proclamation, 1,974 were of Japanese ancestry. These detentions differed from the subsequent evacuation programs, which applied to all Japanese collectively and permitted no individual determina-tions of loyalty until after the detainees reached Relocation Centers.

☆230 Alien Enemies—Japanese: Proclamation of President Franklin D. Roosevelt

55 Stat. 1700 (1941).

AUTHORITY

WHEREAS it is provided by Section 21 of Title 50 of the United States Code as follows:

Whenever there is a declared war between the United States and any foreign nation or government, ... all natives, citizens, denizens, or subjects of the hostile nation or government, being of the age of fourteen years and upward who shall be within the United States and not actually naturalized, shall be liable to be apprehended, restrained, secured, and removed as alien enemies....

PROCLAMATION

NOW, THEREFORE, I, FRANKLIN D. ROOSEVELT, as President of the United States, and as Commander in Chief of the Army and Navy of the United States, do hereby make public proclamation to all whom it may concern that an invasion has been perpetrated upon the territory of the United States by the Empire of Japan.

Conduct to Be Observed by Alien Enemies

... I do hereby further proclaim and direct that the conduct to be observed on the part of the United States toward all natives, citizens, denizens or subjects of the Empire of Japan being of the age of fourteen years and upwards who shall be within the United States or within any territories in any way subject to the jurisdiction of the United States and not actually naturalized, who for the purpose of this Proclamation and under such sections of the United States Code are termed alien enemies, shall be as follows:

All alien enemies are enjoined to preserve the peace towards the United States and to refrain from crime against the public safety, and from violating the laws of the United States and of the States and Territories thereof; and to refrain from actual hostility or giving information, aid or comfort to the enemies of the United States or interfering by word or deed with the defense of the United States or the political processes and public opinions thereof; and to comply strictly with the regulations which are hereby or which may be from time to time promulgated by the President.

*   *   *

Regulations

... I hereby declare and establish the following regulations which I find necessary in the premises and for the public safety:

(1) No alien enemy shall enter or be found within the Canal Zone and no alien enemy shall enter or leave the Hawaiian Islands or the Philippine Islands except under such regulations as the Secretary of War shall from time to time prescribe.

*   *   *

(5) No alien enemy shall have in his possession, custody or control at any time or place or use or operate any of the following enumerated articles:

a. Firearms.

b. Weapons or implements of war or component parts thereof.

c. Ammunition.

d. Bombs.

e. Explosives or material used in the manufacture of explosives.

f. Short-wave radio receiving sets.

g. Transmitting sets.

h. Signal devices.

i. Codes or ciphers.

j. Cameras.

k. Papers, documents or books in which there may be invisible writing; photograph, sketch, picture, drawing, map or graphical representation of any military or naval installations or equipment or of any arms, ammunition, implements of war, device or thing used or intended to be used in the combat equipment of the land or naval forces of the United States or of any military or naval post, camp or station.

All such property found in the possession of any alien enemy in violation of the foregoing regulations shall be subject to seizure and forfeiture.

(6) No alien enemy shall undertake any air flight or ascend into the air in any airplane, aircraft or balloon of any sort whether owned governmentally, commercially or privately, except that travel by an alien enemy in an airplane or aircraft may be authorized by the Attorney General, or his representative, or the Secretary of War, or his representative. . . .

(7) Alien enemies deemed dangerous to the public peace or safety of the United States by the Attorney General or the Secretary of War, as the case may be, are subject to summary apprehension.

*   *   *

(10) With respect to the continental United States, Alaska, Puerto Rico, and the Virgin Islands, an alien enemy shall not change his place of abode or occupation or otherwise travel or move from place to place without full compliance with any such regulations as the Attorney General of the United States may, from time to time, make and declare. . . .

(11) With respect to the Canal Zone, the Hawaiian Islands and the Philippine Islands, an alien enemy shall not change his place of abode or occupation or otherwise travel or move from place to place

without full compliance with any such regulations as the Secretary of War may, from time to time, make and declare. . . .

(12) No alien enemy shall enter or be found in or upon any highway, waterway, airway, railway, railroad, subway, public utility, building, place or thing not open and accessible to the public generally, and not generally used by the public.

(13) No alien enemy shall be a member or an officer of, or affiliated with, any organization, group or assembly hereafter designated by the Attorney General, nor shall any alien enemy advocate, defend or subscribe to the acts, principles or policies thereof, attend any meetings, conventions or gatherings thereof or possess or distribute any literature, propaganda or other writings or productions thereof.

*   *   *

Done at the City of Washington this 7th day of December, in the year of our Lord nineteen hundred and forty-one and of the Independence of the United States of America the one hundred and sixty-sixth.

Franklin D. Roosevelt

231 "every possible protection" (1942)

On February 19, 1942, two months after Pearl Harbor, President Roosevelt issued Executive Order 9066 authorizing the establishment of defense zones within the United States. The order further gave military commanders unbridled discretion to exclude persons from such zones or to restrict their activities therein. Most of the states of California, Oregon, and Washington officially constituted the Pacific Defense Zone.

The speed of the Japanese takeover of the Western Pacific after Pearl Harbor was shocking, and the fear of a Japanese invasion was very strong. False alarms of approaching Japanese submarines and bombers affected West Coast cities. Although no acts of sabotage by Japanese-Americans were ever reported, some believed the racial and cultural loyalties of this easily-identifiable ethnic group would supersede their political allegiance and "a nationwide tornado of destruction" would ensue.

Under the authority of this seemingly simple order, United States military forces evacuated all persons of Japanese ancestry from the Pacific Coast. The armed forces removed 112,000 Japanese, some 70,000 of whom were American citizens (many native-born), from their homes, placed them in temporary collection points, and subsequently shipped them to barbed-wire-enclosed Relocation Centers for internment.

☆ 231 President Roosevelt's Executive
Order 9066

3.C.F.R. 1092 (Feb. 19, 1942).

AUTHORIZING THE SECRETARY OF WAR TO
PRESCRIBE MILITARY AREAS

WHEREAS the successful prosecution of the war requires every possible protection against espionage
and against sabotage to national-defense material,
national-defense premises, and national-defense
utilities. . . .

NOW, THEREFORE, by virtue of the authority
vested in me as President of the United States, and
Commander in Chief of the Army and Navy, I
hereby authorize and direct the Secretary of War,
and the Military Commanders whom he may from
time to time designate, whenever he or any designated Commander deems such action necessary or
desirable, to prescribe military areas in such places
and of such extent as he or the appropriate Military
Commander may determine, from which any or all
persons may be excluded, and with respect to which,
the right of any person to enter, remain in, or leave
shall be subject to whatever restrictions the Secretary of War or the appropriate Military Commander
may impose in his discretion. The Secretary of War
is hereby authorized to provide for residents of any
such area who are excluded therefrom, such transportation, food, shelter, and other accommodations
as may be necessary, in the judgment of the Secretary of War or the said Military Commander, and
until other arrangements are made, to accomplish
the purpose of this order.

*   *   *

FRANKLIN D. ROOSEVELT
The White House, February 19, 1942

232 "offenders against the
law of war" (1942)

Despite the strict standards imposed in the United
States Constitution upon prosecutions for the crime
of treason—considered by the Founding Fathers as
the ultimate political offense—martial law and military justice have provided far less cumbersome procedures for dealing with other classes of political offenders or political suspects. Lincoln's imposition of
martial law and suspension of habeas corpus during
the Civil War permitted the confinement of political
suspects without trial. During World War II, the
government similarly resorted to regulations by military commanders on the West Coast to uproot and
resettle politically suspect Japanese-Americans
without any form of trial.

Two groups of Nazi saboteurs (one member
claiming to be a United States citizen) landed on the
American shores from two submarines during
World War II. After an expedited military trial,
seven of the invaders were summarily convicted and
executed. Both the international law of war and the
United States Articles of War, the Supreme Court
ruled, historically have permitted such military trials of "unlawful belligerents," whether aliens or citizens, without traditional constitutional safeguards.

☆ 232 *Ex Parte Quirin*

317 U.S. 1 (1942).

Mr. Chief Justice STONE delivered the opinion of the
Court.

*   *   *

The question for decision is whether the detention of petitioners by respondent for trial by Military Commission, appointed by Order of the President of July 2, 1942, on charges preferred against
them purporting to set out their violations of the law
of war and of the Articles of War, is in conformity to
the laws and Constitution of the United States.

. . . In view of the public importance of the questions raised by their petitions and of the duty which
rests on the courts, in time of war as well as in time
of peace, to preserve unimpaired the constitutional
safeguards of civil liberty, . . . the public interest required that we consider and decide those questions
without any avoidable delay. . . .

All the petitioners were born in Germany; all
have lived in the United States. All returned to Germany between 1933 and 1941. All except petitioner
Haupt are admittedly citizens of the German Reich,
with which the United States is at war. Haupt came
to this country with his parents when he was five
years old; it is contended that he became a citizen of
the United States by virtue of the naturalization of
his parents during his minority and that he has not
since lost his citizenship. The Government, however,
takes the position that on attaining his majority he
elected to maintain German allegiance and citizenship or in any case that he has by his conduct renounced or abandoned his United States citizenship.
For reasons presently to be stated we do not find it
necessary to resolve these contentions.

After the declaration of war between the United
States and the German Reich, petitioners received
training at a sabotage school near Berlin, Germany,
where they were instructed in the use of explosives
and in methods of secret writing. Thereafter petitioners, with a German citizen, Dasch, proceeded
from Germany to a seaport in Occupied France,
where petitioners Burger, Heinck and Quirin, together with Dasch, boarded a German submarine
which proceeded across the Atlantic to Amagansett
Beach on Long Island, New York. The four were
there landed from the submarine in the hours of

darkness, on or about June 13, 1942, carrying with them a supply of explosives, fuses and incendiary and timing devices. While landing they wore German Marine Infantry uniforms or parts of uniforms. Immediately after landing they buried their uniforms and the other articles mentioned and proceeded in civilian dress to New York City.

The remaining four petitioners at the same French port boarded another German submarine, which carried them across the Atlantic to Ponte Vedra Beach, Florida. On or about June 17, 1942, they came ashore during the hours of darkness wearing caps of the German Marine Infantry and carrying with them a supply of explosives, fuses, and incendiary and timing devices. They immediately buried their caps and the other articles mentioned and proceeded in civilian dress to Jacksonville, Florida, and thence to various points in the United States. All were taken into custody in New York or Chicago by agents of the Federal Bureau of Investigation.

*   *   *

The President, as President and Commander in Chief of the Army and Navy, by Order of July 2, 1942, appointed a Military Commission and directed it to try petitioners for offenses against the law of war and the Articles of War, and prescribed regulations for the procedure on the trial and for review of the record of the trial and of any judgment or sentence of the Commission. On the same day, by Proclamation, the President declared that "all persons who are subjects, citizens or residents of any nation at war with the United States or who give obedience to or act under the direction of any such nation, and who during the time of war enter or attempt to enter the United States . . . through coastal or boundary defenses, and are charged with committing or attempting or preparing to commit sabotage, espionage, hostile or warlike acts, or violations of the law of war, shall be subject to the law of war and to the jurisdiction of military tribunals."

The Proclamation also stated in terms that all such persons were denied access to the courts.

*   *   *

Petitioners' main contention is that the President is without any statutory or constitutional authority to order the petitioners to be tried by military tribunal for offenses with which they are charged; that in consequence they are entitled to be tried in the civil courts with the safeguards, including trial by jury, which the Fifth and Sixth Amendments guarantee to all persons charged in such courts with criminal offenses. . . .

*   *   *

We are not here concerned with any question of the guilt or innocence of petitioners. Constitutional safeguards for the protection of all who are charged with offenses are not to be disregarded in order to inflict merited punishment on some who are guilty. But the detention and trial of petitioners—ordered by the President in the declared exercise of his powers as Commander in Chief of the Army in time of war and of grave public danger—are not to be set aside by the courts without the clear conviction that they are in conflict with the Constitution or laws of Congress constitutionally enacted.

*   *   *

The Constitution thus invests the President as Commander in Chief with the power to wage war which Congress has declared, and to carry into effect all laws passed by Congress for the conduct of war and for the government and regulation of the Armed Forces, and all laws defining and punishing offences against the law of nations, including those which pertain to the conduct of war.

*   *   *

From the very beginning of its history this Court has recognized and applied the law of war as including that part of the law of nations which prescribes, for the conduct of war, the status, rights and duties of enemy nations as well as of enemy individuals. By the Articles of War, and especially Article 15, Congress has explicitly provided, so far as it may constitutionally do so, that military tribunals shall have jurisdiction to try offenders or offenses against the law of war in appropriate cases. . . .

An important incident to the conduct of war is the adoption of measures by the military command not only to repel and defeat the enemy, but to seize and subject to disciplinary measures those enemies who in their attempt to thwart or impede our military effort have violated the law of war. It is unnecessary for present purposes to determine to what extent the President as Commander in Chief has constitutional power to create military commissions without the support of Congressional legislation. For here Congress has authorized trial of offenses against the law of war before such commissions. We are concerned only with the question whether it is within the constitutional power of the national government to place petitioners upon trial before a military commission for the offenses with which they are charged. We must therefore first inquire whether any of the acts charged is an offense against the law of war cognizable before a military tribunal, and if so whether the Constitution prohibits the trial. . . .

*   *   *

By universal agreement and practice the law of war draws a distinction between the armed forces and the peaceful populations of belligerent nations and also between those who are lawful and unlawful combatants. Lawful combatants are subject to capture and detention as prisoners of war by opposing military forces. Unlawful combatants are likewise subject to capture and detention, but in addition they are subject to trial and punishment by military tribunals for acts which render their belligerency unlawful. The spy who secretly and without uniform passes the military lines of a belligerent in time of war, seeking to gather military information and communicate it to the enemy, or an enemy combatant who without uniform comes secretly through the lines for the purpose of waging war by destruction of life or property, are familiar examples of belligerents who are generally deemed not to be entitled to the status of prisoners of war, but to be offenders against the law of war subject to trial and punishment by military tribunals.

*   *   *

Our Government, by . . . defining lawful belligerents entitled to be treated as prisoners of war, has recognized that there is a class of unlawful belligerents not entitled to that privilege, including those who though combatants do not wear "fixed and distinctive emblems." And by Article 15 of the Articles of War Congress has made provision for their trial and punishment by military commission, according to "the law of war."

By a long course of practical administrative construction by its military authorities, our Government has likewise recognized that those who during time of war pass surreptitiously from enemy territory into our own, discarding their uniforms upon entry, for the commission of hostile acts involving destruction of life or property, have the status of unlawful combatants punishable as such by military commission. This precept of the law of war has been so recognized in practice both here and abroad, and has so generally been accepted as valid by authorities on international law that we think it must be regarded as a rule or principle of the law of war recognized by this Government by its enactment of the Fifteenth Article of War.

*   *   *

The law of war cannot rightly treat those agents of enemy armies who enter our territory, armed with explosives intended for the destruction of war industries and supplies, as any the less belligerent enemies than are agents similarly entering for the purpose of destroying fortified places or our Armed Forces. By passing our boundaries for such purposes without uniform or other emblem signifying their belligerent status, or by discarding that means of identification after entry, such enemies become unlawful belligerents subject to trial and punishment.

Citizenship in the United States of an enemy belligerent does not relieve him from the consequences of a belligerency which is unlawful because in violation of the law of war. Citizens who associate themselves with the military arm of the enemy government, and with its aid, guidance and direction enter this country bent on hostile acts are enemy belligerents within the meaning of the Hague Convention and the law of war. . . . It is as an enemy belligerent that petitioner Haupt is charged with entering the United States, and unlawful belligerency is the gravamen of the offense of which he is accused.

*   *   *

But petitioners insist that even if the offenses with which they are charged are offenses against the law of war, their trial is subject to the requirement of the Fifth Amendment that no person shall be held to answer for a capital or otherwise infamous crime unless on a presentment or indictment of a grand jury, and that such trials by Article III, § 2, and the Sixth Amendment must be by jury in a civil court. Before the Amendments, § 2 of Article III, the Judiciary Article, had provided: "The Trial of all Crimes, except in Cases of Impeachment, shall be by Jury," and had directed that "such Trial shall be held in the State where the said Crimes shall have been committed."

Presentment by a grand jury and trial by a jury of the vicinage where the crime was committed were at the time of the adoption of the Constitution familiar parts of the machinery for criminal trials in the civil courts. But they were procedures unknown to military tribunals, which are not courts in the sense of the Judiciary Article, and which in the natural course of events are usually called upon to function under conditions precluding resort to such procedures. As this Court has often recognized, it was not the purpose or effect of § 2 of Article III, read in the light of the common law, to enlarge the then existing right to a jury trial. The object was to preserve unimpaired trial by jury in all those cases in which it had been recognized by the common law and in all cases of a like nature as they might arise in the future, . . . but not to bring within the sweep of the guaranty those cases in which it was then well understood that a jury trial could not be demanded as of right.

*   *   *

[There] are [many] instances of offenses committed against the United States, for which a penalty is imposed, but they are not deemed to be within Article III, § 2 or the provisions of the Fifth and Sixth Amendments relating to "crimes" and "criminal prosecutions." In the light of this long-continued and consistent interpretation we must conclude that § 2 of Article III and the Fifth and Sixth Amendments cannot be taken to have extended the right to demand a jury to trials by military commission, or to have required that offenses against the law of war not triable by jury at common law be tried only in the civil courts.

The fact that "cases arising in the land or naval forces" are excepted from the operation of the

Amendments does not militate against this conclusion. . . .

*   *   *

Section 2 of the Act of Congress of April 10, 1806, derived from the Resolution of the Continental Congress of August 21, 1776, imposed the death penalty on alien spies "according to the law and usage of nations, by sentence of a general court martial." This enactment must be regarded as a contemporary construction of both Article III, § 2, and the Amendments as not foreclosing trial by military tribunals, without a jury, of offenses against the law of war committed by enemies not in or associated with our Armed Forces. It is a construction of the Constitution which has been followed since the founding of our government, and is now continued in the 82nd Article of War. Such a construction is entitled to greatest respect. It has not hitherto been challenged, and so far as we are advised it has never been suggested in the very extensive literature of the subject that an alien spy, in time of war, could not be tried by military tribunal without a jury.

The exception from the Amendments of "cases arising in the land or naval forces" was not aimed at trials by military tribunals, without a jury, of such offenses against the law of war. Its objective was quite different — to authorize the trial by court martial of the members of our Armed Forces for all that class of crimes which under the Fifth and Sixth Amendments might otherwise have been deemed triable in the civil courts. The cases mentioned in the exception are not restricted to those involving offenses against the law of war alone, but extend to trial of all offenses, including crimes which were of the class traditionally triable by jury at common law.

Since the Amendments, like § 2 of Article III, do not preclude all trials of offenses against the law of war by military commission without a jury when the offenders are aliens not members of our Armed Forces, it is plain that they present no greater obstacle to the trial in like manner of citizen enemies who have violated the law of war applicable to enemies. Under the original statute authorizing trial of alien spies by military tribunals, the offenders were outside the constitutional guaranty of trial by jury, not because they were aliens but only because they had violated the law of war by committing offenses constitutionally triable by military tribunal.

We cannot say that Congress in preparing the Fifth and Sixth Amendments intended to extend trial by jury to the cases of alien or citizen offenders against the law of war otherwise triable by military commission, while withholding it from members of our own armed forces charged with infractions of the Articles of War punishable by death. It is equally inadmissible to construe the Amendments —

whose primary purpose was to continue unimpaired presentment by grand jury and trial by petit jury in all those cases in which they had been customary — as either abolishing all trials by military tribunals, save those of the personnel of our own armed forces, or what in effect comes to the same thing, as imposing on all such tribunals the necessity of proceeding against unlawful enemy belligerents only on presentment and trial by jury. We conclude that the Fifth and Sixth Amendments did not restrict whatever authority was conferred by the Constitution to try offenses against the law of war by military commission, and that petitioners, charged with such an offense not required to be tried by jury at common law, were lawfully placed on trial by the Commission without a jury.

Petitioners, and especially petitioner Haupt, stress the pronouncement of this Court in the Milligan case that the law of war "can never be applied to citizens in states which have upheld the authority of the government, and where the courts are open and their process unobstructed." Elsewhere in its opinion the Court was at pains to point out that Milligan, a citizen twenty years resident in Indiana, who had never been a resident of any of the states in rebellion, was not an enemy belligerent either entitled to the status of a prisoner of war or subject to the penalties imposed upon unlawful belligerents. We construe the Court's statement as to the inapplicability of the law of war to Milligan's case as having particular reference to the facts before it. From them the Court concluded that Milligan, not being a part of or associated with the armed forces of the enemy, was a non-belligerent, not subject to the law of war save as — in circumstances found not there to be present and not involved here — martial law might be constitutionally established.

The Court's opinion is inapplicable to the case presented by the present record. . . .

*   *   *

233 Any Act Prescribed by the Military Commander (1942)

When President Roosevelt issued Executive Order 9066 authorizing the establishment of military zones and giving the army authority to regulate and exclude civilians from those zones, no rebellion, invasion, domestic violence, or executive declaration of martial law preceded the order. Thus, as during the Civil War, military authority over civilians was constitutionally suspect. To forestall legal questioning, Congress supplied a legislative foundation for this authority of military orders over civilians by making disobedience to such orders a criminal offense. Unlike the Civil War practice, civilian courts and not military tribunals were to try violations of military regulations.

☆ 233 An Act to Provide a Penalty for Violation of Restrictions

56 Stat. 173 (1942).

Be it enacted by the Senate and House of Representatives of the United States of America in Congress assembled, That whoever shall enter, remain in, leave, or commit any act in any military area or military zone prescribed, under the authority of an Executive order of the President, by the Secretary of War, or by any military commander designated by the Secretary of War, contrary to the restrictions applicable to any such area or zone or contrary to the order of the Secretary of War or any such military commander, shall, if it appears that he knew or should have known of the existence and extent of the restrictions or order and that his act was in violation thereof, be guilty of a misdemeanor and upon conviction shall be liable to a fine of not to exceed $5,000 or to imprisonment for not more than one year, or both, for each offense.

Approved, March 21, 1942.

234 "An armed force which lacks loyalty, morale or discipline" (1943)

Japanese aliens and Americans of Japanese ancestry were not the country's only security concern during this period. Antimilitaristic and revolutionary propaganda of socialist and radical activists continued to threaten the war effort.

Dunne v. United States involved the Smith Act conspiracy convictions of eighteen members of the Socialist Workers Party who, prior to the United States' entry into the war, were arrested and charged with advocating insubordination in the armed forces and the overthrow of the government by force and violence. Dunne challenged the constitutionality of the Smith Act as well as the generality of the indictment. The *Dunne* decision amply demonstrated the potential reach of the Smith Act. Although the court noted the act appeared "on its face to limit exercise of a right specifically protected by the Constitution," it remained unwilling to permit political debate and advocacy to obstruct the country's mobilization for war.

☆ 234 *Dunne v. United States*

138 F.2d 137 (8th Cir. 1943), *cert. denied*, 320 U.S. 790 (1943).

STONE, Circuit Judge.

Twenty-nine persons were indicted in two counts. One died before trial. By direction of the Court, five were found not guilty. The jury found five more not guilty. The jury found the remaining eighteen not guilty on the first count and guilty on the second count. Judgment was entered on the verdicts and sentences imposed. The convicted persons appealed separately. The appeals were consolidated in this Court and presented on a single record.

Count 2 of the indictment charged conspiracy . . . to violate sanctions . . . 1 and 2 [of the Smith Act] in the respects therein set forth.

The issues here have to do with (I) the validity of the Act, (II) the sufficiency of the indictment, and (III) the sufficiency of the evidence.

I. VALIDITY OF THE ACT

* * *

We agree with appellants that, in approaching the problem of validity of a statute, which appears on its face to limit exercise of a right specifically protected by the Constitution, a presumption of validity is narrowed in its scope. In truth, "courts should be astute to examine the effect of the challenged legislation" where it affects the exercise of those fundamental individual rights expressly protected by the Constitution. . . . Here the challenge is that this Act abridges the freedom of speech specifically protected by the First Amendment. Therefore, we approach the problem with the attitude just stated.

Appellants state that "This statute must seek its validating force in the vague and undefined 'right of self-preservation.'" No such extremity exists. The statute is grounded upon specific Constitutional grants of power.

* * *

. . . [A]ppellants recognize the similarity of this section [1] to a part of section 3 of the Espionage Act of 1917, which has been upheld. . . . They rightly urge that this portion of the Espionage Act, by its express terms, was limited to periods when this country might be at war; and that the [*Schenck* and *Debs*] decisions must be construed as ruling authority, with that situation in mind. Also, they rightly contend that this section [1] is, by its terms, also applicable to a state of peace. . . . We agree that these . . . cases do not rule this case as direct decisive authorities. The situation here that section [1] applies to a peace status as well as to war and that the conspiracy claimed here was during time of peace sufficiently differentiates those cases to prevent them from ruling these appeals. . . . On the other hand, it does not follow that those cases contain no expressions which are useful guides for determining the character of questions present here simply because the situation dealt with in those cases was different from that here present. In this connection, a pertinent matter should be stated. . . . [T]here was a situation in 1940 which impressed Congress with the need for this Act. That situation, known to all, was the existence of war in Europe; the apprehension that this country might be drawn into war; the knowledge of the effective use of "fifth column" activities by countries which might be our enemies; and the apprehension that such activities were being or might be used in this country. In stating the purposes of the Bill, it was said in the House: "The officers testified before our committee that they were loath to ask for this provision in peacetime but that conditions had become worse, that propagandists were now gaining a foothold to some extent among the enlisted men of our Army and Navy, and that but for the high character and splendid loyalty that has always obtained among the rank and file of our men they would have had to ask for the enactment of this bill much sooner. So, then, title I interdicts the exertion of subversive influences with the intent to undermine the loyalty, morale, or discipline of our fighting men."

Thus, while this Act is applicable to peace as well as war conditions, it was enacted on the brink of war and to correct existing dangers.

The vital necessity of armed forces to maintain the National and the State governments and the liberties of the citizens is expressly recognized and provided for in the Constitution. The lack of such in the Confederation was one of the cardinal reasons for calling the meeting which became the Constitutional Convention. Congressional enactments having the purposes of raising or maintaining armed forces have high standing because of their importance. At the same time, they must not limit the constitutionally protected individual liberties of the citizen to any greater extent than is reasonably necessary and proper to accomplish the important allowable ends of preserving the life of the Government and the States and their orderly conduct. An armed force which lacks loyalty, morale or discipline or wherein is insubordination, disloyalty, mutiny or refusals to do their duty is far worse than no armed force at all and is positively an active menace to constituted government and to the liberties of the people. Therefore, the question here is whether this section of this Act goes so far beyond what is necessary or proper to effectuate its obviously necessary and proper purposes as to infringe upon protected individual rights.

... [T]he argument centers around the statutory expression "or *in any manner cause* insubordination" (italics added), etc. It is urged that this expression is so broad that it includes "virtually the entire range of civilian expression" since it covers "any utterances whose effect upon any member of the armed forces may be to sow doubts in his mind concerning his duty" even if the forces were not mentioned therein. . . .

*   *   *

This method [of analysis] avoids or slurs over the governing consideration which runs throughout. That is the intent with which the expressions are made. Intent is the cardinal characteristic and vehicle which is necessary to carry any and all interdicted expressions across the boundary line into crime. This is merely an instance of usual criminal law which protects society from evildoers when they do acts—otherwise innocent—with intent to harm. Thus a man may even kill another and he may be entirely unblamed or he may be executed, dependent solely upon the intent motivating the act.

*   *   *

Section [1] is not inherently invalid.

*   *   *

Appellants attack the expression in subsection (a)(1) "advocate, abet, advise, or teach the duty, necessity, desirability, or propriety" as being so vague and sweeping "that they bring within the forbidden area virtually any expression which is considered dangerous or subversive by prosecutor, court or jury." The words attacked are ordinary everyday terms with generally understood meanings. They are not vague. They are "sweeping" only in the sense that they endeavor to cover the different means by which Congress deemed the forbidden result might be brought about. . . . This objection is not well founded.

*   *   *

II. SUFFICIENCY OF INDICTMENT

Appellants contend that the indictment (Count 2) is insufficient "because it merely repeats the words of the statute, fails to allege facts showing the commission of a crime, and is vague and uncertain" and because it "does not allege a conspiracy."

... If the statutory language is, "according to the natural import of the words, fully descriptive of the offense, then ordinarily it is sufficient." The statutory definition here is definitely descriptive. However, this count of the indictment did not stop with stating the broad purposes of the conspiracy. It particularized that the conspirators "would . . . attempt to carry out and accomplish said conspiracy in the manner set out at numbered paragraphs One to Thirteen, inclusive, in the first count of this indictment." Thus, the indictment clearly stated the conspiracy was to do the things forbidden by the statute in the particular manners set forth. . . .

This count of the indictment is sufficient.

III. SUFFICIENCY OF EVIDENCE

*   *   *

Every word of this record of over thirteen hundred pages has been carefully read and considered.

Consideration thereof has required the assembly from the record of the evidence as to each of eighteen defendants and as to four different matters as to each defendant. This has been done. This thorough examination of the record leaves no doubt as to the sufficiency of the evidence and as to the justice of the verdict.

The judgment as to each appellant is affirmed.

235 Compulsory National Unity (1943)

Shortly after the Japanese attack on Pearl Harbor, the West Virginia State Board of Education enacted a regulation requiring public school students to salute and pledge allegiance to the flag of the United States. Members of the Jehovah's Witnesses refused to comply with the regulation on the grounds that it violated the biblical prohibition, in the Second Commandment, against the making of or the bowing down to any graven image. Because of the religious convictions of the challengers, this case is often considered to have been decided under the religious clauses of the First Amendment. Three years earlier, however, in *Minersville School District v. Gobitis*, 310 U.S. 586 (1940), the Supreme Court upheld a similar flag salute law against a Jehovah's Witness's religious challenge. The *Barnette* decision, although overruling *Gobitis*, rests on the broader right of free expression.

☆ 235 *Board of Education v. Barnette*

319 U.S. 624 (1943).

Mr. Justice JACKSON delivered the opinion of the Court:

*   *   *

... What is now required is the "stiff-arm" salute, the saluter to keep the right hand raised with palm turned up while the following is repeated: "I pledge allegiance to the Flag of the United States of America and to the Republic for which it stands; one Nation, indivisible, with liberty and justice for all."

Failure to conform is "insubordination" dealt with by expulsion. Readmission is denied by statute until compliance. Meanwhile the expelled child is "unlawfully absent" and may be proceeded against as a delinquent. His parents or guardians are liable to prosecution, and if convicted are subject to fine not exceeding $50 and jail term not exceeding thirty days.

*   *   *

Children ... have been expelled from school and are threatened with exclusion for no other cause. Officials threaten to send them to reformatories maintained for criminally inclined juveniles. Parents of such children have been prosecuted and are threatened with prosecutions for causing delinquency.

*   *   *

The freedom asserted by these appellees does not bring them into collision with rights asserted by any other individual. It is such conflicts which most frequently require intervention of the State to determine where the rights of one end and those of another begin. But the refusal of these persons to participate in the ceremony does not interfere with or deny rights of others to do so. Nor is there any question in this case that their behavior is peaceable and orderly. The sole conflict is between authority and rights of the individual. The State asserts power to condition access to public education on making a prescribed sign and profession and at the same time to coerce attendance by punishing both parent and child. The latter stand on a right of self-determination in matters that touch individual opinion and personal attitude.

... [W]e are dealing with a compulsion of students to declare a belief. They are not merely made acquainted with the flag salute so that they may be informed as to what it is or even what it means. The issue here is whether this slow and easily neglected route to aroused loyalties constitutionally may be short-cut by substituting a compulsory salute and slogan. ...

There is no doubt that, in connection with the pledges, the flag salute is a form of utterance. Symbolism is a primitive but effective way of communicating ideas. The use of an emblem or flag to symbolize some system, idea, institution, or personality, is a short cut from mind to mind. Causes and nations, political parties, lodges and ecclesiastical groups seek to knit the loyalty of their followings to a flag or banner, a color or design. The State announces rank, function, and authority through crowns and maces, uniforms and black robes; the church speaks through the Cross, the Crucifix, the altar and shrine, and clerical raiment. Symbols of State often convey political ideas just as religious symbols come to convey theological ones. Associated with many of these symbols are appropriate gestures of acceptance or respect: a salute, a bowed or bared head, a bended knee. A person gets from a symbol the meaning he puts into it, and what is one man's comfort and inspiration is another's jest and scorn.

Over a decade ago Chief Justice Hughes led this Court in holding that the display of a red flag as a symbol of opposition by peaceful and legal means to organized government was protected by the free speech guaranties of the Constitution. Here it is the State that employs a flag as a symbol of adherence to government as presently organized. It requires the individual to communicate by word and sign his acceptance of the political ideas it thus bespeaks. Objection to this form of communication when coerced is an old one, well known to the framers of the Bill of Rights.

It is also to be noted that the compulsory flag salute and pledge requires affirmation of a belief and an attitude of mind. It is not clear whether the regulation contemplates that pupils forego any contrary convictions of their own and become unwilling converts to the prescribed ceremony or whether it will be acceptable if they simulate assent by words without belief and by a gesture barren of meaning. It is now a commonplace that censorship or suppression of expression of opinion is tolerated by our Constitution only when the expression presents a clear and present danger of action of a kind the State is empowered to prevent and punish. It would seem that involuntary affirmation could be commanded only on even more immediate and urgent grounds than silence. But here the power of compulsion is invoked without any allegation that remaining passive during a flag salute ritual creates a clear and present danger that would justify an effort even to muffle expression. To sustain the compulsory flag salute we are required to say that a Bill of Rights which guards the individual's right to speak his own mind, left it open to public authorities to compel him to utter what is not in his mind.

Whether the First Amendment to the Constitution will permit officials to order observance of ritual of this nature does not depend upon whether as a voluntary exercise we would think it to be good, bad or merely innocuous. Any credo of nationalism is likely to include what some disapprove or to omit what others think essential, and to give off different overtones as it takes on different accents or interpretations. If official power exists to coerce acceptance of any patriotic creed, what it shall contain cannot be decided by courts, but must be largely discretionary with the ordaining authority, whose power to prescribe would no doubt include power to amend. Hence validity of the asserted power to force an American citizen publicly to profess any statement of belief or to engage in any ceremony of assent to one, presents questions of power that must be considered independently of any idea we may have as to the utility of the ceremony in question.

Nor does the issue as we see it turn on one's possession of particular religious views or the sincerity with which they are held. While religion supplies appellees' motive for enduring the discomforts of making the issue in this case, many citizens who do not share these religious views hold such a compulsory rite to infringe constitutional liberty of the individual. It is not necessary to inquire whether non-conformist beliefs will exempt from the duty to salute unless we first find power to make the salute a legal duty.

*   *   *

1. It was said that the flag-salute controversy confronted the Court with "the problem which Lincoln cast in memorable dilemma: 'Must a government of necessity be too *strong* for the liberties of its people, or too *weak* to maintain its own existence?' " and that the answer must be in favor of strength.

We think these issues may be examined free of pressure or restraint growing out of such considerations.

It may be doubted whether Mr. Lincoln would have thought that the strength of government to maintain itself would be impressively vindicated by our confirming power of the State to expel a handful of children from school. Such oversimplification, so handy in political debate, often lacks the precision necessary to postulates of judicial reasoning. If validly applied to this problem, the utterance cited would resolve every issue of power in favor of those in authority and would require us to override every liberty thought to weaken or delay execution of their policies.

Government of limited power need not be anemic government. Assurance that rights are secure tends to diminish fear and jealousy of strong government, and by making us feel safe to live under it makes for its better support. Without promise of a limiting Bill of Rights it is doubtful if our Constitution could have mustered enough strength to enable its ratification. To enforce those rights today is not to choose weak government over strong government. It is only to adhere as a means of strength to individual freedom of mind in preference to officially disciplined uniformity for which history indicates a disappointing and disastrous end.

The subject now before us exemplifies this principle. Free public education, if faithful to the ideal of secular instruction and political neutrality, will not be partisan or enemy of any class, creed, party, or faction. If it is to impose any ideological discipline, however, each party or denomination must seek to control, or failing that, to weaken the influence of the educational system. Observance of the limitations of the Constitution will not weaken government in the field appropriate for its exercise.

*   *   *

3. . . . [It is argued] that it is constitutionally appropriate to "fight out the wise use of legislative authority in the forum of public opinion and before legislative assemblies rather than to transfer such a contest to the judicial arena," since all the "effective means of inducing political changes are left free."

The very purpose of a Bill of Rights was to withdraw certain subjects from the vicissitudes of political controversy, to place them beyond the reach of majorities and officials and to establish them as legal principles to be applied by the courts. One's right to life, liberty, and property, to free speech, a free press, freedom of worship and assembly, and other fundamental rights may not be submitted to vote; they depend on the outcome of no elections.

*   *   *

4. Lastly, [it is contended] that "National unity is the basis of national security," that the authorities have "the right to select appropriate means for its attainment," and hence reaches the conclusion that such compulsory measures toward "national unity" are constitutional. Upon the verity of this assumption depends our answer in this case.

National unity as an end which officials may foster by persuasion and example is not in question. The problem is whether under our Constitution compulsion as here employed is a permissible means for its achievement.

Struggles to coerce uniformity of sentiment in support of some end thought essential to their time and country have been waged by many good as well as by evil men. Nationalism is a relatively recent phenomenon but at other times and places the ends have been racial or territorial security, support of a dynasty or regime, and particular plans for saving souls. As first and moderate methods to attain unity have failed, those bent on its accomplishment must resort to an ever-increasing severity. As governmental pressure toward unity becomes greater, so strife becomes more bitter as to whose unity it shall be. Probably no deeper division of our people could proceed from any provocation than from finding it necessary to choose what doctrine and whose program public educational officials shall compel youth to unite in embracing. Ultimate futility of such attempts to compel coherence is the lesson of every such effort from the Roman drive to stamp out Christianity as a disturber of its pagan unity, the Inquisition, as a means to religious and dynastic unity, the Siberian exiles as a means to Russian unity, down to the fast failing efforts of our present totalitarian enemies. Those who begin coercive elimination of dissent soon find themselves exterminating dissenters. Compulsory unification of opinion achieves only the unanimity of the graveyard.

It seems trite but necessary to say that the First Amendment to our Constitution was designed to avoid these ends by avoiding these beginnings. There is no mysticism in the American concept of the State or of the nature or origin of its authority. We set up government by consent of the governed, and the Bill of Rights denies those in power any legal opportunity to coerce that consent. Authority here is to be controlled by public opinion, not public opinion by authority.

... We can have intellectual individualism and the rich cultural diversities that we owe to exceptional minds only at the price of occasional eccentricity and abnormal attitudes. When they are so harmless to others or to the State as those we deal with here, the price is not too great. But freedom to differ is not limited to things that do not matter much. That would be a mere shadow of freedom. The test of its substance is the right to differ as to things that touch the heart of the existing order.

If there is any fixed star in our constitutional constellation, it is that no official, high or petty, can prescribe what shall be orthodox in politics, nationalism, religion, or other matters of opinion or force citizens to confess by word or act their faith therein. If there are any circumstances which permit an exception, they do not now occur to us.

We think the action of the local authorities in compelling the flag salute and pledge transcends constitutional limitations on their power and invades the sphere of intellect and spirit which it is the purpose of the First Amendment to our Constitution to reserve from all official control.

[T]he judgment enjoining enforcement of the West Virginia Regulation is

Affirmed.

236 "there has been relatively little social intercourse" (1943)

In *Hirabayashi v. United States*, the Supreme Court examined the case of a Japanese-American citizen, a senior at the University of Washington, convicted of violating a military curfew regulation applicable only to those of Japanese extraction. Hirabayashi had violated the regulation in order to challenge its constitutionality on the grounds of racial discrimination. Although the equal protection clause of the Fourteenth Amendment is not by its terms applicable to the federal government, the federally-applicable due process clause of the Fifth Amendment is considered to require adherence to the same principle of equality. Nevertheless, the court upheld the conviction, reciting the special circumstances of both the war and the Japanese population.

☆ 236 *Hirabayashi v. United States*

320 U.S. 21 (1943).

Mr. Chief Justice STONE delivered the opinion of the Court.

*   *   *

The questions for our decision are whether the particular restriction violated, namely that all persons of Japanese ancestry residing in such an area be within their place of residence daily between the hours of 8:00 P.M. and 6:00 A.M., ... unconstitutionally discriminated between citizens of Japanese ancestry and those of other ancestries in violation of the Fifth Amendment.

The actions taken must be appraised in the light of the conditions with which the President and Congress were confronted in the early months of 1942, many of which, since disclosed, were then peculiarly within the knowledge of the military authorities. . . .

. . . That reasonably prudent men charged with the responsibility of our national defense had ample ground for concluding that they must face the danger of invasion, take measures against it, and in making the choice of measures consider our internal situation, cannot be doubted.

. . . As the curfew was made applicable to citizens residing in the area only if they were of Japanese ancestry, our inquiry must be whether in the light of all the facts and circumstances there was any substantial basis for the conclusion, in which Congress and the military commander united, that the curfew as applied was a protective measure necessary to meet the threat of sabotage and espionage which would substantially affect the war effort and which might reasonably be expected to aid a threatened enemy invasion.

*   *   *

. . . At a time of threatened Japanese attack upon this country, the nature of our inhabitants' attachments to the Japanese enemy was consequently a matter of grave concern. . . .

There is support for the view that social, economic and political conditions which have prevailed since the close of the last century, when the Japanese began to come to this country in substantial numbers, have intensified their solidarity and have in large measure prevented their assimilation as an integral part of the white population. In addition, large numbers of children of Japanese parentage are sent to Japanese language schools outside the regular hours of public schools in the locality. Some of these schools are generally believed to be sources of Japanese nationalistic propaganda, cultivating allegiance to Japan. Considerable numbers, estimated to be approximately 10,000, of American-born children of Japanese parentage have been sent to Japan for all or a part of their education.

Congress and the Executive, including the military commander, could have attributed special significance, in its bearing on the loyalties of persons of Japanese descent, to the maintenance by Japan of its system of dual citizenship. Children born in the United States of Japanese alien parents, and especially those children born before December 1, 1924, are under many circumstances deemed, by Japanese law, to be citizens of Japan. . . .

As a result of all these conditions affecting the life of the Japanese, both aliens and citizens, in the Pacific Coast area, there has been relatively little social intercourse between them and the white population. The restrictions, both practical and legal, affecting the privileges and opportunities afforded to persons of Japanese extraction residing in the United States, have been sources of irritation and may well have tended to increase their isolation, and in many instances their attachments to Japan and its institutions.

*   *   *

[W]e cannot reject as unfounded the judgment of the military authorities and of Congress that there were disloyal members of [the Japanese resident] population, whose number and strength could not be precisely and quickly ascertained. We cannot say that the war-making branches of the Government did not have ground for believing that in a critical hour such persons could not readily be isolated and separately dealt with, and constituted a menace to the national defense and safety, which demanded that prompt and adequate measures be taken to guard against it.

Distinctions between citizens solely because of their ancestry are by their very nature odious to a free people whose institutions are founded upon the doctrine of equality. . . . Because racial discriminations are in most circumstances irrelevant and therefore prohibited, it by no means follows that, in dealing with the perils of war, Congress and the Executive are wholly precluded from taking into account those facts and circumstances which are relevant to measures for our national defense, and for the successful prosecution of the war, and which may in fact place citizens of one ancestry in a different category from others. The adoption by Government, in the crisis of war and of threatened invasion, of measures for the public safety, based upon the recognition of facts and circumstances which indicate that a group of one national extraction may menace that safety more than others, is not wholly beyond the limits of the Constitution and is not to be condemned merely because in other and in most circumstances racial distinctions are irrelevant.

*   *   *

Affirmed.

237 "a fascist form of government should be established in the United States" (1943)

Capping more than a decade of concern about American varieties of fascism and nazism, a grand jury was empaneled on October 26, 1943, and an indictment was returned on January 3, 1944, in Washington, D.C., against an assorted and unrelated group of thirty Nazi sympathizers. The Depression had spawned not only supporters of the socialist and Communist causes but also radicals on the far right.

Beginning in 1934, President Franklin D. Roosevelt had ordered FBI probes of these right-wing critics of his administration, including William Dudley Pelley, chief of the Silver Shirts; Robert Edmondson, a pamphleteer purporting to expose Roosevelt's alleged Jewish ancestry; George E. Deatherage, Grand Commander of the Knights of the White Camelia; and Father Charles E. Coughlin, connected with the Christian Front. America's entry into World War II finally provided an opportunity for more direct action against what were considered the "scurrilous" publications and "Trojan Horse" activities of the Nazi sympathizers. After two earlier aborted indictments, on January 3, 1944, a third indictment was returned against a strange mix of leaders of nativist and isolationist organizations, ranting pro-German and anti-Semitic publicists, and former leaders of the German-American Bund. The prosecution of this group, for participating in an international Nazi conspiracy dedicated to Hitler's program to "destroy democracy" and establish "national Socialist or fascist" governments in the United States, became known as *United States v. McWilliams*, taking the name of the first defendant. Technically the charge was conspiracy to commit sedition under the Smith Act by counseling insubordination in the armed forces.

Chief Justice Edward C. Eicher of the United States district court presided over the trial, which commenced on April 17, 1944. After seven months of proceedings, Judge Eicher died of a heart attack on November 29. A mistrial was declared; and after lingering until 1947, the still outstanding indictments were dismissed on the grounds that the accused had been denied a speedy trial.

☆ 237 *United States v. McWilliams*

Reprinted in M. St. George and L. Dennis, *A Trial on Trial: The Great Sedition Trial of 1944* (National Civil Rights Committee, 1946), 114-21.

District Court of the United States for the District of Columbia

Holding a Criminal Term

District of Columbia, ss:
October Term, A.D. 1943

INDICTMENT

The . . . Grand Jurors for the United States of America, duly empaneled and sworn in the District of Columbia on October 26, 1943, for the October 1943 Term, upon their oaths present that:

In 1933 the National Socialist German Workers Party, also known as the N.S.D.A.P. and the "Nazi Party," came into power in Germany upon a program publicly announced by its leaders to destroy democracy throughout the world and to establish and aid in the establishment of national socialist or fascist forms of government in place of the forms of government then existing in the United States of America and other countries. As a means of accomplishing their objectives, the said Nazi Party and its leaders carried on a systematic campaign of propaganda designed and intended to impair and undermine the loyalty and morale of the military and naval forces of the United States of America and of other countries. The persons hereinafter named as defendants joined in this movement and program and actively cooperated with each other and with leaders and members of the said Nazi Party to accomplish the objectives of said Nazi Party in the United States.

On the 28th day of June, 1940, there w[as] enacted [the Smith Act], and continuously thereafter . . . the defendants, in the District of Columbia and within the jurisdiction of this court, and at divers other places throughout the United States of America, in Germany, and elsewhere, in violation of Section 3 of the aforesaid Act, unlawfully, wilfully, feloniously and knowingly conspired, combined, confederated and agreed together and with each other and with officials of the Government of the German Reich and leaders and members of the said Nazi Party, said persons hereinafter being referred to as "co-conspirators," to commit acts prohibited by Section 1 of said Act in that they, the said defendants and the said co-conspirators, with intent to interfere with, impair and influence the loyalty, morale and discipline of the military and naval forces of the United States, would:

(i) Advise, counsel, urge and cause insubordination, disloyalty, mutiny and refusal to duty by members of the military and naval forces of the United States; and
(ii) Distribute and cause to be distributed written and printed matter, advising, counseling, and urging insubordination, disloyalty, mutiny and refusal of duty by members of the military and naval forces of the United States.

And the Grand Jurors aforesaid, upon their oaths aforesaid, do further present that, as part of said conspiracy and as means and methods of accomplishing the objects thereof, the said defendants and co-conspirators, during the period of said conspiracy, in the District of Columbia and within the jurisdiction of this court and at divers other places throughout the United States, in Germany, and elsewhere would do, and they did, among other things, the following:

1. Print, publish, distribute and circulate, and cause to be printed, published, distributed and circulated, among others, the following newspapers, magazines, books, leaflets, circulars, pamphlets, documents, cartoons, drawings and photographs:

Mein Kampf
The National Socialist Party Programme
Welt Dienst (World Service)
Der Stuermer
News from Germany
Deutsche Wochenschau
Muenchner Neuste Nachrichten
The Free American and Deutscher
Weckruf und Beobachter
The White Knight
The American Nationalist Confederation
  News Bulletin
The Revealer
The Defender
Liberation
The Roll Call
The Galilean
National Liberty Party
Yankee Freemen
Yankee Minute Men
Friends of Progress
Industrial Control Reports
Social Republic Society Bulletin
Comment
The Corporate State
What Prince Lippe Told Me
Patriotic Research Bureau News Letter
Edmondson's Economic Research Service
"American Vigilante" Bulletins
The Christian Mobilizer
The Weekly Foreign Letter
The Dynamics of War and Revolution
Publicity
America in Danger
Nationalist Newsletter
Our Common Cause
The World Hoax
Roosevelt's Jewish Ancestry
History Repeats
The Answer to the Betrayal
America on the March
National Socialism and Its Justification
Card headed *"West Africa Is Not Iceland—It's Anything But a Nice Land!"*
The Miracle of Happiness

2. Organize, support, use, and control, and cause to be organized, supported, and used, among others, the following parties, offices, groups, organizations, publishers and distributors:

National Socialist German Workers Party (N.S.D.A.P.)
Franz Eher Publishing House, Munich
Foreign Organization of The National Socialist Party (A.O.)
Ministry of Public Enlightenment and Propaganda of the German Reich
German Library of Information
Welt Dienst, Erfurt *(World Service)*

German Foreign Institut, Stuttgart *(D.A.I.)*
League of Germandom Abroad (V.D.A.)
Fichte Bund, Hamburg
Terramare Office, Berlin
Transocean News Service
Foreign Office of the German Reich
German Embassy at Washington, D.C., and various
  German Consulates in the United States
German Ministry of Education
Amerika Institut
German-American Bund
Silver Shirts
Silver Legion
Pelley Publishers
Fellowship Press, Inc.
Knights of the White Camelia
American Nationalist Confederation
National Liberty Party
National Workers' League
Friends of Progress
Patriotic Research Bureau
Social Republic Society, also known as *S.O.C.I.S.*
James True Associates
Flanders Hall, Incorporated
Aryan Book Store
The Defenders Publishers
The Christian Mobilizers
The American Destiny Party
American National Socialist Party
National Press Association

3. Disseminate, by the means set forth in the preceding two paragraphs and otherwise, oral, written, and printed statements, representations and charges asserting among other things in substance that:

a. Democracy is decadent; a national socialist or fascist form of government should be established in the United States.

b. A national socialist revolution is inevitable if we are to rid our country of its decadent democracy.

c. The Government of the United States, the Congress and public officials are controlled by Communists, International Jews, and plutocrats.

d. The Democratic and Republican parties and their candidates for public office are tools of International Jewry, and do not represent the will of the American people.

e. The acts, proclamations, and orders of the public officials of the United States and the laws of Congress are illegal, corrupt, traitorous and in direct violation of the Constitution of the United States.

f. The United States is governed, not by the duly elected representatives of the people, but by a group of alien-minded persons opposed to American principles and ideals and seeking to overthrow the Constitution of the United States.

g. President Roosevelt is reprehensible, a war-monger, liar, unscrupulous, and a pawn of the Jews, Communists and Plutocrats.

h. President Roosevelt is a Jew and is working with International Jewry against the interests of the people of the United States.

i. The activities and territorial acquisitions and plans of the Axis Powers constitute no real danger to the national existence and security of the United States or any of its territorial possessions.

j. The Axis Powers are fighting to free the world from domination by Communism and International Jewry, and to save Christianity, hence the United States should give no aid and comfort to the enemies of the Axis.

k. The cause of the Axis Powers is the cause of justice and morality; they have committed no aggressive act against any nation and are fighting a solely defensive war against British Imperialism, American Capitalists, and the desire of American public officials to rule the world, hence any act of war against them is unjust and immoral on the part of the United States.

l. The nations opposed to the Axis, plan to use American lives, money and property to defend their decadent systems of government.

m. The participation of the United States in the war has been deliberately planned by our leaders with the ultimate aim of promoting our enslavement by British Imperialism and International Communism.

n. The public officials of the United States of America are trying deliberately to provoke war with peaceful nations, such as Germany, Italy and Japan, which are seeking only to live at peace with the rest of the world.

o. President Roosevelt and Congress, through a surreptitious and illegal war program against the Axis Powers sold out the United States and forced the Axis Power[s] to wage war upon us.

p. President Roosevelt by his war-mongering policies is draining dry the resources of the United States to save Communist China, Imperialist Britain and Atheistic Russia from inevitable defeat.

q. Our program of giving American arms and equipment to foreign nations results in United States military and naval forces being inadequately armed and equipped and in their being exposed to terrible slaughter.

r. The public officials of the United States are knaves who have deliberately concealed the truth that our unprepared boys, racked by disease and slaughtered like sheep, will be dumped in a million foreign graves to buy a valueless victory.

s. The whole war is the result of a Jew-sponsored money-making scheme to bleed the United States Treasury.

t. As the result of incompetence and corruption in public office, the United States is unprepared to wage war against the Axis Powers, who have the best equipped and most powerful military establishment in the world.

u. The present war is a dishonest war waged at the expense and measured in the blood and dollars of the people of the United States solely for the benefit of and to insure the continuance of world domination by "International Bankers," "International Capitalists," "Mongolian Jews," "Communists," and "International Jewry."

v. The Japanese attack upon Pearl Harbor was deliberately invited by the public officials of the United States, in order to involve the United States in a foreign war.

w. The war with Japan was deliberately provoked by the insane, unjust, aggressive and traitorous policies of officials of the United States.

x. An honorable and just peace could be brought about speedily were it not for the opposition of Communists, International Jewry, and war profiteers.

Contrary to the form of the statute in such case made and provided, and against the peace and dignity of the United States.

EDWARD M. CURRAN
United States Attorney for the
District of Columbia
O. JOHN ROGGE
Special Assistant to the
Attorney General

238 "imprisonment . . . in a concentration camp because of racial prejudice" (1944)

Fred Korematsu challenged his conviction for failing to report for evacuation from the military area in which he resided on the grounds that the evacuation order was racially discriminatory. The government had made no assertion that Korematsu, a native-born citizen of the United States, had been disloyal. Justice Black, writing for the majority, nevertheless upheld the power of the government. He wrote that "[p]ressing public necessity may sometimes justify the existence of such restrictions, racial antagonism never can."

The court stated further that making a determination as to who was loyal would present a tremendous problem, especially when immediate action was necessary in the interest of security. "Our task would be simple, our duty clear, were this a case involving the imprisonment of a loyal citizen in a concentration camp because of racial prejudice . . . [but here] we are dealing specifically with nothing but an exclusion order," Justice Black emphasized. Significantly, only Justice Murphy in this dissent addressed the issue of Japanese-American detention in temporary Relocation Centers. The majority restricted its decision to the issue of exclusion from the military areas.

☆ 238 *Korematsu v. United States*

323 U.S. 214 (1944).

Mr. Justice BLACK delivered the opinion of the Court.

*   *   *

... It should be noted, to begin with, that all legal restrictions which curtail the civil rights of a single racial group are immediately suspect. That is not to say that all such restrictions are unconstitutional. It is to say that courts must subject them to the most rigid scrutiny. Pressing public necessity may sometimes justify the existence of such restrictions; racial antagonism never can.

*   *   *

Exclusion Order No. 34..., issued after we were at war with Japan, declared that "the successful prosecution of the war requires every possible protection against espionage and against sabotage to national-defense material, national-defense premises, and national-defense utilities...."

... [In *Hirabayashi*] [w]e upheld the [Japanese] curfew order as an exercise of the power of the government to take steps necessary to prevent espionage and sabotage in an area threatened by Japanese attack.

... [E]xclusion from the area in which one's home is located is a far greater deprivation than constant confinement to the home from 8 P.M. to 6 A.M. Nothing short of apprehension by the proper military authorities of the gravest imminent danger to the public safety can constitutionally justify either. But exclusion from a threatened area, no less than curfew, has a definite and close relationship to the prevention of espionage and sabotage. The military authorities, charged with the primary responsibility of defending our shores, concluded that curfew provided inadequate protection and ordered exclusion. They did so ... in accordance with Congressional authority to the military to say who should, and who should not, remain in the threatened areas.

In this case the petitioner challenges the assumptions upon which we rested our conclusions in the *Hirabayashi* case. He also urges that by May 1942, when Order No. 34 was promulgated, all danger of Japanese invasion of the West Coast had disappeared. After careful consideration of these contentions we are compelled to reject them.

*   *   *

Like curfew, exclusion of those of Japanese origin was deemed necessary because of the presence of an unascertained number of disloyal members of the group, most of whom we have no doubt were loyal to this country. It was because we could not reject the finding of the military authorities that it was impossible to bring about an immediate segregation of the disloyal from the loyal that we sustained the validity of the curfew order as applying to the whole group. In the instant case, temporary exclusion of the entire group was rested by the military on the same ground.... [This] answers the contention that the exclusion was in the nature of group punishment based on antagonism to those of Japanese origin. That there were members of the group who retained loyalties to Japan has been confirmed by investigations made subsequent to the exclusion....

We uphold the exclusion order as of the time it was made and when the petitioner violated it.... Compulsory exclusion of large groups of citizens from their homes, except under circumstances of direst emergency and peril, is inconsistent with our basic governmental institutions. But when under conditions of modern warfare our shores are threatened by hostile forces, the power to protect must be commensurate with the threatened danger.

*   *   *

It is said that we are dealing here with the case of imprisonment of a citizen in a concentration camp solely because of his ancestry, without evidence or inquiry concerning his loyalty and good disposition towards the United States. Our task would be simple, our duty clear, were this a case involving the imprisonment of a loyal citizen in a concentration camp because of racial prejudice. Regardless of the true nature of the assembly and relocation centers—and we deem it unjustifiable to call them concentration camps with all the ugly connotations that term implies—we are dealing specifically with nothing but an exclusion order. To case this case into outlines of racial prejudice, without reference to the real military dangers which were presented, merely confuses the issue. Korematsu was not excluded from the Military Area because of hostility to him or his race. He *was* excluded because we are at war with the Japanese Empire, because the properly constituted military authorities feared an invasion of our West Coast and felt constrained to take proper security measures, because they decided that the military urgency of the situation demanded that all citizens of Japanese ancestry be segregated from the West Coast temporarily, and finally, because Congress, reposing its confidence in this time of war in our military leaders—as inevitably it must—determined that they should have the power to do just this. There was evidence of disloyalty on the part of some, the military authorities considered that the need for action was great, and time was short. We cannot—by availing ourselves of the calm perspective of hindsight—now say that at that time these actions were unjustified.

Affirmed.

239 "a dangerously disorderly migration" (1944)

The curfew and evacuation programs were not the end of the exercise of war powers over the Japanese-American population. Pursuant to Executive Order 9102, the president established the War Relocation Agency. The agency maintained Relocation Centers, which housed the Japanese (American citizens as well as aliens) excluded from the West Coast by virtue of Executive Order 9066. At the centers, officials were to determine the evacuees' loyalty to the United States, but even those certified as loyal were not free to leave and migrate on their own to less sensitive areas of the United States for fear of popular hostility. Although the court held that the government could not detain Ms. Endo against her will, the decision was narrow in scope. The court did not seriously question Congress's authority to maintain such camps. This seeming assent supported the later argument that the courts would not hold the Emergency Detention Act of 1950 (part of the McCarran Act) to be unconstitutional.

☆ 239 *Ex Parte Endo*

323 U.S. 283 (1944).

Mr. Justice DOUGLAS delivered the opinion of the Court:

*   *   *

Her petition for a writ of *habeas corpus* alleges that she is a loyal and law-abiding citizen of the United States, that no charge has been made against her, that she is being unlawfully detained, and that she is confined in the Relocation Center under armed guard and held there against her will.

It is conceded by the Department of Justice and by the War Relocation Authority that appellant is a loyal and law-abiding citizen. They make no claim that she is detained on any charge or that she is even suspected of disloyalty. Moreover, they do not contend that she may be held any longer in the Relocation Center. They concede that it is beyond the power of the War Relocation Authority to detain citizens against whom no charges of disloyalty or subversiveness have been made for a period longer than that necessary to separate the loyal from the disloyal and to provide the necessary guidance for relocation. But they maintain that detention for an additional period after leave clearance has been granted is an essential step in the evacuation program.

*   *   *

It is argued that such a planned and orderly relocation was essential to the success of the evacuation program; that but for such supervision there might have been a dangerously disorderly migration of unwanted people to unprepared communities; that unsupervised evacuation might have resulted in hardship and disorder; that the success of the evacuation program was thought to require the knowledge that the federal government was maintaining control over the evacuated population except as the release of individuals could be effected consistently with their own peace and well-being and that of the nation; that although community hostility towards the evacuees has diminished, it has not disappeared and the continuing control of the Authority over the relocation process is essential to the success of the evacuation program. It is argued that supervised relocation, as the chosen method of terminating the evacuation, is the final step in the entire process and is a consequence of the first step taken. It is conceded that appellant's detention pending compliance with the leave regulations is not directly connected with the prevention of espionage and sabotage at the present time. But it is argued that ... power [exists] to make regulations necessary and proper for controlling situations created by the exercise of the powers expressly conferred for protection against espionage and sabotage. The leave regulations are said to fall within that category.

First. We are of the view that Mitsuye Endo should be given her liberty. In reaching that conclusion we do not come to the underlying constitutional issues which have been argued. For we conclude that, whatever power the War Relocation Authority may have to detain other classes of citizens, it has no authority to subject citizens who are concededly loyal to its leave procedure.

*   *   *

Such power of detention as the Authority has stems from Executive Order No. 9066. . . .

We approach the construction of Executive Order No. 9066 as we would approach the construction of legislation in this field. That Executive Order must indeed be considered along with the Act of March 21, 1942, which ratified and confirmed it[,] as the Order and the statute together laid such basis as there is for participation by civil agencies of the federal government in the evacuation program. Broad powers frequently granted to the President or other executive officers by Congress so that they may deal with the exigencies of wartime problems have been sustained. And the Constitution when it committed to the Executive and to Congress the exercise of the war power necessarily gave them wide scope for the exercise of judgment and discretion so that war might be waged effectively and successfully. At the same time, however, the Constitution is as specific in its enumeration of many of the civil rights of the individual as it is in its enumeration of the powers of his government. . . .

. . . This Court has quite consistently given a narrower scope for the operation of the presumption of constitutionality when legislation appeared on its face to violate a specific prohibition of the Constitution. We have likewise favored that interpretation of legislation which gives it the greater chance of surviving the test of constitutionality. Those analogies are suggestive here. We must assume that the Chief Executive and members of Congress, as well as the courts, are sensitive to and respectful of the liberties of the citizen. In interpreting a wartime measure we must assume that their purpose was to allow for the greatest possible accommodation between those liberties and the exigencies of war. We must assume, when asked to find implied powers in a grant of legislative or executive authority, that the law makers intended to place no greater restraint on the citizen than was clearly and unmistakably indicated by the language they used.

The Act of March 21, 1942, was a war measure. . . .

. . . The purpose and objective of the Act and of these orders are plain. Their single aim was the protection of the war effort against espionage and sabotage. It is in light of that one objective that the powers conferred by the orders must be construed.

Neither the Act nor the orders use the language of detention. . . . And that silence may have special significance in view of the fact that detention in Relocation Centers was no part of the original program of evacuation but developed later to meet what seemed to the officials in charge to be mounting hostility to the evacuees on the part of the communities where they sought to go.

We do not mean to imply that detention in connection with no phase of the evacuation program would be lawful. The fact that the Act and the orders are silent on detention does not of course mean that any power to detain is lacking. Some such power might indeed be necessary to the successful operation of the evacuation program. At least we may so assume. Moreover, we may assume for the purposes of this case that initial detention in Relocation Centers was authorized. But we stress the silence of the legislative history and of the Act and the Executive Orders on the power to detain to emphasize that any such authority which exists must be implied. If there is to be the greatest possible accommodation of the liberties of the citizen with this war measure, any such implied power must be narrowly confined to the precise purpose of the evacuation program.

A citizen who is concededly loyal presents no problem of espionage or sabotage. Loyalty is a matter of the heart and mind, not of race, creed, or color. He who is loyal is by definition not a spy or a saboteur. When the power to detain is derived from the power to protect the war effort against espionage and sabotage, detention which has no relationship to that objective is unauthorized.

Nor may the power to detain an admittedly loyal citizen or to grant him a conditional release be implied as a useful or convenient step in the evacuation program, whatever authority might be implied in case of those whose loyalty was not conceded or established. If we assume (as we do) that the original evacuation was justified, its lawful character was derived from the fact that it was an espionage and sabotage measure, not that there was community hostility to this group of American citizens. The evacuation program rested explicitly on the former ground not on the latter as the underlying legislation shows. The authority to detain a citizen or to grant him a conditional release as protection against espionage or sabotage is exhausted at least when his loyalty is conceded. If we held that the authority to detain continued thereafter, we would transform an espionage or sabotage measure into something else. That was not done by Executive Order No. 9066 or by the Act of March 21, 1942, which ratified it. What they did not do we cannot do. Detention which furthered the campaign against espionage and sabotage would be one thing. But detention which has no relationship to that campaign is of a distinct character. Community hostility even to loyal evacuees may have been (and perhaps still is) a serious problem. But if authority for their custody and supervision is to be sought on that ground, the Act of March 21, 1942, [and] Executive Order No. 9066 . . . offer no support. And none other is advanced. To read them that broadly would be to assume that the Congress and the President intended that this discriminatory action should be taken against these people wholly on account of their ancestry even though the government conceded their loyalty to this country. We cannot make such an assumption. . . .

Mitsuye Endo is entitled to an unconditional release by the War Relocation Authority.

*   *   *

240 A Failure of Good Moral Character (1945)

In 1942 the nation was at war, and popular sentiment against pacifists was uncordial. Article XII of the Illinois Constitution denominated all able-bodied men between the ages of nineteen and forty-five to be the militia of the state. It also provided that the state would not require those having conscientious scruples against bearing arms to perform militia duty in peacetime. When a recognized conscientious objector applied for admission to the Illinois Bar, the state supreme court refused to admit him on the grounds that his religious scruples disabled him from swearing in good faith to uphold the Illinois Constitution, in particular the provision requiring militia duty in time of war. Summers claimed he could take the oath, but Illinois insisted an incurable incompatibility existed between his conscientious beliefs and the obligations of an attorney.

The United States Supreme Court upheld, 5-4, Illinois' power to ostracize Summers from the legal profession, relying on decisions upholding congressional authority to preclude from naturalization those otherwise eligible aliens whose political allegiance would be suspect because they could not pledge to give military service.

☆ 240 *In re Summers*

325 U.S. 561 (1945).

Mr. Justice REED delivered the opinion of the Court:

*   *   *

... A conscientious belief in non-violence to the extent that the believer will not use force to prevent wrong, no matter how aggravated, and so cannot swear in good faith to support the Illinois Constitution, the [Illinois] Justices contend, must disqualify such a believer for admission.

*   *   *

... Of course, under our Constitutional system, men could not be excluded from the practice of law, or indeed from following any other calling, simply because they belong to any of our religious groups, whether Protestant, Catholic, Quaker or Jewish, assuming it conceivable that any state of the Union would draw such a religious line. We cannot say that any such purpose to discriminate motivated the action of the Illinois Supreme Court.

*   *   *

Illinois has constitutional provisions which require service in the militia in time of war of men of petitioner's age group.[11] The return of the Justices alleges that petitioner has not made any showing that he would serve notwithstanding his conscientious objections. This allegation is undenied in the record and unchallenged by brief. We accept the allegation as to unwillingness to serve in the militia as established. While ... conscientious objectors to participation in war in any form now are permitted to do non-war work of national importance, this is by grace of Congressional recognition of their beliefs. The Act may be repealed. No similar exemption during war exists under Illinois law....

The United States does not admit to citizenship the alien who refuses to pledge military service.

Even the powerful dissents which emphasized the deep cleavage in this Court on the issue of admission to citizenship did not challenge the right of Congress to require military service from every able-bodied man. It is impossible for us to conclude that the insistence of Illinois that an officer who is charged with the administration of justice must take an oath to support the Constitution of Illinois and Illinois' interpretation of that oath to require a willingness to perform military service violates the principles of religious freedom which the Fourteenth Amendment secures against state action, when a like interpretation of a similar oath as to the Federal Constitution bars an alien from national citizenship.

Affirmed.

MR. JUSTICE BLACK, dissenting.

*   *   *

I cannot believe that a state statute would be consistent with our constitutional guarantee of freedom of religion if it specifically denied the right to practice law to all members of one of our great religious groups, Protestant, Catholic, or Jewish. Yet the Quakers have had a long and honorable part in the growth of our nation, and an amicus curiae brief filed in their behalf informs us that under the test applied to this petitioner, not one of them if true to the tenets of their faith could qualify for the bar in Illinois. And it is obvious that the same disqualification would exist as to every conscientious objector to the use of force, even though the Congress of the United States should continue its practice of absolving them from military service. The conclusion seems to me inescapable that if Illinois can bar this petitioner from the practice of law it can bar every person from every public occupation solely because he believes in non-resistance rather than in force. For a lawyer is no more subject to call for military duty than a plumber, a highway worker, a Secretary of State, or a prison chaplain.

It may be, as many people think, that Christ's Gospel of love and submission is not suited to a world in which men still fight and kill one another. But I am not ready to say that a mere profession of belief in that Gospel is a sufficient reason to keep otherwise well qualified men out of the legal profession, or to drive law-abiding lawyers of that belief out of the profession, which would be the next logical development.

Nor am I willing to say that such a belief can be penalized through the circuitous method of prescribing an oath, and then barring an applicant on the ground that his present belief might later prompt him to do or refrain from doing something that might violate that oath. Test oaths, designed to impose civil disabilities upon men for their beliefs rather than for unlawful conduct, were an abomination to the founders of this nation....

... It can be assumed that the State of Illinois has the constitutional power to draft conscientious objectors for war duty and to punish them for a refusal to serve as soldiers. ... But that is not to say that Illinois could constitutionally use the test oath it did in this case. ...

The Illinois Constitution itself prohibits the draft of conscientious objectors except in time of war and also excepts from militia duty persons who are "exempted by the laws of the United States." It has not drafted men into the militia since 1864, and if it ever should again, no one can say that it will not, as has the Congress of the United States, exempt men who honestly entertain the views that this petitioner does. Thus the probability that Illinois would ever call the petitioner to serve in a war has little more reality than an imaginary quantity in mathematics.

I cannot agree that a state can lawfully bar from a semi-public position a well-qualified man of good character solely because he entertains a religious belief which might prompt him at some time in the future to violate a law which has not yet been and may never be enacted. Under our Constitution men are punished for what they do or fail to do and not for what they think and believe. Freedom to think, to believe, and to worship, has too exalted a position in our country to be penalized on such an illusory basis. *West Virginia Board of Education v. Barnette.*

I would reverse the decision of the State Supreme Court.

---

11. "The militia of the state of Illinois shall consist of all able-bodied male persons resident in the state, between the ages of eighteen and forty-five, except such persons as now are, or hereafter may be, exempted by the laws of the United States, or of this state." (Constitution of Illinois, Art. XII, § 1, Ill. Rev. Stat. 1943.)

"No person having conscientious scruples against bearing arms shall be compelled to do militia duty in time of peace; *Provided*, such person shall pay an equivalent for such exemption." (Constitution of Illinois, Art. XII, § 6, Ill. Rev. Stat. 1943.)

241 Exclusion of Named Employees (1945)

On February 1, 1943, Congressman Dies named thirty-nine government employees who were affiliated with "Communist front organizations" as "irresponsible, unrepresentative, crackpot, radical bureaucrats." He urged Congress to refuse to appropriate funds to pay their salaries. Congress did not adopt this proposal but authorized the Appropriations Committee to investigate the charges and report back to Congress. The committee held hearings in executive session and permitted the accused employees to testify. Lawyers were excluded, and only the members of the investigating subcommittee, the witness under examination, and the staff were present. Upon completion of the hearings, the Appropriations Committee concluded that three employees, because of their subversive activities, were unfit to continue in public employment. The House subsequently prohibited, in the Section 304 amendment to a wartime emergency appropriations bill, the payment of the salaries of Robert Morse Lovett, Goodwin B. Watson, and William E. Dodd, Jr., after November 15, 1943. President Truman signed the appropriations bill with reservations that Section 304 was unconstitutional. Denied relief by the Court of Claims, the affected employees appealed to the Supreme Court.

☆ 241 *United States v. Lovett*

328 U.S. 303 (1945).

Mr. Justice BLACK delivered the opinion of the Court:

*   *   *

I

... [W]e cannot agree with the two judges of the Court of Claims who held that § 304 required "a mere stoppage of disbursing routine, nothing more," and left the employer governmental agencies free to continue employing respondents and to incur contractual obligations by virtue of such continued work which respondents could enforce in the Court of Claims. Nor can we agree with counsel for Congress that the section did not provide for the dismissal of respondents but merely forbade governmental agencies to compensate respondents for their work or to incur obligations for such compensation at any and all times. We therefore cannot conclude, as he urges, that § 304 is a mere appropriation measure, and that, since Congress under the Constitution has complete control over appropriations, a challenge to the measure's constitutionality does not present a justiciable question in the courts, but is merely a political issue over which Congress has final say.

... The section's language as well as the circumstances of its passage which we have just described show that no mere question of compensation procedure or of appropriations was involved, but that it was designed to force the employing agencies to discharge respondents and to bar their being hired by any other governmental agency. Any other interpretation of the section would completely frustrate the purpose of all who sponsored § 304, which clearly was to "purge" the then existing and all future lists of government employees of those whom Congress deemed guilty of "subversive activities" and therefore "unfit" to hold a federal job. ...

II

We hold that § 304 falls precisely within the category of congressional actions which the Constitution barred by providing that "No Bill of Attainder or ex post facto Law shall be passed." In *Cummings v. Missouri* this Court said, "A bill of attainder is a legislative act which inflicts punishment without a judicial trial. If the punishment be less than death, the act is termed a bill of pains and penalties. Within the meaning of the Constitution, bills of attainder include bills of pains and penalties." ... [L]egislative acts, no matter what their form, that apply either to named individuals or to easily ascertainable members of a group in such a way as to inflict punishment on them without a judicial trial are bills of attainder prohibited by the Constitution. Adherence to this principle requires invalidation of § 304. We do adhere to it.

Section 304 was designed to apply to particular individuals.... [I]t "operates as a legislative decree of perpetual exclusion" from a chosen vocation. This permanent proscription from any opportunity to serve the Government is punishment, and of a most severe type. It is a type of punishment which Congress has only invoked for special types of odious and dangerous crimes, such as treason[,] acceptance of bribes by members of Congress or by other government officials, and interference with elections by Army and Navy officers.

Section 304, thus, clearly accomplishes the punishment of named individuals without a judicial trial. The fact that the punishment is inflicted through the instrumentality of an Act specifically cutting off the pay of certain named individuals found guilty of disloyalty, makes it no less galling or effective than if it had been done by an Act which designated the conduct as criminal. No one would think that Congress could have passed a valid law, stating that after investigation it had found Lovett, Dodd, and Watson "guilty" of the crime of engaging in "subversive activities," defined that term for the first time, and sentenced them to perpetual exclusion from any government employment. Section 304, while it does not use that language, accomplishes that result. The effect was to inflict punishment without the safeguards of a judicial trial and "determined by no previous law or fixed rule." The Constitution declares that that cannot be done either by a State or by the United States.

... When our Constitution and Bill of Rights were written, our ancestors had ample reason to know that legislative trials and punishments were too dangerous to liberty to exist in the nation of free men they envisioned. And so they proscribed bills of attainder. Section 304 is one. Much as we regret to declare that an Act of Congress violates the Constitution, we have no alternative here.

Section 304 therefore does not stand as an obstacle to payment of compensation to Lovett, Watson, and Dodd.

The judgment in their favor is affirmed.

242 " 'He that would make his own liberty secure must guard even his enemy from oppression' " (1945)

Anthony Cramer was a German-born naturalized American citizen. Prior to the United States' entry into World War II, Cramer had been a strong German sympathizer openly opposing this nation's participation in the hostilities against Germany. Cramer met with known German saboteurs, one of whom was a prewar friend, and was subsequently indicted and convicted of treason.

Although it was still wartime, the Supreme Court narrowly concluded that the assistance given by Cramer did not support the charge. It should be noted how carefully the court reviewed the evidence and strictly construed the constitutional offense of treason—unlike its treatment of cases arising out of prosecutions handled under military authority. The difference in treatment illuminates the preference of the executive branch for military rather than civilian law in the trial and punishment of political offenders.

☆242 *Cramer v. United States*

325 U.S. 1 (1945).

MR. JUSTICE JACKSON delivered the opinion of the Court.

Anthony Cramer, the petitioner, stands convicted of violating Section 1 of the Criminal Code, which provides: "Whoever, owing allegiance to the United States, levies war against them or adheres to their enemies, giving them aid and comfort within the United States or elsewhere, is guilty of treason."

... Prosecution resulted from his association with two of the German saboteurs, ... Werner Thiel and Edward Kerling....

*   *   *

Cramer ... had known intimately the saboteur Werner Thiel while the latter lived in this country....

*   *   *

Coming down to the time of the alleged treason, the main facts, as related on the witness stand by Cramer, are not seriously in dispute. He was living in New York; and in response to a cryptic note left under his door, which did not mention Thiel, he went to the Grand Central Station. There Thiel appeared. Cramer had supposed that Thiel was in Germany, knowing that he had left the United States shortly before the war to go there. Together they went to public places and had some drinks. Cramer denies that Thiel revealed his mission of sabotage. Cramer said to Thiel that he must have come to America by submarine, but Thiel refused to confirm it, although his attitude increased Cramer's suspicion. Thiel promised to tell later how he came to this country. Thiel asked about a girl who was a mutual acquaintance and whom Thiel had engaged to marry previous to his going to Germany. Cramer knew where she was, and offered to and did write to her to come to New York, without disclosing in the letter that Thiel had arrived. Thiel said that he had in his possession about $3,600, but did not disclose that it was provided by the German Government, saying only that one could get money in Germany if he had the right connections. Thiel owed Cramer an old debt of $200. He gave Cramer his money belt containing some $3,600, from which Cramer was to be paid. Cramer agreed to and did place the rest in his own safe-deposit box, except a sum which he kept in his room in case Thiel should want it quickly.

*   *   *

Cramer's case raises questions as to application of the constitutional provision that "Treason against the United States shall consist only in levying War against them, or in adhering to their Enemies, giving them Aid and Comfort. No person shall be convicted of Treason unless on the Testimony of two Witnesses to the same overt Act, or on Confession in open Court."

Cramer's contention may be well stated in words of Judge Learned Hand in *United States v. Robinson*:

"Nevertheless a question may indeed be raised whether the prosecution may lay as an overt act a step taken in execution of the traitorous design, innocent in itself, and getting its treasonable character only from some covert and undeclared intent. It is true that in prosecutions for conspiracy under our federal statute it is well settled that any step in performance of the conspiracy is enough, though it is innocent except for its relation to the agreement. I doubt very much whether that rule has any application to the case of treason, where the requirement affected the character of the pleading and proof, rather than accorded a season of repentance before the crime should be complete. Lord Reading in his charge in *Casement's Case* uses language which accords with my understanding:

" 'Overt acts are such acts as manifest a criminal intention and tend towards the accomplishment of the criminal object. They are acts by which the purpose is manifested and the means by which it is intended to be fulfilled.' "

The Government, however, contends for, and the court below has affirmed, this conviction upon a contrary principle. It said: "We believe in short that no more need be laid for an overt act of treason than for an overt act of conspiracy.... Hence we hold the overt acts relied on were sufficient to be submitted to the jury, even though they perhaps may have appeared as innocent on their face." A similar conclusion was reached in *United States v. Fricke*; it is: "An overt act in itself may be a perfectly innocent act standing by itself; it must be in some manner in furtherance of the crime."

I

*   *   *

... [T]he revolutionary doctrine that the people have the right to alter or abolish their government relaxed the loyalty which governments theretofore had demanded—dangerously diluted it, as the ruling classes of Europe thought, for in their eyes the colonists not only committed treason, they exalted it. The idea that loyalty will ultimately be given to a government only so long as it deserves loyalty and that opposition to its abuses is not treason has made our government tolerant of opposition based on differences of opinion that in some parts of the world would have kept the hangman busy. But the basic law of treason in this country was framed by men who, as we have seen, were taught by experience and by history to fear abuse of the treason charge almost as much as they feared treason itself....

II

*   *   *

Distrust of treason prosecutions was not just a transient mood of the Revolutionists. In the century and a half of our national existence not one execution on a federal treason conviction has taken place. Never before has this Court had occasion to review a conviction. In the few cases that have been prosecuted the treason clause has had its only judicial construction by individual Justices of this Court presiding at trials on circuit or by district or circuit judges. After constitutional requirements have been satisfied, and after juries have convicted and courts have sentenced, Presidents again and again have intervened to mitigate judicial severity or to pardon entirely. We have managed to do without treason prosecutions to a degree that probably would be impossible except while a people was singularly confident of external security and internal stability.

III

Historical materials aid interpretation chiefly in that they show two kinds of dangers against which the framers were concerned to guard the treason offense: (1) perversion by established authority to repress peaceful political opposition; and (2) conviction of the innocent as a result of perjury, passion, or inadequate evidence. The first danger could be diminished by closely circumscribing the kind of conduct which should be treason.... The second danger lay in the manner of trial and was one which would be diminished mainly by procedural requirements.... The concern uppermost in the framers' minds, that the mere mental attitudes or expressions should not be treason, influenced both definition of the crime and procedure for its trial....

Treason or adherence to an enemy was old in the law.... It might be predicated on intellectual or emotional sympathy with the foe, or merely lack of zeal in the cause of one's own country. That was not the kind of disloyalty the framers thought should constitute treason. They promptly accepted the proposal to restrict it to cases where also there was conduct which was "giving them aid and comfort."

*   *   *

Thus the crime of treason consists of two elements: adherence to the enemy; and rendering him aid and comfort. A citizen intellectually or emotionally may favor the enemy and harbor sympathies or convictions disloyal to this country's policy or interest, but so long as he commits no act of aid and comfort to the enemy, there is no treason. On the other hand, a citizen may take actions which do aid and comfort the enemy — making a speech critical of the government or opposing its measures, profiteering, striking in defense plants or essential work, and the hundred other things which impair our cohesion and diminish our strength — but if there is no adherence to the enemy in this, if there is no intent to betray, there is no treason.

While to prove giving of aid and comfort would require the prosecution to show actions and deeds, if the Constitution stopped there, such acts could be inferred from circumstantial evidence. This the framers thought would not do. So they added what in effect is a command that the overt acts must be established by direct evidence, and the direct testimony must be that of two witnesses instead of one. In this sense the overt act procedural provision adds something, and something important, to the definition.

Our problem begins where the Constitution ends. That instrument omits to specify what relation the indispensable overt act must sustain to the two elements of the offense as defined: viz., adherence and giving aid and comfort. It requires that two witnesses testify to the same overt act, and clearly enough the act must show something toward treason, but what? Must the act be one of giving aid and comfort? If so, how must adherence to the enemy, the disloyal state of mind, be shown?

The defendant especially challenges the sufficiency of the overt acts to prove treasonable inten-

tion. Questions of intent in a treason case are even more complicated than in most criminal cases because of the peculiarity of the two different elements which together make the offense.... [T]o make treason the defendant not only must intend the act, but he must intend to betray his country by means of the act. It is here that Cramer defends. The issue is joined between conflicting theories as to how this treacherous intention and treasonable purpose must be made to appear.

*   *   *

Since intent must be inferred from conduct of some sort, we think it is permissible to draw usual reasonable inferences as to intent from the overt acts. The law of treason, like the law of lesser crimes, assumes every man to intend the natural consequences which one standing in his circumstances and possessing his knowledge would reasonably expect to result from his acts. Proof that a citizen did give aid and comfort to an enemy may well be in the circumstances sufficient evidence that he adhered to that enemy and intended and purposed to strike at his own country....

While of course it must be proved that the accused acted with an intention and purpose to betray or there is no treason, we think that in some circumstances at least the overt act itself will be evidence of the treasonable purpose and intent. But that still leaves us with exceedingly difficult problems.... Must the overt act be appraised for legal sufficiency only as supported by the testimony of two witnesses, or may other evidence be thrown into the scales to create inferences not otherwise reasonably to be drawn or to reinforce those which might be drawn from the act itself?

It is only overt acts by the accused which the Constitution explicitly requires to be proved by the testimony of two witnesses. It does not make other common-law evidence inadmissible nor deny its inherent powers of persuasion....

It would be no contribution to certainty of judgment, which is the object of the provision, to construe it to deprive a trial court of the aid of testimony under the ordinary sanctions of verity, provided, of course, resort is not had to evidence of less than the constitutional standard to supply deficiencies in the constitutional measure of proof of overt acts. For it must be remembered that the constitutional provision establishes a minimum of proof of incriminating acts, without which there can be no conviction, but it is not otherwise a limitation on the evidence with which a jury may be persuaded that it ought to convict....

From duly proven overt acts of aid and comfort to the enemy in their setting, it may well be that the natural and reasonable inference of intention to betray will be warranted.... But the protection of the two-witness rule extends at least to all acts of the defendant which are used to draw incriminating inferences that aid and comfort have been given.

The controversy before us has been waged in terms of intentions, but this, we think, is the reflection of a more fundamental issue as to what is the real function of the overt act in convicting of treason. The prisoner's contention that it alone and on its face must manifest a traitorous intention, apart from an intention to do the act itself, would place on the overt act the whole burden of establishing a complete treason. On the other hand, the Government's contention that it may prove by two witnesses an apparently commonplace and insignificant act and from other circumstances create an inference that the act was a step in treason and was done with treasonable intent really is a contention that the function of the overt act in a treason prosecution is almost zero. It is obvious that the function we ascribe to the overt act is significant chiefly because it measures the two-witness rule protection to the accused and its handicap to the prosecution. If the overt act or acts must go all the way to make out the complete treason, the defendant is protected at all points by the two-witness requirement. If the act may be an insignificant one, then the constitutional safeguards are shrunken so as to be applicable only at a point where they are least needed.

The very minimum function that an overt act must perform in a treason prosecution is that it show sufficient action by the accused, in its setting, to sustain a finding that the accused actually gave aid and comfort to the enemy. Every act, movement, deed, and word of the defendant charged to constitute treason must be supported by the testimony of two witnesses. The two-witness principle is to interdict imputation of *incriminating acts* to the accused by circumstantial evidence or by the testimony of a single witness. The prosecution cannot rely on evidence which does not meet the constitutional test for overt acts to create any inference that the accused did other acts or did something more than was shown in the overt act, in order to make a giving of aid and comfort to the enemy. The words of the Constitution were chosen, not to make it hard to prove merely routine and everyday acts, but to make the proof of acts that convict of treason as sure as trial processes may.... [I]n this and some cases we have cited where the sufficiency of the overt acts has been challenged because they were colorless as to intent, we are persuaded the reason intent was left in question was that the acts were really indecisive as a giving of aid and comfort....

We proceed to consider the application of these principles to Cramer's case.

IV

*   *   *

... By direct testimony of two or more agents it was established that Cramer met Thiel and Kerling on the occasions and at the places charged and that they drank together and engaged long and earnestly in conversation. This is the sum of the overt acts as established by the testimony of two witnesses. There is no two-witness proof of what they said nor in what language they conversed. There is no showing that Cramer gave them any information whatever of value to their mission or indeed that he had any to give. No effort at secrecy is shown, for they met in public places. Cramer furnished them no shelter, nothing that can be called sustenance or supplies, and there is no evidence that he gave them encouragement or counsel, or even paid for their drinks.

The Government recognizes the weakness of its proof of aid and comfort, but on this score it urges: "Little imagination is required to perceive the advantage such meeting would afford to enemy spies not yet detected...." The difficulty with this argument is that the whole purpose of the constitutional provision is to make sure that treason conviction shall rest on direct proof of two witnesses and not on even a little imagination. And without the use of some imagination it is difficult to perceive any advantage which this meeting afforded to Thiel and Kerling as enemies or how it strengthened Germany or weakened the United States in any way whatever.... Meeting with Cramer in public drinking places to tipple and trifle was no part of the saboteurs' mission and did not advance it. It may well have been a digression which jeopardized its success.

The shortcomings of the overt act submitted are emphasized by contrast with others which the indictment charged but which the prosecution withdrew for admitted insufficiency of proof.... That Thiel would be aided by having the security of a safe-deposit box for his funds, plus availability of smaller amounts, and by being relieved of the risks of carrying large sums on his person—without disclosing his presence or identity to a bank—seems obvious. The inference of intent from such act is also very different from the intent manifest by drinking and talking together. Taking what must have seemed a large sum of money for safekeeping is not a usual amenity of social intercourse. That such responsibilities are undertaken and such trust bestowed without the scratch of a pen to show it, implies some degree of mutuality and concert from which a jury could say that aid and comfort was given and was intended. If these acts had been submitted as overt acts of treason, and we were now required to decide whether they had been established as required, we would have a quite different case.... But this transaction was not proven as the Government evidently hoped to do when the indictment was obtained. The overt acts based on it were expressly withdrawn from the jury, and Cramer has not been convicted of treason on account of such acts. We cannot sustain a conviction for the acts submitted on the theory that, even if insufficient, some unsubmitted ones may be resorted to as proof of treason. Evidence of the money transaction serves only to show how much went out of the case when it was withdrawn.

The Government contends that outside of the overt acts, and by lesser degree of proof, it has shown a treasonable intent on Cramer's part in meeting and talking with Thiel and Kerling. But if it showed him disposed to betray, and showed that he had opportunity to do so, it still has not proved in the manner required that he did any acts submitted to the jury as a basis for conviction which had the effect of betraying by giving aid and comfort. To take the intent for the deed would carry us back to constructive treasons.

It is outside of the commonplace overt acts as proved that we must find all that convicts or convinces either that Cramer gave aid and comfort or that he had a traitorous intention. . . .

It is not relevant to our issue to appraise weight or credibility of the evidence apart from determining its constitutional sufficiency. . . . At all events much of the evidence is of the general character whose infirmities were feared by the framers and sought to be safeguarded against.

Most damaging is the testimony of Norma Kopp, a friend of Cramer's and one with whom, if she is to be believed, he had been most indiscreetly confidential. . . . To the extent that his conviction rests upon such evidence, and it does to an unknown but considerable extent, it rests upon the uncorroborated testimony of one witness not without strong emotional interest in the drama of which Cramer's trial was a part. Other evidence relates statements by Cramer before the United States was at war with Germany. At the time they were uttered, however, they were not treasonable. To use pre-war expressions of opposition to entering a war to convict of treason during the war is a dangerous procedure at best. The same may be said about the inference of disloyal attitude created by showing that he refused to buy bonds and closed the door in the salesman's face. Another class of evidence consists of admissions to agents of the Federal Bureau of Investigation. They are, of course, not "confessions in open court." . . .

V

* * *

The framers' effort to compress into two sentences the law of one of the most intricate of crimes gives a superficial appearance of clarity and simplicity which proves illusory when it is put to practical application. There are few subjects on which the temptation to utter abstract interpretation generalizations is greater or on which they are more to be distrusted. The little clause is packed with controversy and difficulty. The offense is one of subtlety, and it is easy to demonstrate lack of logic in almost any interpretation by hypothetical cases, to which real treasons rarely will conform. . . .

* * *

It is not difficult to find grounds upon which to quarrel with this constitutional provision. . . . Certainly the treason rule, whether wisely or not, is severely restrictive. It must be remembered, however, that the Constitutional Convention was warned by James Wilson that "Treason may sometimes be practiced in such a manner, as to render proof extremely difficult — as in a traitorous correspondence with an Enemy." The provision was adopted not merely in spite of the difficulties it put in the way of prosecution but because of them. And it was not by whim or by accident, but because one of the most venerated of that venerated group considered that "prosecutions for treason were generally virulent." Time has not made the accusation of treachery less poisonous, nor the task of judging one charged with betraying the country, including his triers, less susceptible to the influence of suspicion and rancor. The innovations made by the forefathers in the law of treason were conceived in a faith such as Paine put in the maxim that "He that would make his own liberty secure must guard even his enemy from oppression; for if he violates this duty he establishes a precedent that will reach himself." We still put trust in it.

We hold that overt acts 1 and 2 are insufficient as proved to support the judgment of conviction, which accordingly is

Reversed.

243 "the military authorities took over the government of Hawaii" (1946)

On the day that the Japanese attacked Pearl Harbor, Hawaii's governor declared martial law and suspended the writ of habeas corpus, as authorized by the Hawaiian Organic Act in cases of rebellion, invasion, or imminent danger thereof. Under this authority military tribunals (which did not observe the strictures of the Bill of Rights) took over the function of the civilian courts. Duncan petitioned for a writ of habeas corpus after being convicted by one of these tribunals.

Without addressing the constitutional issues, the Supreme Court recognized the imposition of martial law but denied the legitimacy of the military tribunals. Justice Murphy, in concurrence, admonished the court for not being more forceful in its condemnation of military usurpation of governmental power.

☆ 243 *Duncan v. Kahanamoku*

327 U.S. 304 (1946).

Mr. Justice BLACK delivered the opinion of the Court.

*   *   *

... The President approved the Governor's action on December 9th. The Governor's proclamation also authorized and requested the Commanding General, "during ... the emergency and until danger of invasion is removed, to exercise all the powers normally exercised" by the Governor and by "the judicial officers and employees of the Territory."

*   *   *

... Thus the military authorities took over the government of Hawaii. They could and did, by simply promulgating orders, govern the day to day activities of civilians who lived, worked, or were merely passing through there. The military tribunals interpreted the very orders promulgated by the military authorities and proceeded to punish violators. The sentences imposed were not subject to direct appellate court review, since it had long been established that military tribunals are not part of our judicial system....

*   *   *

Duncan ... was a civilian shipfitter employed in the Navy Yard at Honolulu. On February 24th, 1944, more than two years and two months after the Pearl Harbor attack, he engaged in a brawl with two armed Marine sentries at the yard. He was arrested by the military authorities. By the time of his arrest the military had to some extent eased the stringency of military rule. Schools, bars and motion picture theatres had been reopened. Courts had been authorized to "exercise their normal functions." They were once more summoning jurors and witnesses and conducting criminal trials. There were important exceptions, however. One of these was that only military tribunals were to try "Criminal Prosecutions for violations of military orders." ... He was therefore tried by a military tribunal rather than the Territorial Court, although the general laws of Hawaii made assault a crime.... A conviction followed and Duncan was sentenced to six months imprisonment.

*   *   *

We believe that when Congress passed the Hawaiian Organic Act and authorized the establishment of "martial law" it had in mind and did not wish to exceed the boundaries between military and civil-

ian power, in which our people have always believed, which responsible military and executive officers had heeded, and which had become part of our political philosophy and institutions prior to the time Congress passed the Organic Act. The phrase "martial law" as employed in that Act, therefore, while intended to authorize the military to act vigorously for the maintenance of an orderly civil government and for the defense of the island against actual or threatened rebellion or invasion, was not intended to authorize the supplanting of courts by military tribunals. Yet the government seeks to justify the punishment of ... Duncan on the ground of such supposed Congressional authorization. We hold that [petitioner is] now entitled to be released from custody.

Reversed.

Mr. Justice MURPHY, concurring.

The Court's opinion, in which I join, makes clear that the military trials in these cases were unjustified by the martial law provisions of the Hawaiian Organic Act. Equally obvious, as I see it, is the fact that these trials were forbidden by the Bill of Rights of the Constitution of the United States, which applies in both spirit and letter to Hawaii. Indeed, the unconstitutionality of the usurpation of civil power by the military is so great in this instance as to warrant this Court's complete and outright repudiation of the action.

Abhorrence of military rule is ingrained in our form of government. Those who founded this nation knew full well that the arbitrary power of conviction and punishment for pretended offenses is the hallmark of despotism. History had demonstrated that fact to them time and again. They shed their blood to win independence from a ruler who they alleged was attempting to render the "military independent of and superior to the civil power" and who was "depriving us of the benefits of trial by jury." In the earliest state constitutions they inserted definite provisions placing the military under "strict subordination" to the civil power at all times and in all cases. And in framing the Bill of Rights of the Federal Constitution they were careful to make sure that the power to punish would rest primarily with the civil authorities at all times. They believed that a trial by an established court, with an impartial jury, was the only certain way to protect an individual against oppression. The Bill of Rights translated that belief into reality by guaranteeing the observance of jury trials and other basic procedural rights foreign to military proceedings. This supremacy of the civil over the military is one of our great heritages. It has made possible the attainment of a high degree of liberty regulated by law rather than by caprice. Our duty is to give effect to that heritage at all times, that it may be handed down untarnished to future generations.

... There is a very necessary part in our national life for the military; it has defended this country well in its darkest hours of trial. But militarism is not our way of life. It is to be used only in the most extreme circumstances.

244 "an uninterrupted record of economic aggression" (1946)

Ezra Pound was born in Hailey, Idaho, on October 30, 1885. In 1907 he traveled extensively throughout Europe, eventually settling in England. Considered a brilliant and erudite poet and translator, Pound exerted great influence on several poetic movements. His *Cantos* represented the greatest body of his work. After emigrating to Italy in 1924, he broadcast Fascist propaganda to the United States up to and during World War II. After Pound was indicted for treason, a potentially difficult and controversial trial on the charge was avoided when, upon the testimony of physicians, a jury found him to be incompetent to stand trial. The court confined him to St. Elizabeth's mental hospital in Washington, D.C. *Pisan Cantos*, published during his confinement, won him the Bollingen Prize, an important literary award, in 1949. He remained under guard at St. Elizabeth's for twelve years. Upon his release in 1958 he returned to Italy, where he died in 1972. Other United States citizens, however, were convicted of treason for conducting "psychological warfare" against the United States through propaganda broadcasts. *Gillars v. United States*, 182 F.2d 902 (D.C. Cir. 1950).

☆ 244 The Trial of Ezra Pound

Reprinted in J. Cornell, *The Trial of Ezra Pound: A Documented Account of the Treason Case by the Defendant's Lawyer* (New York: John Day, 1966).

☆ 244a Transcript of Short Wave Broadcast, May 15, 1943. Cornell, 141-44.

Europe calling, Ezra Pound speaking.

About economic aggression. Mr. Sumner Welles' speech at Toledo was a serious matter....

*   *   *

... Had Mr. Welles been ready to make such a speech three years ago, this distressing war might have been quite well avoided. Mr. Welles appeared to be renouncing dollar diplomacy. A few months sooner, a good deal of bloodshed might have been spared us. Mr. Welles also spoke of misapprehension, of incomplete knowledge, of heedlessness, inconsideration.

I'm perfectly ready to take Mr. Welles' speech at its face value. If the United States has been ill informed, or tardily informed of the conditions of Europe, there is no reason for you to remain voluntarily in that condition. But, it is now extremely hard for the people inside any country to get accurate impressions of the state of mind of people inside any other. It has been for years, extremely hard to get news into America.... It is not to be supposed that even now, Mr. Welles would listen to me over a cable, or answer what I intend to say to him during the next five minutes.

*   *   *

... Now to the outer world, the American history of the past 30 years appears to be an uninterrupted record of economic aggression on the part of the United States. The United States is the hometown of the Rockefellers, Guggenheims, Morgan. The world has had on its news stalls the works of Vishka (?), I suppose he's a Polish author. Anyhow he wrote the "War for Oil," "War for Cotton," and so on. And we have heard of wars for commodities and wars for gold. We have heard much less of a sacred war that the United States lost in 1863.

While the boys in blue and the boys in grey were obligingly dying and taking the spotlight, the Civil War was, at that time, a world record for carnage and both sides well vanquished. The control of the national credit, control of the national currency, the national purchasing power, passes right away from the people and right out of the control of the national and responsible government. That is why many of Mrs. Welles' foreign auditors will think there is a nigger in Mr. Welles' woodshed. Suddenly a coalition of the three most aggressive powers, economically aggressive powers, on earth, put forth not an official statement, but a statement by the most authoritative member of the State Department to the effect that economic aggression is, after all, a factor in causing wars, and that to obtain a durable peace we must lay off it.

England, Mr. Welles tell us, is aggressive, economically. The United States, has in the past been aggressive, Russia has made up for lost time and been extremely aggressive. Quite economically. It does sound to the European almost as if Legs Diamond, or Billy the Kid or Jesse James had suddenly decided to change his habits. I mean, economic aggression has been for so long considered the very breath of life for the American system, the bone of its bone, its inner and intimate fiber. And then again, when a nation's inner life is so palpably made up of the economic aggression of one class or group against the whole rest of the population, it is very difficult for any foreigner, or indeed for anyone not carried away by political heat of the moment, to see why that particular nation should be entrusted with the latch key of any other.

I will return to this subject.

Ezra Pound, speaking.

☆ 244b Indictment. Cornell, 145-48.

In the District Court of the United States for the District of Columbia
October Term A.D. 1945

The Grand Jurors for the United States of America duly impaneled and sworn in the District Court of the United States for the District of Columbia and inquiring for that District upon their oath present:

*   *   *

2. That the defendant, Ezra Pound, at Rome, Italy and other places within the kingdom of Italy . . . in the manner and by the means hereinafter set forth, then and there being a citizen of the United States, and a person owing allegiance to the United States, in violation of said duty of allegiance, knowingly, intentionally, wilfully, unlawfully, feloniously, traitorously and treasonably did adhere to the enemies of the United States, . . . giving to the said enemies of the United States aid and comfort within the United States and elsewhere, that is to say:

3. . . . (a) Of accepting employment from the Kingdom of Italy in the capacity of a radio propagandist and in the performance of the duties thereof which involved the composition of texts, speeches, talks and announcements and the recording thereof for subsequent broadcast over short-wave radio on wave lengths audible in the United States and elsewhere on ordinary commercial radio receiving sets having short-wave reception facilities. . . .

That the aforesaid activities of the said defendant, Ezra Pound, were intended to persuade citizens and residents of the United States to decline to support the United States in the conduct of the said war, to weaken or destroy confidence in the Government of the United States and in the integrity and loyalty of the Allies of the United States, and to further bind together and increase the morale of the subjects of the Kingdom of Italy in support of the prosecution of the said war by the Kingdom of Italy and its military allies.

4. And the Grand Jurors aforesaid upon their oath aforesaid do further present that the said defendant, Ezra Pound, in the prosecution, performance and execution of said treason . . . did do, perform, and commit certain overt and manifest acts, that is to say:

[Here the indictment alleges overt acts consisting of broadcasts by Pound over a radio station of the Italian government at Rome, Italy on September 11, 1942; December 10, 1942; February 4, 1943; March 19, 1943; May 12, 1943; May 14, 1943; May 15, 1943; and recording of broadcasts on various dates.]

*   *   *

A TRUE BILL

☆ 244c Report to the Court of Examining Psychiatrists [Read in court 12/21/45]. Cornell, 36-37.

SIR:

The undersigned hereby respectfully report the results of their mental examination of Ezra Pound, now detained in Gallinger Hospital by transfer for observation from the District Jail on a charge of treason. Three of us (Drs. Gilbert, King, and Overholser) were appointed by your Honor to make this examination. At our suggestion, and with your approval, Dr. Wendell Muncie, acting upon the request of counsel for the accused, made an examination with us and associates himself with us in this joint report. Dr. Muncie spent several hours with the defendant, both alone and with us, on December 13, 1945, and the others of us have examined the defendant each on several occasions, separately and together, in the period from his admission to Gallinger Hospital on December 4, 1945, to December 13, 1945. We have had available to us the reports of laboratory, psychological and special physical examinations of the defendant and considerable material in the line of his writings and biographical data.

The defendant, now 60 years of age and in generally good physical condition, was a precocious student, specializing in literature. He has been a voluntary expatriate for nearly 40 years, living in England and France, and for the past 21 years in Italy, making an uncertain living by writing poetry and criticism. His poetry and literary criticism have achieved considerable recognition, but of recent years his preoccupation with monetary theories and economics has apparently obstructed his literary productivity. He has long been recognized as eccentric, querulous, and egocentric.

At the present time he exhibits extremely poor judgment as to his situation, its seriousness and the manner in which the charges are to be met. He insists that his broadcasts were not treasonable, but that all of his radio activities have stemmed from his self-appointed mission to "save the Constitution." He is abnormally grandiose, is expansive and exuberant in manner, exhibiting pressure of speech, discursiveness, and distractibility. In our opinion, with advancing years his personality, for many years abnormal, has undergone further distortion to the extent that he is now suffering from a paranoid state which renders him mentally unfit to advise properly with counsel or to participate intelligently and reasonably in his own defense. He is, in other words, insane and mentally unfit for trial, and is in need of care in a mental hospital.

Respectfully submitted,

JOSEPH L. GILBERT, M.D.
MARION R. KING, M.D.
WENDELL MUNCIE, M.D.
WINFRED OVERHOLSER, M.D.

☆ 244d Transcript of Hearing, February 13, 1946. Cornell, 188-96.

[Direct Examination, JULIAN CORNELL, Defense Counsel:]

Q. Will you tell us the reasons which lead you to the conclusion that he is unable to participate in the trial of this indictment intelligently? A. [DR. WIN-FRED OVERHOLSER, Superintendent of St. Elizabeth's Hospital, Washington, D.C.] Yes, and other things in addition. In the first place, it is quite obvious that the man has always been unusually eccentric through the years. He has undoubtedly a high regard of his own opinion, and has been extremely vituperative of those who disagree with him.

He has a very high degree of intelligence, there is no question on that score, and his relations with the world and other people during practically all his life have been those of a person who was very skeptical to say the least.

He is extremely free in his conversation; he has not been reticent by any stretch of the imagination, but his production has been unusually hard to follow. He speaks in bunches of ideas.

Q. You mean his production of speech? A. Yes, and rambling and illogical.

*   *   *

The ideas, perhaps, which he expresses indicate some of his views in connection with the war. In the first place, he is thoroughly convinced that if he had been allowed to send his messages to the Axis, which he wished to send, prior to 1940, there would have been no Axis even. In other words, that if given a free hand by those who were engaged in stultifying him, he could have prevented the war.

He lays a great deal of his difficulty at the door of British Secret Service, and other groups, which have opposed him.

He assures me, too, that he served a very useful purpose to the United States by remaining at the Italian prison camp to complete his translation of Confucius, which he regards as the greatest contribution to literature.

He is sure that he should not have been brought to this country in the capacity of a prisoner, but in the capacity of someone who was to be of great benefit to the United States in its post-war activities.

I might state that this constitutes a grandiosity of ideas and beliefs that goes far beyond the normal, even in a person who is as distraught in his mind as he is.

From a practical view of his advising with his attorney, there would be the fact that you cannot keep him on a straight line of conversation; he rambles around, and has such a naive grasp of the situation in which he finds himself, it would not be fair to him or his attorney to put him on trial.

*   *   *

Q. You mentioned his naive reasoning. Will you expand on that? A. For example, he did not expect to be brought here. He did not expect to be put in prison when he got here. He thought he was double-crossed. He thought he was to be used by the government in any movement for the organization of the world. He is sure that his connections with Japan would enable him to deal with the delicate post-war situation. I think "naive" is a mild word to apply to that line of reasoning.

Q. Based upon your knowledge and understanding of the situation, how do you regard his ability to understand the situation and to answer questions in connection with the presentation of his defense? A. Well, with an infinite amount of patience, and an infinite amount of time, it might be possible sometime in the future to get a lucid answer to a question.

Q. In other words, would his discursiveness and inability to answer questions prevent his attorney from presenting his side of the picture in defense of this indictment? A. It would.

MR. CORNELL: Your witness.

*   *   *

[Cross-examination by MR. MATLACK:]

*   *   *

Q. What is your opinion as to the chances of improvement for this patient? A. As far as the basic sub-strata beneath these ideas of persecution, and so on, I should say not particularly good. . . . [W]hile he is in this particular condition I do not look for any fundamental change in his condition.

*   *   *

Q. Now, what part does his background history play in your opinion as to his present sanity? A. It shows that we are dealing now with the end-product of an individual who throughout his lifetime has been highly antagonistic, highly eccentric, the whole world has revolved around him, he has been a querulous person, he has been less and less able to order his life. This has been a gradual evolution through his life, so that now we are dealing with the end-product, so to speak.

Q. Do you think that because he is eccentric that makes him unable to consult counsel? A. Oh, no.

Q. That is true of many people? A. Yes.

Q. That does not make him unable to consult with counsel? A. It might make him a nuisance.

Q. Make him a nuisance but not insane? A. Yes.

Q. I think you said one of the characteristics was that he was very vituperative to one who opposed his will? A. He has been.

Q. Do you think that, in itself, displays a person who could not be able to consult with counsel? A. Not in itself. I haven't said that any one of these things in itself would.

Q. I am going to come to that. I have forgotten what other thing you did say. I did understand you to say that he is vituperative, and eccentric; I don't know whether you used the word "sensitive" or not. A. No, but he is highly supersensitive.

Q. Now, couldn't a man who was eccentric, and vituperative, and all the other attributes that you have given to him rolled into one, still be able to consult with counsel? A. Even with all those three, and with nothing else, very likely, yes.

* * *

Q. Did he give you in his general history anything about his belief in Fascism? A. I did not discuss that with him particularly.

THE DEFENDANT: I never did believe in Fascism, God damn it; I am opposed to Fascism.

* * *

Q. Did he ever discuss with you his advocacy of Mussolini and his politics? A. In the most general terms. I didn't go into that in great detail, either. I looked upon that as a political matter.

Q. Well; that is what I am beginning to get at. Did you read his book entitled Jefferson and Mussolini? A. No.

Q. Did you take into consideration the fact that living in Italy, where the political philosophy was Fascism, that he may have become imbued with that philosophy?

MR. CORNELL: Your Honor, I object to this line of questioning and characterization of Mr. Pound, which I think is very distressing to him.

THE COURT: I will give you a certain latitude, but try not to disturb him if you can help it.

MR. MATLACK: I will strike the question and ask it again.

By MR. MATLACK: Q. Did the fact that living in Italy, where Fascism was a political philosophy, and where most of the people in Italy had adopted the Mussolini Government, have any influence, do you think, on the question of whether he is sane or insane? A. No, I should not say so.

Q. Well, would the fact that somebody believed like Mussolini in his theories, or political philosophies, and the fact that others joined in his beliefs, and were otherwise normal, make them abnormal? A. I think that is a question of politics rather than psychiatry.

Q. Now, on the same theory, if somebody believes in an economic theory such as social credit, and is able to write and broadcast his theories about social credit, does the fact that he is imbued with a belief in social credit, if he is otherwise normal, make him abnormal or insane? A. I don't know that I mentioned his views on social credit. There are a great many people who take stock in that view of economics, but I do not think that because one believes in it stamps him any more than out of agreement with most people in this country at least.

Q. If I understand your testimony, he has certain

grandiose ideas of saving the Constitution through the money clause in the Constitution, and that on certain economic theories if he could get to Japan he might have been of some service to the United States, and so on; I think that is what you testified to. A. I am not sure on the economic phase of the theories and, in fact, I never did get to the end of the explanation.

Q. Now, just how was he going to save the Constitution? A. There was some discussion about the money clause of the Constitution, but just what it had to do with saving the Constitution I was not quite clear.

* * *

Q. On what do you base your conclusion that he is in a paranoid state if it isn't based on his theories about saving the Constitution, and so on? A. The matter of his saving the Constitution, the mention about saving the Constitution is one of the factors. I don't remember that I mentioned that. I did mention particularly his idea that he could have prevented the formation of the Nazis; that he was the victim of machinations of the British Secret Service and antagonistic groups; that he was of far more use as an adviser to the Government than as a defendant in a criminal case.

* * *

Q. On the other hand, you think that under those circumstances, he thought he would be of service to the United States? A. As I say, he was unable to explain what that was, or how it would be accomplished. It was the fact he felt he was so important and of such value to the United States that I put him down as suffering a mental disorder.

Q. Did you talk to him at all about the charge of treason he is under? A. Yes.

Q. Did he understand that he had done anything treasonable? A. Apparently not, because he denied that he had done anything in connection with the Government of Italy against the United States. There was no significance apparently to that charge.

* * *

Q. Did he realize that he was subject to trial and possible conviction and punishment? A. I should say that his attitude was that the reasons for his being brought over as a prisoner was a part of the plot against him on the part of the British Secret Service and the Communist groups that he mentioned; in other words, that they were instigating the Department of Justice in the prosecution. That sounded to me pathological.

Q. Do you think that that could be without any foundation of fact when shortly before that he had given a statement to the Department as to his activities in which he recognized that he had been charged with treason? A. Oh, he knew he had been charged with treason. He told me that.

Q. And he knew it before he was brought to this country? A. Oh, yes.

Q. But did I understand you to say that notwithstanding that, that he thought he was coming over here to be of assistance to the United States in some other capacity? A. Yes.

Q. Do you think that that was something he might have told you out of whole cloth? A. It did not appear that way to me; taking into consideration the whole line of examination, I am quite convinced that there was no question of malingering.

Q. No malingering in that statement or any other, but in that particular statement you did not think that there was any question of malingering? A. No.

*   *   *

Q. Do you feel that he was so imbued with his economic theories, or whatever his message might have been, that even if he had realized the consequences of his treasonable act that he still would have broadcast? A. I haven't an opinion on it.

Mr. Matlack: I think that is all.

*   *   *

☆ 244e *New York Herald Tribune* Account (February 14, 1946). Cornell, 44-45.

Washington, Feb. 13, 1946.—The treason case against Ezra Pound, expatriate American poet, was pigeon-holed today when a specially impaneled Federal jury returned a verdict that Pound is "mentally unsound" and unfit to stand trial on treason charges arising out of his war-time writings and broadcasts in Fascist Italy. This is the first time an accused war criminal has escaped trial because of insanity.

The sixty-year-old poet will be confined here at the St. Elizabeths Federal Hospital for the Insane. He may again face trial if he recovers from his present "paranoiac state," government prosecutors said, pointing out that a treason charge has no limitation, being valid until the defendant dies. They virtually conceded defeat, however, by announcing that the government will send back to Italy seven Fascist radio announcers who were to have been key witnesses against Pound.

The jury deliberated only five minutes after hearing four and a half hours' testimony by four psychiatrists. Chief Justice Bolitha Laws, of the Federal District Court hearing the case, called the jury at the request of the prosecution.

The same psychiatrists had filed affidavits with the court on Dec. 14 declaring the poet unfit for trial, but government attorneys had demanded a public jury hearing of their findings.... All four experts agreed that Pound is mentally unsound, probably permanently. They all attested a prevailing "grandiosity" in the poet, which they said indicated his abnormal mental state.

Pound was not called to testify, but he sprang to his feet at one point, shouting, "I've never been a Fascist, Goddamit! I've always opposed them." He did this when a government attorney asked a witness if he had ever heard Pound speak of his views on Fascism.

Throughout the rest of the hearing, the bearded defendant moved nervously in his seat, held his head in his hands or leaned back and stared at the ceiling.

The psychiatrists reported that nearly two months' observation of Pound's mental condition revealed a number of "fixed ideas" held by the poet: That his mission in life was to save the United States Constitution, that the only way to world peace was through the teachings of Confucius, that he could have prevented the formation of the Axis and the war by uniting intellectual groups of the world and that he was persecuted by bureaucrats.

All four agreed that, in their observation, Pound was not able to explain his reasons for holding these views, and that he could not confer logically on any subject for even a brief period. They said they believed, therefore, that he would not be able to consult with his counsel on defense against the treason charges.

245 "a thoroughgoing Nazi" (1946)

The relationship between citizen and sovereign is based on allegiance by the former and proffered protection by the latter. When the relationship fails, how is it dissolved?

The United States informally has long recognized the rights of voluntary expatriation, that is, the right to renounce one's citizenship. England's refusal to recognize that right and its belief that American sailors were British subjects available for impressment into the British navy was a major impetus for the War of 1812. In 1868, the United States formally recognized the right of voluntary expatriation.

Forced expatriation stands on different footing. In 1940, and in subsequent legislation, Congress provided that a citizen, born here or naturalized, would lose United States citizenship involuntarily by performing certain acts that Congress deemed to be inconsistent with the obligations of allegiance. In *Afroyim v. Rusk*, 387 U.S. 253 (1967), the Supreme Court held Congress had no power to expatriate citizens without their consent regardless of the offense committed. In contrast, the process of "denaturalization," described below, continues to be available to challenge and revoke citizenship obtained by the foreign-born through alleged fraud in his or her oath of allegiance.

☆ 245 *Knauer v. United States*

328 U.S. 654 (1946).

MR. JUSTICE DOUGLAS delivered the opinion of the Court.

Knauer is a native of Germany. He arrived in this country in 1925 at the age of 30. He had served in the German army during World War I and was decorated. He had studied law and economics in Germany. He settled in Milwaukee, Wisconsin, and conducted an insurance business there. He filed his declaration of intention to become a citizen in 1929 and his petition for naturalization in 1936. He took his oath of allegiance and was admitted to citizenship on April 13, 1937. In 1943 the United States instituted proceedings under § 338(a) of the Nationality Act of 1940 to cancel his certificate of naturalization on the ground that it had been secured by fraud in that (1) he had falsely and fraudulently represented in his petition that he was attached to the principles of the Constitution and (2) he had taken a false oath of allegiance. The District Court was satisfied beyond a reasonable doubt that Knauer practiced fraud when he obtained his certificate of naturalization. It found that he had not been and is not attached to the principles of the Constitution and that he took a false oath of allegiance. It accordingly entered an order cancelling his certificate and revoking the order admitting him to citizenship. The Circuit Court of Appeals affirmed. . . .

I. In the oath of allegiance which Knauer took, he swore that he would "absolutely and entirely renounce and abjure all allegiance and fidelity to any foreign prince, potentate, state, or sovereignty, and particularly to the German Reich," that he would "support and defend the Constitution and laws of the United States of America against all enemies, foreign and domestic"; that he would "bear true faith and allegiance to the same" and that he took "this obligation freely without any mental reservation or purpose of evasion." The first and crucial issue in the case is whether Knauer swore falsely and committed a fraud when he promised under oath to forswear allegiance to the German Reich and to transfer his allegiance to this nation. Fraud connotes perjury, falsification, concealment, misrepresentation. When denaturalization is sought on this as well as on other grounds, the standard of proof required is strict. . . .

That strict test is necessary for several reasons. Citizenship obtained through naturalization is not a second-class citizenship. It has been said that citizenship carries with it all of the rights and prerogatives of citizenship obtained by birth in this country "save that of eligibility to the Presidency." There are other exceptions of a limited character. But it is plain that citizenship obtained through naturalization carries with it the privilege of full participation in the affairs of our society, including the right to speak freely, to criticize officials and administrators, and to promote changes in our laws including the very Charter of our Government. Great tolerance and caution are necessary lest good faith exercise of the rights of citizenship be turned against the naturalized citizen and be used to deprive him of the cherished status. Ill-tempered expressions, extreme views, even the promotion of ideas which run counter to our American ideals, are not to be given disloyal connotations in absence of solid, convincing evidence that that is their significance. Any other course would run counter to our traditions and make denaturalization proceedings the ready instrument for political persecutions. "Were the law otherwise, valuable rights would rest upon a slender reed, and the security of the status of our naturalized citizens might depend in considerable degree upon the political temper of majority thought and the stresses of the times."

These are extremely serious problems. They involve not only fundamental principles of our political system designed for the protection of minorities and majorities alike. They also involve tremendously high stakes for the individual. For denaturalization, like deportation, may result in the loss "of all that makes life worth living." . . . "Forswearing past political allegiance without reservation and full assumption of the obligations of American citizenship are not at all inconsistent with cultural feelings imbedded in childhood and youth." Human ties are not easily broken. Old social or cultural loyalties may still exist, though basic allegiance is transferred here. The fundamental question is whether the new citizen still takes his orders from, or owes his allegiance to, a foreign chancellory. Far more is required to establish that fact than a showing that social and cultural ties remain. And even political utterances, which might be some evidence of a false oath if they clustered around the date of naturalization, are more and more unreliable as evidence of the perjurious falsity of the oath the further they are removed from the date of naturalization.

We have read with care the voluminous record in this case. . . . We conclude with the District Court and the Circuit Court of Appeals that there is solid, convincing evidence that Knauer before the date of his naturalization, at that time, and subsequently was a thoroughgoing Nazi and a faithful follower of Adolph Hitler. The conclusion is irresistible, therefore, that when he forswore allegiance to the German Reich he swore falsely. The character of the evidence, the veracity of the witnesses against Knauer as determined by the District Court, the corroboration of challenged evidence presented by the Government, the consistent pattern of Knauer's conduct before and after naturalization convince us that the two lower courts were correct in their conclusions. The standard of proof . . . is therefore plainly met here.

We will review briefly that we, as well as the two lower courts, accept as the true version of the facts.

As early as 1931, Knauer told a newly arrived immigrant who came from the same town in Germany that in his opinion the aim of Hitler and the Nazi party was good, that it would progress, and that it was necessary to have the same party in this country because of the Jews and the Communists. During the same period, he told another friend repeatedly that he was opposed to any republican form of government and that Jewish capital was to blame for Germany's downfall. He visited Germany for about six months in 1934 and while there read Hitler's Mein Kampf. On his return he said with pride that he had met Hitler, and that he had been offered a post with the German government at 600 marks per month, that Hitler was the savior of Germany, that Hitler was solving the unemployment problem while this country was suffering from Jewish capitalism, that the Hitler youth organization was an excellent influence on the children of Germany. On occasions in 1936 and 1937 he was explosive in his criticism of those who protested against the practices and policies of Hitler.

The German Winter Relief Fund was an official agency of the German government for which German consulates solicited money in the United States. In the winter of 1934-1935 Knauer was active in obtaining contributions to the Fund and forwarded the money collected to the German consulate in Chicago.

*   *   *

Knauer participated in Bund meetings in 1936. In the summer of 1936 he and his family had a tent at the Bund camps. In the fall of 1936 he enrolled his young daughter in the Youth Movement of the Bund—a group organized to instill the Nazi ideology in the minds of children of German blood. They wore uniforms, used the Nazi salute, and were taught songs of allegiance to Hitler. Knauer attended meetings of this group.

The Federation of German-American Societies represented numerous affiliated organizations consisting of Americans of German descent and sought to coordinate their work. It was the policy of the Bund to infiltrate older German societies. This effort was made as respects the Federation. Knauer assisted Froboese and others between 1933 and 1936 in endeavoring to have the swastika displayed at celebrations of the Federation. In 1935 Knauer reprimanded a delegate to the Federation for passing out pamphlets opposing the Nazi government in Germany. At a meeting of the Federation in 1935, Knauer moved to have the Federation recognize the swastika as the flag of the German Reich. The mo-

tion failed to carry. . . . Froboese and others proposed the formation of the German-American Citizens Alliance to compete with the Federation. It was organized early in 1937. The constitution and articles of incorporation of the Alliance provided that all of its assets on dissolution were to become the property of a German government agency for the dissemination of propaganda in foreign countries—the Deusches Auslands-Institut. The Alliance was a front organization for the Bund. It was designed to bring into its ranks persons who were sympathetic with the objectives of the Bund but who did not wish to be known as Bund members.

On February 22, 1937—less than two months before Knauer took his oath of naturalization—he was admitted to membership in the Alliance and became a member of its executive committee. . . . In 1938 Knauer was elected vice-president of the Alliance and subsequently presided over most of its meetings. He was the dominant figure in the Alliance. In May 1937 the German consul presented to the Alliance the swastika flag which had been torn down at the Federation celebration the year before. Not long after his naturalization Knauer urged that the Alliance sponsor a solstice ceremony, a solemn rite at which a wooden swastika is burned to symbolize the unity of German people everywhere. In August 1937 the Alliance refused to participate in an affair sponsored by a group which would not fly the swastika flag. In May 1938 Knauer at a meeting of the Alliance read a leaflet entitled "America, the Garbage Can of the World." In 1939 he arranged for public showings of films distributed by an official German propaganda agency and depicting the glories of Nazism.

*   *   *

In May 1938 Knauer and Froboese formed the American Protective League with a secret list of members. Knauer was elected a director. A constitution and bylaws were adopted and copies mailed by Knauer and Froboese to Hitler. . . .

Important evidence implicating Knauer in promoting the cause of Hitler in this country was given by a Mrs. Merton. She testified that, prompted solely by patriotic motives, she entered the employ of Froboese in 1938 in order to obtain evidence against the Bund and its members. . . .

Her testimony may be summarized as follows: She acted as secretary to Froboese in 1938. During the period of her employ Froboese and Knauer worked closely together on Bund matters. He helped Froboese in the preparation of articles for the Bund newspaper, of speeches, and of Bund correspondence. He helped Froboese prepare resolutions to be offered at the 1938 Bund convention calling for a white-gentile-ruled America. When Froboese left the city to attend the convention, he told her to contact Knauer for advice concerning Bund matters.

Letters signed by Froboese and Knauer jointly were sent to Hitler and other Nazi officials. One contained a list of 700 German nationals. One was the constitution and by-laws of the American Protective League which we have already mentioned. One to Hess said they had to lay low for awhile, that there was an investigation on. A birthday greeting to Hitler from Froboese and Knauer closed with the phrase, "In blind obedience we follow you." Knauer told her never to reveal that the Alliance and the Bund were linked together. One day she asked Knauer what the Bund was. His reply was that the Bund "was the Fuehrer's grip on American democracy." She reminded Knauer that he was an American citizen. He replied, "That is a good thing to hide behind."

We have given merely the highlights of the evidence. Much corroborative detail could be added. But what we have related presents the gist of the case against Knauer. If isolated parts of the evidence against Knauer were separately considered, they might well carry different inferences. His alertness to rise to the defense of Germans or of Americans of German descent could well reflect, if standing as isolated instances, attempts to protect a minority against what he deemed oppressive practices. Social and cultural ties might be complete and adequate explanations. Even utterances of a political nature which reflected tolerance or approval of the Nazi program in Germany might carry no sinister connotation, if they were considered by themselves. For many native-borns in this country did not awaken to the full implications of the Nazi program until war came to us. . . .

But we have here much more than political utterances, much more than a crusade for the protection of minorities. This record portrays a program of action to further Hitler's cause in this nation—a program of infiltration which conforms to the pattern adopted by the Nazis in country after country. The ties with the German Reich were too intimate, the pattern of conduct too consistent, the overt acts too plain for us to conclude that Knauer was merely exercising his right of free speech either to spread tolerance in this country or to advocate changes here.

*   *   *

The District Court properly ruled that membership in the Bund was not in itself sufficient to prove fraud which would warrant revocation of a degree of naturalization. Otherwise, guilt would rest on implication. But we have here much more than that. We have a clear course of conduct, of which membership in the Bund was a manifestation, designed to promote the Nazi cause in this country. This is not a case of an underling caught up in the enthusiasm of a movement, driven by ties of blood and old associations to extreme attitudes, and perhaps unaware of

the conflict of allegiance implicit in his actions. Knauer is an astute person. He is a leader—the dominating figure in the cause he sponsored, a leading voice in the councils of the Bund, the spokesman in the program for systematic agitation of Nazi views. His activities portray a shrewd, calculating, and vigilant promotion of an alien cause. The conclusion seems to us plain that when Knauer forswore allegiance to Hitler and the German Reich he swore falsely.

II. [W]hen an alien takes the oath with reservations or does not in good faith forswear loyalty and allegiance to the old country, the decree of naturalization is obtained by deceit. The proceeding itself is then founded on fraud. A fraud is perpetrated on the naturalization court. We have recently considered the broad powers of equity to set aside a decree for fraud practiced on the court which granted it. The present suit is an equity suit. But we need not consider in this case what the historic powers of equity might be in this situation. For Congress has provided that fraud is a basis for cancellation of certificates of naturalization in proceedings instituted by the United States. The legislative history of that enactment shows that false swearing was one of the evils included in the statutory grounds for denaturalization. That power was granted to give added protection against fraud committed on the naturalization courts. Cancellation of a certificate on the grounds of fraud includes cancellation for falsely swearing that the applicant forswore allegiance to his native country. Though the making of a false oath be called intrinsic fraud, it is within the reach of the statute.

We have no doubt of the power of Congress to provide for denaturalization on the ground of fraud. . . . We adhere to the prior rulings of this Court that Congress may provide for the cancellation of certificates of naturalization on the ground of fraud in their procurement and thus protect the courts and the nation against practices of aliens who by deceitful methods obtain the cherished status of citizenship here, the better to serve a foreign master.

Since fraud in the oath of allegiance which Knauer took is sufficient to sustain the judgment below, we do not reach the other questions which have been argued.

Affirmed.

MR. JUSTICE RUTLEDGE, dissenting.

*   *   *

My concern is not for Paul Knauer. The record discloses that he has no conception of, much less attachment to, basic American principles or institutions. He was a thorough-going Nazi, addicted to philosophies altogether hostile to the democratic framework in which we believe and live. Further, he was an active promoter of movements directed to securing acceptance of those ideas here and incorporating them in our institutions. And in this case . . . it would be hard to say that the evidence would not sustain a finding that he falsely took the oath of allegiance or that he never in his heart renounced his prime fealty to Adolph Hitler and Nazi Germany. Nor, in my opinion, can it be thought unequal to supporting a conclusion that, from a time prior to his admission to citizenship in 1935 until at any rate the assault on Pearl Harbor, Knauer was in the active service of the Nazi regime, promoting its cause here, and also for a short time in Germany, as the object of his first loyalty.

If therefore in any case a naturalized citizen's right and status can be revoked, by the procedure followed here or perhaps at all, it would be in such a case as this. But if one man's citizenship can thus be taken away, so can that of any other. And even in this case it would be in large part for his political convictions and acts done openly in espousal of them. Not merely Knauer's rights, but those of millions of naturalized citizens in their status and all that it implies of security and freedom, are affected by what is done in this case. By the outcome they are made either second-class citizens or citizens having equal rights and equal security with others.

No native-born American's birthright could be stripped from him for such a cause or by such a procedure as has been followed here. Nor could he be punished with banishment. To suffer that great loss he must forfeit citizenship by some act of treason or felony and be adjudged guilty by processes of law consistent with all the great protections thrown around such trials. Not yet has attempt been made to do this otherwise. Nor in my opinion could it be done, except for some such cause or by any less carefully safeguarded procedure.

In no instance thus far has our system tolerated destruction of that right of the native-born, except by voluntary surrender, on account of convictions held, views expressed, or acts done in promoting their acceptance falling short of treason as defined in the Constitution or conviction for felony. Nor has it thus far brought about that extinction by forms of trial other than those provided for such offenses. Moreover, even in such cases, although the penalty may be death or loss of the rights of citizenship, we have not yet imposed those penalties altogether foreign to our institutions, namely, deportation and exile. For one cause and one only have they been provided, namely, the loss of the naturalized citizen's status.

I do not find warrant in the Constitution for believing that it contemplates two classes of citizens, excepting only for two purposes. . . .

Congress, it is true, is empowered to lay down the conditions for admission of foreign-born persons to citizenship. In this respect it has wide authority. But it is not unlimited. Nor is Congress given power to take away citizenship once it is conferred, other than for some sufficient act of forfeiture taking place afterward. Naturalized citizens are no more free to become traitors or criminals than others and may be punished as they are when they commit the same offense. But any process which takes away their citizenship for causes or by procedures not applicable to native-born citizens places them in a separate and an inferior class. That dilemma is inescapable, though it is one not heretofore faced squarely. Unless it is the law that there are two classes of citizens, one superior, the other inferior, the status of no citizen can be annulled for causes or by procedures not applicable to all others.

. . . In my opinion the power to naturalize is not the power to denaturalize. The act of admission must be taken as final, for any cause which may have existed at that time. Otherwise there cannot but be two classes of citizens, one free and secure except for acts amounting to forfeiture within our tradition; the other, conditional, timorous and insecure because blanketed with the threat that some act or conduct, not amounting to forfeiture for others, will be taken retroactively to show that some prescribed condition had not been fulfilled and be so adjudged. I do not think such a difference was contemplated when Congress was authorized to provide for naturalization and the terms on which it should be granted.

But if I may be wrong in this, certainly so drastic a penalty as denaturalization, with resulting deportation and exile and all the attendant consequences, should not be imposed by any procedure less protective of the citizen's most fundamental right, comprehending all others, than must be employed to take away the native-born citizen's status or the lesser rights of the foreign-born citizen. If strings may be attached to citizenship and pulled retroactively to annul it, at the least this should be done only by those forms of proceeding most fully surrounded with the constitutional securities for trial which are among the prized incidents of citizenship. It is altogether anomalous that those safeguards are thrown about the foreign-born citizen when, for some offense, his liberty even for brief periods is at stake, but are withdrawn from him when all that gives substance to that freedom is put in jeopardy.

The right of citizenship is the most precious of all. The penalty of denaturalization is always harsh. Often it is more drastic than any other. It is also unique for this situation. For the required measure of security, the native-born citizen can be deprived of his status only by the rigidly safeguarded trial for treason or for conviction of a criminal offense which brings loss of rights as a citizen. To those procedures, with the same penalties and for the same causes, the foreign-born citizen is subject; but also by them he is protected. He should not be less secure when it is sought to annul his citizenship than when the effort is to bring about its forfeiture. Nor, in either event, should his procedural safeguards be less than when the same consequence, in substance, is inflicted upon the citizen native born.

The procedure prescribed for and followed in this case was not in accord with those standards. I think nothing less is adequate, or consistent with the constitutional status of citizenship, for the purpose of taking it away.

If this means that some or even many disloyal foreign-born citizens cannot be deported, it is better so than to place so many loyal ones in inferior status. And there are other effective methods for dealing with those who are disloyal, just as there are for such citizens by birth.

Accordingly, I would reverse the judgment.

MR. JUSTICE MURPHY joins in this dissent.

Bibliography

Abalone Alliance. *Diablo Canyon/Encampment Handbook.* Santa Cruz, Calif.: Northern California Preparers' Collective, 1980.

Abbey, Edward. *The Monkey Wrench Gang.* Philadelphia: Lippincott, 1975.

Abels, Jules. *Man on Fire: John Brown and the Cause of Liberty.* New York: Macmillan, 1971.

Abernathy, Thomas P. *The Burr Conspiracy.* New York: Oxford University Press, 1954.

The Acts of Assembly Now in Force in the Colony of Virginia, 1661-1769. Williamsburg: Rind, Purdie, and Dixon, 1769.

Adams, C. F., ed. *The Works of John Adams.* Vols. 3, 7-10, *Official Letters, Messages and Public Papers, Correspondence.* 1851, 1854 eds. Reprint. New York: AMS Press, 1971.

Adams, James Truslow. *The Epic of America.* Garden City, N.Y.: Blue Ribbon Books, 1941.

Agee, Philip, and Wolf, Louis, eds. *Dirty Work: The CIA in Western Europe.* Secaucus, N.J.: Stuart, 1978.

Albright, Joseph. *What Makes Spiro Run: The Life and Times of Spiro T. Agnew.* New York: Dodd, Mead, 1972.

Alexander, James. *A Brief Narrative of the Case and Trial of John Peter Zenger.* Cambridge, Mass.: Harvard University Press, Belknap Press, 1963.

Alexander, Yonah; Browne, Marjorie A.; and Nanes, Allan S., eds. *Control of Terrorism: International Documents.* New York: Crane, Russak, 1979.

Ali, Tariq, ed. *The New Revolutionaries: A Handbook of the International Radical Left.* New York: Morrow, 1969.

Alinsky, Saul D. *Reveille for Radicals.* Chicago: University of Chicago Press, 1946.

Allen, Francis A. *The Crimes of Politics: Political Dimensions of Criminal Justice.* Cambridge, Mass.: Harvard University Press, 1974.

Allen, W. *Governor Chamberlain's Administration in South Carolina.* New York: Negro Universities Press, 1969.

Anderson, Eric. *Race and Politics in North Carolina, 1872-1901.* Baton Rouge: Louisiana State University Press, 1981.

Andrews, Charles McLean, ed. *Narratives of the Insurrections, 1675-1690.* New York: Scribner, 1915.

Anthony, Earl. *Picking Up the Gun: A Report on the Black Panthers.* New York: Dial Press, 1970.

Aptheker, Herbert. *American Negro Slave Revolts.* New York: International Publishers, 1978.

Arber, E. *Travels and Works of Captain John Smith.* New York: Burt Franklin, 1910.

Archer, Jules. *Treason in America: Disloyalty versus Dissent.* New York: Hawthorn Books, 1971.

Arendt, Hannah. *On Revolution.* New York: Viking Press, 1970.

Arens, Richard, and Lasswell, Harold D. *In Defense of Public Order: The Emerging Field of Sanction Law.* New York: Columbia University Press, 1961.

Avrich, Paul. *The Haymarket Tragedy.* Princeton: Princeton University Press, 1984.

Babcox, Deborah; Babcox, Peter; and Abel, Bob, eds. *The Conspiracy.* New York: Dell, 1969.

Bailyn, Bernard. *The Ideological Origins of the American Revolution.* Cambridge, Mass.: Harvard University Press, 1967.

Bakeless, John. *Turncoats, Traitors, and Heroes.* New York: Lippincott, 1959.

Baldwin, Leland Dewitt. *Whiskey Rebels: The Story of a Frontier Uprising.* Pittsburgh: University of Pittsburgh Press, 1939.

Banner, James M. *To the Hartford Convention: The Federalists and the Origins of Party Politics in Massachusetts, 1789-1815.* New York: Knopf, 1970.

Barnes, Gilbert Hobbs. *The Antislavery Impulse, 1830-1844.* New York: Harcourt Brace & World, 1964.

Barsh, Russel Lawrence, and Henderson, James Youngblood. *The Road.* Berkeley and Los Angeles: University of California Press, 1980.

Barton, William E. *The Life of Abraham Lincoln.* Indianapolis: Bobbs-Merrill, 1925.

Baskir, Laurence M., and Strauss, William A. *Chance and Circumstance: The Draft, the War, and the Vietnam Generation.* New York: Knopf, 1978.

Basler, R. P., ed. *The Collected Works of Abraham Lincoln.* Vols. 4-8. New Brunswick, N.J.: Rutgers University Press, 1959.

Bassiouni, M. Cheriff, ed. *International Terrorism and Political Crimes.* Springfield, Ill.: Charles C Thomas, 1975.

Beck, Carl. *Contempt of Congress: A Study of the Prosecutions Initiated by the Committee on Un-American Activities, 1945-1957*. New Orleans: Hauser Press, 1959.

Becker, Carl Lotus. *The Eve of the Revolution: A Chronicle of the Breach with England*. New Haven: Yale University Press, 1918.

——. *The Declaration of Independence: A Study in the History of Political Ideas*. 3d ed. Reprint. New York: Vintage Books, 1958.

Becker, Theodore L., ed. *Political Trials*. Indianapolis: Bobbs-Merrill, 1971.

Bedau, Hugo Adam, ed. *Civil Disobedience: Theory and Practice*. New York: Pegasus, 1969.

Belfrage, Cedric. *The American Inquisition, 1945-1960*. Indianapolis: Bobbs-Merrill, 1973.

Belknap, Michal R. *Cold War Political Justice: The Smith Act, the Communist Party and American Civil Liberties*. Westport, Conn.: Greenwood Press, 1977.

Bell, Derrick, ed. *Shades of Brown: New Perspectives on School Desegregation*. New York: Teachers College Press, Columbia University, 1980.

Bell, Jason S. "Violation of International Law and Doomed United States Policy: An Analysis of the Cuban Democracy Act." 25 *U. Miami Inter-Am. L. Rev.* 77 (1993).

Bemis, Samuel Flagg. *The Diplomacy of the American Revolution*. Bloomington: Indiana University Press, 1957.

Ben-Dak, Joseph D., ed. *The Future of Collective Violence: Societal and International Perspectives*. Lund: Student Litteratur, 1974.

Bennett, Lerone. *Before the Mayflower: A History of the Negro in America, 1619-1966*. 3d ed. Chicago: Johnson, 1966.

Bentley, Eric, ed. *Thirty Years of Treason: Excerpts from Hearings before the House Committee on Un-American Activities, 1938-1968*. New York: Viking Press, 1971.

Berrigan, Daniel. *The Trial of the Catonsville Nine*. Boston: Beacon Press, 1970.

——. *The Dark Night of Resistance*. Garden City, N.Y.: Doubleday, 1971.

Berrigan, Daniel, and Coles, Robert. *The Geography of Faith*. New York: Bantam Books, 1972.

Berrigan, Philip. *Prison Journals of a Priest Revolutionary*. New York: Holt, Rinehart and Winston, 1969.

Blanchard, Dallas A., and Prewitt, Terry J. *Religious Violence and Abortion: The Gideon Project*. Gainesville: University Press of Florida, 1993.

Blaustein, Albert P. *Desegregation and the Law: The Meaning and Effect of the School Desegregation Cases*. New Brunswick, N.J.: Rutgers University Press, 1957.

Blaustein, Albert P., and Zangrando, Robert, eds. *Civil Rights and the American Negro: A Documentary History*. New York: Trident Press, 1968.

Blumenthal, Monica D.; Kahn, Robert L.; Andrews, Frank M.; and Head, Kendra B. *Justifying Violence: Attitudes of American Men*. Ann Arbor: Institute for Social Research, University of Michigan, 1975.

Blumenthal, Walter Hart. *American Indians Dispossessed*. 1955 ed. Reprint. New York: Arno Press, 1975.

Boesel, David, and Rossi, Peter H. *Cities under Siege: An Anatomy of the Ghetto Riots, 1964-1968*. New York: Basic Books, 1971.

The Book of the General Laws of the Inhabitants of the Jurisdiction of New Plymouth. Boston: Samuel Green, 1685.

Boorstin, Daniel J. *The Americans: The Colonial Experience*. New York: Random House, 1958.

Bowers, Claude G. *Jefferson and Hamilton: The Struggle for Democracy in America*. Boston: Houghton Mifflin, 1926.

Boyd, J., ed. *The Papers of Thomas Jefferson*. Princeton: Princeton University Press, 1950.

Brackenridge, Henry M. *History of the Western Insurrection in Western Pennsylvania, Commonly Called the Whiskey Insurrection, 1794*. Pittsburgh: W. S. Haven, 1859.

Bradford, William. *Of Plymouth Plantation, 1620-1647*. 1898 ed. Reprint. New York: Knopf, 1953.

Breen, T. H. *Puritans and Adventurers: Change and Persistence in Early America*. New York: Oxford University Press, 1980.

Breitman, G., ed. *Malcolm X Speaks*. New York: Grove Press, 1965.

Bremer, Arthur. *An Assassin's Diary*. New York: Harper's Magazine Press, 1972.

Brinton, Crane. *The Anatomy of Revolution*. New York: Random House, 1952.

——. *A Decade of Revolution, 1789-1799*. New York: Harper & Row, 1963.

Brissenden, Paul F. *The I.W.W.: A Study of American Syndicalism*. 2d ed. New York: Columbia University, 1920.

Brock, William R. *An American Crisis: Congress and Reconstruction, 1865-1867*. New York: St. Martin's Press, 1963.

Brodie, Fawn M. *Thomas Jefferson: An Intimate History*. New York: Bantam Books, 1974.

Brogan, D. W. *The American Character*. New York: Random House, 1956.

Brooks, Thomas R. *Toil and Trouble: A History of American Labor*. New York: Dell, 1964.

Brower, Brock. *Other Loyalties*. New York: Atheneum, 1968.

Brown, Ralph S. *Loyalty and Security: Employment Tests in the United States*. New Haven: Yale University Press, 1958.

Brown, Richard M. *Strain of Violence*. New York: Oxford University Press, 1975.

Brown, W., ed. *Proceedings and Acts of the General Assembly of Maryland, January 1637-1658*. Baltimore: Press of Isaac Friedenwald, 1883.

Brownlie, Ian. *The Law Relating to Public Order*. London: Butterworth, 1968.

Bryan, George S. *The Spy in America*. Philadelphia: Lippincott, 1943.

Buckley, William F. *The Committee and Its Critics: A Calm Review of the House Committee on Un American Activities*. New York: Putnam, 1962.

Buckman, Peter. *The Limits of Protest*. Indianapolis: Bobbs-Merrill, 1970.

Buncher, Judith F., ed. *The CIA and the Security Debate, 1975-1976*. New York: Facts on File, 1977.

Bunzel, John H. *Anti-Politics in America*. New York: Vintage Books, 1970.

Burke, Edmund. *Reflections on the Revolution in France*. Baltimore: Penguin Books, 1969.

Burton, Anthony. *Revolutionary Violence*. New York: Crane, Russak, 1978.

Calhoon, Robert McCluer. *The Loyalists in Revolutionary America, 1760-1781*. New York: Harcourt Brace Jovanovich, 1973.

Califano, Joseph A., Jr. *The Student Revolution: A Global Confrontation*. New York: Norton, 1970.

Cameron, Jenks. *The Development of Governmental Forest Control in the United States*. 1928; reprint, New York: DaCapo Press, 1972.

Campbell, James S.; Sahid, Joseph R.; and Stang, David P. *Law and Order Reconsidered*. Washington, D.C.: U.S. Government Printing Office, 1969.

Campbell, Stanley W. *The Slave Catchers: Enforcement of the Fugitive Slave Law, 1850-1860*. Chapel Hill: University of North Carolina Press, 1970.

Camus, Albert. *Resistance, Rebellion, and Death*. New York: Random House, 1960.

Canby, Courtland. *Lincoln and the Civil War: A Profile and a History*. New York: Braziller, 1960.

Candler, A., ed. *The Confederate Records of the State of Georgia*. Atlanta: C. P. Byrd, 1909.

Carlson, Peter. *Roughneck: The Life and Times of Big Bill Haywood*. New York: Norton, 1983.

Carmichael, Stokely. *Stokely Speaks: Black Power Back to Pan-Africanism*. New York: Random House, 1971.

Carter, H.; Stone, W.; and Gould, M., eds. *Reports of the Proceedings and Debates of the Convention of 1821*. New York: Da Capo Press, 1970.

Catton, William B. *Two Roads to Sumter*. New York: McGraw-Hill, 1963.

Caute, David. *The Great Fear: The Anti-Communist Purge under Truman and Eisenhower*. New York: Simon & Schuster, 1978.

Chafee, Zechariah. *How Human Rights Got into the Constitution*. Boston: Boston University Press, 1952.

Chalmers, David M. *Hooded Americanism: The First Century of the Ku Klux Klan, 1865-1965*. Garden City, N.Y.: Doubleday, 1965.

The Chicago Martyrs: The Famous Speeches of Eight Anarchists in Judge Gary's Court. San Francisco: Free Society, 1899.

Chomsky, Noam, et al. *Trials of the Resistance*. New York: Vintage Books, 1970.

Clavir, Judy, and Spitzer, John, eds. *The Conspiracy Trial*. Indianapolis: Bobbs-Merrill, 1970.

Cleaver, Eldridge. *Soul on Ice*. New York: Dell, 1972.

Clinard, Marshall B., and Quinney, Richard. *Criminal Behavior Systems: A Typology*. New York: Holt, Rinehart and Winston, 1967.

Cohen, Nathan, ed. *The Los Angeles Riots: A Psychological Study*. New York: Praeger, 1970.

Commager, H. S., ed. *Documents of American History*. New York: Meredith Corp., 1973.

Commins, S., ed. *Basic Writings of George Washington*. New York: Random House, 1948.

Commission on CIA Activities within the United States. *Report to the President by the Commission on CIA Activities within the United States*. Washington, D.C.: U.S. Government Printing Office, 1975.

Commons, J. R., and Gillmore, E., eds. *A Documentary History of American Industrial Society*. Vol. 4. New York: Russell & Russell, 1958.

Connery, Robert H., ed. *Urban Riots: Violence and Social Change*. New York: Vintage Books, 1969.

Cook, Adrian. *The Armies of the Streets: The New York City Draft Riots of 1863*. Lexington: University Press of Kentucky, 1974.

Cooper, T., ed. *Statutes of South Carolina, 1682-1716*. Vol. 2. Columbia, S.C.: A. S. Johnston, 1837.

Cooper, William J. *The Conservative Regime: South Carolina, 1877-1890*. Baltimore: Johns Hopkins Press, 1968.

Cornell, J. *The Trial of Ezra Pound: A Documented Account of the Treason Case by the Defendant's Lawyer*. New York: John Day, 1966.

Cover, Robert. *Justice Accused: Antislavery and the Judicial Process*. New Haven: Yale University Press, 1975.

Crelinsten, Ronald D.; Laberge-Altmejd, Danielle; and Szabo, Denis. *Terrorism and Criminal Justice*. Lexington, Mass.: Heath, 1978.

Crook, Wilfred H. "The Revolutionary Logic of the General Strike." *American Political Science Review* 28 (1934): 655-63.

Currie, David P. *The Constitution of the Federal Republic of Germany*. Chicago: University of Chicago Press, 1994.

Cushing, J. D., ed. *The Earliest Laws of the New Haven and Connecticut Colonies, 1639-1673*. Wilmington, Del.: Michael Glazier, 1977.

——. *Laws of the Province of Maryland (1718)*. Wilmington, Del.: Michael Glazier, 1977.

——. *Rhode Island Colony Laws, 1647-1719*. Wilmington, Del.: Michael Glazier, 1977.

Daniels, Roger. *The Bonus March: An Episode of the Great Depression*. Westport, Conn.: Greenwood Press, 1971.

Darvall, Frank O. *Popular Disturbances and Public Order in Regency England*. London: Oxford University Press, 1934.

David, H. *The History of the Haymarket Affair*. New York: Farrar & Rinehart, 1936.

Davis, Allen F., and Woodman, Harold D., eds. *Conflict and Consensus in Modern American History*. Lexington, Mass.: Heath, 1980.

Davis, Angela Y. *If They Come in the Morning*. New York: Joseph Okpaku, 1971.

Davis, David B. *The Fear of Conspiracy: Images of Un-American Subversion from the Revolution to the Present*. Ithaca: Cornell University Press, 1971.

Davis, D. *The Billy Mitchell Affair*. New York: Random House, 1967.

Davis, William W. H. *The Fries Rebellion, 1798-1799: An Armed Resistance to the House Tax Law, Passed by Congress, July 9, 1798, in Bucks and Northampton Counties, Pennsylvania*. Doylestown, Pa.: Doylestown, 1899.

Dawson, Frank Griffith, and Head, Ivan L. *International Law, National Tribunals, and the Rights of Aliens*. New York: Procedural Aspects of International Law Institute, 1971.

Debo, Angie. *The Road to Disappearance*. Norman: University of Oklahoma Press, 1941.

——. *A History of the Indians of the United States*. Norman: University of Oklahoma Press, 1971.

Debray, Regis. *Revolution in the Revolution: Armed Struggle and Political Struggle in Latin America*. New York: Grove Press, 1967.

Dell, Christopher. *Lincoln and the War Democrats: The Grand Erosion of Conservative Tradition*. Rutherford, N.J.: Fairleigh Dickinson University Press, 1975.

Dellinger, Dave. *Revolutionary Nonviolence*. New York: Doubleday, 1971.

Deloria, Vine. *A Brief History of the Federal Responsibility to the American Indians*. Washington, D.C.: U.S. Government Printing Office, 1979.

Deloria, Vine, and Lytle, Clifford M. *American Indians, American Justice*. Austin: University of Texas Press, 1983.

De Silva, Peer. *Sub Rosa: The CIA and the Uses of Intelligence*. New York: Times Books, 1978.

Dillon, Martin, and Lehane, Denis. *Political Murder in Northern Ireland*. Middlesex: Penguin Books, 1973.

Dobrouir, William A. *Justice in Time of Crisis*. Washington, D.C.: U.S. Government Printing Office, 1969.

Donner, Frank J. *The Age of Surveillance*. New York: Knopf, 1980.

Dowell, Eldridge F. *A History of Criminal Syndicalism Legislation in the United States*. New York: Da Capo Press, 1969.

Dubofsky, Melvyn. *We Shall Be All: A History of the Industrial Workers of the World*. Chicago: Quadrangle Books, 1969.

Dubois, W. E. B. *John Brown*. New York: International Publishers, 1962.

Duff, John B., and Mitchell, Peter M., eds. *The Nat Turner Rebellion: The Historical Event and the Modern Controversy*. New York: Harper & Row, 1971.

Dwight, T. *History of the Hartford Convention*. 1833 ed. Reprint. New York: Da Capo Press, 1970.

Eddowes, Michael. *The Oswald File*. New York: C. N. Potter, 1977.

Edelman, Murray. *The Symbolic Uses of Politics*. Urbana: University of Illinois Press, 1970.

Edwards, Samuel. *Rebel! A Biography of Tom Paine*. New York: Praeger, 1974.

Ehrlich, Walter. *They Have No Rights: Dred Scott's Struggle for Freedom*. Westport, Conn.: Greenwood Press, 1979.

Ehrmann, Herbert. *The Case That Will Not Die: Commonwealth vs. Sacco and Vanzetti*. Boston: Little, Brown, 1969.

Elliot, J., ed. *Debates in the Several State Conventions on the Adoption of the Federal Constitution*. 5 vols. Philadelphia: Lippincott, 1907.

Elliot, John D., and Gibson, Leslie K., eds. *Contemporary Terrorism: Selected Readings*. Gaithersburg, Md.: International Association of Chiefs of Police, 1978.

Ellis, George William, and Morris, John E. *King Philip's War*. New York: Grafton Press, 1906.

Emerson, Thomas I. *The System of Freedom of Expression*. New York: Random House, 1970.

Emerson, Thomas I.; Haber, David; and Dorsen, Norman, eds. *Political and Civil Rights in the United States*. Boston: Little, Brown, 1967.

Endleman, Shalom, ed. *Violence in the Streets*. Chicago: Quadrangle Books, 1968.

Erm, Rene, II. "The 'Wise Use' Movement: The Constitutionality of Local Action on Federal Lands under the Preemption Doctrine." 30 *Idaho L. Rev.* 631 (1993-94).

Ernst, Morris L. *The First Freedom*. New York: Macmillan, 1946.

Fall, Bernard B., ed. *Ho Chi Minh on Revolution*. New York: Praeger, 1968.

Fanon, Frantz. *The Wretched of the Earth*. New York: Grove Press, 1968.

Farrell, William R. *The U.S. Government Response to Terrorism*. Boulder, Colo.: Westview Press, 1982.

Fehrenbacker, Don E. *The Dred Scott Case: Its Significance in American Law and Politics*. New York: Oxford University Press, 1978.

——. *Slavery, Law, and Politics: The Dred Scott Case in Historical Perspective*. New York: Oxford University Press, 1981.

Ferber, Michael. *The Resistance*. Boston: Beacon Press, 1971.

Feuerlicht, Roberta S. *Justice Crucified: The Story of Sacco and Vanzetti*. New York: McGraw-Hill, 1977.

Fifty Mutinies, Rebellions, and Revolutions. London: Odhams Press, n.d.

Filler, Louis. *The Crusade against Slavery, 1830-1860*. New York: Harper & Row, 1960.

Filler, Louis, and Guttmann, Allen, eds. *The Removal of the Cherokee Nation: Manifest Destiny or National Dishonor?* Problems in American Civilization, vol. 48. Boston: Heath, 1962.

Fink, Leon. *Workingmen's Democracy: The Knights of Labor and American Politics*. Urbana: University of Illinois Press, 1983.

Finn, James, ed. *A Conflict of Loyalties*. New York: Western Publishing, 1968.

Fleming, W. L., ed. *The Ku Klux Klan: Its Origin, Growth, and Disbandment*. New York: Neale, 1905.

Fleming, W. L., ed. *Documents Relating to Reconstruction*. Morgantown: University of West Virginia, 1904.

Flynn, Elizabeth Gurley. *The Rebel Girl: An Autobiography, My First Life (1906-1926)*. New York: International Publishers, 1979.

Foner, Eric. *Nothing but Freedom: Emancipation and Its Legacy*. Baton Rouge: Louisiana State University Press, 1983.

Foner, Philip S. *History of the Labor Movement in the United States*. New York: International Publishers, 1947.

——. *The Case of Joe Hill*. New York: International Publishers, 1975.

——, ed. *The Black Panthers Speak*. Philadelphia: Lippincott, 1970.

Foreman, Dave. *Confessions of an Ecowarrior*. New York: Harmony Books, 1991.

Foreman, Dave, and Haywood, Bill, eds. *Ecodefense: A Field Guide to Monkeywrenching*. 3d ed. Chico, Calif.: Abbzug Press, 1993.

Force, P., ed. *American Archives: 4th series*. Vol. 3. Washington, D.C.: M. St. Clair Clarke & P. Force, 1853.

Force, W. C., ed. *Writings of George Washington*. New York: Putnam, 1889.

Ford, Gerald R., and Stiles, John R. *Portrait of the Assassin*. New York: Ballantine Books, 1966.

Ford, W. C., ed. *Journals of the Continental Congress*. 34 vols. Washington, D.C.: U.S. Government Printing Office, 1906.

Ford, W. J. *Resistance Movements and International Law*. Geneva: 1967, 1968.

Foreman, Grant. *Indian Removal: The Emigration of the Five Civilized Tribes of Indians*. Norman: University of Oklahoma Press, 1966.

Fortas, Abe. *Concerning Dissent and Civil Disobedience*. New York: New American Library, 1968.

Fraenkel, O. K. *The Sacco-Vanzetti Case*. New York: Knopf, 1931.

Frankfurter, M. D., and Jackson, G., eds. *The Letters of Sacco and Vanzetti*. New York: Viking Press, 1928.

Fritz, Henry E. *The Movement for Indian Assimilation, 1860-1890*. Philadelphia: University of Pennsylvania Press, 1963.

Fromm, Erich. *Escape from Freedom*. 1941 ed. Reprint. New York: Avon Books, 1969.

Frost, R. *The Mooney Case*. Stanford: Stanford University Press, 1968.

Furniss, Norman F. *The Mormon Conflict, 1850-1859*. New Haven: Yale University Press, 1966.

Gage, Thomas. *The Correspondence of General Thomas Gage*. Edited by Clarence Edwin Carter. 2 vols. New Haven: Yale University Press, 1931-33.

Gambill, Edward L. *Conservative Ordeal: Northern Democrats and Reconstruction, 1865-1868*. Ames: Iowa State University Press, 1981.

Gambs, John S. *The Decline of the I. W. W.* New York: Columbia University Press, 1932.

Garrison, W., and Garrison, F. *William Lloyd Garrison, 1805-1879: The Story of His Life Told by His Children*. 4 vols. 1884-89 ed. Reprint. New York: Arno Press, 1969.

Gates, Paul W. *History of Public Land Law Development*. North Stratford, N.H.: Ayer Publishers, 1972.

Gaylin, Willard. *In the Service of Their Country: War Resisters in Prison*. New York: Grosset & Dunlap, 1970.

Gellhorn, Walter. *Security, Loyalty, and Science*. Ithaca: Cornell University Press, 1950.

Gentry, Curt. *Frame-Up: The Incredible Case of Tom Mooney and Warren Billings*. New York: Norton, 1967.

Gerhardt, James M. *The Draft and Public Policy: Issues in Military Manpower Procurement, 1945-1970*. Columbus: Ohio State University Press, 1971.

Geschwender, James A. *The Black Revolt*. Englewood Cliffs, N.J.: Prentice-Hall, 1971.

Gillette, William. *Retreat from Reconstruction, 1869-1879*. Baton Rouge: Louisiana State University Press, 1982.

Goldman, E. *Anarchism and Other Essays*. Port Washington, N.Y.: Kennikat Press, 1969.

Goldstein, Alvin H. *The Unquiet Death of Julius and Ethel Rosenberg*. New York: Lawrence Hill, 1975.

Goldstein, Robert J. *Political Repression in Modern America*. Cambridge, Mass.: Schenkman, 1977.

Goodell, Charles E. *Political Prisoners in America*. New York: Random House, 1973.

Goodman, Walter. *The Committee: The Extraordinary Career of the House Committee on Un-American Activities*. New York: Farrar, Straus & Giroux, 1968.

Goodspeed, D. J. *The Conspirators: A Study of the Coup d'Etat*. New York: Viking Press, 1962.

Graglia, Lino A. *Disaster by Decree: The Supreme Court Decisions on Race and the Schools*. Ithaca: Cornell University Press, 1976.

Graham, Hugh Davis, and Gurr, Ted Robert. *Violence in America: Historical and Comparative Perspectives*. Washington, D.C.: U.S. Government Printing Office, 1969.

Grathwohl, Larry, as told to Frank Reagan. *Bringing down America: An FBI Informer with the Weathermen*. New Rochelle, N.Y.: Arlington House, 1976.

Greenberg, Douglas. *Crime and Law Enforcement in the Colony of New York, 1691-1761*. Ithaca: Cornell University Press, 1976.

Greene, Jack P., ed. *Colonies to Nation, 1763-1789: A Documentary History of the American Revolution*. New York: Norton, 1975.

Grey, Zane. *To the Last Man*. New York: Harper & Bros., 1921.

Guerrilla War in the U.S.A. Scanlan's Monthly, January 1971.

Gurr, Ted Robert. *Why Men Rebel*. Princeton: Princeton University Press, 1971.

——. *Rogues, Rebels, and Reformers: A Political History of Urban Crime and Conflict*. Beverly Hills, Calif.: Sage, 1976.

Gusfield, Joseph R. *Protest, Reform, and Revolt*. New York: Wiley, 1970.

Guttmann, Allen, ed. *Communism, the Courts, and the Constitution*. Boston: Heath, 1964.

Halperin, Morton H. *The Lawless State: The Crimes of the U.S. Intelligence Agencies*. New York: Penguin Books, 1976.

Hansen, Klaus J. *Quest for Empire: The Political Kingdom of God and the Council of Fifty in Mormon History*. East Lansing: Michigan State University Press, 1967.

Hanser, Richard. *A Noble Treason*. New York: Putnam, 1979.

Hardt, Scott W. "Federal Land Management in the Twenty-first Century: From Wise Use to Wise Stewardship." 18 *Harv. Env. L. Rev.* 345 (1994).

Hartogs, Dr. Renatus, and Artzt, Eric. *Violence: Causes and Solutions*. New York: Dell, 1970.

Haskins, George Lee. *Law and Authority in Early Massachusetts: A Study in Tradition and Design.* New York: Macmillan, 1960.

Havens, Murray Clark; Leiden, Carl; and Schmitt, Karl M. *The Politics of Assassination.* Englewood Cliffs, N.J.: Prentice-Hall, 1970.

Hayden, Tom. *Trial.* New York: Holt, Rinehart and Winston, 1970.

Haywood, William D. *The Autobiography of Big Bill Haywood.* New York: International Publishers, 1974.

Heffner, R., ed. *A Documentary History of the United States.* New York: Mentor, 1952.

Hendel, Samuel, ed. *The Politics of Confrontation.* New York: Meredith Corp., 1971.

Hendrick, Burton J. *Statesmen of the Lost Cause: Jefferson Davis and His Cabinet.* Boston: Little, Brown, 1939.

——. *Lincoln's War Cabinet.* Garden City, N.Y.: Doubleday, 1961.

Hening, W., ed. *Virginia Statutes at Large.* Vol. 1, *Virginia Statutes at Large, 1619-1660.* Vol. 2, *Virginia Statutes at Large, 1660-1682.* Vol. 3, *Virginia Statutes at Large, 1682-1710.* 1823 ed. Reprint. Charlottesville: University Press of Virginia, 1969.

Hennacy, A., ed. *Two Agitators: Peter Maurin—Ammon Hennacy.* New York: Catholic Worker, 1959.

Henty, G. A. *Through the Fray: A Tale of the Luddite Riots.* New York: Hurst, c. 1890.

Higham, John. *Strangers in the Land: Patterns of American Nativism, 1860-1925.* New York: Atheneum, 1965.

Hofstadter, Richard, and Wallace, Michael, eds. *American Violence: A Documentary History.* New York: Knopf, 1970.

Holden, Matthew, Jr. *The Politics of the Black "Nation."* New York: Chandler, 1973.

Holt, Thomas. *Black over White: Negro Political Leadership in South Carolina during Reconstruction.* Urbana: University of Illinois Press, 1977.

Honderich, Ted. *Three Essays on Political Violence.* Oxford: Basil Blackwell, 1976.

Hoopes, Townsend. *The Limits of Intervention.* New York: McKay, 1970.

Horn, Stanley F. *Invisible Empire: The Story of the Ku Klux Klan, 1866-1871.* Montclair, N.J.: Patterson Smith, 1969.

Horowitz, Irving Louis, ed. *The Anarchists.* New York: Dell, 1970.

Hubbard, David G. *The Skyjacker.* New York: Macmillan, 1971.

Huffman, James L., "The Inevitability of Private Rights in Public Lands." 65 *U. Colo. L. Rev.* 241 (1994).

Hughes, Rupert. *George Washington: The Rebel and the Patriot, 1762-1777.* New York: Morrow, 1927.

Humphrey, Hubert H., ed. *School Desegregation: Documents and Commentaries.* New York: Crowell, 1962.

Hurd, Rollin C. *A Treatise on the Right of Personal Liberty and on the Writ of Habeas Corpus.* 2d ed., rev., with notes by Frank H. Hurd. New York: Da Capo Press, 1972.

Hurst, Charles G. *Passport to Freedom: Education, Humanism, and Malcolm X.* Hamden, Conn.: Linnet Books, 1972.

Hurwood, Bernhardt J. *Society and the Assassin: A Background Book on Political Murder.* New York: Parents Magazine Press, 1970.

Hyams, Edward. *Terrorists and Terrorism.* New York: St. Martin's Press, 1975.

Hyman, Harold M. *Era of the Oath: Northern Loyalty Tests during the Civil War and Reconstruction.* Philadelphia: University of Pennsylvania Press, 1954.

——. *To Try Men's Souls: Loyalty Tests in American History.* Berkeley and Los Angeles: University of California Press, 1959.

Hyneman, Charles S., and Lutz, Donald S., eds. *American Political Writings during the Founding Era.* Indianapolis: Liberty Press, 1983.

Inglis, Brian. *Roger Casement.* London: Hodder Paperbacks, 1974.

Irons, Peter H. *Justice at War.* New York: Oxford University Press, 1983.

Jackson, Curtis, and Galli, Marcia J. *A History of the Bureau of Indian Affairs and Its Activities among Indians.* San Francisco: R & E Research Associates, 1977.

Jackson, George. *Soledad Brother: The Prison Letters of George Jackson.* New York: Bantam Books, 1970.

Jackson, Kenneth T. *The Ku Klux Klan in the City, 1915-1930.* New York: Oxford University Press, 1977.

Jacobs, Harold, ed. *Weatherman.* Berkeley: Ramparts Press, 1971.

Jacobs, Wilbur R. *Dispossessing the American Indian: Indians and Whites on the Colonial Frontier.* New York: Scribner, 1972.

James, Edward T., ed. *The American Plutarch: Eighteen Lives Selected from the Dictionary of American Biography.* New York: Scribner, 1964.

Jameson, John Franklin, ed. *Essays in the Constitutional History of the United States in the Formative Period, 1775-1789, by Graduates and Former Members of The Johns Hopkins University.* Boston: Houghton Mifflin, 1889.

Johnson, F. Roy, *The Nat Turner Slave Insurrection.* Murfreesboro, N.C.: Johnson Publishing Co., 1966.

Josephy, Alvin M., Jr. *Red Power.* New York: McGraw-Hill, 1971.

——. *The Patriot Chiefs.* New York: Penguin Books, 1978.

Joughin, Louis, and Morgan, E. M. *The Legacy of Sacco and Vanzetti.* New York: Harcourt, Brace, 1948.

Joyner, Nancy D. *Aerial Hijacking as an International Crime.* Dobbs Ferry, N.Y.: Oceana Publications, 1974.

Kaiser, R. B. *RFK Must Die.* New York: Dutton, 1970.

Karalekas, Anne. *History of the Central Intelligence Agency.* Laguna Hills, Calif.: Aegean Park Press, 1977.

Kariel, Henry S. *The Decline of American Pluralism.* Stanford: Stanford University Press, 1967.

Katkov, George. *The Trial of Bukharin.* London: B. T. Batsford, 1969.

Keller, Allan. *Thunder at Harper's Ferry.* Englewood Cliffs, N.J.: Prentice-Hall, 1958.

Kennedy, Robert F. *The Enemy Within.* New York: Popular Library, 1960.

Kimmel, Stanley. *The Mad Booths of Maryland.* 2d ed., rev. and enl. New York: Dover, 1969.

King, Dan. *The Life and Times of Thomas Wilson Dorr, with Outlines of the Political History of Rhode Island.* Freeport, N.Y.: Books for Libraries Press, 1969.

King, Duane H., ed. *The Cherokee Indian Nation: A Troubled History.* Knoxville: University of Tennessee Press, 1979.

King, Martin Luther, Jr. *Why We Can't Wait.* New York: Harper & Row, 1963.

Kirchheimer, Otto. *Political Justice.* Princeton: Princeton University Press, 1961.

Kirkham, James; Levy, Sheldon G.; and Crotty, William J. *Assassination and Political Violence.* Vol. 8 of *The National Commission on the Causes and Prevention of Violence Staff Study Series.* Washington, D.C.: U.S. Government Printing Office, 1969.

Kittrie, Nicholas N. "Reconciling the Irreconcilable: The Quest for Internationl Agreement over Political Crime and Terrorism." In *The Year Book of World Affairs, 1978.* London: Stevens & Sons, 1978.

Kommers, Donald P. *The Constitutional Jurisprudence of the Federal Republic of Germany.* Durham, N.C.: Duke University Press, 1989.

Konitz, Milton R. *A Century of Civil Rights.* New York: Columbia University Press, 1961.

Kornbluh, Joyce L., ed. *Rebel Voices: An I. W. W. Anthology.* Ann Arbor: University of Michigan Press, 1964.

Kraditor, Aileen S. *The Ideas of the Woman Suffrage Movement, 1890-1920.* New York: Columbia University Press, 1965.

——. *Means and Ends in American Abolitionism: Garrison and His Critics on Strategy and Tactics, 1834–1850.* New York: Pantheon Books, 1969.

Kutler, Stanley I. *The American Inquisition: Justice and Injustice in the Cold War.* New York: Hill & Wang, 1982.

Labaree, Benjamin W. *The Boston Tea Party.* New York: Oxford University Press, 1964.

Lane, Mark. *Rush to Judgment: A Critique of the Warren Commission's Inquiry into the Murders of President John F. Kennedy, Officer J. D. Tippit, and Lee Harvey Oswald.* New York: Holt, Rinehart and Winston, 1966.

Larsen, Otto N., ed. *Violence and the Mass Media.* New York: Harper & Row, 1968.

Lattimore, Owen. *Ordeal by Slander.* Boston: Little, Brown, 1950.

Lauber, Almon Wheeler. *Indian Slavery in Colonial Times within the Present Limits of the United States.* New York: Columbia University, 1913.

Laws of the Colonial and State Governments, Relating to Indians and Indian Affairs, 1633-1831, Inclusive: With an Appendix Containing the Proceedings of the Congress of the Confederation and the Laws of Congress from 1800 to 1830 on the same subject. 1932 ed. Reprint. Standfordville, N.Y.: E. M. Coleman, 1979.

Laws of the State of New York. Vol. 1, *1777-1784.* Albany: Weed, Parsons, 1886.

Lawson, J. D., ed. *American State Trials.* Vol. 15. St. Louis: Thomas Lawbook Co., 1856.

Leach, Douglas Edward. *Flintlock and Tomahawk: New England in King Philip's War.* New York: Macmillan, 1958.

Leary, Timothy. *Flashbacks: An Autobiography.* Boston: Houghton Mifflin, 1983.

Leary, William L., ed. *The Central Intelligence Agency: History and Documents.* University, Ala.: University of Alabama Press, 1984.

Lee, R. Alton. *Truman and Taft-Hartley: A Question of Mandate.* Lexington: University of Kentucky Press, 1966.

Leech, Margaret. *In The Days of McKinley.* New York: Harper & Bros., 1959.

Lehey, John D. "Unraveling the Sagebrush Rebellion: Law, Politics, and Federal Lands." 14 *U. Cal. Dav. L. Rev.* 317 (1980).

Levy, Leonard W. *The Law of the Commonwealth of Chief Justice Shaw.* New York: Harper & Row, 1957.

——. *Legacy of Suppression: Freedom of Speech in Early American History.* Cambridge, Mass.: Harvard University Press, Belknap Press, 1960.

Lewis, Anthony. *Gideon's Trumpet.* New York: Vintage Books, 1964.

Lewy, Guenter. *The Federal Loyalty Security Program: The Need for Reform.* Washington, D.C.: American Enterprise Institute for Public Policy Research, 1983.

Lieberman, Jethro K. *How the Government Breaks the Law.* New York: Stein & Day, 1972.

Lindner, Robert. *Must You Conform?* New York: Holt, Rinehart and Winston, 1956.

Linton, Calvin D., ed. *The Bicentennial Almanac.* New York: Thomas Nelson, 1975.

Lipset, Seymour M. *Political Man: The Social Bases of Politics.* Garden City, N.Y.: Doubleday, 1963.

Lisio, Donald J. *The President and Protest: Hoover, Conspiracy, and the Bonus Riot.* Columbia: University of Missouri Press, 1974.

Liston, Robert A. *Dissent in America.* New York: McGraw-Hill, 1971.

Littlefield, Daniel F. *Africans and Creeks: From the Colonial Period to the Civil War.* Westport, Conn.: Greenwood Press, 1979.

Lockridge, Kenneth A. *Settlement and Unsettlement in Early America: The Crisis of Political Legitimacy before the Revolution.* New York: Cambridge University Press, 1981.

Lockwood, Lee. *Conversation with Eldridge Cleaver.* New York: Dell, 1970.

Lowi, Theodore, ed. *The Politics of Disorder.* New York: Norton, 1974.

——, ed. *The End of Liberalism: The Second Republic of the United States.* New York: Norton, 1979.

Lucas, Jim. *Agnew: Profile in Conflict.* New York: Universal Publishing, 1970.

Lumpkin, Wilson. *The Removal of the Cherokee Indians from Georgia.* New York: Dodd, Mead, 1907.

Lundberg, Ferdinand. *Cracks in the Constitution.* Secaucus, N.J.: Stuart, 1980.

Lutz, Alma. *Susan B. Anthony: Rebel, Crusader, Humanitarian.* Boston: Beacon Press, 1959.

Lynd, S., ed. *Nonviolence in America: A Documentary History.* New York: Bobbs-Merrill, 1966.

Mabee, Carleton. *Black Freedom.* London: Macmillan, 1970.

McCague, James. *The Second Rebellion: The Story of the New York City Draft Riots of 1863.* New York: Dial Press, 1968.

McCaleb, Walter F. *The Aaron Burr Conspiracy; and, A New Light on Aaron Burr.* 2 vols in 1. 1903 ed., enl. New York: Argosy-Antiquarian, 1966.

McDonald, Forrest. *Alexander Hamilton: A Biography.* New York: Norton, 1982.

McHenry, Robert, ed. *Liberty's Women.* Springfield, Mass.: Merriam, 1980.

Mackenzie, Compton. *Certain Aspects of Moral Courage.* Garden City, N.Y.: Doubleday, 1962.

Macknight, Gerald. *The Terrorist Mind.* Indianapolis: Bobbs-Merrill, 1974.

McDougall, Mary Lynn, ed. *The Working Class in Modern Europe.* Lexington, Mass.: Heath, 1975.

McLellan, Vin, and Avery, Paul. *The Voices of Guns: The Definitive and Dramatic Story of the Twenty-Two-Month Career of the Symbionese Liberation Army, One of the Most Bizarre Chapters in the History of the American Left.* New York: Putnam, 1977.

McPherson, E., ed. *The Political History of the United States during the Great Rebellion.* Washington, D.C.: Philip and Solomons, 1865.

McPherson, James M. *Ordeal by Fire: The Civil War and Reconstruction.* New York: Knopf, 1981.

Madison, James, and Jefferson, Thomas. *Resolutions of Virginia and Kentucky.* Richmond, Va.: Shepherd, 1835.

Major, John. *The New Deal.* London: Longmans, Green, 1968.

Major, Reginald. *Justice in the Round: The Trial of Angela Davis.* New York: Third Press, 1973.

Malcolm X, and Haley, Alex. *The Autobiography of Malcolm X.* New York: Grove Press, 1969.

Malone, Dumas. *Jefferson the Virginian.* Boston: Little, Brown, 1948.

Marchetti, Victor, and Marks, John D. *The CIA and the Cult of Intelligence.* New York: Dell, 1974.

Marine, Gene. *The Black Panthers.* New York: New American Library, 1969.

Mark, Irving. *Agrarian Conflicts in Colonial New York, 1711-1775.* 2d ed. Port Washington, N.Y.: I. J. Friedman, 1965.

Martin, James Kirby. *Men in Rebellion.* New York: Macmillan, 1973.

Marx, Karl. *The Civil War in France.* Peking: Foreign Languages Press, 1966.

Mason, Alpheus T. *The States Rights Debate: Antifederalism and the Constitution.* 2d ed. New York: Oxford University Press, 1972.

Masotti, Louis H., and Bowen, Don R., eds. *Riots and Rebellion: Civil Violence in the Urban Community*. Beverly Hills, Calif.: Sage, 1968.

Mayo, Bernard, ed. *Jefferson Himself: The Personal Narrative of a Many-Sided American*. Charlottesville: University Press of Virginia, 1976.

Mazlish, Bruce; Kaledin, Arthur D.; and Ralston, David B., eds. *Revolution: A Reader*. New York: Macmillan, 1971.

Meltzer, Milton. *Hunted Like a Wolf: The Story of the Seminole War*. New York: Farrar, Straus & Giroux, 1972.

Merrill, W. M., ed. *The Letters of William Lloyd Garrison*. 6 vols. Cambridge, Mass.: Harvard University Press, Belknap Press, 1971-1981.

Methuin, Eugene H. *The Riot Makers*. New Rochelle, N.Y.: Arlington House, 1970.

Middlekauff, Robert, ed. *Bacon's Rebellion*. Chicago: Rand McNally, 1964.

Miller, Helen Hill. *The Case for Liberty*. Chapel Hill: University of North Carolina Press, 1965.

Miller, John C. *Crisis in Freedom: The Alien and Sedition Acts*. Boston: Little, Brown, 1951.

Miller, Michael V., and Gilmore, Susan, eds. *Revolution at Berkeley*. New York: Dell, 1965.

Miller, Sally M. *Victor Berger and the Promise of Constructive Socialism, 1910-1920*. Westport, Conn.: Greenwood Press, 1973.

Miner, Craig H., and Unrau, William E. *The End of Indian Kansas: A Study of Cultural Revolution, 1854-1871*. Lawrence: Regents Press of Kansas, 1978.

Minor, Clarence E. *The Ratification of the Federal Constitution by the State of New York*. New York: Columbia University Press, 1921.

Minot, G. R. *History of the Insurrection in Massachusetts*. Boston: James W. Burditt, 1810.

Mississippi Violence vs. Human Rights. Atlanta: Committee for the Distribution of the Mississippi Story, 1963.

Mitchell, Broadus. *The Price of Independence: A Realistic View of the American Revolution*. New York: Oxford University Press, 1974.

Mitford, Jessica. *The Trial of Dr. Spock*. New York: Random House, 1970.

Mode, P., ed. *Source Book and Bibliographical Guide for American Church History*. Menasha, Wis.: George Banta, 1921.

Montgomery, Robert H. *Sacco-Vanzetti: The Murder and the Myth*. New York: Devin-Adair, 1960.

Montross, Lynn. *The Reluctant Rebels: The Story of the Continental Congress, 1774-1789*. New York: Harper, 1950.

Moore, Barrington, Jr. *Social Origins of Dictatorship and Democracy*. Boston: Beacon Press, 1969.

Moore, F., ed. *The Rebellion Record*. 12 vols. New York: Putnam, 1861-63.

Morgan, David. *Suffragists and Democrats: The Politics of Woman Suffrage in America*. East Lansing: Michigan State University Press, 1972.

Morgan, Edmund Sears, ed. *Prologue to Revolution: Sources and Documents on the Stamp Act Crisis, 1764-1766*. Chapel Hill: University of North Carolina Press, 1959.

Morison, Samuel Eliot; Merk, Frederick; and Freidel, Frank. *Dissent in Three American Wars*. Cambridge, Mass.: Harvard University Press, 1970.

Morris, Richard B. *Seven Who Shaped Our Destiny: The Founding Fathers as Revolutionaries*. New York: Harper & Row, 1973.

Motley, James B. *U.S. Strategy to Counter Domestic Political Terrorism*. Washington, D.C.: National Defense University Press, 1983.

Mowry, George E. *The Era of Theodore Roosevelt and the Birth of Modern America, 1900-1912*. New York: Harper & Row, 1962.

Muller, Charles G. *The Proudest Day: Macdonough on Lake Champlain*. New York: John Day, 1960.

Mullin, Gerald W. *Flight and Rebellion: Slave Resistance in Eighteenth-Century Virginia*. New York: Oxford University Press, 1975.

Muse, Benjamin. *Ten Years of Prelude: The Story of Integration since the Supreme Court's 1954 Decision*. New York: Viking Press, 1964.

Myles, W., ed. *The State Papers and Other Public Writings of Herbert Hoover*. Garden City, N.Y.: Doubleday, Doran, 1934.

Nammack, Georgiana. *Fraud, Politics, and the Dispossession of the Indians: The Iroquois Frontier in the Colonial Period*. Norman: University of Oklahoma Press, 1969.

Nash, Howard P. *Andrew Johnson: Congress and Reconstruction*. Rutherford, N.J.: Fairleigh Dickinson University Press, 1972.

National Advisory Commission on Civil Disorders. *Report of the National Advisory Commission on Civil Disorders*. New York: Bantam Books, 1968.

National Advisory Commission on Civil Disorders. *Supplemental Studies for the National Advisory Commission on Civil Disorders.* Washington, D.C.: U.S. Government Printing Office, 1968.

National Commission on the Causes and Prevention of Violence Task Force on Law and Law Enforcement. *Rights in Concord.* Washington, D.C.: U.S. Government Printing Office, 1969.

National Commission on the Causes and Prevention of Violence. *To Establish Justice, to Insure Domestic Tranquillity.* Washington, D.C.: U.S. Government Printing Office, 1969.

Nelson, Jack, and Ostrow, Ronald J. *The FBI and the Berrigans: The Making of a Conspiracy.* New York: Coward, McCann & Geoghegan, 1972.

Nelson, Truman J. *Documents of Upheaval: Selections from William Lloyd Garrison's "The Liberator," 1831–1865.* New York: Hill & Wang, 1966.

Newman, Graeme. *Understanding Violence.* New York: Harper & Row, 1979.

Nichols, David A. *Lincoln and the Indians: Civil War Policy and Politics.* Columbia: University of Missouri Press, 1978.

Nicolay, J., and Hay, J., eds. *Complete Works of Lincoln.* 12 vols. New York: F. D. Tandy, 1905.

Niles, Hezekiah. *Chronicles of the American Revolution.* Edited by Alden T. Vaughn. (Reprint of Niles, *Principles and Acts of the Revolution in America,* 1822.) Grosset & Dunlap, 1965.

Nizer, Louis. *The Implosion Conspiracy.* Garden City, N.Y.: Doubleday, 1973.

North, Oliver L., et al. *Taking the Stand.* Edited by Daniel Schorr. New York: Pocket Books, 1987.

Nozick, Robert. *Anarchy, State, and Utopia.* New York: Basic Books, 1974.

Oates, Stephen B. *To Purge This Land with Blood: A Biography of John Brown.* New York: Harper & Row, 1970.

——. *The Fires of Jubilee: Nat Turner's Fierce Rebellion.* New York: Harper & Row, 1975.

O'Gorman, Ned, ed. *Prophetic Voices.* New York: Random House, 1969.

Overstreet, Harry, and Overstreet, Bonaro. *The Strange Tactics of Extremism.* New York: Norton, 1964.

Palmer, Stuart. *The Violent Society.* New Haven, Conn.: College and University Press Services, 1972.

Parker, J. A. *Angela Davis.* New Rochelle, N.Y.: Arlington House, 1973.

Parker, W., ed. *Letters and Addresses of Thomas Jefferson.* New York: United Book Publishing Co., 1905.

Parry, Albert. *Terrorism from Robespierre to Arafat.* New York: Vanguard Press, 1976.

Payne, Les, and Findley, Tim. *The Life and Death of the SLA.* New York: Ballantine Books, 1976.

Peare, Catherine Owens. *William Penn: A Biography.* Ann Arbor: University of Michigan Press, 1956.

——. *The Woodrow Wilson Story: An Idealist in Politics.* New York: Crowell, 1963.

Pekelis, Alexander H. *Law and Social Action.* Ithaca: Cornell University Press, 1950.

Perkus, Cathy, ed. *Cointelpro: The FBI's Secret War on Political Freedom.* New York: Monad Press, 1975.

Philbrick, Herbert A. *I Led Three Lives.* Washington, D.C.: Capitol Hill Press, 1972.

Phillips, Donald E. *Student Protest, 1960-1969: An Analysis of the Issues and Speeches.* Washington, D.C.: University Press of America, 1980.

Pierce, William L. [Andrew Macdonald]. *The Turner Diaries.* Hillsboro, W. Va.: National Vanguard, 1979.

Pinkney, Alphonso. *The American Way of Violence.* New York: Random House, 1972.

Pitman, B., ed. *The Assassination of President Lincoln and the Trial of the Conspirators.* Cincinnati: Moore, Wilstach & Baldwin, 1865.

Plechanoff, George. *Anarchism and Socialism.* Translated by Eleanor Marx Aveling. London: Twentieth Century Press, 1906.

Poore, B. P., ed. *The Federal and State Constitutions, Colonial Charters, and Other Organic Laws of the United States.* Washington, D.C.: U.S. Government Printing Office, 1877.

Powderly, T. V. *Thirty Years of Labor.* Columbus, Ohio: Excelsior, 1980.

Powers, E. *Crime and Punishment in Early Massachusetts, 1620-1692.* Boston: Beacon Press, 1966.

Powers, Thomas. *Diana: The Making of a Terrorist.* Boston: Houghton Mifflin, 1971.

The Presidential Clemency Board's Report to the President. Washington, D.C.: U.S. Government Printing Office, 1975.

President's Commission on Campus Unrest. *The Report of the President's Commission on Campus Unrest.* New York: Avon Books, 1971.

Preston, William, Jr. *Aliens and Dissenters.* New York: Harper & Row, 1966.

Price, Glenn W. *Origins of the War with Mexico: The Polk-Stockton Intrigue.* Austin: University of Texas Press, 1970.

Priest, Loring B. *Uncle Sam's Stepchildren: The Reformation of United States Indian Policy, 1865-1887.* New Brunswick, N.J.: Rutgers University Press, 1942.

Prucha, Francis Paul, ed. *Documents of United States Indian Policy.* Lincoln: University of Nebraska Press, 1975.

Rable, George C. *But There Was No Peace: The Role of Violence in the Politics of Reconstruction.* Athens: University of Georgia Press, 1984.

Radosh, Ronald, and Milton, Joyce. *The Rosenberg File: A Search for the Truth.* New York: Holt, Rinehart and Winston, 1983.

Randall, James G. *Constitutional Problems under Lincoln.* Urbana: University of Illinois Press, 1951.

Rapoport, David C. *Assassination and Terrorism.* Toronto: T. H. Best, 1971.

Raschhofer, Hermann. *Political Assassination.* Tübingen: Fritz Schlichtenmayer, 1964.

Reed, Scott W. "The County Supremacy Movement: Mendacious Myth Marketing." 30 *Idaho L. Rev.* 525 (1993-94).

Reich, Charles A. *The Greening of America.* New York: Random House, 1970.

Reid, John P. *In a Defiant Stance.* University Park: Pennsylvania State University Press, 1977.

Renshaw, Patrick. *The Wobblies: The Story of Syndicalism in the United States.* Garden City, N.Y.: Anchor Books, 1968.

Report of the President's Commission on the Assassination of President John F. Kennedy. Washington, D.C.: U.S. Government Printing Office, 1964.

Report to the President by the Commission on CIA Activities within the United States. Washington, D.C.: U.S. Government Printing Office, 1975.

Revolutionary Communist Party, USA. *Revolution and Counter-Revolution.* Chicago: RCP Publications, 1978.

——. *News Programme and New Constitution of the Revolutionary Communist Party, USA.* Chicago: RCP Publications, 1980.

Richardson, J., ed. *A Compilation of Messages and Papers of the Confederacy.* 2 vols. Nashville: United States Publishing Co., 1905.

Richardson, J., ed. *A Compilation of the Messages and Papers of the Presidents.* 20 vols. New York: Bureau of National Literature, 1897-1917.

Rivera, Mario A. *Decision and Structure: United States Refugee Policy in the Mariel Crisis.* Lanham, Md.: University Press of Maryland, 1991.

Robertson, A. H., ed. *Human Rights in National and International Law.* Manchester: Manchester University Press, 1968.

Roebuck, Julian, and Weeber, Stanley C. *Political Crime in the United States.* New York: Praeger, 1978.

Rojo, Ricardo. *My Friend Che.* New York: Grove Press, 1968.

Rosenberg, Charles E. *The Trial of the Assassin Guiteau: Psychiatry and Law in the Gilded Age.* Chicago: University of Chicago Press, 1968.

Rostow, Eugene V., ed. *Is Law Dead?* New York: Simon & Schuster, 1971.

Roszak, Theodore. *The Cult of Information: A Neo-Luddite Treatise on Higher Technology, Artificial Intelligence, and the True Art of Thinking.* 2d ed. Berkeley: University of California Press, 1994.

Rozwenc, Edwin C., ed. *The Causes of the American Civil War.* Boston: Heath, 1965.

Rubenstein, Richard E. *Rebels in Eden: Mass Political Violence in the United States.* Boston: Little, Brown, 1970.

Rubin, Jerry. *Growing Up at Thirty-seven.* New York: M. Evans, 1976.

Ruchames, L. *John Brown: The Making of a Revolutionary.* New York: Grosset & Dunlap, 1969.

Rushton, Reginald M. *The Rushton Report: Right-Wing Extremism in the Federal Republic of Germany, 1973-1995.* Diss., Department of German Studies, University of Birmingham, U.K., June 1995. Available at http://www.almanac.bc.ca/web/people/z/zundel-ernst/rushton-report.html.

Ruthland, Robert A. *The Ordeal of the Constitution: The Antifederalists and the Ratification Struggle of 1787-1788.* Norman: University of Oklahoma Press, 1966.

Said, Abdul A., and Collier, Daniel M. *Revolutionism.* Boston: Allyn & Bacon, 1971.

St. George, M., and Dennis, L. *A Trial on Trial: The Great Sedition Trial of 1944.* National Civil Rights Committee, 1946.

Sale, Kirkpatrick. *Rebels against the Future: The Luddites and Their War on the Industrial Revolution.* Reading, Mass.: Addison-Wesley, 1995.

Salisbury, H., ed. *The Eloquence of Protest: Voices of the 70's.* Boston: Houghton Mifflin, 1972.

Sandburg, Carl. *Abraham Lincoln: The War Years.* New York: Harcourt, Brace, 1939.

Sanders, Ronald. *Lost Tribes and Promised Lands.* Boston: Little, Brown, 1978.

Sargent, W. *The Loyalist Poetry of the Revolution*. Boston: Milford House, 1972.

Saunders, W., ed. *The Colonial Records of North Carolina*. 10 vols. Raleigh: Josephus Daniel, 1890.

Schafer, Stephen. *The Political Criminal*. New York: Free Press, 1974.

Scheer, Robert, ed. *Eldridge Cleaver*. New York: Random House, 1969.

Schiff, Zeev, and Rothstein, Raphael. *Fedayeen*. New York: McKay, 1972.

Schindler, D., and Toman, J., eds. *The Laws of Armed Conflicts*. Alphen aan den Rijn, The Netherlands: Sijthoff & Noordhoff, 1981.

Schlissel, Lillian, ed. *Conscience in America: A Documentary History of Conscientious Objection in America, 1757-1967*. New York: Dutton, 1968.

Schneebeck, Richard. "State Participation in Federal Policy for the Yellowstone Ecosystem: A Meaningful Solution or Business as Usual." 21 *Land & Water L. Rev.* 397 (1986).

Schwartz, David C. *Political Alienation and Political Behavior*. Chicago: Aldine, 1973.

Seidman, Joel. *Sit Down*. New York: League for Industrial Democracy, 1937.

1777-80 Maryland Laws. Annapolis: Frederick Green, 1777.

Shaw, Peter. *The Character of John Adams*. New York: Norton, 1976.

Shearer, I. A. *Extradition in International Law*. Manchester: Manchester University Press, 1971.

Sheehan, Bernard W. *Seeds of Extinction: Jeffersonian Philanthropy and the American Indian*. New York: Norton, 1974.

Shoham, Shlomo. *Crime and Social Deviation*. Chicago: Henry Regnery, 1966.

Short, James F., Jr., and Wolfgang, Marvin E., eds. *Collective Violence*. Chicago: Aldine-Atherton, 1972.

Shuman, Samuel I., ed. *Law and Disorder: The Legitimation of Direct Action as an Instrument of Social Policy*. Detroit: Wayne State University Press, 1971.

Silver, David M. *Lincoln's Supreme Court*. Urbana: University of Illinois Press, 1956.

Simkins, Francis B., and Woody, Robert H. *South Carolina during Reconstruction*. Chapel Hill: University of North Carolina Press, 1932.

Sims, Patsy. *The Klan*. New York: Stein & Day, 1978.

Sink, John M. *Political Criminal Trials: How to Defend Them*. New York: Clark Boardman, 1974.

Sirica, John J. *To Set the Record Straight: The Break-in, The Tapes, The Conspirators, The Pardon*. New York: Norton, 1979.

Skolnick, Jerome H. *The Politics of Protest*. New York: Ballantine Books, 1970.

Smith, Colin. *Carlos: Portrait of a Terrorist*. London: André Deutsch, 1976.

Smith, Gibbs M. *Joe Hill*. Salt Lake City: University of Utah Press, 1969.

Snow, Peter, and Phillips, David. *The Arab Hijack War*. New York: Ballantine Books, 1971.

Sonn, Richard D. *Anarchism*. New York: Twayne, 1992.

Sowell, Thomas. *Civil Rights: Rhetoric or Reality?* New York: Morrow, 1984.

Stanton, E.; Anthony, S.; and Gage, M., eds. *History of Woman Suffrage*. 6 vols. New York: Fowler & Wells, 1881.

Stein, Leon. *The Pullman Strike*. New York: Arno Press, 1969.

Steinberg, Peter L. *The Great "Red Menace": United States Prosecution of American Communists, 1949-1952*. Westport, Conn.: Greenwood Press, 1984.

Stephenson, C., and Marcham, F., eds. *Sources of English Constitutional History*. New York: Harper & Bros., 1937.

Stevens, D. *Jailed for Freedom*. New York: Boni and Liveright, 1920.

Stewart, James Brewer. *Holy Warriors: The Abolitionists and American Slavery*. New York: Hill & Wang, 1976.

Stone, Irving. *Clarence Darrow for the Defense*. Garden City, N.Y.: Garden City Publishing Co., 1943.

Stormer, John A. *None Dare Call It Treason*. Florissant, Mo.: Liberty Bell Press, 1964.

Styron, William. *The Confessions of Nat Turner*. New York: Random House, 1967.

Summers, Marvin, ed. *Free Speech and Political Protest*. Boston: Heath, 1967.

Szatmary, David P. *Shays's Rebellion: The Making of an Agrarian Insurrection*. Amherst: University of Massachusetts Press, 1980.

Tannenbaum, Frank. *Darker Phases of the South*. New York: Putnam, 1924.

Tatum, Laurie. *Our Red Brothers and the Peace Policy of President Ulysses S. Grant*. Philadelphia: J. C. Winston, 1899.

Taylor, Telford. *Grand Inquest*. New York: Ballantine Books, 1961.

Theoharis, Athan G., ed. *Beyond the Hiss Case: The FBI, Congress, and the Cold War*. Philadelphia: Temple University Press, 1982.

Thomas, Donald, ed. *Treason and Libel*. Vol. 1 of *State Trials*. Boston: Routledge & Kegan Paul, 1972.

Thomas, Gordon, and Witts, Max Morgan. *The Voyage of the Damned*. New York: Stein & Day, 1974.

Thomas, N. *The Conscientious Objector in America*. New York: B. W. Heubsch, 1923.

Thomis, Malcolm I., ed. *Luddism in Nottinghamshire*. London: Phillimore, 1972.

Thompson, E. P. *The Making of the English Working Class*. New York: Pantheon Books, 1963.

Thompson, Francis H. *The Frustration of Politics: Truman, Congress, and the Loyalty Issue, 1945-1953*. Rutherford, N.J.: Fairleigh Dickinson University Press, 1979.

Thompson, Henry T. *Ousting the Carpetbagger from South Carolina*. Columbia, S.C.: Press of the R. J. Bryan Co., 1926.

Thoreau, Henry David. *"Walden" and the "Essay on Civil Disobedience."* New York: Lancer Books, 1968.

Thornton, J. W., ed. *The Pulpit of the American Revolution: Or the Political Sermons of the Period of 1776*. Boston: Gould & Lincoln, 1860.

Thorpe, F., ed. *Federal and State Constitutions*. 7 vols. 59th Cong., 2d sess., 1906. H. Doc. 357. Washington, D.C.: U.S. Government Printing Office, 1909.

Toch, Hans. *Violent Men*. Chicago: Aldine, 1969.

Toplin, Robert Brent. *Unchallenged Violence*. Westport, Conn.: Williamhouse-Regency, 1975.

Trager, James, ed. *The People's Chronology: A Year-by-Year Record of Human Events from Prehistory to the Present*. New York: Holt, Rinehart and Winston, 1979.

Tragle, Henry I. *The Southampton Slave Revolt of 1831: A Compilation of Source Material*. Amherst: University of Massachusetts Press, 1971.

Turk, Austin T. *Political Criminality*. Beverly Hills, Calif.: Sage, 1982.

Turner, Nat. *The Confession, Trial, and Execution of Nat Turner, The Negro Insurrectionist*. 1881 ed. Reprint. New York: AMS Press, 1975.

Turner, William W., and Christian, John G. *The Assassination of Robert F. Kennedy: The Conspiracy and the Cover-Up, 1968-1978*. New York: Random House, 1978.

Tyler, Alice Felt. *Freedom's Ferment*. New York: Harper & Row, 1961.

Tyler, Lyman S. *Indian Affairs: A Study of the Changes in Policy of the United States toward Indians*. Provo, Utah: Institute of American Studies, Brigham Young University, 1964.

——. *A History of Indian Policy*. Washington, D.C.: Bureau of Indian Affairs, 1973.

Tyler, Lyon Gardiner, ed. *Narratives of Early Virginia, 1606-1625*. New York: Barnes & Noble, 1952.

Ulam, Adam B. *The Unfinished Revolution*. New York: Random House, 1964.

U.S. Commission on Wartime Relocation and Internment of Civilians. *Personal Justice Denied: Report of the Commission on Wartime Relocation and Internment of Civilians*. Washington, D.C.: U.S. Government Printing Office, 1983.

U.S. Congress. House. Committee on Internal Security. *Terrorism*, pts. 1 & 2. 93d Cong., 2d sess. Washington, D.C.: U.S Government Printing Office, 1974.

U.S. Congress. Senate. Subcommittee to Investigate the Administration of the Internal Security Act and Other Internal Security Laws of the Committee on the Judiciary. *Communist Global Subversion and American Security*. 92d Cong., 2d sess. Committee Print. Washington, D.C.: U.S. Government Printing Office, 1972.

U.S. Library of Congress. Legislative Reference Service. *Internal Security and Subversion: Principal State Laws and Cases*. Washington, D.C.: U.S. Government Printing Office, 1965.

Upton, L. F. S., ed. *Revolutionary versus Loyalist: The First American Civil War, 1774-1784*. Waltham, Mass.: Blaisdell, 1968.

Useem, Michael. *Conscription, Protest, and Social Conflict: The Life and Death of a Draft Resistance Movement*. New York: Wiley, 1973.

Utley, Robert M., and Washburn, Wilcomb E. *The American Heritage History of the Indian Wars*. New York: American Heritage, 1977.

Van Doren, Carl C. *Secret History of the American Revolution: An Account of the Conspiracies of Benedict Arnold and Numerous Others, Drawn from the Secret Service Papers of the British Headquarters in North America, Now for the First Time Examined and Made Public*. New York: Viking Press, 1941.

Viorst, Milton. *Fire in the Streets: America in the 1960s*. New York: Simon & Schuster, 1979.

Walker, Daniel. *Rights in Conflict*. New York: New American Library, 1968.

The Walker Report to the National Commission on The Causes and Prevention of Violence. *Rights in Conflict*. New York: Bantam Books, 1968.

Ward, Barbara. *Faith and Freedom*. Garden City, N.Y.: Doubleday, 1958.

Ware, Norman J. *The Labor Movement in the United States, 1860-1895: A Study in Democracy*. New York: Appleton, 1929.

Warfield, Ethelbert D. *The Kentucky Resolutions of 1798: An Historical Study*. New York: Putnam, 1894.

Warne, Colston E. *The Pullman Boycott of 1894*. Boston: Heath, 1955.

Wasby, Stephen L.; D'Amato, Anthony A.; and Metrailer, Rosemary. *Desegregation from Brown to Alexander: An Exploration of Supreme Court Strategies*. Carbondale: Southern Illinois University Press, 1977.

Washburn, Wilcomb E. *The Governor and the Rebel: A History of Bacon's Rebellion in Virginia*. Chapel Hill: University of North Carolina Press, 1957.

——. *The American Indian and The United States: A Documentary History*. New York: Random House, 1973.

Webb, Stephen Saunders. *1676, the End of American Independence*. New York: Knopf, 1984.

Weber, David R., ed. *Civil Disobedience in America*. Ithaca: Cornell University Press, 1978.

Weglyn, Michi. *Years of Infamy: The Untold Story of America's Concentration Camps*. New York: Morrow, 1976.

Weichmann, L. A. *A True History of the Assassination of Abraham Lincoln and of the Conspiracy of 1865*. New York: Knopf, 1975.

Weinberg, A., ed. *Attorney for the Damned*. New York: Simon & Schuster, 1957.

Weyl, Nathaniel. *Treason*. Washington, D.C.: Public Affairs Press, 1950.

Whittaker, Charles E., and Griffin, William Sloane, Jr. *Law and Order and Civil Disobedience*. Washington, D.C.: American Enterprise Institute for Public Policy Research, 1967.

Whitten, Woodrow C. *Criminal Syndicalism and the Law in California, 1919-1927*. Philadelphia: American Philosophical Society, 1969.

Wilbur, William H. *The Making of George Washington*. Deland, Fla.: Patriotic Education, 1973.

Williams, Roger Neville. *The New Exiles: American War Resisters in Canada*. New York: Liveright, 1971.

Wills, Garry. *The Second Civil War: Arming for Armageddon*. New American Library, 1968.

Wolfenstein, Victor E. *The Victims of Democracy: Malcolm X and the Black Revolution*. Berkeley and Los Angeles: University of California Press, 1981.

Wright, Esmond. *Fabric of Freedom, 1763-1800*. New York: Hill & Wang, 1964.

Yarmolinsky, Adam; Liebman, Lance; and Schelling, Corinne S., eds. *Race and Schooling in the City*. Cambridge, Mass.: Harvard University Press, 1981.

Young, Alfred F., ed. *Dissent: Explorations in the History of American Radicalism*. De Kalb: Northern Illinois University Press, 1968.

Zimmerman, Bill. *Airlift to Wounded Knee*. Chicago: Swallow Press, 1976.

Zinn, Howard. *Disobedience and Democracy*. New York: Random House, 1968.

Zobel, Hiller B. *The Boston Massacre*. New York: Norton, 1970.

Concordance and User's Guide

All numbers refer to documents.

Table of Cases

All numbers refer to documents.

Proper Name Index

All numbers refer to documents.